Ramazan Yildirim

Capital Structure and Shari'ah Compliance of non-Financial Firms

De Gruyter Studies in Islamic Economics, Finance and Business

Edited by
Abbas Mirakhor and Idris Samawi Hamid

Volume 9

Ramazan Yildirim

Capital Structure and Shari'ah Compliance of non-Financial Firms

DE GRUYTER

ISBN 978-3-11-071350-3
e-ISBN (PDF) 978-3-11-071366-4
e-ISBN (EPUB) 978-3-11-071371-8
ISSN 2567-2533

Library of Congress Control Number: 2020950241

Bibliographic information published by the Deutsche Nationalbibliothek
The Deutsche Nationalbibliothek lists this publication in the Deutsche Nationalbibliografie; detailed bibliographic data are available on the Internet at http://dnb.dnb.de.

Cover image: nnnnae/iStock/Getty Images Plus
Typesetting: Integra Software Services Pvt. Ltd.
Printing and binding: CPI books GmbH, Leck

www.degruyter.com

To my parents ***Cuma*** *and* ***Sıdıka (Biter)***
and sons ***Jumaa Elijah*** *and* ***Yaseen Ramazan***

Foreword

This book is a solid contribution to the literature on the theory and empirics of the design, development and implementation of screening devices in "Islamic finance". Its analytic underpinnings rely on capital structure literature in conventional finance but innovate beyond this pedigree. To understand the importance of this contribution, it would be helpful to place it within the theoretical and empirical topography of issues in "Islamic finance." Spurred by a variety of motivations, the mid-1980s marked the beginning of intensified efforts at finding alternatives to the conventional, interest-rate-based debt finance (IRBDF). Much of this effort was exerted by Muslim scholars and financiers that had, as early as the 1960s, started in earnest to define and implement an Islamic approach to banking and finance. From the outset, this effort recognized that, given the long history of operation of interest-based finance and banking (IRBF) in Muslim countries, a long period of transition was necessary before an Ideal Islamic finance (IIF) could be implemented fully.

As a transitional arrangement, Muslim scholars and financiers accepted a proposal designed originally by the Iraqi scholar, M. B. Al-Sadr. The idea was that the interest rate in financial transactions could be replaced by the rate of markup on trade transactions. Moreover, Al-Sadr argued that it is possible to organize a banking system in which decisions would be based on this rate as the operating mechanism which would then effectively replace the interest rate mechanism (IRM). The proposed mechanism served a number of requirements demanded, inter alia, by IIF. First, it would establish a closer relationship between ROR to finance and the ROR to real economic activities. Second, it would not be *ex ante* determined and fixed, as is IRM. Third, this rate would not be related to the amount of principal involved, as is the case in the IRBF.

At the time it was hoped that the adoption and operationalization of this idea would in time pave the way for the emergence of the IIF system in which there would be no interest-rate-based debt financing and all risks and gains/losses of economic activities would be shared among participants. This dimension of the IIF had been proposed already by Al-Sadr in the 1960s; he had argued that risk/reward sharing would be an effective basis for medium-to-long-term investment projects in which ROR to finance would be based on the prospective ROR of these projects. In the event, the model of trade financing based on markups dominated "Islamic banking and finance" activities. An important issue emerging from application of this model was that in practice the ROR of this model was closely related to some index of international interest rates, such as Libor. Since then, a number of empirical studies have confirmed that the ROR prevailing in the present form of "Islamic banking and finance" closely tracks interest rates – close enough to suggest equivalency of the two. In the mid-1980s, even this model was subjected to a major change based upon which the current configuration of "Islamic banking and finance" has been structured.

https://doi.org/10.1515/9783110713664-202

This major modification was the introduction of ways and means of legitimizing debt instruments to be included in the portfolio of Muslim investors. This was done through the device of "Shari'ah Compliance" mechanism which included determination by religious scholars whether a particular investment met "Shari'ah" requirements – among which were criteria to declare a particular economic activity prohibited. Investments in firms that engaged in "permissible" activities and reliance on IRBDF were legitimate so long as the level of debt did not exceed a maximum threshold – set at 30 percent – in the firm's capital structure.

It should be noted that under IIF, question of capital structure – mixture of debt and equity as defined by Modigliani-Miller – would have no relevance due to the absence of IRM. But the moment IRBDF is allowed, capital structure and its relation to the profit of firms assumes crucial importance. In the event, beginning in the 1990s, researchers and financiers focused on the issue of classification of firms according to their capital structure as the idea was actively promoted that, ostensibly, Muslim investors needed guidance regarding the optimal structure of their investment portfolios. That guidance was to be provided by the mechanism of "Shari'ah Compliance," hence there was perceived the need for "Shari'ah Screening" algorithms and indices. It is in this context that Dr. Yildirim's uniquely innovative contribution assumes its importance.

To date a number of such screening devices have been developed and are currently in use. One of the notable features of the present book is its analytic assessment of the methodologies, their underpinning theoretical roots, and the applications of these devices. This provides a basis for the comparative analysis of the book that differentiates Dr. Yildirim's contribution from all other screening devices available in the market. Another important feature of the book worth noting is that at a time when even relatively simple but innovative ideas form the foundation of startups – which maintain full proprietary claims – Dr. Yildirim's book provides technical details of his methodology as well as religious justifications to underpin the legitimacy of his innovative and unique approach to specialized screening devices.

Dr. Yildirim's book is based on his dissertation supervised on the theory side by one of Asia's foremost capital market experts, Professor Dr. Obiyathulla Ismath Bacha, while the econometric part was supervised by one of the most accomplished contemporary econometricians, Professor Dr. Mansur Masih. This fact enhances confidence in the quality of Dr. Yildirim's proposed screening methodology in terms of its theoretical and empirical quality and validity.

On a personal note, as a member of the faculty that granted Dr. Yildirim his Doctorate, I have had the opportunity to observe his dedication, conviction and admirable tenacity in pursuing the goal of developing his unique screening index despite the many obstacles, frustrations and challenges faced in the acceptability of innovative ideas. The present book is a shining result of this effort which is certain to be recognized as an important contribution to the field. The publisher, De Gruyter, deserves commendation for perceiving the value of this unique effort and for its willingness to present it to the interested audiences.

Abbas Mirakhor
Retired Professor of Economics and Finance

Preface

Islamic finance is relatively new compared to conventional finance. It has undergone tremendous growth and advancement in the global financial sector over the last half a century, showing no signs of slowing down. Especially after the Global Financial Crisis (GFC), when the Islamic financial industry revealed its robustness, it has reached its climax in terms of attention at all levels, covering financial and non-financial sectors, capital markets, academia up to the individuals. Most of the stakeholders joined the hype as they saw an alternative to the status quo. As one of the main intermediates between various stakeholders, capital markets adjusted and enhanced their existing product and service portfolio by introducing Islamic indices. These Islamic indices' core element is the integrated *Shari'ah screening methodology*, a tool applied in the equity markets to differentiate Shari'ah compliant (SC) from the Shari'ah non-compliant (SNC) firms.

Although these methodologies aim the same, i.e., adhering to the teachings of the *Qur'an* and *Sunnah*, its definition and application are disputed among the Shari'ah scholars as they differ among various index providers. Long-lasting debates continue, and the signs of standardization and harmonization are still a long way off. Controversial views shouldn't be perceived as a flaw or weakness instead considered as incomplete. The diversified opinions of Shari'ah scholars is the dynamic element required during the stages of development of the Islamic financial system. The future growth and success of Islamic Finance depend on, among others, the international *fatwa* committees, such as IIFA (International Islamic Fiqh Academy), the regulators such as AAOIFI (Accounting and Auditing Organization for Islamic Financial Institution), and policymakers. Lately, innovations and *fatwas* have not been seen by the major international committees, similarly also not from the Islamic index provider, Islamic financial institutions, and other providers.

This book came into existence because I felt the urge to contribute to the Islamic finance industry with the hope of igniting the innovation-wheel again. What is unique about this book (compared to my PhD dissertation) is the combined coverage of three elements, (i) religious discussion of *Shari'ah screening methodologies*, (ii) the theoretical background of capital structure, and (iii) the practical application of statistical methods (econometrics). As far as the *Shari'ah screening methodologies* are concerned, during my PhD study, an extraordinary moment forced me not to accept my research results blindly. Instead, I couldn't stop digging deeper and deeper until I believed to have found a) the origin of the issue and b) a potential solution. The moment of truth came when I presented my solution as an exhibitor at the 1st IF Innofest 2016 (Islamic Finance Innovation Festival/Competition) sponsored and organized by the Central Bank of Malaysia (Bank Negara) and INCEIF (International Centre for Education in Islamic Finance), respectively. Titled as *Shari'ah Screening Methodology – New Shari'ah Compliant Approach*, my proposed solution received the 1st Prize as an Idea Pitch.

https://doi.org/10.1515/9783110713664-203

In this book, I am sharing the full details of my proposed solution in Chapter 3, which is the heart of this book and has the potential to close the long-lasting gap in Islamic literature. I have designed this book primarily for (advanced) undergraduate and postgraduate students interested in the capital structure's theoretical and practical research. Furthermore, I have discussed all research steps, including all shortcomings/limitations, in detail (with important highlights and notes) and referred to the respective tables/figures. All tables and figures, especially those in the appendices, are intended to improve students' understanding and keep them interested in the subject matter. I am also sharing the research data and Stata codes (Appendix G) for replication purposes. This way, lecturers and research students can utilize it as a practical handbook for various research projects and studies (not limited to corporate finance). Financial professionals and practitioners may also find this book interesting and useful as it sheds more light on the factors affecting firms' capital structure. Last, this book might serve as an investment and financing guideline for international investors and CFOs interested in operating under Islamic principles. They all, including the general reader, can benefit from it since it is written in an easy-to-read manner.

Ramazan Yildirim

Structure of the Book

The following chapter outlines explain the structure and arrangement of the book.

Chapter 1 outlines the background and provides information about the Shari'ah screening methodology applied by the Islamic index providers. Furthermore, it identifies the essential research needs, motivates the objectives, and highlights the research questions.

Chapter 2 focuses on the main notion of capital structure and reviews the relevant underpinning theories proposed by academic research to explain companies' financing decisions. Specifically, after brief elaboration on (Modigliani and Miller, 1958, 1963)'s Irrelevance Theory, this chapter investigates both the *static* and *dynamic* approach of the Trade-Off Theory on firms' capital structure decisions followed by the Pecking Order Theory. Furthermore, this chapter provides the core debt determinants of the capital structure decision, differentiating between firm-specific and macroeconomic factors.

Chapter 3 illuminates the historical background of the newly implemented stocks screening procedure and shows the Shari'ah screening methodologies development with its screening criterion set by the DJIMI (Dow Jones Islamic Market Index). Following a critical assessment of the currently applied Shari'ah screening methodologies, this chapter discusses the notion of Shari'ah screening methodologies in general. It looks behind the scene at the financial screening criterion *debt-to-equity* ratio. Finally, this chapter addresses the major criticism and attempts to propose a unique Shari'ah screening solution, named *RIEM* (Ramy Islamic Equity Market) methodology and a financing hierarchy to firms interested in operating under Islamic principles.

Chapter 4 outlines the research methodologies applied in this study. Specifically, this study employs advanced econometric techniques such as *static* and *dynamic* models using unbalanced panel datasets. Additionally, this chapter provides the sample selection procedure to identify Shari'ah compliant (SC) firms and their Shari'ah non-compliant (SNC) peers. Furthermore, this chapter discusses the developed hypotheses that will be tested and finally specifies the regression model and research design.

Chapter 5 details the empirical data used in testing the theoretical framework and hypotheses and provides a sample description and summary statistics of SC and SNC firms' debt determinants. Moreover, this chapter offers an in-depth empirical analysis for *overall (pooled)*, cross-*country*, cross-*industry* sample results, including a time-breakdown analysis for the *overall (pooled)* sample.

Chapter 6 aims to validate the findings obtained in Chapter 5 by directly measuring each capital structure theory. This chapter concludes with the sample group, i.e., SC *(RIEM)* and SNC *(RIEM)* firms identified based on our proposed *RIEM* methodology from Chapter 3.

Chapter 7 discusses the implications, contributions, and limitations of the study, offers possible future research, and finally summarizes it.

https://doi.org/10.1515/9783110713664-204

Additional Materials

For lecturers and research students using this book, the following supporting data are available:

- SC and SNC firm sample (used throughout the book)
- SC *(RIEM)* and SNC *(RIEM)* firm sample (used in Section 6.3)

For more information and to download the sample data please visit the following page: https://www.degruyter.com/document/isbn/9783110713664/html

https://doi.org/10.1515/9783110713664-205

Acknowledgment

Any work to this extent is not possible without the support of others. I am grateful to those who encouraged me and provided me with feedback throughout the entire idea-to-dissertation-to-book process.

First and foremost, I would like to express my sincere recognition to my mentors Prof. Obiyathulla (Obiya) Ismath Bacha and Prof. Mansur Masih. I owe Prof. Obiya the utmost since he allowed me to join the PhD program in Islamic Finance at INCEIF in the first place. Throughout my journey, he provided comprehensive and insightful guidance, assistance, and support. Prof. Mansur Masih provided me the most inspiring advice, statistical/econometrical insights, and valuable suggestions to make this research more rewarding. I cannot thank them enough for their significant contribution, inspiration, and encouragement throughout my study.

I want to thank Prof. Abbas Mirakhor, who encouraged me to convert my dissertation into this book. I have learned from him the fundamentals of Islamic Economics in many ways. I owe many thanks to Dr. Ahcene Lahsasna, from whom I have learned the fundamentals of *Usul Al-Fiqh and Fiqh Al-Muamalat,* and Dr. Hazik Mohamed, who provided me with initial encouragement to start the writing process. Special mentions are due to Dr. Bilal Ilhan, Dr. Alam Asadov, Dr. Ruslan Nagayev (Dr. Adam), Gerd-Mathias (Ibrahim) Rehner, Ertuğrul Başer, and Safwan Butt for their ad-hoc unlimited support.

This book would not have been possible without my parents' mental and motivational support; (my late father) Cuma and Sıdıka, and my siblings, Fatma, Sevim, and Muhammet Bilal.

May Allah bless you all with His bounties and blessings.

Allah ömrünüzü uzun eylesin – Amin!

https://doi.org/10.1515/9783110713664-206

Contents

1 Introduction

1.1 Context and Background

The capital structure, which is the mixture of debt and equity capital of a company, is very important since it is related to its ability to fulfill its stakeholders' needs. While capital structure determinants are not a new question, the optimal capital structure has been one of the past decades' concerned topics. The recent Global Financial Crisis (GFC) in 2007–2008 also has been called the worst financial crisis since the one related to the Great Depression by the top economists.[1] It triggered companies to focus more on firms' capital structure, as many company bankruptcies have followed in the wake of the financial crisis.[2] The focus of capital structure is not merely of interest to academics but also to various stakeholders such as financial managers, shareholders, debt holders, etc. The financial crisis has generated a renewed focus and needs for companies to evaluate the financing decisions to maximize firm value critically.

Theories of capital structure seek to provide a framework for understanding how financing decisions are made and how they may influence a company's value. Since Modigliani and Miller published their paper on the cost of capital, corporate finance, and investment theory in 1958, many academic works emerged. Several competing theories developed to arrive at one that can explain companies' financing behavior and establish whether an optimal capital structure exists. Michaelas et al. (1999) partition the theory of capital structure into three categories. These categories are the *tax-based*, the *agency cost*, and the *asymmetric information and signaling* theories. The main theory that considers both taxes and agency costs is the Trade-Off Theory. In contrast, the main theory under asymmetric information and signaling seems to be the Pecking Order Theory. Trade-Off Theory predicts that firms should balance the tax benefits of debt against the cost of debt. Therefore, firms should have an optimal capital structure. In contrast to Trade-Off Theory, Pecking Order Theory does not imply that firms' capital structure decision is driven by the notion of optimal capital structure, but rather simply based on the firms' willingness to reduce information asymmetry. Consequently, firms tend to exhaust their internal funds first through retained earnings, followed by secured debt, and use riskier equity financing as a last resort.

1 "Top Economists Agree 2009 Worst Financial Crisis Since Great Depression" by Nourial Roubini (2009). Retrieved from: https://www.businesswire.com/news/home/20090213005161/en/Top-Economists-Agree-2009-Worst-Financial-Crisis, (accessed July 30, 2020).
2 "The US Financial and Economic Crisis: Where Does It Stand and Where Do We Go From Here? Initiative on Business and Public Policy" by Baily and Elliott (2009) at Brookings. Retrieved from: https://www.brookings.edu/wp-content/uploads/2016/06/0615_economic_crisis_baily_elliott.pdf, (accessed July 30, 2020).

https://doi.org/10.1515/9783110713664-001

Kraus and Litzenberger (1973) stated that the capital structure decision impacts the firm value under capital market imperfection. According to the Trade-Off Theory, at the optimal debt level of firms, debt financing's tax advantages are balanced with the cost of financial distress Modigliani and Miller (1963). Financial distress arises from the bankruptcy risks, agency costs, and signaling; see the seminal works of Hart and Moore (1995), Jensen and Meckling (1976), Kraus and Litzenberger (1973), Myers (1977), and Stulz (1990). Consequently, as Myers (1984) states, firms following the Trade-Off Theory aim to have their target debt-to-equity ratio to reach their optimal capital structure. The static Trade-Off Theory is named after. Academic studies have shown that firms seek to maintain their optimal leverage ratio, although firms tend to deviate from it occasionally underline the dynamic settings of the capital structure decision of firms Antoniou et al. (2008), Hennessy and Whited (2005), R. Huang and Ritter (2009), and Kayhan and Titman (2007). Specifically, while some academic studies report that firms quickly adjust to their target ratio Flannery and Rangan (2006), other studies state that the adjustment speed is pretty slow Fama and French (2002) and R. Huang and Ritter (2009).

In Myers and Majluf (1984) seminal work, the authors claim that firms follow a preferred hierarchy for financing decisions. Following the top-down approach, firms prefer to use retained earnings (internal financing) before seeking any form of external funds (external financing). Myers (1984) states that if a firm must utilize external funds, the following order of financing sources is used: *debt*, *convertible securities*, *preferred stock*, and *common stock*. The Pecking Order Theory is named after it. Many academic studies such as Beattie et al. (2006), Booth et al. (2001), and Shyam-Sunder and Myers (1999) have found evidence of the Pecking Order Theory. Other studies such as Fama and French (2002, 2005) and Frank and Goyal (2003) find counter-evidence for the Pecking Order Theory. A more recent study by Gaud et al. (2007) investigates firms' financing decisions in European countries. It shows that none of the mentioned theories, namely Trade-Off nor Pecking Order, can fully explain their results.

Despite many academic studies, there is still no agreement among scholars on which determinants are reliably important. Firms generally differ in profitability, growth opportunities, asset structure, operational risk, competitiveness, the country's legal and tax frameworks, etc. Therefore, firms must consider all these factors to remain operative in the current competitive environment. Consequently, firms' capital structure ratio is expected to be dynamic and vary between countries, industries, and firm sizes.

During the last decades, Islamic finance experienced enormous growth and innovation within the currently overpowered global (conventional) financial industry. According to HSBC, the Islamic finance industry showed an annual growth rate of 28% during 2006–2009 (despite the Global Financial Crisis in 2007–08).[3] However,

3 "Reuters Islamic Banking and Finance Summit 2010" Thomson Reuters. Retrieved from: https://customers.reuters.com/wetfetch/index.aspx?CID=30887anddoc=Reuters_Islamic_Banking_and_Finance_Summit_10.pdfandbase=/community/summits/previous.asp, (accessed July 30, 2020).

growth in the Islamic finance industry is expected further as of late, at a slower pace. We believe this is attributed to two factors. First, the sharp fall in oil price, which showed its impact on Islamic Banking and Capital Market activities within GCC, and second, the natural reduction in growth as asset size becomes large. For instance, Thomson Reuters reports an average growth rate of 9.5% per year, with the total assets under management around USD 2,200 Billion in 2016 and USD 3,800 Billion by 2022.[4] A reduction in growth after many years of rapid growth is expected, as no financial sector can keep growing at double-digit rates over a prolonged period. In line with this growth, innovative Islamic finance products have been introduced in the Islamic financial market. This is attributed to the increasing demand for such products by the rapidly expanding Muslim population who require finance products compatible with their beliefs Grais and Pellegrini (2006). One of the areas that have affected Islamic finance's recent growth is international stock markets' investment. In the same report, Thomson Reuters shows an annual growth rate of approximately 28% of Islamic funds with assets under management of USD 90 Billion and USD 400 Billion by 2016 and 2022, respectively.[5]

Many individual and institutional investors, mainly from Islamic countries, seek to invest only in stocks compliant with the Shari'ah, i.e., Islamic law. Different index providers started to develop their Islamic indices based on their proprietary screening algorithm to address the increasing demand. Specifically, in 1999, Dow Jones launched its first Islamic index, namely the Dow Jones Islamic Market Index (DJIMI), and introduced its applied *Shari'ah screening methodology*. Other index providers relied on the same principle and launched their screening methodologies upon approval of each index provider's individual Shari'ah board. Each Shari'ah index provider applies their screening methodology; some have similar selection criteria, while others are different. Firms are screened on two aspects, namely, *qualitative* and *quantitative*. It first applies the *qualitative screening* in which the company's primary business operations are scrutinized. Companies involved in prohibited activities such as conventional financial services, pork, alcohol, tobacco, gaming, pornography, etc., are deemed non-compliant by Shari'ah law. Once firms pass the first check successfully, it triggers the *quantitative screening*, which focuses on a set of pre-defined financial ratios and a maximum threshold. For instance, the debt-to-equity ratio must be less than 33%. Companies classified as being Shari'ah compliant (SC) are those who pass both screenings successfully. Failing in any screening criteria will lead companies to be considered Shari'ah non-compliant (SNC).

Authors such as Derigs and Marzban (2008) and others addressed the dilemma of having different screening criteria. They highlighted the importance of harmonizing

---

4 See Islamic Finance Development Report 2017, ICD-Thomson Reuters. Available at: https://www.zawya.com/mena/en/ifg-publications/231017094152F/, (accessed July 30, 2020).

5 See Islamic Finance Development Report 2017, ICD-Thomson Reuters. Available at: https://www.zawya.com/mena/en/ifg-publications/231017094152F/, (accessed July 30, 2020)

the screening criterion and the discrepancies resulting from different screening, i.e., a company could be screened as compliant according to one index criteria and might be rejected and considered non-compliant following another index criterion. Among others, Derigs and Marzban (2008), Gamaleldin (2015), Habib and Ahmad (2017), Khatkhatay and Nisar (2007a), Mahfooz and Ahmed (2014), Raghibi and Oubdi (2020), and Saiti and Ahmad (2017) have tried to discuss the rationale behind these pre-defined financial ratios and further attempt to offer a revised version of a *Shari'ah screening methodology*. A satisfactory justification of the screens (i.e., financial ratios), especially from the Shari'ah perspective, and a solution for the long-lasting urge for harmonization have not yet been provided.

A significant amount of literature exists on firms' capital structure and financing behavior. Compared to the conventional studies, the capital structure studies applied to SC firms per se are limited in number and scope. For instance, Haron and Ibrahim (2012) and Thabet and Hanefah (2014) use a data set of SC firms only operating in Malaysia. The authors investigate selected debt determinants and find inconsistent results. While Haron and Ibrahim (2012) find support for the existence of target capital structure (the *dynamic* version of Trade-Off Theory), Thabet and Hanefah (2014) find support for the Pecking Order Theory. In Ramli and Haron (2017a), the authors attempt to identify the target capital structure and the speed of adjustment of SC firms listed on Bursa Malaysia, which consistently maintain their Shari'ah compliance status. The authors find that SC firms opt for adjusting towards an optimal capital structure; however, they find evidence for these firms being under-adjusted. Akinsomi et al. (2019) enhanced the scope by conducting a comparative analysis among property firms operating in the GCC countries. Analyzing SC firms against the conventional property firms, even though the authors find partially inconsistent results, they conclude that the Pecking Order Theory may explain SC property firms' capital structure. While all the authors apply quantitative analysis, Ahmed (2007) uses an exploratory approach. He suggests that Islamic firms should follow a slightly revised version of the Pecking Order Theory to seek the least costly financing alternative. This is in line with Obaidullah (2007), a proponent of a pecking order financing approach, in case SC firms aim to minimize total costs. However, the author advocates that the Trade-Off Theory is irrelevant for the firms operating under Shari'ah principles due to the non-existence of a tax shield on interest from an Islamic perspective.

This comparative study is the first attempt to identify which of both capital structure theories (i.e., Trade-Off Theory and Pecking Order Theory) best explains SC and SNC firm's financing decisions. We estimated the relationship of the most reliable debt determinants, namely, *profitability*, *growth opportunity*, *firm size*, *tangibility*, *business risk*, and *GDP growth* and the capital structure decision of both firm types. We have explicitly selected those debt determinants which have predictions made by both capital structure theories under study. It is important to note that all capital structure theories are based on the conventional financial system in which debt and interest is the basis for its core belief. In contrast, the Islamic economic and financial system is based on the principles of risk-sharing and equity-based transactions (i.e., promotes entrepreneurship) and compared to the conventional system, as stated in Bacha and Mirakhor (2013), "debt financing" does not exist. Consequently, an Islamic capital structure theory and its hypotheses around "equity" determinants per se do not exist. Considering the enormous growth of Islamic finance globally, to contribute to the respective Body of Knowledge, we believe it is evident that diversified studies are required to increase its maturity level. Yildirim et al. (2018) state that a certain maturity level to establish an Islamic capital structure theory that would explain firms' financing behavior under Shari'ah principles has not been reached yet. This, for instance, clearly demonstrates the importance of capital structure studies by utilizing the SC firm dataset. Additionally, the inconclusive results derived from the previous studies have further motivated this research.

1.2 Motivation and Research Questions

As mentioned, there has always been controversy in the literature regarding the subject of capital structure. Specifically, a consensus has not been reached yet on the optimal capital structure of firms. Besides, the use of financial leverage varies significantly by country, industry, and company. SC firms are expected to have lower leverage by default. Due to this limitation imposed on them, SC firms are not likely to benefit through the debt tax shield to their SNC peers' extent. Consequently, it is expected that SC firms exhibit different financing behavior. Even though limited in numbers, academic studies have been conducted to examine the significance of the existing capital structure theories and the debt determinants in explaining SC firms' financing decision operating in Malaysia, Indonesia, or Saudi Arabia (i.e., limited to one country). Therefore, the need to look beyond these countries is obvious. This study aims to fill the gap by conducting a comprehensive comparative analysis among SC and SNC peers, with *overall (pooled)*, cross-*country*, and cross-*industry* dimensions. Consequently, in this study, we intended to find answers to the research questions (RQs) derived from the research objectives (ROs).[6]

In light of the preceding discussions about *Shari'ah screening methodology* and *capital structure*, the following research objectives are proposed:

RO 1. Investigating the primary sources of Islam (i.e., *Qur'an* and *Sunnah*) to find any specific guidance to provide a unique solution of Shari'ah screening methodology for future standardization.

RO 2. Understanding the debt determinants that influence the capital structure decision in the context of SC and SNC firms.

6 The ranking of the research questions is in line with the research objectives and mirror the hierarchical study of these questions.

RO 3. Investigating the effect of time on the capital structure decision of SC and SNC firms.
RO 4. Understanding the capital structure differs between different countries and industries in the context of SC and SNC firms.
RO 5. Investigating the significance of different capital structure theories on the financial decision behavior of SC and SNC firms.

Based on the research objectives, the goal of this study is to address the following research questions:
RQ 1. Do the *quantitative screens* in the current Shari'ah screening methodologies support the Islamic finance's main notion by following the principles of Shari'ah itself?
RQ 2. What are the significant determinants of capital structure in the context of SC and SNC firms?
RQ 3. Are certain capital structure determinants only temporarily important in SC and SNC firms' leverage decisions, or do they exhibit a consistent impact over time?
RQ 4. Are certain capital structure determinants, for SC and SNC firms, more important in some countries yet unimportant elsewhere?
RQ 5. Are certain capital structure determinants, for SC and SNC firms, more important in some industries yet unimportant elsewhere?
RQ 6. Does a universal theory exist that best explains the financing decision of SC and SNC firms?
RQ 7. Do SC firms follow a financing pattern that resembles the principles postulated by the Shari'ah by issuing equity more than debt when facing financial deficits?

Our approach to providing an answer to all these research questions was straight forward. First, we presented an in-depth discussion of the long-lasting criticism of the various Shari'ah screening methodologies. We then provided a new screening solution, discussed, and derived information from the primary sources of Islamic (i.e., *Qur'an* and *Sunnah*). Second, we regressed the impact of selected debt determinants (i.e., independent variables) against the book and market leverage separately for SC and SNC firms, using the *overall (pooled)* sample. Third, we split our pooled sample into the *country* and *industry* sub-samples to identify possible cross-sectional differences and separately repeated our regression for SC and SNC firms. The reason for the "separate" regression approach was that we were interested in identifying the significance of each debt determinant on each firm type *individually* (i.e., "SC" and "SNC") and not in the context of *direct comparison* (i.e., "SC compared to SNC"). Fourth, we consolidated all significant debt determinants and identified the explanatory power of capital structure theories. Specifically, we provided evidence whether the Trade-Off Theory or the Pecking Order Theory has a better explanatory power of each firm type's financing behavior. Last, we provided direct measures of both capital structure theories to support and strengthen our previous findings and understand the financing pattern among SC and SNC firms. However, we finalized our study with a proof-of-concept merely to determine whether the new SC firm sample, filtered based on our proposed *RIEM* methodology, follows a financing pattern common with the Islamic finance principles.

2 Capital Structure Theories and its Determinants

This chapter highlights the main notion of capital structure. It reviews various theories advocated and proposed by academic research to explain companies' financing decisions. This chapter starts with a brief introduction and definition of the capital structure followed by reviewing the development in capital structure theory since Modigliani and Miller's seminal work in 1958 and highlights the leading capital structure theories that have mainly been discussed in the literature. These capital structure theories have been classified into three main categories, namely *tax-based*, *agency cost*, and *asymmetric information and signaling* theories, respectively. The leading theory that considers both taxes and agency costs is the Trade-Off Theory. In contrast, the main theory considering asymmetric information and signaling appears to be the Pecking Order Theory. Finally, with the support of the academic literature and research findings, we discussed the most reliable determinants of capital structure.

2.1 Introduction

How do companies finance their assets/investments? One of the most important questions in Corporate Finance that ultimately influences the capital structure of a company. Myers (2001, p. 81) states, *"The study of capital structure attempts to explain the mix of securities and financing sources used by corporations to finance real investments."* The choice and decision between debt and equity are indisputable facts companies face in practice.

Indeed, the main advantages of debt financing lie in its relative cost compared to equity financing. The main reason why debt financing might be superior to equity financing can be explained by the fact that the cost of debt financing is lower than the cost of equity financing, which is justified mainly due to three reasons. First, the pre-tax rate of interest is consistently lower than the return requested by shareholders (risk premium).[7] This is because of the better legal position of creditors compared to the shareholders. While creditors have a prior claim on the distribution of a company's income, shareholders possess the weakest claim. Moreover, in insolvency, creditors are preferred over common shareholders in the line for the settlement claims. Second, the cost of debt (i.e., paid interest) can be used as a tax shield, leading to a tax advantage.[8] Finally, the costs involved in the administration and issuing debt are generally not as high for equity financing.[9]

7 See Berk and DeMarzo (2014, pp. 479–482).
8 See Berk and DeMarzo (2014, pp. 509–510).
9 See Berk and DeMarzo (2014, p. 824).

https://doi.org/10.1515/9783110713664-002

Given that higher leverage is associated with considerable tax advantages, *why do firms not max-out their debt level and utilize debt more exclusively?* Graham (2000) reports that firm value will increase by up to 7.5% when firms engage in debt financing until the marginal tax benefit starts to decline. Until now, a large number of academic studies in the field of corporate finance have attempted to deal with the issue of how companies should optimally choose their capital structure. However, a comprehensive and consistent capital structure theory that best explains companies' financing decisions remains a puzzle.[10]

Since this book's focus lies in capital structure per se, it is of utmost importance to define what capital structure is all about. In brief, the term "Capital Structure" refers to the combination of different securities (debt, equity, or hybrid) issued by a firm to finance its assets. Firms without debt issues are classified as unleveraged, and firms with debt issues are being leveraged.

Leverage is differentiated further between operational- and financial leverage. The former is related to firms' fixed operating costs and its associated increase in business risk. The latter is related to firms' fixed debt cost and its associated increase in financial risk. Total leverage is then given by a firm's use of both the fixed operating costs and the fixed debt costs, implying that a firm's total risk equals business risk plus financial risk.[11] The term leverage is used in this book to represent financial leverage only.

2.2 Development of Capital Structure Theories

Even though the Modigliani-Miller theorem is considered purely theoretical, the seminal work of Modigliani and Miller (1958, 1963) formed the basis for modern thinking on capital structure. The theorem applies arbitrage arguments and illustrates that the impact of a firm's capital structure decision on firm value becomes irrelevant due to the restrictive assumptions. Specifically, firms do not have to be concerned about their debt or equity financing and instead should emphasize the future cash flows that the assets in place generate.[12]

The authors were able to derive this extreme conclusion only after incorporating a large set of assumptions. Copeland et al. (2005, p. 559) provide a list of the explicit

10 Important academic studies on capital structure theories have contributed to corporate finance after the seminal work of Modigliani and Miller (1958, 1963). For instance, Baker and Wurgler (2002), Fama and French (2002), Frank and Goyal (2008, 2009), Jensen (1986), Jensen and Meckling (1976), Kraus and Litzenberger, (1973), Leland and Pyle, (1977), Myers, (1977, 1984), Myers and Majluf, (1984), Ross, 1977), Shyam-Sunder and Myers (1999), and Welch (2004, 2011).

11 See Brealey et al. (2010) for the treatment of leverage and risk.

12 See Modigliani and Miller (1958, p. 261).

and implicit assumptions that Modigliani and Miller (1958, 1963) have taken. More specifically:
- Capital markets are frictionless.
- Individuals can borrow and lend at the risk-free rate.
- There are no costs to bankruptcy or business disruption.
- Firms only issue two types of claims: risk-free debt and (risky) equity.
- All firms are assumed to be in the same risk class (i.e., operating risk).
- Corporate taxes are the only form of government levy (i.e., there are no wealth taxes on corporations and no personal taxes).
- All cash flow streams are perpetuities (i.e., no growth).
- Corporate insiders and outsiders have the same information (i.e., no signaling opportunities).
- Managers always maximize shareholders' wealth (i.e., no agency costs).
- Operating cash flows are completely unaffected by changes in the capital structure.

Even though their assumptions only hold in a capital market without any market imperfection, MM's Irrelevance Theory can be considered the "beginning" of all persistent capital structure debates. Since many academic studies have emerged and developed several competing theories, in which capital market imperfections were introduced and incorporated, such theories aim to provide evidence that the impact of a firm's capital structure decision on firm value – in reality – does matter.

Several theories have attempted to explain firms' capital structure and find an optimal structure, a mix of internal and external finance (debt, equity, or hybrid) that optimizes a firm's value. In Michaelas et al. (1999), the authors partition the capital structure theory into three categories. These categories are the *tax-based*, the *agency cost*, and the *asymmetric information and signaling* theories.

2.2.1 Tax-based Theories

After introducing the Irrelevance Theorem Modigliani and Miller (1958, 1963), Kraus and Litzenberger (1973) introduced the two basic capital market frictions that strongly impact firms' capital structure decisions. The authors show that firms should trade-off the tax-saving benefits against the financial distress costs associated with too much leveraging.[13] Mackie-Mason (1990) and Graham (1996, 2000) conclude that debt's "tax shield benefit" influences firms' financing decisions.

According to tax-related theories, the primary force influencing firms' capital structure decision is tax and bankruptcy considerations. The amount paid for debt interest provides a tax shield and is generally tax-deductible; consequently, profitable

13 See Kraus and Litzenberger (1973, p. 911).

firms should utilize more debt since it shields a firm's income from taxation. Therefore, tax-paying firms are expected to use debt rather than equity to benefit from the tax savings up to a point in which the probability of financial distress (bankruptcy cost) starts to be important (Michaelas et al., 1999).

Similarly, firms determine their optimal capital structure by weighing the benefits and costs of debt (Fama and French, 2002). The authors further argue that taxes consist of two offsetting effects on optimal capital structure. First, interest payments' tax-deductibility drives firms towards higher target leverage, whereas the higher personal tax rate on debt relative to equity pushes firms towards lower leverage targets. Second, the existence of financial distress costs, which arise, among other reasons, when profitability declines,[14] pushing firms towards lower leverage targets.

2.2.2 Agency Cost Theories

The pioneers of agency cost theory go back to Fama and Miller (1972) and Jensen and Meckling (1976). The authors highlight two types of conflict of interest between different firm stakeholders: the conflict between *managers and shareholders* and the conflict between *debtholders and shareholders*.

Since managers are not the exclusive beneficiaries of the firms' profit (due to the managers' hard work), the conflict between managers and shareholders arises. For instance, instead of returning free cash to shareholders, managers conduct negative net present value (NPV) projects to let the firm become bigger (leading to overinvestment).[15] As a result, as stated in Harris and Raviv (1991), managers prefer to consume more "perquisites" such as corporate jets, plush offices, building "empires", self-interested investments, etc., rather than increasing firm value and shareholders' wealth.

In Stulz (1990), the author shows that the agency conflict between managers and shareholders can also cause underinvestment. Specifically, when free cash is insufficient to utilize all positive NPV projects, the informational asymmetry between managers and shareholders ultimately leads to sub-optimal investments.[16] Since the shareholders cannot value the different investment opportunities fairly, the shareholders never believe management's assertion that cash flow is too low because management always benefits from increasing investment (Stulz, 1990). Therefore, management cannot invest in all the different valuable projects optimally, implying

---

14 Bankruptcy costs are higher for firms with more volatile earnings. For instance, more diversified firms (usually medium-to-large size) have steady earnings than less diversified firms (small-to-low medium size). As such, less diversified firms should drive towards less leverage.

15 See Stulz (1990, p. 4).

16 The underinvestment cost equals the net present value of the profitable investments that have not been undertaken by management. See Stulz (1990, p. 9).

that the firm underinvests. The paper of Stulz (1990) illustrates that managerial discretion comes at two costs. First, an *overinvestment cost* that occurs due to the circumstances that management often engages in self-interested investments. Second, the *underinvestment cost* occurs when the available internal funds prevent management from exhausting positive NPV investment opportunities.

The conflict between debtholders and shareholders arises because debt contracts give shareholders an incentive to invest suboptimally. Specifically, in case if an investment yields higher returns (above the face value of the debt), shareholders are the ones who benefit from this successful investment. In case an investment fails (because of limited liability), debtholders are the ones who bear most of the costs. Harris and Raviv (1991) state that risk-sharing asymmetry triggers debtholders to prefer less risky projects, while the shareholders prefer the opposite, i.e., very risky projects with high returns.

Both conflicts of interest can be mitigated, as stated in, among others, Jensen and Meckling (1976), by trading off the benefits and costs of debt and reaching an optimal capital structure. Jensen and Meckling (1976) argue that debt increases managers' ownership of the firm. Specifically, if a firm is financed continuously through debt, this would imply that the firm relies less on equity. This further implies that the ownership of managers (instead of shareholders) in the firm increases.[17] Consequently, managers will perform in the firm's interest and subsequently benefit more from their "profit improvement activities" than the shareholders. Furthermore, firms with high leverage use free cash to repay their debt obligations. As a result, less cash will be available to managers to engage in activities for their interest. Consequently, a higher debt level increases managers' ownership in the firm and provides managers' commitment to firms' interest.

2.2.3 Asymmetric Information Theories

Managers (insider) do have more information about the true value of the firm and its riskiness. This notion was developed initially by Ross (1977), and the rationale behind it is that due to information asymmetry, firms that issue equity will face underpricing. Myers (1984) and Myers and Majluf (1984) extended the asymmetric information framework. The authors proposed a new model that the managers (i.e., insider) know about the firm's future returns, whereas the investors (i.e., outsider) do not. In this regard, investors' perception towards a firm's high level of debt is positive; hence it explains the firm's preference for debt financing rather than equity financing.

17 The basic assumption here is the existence of a trade-off between managers' and shareholders' ownership. Thus, if the managers' ownership in the firm decreases, consequently, the shareholders' ownership increases, and the other way around.

Furthermore, it signals to investors a firm's ability to fulfill their debt obligations; thus, indicating that a firm's investment will pay off. Additionally, a high level of leverage conveys a positive signal to the market because it implies managers opt for debt when bankruptcy risk is low. Therefore, investors regard firms with a high level of debt as favorable.

Firms' announcement of new equity issues will cause a fall in firms' existing shares' market value.[18] Harris and Raviv (1991) state that internal funds, riskless debt, or both is preferred as there is no undervaluation involved. Furthermore, in Myers (1984), the author shows that firms should use a hierarchical financing decision due to high adverse selection costs. Myers (1984) claims that, in general, firms should give priority to internal funds over external funds. In case the internal funds are fully utilized, debt financing over equity financing should be the hierarchical order. In other words, equity financing should be chosen as a financing means of last resort when all other financing options are exhausted. This financing behavior of the capital structure is known as the Pecking Order Theory.

Above, we have discussed three broad categories of capital structure: *tax-based*, *agency cost*, and *asymmetric information and signaling* theories. The first two categories cannot be treated individually, as they have many factors in common. Both theories attempt to explain the reason why firms use debt in their capital structure. While tax-based theories show the benefit that comes with debt in the form of a tax shield for income, agency cost theories regard debt as a mechanism to mitigate potential conflicts and control managers' behavior. Specifically, both theories promote and favor debt financing and attempt to find suitable justification and explanation for leveraging. With the first two theories, this study focuses on the Trade-Off Theory. In contrast, in the third theory (i.e., asymmetric information and signaling), the focus will mainly revolve around the Pecking Order Theory.

2.3 Trade-Off Theory

The Trade-Off Theory addresses the gap in Irrelevance Theory by combining the impact of the cost (bankruptcy) and the benefits (tax shield) of debt in firms' capital structure decisions. The Trade-Off Theory states that firms can find their optimal leverage ratio (i.e., debt-to-equity) by balancing the debt tax savings benefits against the financial distress costs that arise from bankruptcy risk and agency costs. Jensen and Meckling (1976) and Kraus and Litzenberger (1973) The Trade-Off Theory further can be distinguished between the "*static*"[19] and the "*dynamic*", in which the optimal leverage varies over time due to time-varying determinants. Myers (1984) states that

18 See, among others, Myers and Majluf (1984, p. 203) and Lucas and McDonald (1990, p. 1019).
19 Bradley et al. (1984) and Myers (1984) provide a detailed overview of the static Trade-Off Theory.

firms should adjust their capital structure if the optimal level differs from the target level due to unexpected events. Nevertheless, academic evidence of the Trade-Off Theory is inconclusive. For instance, while some academic studies[20] do not confirm the existence of the Trade-Off Theory, other studies[21] confirm the theory's validity.

2.3.1 Static Trade-Off Theory

Kraus and Litzenberger (1973), one of the pioneers in developing the Trade-Off Theory, showed that optimal capital structure (leverage) reflects a trade-off between the tax benefits of debt and the bankruptcy costs of debt. Other authors such as Baxter (1967), Bradley et al. (1984), DeAngelo and Masulis (1980), Fama and French (2002), Frank and Goyal (2008), Miller (1977), and Shyam-Sunder and Myers (1999), etc. had an extensive contribution to the development of the Trade-Off Theory.

Frank and Goyal (2008, p. 142) state in their study that "*a firm is said to follow the static Trade-Off Theory if the firm's leverage is determined by a single period trade-off between the tax benefits of debt and the deadweight costs of bankruptcy.*" In the same notion, Myers (1984, p. 577) states that "*the firm is supposed to substitute debt for equity, or equity for debt until the value of the firm is maximized.*". Myers (1984) extends his arguments and highlights the difficulty of identifying the tax benefits and financial distress costs' true value.

Among others, J. P. H. Fan et al. (2012) and Frank and Goyal (2009) emphasize that firms should base their financing decision on observable firm-specific determinants such as earnings volatility (business risk) and firms' asset structure. For instance, younger firms with large intangible assets frequently face higher financial distress costs than older and mature firms with tangible assets. Firms use these physical (tangible) assets as collateral. Therefore, according to the static Trade-Off Theory, firms with larger intangible assets should make less use of debt and keep their leverage ratio low. The authors DeAngelo and Masulis (1980), Leland (1994), and Ross (1985) have reported that especially profitable firms with constant cash flows and fixed assets face lower financial distress cost. Consequently, these firms should have utilized more debt financing and increase their leverage ratio to trade-off the tax benefits against the financial distress cost. The static Trade-Off Theory confirms and predicts a negative relationship between earnings volatility (business risk) and leverage.[22] Therefore, it could be argued that firms' capital structure varies among industries since business risk typically differs among industries.[23]

---

20 For instance, Bradley et al. (1984, pp. 857–878).

21 For instance, Trezevant (1992, pp. 1557–1568).

22 See Frank and Goyal (2009) for a detailed overview of the relationship between business risk and leverage.

23 See Matlay (2005, p. 162).

Graham (2000) argues that a firm's value increases due to higher leverage because debt enables the possibility to deduct interest charges and hence raises the incentive for higher leverage to increase tax shields. Therefore, according to the Trade-Off Theory, an optimal debt level that maximizes the firm value does indeed exist when attaining a trade-off as balancing the tax benefits of debt against the cost of financial distress (Figure 2.1). Consequently, it is in each firm's interest to find an optimal balance between internal and external financing. Frank and Goyal (2008) state that firms with target debt level and a deviation from that target if the firm reverts are said to exhibit a so-called *target adjustment behavior.*

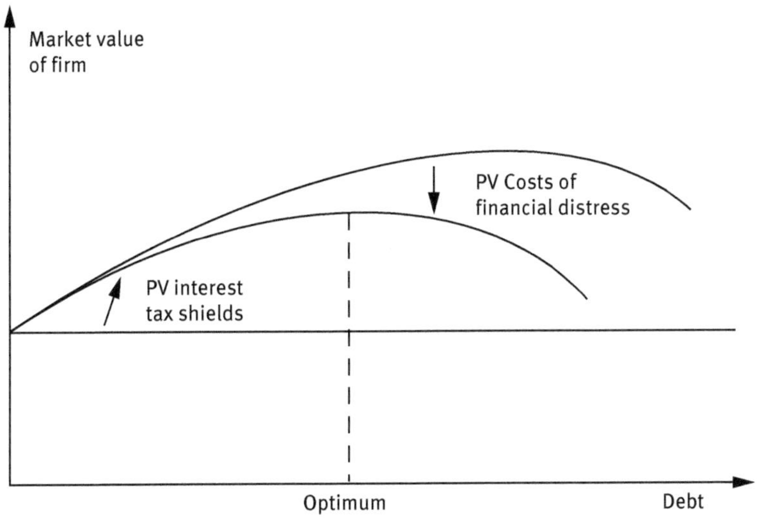

Figure 2.1: The static Trade-Off Theory of Capital Structure.
Source: Myers (1984, p. 577).

2.3.2 Dynamic Trade-Off Theory

In contrast to the static Trade-Off Theory,[24] Myers (1984) describes the dynamic Trade-Off Theory because firms define their specific target leverage and *gradually adjust* their capital structure to that target when deviations (i.e., due to unexpected events) occur.[25] Among others, Brennan and Schwartz (1984) and Kane et al. (1984) developed the first *dynamic* models analyzing continuous-time models considering uncertain-

24 Static Trade-Off Theory states that firms should hold on their pre-defined target leverage all the time to max-out the benefits driven from being at their optimum leverage level.
25 See Myers (1984, p. 585).

ties, taxes, bankruptcy costs, etc. but not transaction costs. These *dynamic* models enable firms to rebalance their capital structure towards their target leverage without considering transaction costs in adverse shocks.

Fischer et al. (1989) introduced a *dynamic* model and show that firms allow their capital structure to have deviated from their target leverage due to transaction costs. In other words, for some time, firms hold to rebalance as long as the adjustment costs (transaction cost) exceed the value lost due to sub-optimal leveraging. In Fischer et al. (1989), the authors suggest that firms have an optimal capital structure range instead of an optimal capital structure (target leverage). They let the capital structure fluctuate. The notion behind this is, as the cost of adjusting within this range is lower than the benefits, firms do adjust their capital structure immediately when sudden deviations in their assets occur. Figure 2.2 illustrates the basic idea behind the dynamic Trade-Off Theory model:

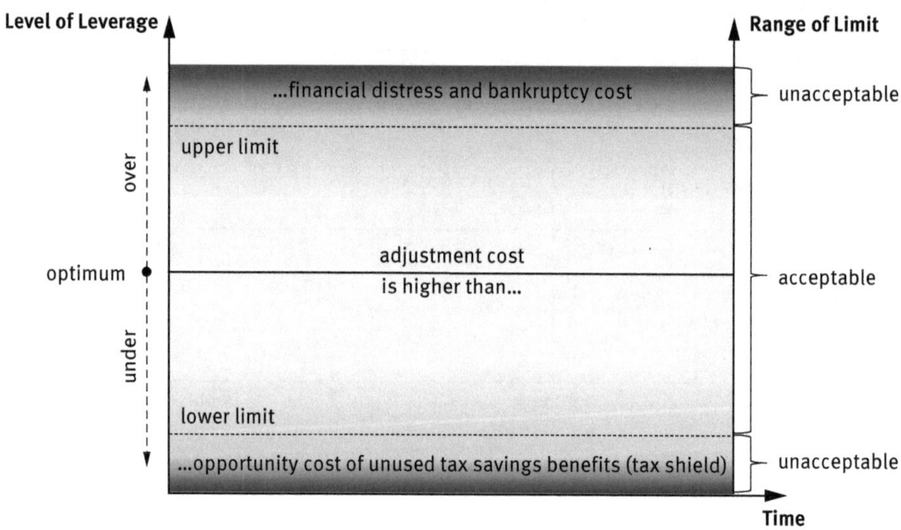

Figure 2.2: The Dynamic Capital Structure with Transaction Costs.
Source: own contribution, in reference to Fischer et al. (1989).

Companies will let their leverage level vary within the range of over-/ and under-leveraged (in other words, within the upper and lower leverage limit), which is represented by the grey shaded area. Within this "acceptable" range, the costs of adjusting the leverage ratio (transaction costs) are higher than the costs that occur of being over-/ underleveraged. If a company is overleveraged, but within the "acceptable" range, the company will not adjust to its target leverage (optimum) as the cost of adjustment is higher than the costs of financial distress and potential bankruptcy. The other way around, if a company is underleveraged but within the "acceptable" range, the company will not adjust to its target leverage (optimum) as the cost of adjustment is higher than the potential tax savings (tax shield). The adjustment cost is below the financial distress and bankruptcy cost and unused tax savings outside the acceptable range. Firms in both "unacceptable" ranges, whether being over-/ or under-leveraged, will actively rebalance their capital structure towards the optimum. This is in line with Frank and Goyal (2008), who analyzed a large panel of data and found that most of the data show firms are not actively rebalancing. This finding could be explained by the existence of transaction costs in the real world.

2.3.3 Review of Earlier Studies on Trade-Off Theory

One of the first papers that attempted to formulate models of optimal capital structure is DeAngelo and Masulis (1980), Fama and French (2002), Frank and Goyal (2008), Miller (1977), Shyam-Sunder and Myers (1999), and Taggart (1977), which show the popularity and the dominance of the Trade-Off Theory among academics. However, at the same time, it was also under severe debate. The notion of the static Trade-Off Theory states that firms should weigh the tax shield benefits of debt against the higher bankruptcy risk costs. Based on this rationale, firms should set their leverage level to its optimum, as shown in Figures 2.1 and 2.2.

Since then, academic studies have emerged that reported contrasting results to the static Trade-Off Theory's main notion. For example, in Myers (1993, p. 83), the author states that "*The most telling evidence against the static trade-off theory is the strong inverse correlation between profitability and financial leverage.*" In Graham (2000, p. 1901), the author states, "*[...] large, liquid, profitable firms with low expected distress costs use debt conservatively.*" In a more recent study by Baker and Wurgler (2002), the authors examine the Market-Timing Theory of capital structure and disapprove of the Trade-Off Theory concept. They claim that "*The trade-off theory predicts that temporary fluctuations in the market-to-book ratio or any other variable should have temporary effects.*"[26] These three quotations confirm that firms do not sufficiently issue debt to max-out the tax shield benefits of debt financing.

In Miller (1977), the author contradicts the Trade-Off Theory's main notion by considering it as one of a horse-and-rabbit stew, in which the horse represents the tax shield, and the rabbit represents the bankruptcy costs. Miller (1977, p. 264) states that "*The supposed trade-off between tax gains and bankruptcy costs looks suspiciously like the recipe for the fabled horse-and-rabbit stew – one horse, one rabbit.*" Miller's message indicates that taxes are large and certain, while bankruptcy is infrequently and has low deadweight costs. Consequently, the author suggests that if the Trade-Off Theory were true, then firms would have much higher debt levels than what is observed in reality.

26 See Baker and Wurgler (2002, p. 3).

Miller's (1977) suggestion finds support by Haugen and Senbet (1978), in which the authors report the insignificance of bankruptcy costs to the main notion of the Trade-Off Theory. Furthermore, Hart and Moore (1995, p. 567) claim that the existing trade-off models "*cannot explain the types of debt claims observed in practice.*" Specifically, trade-off models such as those developed by Fischer et al. (1989) and Titman and Tsyplakov (2006) do not address firms' debt structure. New evidence on the Trade-Off Theory is provided by a more recent study of Sabiwalsky (2010), in which the author applied a non-linear structural equation framework. Sabiwalsky (2010) reports that the optimal capital structure theory is existent and more suitable for small and medium-sized companies. However, Hackbarth et al. (2007) are in line with the Hart and Moore (1995) opinion. They argue that most of the existing trade-off models only analyze the optimal debt level a firm should hold but do not provide any guidance on firms' debt structure.

The sources of debt are either through the market (e.g., a capital bond) or bank (e.g., loans). When firms identify their optimal debt level, the question of HOW much from WHICH of both sources arises. Studies such as H. Fan and Sundaresan (2000) and Mella-Barral (1999) consider both the market debt and bank debt and try to find the optimal debt structure. For instance, Hackbarth et al. (2007) analyze the optimal mixture of market debt and bank debt. The authors report that especially small and young firms should exclusively use bank debt compared to large and mature firms. Larger and mature firms have better access to the market. Hence they should utilize a mix of both the market and bank debt.[27] Among others, De Jong et al. (2008) and Titman and Wessels (1988) find that the amount of market debt utilized by a company increases with its maturity and firm size. In Welch (2011, p. 16), the author refers to the relevance of tax benefit and bankruptcy costs of the optimal capital structure decision and states that the managerial capital structure "*remains largely a mystery.*" The main reason for this mystery is that the first-order friction that provides a counterbalance to the tax shield is almost impossible to identify, limiting the benefits of leverage.

2.3.4 Critical Comments on Trade-Off Theory

In contrast to Modigliani and Miller (1958) Irrelevance Theory, the Trade-Off Theory's objective is to point out the true significance of firms' capital structure decisions. As mentioned above, the Trade-Off Theory incorporates the two market imperfections, which transmits the following simple rationale: Firms should always weigh both tax shield benefits and the bankruptcy costs, which come with debt before making capital structure decisions. This rationale leads firms to find their optimal capital structure, and deviations from this optimal target are temporary.

27 See Hackbarth et al. (2007, p. 1396).

Although the basic notion of the Trade-Off Theory reached many academic proponents, in the beginning,[28] a large number of academic studies were conducted on firms' capital structure, showing that firms do not pursue the basic notion of the Trade-Off Theory.[29] The rationale behind the criticism is, implementing the Trade-Off Theory, in reality, is not an easy task. While the estimation of the tax shield benefits is generally unproblematic, the exact determination of the bankruptcy costs is comparatively unrealistic.

Some academic studies have shown contradicting results in the Trade-Off Theory's basic notion due to its shortcomings. Weigl (2011) highlights these as follows:

i. First, the most critical point that runs against this theory's validity is the negative correlation between profitability and the firm leverage, as shown by most academic findings. The Trade-Off Theory posits a positive relationship between *profitability* and leverage. It is argued that profitable firms can utilize the tax benefits (through increased tax shield) by engaging in massive debt financing as they are exposed to less financial distress. However, academic studies contradict this rationale and report that profitable firms tend to have a higher equity ratio (consequently lower debt ratio) than non-profitable firms.[30]
ii. Second, for instance, historians such as Braudel (1982) report that firms were engaged in debt financing long before corporate income taxes existed. Therefore, corporate income tax cannot explain the use of debt contracts, which was the practice centuries before such taxes had been introduced.[31] For instance, Copeland et al. (2005, p. 594) have reported that US companies' capital structure did not change much after corporate income tax had been implemented. A similar statement is found in Brealey, Myers, and Allen (2010, p. 459), who states, *"Debt ratios today are no higher than they were in the early 1900s when income tax rates were low (or zero)."*

Due to many academic studies contradicting the basic idea of the Trade-Off Theory, it can be concluded that the Trade-Off Theory cannot exclusively determine the capital structure decision of firms.

---

28 It originated with the seminal work of Kraus and Litzenberger (1973), followed by, among others, E. H. Kim (1978), Scott (1976), and Taggart (1977).

29 Criticism of the Trade-Off Theory is made by, for instance, Baker and Wurgler (2002), DeAngelo and Masulis (1980), and Myers (1993).

30 In Section 4.3.2, an overview of academic studies dealing with the effect of various debt determinants (e.g., profitability) on the leverage decision of firms will be provided.

31 See Braudel (1982, p. 385), "*Civilization and Capitalism 15th–18th Century. The Wheels of Commerce.*".

2.4 Pecking Order Theory

As highlighted in Chapter 2.3, the notion of the Trade-Off Theory of capital structure supports and favors debt financing within the category of tax-based and agency cost theories and tries to find a suitable explanation for leveraging. An alternative theory exists, the Pecking Order Theory, which tries to explain firms' financing behavior driven from the notion of asymmetric information and signaling theories.

2.4.1 Basic Notion of Pecking Order Theory

The Pecking Order Theory originates from uncertainty about a given product (performance of an investment). This goes back to the article published by Akerlof (1970). The author discusses the adverse selection problem caused due to the asymmetric information between the sellers and buyers regarding the quality of a given product. Akerlof (1970) illustrates the adverse selection problem using an example of second-hand cars. The idea behind this is that there is a mixed quality of second-hand cars, the good ones (quality) and the bad ones (lemons). When the price between the good and the bad quality cars differs much, e.g., USD 12,000 and USD 4,000, respectively, then the buyers will face the problem of not being able to distinguish the quality between these cars; hence, they are not willing to pay USD 12,000 for any car. In this case, the number of good and bad cars are equal; the buyers are willing to pay USD 8,000 for a car. However, this time, the sellers of the "quality" cars are not willing to sell at this price. Consequently, the buyers get only attracted to the "lemons".[32]

The problem of adverse selection is similarly present in the relationship between the different stakeholders.[33] In general, managers (insider) have more information about its (i.e., firms) true value and riskiness than less-informed investors (outsiders). This imbalance of information might ultimately lead to a mispricing of equity by the market. Therefore, potential investors may have difficulties distinguishing good quality companies from bad (lemons) quality companies. Therefore, potential investors will account for this uncertainty by requiring a higher return rate, making the funding more expensive for the companies. Myers and Majluf (1984) state that such an imbalance of information (as described above) might ultimately lead to an underpricing of the equity. In this way, new shareholders gain more than the net present value (NPV) of a new project, thus will lead to a net loss to the existing shareholders. However, this scenario can even result in companies' decision to reject a new project with positive NPV (underinvestment problem). One way to mitigate the underinvestment problem

32 See the famous article "Market for Lemons" by Akerlof (1970).

33 An overview of the Pecking Order Theory per se and the contributions of Myers to the corporate finance theory can be found in F. Allen and Rajan (2008).

is that companies prefer internal funds (if available), less risky debt, or both. These financial instruments are characterized by not facing any market undervaluation.[34] In contrast to Trade-Off Theory, Pecking Order Theory does not imply that firms' capital structure decision is driven by the notion of target leverage (optimal capital structure), but rather simply based on the firm's willingness to reduce information asymmetry.

Figure 2.3 illustrates the financing hierarchy of the Pecking Order model. This is the basic notion of the Pecking Order Theory as introduced by Myers (1984) and Myers and Majluf (1984) and further developed by Lucas and McDonald (1990).

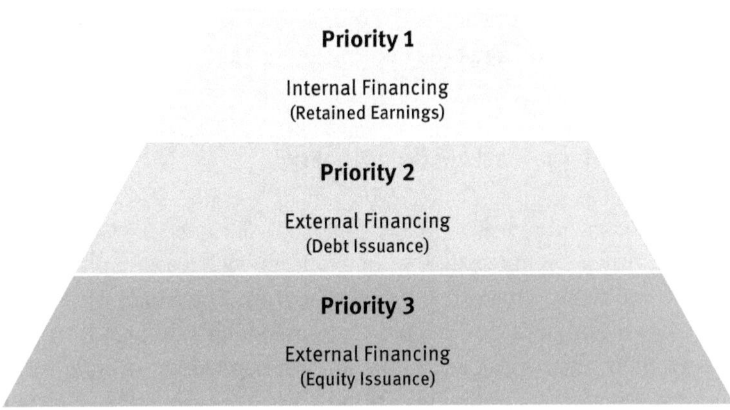

Figure 2.3: Pecking Order of Financing Hierarchy (Stewart Myers).
Source: own contribution, in reference to Myers (1984).

A firm following the Pecking Order Theory prefers internal financing over external financing. If they require external funding, firms will first issue debt, and if further funds are needed, then issue equity.[35] However, looking closer to the financial hierarchy, Pecking Order Theory's prediction about leverage itself is that debt typically grows when investment exceeds internal funds available. The other way around, debt falls when investment falls behind the available internal funds. Fama and French (2002) have tested some qualitative predictions of the Pecking Order Theory. They found that more profitable firms are less leveraged, and this is consistent with the Pecking Order. This is because of such asymmetric information among the firm's stakeholders, i.e., issues of adverse selection or moral hazard.[36] In other words, the main objective of the Pecking Order Theory is to point out that asymmetric information and signaling problems exist between managers and less-informed outside investors. In this order,

34 Additionally, even risky debts (rather than equity) are frequently financed by firms to mitigate the problem associated with asymmetric information.

35 See Myers (1984, p. 9).

36 See Frank and Goyal (2008).

firms tend to exhaust their internal funds first through retained earnings, followed by secured debt, and as a last resort, use riskier equity financing. A financial hierarchy is apparent, demonstrating that when firms face financial deficits (insufficient internal funds), they tend to go further down the pecking order.

Academic studies have shown a negative relation between firms' profitability and leverage, which can be explained by the Pecking Order Theory. According to Brealey et al. (2010), the Pecking Order Theory works best for larger firms because they have better access to capital bond markets, prefer internal financing, and hardly issue equity. The empirical findings for small growth firms compared to large firms seem to be inconsistent. Smaller firms are more likely to rely on equity issuance when external financing is required, which runs against the Pecking Order Theory.[37]

2.4.2 Review of Earlier Studies on Pecking Order Theory

Next to the Trade-Off Theory, the Pecking Order Theory is the most cited and most accepted in explaining firms' capital structure. Its comprehensive assumptions and consequences mainly drive the popularity of both theories. The Trade-Off Theory claims the existence of an optimal target capital structure subject to the advantages and disadvantages of debt financing, i.e., tax shield and bankruptcy costs, respectively. If a firms' leverage level varies from its optimum, management adjusts its debt structure accordingly to revert to its optimal capital structure.

In the following, an overview of the different empirical evidence on the Pecking Order Theory notion will be provided. As mentioned in Section 2.2.3 and Section 2.4.1, the announcement of equity issuance sends out a negative signal to the capital market, leading to an undervaluation of the stock price. In contrast, debt issuance sends out a less negative signal to the capital market, leading to less undervaluation of the stock price. Thus, the less negative signaling effect of debt makes debt financing more favorable compared to equity financing. This is in line with the notion of the Pecking Order Theory. Its validity was shown, for instance, in McDaniel et al. (1994). The authors have shown that firms primarily use internal financing when they need capital for their projects. Only about 20% of the capital is from external financing, with debt playing a more dominant role than equity.

Further, positive results of the Pecking Order Theory have been reported in the literature. For instance, in Shyam-Sunder and Myers (1999), the authors report the validity of the Pecking Order Theory by empirically analyzing 157 US firms during the period 1971–1989. They provide evidence that firms with higher financial deficits issue more debt to increase their leverage ratio. Tong and Green (2005) analyze 47 listed Chinese companies and find that the Pecking Order Theory best explains these

37 See Brealey et al. (2010, p. 463).

firms financing behavior. Furthermore, in Kayhan and Titman (2007), the authors show that firms with higher financial deficits ultimately increase their leverage level. Hence their result supports the essence of the Pecking Order Theory. A more recent study by Lemmon and Zender (2010) finds that companies with excess debt capacity use debt primarily when external financing is required. Bartoloni (2013) supports the Pecking Order Theory as the firms show less indebtedness when operating profitability increases.[38]

On the contrary, the Pecking Order Theory's negative results can be found in the literature as reality also shows equity financing dominance. For instance, Helwege and Liang (1996) analyze firms' financing decisions during the period 1984–1992 and found that firms that access the capital markets do not follow the pecking order when choosing the type of security to offer. Fama and French (2005) find that especially small firms face the most serious asymmetric information problem. The authors analyze firms' financing decisions from 1983–2002; although these small firms still had not utilized their debt capacity, equity was their primary external financing.

Recall, according to the Pecking Order Theory, the most serious asymmetric information problems are faced by small and high growth firms. Therefore, these firms should employ more debt and use a large degree of leverage. However, this contrasts with Barclay et al. (2006) findings, which report that firms with high growth opportunities continuously use less debt financing.[39] The authors Seifert and Gonenc (2008) analyze the validity of the Pecking Order Theory on firms operating in the selected developed countries such as the US, UK, Germany, and Japan. Their result shows equity as the primary external financing in all four countries, which runs against the Pecking Order Theory's basic idea.[40] In Autore and Kovacs (2010), the authors show that firms are more provoked, engaging in equity financing when firms' information asymmetry decreases compared to their recent past. This relation is only valid for firms exposed to high information asymmetry, hence exposed to adverse selection costs. Consequently, they will benefit more when through equity issuance.[41]

In the literature, partial support of the Pecking Order Theory can be found, for instance, in Rajan and Zingales (1995). The authors analyze the cross-sectional relation between firm-specific determinants and debt for multiple countries. The Pecking Order Theory foresees firms with larger asset tangibility that would engage in less debt financing (facing low asymmetric information problems). Consequently, firms with lower tangible assets would engage in more debt. However, the authors find that

38 Other studies such as Aggarwal and Zong (2006), Baskin (1989), Beck et al. (2002), Chaplinsky and Niehaus (1993), L. Chen and Zhao (2005), Cotei and Farhat (2013), D'Mello and Ferris (2000), Daude and Fratzscher (2006), De Jong et al. (2007), and Lin et al. (2008) find evidence for the Pecking Order Theory.

39 See Barclay et al. (2006, p. 37).

40 See Seifert and Gonenc (2008, pp. 252–259).

41 See Autore and Kovacs (2010, pp. 15–18).

firms with fewer tangible assets are, in fact, more involved in equity financing rather than in leveraging.[42]

Jung et al. (1996) report that firm announcements are negative and significant for stocks and insignificant for bonds, aligning with the Pecking Order Theory notion. However, contrary to the Pecking Order Theory, the authors observe that firms with large asymmetric information are indeed engaged more in equity financing. The authors also find an interesting phenomenon that firms with large total assets, being closely followed by financial analysts and face lower asymmetric information, are more likely to issue debt than equity.[43]

Frank and Goyal (2003), in which the authors apply a similar methodology to Shyam-Sunder and Myers (1999) on publicly traded US firms during 1971–1998. The authors find a strong positive relationship between a firm's financial deficit and leverage. This relationship is attributed to rather larger and mature firms, which, by definition, have much lower asymmetric information issues than smaller and younger firms. The differences in both studies can be explained by using firm data of different periods.[44] Consequently, Frank and Goyal's (2003) findings only partially support the Pecking Order Theory notion.

Gaud et al. (2007) analyzed the financing decision of more than 5,000 European firms over 1988–2000 and did not find any supporting evidence for the Pecking Order Theory. Ni and Yu (2008) show a mix of results of the Pecking Order Theory. Specifically, the authors find that while relatively large firms follow a pecking order, small firms do not, which is a contrary finding to Myers (1984). A more recent study of D.-H. Chen et al. (2013) analyze Taiwanese firms' financing decisions over 1990–2005. Their findings do not support the Pecking Order Theory since firms' equity issues track the financing decision more closely than the debt issues. However, D.-H. Chen et al. (2013) find the opposite and confirm that firms in Taiwan prefer debt issuance over equity issuance in the sub-period 2002–2005, which again supports the Pecking Order Theory notion.[45]

42 See Rajan and Zingales (1995, p. 1440).

43 See Jung et al. (1996, pp. 180–182).

44 Before 1990, firm data supports the pecking order hypothesis than firm data after 1990 when many small companies became publicly traded.

45 Other studies also find evidence and mixed results for the Pecking Order Theory. Among others, see D. E. Allen (1993) for Australia, Bontempi (2002) for Italy, Adedeji (2002) for the UK, De Miguel and Pindado (2001) and López-Gracia and Sogorb-Mira (2008) for Spain, Booth et al. (2001) and Mitton (2008) for developing countries, J. J. Chen (2004) for China, Deesomsak et al. (2004) for Asian countries, Drobetz and Fix (2005) for Switzerland, Delcoure (2007) for European countries, Eldomiaty and Ismail (2009) for Egypt, Vasiliou and Daskalakis (2009) for Greece, Sakai (2009) for Japan, Tsuji (2011), and Alves and Francisco (2013) for selected developed and developing countries.

Above, we have shown mixed findings of the validity of the Pecking Order Theory. This accounts for the main problems derived from the asymmetric information among the different stakeholders, i.e., adverse selection or moral hazard.[46]

2.4.3 Critical Comments on Pecking Order Theory

As mentioned above, the agency theory tries to find a mixture of debt and equity financing to mitigate such agency costs. In contrast, the Pecking Order Theory rationale does not arise from a given capital structure, but rather from asymmetric information between managers (insider) and potential investors (outsider).

Pecking Order Theory rejects the idea of a firm's optimal target capital structure. It suggests a flexible approach in which firms can consider structuring their capital at any point in time. In the words of Myers (2001, p. 93), "*Each firm's debt ratio[,] therefore reflects its cumulative requirement for external financing.*" This indicates that the number of investment opportunities with positive NPV and the available cash and securities dictates the capital structure. Consequently, profitable firms with only a few investment opportunities have no benefit of issuing debt, thus keep their leverage ratio low. The more profitable a firm, the more internal funds, aka cash, can be generated. Upcoming investment opportunities can be financed internally that consequently keep their leverage ratio low. Firms with the limited use of external financing can maintain "*financial flexibility*", which is considered one of the most important capital structure determinants, according to Graham and Harvey (2001) study. Empirical studies have shown the firm's preferences for internal financing compared to equity as external financing.[47] For instance, McDaniel et al. (1994) report that around 80% of US firms do not issue equity or issue equity once. Pecking Order Theory also best explains the stock price experience, i.e., price drop when firms announce equity issuance.

Even though the Pecking Order Theory provides answers and explanations for firms' certain financing patterns, it also comes with shortcomings. Weigl (2011) classifies these shortcomings broadly in the following categories:

i. The notion of the Pecking Order Theory assumes that managers act in the interest of the existing shareholders. Consequently, it could be expected that firms progress on optimal capital investment decisions, and the existing shareholders would benefit from greater financial gains. In Myers and Majluf (1984), the authors fail to prove why managers do not aim for firm maximization. Dybvig and Zender (1991) studied that weakness and highlights that firms must choose optimal managerial compensation to boost managers' habits to maximize firm value. As a consequence, agency

46 See Frank and Goyal (2008).
47 See for instance, McDaniel et al. (1994).

problems disappear, and the underinvestment problems[48] of Myers and Majluf will be mitigated.[49]

ii. Another weakness of the theory is its inflexibility on the negative consequences of the asymmetric information problem between managers (insider) and investors (outsiders). Various financing strategies or mechanisms could be developed to overcome such adverse effects.[50] For instance, Fama and French (2005) suggest integrating equity issues to the compensation plan (e.g., employee stock options) or issuing equities to the existing shareholders to maintain the ownership structure and control.[51]
iii. A further weakness of the theory is based on its simplicity. Specifically, the Pecking Order Theory only considers the choice of debt and equity when external financing is required. Ibrahimo and Barros (2009) detected this weakness and developed a capital market model in which the mix of "debt and equity"[52] serves as a financial arrangement.[53] Among others, Brennan and Kraus (1987) test the Pecking Order Theory with more complicated financing settings. They argue that Myers and Majluf's (1984) initial theory does not hold when the financing decision instruments have been extended, for instance, if the firm also chooses between straight- and convertible bonds.
iv. Finally, academic studies cannot fully support the Pecking Order Theory since it is difficult to identify in practice. For instance, as mentioned in Section 2.3.4. the relationship between firms' profitability and leverage is mostly found as being negative. Interestingly, these phenomena lead some academic studies to point out that the most significant capital structure theory explaining firms' financing patterns is the Pecking Order Theory. However, other academic studies found contrasting evidence to the Pecking Order Theory. For instance, Fama and French (2002) show that young firms (especially start-ups) prefer equity over debt financing.

Due to many academic studies contradicting the basic idea of the Pecking Order Theory, it can be concluded that the Pecking Order Theory cannot exclusively determine firms' capital structure decisions.

---

48 See Section 2.2.2.
49 See Dybvig and Zender (1991).
50 For example, firms could issue equities that are less sensitive to information asymmetry and do not send out any adverse signals to investors, such as convertibles or deferred equity.
51 See Fama and French (2005, p. 560).
52 Williamson (1988) shows that an optimal mix of debt and equity, which is termed "dequity", may supersede both debt and equity.
53 For more details, see Ibrahimo and Barros (2009, pp. 473–479).

2.5 Capital Structure Determinants

Despite many academic studies, there is still no agreement among scholars on which determinants are reliably important. Firms generally differ in profitability, growth opportunities, asset structure, operational risk, competitiveness, the country's legal and tax frameworks, etc. Therefore, firms must consider all these factors to remain operative in the current competitive environment. Consequently, firms' capital structure ratio is expected to be *dynamic* and vary between countries, industries, and firm sizes.

In this section, the most relevant determinants that significantly impact firms' capital structure decisions will be discussed briefly, guided by the existing empirical literature.[54] Section 4.3.2 offers an in-depth empirical analysis and hypothesis development on those capital structure determinants that have predictions made by both the Trade-Off Theory and Pecking Order Theory.

2.5.1 Firm-Specific Determinants (Endogenous)

2.5.1.1 Profitability

As mentioned in Section 2.3, profitable firms should utilize the benefits of debt offered through tax shield by increasing their debt level since they are exposed to less financial distress. Accordingly, the Trade-Off Theory predicts a positive relationship between profitability and leverage. This finding is in line with the results of Deesomsak et al. (2009), Delcoure (2007), Graham (2000), Halim et al. (2019), Haron and Ibrahim (2012), and Piaw and Jais (2014a). However, in contrast to the same theory, the *dynamic* version of the Trade-Off Theory argues that existing transaction costs will prevent firms from immediate adjustment to firms' optimal capital structure. Consequently, a negative relationship between leverage and profitability is expected. Furthermore, the Pecking Order Theory predicts a negative relationship between profitability and leverage because profitable firms are associated with a higher amount of internal funds and therefore prevent external financing. This finding has been reported, among others, by Alnori and Alqahtani (2019), Ariff et al. (2008), Cekrezi (2013), Fama and French (2002), Flannery and Rangan (2006), Guney et al. (2011), Kayhan and Titman (2007), Rahim et al. (2020), and Shyam-Sunder and Myers (1999).

2.5.1.2 Growth Opportunity

The more growth opportunities a firm has, the less leverage it applies. Hence, the relationship between growth opportunities of a firm and leverage is negative. This has also been reported and confirmed, for instance, by Alnori and Alqahtani (2019), Ariff

54 The number of various determinants used in academic studies is large. Therefore in this section, we only focus on those most reliable determinants following mostly (Frank and Goyal, 2009).

et al. (2008), Baker and Wurgler (2002), Flannery and Rangan (2006), Ibrahim et al. (2015), Kayo and Kimura (2011), MacKay and Phillips (2005), Mai (2019), Rajan and Zingales (1995), and Shyam-Sunder and Myers (1999). This academic finding seems to support the prediction made by the Trade-Off Theory, which states that firms with large growth opportunities might increase the financial distress costs, which in turn leads to lower leverage. Nevertheless, this prediction stays in contrast to the Pecking Order Theory's basic idea, which states that firms with growth opportunities should utilize external financing in the form of debt (not equity), leading to an increase in firms' debt level. A positive relationship has been confirmed in academic studies such as Akinsomi et al. (2019), Andres et al. (2014), Cheng and Shiu (2007), Deesomsak et al. (2009), Guney et al. (2011), Kremp et al. (1999), Mai (2019).

2.5.1.3 Firm Size

In most academic studies, firm size is found positively related to leverage. Hence, the larger and mature a firm, the more leverage it utilizes. This is in line with the Trade-Off Theory notion, which argues that larger and mature firms are exposed to less bankruptcy risk than smaller and younger firms. Moreover, it is expected that larger and mature firms can provide a sound record of success, which might further help them establish a certain creditability level. Firms with a high creditability level enjoy more top recognition from financial analysts and credit rating agencies, which favors more debt financing.[55] This prediction is in line with the findings of Alnori and Alqahtani (2019), Ariff et al. (2008), Baker and Wurgler (2002), Booth et al. (2001), Cekrezi (2013), Flannery and Rangan (2006), Guney et al. (2011), Hovakimian et al. (2004), Ibrahim et al. (2015), and Rajan and Zingales (1995). In contrast, the Pecking Order Theory argues that especially larger and mature firms are exposed to more monitoring, thus decreases asymmetric information. Consequently, larger firms can issue equity at a lower cost, leading to a decreased level ratio. For instance, Arif and Mai (2020), Chakraborty (2010), Haron and Ibrahim (2012), Rajan and Zingales (1995), Sahudin et al. (2019), and Titman and Wessels (1988) found a negative relationship between firm size and leverage, which support the notion of the Pecking Order Theory.

2.5.1.4 Tangibility

Most studies identified a positive relationship between the tangibility and leverage ratio of a firm. Assets tangibility more often serves as collateral for debt financing, which leads to a decrease in financial distress cost and consequently supports firms in raising more external financing. See, among others, Andres et al. (2014), Arif and Mai

55 In Beck et al. (2008), the authors report the significant role of firm size in firms' financing decisions. Specifically, this study applied a firm-level survey database on an international level covering 48 countries. It proved that small firms and firms in countries with poor institutions are using less external financing and, in particular, less bank financing (i.e., debt).

(2020), Ariff et al. (2008), Baker and Wurgler (2002), Cekrezi (2013), Gajurel (2005), Hanousek and Shamshur (2011), Long and Malitz (1985), Mai (2019), and Rajan and Zingales (1995). They found a positive relationship between tangibility and firm leverage. This is in line with the basic idea of the Trade-Off Theory. On the contrary, Bas et al. (2009), Cheng and Shiu (2007), Graham (2000), Piaw and Jais (2014a), and Sahudin et al. (2019) found a negative relationship between tangibility and leverage, which supports the notion of the Pecking Order Theory. It is argued that tangibility generates fewer information asymmetries between potential investors and shareholders. This leads the firm to prefer equity financing due to a fall in the cost of equity, resulting in lower debt-financing levels.

2.5.1.5 Business Risk (Earnings Volatility)

The Trade-Off Theory assumes that companies with higher risk indicate higher volatility of earnings, which leads to a higher probability of bankruptcy. Frank and Goyal (2009) state that volatility in earnings may limit the probability of fully utilizing the benefits from tax shields, leading to lower debt levels. See, among others, De Jong et al. (2008), Deesomsak et al. (2009), Kremp et al. (1999), Mai (2019), Marsh (1982), Thabet and Hanefah (2014), and Titman and Wessels (1988). As expected, the Pecking Order Theory argues from another angle that higher business risk leads to an increase in leverage. The reason behind is that volatility in earnings will lead investors to require a higher rate of return, making it more expensive to issue equity Ariff et al. (2008), Cekrezi (2013), Deesomsak et al. (2004), Gaud et al. (2005), and Haron and Ibrahim (2012).

2.5.1.6 Research and Development Expenses

The Pecking Order Theory posits R&D expenses correlate positively to firms' leverage. This is mainly explained by the fact that these expenses can better be evaluated by firms' insiders, which leads to adverse selection problems (Frank and Goyal, 2009). A positive relationship is reported in Graham (2000), Halim et al. (2019), and Piaw and Jais (2014b). In contrast, the Trade-Off Theory assumes that outsiders fail to evaluate accurately due to less information availability. Compared with tangible assets, the R&D expenditures (intangible assets) cannot be collateralized, as they are immediately expensed. Therefore, it is expected to observe a negative relationship between R&D expenditures and leverage. This is in line with the findings of Byoun (2008), Dang et al. (2014), Dang and Garrett (2015), Flannery and Rangan (2006), and Frank and Goyal (2009).

2.5.1.7 Tax-related

The tax rate effect on capital structure is two-fold: First, according to the Trade-Off Theory, higher tax rates enable larger tax shield benefits, which attracts debt financing to companies. A positive relationship is expected as higher tax rates lead to an increase in firms' leverage, see among others, Bradley et al. (1984), Dang and Garrett (2015), Delcoure (2007), and Mackie-Mason, (1990). According to Antoniou et al. (2002), this argument only holds if firms have a sufficient amount of taxable income. On the other hand, higher corporate tax rates would result in lower internal funds and a higher cost of capital. As a result, fixed capital formation and demand for external funds would decrease (Kremp et al., 1999). This implies an inverse relationship between the level of debt and the effective tax rate, as reported in Andres et al. (2014); Booth et al. (2001), and Byoun (2008). However, Titman and Wessels (1988), among others, find the insignificant effect of corporate tax on leverage. Due to these complexities, the overall relationship between effective tax rate and leverage remains unclear.

Second, non-debt tax shields (NDTS) stay in stark contrast to the tax benefits of leverage, and consequently, a negative relationship is expected. In DeAngelo and Masulis (1980), the authors argue that firms have less need for tax shield provided through debt financing when many non-debt tax shields already exist. Therefore, the Trade-Off Theory predicts a negative relationship between non-debt tax shields and leverage (Titman and Wessels, 1988). The findings in academic studies such as in Ariff et al. (2008), DeAngelo and Masulis (1980), Deesomsak et al. (2004), González and González (2014), Guney et al. (2011), Haron (2017), Haron and Ibrahim (2012), and Mackie-Mason (1990) support the notion of Trade of Theory.

While the Trade-Off Theory predicts a positive (negative) relationship between tax rates (non-debt tax shield), the Pecking Order Theory does not make any prediction for tax-related determinants.

2.5.1.8 Bankruptcy (Financial Constraints)

The Trade-Off Theory's main notion is the trade-off between the tax benefits of debt (tax shield) and bankruptcy cost (financial distress). The costs of financial distress can offset the tax benefits by issuing debts. Therefore, the Trade-Off Theory predicts a negative relationship between bankruptcy and leverage. In Graham (2000), the author uses Altman's z-score,[56] which implies that firms using less debt can avoid financial distress. This finding is in line with the findings of Byoun (2008), Dang and Garrett (2015), Piaw and Jais (2014b), Ramli and Haron (2017b), Sahudin et al. (2019), and Stöter (2013). Similar to NDTS, Pecking Order Theory does not make any prediction.

---

56 Altman Z-score is a control measure for financial distress/bankruptcy. It uses multiple corporate income and balance sheet values to measure the financial health of a company. Retrieved from: https://en.wikipedia.org/wiki/Altman_Z-score, (accessed July 30, 2020).

2.5.2 Macroeconomic Determinants (Exogenous)

2.5.2.1 GDP Growth

Business activities usually go along with the economic growth of a country. During peak times, companies take opportunities in expansion and investment programs to generate more profits. Academic studies show that the higher the economic growth, the higher the firm's willingness to increase its leverage to finance new projects (De Jong et al., 2008). This is in line with the Trade-Off Theory and supported by the findings of Arif and Mai (2020), Bas et al. (2009), Cekrezi (2013), Hanousek and Shamshur (2011), and Haron et al. (2011). In contrast, Pecking Order Theory postulates that the higher the economic growth, the firms can generate and make use of internal funds, hence makes debt financing unnecessary. The negative relationship between GDP growth and leverage is in line with the findings of Ariff et al. (2008), Cheng and Shiu (2007), Halim et al. (2019), and Piaw and Jais (2014b).

2.5.2.2 Inflation

Cross-sectional studies show that the connection between expected inflation and the level of debt is positive. This positive relationship supports the central notion of the Market-Timing Theory, which predicts that managers will time the market (when inflation is expected) and focus on debt issues; consequently, increase their leverage to pay off the debt in devalued currency. Tax considerations in the Trade-Off Theory make the debt more attractive due to apparent inflation (Frank and Goyal, 2009). However, Piaw and Jais (2014b) argue that companies operating in a highly inflationary environment tend to raise funds via new equity issuance to maintain some flexibility and preserve some unused debt capacity for the future when the business environment declines. Besides, debt contracts generally are stated in the nominal rate. High uncertainty about future inflation may cause firms to avoid long-term debt. Hence, there should be an inverse relationship between the Consumer Price Index and the debt ratio (Hatzinikolaou et al., 2002). This negative prediction is supported in Antoniou et al. (2002), Bas et al. (2009), Cekrezi (2013), Deesomsak et al. (2009), and Ramli and Haron (2017a). Pecking Order Theory does not make any prediction.

2.5.2.3 Interest Rate

The prime lending rate is the basis to calculate the cost of debt that the borrower must pay. That means, as soon the lending rate increases, issuing debt becomes more expensive; thus, a higher lending rate increases the probability of financial distress. The other way around, companies will use more debt if the current interest rate is lower than past interest rates (Barry et al., 2008). Consistent with the shareholders' maximization goal, Antoniou et al. (2008) argued that managers are reluctant to use debt as long-term interest rates are relatively high. Ariff et al. (2008), among others, have found a negative correlation between the interest rate and leverage across distressed and healthy companies. Therefore, in line with the Trade-Off Theory, interest rates are expected to be negatively related to leverage; see Antoniou et al. (2008), Deesomsak et al. (2009), and Haron and Ibrahim (2012). Like Inflation, Pecking Order Theory does not make any prediction.

2.5.2.4 Stock Market Development

Companies' choice of financing is associated with the role of financial market development (Baker and Wurgler, 2002). Companies prefer equity financing rather than debt financing when the stock market's activity increases, which is in the notion of Market-Timing Theory. Demirgüç-Kunt and Maksimovic (1999) study the effects of stock market development on firms' financing choices and conclude that financial market development plays a crucial part in a firm's financing choice. The more developed the stock market, the lower the firms' leverage as the cost of equity is lower. Among others, De Jong et al. (2008), Deesomsak et al. (2009), and Haron et al. (2011) find that there is a significant negative relationship between stock market development and firms' leverage, which is in line with the Trade-Off Theory. Pecking Order Theory does not make any prediction.

2.5.2.5 Debt Market Development

Companies tend to utilize more debt financing as the capital markets focus on debt market development. As mentioned before, as the stock market develops, firms prefer equity financing over debt. Booth et al. (2001) and De Jong et al. (2008) conclude a positive relationship between debt market development and firm leverage. They find that a country with a highly developed debt market will have a higher private-sector debt ratio. Another study by Agarwal and Mohtadi (2004) focusing on financial market development and financing choice of firms in developing countries finds that a developed banking sector (for instance, Germany) is significantly and positively associated with firm leverage. Studies by Booth et al. (2001), De Jong et al. (2008), Haron et al. (2011), Mitton (2008), and Piaw and Jais (2014b) also support the positive relationship between debt market development and firms' leverage, which confirms the prediction made by the Trade-Off Theory. Like Stock Market Development, Pecking Order Theory does not make any prediction as well.

2.5.2.6 Country Governance

For country governance, academic studies such as De Jong et al. (2008), among others, have shown that the legislative and governance setting of a country has a strong effect on debt financing. A recent study with a sample of firms across 45 countries conducted by Cheng and Shiu (2007) found that investor protection plays a vital role in capital structure determinants. Hence, firms in countries with better creditor protection have higher leverage, while firms in countries where shareholder rights are better-protected use more equity funds. Therefore, country governance is positively related to companies' capital structure. As a proxy, Haron and Ibrahim (2012) and Piaw and Jais (2014b) determine country governance according to the average of six World Bank governance indicators (voice and accountability, political stability, government effectiveness, regulatory quality, the rule of law, and control of corruption).[57] Pecking Order Theory does not make any prediction.

2.5.2.7 Industry Median

It is questionable whether or not peer groups might influence the leverage decision of companies. Ronn and Senbet (1995) state that firms' debt structure depends on the industry; firms with low-risk and solvent industries opt for higher leverage while high-risk industries opt for lower leverage. Companies within the same industry are often exposed to joint forces, or in other words, to similar micro-/ and macro conditions. Competition within these industries might prompt companies "to mimic"[58] the capital structure of their competitors. Frank and Goyal (2009) state that managers use industry median leverage as a point of reference within the industry or some kind of target capital structure to which they adjust.[59] Under the Trade-Off Theory, a positive correlation between the industry median leverage and the company's debt level is expected, while the Pecking Order Theory does not make a clear prediction. Empirical findings have shown that companies competing in industries in which the median company has high leverage tend to employ more debt, see Andres et al. (2014), Dang and Garrett (2015), De Jong et al. (2008), Frank and Goyal (2003), Hovakimian et al. (2004), Ramli and Haron (2017b), and Sahudin et al. (2019).

Table 2.1 summarizes the most relevant capital structure determinants (explanatory variables). These results are based on both the Trade-Off Theory and the Pecking Order Theory's theoretical foundations. While the Trade-Off Theory developed its predictions for all the above-listed determinants, Pecking Order Theory's prediction is limited to *profitability*, *growth opportunity*, *firm size*, *tangibility*, *business risk*, and *GDP growth*. The predicted correlation between each determinant and firm leverage is presented in Table 2.1.[60]

57 The six governance indicators are measured in units ranging from about −0.5 to +2.5, with higher values corresponding to better governance outcomes. (source: World Bank database).

58 The positive relationship between industry leverage and firms' leverage is in line with the notion of the capital structure theory called "herding behavior" and "follow the leader" under Corporate Behavioral Finance.

59 For instance, among others, Hovakimian et al. (2004) find that firms adjust their leverage towards the industry median.

60 See, for instance, Frank and Goyal (2009).

Table 2.1: Capital Structure Determinants – Prediction on Leverage.

Determinants	Description	Trade-Off Theory	Pecking Order Theory
Firm-Specific		*Prediction on Leverage*	
Profitability	Return on Assets (ROA)	positive/negative*	negative
Growth Opportunity	Market-to-Book Value	negative	positive
Firm Size	Firm Size (in Sales)	positive	negative
Tangibility	Fixed Assets (Collateral)	positive	negative
Business Risk	Earnings Volatility	negative	positive
R&D Expenses	Research and Development	negative	positive
Tax Rate	Effective Tax Rates	positive	–
NDTS	Non-Debt Tax Shield	negative	–
Bankruptcy	Fin. Distress (Altman Z-Score)	negative	–
Macroeconomic			
GDP	GDP growth (annual %)	positive	negative
Inflation	Consumer Prices (annual %)	positive	–
Interest Rate	Lending Interest Rate (%)	negative	–
Stock Market Dev.	Stock Market Development	negative	–
Debt Market Dev.	Debt/Bond Market Development	positive	–
Country Governance	Govern. Indicator (WorldBank)	positive	–
Industry Leverage	Median Industry Leverage	positive	–

*Dynamic Trade-Off Theory.
Source: own contribution.

2.6 Review of Earlier Capital Structure Studies on Shari'ah Compliant Companies

The classification of firms in being SC and SNC is relatively new. Therefore, studies on the capital structure of especially on SC companies are still limited, and such comprehensive academic studies on this field are still behind in the literature. As of today, only a few studies have focused on the capital structure of SC firms, e.g., Ahmed (2007), Akinsomi et al. (2019), Alnori and Alqahtani (2019), Arif and Mai (2020), Haron et al. (2011), Ibrahim et al. (2015), Rahim et al. (2020), Thabet et al. (2017), and Thabet and Hanefah (2014).

In Sections 2.3 and 2.4, we have discussed the most dominant and influential capital structure theories, namely, Trade-Off Theory and the Pecking Order Theory. Within these theoretical frameworks, Ahmed (2007) suggests that the capital structure of firms operating under the Islamic principle (i.e., Islamic firms) should be very similar to the Pecking Order Theory (see Figure 2.4). Specifically, to seek the least costly financing alternative, these firms should rely on internal financing (retained earnings) over external financing (debt and equity). If the latter is required, firms should first issue debt in the form of *murabahah*,[61] *ijarah*,[62] *salam*,[63] or *istisna*,[64] and

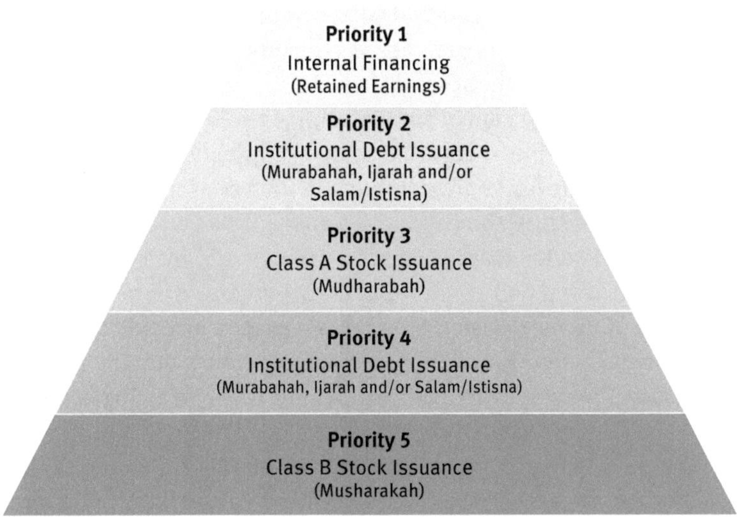

Figure 2.4: Pecking Order of Financing Hierarchy (Habib Ahmed).
Source: own contribution, suggested by Ahmed (2007).

61 *Murabahah/Bay Muajjal:* A *murabahah* contract refers to a sales contract whereby the IFI (Islamic Financial Institutions) sells its customers a specified kind of asset that is already in their possession at an agreed profit margin plus cost (selling price). The cost and profit must be disclosed. See Bacha and Mirakhor (2013, pp. 69–71).

62 *Ijarah:* An *ijarah* contract refers to an agreement made by IFI to lease to its customer for an agreed period against specified installments of ease rental. An *ijarah* contract commences with a promise to lease that is binding on the part of the potential lessee prior to entering the *ijarah* contract. See Bacha and Mirakhor (2013, pp. 69–71).

63 *Salam:* A *salam* contract refers to an agreement to purchase, at a predetermined price, a specified kind of commodity not available with the seller, which is to be delivered on a specified future date in a specified quantity and quality. See Bacha and Mirakhor (2013, pp. 69–71).

64 *Istisna:* An *istisna* contract refers to an agreement to sell to a customer a nonexistent asset, which is to be manufactured or build according to the buyer's specifications and is to be delivered on a specified future date at a predetermined selling price. See Bacha and Mirakhor (2013, pp. 69–71).

finally, issue equity in the form of *mudharabah,*[65] *musharakah,*[66] or both. Ahmed (2007) emphasizes that the firms' debt under Islamic principles must be asset-backed and cannot exceed firms' tangible assets. Consequently, firms with more tangible assets will have a higher debt level, and the other way around, firms with less tangible assets will have a lower debt level.

Haron and Ibrahim (2012) investigate the *dynamic* aspects of the capital structure, looking particularly at the existence of target capital structure, the speed of adjustment, and the determinants of the target capital structure of Shari'ah compliant firms in Malaysia. Contrary to Ahmed's (2007) suggestion, this study confirms the existence of dynamic Trade-Off Theory and finds that certain firm- and country-level determinants significantly affect the target capital structure of Shari'ah compliant firms in Malaysia. The magnitude of the speed of adjustment suggests a rapid adjustment towards firms' optimum target capital structure.

Thabet and Hanefah (2014) investigate the relationship between the determinants of capital structure and leverage to determine the effect of managerial ownership on SC firms' capital structure choice in Malaysia for 2006–2011. The result of this study is consistent with certain capital structure theory and inconsistent with others. For instance, the authors find that profitability, liquidity, and risk have an inverse relationship with SC firms' decision on issuing new debt as predicted by the Pecking Order and Agency Theory. Therefore, the study concludes that the Pecking Order Theory and Agency Theory are predominant in Malaysia's financing behavior and, consequently, reject the Trade-Off Theory.

In Ramli and Haron (2017b), the authors attempt to identify the target capital structure and the speed of adjustment of SC firms listed on Bursa Malaysia (Central Bank of Malaysia), which consistently maintain their Shari'ah compliance status. The authors find that SC firms opt for adjusting towards an optimal capital structure; however, they find evidence for these firms being under-adjusted. Halim et al. (2019) also find support for the Trade-off Theory with the existence of the target debt ratio and significantly fast speed of adjustments in SC firms operating in Malaysia.

---

65 *Mudarabah (or qirad or muqadarah).* A *mudarabah* is a partnership contract in profit between the capital provider and a skilled entrepreneur through contribution whereby the capital provider would contribute capital to an enterprise or activity, which is to be managed by the entrepreneur as the *mudarib* (or labor provider). Profits generated by that enterprise or activity are shared in accordance with the percentage specified in the *mudarabah* agreement, while losses are to borne solely by the capital provider unless the losses are due to the *mudarib's* misconduct, negligence, or breach of contracted terms. (similar to the concept of silent partnership). See Bacha and Mirakhor (2013, pp. 69–71).

66 *Musharakah:* A *musharakah* is a contact between the IFI and a customer to contribute capital to an enterprise (whether existing or new) or ownership of a real estate or moveable asset, either on a temporary or permanent basis. Profits generated by that enterprise or real estate/asset are shared in accordance with a percentage specified in the *musharakah* agreement, while losses are shared in proportion to each partner's share of capital. See Bacha and Mirakhor (2013, pp. 69–71).

In Akinsomi et al. (2019), the authors study the determinants of property firms' capital structure decisions operating in the Gulf Cooperation Council (GCC) countries. Analyzing the quarterly data from 2004–2009 of SC, Islamic, and general property firms,[67] the author concludes that the Pecking Order Theory may explain the capital structure of property firms in GCC. The study shows a negative correlation between profitability and leverage and a positive relationship between growth and leverage; both results support the Pecking Order Theory notion. Furthermore, it concludes that SC firms are more levered, and the Islamic firms are less levered than general property firms. The results of the former firms are inconsistent, while the results of latter firms are consistent. As both types of firms operate under the principles of Shari'ah, it is expected to be less levered than the general property firms, as these firms are not exposed to any debt restriction.

According to the study of Arif and Mai (2020), SC firms operating in Indonesia's manufacturing sector tend to apply the Pecking Order Theory as these firms use retained earnings to develop their capital structure. The authors highlight that the regulation imposed on SC firms forces the management to limit interest-bearing debt.

As of today, and to our best knowledge, only view studies, as mentioned above, have analyzed the capital structure of firms operating under the Shari'ah principles.

2.7 Conclusion

This chapter has discussed and shown the most dominant and influential capital structure theories, namely, Trade-Off Theory and the Pecking Order Theory. Both theories are manifested considering real-life market imperfections such as taxes, bankruptcy costs, transaction costs, agency costs, and asymmetric information.[68] Academic studies have shown that firms' financing decision is greatly influenced by firm-specific (endogenous) and macroeconomic (exogenous) factors. Key determinants shown in Table 2.1 are used by both theories on the racecourse with the same objective to explain the financing behavior of firms best. In other words, the Trade-Off Theory and the Pecking Order Theory are often characterized as the two main competing theories to provide different views and explanations on the firm's leverage decision. Answering the question of which theory best explains firms' financing behavior, the following two citations perfectly fit both theories' different results.

67 Akinsomi et al. (2019) sourced the Shari'ah compliant property firms as listed in the DJIMI. Property firms that appoint an internal Shari'ah board are considered an "Islamic firm". The Shari'ah board, whose responsibility includes ensuring that the firms operate in accordance with the Shari'ah laws. Property firms, not listed in DJIMI and without an internal Shari'ah board, are classified as "general" property firms.

68 See, among others, Hatfield et al. (1994), Jensen and Meckling (1976), Miller (1977), Modigliani and Miller (1963), Myers (1984), and Myers and Majluf (1984).

> *In sum, we identify one scar on the tradeoff model (the negative relation between leverage and profitability), one deep wound on the pecking order (the large equity issues of small low-leverage growth firms), and one area of conflict (the mean reversion of leverage) on which the data speak softly. The many shared predictions of the two models tend to do well in our tests. But when shared predictions are confirmed, attributing causation is elusive: we cannot tell whether the results are due to tradeoff forces, pecking order forces, or indeed other factors overlooked by both.*
>
> Fama and French (2002, p. 31)

> *In short, both the tradeoff model and the pecking order model have serious problems. Thus, it is probably time to stop running empirical horse races between them as stand-alone stories for capital structures. Perhaps it is best to regard the two models as stable[-]mates, with each having elements of truth that help explain some aspects of financing decisions.*
>
> Fama and French (2005, pp. 580–581)

The racecourse continues, and as of today, only a few capital structure literature exists on firms operating under the Shari'ah principles. Therefore, this study aims to fill the gap through a comprehensive analysis with a widening scope, i.e., overall *(pooled)* and cross-section (*country/industry*) analysis, including a comparative examination between Shari'ah compliant and their non-compliant peers.

3 Shari'ah Compliant Equities and Capital Structure

This chapter deals with the methodology applied by various Islamic index providers to distinguish between SC and SNC firms, namely the Shari'ah screening methodology. Since a "decision/judgment" is made in the name of Shari'ah, it is of utmost importance not only to have a robust screening criterion but also to ensure that Shari'ah screening methodologies themselves are compliant with the principles of Shari'ah. After providing a brief historical background, we show the rise and development of the Shari'ah screening methodology and elaborate on the screening criterion set by the Dow Jones Islamic Market Index (DJIMI). From its inception until now, the opinion of Shari'ah scholars differs, let alone supports the aimed standardization. A look behind the scene revealed that all Shari'ah screening methodologies not only have common shortcomings, but some have elements that are non-compliant with Shari'ah intrinsically. In this chapter, we aim to provide evidence derived from the Islamic sources (*Qur'an* and *Sunnah*) and offer a potential solution for the harmonization of Shari'ah screening methodologies.[69] Along with it, we attempt to provide a pecking order-like financing hierarchy to firms interested to operate under Islamic principles. Both solutions support the central notions of Islamic finance and adhere to the essence of the *Qur'an* Surah Al-Baqarah, 2:275.

3.1 Historical Background

As highlighted in Section 1.1, Islamic finance has undergone tremendous growth (in double digit rates) and advancement in the global financial sector over the last few decades. Even though a reduction in the growth is witnessed (about 2% in 2018 compared with 10% in 2017), product-structuring and innovation are in full swing within the Islamic finance industry, focusing on Standardization, Fintech Disruption, and ESG Opportunities.[70] One of the drivers that affect Islamic finance's growth is international stock markets' investment. With increased global awareness, many individual and institutional investors worldwide seek to invest only in stocks compliant with the Shari'ah (i.e., Islamic law). The investment in companies compliant with Islamic laws can be considered a form of ethical and socially responsible investment since investors select their stocks based on their religious beliefs.[71]

---

69 An earlier version of this chapter was published as Yildirim and Ilhan (2018).

70 "Islamic Finance Outlook 2020 Edition" S&P Global Ratings. Retrieved from: https://www.spglobal.com/ratings/en/research/pdf-articles/islamic-finance-outlook-2020-edition, (accessed July 30, 2020).

71 However, the differences between Shari'ah compliant investment from ethical and socially responsible investments were highlighted by Forte and Miglietta (2007). The authors argue that Islamic investments, as faith-based investments, should be excluded from the general grouping of socially responsible investment practices, as they differ in asset allocation and econometric profile.

https://doi.org/10.1515/9783110713664-003

Islam, with Shari'ah as its core, is a religion that guides all aspects of a Muslim. Hence, Muslims' actions are required to be under Islam's teachings, including economic affairs. The idea of "screening" companies before making investments in them is derived from the Shari'ah principle that Muslims should not participate in an activity that does not comply with Islam's teachings.[72]

Muslims worldwide have been seeking the guidance of Shari'ah scholars on the permissibility of investment in stock markets. In practice, however, as Mian (2008) states, it "*[...] has evolved from an informal consultation with a local mosque leader to the development of a methodology approved by renowned religious scholars and used by financial institutions around the globe.*" Mian (2008) continues by stating that "*[...] awareness of potential Muslim investors played an essential role in the development of the Shari'ah screening methodology.*" Prominent Shari'ah scholars, namely, Prof. Salih Tuğ (Turkey), Sheikh Mohammad Al Tayyeb Al Najar (Egypt), and Sheikh Muhammad Taqi Usmani (Pakistan), teamed up in 1987 to find a solution that would allow Muslim investor to own shares of listed companies.[73]

Sheikh Nizam Yaqoubi, who issued the *fatwa*[74] for DJIMI in 1998, is the key player in the area of SC stocks screening. In an interview with Sheikh Nizam Yaqoubi in 2015,[75] he explained the historical motivation, which can be dated back to the 1990s. The dot.com boom attracted many Muslims worldwide to make investments by using their families' wealth to benefit from the economic hype with high returns. Potential Muslim investors around the world inquired about the permissibility of investment in individual stocks. However, Sheikh Nizam Yaqoubi could not respond to all inquiries because the process requires thorough analysis, time and resource allocation, and final judgment for each company. He proposed a general criterion applicable to identifying those operating within the acceptable range of Shari'ah principles (Gamaleldin, 2015).

3.2 Shari'ah Screening Methodology

In recent years, several stock exchanges and financial institutions have established Shari'ah indices to increase Muslim investors' participation. The first Islamic equity

72 See *Shari'ah Screening and Islamic Equity Indices*, by Mian (2008). Retrieved from: http://www.eurekahedge.com/NewsAndEvents/News/687/Shariah_Screening_and_Islamic_Equity_Indices, (accessed July 30, 2020).

73 See *Shari'ah Screening and Islamic Equity Indices*, by Mian (2008). Retrieved from: http://www.eurekahedge.com/NewsAndEvents/News/687/Shariah_Screening_and_Islamic_Equity_Indices, (accessed July 30, 2020).

74 *Fatwa* is a jurisconsult's evidence-based clarification of the Shari'ah ruling in response to a question about a specific issue. See ISRA (2016, p. 903).

75 See Gamaleldin (2015). Unstructured Interview on "*Background of Shariah Compliance Stocks Screening and Purification Fatwa*" with Sheikh Yaqoubi, interview conducted in person by Farid Gamaleldin on 2. February 2015.

index was introduced in Malaysia by RHB Unit Trust Management Bhd in 1996. Following DJIMI[76] in 1999 and relying on the same principles, the Kuala Lumpur Shariah Index and FTSE Islamic Index were launched in the same year, 1999, respectively.[77] Since then, global players introduced their Shari'ah indices, such as Morgan Stanley Capital International World Islamic Index (MSCI) in 2007, Karachi Meezan Index in 2009, and STOXX Europe Islamic Index in 2011.

A recent study of Ho (2015) reviews the Shari'ah screening methodologies of well-known global Islamic financial institutions. The author suggests setting globally acceptable Shari'ah screening methodologies for greater harmonization, which would provide a more precise understanding of Islamic investing, supporting the Islamic finance sector's growing trend. All of the different Shari'ah index provider have in common the aim of identifying the elements that violate the rules and guidelines of Shari'ah law, as contained in the *Qur'an* (considered by Muslims to be the revealed word of God) and the *Sunnah* (the sayings and practices of the Islamic prophet and messenger Muhammad (ﷺ)).[78] Shari'ah law prohibits *riba* (usury/interest), *gharar fahish* (unnecessary/excessive risk, uncertainty), and *maysir* (gambling/speculation), etc. These elements are common and present in many conventional financial activities.

Alhabshi (2008), cited in Adam and Bakar (2014, p. 113), has argued that *"stocks have to be either Shari'ah compliant [SC] or non-compliant [SNC]."* Khatkhatay and Nisar (2007a, p. 47) support this opinion by stating that *"fully Shari'ah compliant equities are extremely rare."* Many academicians have questioned the feasibility of not being involved in SNC activities. Since most countries do have conventional financial institutions, companies are exposed to riba-related activities when dealing with these institutions by default. Donia and Marzban (2008, p. 1) strengthen this argument by stating that *"[...] it is almost impossible to find companies which are not dealing with conventional banks and either earn or pay interest [...]."*[79] As reported by Adam and Bakar (2014, p. 114), *"To overcome this problem, Shariah scholars have agreed on certain acceptable level[s] to which companies can involve in such [non-compliant] practices and outline the steps to purify the sinful earnings."*

---

76 The DJIMI is a subset of Dow Jones Global Indexes (DJGI) group, which includes indexes for 10 economic industries, 20 supersectors, 41 sectors, and 114 subsectors defined by the Dow Jones Global Classification Standard. Information can be retrieved: https://www.spglobal.com/spdji/en/indices/equity/dow-jones-islamic-market-world-index/#overview, (accessed July 30, 2020).

77 See Gamaleldin (2015, p. 19).

78 Primary Sources (*Qur'an* and *Sunnah*): *Qur'an* is the primary source of the Shari'ah upon which all other sources founded their authority. The second source of Shari'ah is the *Sunnah*. The word *Sunnah* literally means a clear path or beaten track. It also refers to the normative practice or an established course of conduct/behavior passed on from generation to generation. Technically, the *Sunnah* is what is narrated from the messenger Muhammad (ﷺ), including his actions, sayings, and tacit approvals. See ISRA (2016, pp. 155–157).

79 See *Identifying Shariah-compliant equities a challenging task*, by Donia and Marzban (2008). Retrieved from: http://ir-media.s3.amazonaws.com/IBTimes_Oct2008.pdf (accessed July 30, 2020).

From the Shari'ah perspective, publicly listed companies are categorized into three groups regarding their operations and transactions: see Gamaleldin (2015)
1. Companies with *permissible operations* and *transactions*
2. Companies with *forbidden operations* and *transactions*
   (see *Qualitative Aspect* in Table 3.1)
3. Companies with *permissible operations* and *directly or indirectly impermissible transactions* (see *Quantitative Aspect* in Table 3.1)

Table 3.1: Dow Jones Islamic Index – Shari'ah Compliance Criteria.

Screening		Definition/Ratio			Threshold
i	*Qualitative Aspect*	Alcohol, tobacco, pork-related products, weapons and defense, conventional financial services[a] (banking, insurance, etc.), entertainment (hotels, casinos/gambling, cinema, pornography, music, etc.)			
ii	*Quantitative Aspect*	– Impermissible Revenue	/	Total Revenue	≤ 5%[b]
		– Interest-Bearing Debt – Cash and Interest-Bearing Securities – Accounts Receivables	/	Market Capitalization (trailing 24-month average)[c]	< 33%

[a] Islamic Banks and Takaful Insurance Companies are excluded.
[b] Maximum tolerable impermissible (Shari'ah non-compliant) income is subject to purification (e.g., donation).
[c] Trailing period was 12–month in 2003 and increased to 24–month in 2011.
Source: own contribution, in reference to DJ Islamic Market Indices Methodology (2020).[80]

Regarding the first and second group of companies, Shari'ah scholars are in full agreement. While the companies' shares in the first group can be owned and traded, the second group's shares cannot. However, concerning the third group of companies, opinions diverge. Most of the Shari'ah scholars permit owning and trading the companies' stocks from the third group,[81] however, subject to the passing of the "Shari'ah screening".

The DJIMI can be considered the pioneer among all Shari'ah indices in the definition and application of Shari'ah screening methodology. The Dow Jones Global Index (DJGI) is the central pool where the stocks are filtered and selected as per Shari'ah criteria. Based on the DJIMI Shari'ah supervisory board, companies' stocks are subject

80 See (Standard and Poor's, 2020) *Dow Jones Islamic Market Indices Methodology*. Retrieved from: https://www.spglobal.com/spdji/en/documents/methodologies/methodology-dj-islamic-market-indices.pdf (accessed July 30, 2020).
81 For more detail, please see (Gamaleldin, 2015, pp. 13–18).

to two primary screening levels, the *qualitative* and *quantitative* screens, to determine the indices' eligibility, as shown in Table 3.1.

i. In qualitative screening, the business operation (sector/industry) of each company is assessed. Companies involved in activities prohibited by Shari'ah law are deemed SNC. Activities generally considered non-compliant include conventional financial services, pork, alcohol, tobacco, weapon, defense, entertainment (including gambling, cinema, and adult entertainment).[82]

   As discussed above, since companies are exposed to riba-related activities by default (due to the current capitalistic-oriented economic and finance system), Shari'ah scholars have set a "tolerance level" of income generated through SNC activities. The respective financial ratio (as a part of qualitative screening) is as follows (and subject to purification): Income from "impermissible" transactions divided by total revenue; must be less than 5%.

ii. After removing companies with non-compliant activities, the remaining companies are screened further for compliance with the pre-determined financial ratios (quantitative screening). These ratios test the level of debt (leverage), cash and interest-bearing securities, and accounts receivables against the threshold determined by the Dow Jones Shari'ah supervisory board. All of the following financial ratios in Table 3.1 must be less than 33%

Companies, which pass all the screening criteria, are classified as SC.

3.3 Critical Comments on Shari'ah Screening Methodology

As mentioned in Section 3.2, the Shari'ah scholars and Shari'ah index providers have defined screening methodologies that can be applied to address Muslim investors' concerns regarding the permissibility of investment in individual stocks. Regularly (e.g., annually, semi-annually, quarterly), Shari'ah index provider apply their screening methodology to each publicly listed company within their index universe to ensure ongoing compliance. Companies classified as SC or SNC, therefore, become "*halal*" or "*haram*" for Muslim investors to invest in, respectively.

The Shari'ah screening results of various Shari'ah index provider may or may not be similar to other Shari'ah index providers. For instance, in Mohd-Sanusi et al. (2015),

82 Although no universal consensus exists among contemporary Shari'ah scholars on the prohibition of tobacco companies, hotels, and the defense industry, most Shari'ah boards have advised against investment in companies involved in these activities. See Standard and Poor's (2020) *Dow Jones Islamic Market Indices Methodology*. Retrieved from: https://www.spglobal.com/spdji/en/documents/methodologies/methodology-dj-islamic-market-indices.pdf (accessed July 30, 2020).

the authors applied the DJIMI criteria to the companies classified as SC based on the Bursa Malaysia criteria. The authors concluded that most of the companies screened as SC under the Shari'ah Advisory Council (SAC) of Bursa Malaysia did not meet DJIMI criteria. The study highlighted the importance of harmonizing the screening criteria and the discrepancies resulting from different screening criteria.[83] Briefly stated, the following criticism has been made relating to the current screening methodologies[84]:

a) Khatkhatay and Nisar (2007b) examined the criteria set by DJIMI in the Bombay Stock Exchange (BSE 500) context. They criticized the use of market capitalization as part of the screening ratios as they consider it not relevant. They proposed using total assets as being more rational. The authors also criticized the absence of a different ratio for interest income and argued that the debt and liquid assets ratio threshold needed to be tightened. The level of receivables was shown to have little relevance.
b) Derigs and Marzban (2008) reviewed major Islamic indices to identify Shari'ah compliant companies. They analyzed the similarities and differences between Islamic index providers and conducted a comparative survey of nine Islamic indices with the ratio thresholds set by each index provider. The authors conclude that a company could be screened as permissible by one index criteria and might be rejected and considered impermissible under another index criterion. The authors addressed the dilemma of having different screening criteria.
c) Htay et al. (2013) examined the criteria set by various indices. They criticized the inconsistency, and that may adversely affect Muslim investors.
d) Sani and Othman (2013) applied Morgan Stanley Capital International (MSCI) screening criteria on Malaysian firms to examine the results with SAC (Securities Commission of Malaysia) criteria. They compared different thresholds used by both providers and the composition of the financial ratio. The authors urged for the harmonization of various screening methodologies.
e) Najib et al. (2014, p. 12) compared the screening criterion of SAC and DJIMI. They highlighted all the differences and inconsistencies and strongly recommended that "*the relevant authority should set a universal standard with clear guidelines and understanding to be applicable to all.*"[85] Similar to Sani and Othman (2013), the authors urge and call for standardization.
f) Zandi et al. (2014) examined the stocks approved by the SAC against the criteria of DJIMI, MSCI, and Standard and Poor's (S&P). The authors recommended adding leverage and liquidity ratio to Malaysian's screening criteria and using total assets instead of market capitalization as in DJIMI and S&P.

83 See Mohd-Sanusi et al. (2015, p. 191).
84 For more details on critical comments from various studies, please see Gamaleldin (2015, pp. 6–10).
85 See Najib et al. (2014, p. 12).

g) In an interview in 2015, Dr. Abdul Hameed El Baaly[86] states that using the *hadith* of "*one-third is big*" is improper analogical reasoning. Sheikh Nizam Yaqoubi's opinion differs from Dr. El Baaly and justifies using it as *istinbath.*[87]
h) Habib and Ahmad (2017) scrutinized the currently applied financial screening ratios' applicability and suggested removing all three financial ratios. The authors proposed two new ratios that aim to control businesses from receiving interest and other impermissible income types and limiting their involvement in paying interest.
i) Saiti and Ahmad (2017) called for a universal model by justifying that newcomers in Islamic stock investment might get confused about which methodology to follow and adapt. Furthermore, they suggest that a standardized and universal model might guide Islamic investment for many living in non-Muslim countries.
j) Raghibi and Oubdi (2020) criticized current methodologies due to their rigid ratios and irrelevant thresholds. The authors highlighted that a universal threshold applied to all companies lacks flexibility and proposed a new threshold based on each industry's optimal capital structure.

It is important to note that this mentioned *hadith* of "*one-third is big*" is unanimously used to justify the 33% criterion set on the quantitative screening level. Several ahadith narrated about the same incident reported in Sahih Muslim, Book 13 *Kitab Al-Wasiyya* (Bequest) No: 3991, 3996, and 3997.[88]

> i. *Amir b. Sa'd reported on the authority of his father (Sa'd b. Abi Waqqas): Allah's Messenger (may peace be upon him) visited me in my illness[,] which brought me near death in the year of Hajjat-ul-Wada' (Farewell Pilgrimage). I said: Allah's Messenger, you can well see the pain with which I am afflicted[,] and I am a man possessing wealth, and there is none to inherit me except only one daughter. Should I give two-thirds of my property as Sadaqa? He said: No. I said: Should I give half (of my property) as Sadaqa? He said: No. He (further) said: Give one-third (in charity)[,] and that is quite enough. To leave your heirs rich is better than to leave them poor, begging from people; that you would never incur an expense seeking therewith the pleasure of Allah, but you would be rewarded therefor, even for a morsel of food that you put in the mouth of your wife. I said: Allah's Messenger. [W]ould I survive my companions? He (the Holy Prophet) said: If you survive them, then do such a deed by means of which you seek the pleasure of Allah, but you would increase in your status (in religion) and prestige;*

86 See Gamaleldin (2015, p. 8).

87 In *fiqh* (Islamic jurisprudence), *istinbath* (domestication) is a well-established and widely applied approach used by a *mujtahid* (a qualified Muslim scholar who performs *ijtihad*). It allows the *mujtahid* to derive *hukm* (Islamic legal ruling) by relying on primary sources, even though these sources' content may be unrelated to the content of the issue being examined. Note: *Istinbath* itself has its legitimation, among other primary sources, from *Qur'an* Surah An-Nisa, 4:83. *Ijtihad* is the intellectual endeavor of a qualified jurist (Muslim scholar) to derive or formulate a rule of law on a matter which is not explicitly found in the *Qur'an* or the *Sunnah*. See ISRA (2016, pp. 904–905).

88 See *Sahih Muslim, Book 13*. Retrieved from: https://sunnah.com/muslim/25 (accessed July 30, 2020).

you may survive so that people would benefit from you, and others would be harmed by you. (The Holy Prophet) further said: Allah, complete for my Companions their migration, and not cause them to turn back upon their heels. Sa'd b. Khaula is, however, unfortunate. Allah's Messenger (may peace be upon him) felt grief for him as he had died in Mecca.

Sahih Muslim, Book 13 *Kitab Al-Wasiyya* No: 3991

ii. *Ibn Sa'd reported his father as saying: Allah's Apostle (may peace be upon him) visited me during my illness. I said: I am willing away the whole of my property. He said: No. I said: Then half? He said: No. I said: Should I will away one-third? He said: Yes, and even one-third is enough.*

Sahih Muslim, Book 13 *Kitab Al-Wasiyya* No: 3996

iii. *Humaid b. 'Abd al-Rahman al-Himyari reported from three of the sons of Sa'd[,] all of whom reported from their father that Allah's Apostle (may peace be upon him) visited Sa'd as he was ill in Mecca. He (Sa'd) wept. He (the Holy Prophet) said: What makes you weep? He said: I am afraid I may die in the land from where I migrated as Sa'd b. Khaula had died. Thereupon Allah's Apostle (may peace be upon him) said: O Allah, grant health to Sa'd. O Allah, grant health to Sad. He repeated it three times. He (Sa'd) said: Allah's Messenger, I own a large property[,] and I have only one daughter as my inheritor. Should I not will away the whole of my property? He (the Holy Prophet) said: No. He said: (Should I not will away) two-thirds of the property? He (the Holy Prophet) said: No. He (Sa'd) (again) said: (Should I not will away) half (of my property)? He said: No. He (Sa'd) said: Then one-third? Thereupon he (the Holy Prophet) said: (Yes), one-third, and one-third is quite substantial. And what you spend as charity from your property is Sadaqa and flour spending on your family is also Sadaqa, and what your wife eats from your property is also Sadaqa, and that you leave your heirs well off (or he said: prosperous) is better than to leave them (poor and) begging from people. He (the Holy Prophet) pointed this with his hands.*

Sahih Muslim, Book 13 *Kitab Al-Wasiyya* No: 3997

3.4 Proposed Solution for Shari'ah Screening Methodology

In Section 3.3, we have referred to the criticism of Shari'ah screening methodologies currently applied by many Islamic index providers and financial institutions globally. Islamic index providers use their screening methodology based on the *fatwa* issued by their Shari'ah supervisory board.[89] Some index providers may share similar selection criteria, while others may have stark differences. In Derigs and Marzban (2008), the authors stress the different definitions of the threshold criteria (as applied in quantitative screens) and conclude that companies screened as compliant by an index criterion might be non-compliant under another index criterion.

In contrast to Derigs and Marzban (2008), among others, Gamaleldin (2015), Khatkhatay and Nisar (2007b), Saiti and Ahmad (2017), and Zandi et al. (2014) criticize the

89 See "*STOXX Europe Islamic Index*" Fatwa as of February 21, 2011. Retrieved from: https://www.stoxx.com/document/Bookmarks/CurrentFactsheets/fatwa.pdf, (accessed July 30, 2020).

different definitions of the ratio per se. They strongly recommend using total assets in the denominator for quantitative screens instead of market capitalization used by DJIMI, S&P, and AAOIFI,[90] etc. In this way, the authors make the same case as that contained in the FTSE Factsheet:

> *Unlike other competitor methodologies, a more conservative approach to Shari'ah compliance is ensured by rating debt ratio limits that are measured as a percentage of total assets, rather than more volatile measures that use 12[-] month trailing market capitalisation. This ensures companies do not pass the screening criteria due to market price fluctuation, allowing the methodology to be less speculative and more in keeping with Shariah principles.*[91]
>
> FTSE Russell Factsheet (2020, p. 2)

Consequently, the number of SC companies fluctuates even within the same index provider over a short period.

We can narrow down all the above-discussed criticism of Shari'ah screening methodologies to two points: the *financial ratio* per se and the *threshold criteria*. In the next two sub-sections, we will first discuss the rationale and the basis for the Shari'ah compliance classification/judgment, then address the two base criticism made on the quantitative screens (e.g., leverage/debt ratio). Our analysis requires us to think *out-of-the-box*, and with an appropriate level of rational interpretation, our approach will lead us in answering RQ 1. Additionally, we will attempt to provide a unique solution that we believe can be used as a foundation for future standardization.

Important Note: We rely on the information provided and derived from Islam's primary sources. There is no reason or necessity to provide scientific proof for the injunctions contained in the *Qur'an* or *Sunnah*.

3.4.1 Shari'ah Compliance (SC) vs. Shari'ah Non-Compliance (SNC): The Judgment per se

One of the most important questions that should be asked in the field of Shari'ah-compliant screening is: *What is the basis behind these compliance screens, and does it achieve justice?* Until now, Islamic index providers provide only their screening methodology, as per the *fatwa* issued by their Shari'ah supervisory board, while

90 AAOIFI stands for Accounting and Auditing Organization for Islamic Financial Institutions, a leading international standard-setting body that serves the global Islamic finance industry. Although its standards are generally non-binding, they have been accepted by many Islamic financial institutions and jurisdictions either on a compulsory or voluntary basis.

91 See *FTSE Global Equity Shariah Index Series*. FTSE Russell Factsheet as of June 30, 2020. Retrieved from: http://www.ftse.com/products/indices/Global-Shariah, (accessed July 30, 2020).

academics apply these screening methodologies to identify SC companies for their research studies. However, both the index provider and many scholars fail to provide the rationale behind these applied criteria satisfactorily. The following statement addresses this issue and builds the bridge to our argument:

> *There are different opinions about such investment as there is no scriptural basis in [the] Qur['] an or Prophet Mohamed (PBUH) traditions regarding investment in stock markets. Contemporary scholars have contributed through exercising analogical reasoning and referring to primary objectives and jurisprudence rules in providing methodologies by which international and locally listed securities are filtered in agreement with Islamic Shari'ah.*
>
> Gamaleldin (2015, p. 2)

In other words, since there is no direct provision from the main sources of Islam regarding investment in stock markets, Shari'ah scholars' (Shari'ah supervisory boards) perform *ijtihad* and issue *fatwa* to provide solutions, relying on the *Maqasid Al-Shari'ah.*[92] Recap: A *fatwa* is a religious decree, edict, opinion, or *judgment* based on scholarly discussions derived from religious sources. As mentioned before, Shari'ah scholars, being the guardians of the Islamic religious sciences, also serve the judicial function as judges and interpreters of Islamic Law. The *hukm* (Islamic legal ruling) issued by the Shari'ah scholars has to ensure fairness and impartiality in the delivery of justice. Next, we cautiously want to demonstrate critical thinking that is not only permissible but encouraged in Islam.[93]

Let's start and straight to the point! The questions arise *Who is the best judge we can learn from? Who assures ultimate justice? Or,* even further, *Who is the owner of The Day of Judgment?* The answer, without any hesitation, is Allah (ﷲ), God in Islam! One of God's names is *Al-Hakam* (The Judge/Arbitrator/All-Decree/Possessor of Authority of Decisions and Judgment). Every Muslim believes that all humankind (without exception) is subject to being judged by God himself on Judgment Day.[94] The *Qur'an*

---

92 *Maqasid Al-Shariah* means literally "the objectives of the Shari'ah" and technically "the deeper meanings and inner aspects of wisdom (*hikam*) considered by the Lawgiver in all or most of the areas and circumstances of legislation". See ISRA (2016, p. 906).

93 See *Does Islam permit critical thinking?* By M. Qasmi, Islamic Research Foundation International, Inc. Retrieved from: http://www.irfi.org/articles/articles_351_400/does_islam_permit_critical_think.htm, (accessed August 1, 2020).

94 All monotheistic religions, e.g., Judaism, Christianity, and Islam, share the doctrine of the "Day of Judgement" in common. For instance, Christianity in the Books of Daniel, Isaiah, and Revelation, it is said *"Then I saw a great white throne and the one who sat on it; the earth and the heaven fled from his presence, and no place was found for them. And I saw the dead, great and small, standing before the throne, and books were opened. Also[,] another book was opened, the book of life. And the dead were judged according to their works, as recorded in the books." See Bible, Revelation (20:11–12).* Retrieved from: https://www.biblegateway.com/passage/?search=Rev+20%3A11%E2%80%9312and-version=NRSV, (accessed August 1, 2020).

and the *Sunnah* evidence this. For this discussion, we limit ourselves to a few *ayat*[95] from the *Qur'an* or *hadith*, which suffice to prove our point:

وَمَا تَكُونُ فِي شَأْنٍ وَمَا تَتْلُو مِنْهُ مِن قُرْآنٍ وَلَا تَعْمَلُونَ مِنْ عَمَلٍ إِلَّا كُنَّا عَلَيْكُمْ شُهُودًا إِذْ تُفِيضُونَ
فِيهِ ۚ وَمَا يَعْزُبُ عَن رَّبِّكَ مِن مِّثْقَالِ ذَرَّةٍ فِي الْأَرْضِ وَلَا فِي السَّمَاءِ وَلَا أَصْغَرَ مِن ذَٰلِكَ وَلَا
أَكْبَرَ إِلَّا فِي كِتَابٍ مُّبِينٍ ○

And thou (Muhammad) art not occupied with any business and thou recitest not a Lecture from this (Scripture), and ye (mankind) perform no act, but We are Witness of you when ye are engaged therein. And not an atom's weight in the earth or in the sky escapeth your Lord, nor what is less than that or greater than that, but it is (written) in a clear Book.

(*Qur'an* Surah Yunus [Jonah], 10:61; translated from Arabic to English by Pickthall)

فَأَمَّا مَنْ أُوتِيَ كِتَابَهُ بِيَمِينِهِ ○ فَسَوْفَ يُحَاسَبُ حِسَابًا يَسِيرًا ○ وَيَنقَلِبُ إِلَىٰ أَهْلِهِ مَسْرُورًا ○
وَأَمَّا مَنْ أُوتِيَ كِتَابَهُ وَرَاءَ ظَهْرِهِ ○ فَسَوْفَ يَدْعُو ثُبُورًا ○

Then whoso is given his account in his right hand. He truly will receive an easy reckoning. And will return unto his folk in joy. But whoso is given his account behind his back, He surely will invoke destruction.

(*Qur'an* Al-Inshiqaq [The Sundering], 84:7–11; translated from Arabic to English by Yusuf Ali)

فَمَن يَعْمَلْ مِثْقَالَ ذَرَّةٍ خَيْرًا يَرَهُ ○ وَمَن يَعْمَلْ مِثْقَالَ ذَرَّةٍ شَرًّا يَرَهُ ○

Then shall anyone who has done an atom's weight of good see it! And anyone who has done an atom's weight of evil shall see it.

(*Qur'an* Az-Zalzala [The Earthquake], 99:7–8; translated from Arabic to English by Yusuf Ali)

The first *ayah* informs us that every single act one performs (*even an "atom" of a thing*), whether good or bad, is recorded in the *Lauh Mahfuzh* (preserved book). Specifically, from a silent whisper to the most audacious act, all deeds during one's life in *dunya* (world), with no exception, are recorded in his/her book (i.e., the book of deeds).

The second *ayah* informs us of a particular procedure on the Day of Resurrection. It says that one will receive his/her book of deeds, and whoever receives it on his/her right hand is considered fortunate. Those who receive it from behind his/her back is set for doom.[96] From the two *ayat*, it is believed that one will take his/her book of deeds to his/her own grave.[97]

---

95 *Ayah/ayah* = verse, (plural form: *Ayat/ayat* = verses), whereby ○ denotes to *End of Ayah.*

96 See *How will the sinful Muslim take his book of deeds on the Day of Resurrection? By* Sheikh Muhammad Saalih Al-Munajjid, *Fatwa*: 52887. Retrieved from: https://islamqa.info/en/52887 (accessed August 1, 2020).

97 Islam is one of the few religions in the world that openly speaks about the hereafter. Muslim parents even pass this undeniable fact to their children in their childhood. For instance, Islam teaches whatever someone possesses (e.g., wealth), everything will be left in this world, except his/her book of deeds.

In the third *ayah*, God informs humankind that everyone is judged based on the values (deeds) written in his/her book. God will then ultimately make His decision on whether someone will enter Jannah (Paradise) or will enter *Jahannam* (Hell). In other words, on the Day of Judgment, God *Al-Hakam* will exercise His judgment based on the values (deeds) recorded in one's book that is generated by one's *irada* (free will), i.e., actions performed within one's control. Consequently, everyone is entirely responsible and accountable for his/her deeds on that day. In the language of Finance or Econometrics, ***God's judgment is based purely on everyone's endogenous factors***. Consequently, we cautiously claim that many Shari'ah scholars have erroneously issued their *fatwas* related to Shari'ah screening by integrating an ***exogenous factor***.

Specifically, Table 3.2 shows the frequently applied financial items in forming the leverage (debt-to-equity) ratio. In Part A, we have divided these items into numerators and denominators, and in Part B, we have classified these items as *endogenous* or *exogenous*. Interestingly, all of these financial items, **except for market capitalization**, are classified as *endogenous*. Short-term debt, long-term debt, total debt, total liabilities, book debt, total assets, total capital, and total equity are *endogenous* and, therefore, within the company's control. In other words, each of these factors is the result of companies' management performance (i.e., actions and decisions made by their executives) and are (under normal circumstances) annually recorded in their accounting books; the so-called book values.

Table 3.2: Overview of financial items frequently used on leverage ratios.

Part A: Financial items applied*		**Part B: Financial items classified**		**Part C: Dow Jones Islamic Index**
Numerator	**Denominator**	**Endogenous**	**Exogenous**	**Leverage Ratio**
Short-Term Debt	Total Assets	Short-Term Debt	***Market Capitalization***	Total Debt/***Market Capitalization***
Long-Term Debt	Total Capital	Long-Term Debt		
Total Debt	Total Equity	Total Debt		
Total Liabilities	Market Capitalization	Total Liabilities		
		Total Assets		
		Total Capital		
		Total Equity		

* not limited to.
Source: own contribution.

In Part C, one notes that market capitalization, an *exogenous factor* that is not within the company's control, has been applied in the debt-to-equity ratio in the Shari'ah screens of Dow Jones.[98] Any change in the market values may change the leverage

98 Financial institutions such as S&P, Al-Rajhi, AAOIFI, STOXX, and others also apply market capitalization in their Shari'ah Screening Methodology.

ratio without any active changes in its debt or equity structure. More specifically, when a company's market capitalization value varies, its leverage ratios vary by default. Since there is a 33% threshold on debt ratio, companies may cross this threshold (restriction) by coincident without any financing decisions or actions taken by their senior management. Consequently, these companies suddenly would be classified as SNC (see the criticized points listed in Section 3.3).

Conventional finance literature provides the pros and cons of the book-/ and market value of leverage. Briefly, it is argued that book leverage is past-oriented and is influenced by the firm's choice of selecting an accounting method. In contrast, market leverage is future-oriented and better reflect the intrinsic firm value. Even though market capitalization is subject to high volatility and impacts Shari'ah screening results, proponents of using market capitalization in the denominator, such as Sheikh Nizam Yaqoubi, argue that in the case a company's assets and liabilities are valued at market value, it should equate market capitalization value.[99]

As stated in Section 3.2., the purpose of applying a Shari'ah screening methodology is to judge and classify companies as either SC or SNC. As the *Qur'an* teaches us, the most righteous and fair judgment is when only *endogenous factors* are applied. In other words, to align with Islamic principles and *Maqasid Al-Shari'ah*, the Shari'ah supervisory board has to consider in their *fatwas* only factors that are entirely in each company's control. Consequently, the application of *exogenous factors* as a part of Shari'ah screens is injustice per se. Shari'ah scholars (those who are the proponents of using *exogenous factors*) can adopt the "*endogenous* factors" approach in their quantitative screens on all ratios, including the leverage ratio.

We are not against, nor decline, nor reject the concept of market values of leverage in corporate finance. We even think it is an important measure that should run parallel with the book value of leverage (e.g., comparative purposes). However, in terms of classifying/judging companies from an Islamic perspective *(i.e., into SC or SNC)*, as elucidated in the derivation process above, we strongly suggest using book values (e.g., retrieved from the balance sheet items).

3.4.2 The Ratio and Threshold Criterion

In Section 3.4.1, we have addressed the long-lasting discussion in the literature about total assets vs. market capitalization value used in the Shari'ah screens. We have shown that all screening ratios must consist of "*endogenous*" values to align with Islamic principles. Consequently, consideration only can be given to the financial items recorded in companies' financial statements, e.g., the balance sheet. For the

99 See Gamaleldin (2015, p. 32). Interview on "*Background of Shariah Compliance Stocks Screening and Purification Fatwa*" with Sheikh Yaqoubi, conducted in person by Farid Gamaleldin on 2. February 2015.

Table 3.3: Simplified Balance Sheet.

Balance Sheet	
	non-interest-bearing
	interest-bearing
	Total Liabilities
	Total Equity
Total Assets	**Total Liability and Equity**

Source: own contribution.

sake of our approach, we have simplified the balance sheet in Table 3.3 for demonstration purposes. As a general accounting rule, the left side (total assets) and the right side (total liabilities and total equity) must balance out. In other words, a company has to finance its total assets (which they own) either through liabilities (which they owe), equity (own capital provided), or a mix of both. We have further divided the total liabilities into interest- and non-interest-bearing liabilities.

In the following discussion, we ask, *What is the rationale behind these ratios and their threshold?* The answer to this question ultimately will influence the results of the Shari'ah screens applied to companies. Referring to the previous argument that there is no direct provision from the Islamic sources regarding stock investments, Shari'ah scholars use the "*one-third is big*" *hadith* to justify the 33% threshold criteria set on the quantitative screening. However, the financial screening criterion consists of two parts – the *ratio* per se and the *threshold*. The ratio further consists of a numerator and denominator. Current Shari'ah screens have unanimously and implicitly accepted to apply *negative screening* using total debt (i.e., interest-bearing debt) in the numerator (see Table 3.4), and variations only exist in the denominator and the threshold criteria. As stated earlier, the criticism focuses mainly on two points, except the criticism of Dr. El-Baaly. He even goes beyond the ordinary criticism and states that relying on this "*one-third is big*" *hadith* as a justification for the Shari'ah screens is improper by itself. On the contrary, Sheikh Yaqoubi justifies using this *hadith* as *istinbath* (domestication) (see Section 3.3). In the same line of thought, we think *out-of-the-box* and address these common issues differently.

Straight to the point! *Which primary source of Islamic could potentially support the application of the Shari'ah screens?* Since neither the *Qur'an* nor the *ahadith* offer direct provision regarding stock investments, we thus rely on and analyze the same "*one-third is big*" *hadith*. Our findings are promising, as we have found a "provision", which leads us to derive a new screening solution. Not only do our findings respond to all existing points of criticism, but Shari'ah scholars can even apply our proposed solution as a framework for further development towards the standardization of the current Shari'ah screening methodologies. We have divided the process of analyzing the *hadith* narrated in Sahih Muslim, Book 13 *Kitab Al-Wasiyya* No: 3996, into three steps.

Ibn Sa'd reported his father [Ibn Waqqas] as saying: Allah's Apostle (may peace be upon him) visited me during my illness. I said: I am willing away [sadaqah] ***the whole of my property****. He said: No. I said: Then half? He said: No. I said: Should I will away one-third?* ***He said: Yes, and even one-third is enough.***

a. In the first step, we have read the *hadith* ***as-is*** (i.e., literally). The following implication took our attention: It is clear that this *hadith* is related to a personal (i.e., individual) affair and not related to any business or governmental affairs. Furthermore, the expression *"the whole of my property"* indicates something that Ibn Waqqas possessed, i.e., physical assets, cash, etc. As pointed in Section 3.4.1, we only consider financial items recorded in companies' balance sheets. Therefore, we raise the question: *Would his "whole property" closely represent today's total value of assets or equity?* Before answering this question, the next question is: *What if Ibn Waqqas had debt?* With the highest certainty, we can conclude the following:
   i. His debt was not interest-based.
   ii. Ibn Waqqas would have already considered paying off all his debt before approaching the Messenger (ﷺ) with such a request.
   iii. The Messenger (ﷺ) would have requested that he seeks his freedom first by paying ALL of his debt[100] before giving any *sadaqah* (charity).

   We conclude that Muhammad's (ﷺ) judgment, reported in the *hadith*, was based on Ibn Waqqas' total value of equity.[101] Consequently, this *hadith* could be interpreted, by relying on the direction highlighted in Section 3.4.1, that this judgment undoubtedly was based on the "book value".
b. In the second step, we have read the *hadith* ***as-is*** (i.e., literally) again. The following implication took our attention: As mentioned in Section 3.4.1, Islamic index providers have used the maximum threshold criterion of 33% by relying on this *hadith* as a justification (note that the name "*one-third is big*" is derived from the last statement of this *hadith*). In *fiqh* (Islamic jurisprudence), from this *hadith,* it is interpreted that the minimal portion (subset) of the full entity (set) cannot exceed 33.33%. The critical question here arises *What represents the full entity (set) in firms' financials?* The Shari'ah scholars' opinion differs as some Islamic index providers considered *total assets*, *market capitalization*, or both as the full entity (set). Table 3.4 provides an overview of the leverage ratio and its threshold used by the major Islamic index provider and financial institutions. It is interesting to

100 "Freedom from liability is a fundamental principle." see Majallah Al-Ahkam Article 8. Retrieved from: http://legal.pipa.ps/files/server/ENG%20Ottoman%20Majalle%20(Civil%20Law).pdf (accessed August 1, 2020).
101 In the absence of total liability, total equity equals total assets.

observe that all leverage screens are based on the *minimal* portion[102] principle. Furthermore, it is notable how one-third has been interpreted and implemented as ranging from 30%–37%.

There are two significant reasons for us to declare and use either *total assets* or *total equity* as the "full entity". Again, as pointed in Section 3.4.1, we only consider financial items recorded in companies' balance sheets. Furthermore, as Mian (2014, p. 44) stated, "*Market capitalization does not give the true value of the company. It rather reflects, [...], the market sentiments [...] due to factors that are totally unconnected to the company (e.g., the poor performance of another company in the same industry sector).*"[103]

Table 3.4: Leverage criteria applied in Shari'ah screening methodologies.

Islamic Index (Provider)	Numerator	Denominator	Threshold
FTSE	Total Debt	Total Assets	<33.33%
KSE Meezan	Total Debt	Total Assets	<37%
Malaysia SC	Total Debt	Total Assets	<33%
MSCI	Total Debt	Total Assets	<30%
AAOIFI	Total Debt	Market Capitalization	<30%
Al-Rajhi	Total Debt	Market Capitalization	<30%
Borsa Istanbul	Total Debt	Market Capitalization	<30%
Dow Jones	Total Debt	24–month trailing Market Capitalization	<33%
S&P	Total Debt	36–month trailing Market Capitalization	<33%
STOXX*	Total Debt	Market Capitalization/Total Assets	<33%

* STOXX denominator considers both, Total Assets or Market Capitalization (whichever is greater).[104]
Islamic index providers are listed alphabetically within Total Assets/Market Capitalization classes.
Source: own compilation, from the information available on the websites of each index provider

c. In the third step, we have read the *hadith* ***not as-is*** (i.e., not literally) to find a spiritual understanding of this narration. The content of this *hadith* is about the inner meaning of giving *sadaqah*. Charity is a highly preached act of worship that is emphasized and encouraged in Islam. It is not clear how this *hadith* got associated with something entirely discouraged in Islam, i.e., debt. We partially agree with both the criticism by Dr. El Baaly and the interpretation of Sheikh

102 Here, the minimal portion (subset) principle is set on forbidden elements by the Shari'ah scholars, namely interest-bearing debt.

103 See *IFRS 13 Fair Value Measurement*, in IFRS Standards. This standard requires firms fair value measurements or disclosures. In other words, firms are required/strongly encouraged to adjust their total assets annually, reflecting the company's intrinsic value (fair value) better. Retrieved from: http://www.ifrs.org/IFRSs/Pages/IFRS.aspx (accessed August 1, 2020).

104 See "*STOXX Europe Islamic Index*" Fatwa as of February 21, 2011. Retrieved from: https://www.stoxx.com/document/Bookmarks/CurrentFactsheets/fatwa.pdf, (accessed July 30, 2020).

Nizam Yaqoubi. Since no direct provision from the *Qur'an* nor the *ahadith* exists, Shari'ah scholars have no other choice but to rely on a source that can be taken as *istinbath* (domestication), as Sheikh Yaqoubi has termed it. However, applying the *hadith*, narrated in Sahih Muslim in Book 13 *Kitab Al-Wasiyya* No: 3996, as *istinbath*, should not be limited to its last statement only (such in the case of existing Shari'ah screenings, see Table 3.4). Rather we recommend deriving as much as valuable information from it. Supporting this suggestion and looking at the current Shari'ah screening ratio with its threshold criteria, we disagree with how this hadith has been applied.

The *Qur'an* says:

الَّذِينَ يَأْكُلُونَ الرِّبَا لَا يَقُومُونَ إِلَّا كَمَا يَقُومُ الَّذِي يَتَخَبَّطُهُ الشَّيْطَانُ مِنَ الْمَسِّ ۚ ذَٰلِكَ بِأَنَّهُمْ قَالُوا إِنَّمَا
الْبَيْعُ مِثْلُ الرِّبَا ۗ **وَأَحَلَّ اللَّهُ الْبَيْعَ** وَحَرَّمَ الرِّبَا ۚ فَمَن جَاءَهُ مَوْعِظَةٌ مِّن رَّبِّهِ فَانتَهَىٰ فَلَهُ مَا سَلَفَ
وَأَمْرُهُ إِلَى اللَّهِ ۖ وَمَنْ عَادَ فَأُولَٰئِكَ أَصْحَابُ النَّارِ ۖ هُمْ فِيهَا خَالِدُونَ ۝

Those who devour usury will not stand except as stand one whom the Evil one by his touch Hath driven to madness. That is because they say: "Trade is like usury," but Allah hath ***permitted trade*** *and forbidden usury. Those who after receiving direction from their Lord, desist, shall be pardoned for the past; their case is for Allah (to judge), but those who repeat (The offence) are companions of the Fire: They will abide therein (for ever).*

(*Qur'an* Surah Al-Baqarah [The Cow], 2:275; translated from Arabic to English by Yusuf Ali)

This *ayah* is the basis of the entire Islamic financial system. It comes with two provisions:

i. First, it approves and legalizes direct engagement in exchange and trade ***(al-bay)*** while encouraging risk-sharing and equity-based transactions (investment operations) such as *mudharabah* and *musharakah* and promotes entrepreneurship ***(bold)***.
ii. Second, it disapproves and prohibits the payment or receipt of interest *(ar-riba/usury)* and the involvement in any interest-related transactions *(grey-colored)*.

There are two approaches that the Islamic financial system (including its financial instruments, screening methodologies, procedures, goods, and services, etc.) can derive and adopt from this *ayah*. Either promote equity-based and risk-sharing instruments (such as *Mudharabah* and *Musharakah*) or demote usury and interest-based instruments. Figure 3.1 illustrates the potential impact of using risk-sharing instruments on debt-based instruments.

The bottom line is that the more Islamic finance promotes and implements equity-based instruments, the lesser room will be available for debt-based instruments. Consequently, the power of interest, which is the conventional financial system's primary tool, will eventually diminish over time. Enhancing the line of thought, all Islamic financial instruments, including screening methodologies, procedures,

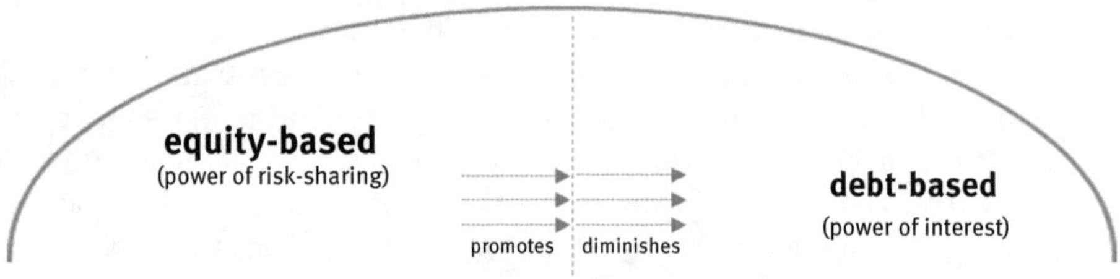

Figure 3.1: Impact of promoting equity-based instruments on interest-based instruments. Source: own contribution.

goods, and services, should primarily aim to reflect the higher purpose of the first provision of this the *ayah*, i.e., promoting *al-bay*. Consequently, to support the notion of Islamic finance and adhere to this *ayah*'s essence, we positively frame the Shari'ah compliance criteria that necessarily reflect the Islamic ideology. As supported by Tversky and Kahneman (1981), framing is an important factor affecting human decisions' perception and behavior (i.e., investment decision).

Since our principal purpose is to promote risk-sharing-based financing behavior, i.e., equity-based financing, we focus on exploring this hadith's inner meaning by understanding the *hikmah* (wisdom) provided in the longer version of this *hadith*. After Muhammad (ﷺ) rejected his companions request twice, he finally permitted to give away one-third as a maximum. But *Why did he reject in the first place?* In the longer version of the *hadith* (Sahih Muslim, Book 13 *Kitab Al-Wasiyya* No: 3997 and 3991, see Section 3.3), he explained *"to leave your[the] heirs rich is better"* and indicated that it is better to *keep one's property/wealth/equity* for his wellbeing and that of his family members, instead of depriving them in favor of non-family members. Therefore, we emphasize the converse statement, i.e., *keep a minimum of two-thirds* rather than *give a maximum of one-third.*[105]

Next, we attempt to derive a ratio that potentially serves as a screening criterion. We want to highlight that we mimic the current practice by relying on the same *hadith* applying *istinbath* (domestication). Let's start! First, we have to define the *denominator*, and for this, we need to understand and decide *What represents the full entity (set) in firms' financials?* Let's go back to the *hadith*. It is all about *wasiyya* (bequest) or charity, which can be given only from one's equity. Another way around, one cannot give away something from what he/she does not own. We have two perspectives to approach and answer that question:

i. From an *individual* perspective, it is clear that he/she can give a maximum of *one-third* only from equity after deducting all outstanding debts/liabilities. Consequently, the denominator has to be total equity *TE*. The *hikmah* lies in *keeping*

105 Our approach is two-fold: First, it allows us to utilize the direct statement made by the Messenger (ﷺ) that can be extracted from the more extended version of this *hadith*. Second, it allows us to adhere more to the inner meaning of this *hadith*.

a minimum of two-thirds of the wealth (i.e., pure equity) as a protective measure for the heir, from which we derive the necessary threshold measure. So far, this assumption can be expressed as:

$$\frac{x}{TE} \geq \frac{2}{3} \qquad \text{SC(1)}$$

Since we have both the denominator and the threshold defined, the criticality lies in identifying the respective numerator, indicated here as x. Now, we need to subtract an element that reflects the *giveaway*, and at the same time, assures a leftover (for the heirs), call it *pure equity*. We suggest that the element needs to be subtracted from the total equity per se and propose two options, as shown in the equations SC(2) and SC(3), and with this, we continue with an exploratory approach. In the first option, we deduct only the interest-bearing debts, and in the second option, the total liabilities from the total equity. The former is defined as the sum of all interest-bearing short-term debt and long-term debt, i.e., total debt *TD*. This form of debt is *haram* (forbidden) in Islam. The latter, i.e., total liabilities *TL*, equals total debt *TD* and all non-interest-bearing debt, which is highly discouraged in Islam.

$$\frac{TE - TD}{TE} \geq \frac{2}{3} \qquad \text{SC(2)}$$

$$TE \geq 3TD \qquad \text{SC(2')} \ \textit{(simplified)}$$

The equation SC(2) reflects the *giveaway* portion only on the element that is absolutely *haram*. In this case, the "heirs" would partially pay off their debt (i.e., only interest-bearing debt) and ignore the non-interest-bearing debt. By not controlling for the non-interest-bearing debt, using this ratio as part of the screening would allow firms to comply and pass Shari'ah compliance by ensuring that its total equity *TE* is at least three times higher than its interest-bearing debts *TD*. We believe that this option would not support the notion of Islamic Finance since companies have an alternative to equity, which is non-interest-bearing debt. Table 3.7 represents the non-interest-bearing debt of the DJIMI SC firms. It is interesting to observe that some SC firms passed the screening, although they are highly indebted (see maximum percentile values).

The second option is straightforward. As discussed earlier, the preliminary step before any *giveaway* is that one must pay off all debts/liabilities entirely in the first place. In equation SC(3), we have replaced *TD* with *TL*, i.e., total liability. Thus, following the famous *"one-third is big" hadith*, analyzing it from an individual perspective, using analogical reasoning, and applying it to a corporate structure, we derive *Total Equity over Total Assets* ≥75% as the ratio derived in SC(3‴). This ratio exists and is known as the equity ratio.

$$\frac{TE-TL}{TE}\geq\frac{2}{3} \qquad \text{SC(3)}$$

$$TE\geq 3TL \qquad \text{SC(3')} \; (\textit{simplified})$$

$$TE\geq 3(TA-TE) \qquad \text{SC(3'')} \; (\textit{substituted})$$
$$TL = \textit{Total Assets minus Total Equity } (TA-TE)$$

$$\frac{TE}{TA}\geq\frac{3}{4} \qquad \text{SC(3''')} \; (\textit{simplified})$$

ii. From an *institutional* perspective, if we refer to a company as an artificial being (a judicial person or legal entity), its assets can be considered its property. In this case, the denominator has to be *total assets* as the total assets represent the full entity (set) of firms' financials. Consequently, and analogically, we transmit this protective measure to the company's heirs, i.e., shareholders, by *applying a minimum of two-thirds* of shareholders' wealth as a threshold. Thus, this assumption can be expressed directly as:

$$\frac{TE}{TA}\geq\frac{2}{3} \qquad \text{SC(4)}$$

Both perspectives, *individual* and *institutional*, let us derive equity ratios with different threshold values, as illustrated in Table 3.5.

Table 3.5: Proposed Index Screening Methodologies (one-criterion approach).

Screening Type	Equation	Ratio	Threshold
Strict	SC(3‴)	***TE / TA***	**≥75%**
Lenient	SC(4)	***TE / TA***	**≥66.67%**

Source: own contribution.

If the Shari'ah scholars prefer to control the *haram* element (as the current practice), they might introduce an additional criterion, e.g., SC(2′), as shown in Table 3.6. Specifically, after applying the SC(4), SC(2′) can serve as a secondary criterion. This way, firms have to keep a minimum of 66.67% *TE* and a maximum of 33.33% *TD* compared to their *TE*. Any form of (re-)structuring and combinations are possible as long as it is appropriately, i.e., Islamically, justified. It is up to the individual index provider to add additional criteria for instance, to control interest-bearing or non-interest-bearing debt as long as they assure that firms hold a minimum amount of equity in their capital structure in the first place.[106] (see Tables 3.5 and 3.6, *grey-colored*)

Table 3.6: Proposed Index Screening Methodologies (two-criterion approach).

Screening Type	Equation	Ratio		Threshold
Moderate	SC(4)	I	***TE / TA***	**≥66.67%**
	SC(2′)	II	***TD / TE***	**≤33.33%**

Source: own contribution.

We believe that all screening types represented in Tables 3.5 and 3.6 can serve in Shari'ah screening. They are practical, especially when introducing screenings for various countries or industries, as the universally applied ratios do not consider country/industry-specific requirements. For instance, depending on the relative proportion of finance channeled through banks or markets, countries and their financial systems are often classified as being bank-based or market-based. In bank-based financial systems, banks are the main driver of capital allocation and investment. In contrast, in a market-based financial system, equity capital markets are equally (or more) significant than banks for transferring the necessary funding towards firms. The application of strict screening type, i.e., SC(3‴), is deemed more appropriate in market-based countries such as the US, UK, or Canada since firms have better access to their well-developed equity markets. On the other hand, to ease the burden of firms operating in bank-based countries such as Japan and Germany, which have already established historically strong relationships with their home banks, the lenient screening type would be more appropriate, i.e., SC(4).

As far as industry-specific requirements are concerned, capital-intensive industries such as Oil and Gas, Automobile, or Telecommunications require a significant amount of financial resources to establish their infrastructure and produce goods or services. For companies operating in these industries, the lenient screening criteria would be more appropriate, i.e., SC(4). Another way around, companies operating in less capital-intensive industries (e.g., Technology), the strict screening type would be more appropriate, i.e., SC(3‴).

Next, taking the lenient type of our methodology, i.e., SC(4), we want to illustrate its impact on SC companies' capital structure. The proposed solution's application ensures the following capital structure, as shown in Figure 3.2. Intuitively, we believe it is closer to what we would have expected in the first place. That is, with the

106 In the case equation SC(3‴) is applied, the two-criterion approach becomes obsolete, because the criterion of SC(2′) is by default fulfilled.

Figure 3.2: Future SC companies' capital structure (simplified and demonstrative purposes). Source: own contribution

minimum threshold of 66.67% of equity, SC companies have to consider equity-based financing as a higher priority rather than debt-based financing.

Every company's source of funds is either through interest-bearing debt, non-interest-bearing debt, or equity. Welch (2011) states that for the average publicly-traded company, both the interest-bearing and non-interest-bearing debt almost equal in amount.[107] With the non-interest-bearing debt (which is not prohibited by Islam), the room in engaging in interest-bearing debt will be less for companies by default. The proposed solution further ensures that we can implement an instrument that is itself Shari'ah compliant by adhering to the essence of the *ayah* (*Qur'an* Surah Al-Baqarah, 2:275). Furthermore, it supports the Islamic financial system's notion since we have derived the ratio and its threshold through this given "*one-third is big*" *hadith*.

Figure 3.3 attempts to illustrate the impact of the currently applied Shari'ah screens on the current DJ SC companies' capital structure. Considering and controlling only interest-bearing debt in the Shari'ah screening methodologies sounds reasonable; however, as illustrated in Figure 3.3, companies also utilize non-interest-bearing debt to finance their assets approximately in the same amount. Hence, they can increase their non-interest-bearing debt (which is not prohibited but discouraged by Islam) without any limitation. Table 3.7 shows the mean values of the non-interest-bearing debt of the DJ SC companies and supports our arguments. Replacing the "xx.xx%" in Figure 3.3 with the mean values (*let alone with the maximum values*) reveals that companies can pass the Shari'ah screens even despite being highly indebted, as long as their interest-bearing debt level is within the maximum threshold of 33%. Along the same line of thought, the next question arises: *What would be left for equity financing*?

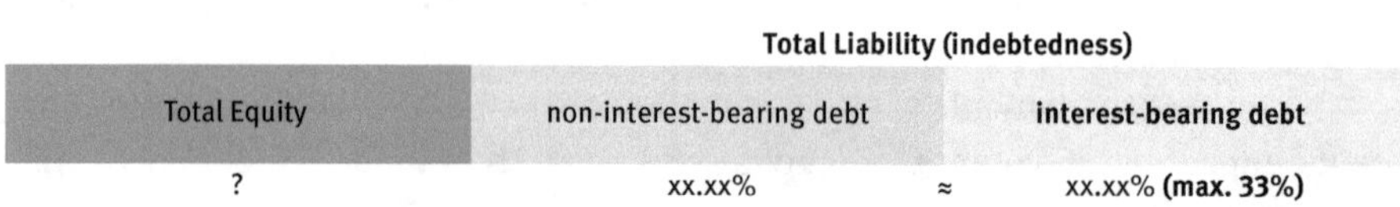

Figure 3.3: Current SC companies' capital structure (simplified and demonstrative purposes). Source: own contribution

107 See Welch (2011, p. 4).

Table 3.7: Descriptive Statistics for Non-Interest-Bearing Debt of SC companies.[108]

Non-Interest-Bearing Debt*	Mean	Std.Dev	Min	Max	Obs
Overall	0.296	0.123	0.078	0.687	6618
United States	0.300	0.123	0.078	0.687	3518
United Kingdom	0.352	0.124	0.078	0.687	606
Canada	0.251	0.103	0.078	0.680	441
Japan	0.267	0.093	0.078	0.594	931
South Korea	0.259	0.095	0.078	0.548	217
Taiwan	0.229	0.132	0.078	0.687	263
India	0.331	0.142	0.078	0.687	642
Oil and Gas	0.283	0.107	0.078	0.669	556
Basic Materials	0.248	0.104	0.078	0.588	527
Industrials	0.332	0.136	0.078	0.687	1668
Consumer Goods	0.315	0.109	0.078	0.687	1150
Technology	0.273	0.130	0.078	0.687	1089
Health Care	0.244	0.100	0.078	0.664	867
Consumer Services	0.322	0.112	0.078	0.687	761

** whereby, Non-Interest-Bearing Debt = (Total Liabilities – Total Debt**)/Total Assets*
*** whereby, Total Debt = Short-Term Debt + Long-Term Debt (all interest-bearing debt)*
Source: own contribution.

One could plausibly finalize the Shari'ah screens' ratio by adding Total Liability in the numerator and using the one-third as threshold criteria, which would finally lead to Total Liability over Total Assets ≤ 33.33%. However, since we suggest drawing attention to the equity financing for the reasons mentioned above, the ratio should be equity-oriented with having Total Equity in the numerator rather than any debt-oriented element (see Table 3.4 vs. Tables 3.5/3.6). We follow the suggestions made by Tversky and Kahneman (1981) and "frame" the proposed criterion for *positive screening.*

In this section, we have attempted to address our RQ 1 and found strong evidence from the *Qur'an* that most righteous and fair judgment exists when "endogenous factors" are considered in the screening criterion. Furthermore, we have highlighted the importance of implementing a tool (i.e., Shari'ah screening methodology) that supports the notion of Islamic finance and emphasizes the integration of equity-based rather than debt-based concept. Hence RQ 1 cannot be affirmed. In the following section, we propose a revised version of the currently applied Shari'ah screening methodology.

108 This table shows the mean values of the variable non-interest-bearing debt of the Dow Jones SC firms operating in seven countries and seven industries for the period 2004–2014. The variable is winsorized at the 1% and 99% level.

3.4.3 *RIEM* Methodology (Revised Shari'ah Screening Methodology)

Earlier in this section, we have pointed out that providing a unique solution can be used as a foundation for standardization. Bearing in mind to have an Islamic financial stock market in which the activities are entirely in compliance with Shari'ah, as stated by Sheikh Yaqoubi,[109] we propose ***RIEM (Ramy Islamic Equity Market)*** **methodology** with *RIEM 75, RIEM 66-33, and RIEM 66 stock indices.*

Similar to the current practice, companies' stocks are subject to two primary screening levels, *qualitative* and *quantitative*, as represented in Table 3.8.

Table 3.8: Proposed *RIEM* (Ramy Islamic Equity Market) Methodologies.

<table>
<tr><th colspan="2">Islamic Stock Indices</th><th colspan="2">RIEM 75 Index ●(*)</th><th colspan="2">RIEM 66-33 Index ●(**)</th><th colspan="2">RIEM 66 Index ●(*)</th></tr>
<tr><td colspan="2">Index Classes</td><td colspan="2">Class A</td><td colspan="2">Class B</td><td colspan="2">Class C</td></tr>
<tr><td colspan="2">Screening Type</td><td colspan="2">strict</td><td colspan="2">moderate</td><td colspan="2">lenient</td></tr>
<tr><td>i</td><td>Qualitative Aspect</td><td colspan="6">Alcohol, tobacco, pork-related products, weapons and defense, conventional financial services (banking, insurance, etc.)[a], entertainment (hotels, casinos/gambling, cinema, pornography, music, etc.)</td></tr>
<tr><td rowspan="3">ii</td><td rowspan="3">Quantitative Aspect</td><td colspan="6">Impermissible Revenue/Total Revenue ≤ 5%[b]</td></tr>
<tr><td rowspan="2">I</td><td rowspan="2">TE/TA ≥ 75%</td><td>I</td><td>TE/TA ≥ 66.67%</td><td rowspan="2">I</td><td rowspan="2">TE/TA ≥ 66.67%</td></tr>
<tr><td>II</td><td>TD/TE ≤ 33.33%</td></tr>
</table>

● *(proposed name)* (*) *one-criterion approach* (**) *two-criterion approach*
[a] Islamic Banking and Takaful Insurance Companies are excluded.
[b] Maximum tolerable impermissible (Shari'ah non-compliant) income is subject to purification (e.g., donation).
Source: own contribution.

i. *Qualitative:* In the first screens, each company's business operation (industry/sector) is assessed. Companies involved in activities prohibited by Shari'ah law are deemed SNC. Furthermore, income generated through SNC activities, companies should be controlled with the threshold-criterion *impermissible revenue* divided by *total revenue* less than 5% and subject to purification.
Rationale: The unlawful income criterion is meant to ensure that any impermissible income is limited, whether generated through interest or other prohibited activities. As mentioned in Section 3.2, firms are exposed to riba-related activities by default. However, it is not allowed, to any extent, to benefit from the

109 See Gamaleldin (2015, p. 32). Interview on "*Background of Shariah Compliance Stocks Screening and Purification Fatwa*" with Sheikh Yaqoubi, conducted in person by Farid Gamaleldin on 2. February 2015.

impermissible income.[110] Thus it should be donated to charitable activities as a part of their income purification activities, but not to be used in paying taxes, alms, advertising, etc.[111] There is no Islamic rationale for the set threshold-criterion of 5% for impermissible income.[112] Consequently, we adopt the common practice applied in current Shari'ah screening and purification methodologies and rely on the definitions and suggestions of the Shari'ah scholars. Similarly, we rely on the Shari'ah scholars regarding the qualitative screens on the rationale that Muslims are commanded to participate in good things and to work for righteousness (*Qur'an* Surah Al-Mu'Minun, 23:51). According to Muhammad's (ﷺ) companion Abdullah ibn Masud, the Messenger (ﷺ) once remarked: "*It is Obligatory to seek to earn Halal after other Obligatory observations, i.e., Prayers, etc.*"[113] The industries and their products and services mentioned in Section 3.2 have been specifically prohibited in Islamic teaching (in *Qur'an* Surah Al-Baqarah, 2:168 and 2:275, *Qur'an* Surah Al-Maida, 5:90, etc.).

ii. *Quantitative:* After passing the first screens, the companies are further screened for compliance with the pre-determined financial ratio set in the proposed *RIEM XX Index* to test the level of equity. (The rationale for this has been set out in previous Sections 3.4.1 and 3.4.2).

The formation of investment portfolios from common stocks of listed companies could be sufficient with two basic criteria: *legitimate economic activity and active participation in risk-sharing activities.*[114] Specifically, to pass the screening process, companies must engage in producing legitimate goods and services. Furthermore, companies should actively engage in equity financing to keep equity dominant in their capital structure.[115]

110 See *Shari'ah Standard No. (21) Financial Paper (Shares and Bonds)*, AAOIFI Shari'ah Standards (2017, pp. 564–565). Retrieved from: https://aaoifi.com/shariaa-standards/?lang=en#., (accessed August 2, 2020).

111 See Gamaleldin (2015, p. 21), (refers to the criterion set by Al Rajhi Bank Shariah Board *Fatwa* numbers 53/1990, 182/1994, 310/1998 and 485/2001).

112 AAOIFI does not provide Shari'ah justification for the 30% for their (financial) screens, nor the 5% benchmark. See *Shari'ah Standard No. (21) Financial Paper (Shares and Bonds)*, in AAOIFI Shari'ah Standards (2017, pp. 572–579). Retrieved from: https://aaoifi.com/shariaa-standards/?lang=en#., (accessed August 2, 2020).

113 See *Earning Halal in Islam*, by Khan (2010, p. 2), (further referring to *hadith* reported in Sunan Al-Baihaqi, 6:126). Retrieved from http://pragmaticwealth.net/KnowledgeCentre/PDF/EarningHalal inIslam.pdf, (accessed August 4, 2020).

114 See "*Risk-sharing in Finance: The Islamic Finance Alternative*", Askari et al. (2012) The authors emphasize the role of vibrant stock markets for the success of risk-sharing and equity finance and further consider the stock markets as a fundamental driver of Islamic finance.

115 Since a company's shares represent equity rights in its assets, the assets should be ideally in the form of "real assets" as they can be sold freely at a profit like real assets (e.g., tangible goods, real estate, and machinery).

Table 3.9 represents the future projections and outlook of the *RIEM* methodology compared with the leading Islamic index provider. We ranked each provider (including *RIEM*) in index classes to better understand their Shari'ah compliance level. Shari'ah index classes range from A to E, whereby Class A represents the most Shari'ah compliance. In this sub-section, we highlighted the importance of implementing a screening methodology that supports the notion of Islamic finance and emphasizes the integration of equity-based rather than debt-based concept. It is evident that indices based on the *RIEM* methodology are equity-driven and ensure full Shari'ah compliance by yielding a firm capital structure with equity ranging from a minimum of 66.67% and above; hence, rank in Class C, Class B, and Class A, respectively. All other Islamic index providers with debt-driven indices are represented consequently in Class D and Class E.

Table 3.9: Projections/Classifications of the Islamic Stock Market Indices.

Index Classes	Islamic Index (Provider)		Numerator	Denominator	Threshold
Class A	RIEM 75		Total Equity	Total Assets	≥75%
Class B	RIEM 66-33[(*)]	I	Total Equity	Total Assets	≥66.67%
		II	Total Debt	Total Equity	≤33.33%
Class C	RIEM 66		Total Equity	Total Assets	≥66.67%
Class D	FTSE		Total Debt	Total Assets	<33.33%
	KSE Meezan		Total Debt	Total Assets	<37%
	Malaysia SC		Total Debt	Total Assets	<33%
	MSCI		Total Debt	Total Assets	<30%
Class E	AAOIFI		Total Debt	Market Capitalization	<30%
	Al-Rajhi		Total Debt	Market Capitalization	<30%
	Borsa Istanbul		Total Debt	Market Capitalization	<30%
	Dow Jones		Total Debt	24–month trailing Market Capitalization	<33%
	S&P		Total Debt	36–month trailing Market Capitalization	<33%
	STOXX[(**)]		Total Debt	Market Capitalization/Total Assets	<33%

Source: Own compilation from the documentation available on the websites of each index provider.
[(*)] two-criterion approach.
[(**)] STOXX denominator considers both Total Assets or Market Capitalization (whichever is greater).
Note: Islamic index providers within the same class are listed alphabetically; hence they are not ranked.
Source: own contribution.

The application of the proposed *RIEM Indices* is two-fold, either complementary to the existing Islamic indices or substitute of the current screening methodologies. In the former case, i.e., co-existence, the minimum investments for an investor would be Shari'ah stocks from classes D and E; however, with the inspiration, these (individual/

institutional) investors aim to move up the latter towards Class A to ensure most Shari'ah compliance. With the aim to offer investors better awareness and confidence regarding Shari'ah compliance in stock investments, we believe *RIEM* methodology with its *RIEM 75, RIEM 66-33,* and *RIEM 66 Indices* are practical and straightforward, and foremost all three are fully justified from the Shari'ah perspective.

3.4.4 The Journey towards *Islamic Firms*

In general, all screening criteria, including our proposed solution, aim to identify whether a company's stock can be obtained or traded from an Islamic investors/ investment perspective.[116] However, if the screening methodologies' ultimate goal is to identify whether firms are fully operating with Islamic principles (maybe to be called *Islamic firms* analogy to *Islamic banks*), next to the pre-defined financial ratios, other factors in a holistic framework are inevitable. In other words, to identify firms in terms of being *Islamic*, the following eight additional screening factors are suggested for consideration (not limited to):

I. *Shari'ah Board*: Firms should establish similar to Islamic financial institutions or Islamic REITs in GCC, a supervisory and consultative function, as a part of corporate governance.
II. *Certification*: Firms should obtain "*Halal*" and other related certificates (if available) for the goods and services they offer.
III. *Processes*: Firms should implement and standardize their business processes (including workflows) according to AAOIFI and/or other globally accepted Shari'ah and Accounting standards, where applicable, supported by IT.
IV. *Governance*: Firms should implement a holistic Enterprise Risk Management framework, including Governance, Risk and Compliance (GRC), ensuring compliance with the local and international statutory requirements.
V. *Marketing*: Firms should adhere to the principles of Islamic Marketing in marketing and related activities.
VI. *HCM*: Firms should adhere to the principles of Islamic Human Capital Management in HR-related activities such as planning, recruitment, selection, orientation, performance appraisal, training and development, compensations and benefits, and career development.
VII. *Reputation*: Firms should ensure to have a good image and positive perception by the public and that the core activities of the company realize "*Maslaha*"

116 As far as cash and receivable ratios are concerned, Habib and Ahmad (2017, p. 163) state "*[...] that since cash and receivables are subordinate to a principal asset which is non-cash and non-debt in nature, their amount should not be restricted by any percentage.*" We agree with the authors and consider both cash and receivable ratios as irrelevant for Shari'ah screening.

(benefit) to the Muslim *ummah* (people) and the community in general (for instance, as practiced in Kuala Lumpur Shari'ah Index).

VIII. *Sustainability*: Firms should incorporate and improve with environmental, social, and governance issues (ESG) as a part of sustainability standards (e.g., Principles for Responsible Investment (PRI).[117]

3.5 *Islamic Pecking Order* Model (Financing Hierarchy)

In Islam, since there would be no interest in the tax-shield and similar benefits, an analogy to the first MM Preposition (see Section 2.2), whether firms finance through debt or equity, becomes irrelevant. However, since Islam does not emphasize and promote any form of debt (interest or non-interest-bearing debt), the preference is given to equity financing. In line with these arguments, it is essential to define a financing hierarchy that serves as a guide in making financing decisions and, at the same time, supports firms that are interested in operating under the Shari'ah principles (Islamic law). Figure 3.4 illustrates the proposed financing hierarchy that reflects the Islamic alternative and resembles the conventional Pecking Order model and the financing hierarchy illustrated in Section 2.6.

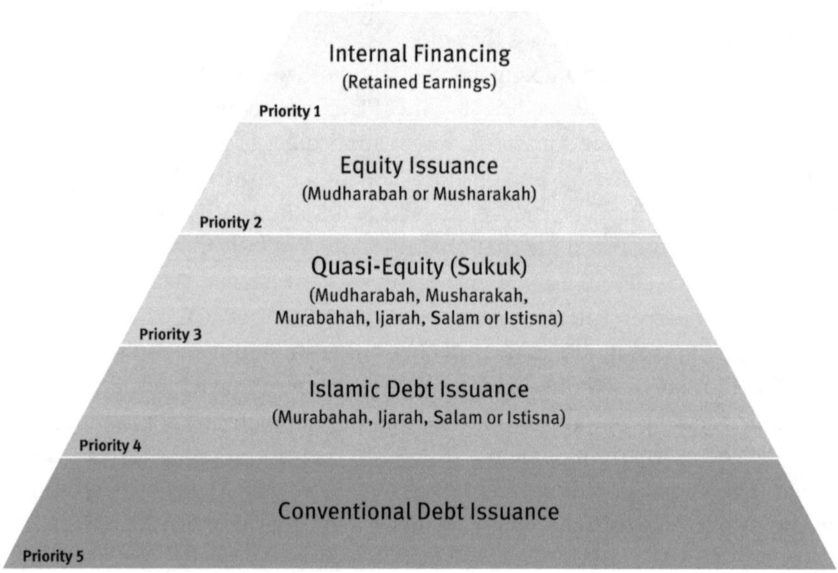

Figure 3.4: Islamic Pecking Order Model.
Source: own contribution.

117 See Gamaleldin (2015, p. 32).

Firms following such a financing order prefer internal over external financing. If they face a financial deficit (insufficient internal funds), to close the gap, these firms would first issue equity in the form of *mudharabah* (Class A shares), *musharakah* (Class B shares), or both instruments. If further funds are required, quasi-equity instruments such as *sukuk* (Islamic Bond) would be the next option. *sukuk*, in general, can be in the form of equity or debt financing. The underlying Islamic contracts for the equity-based *sukuk* are *mudharabah* and *musharakah*. In comparison, the debt-based *sukuk* is designed with Shari'ah-based contracts such as *murabahah*, *ijarah*, *salam*, and *istisna*. When firms exhaust their equity-based financing options, and if further funds are still required, they would go down the latter and engage in debt financing in the form of *murabahah*, *ijarah*, *salam*, and *istisna*, offered by Islamic Financial Institutions.[118] However, if necessity *(darurah)*[119] is evident, tolerance is shown if firms engage in conventional debt financing. The external financing sequence is contrary to the Pecking Order Theory, which seeks the least costly financing alternative and favors debt over equity financing.

On the contrary, Islam discourages any kind of debt except *qard hassan* (benevolent loan), which is not related to any business affairs.[120] Specifically, it is important to highlight, all verses in the *Qur'an* and all narrated *ahadith* related to *qard hassan* always are linked with *darurah*. The following *hadith* narrated in Sunan Ibn Majah, Volume 3, Book 15 *The Chapters on Charity* No: 2431,[121] serves as an example:

> *On the night on which I [Muhammad] was taken on the Night Journey (Isra) [Miraj], I [Muhammad] saw written at the gate of Paradise: Charity brings a tenfold reward and a loan brings an eighteen fold reward. I [Muhammad] said: O Jibril! Why is a loan better than charity?' He [Jibril] said: 'Because the beggar asks when he has something, but the one* ***who asks for loan*** *does so only because he* ***is in need****.'*

We believe that firms operating under normal circumstances do not fall into the category *darurah* (unless bankruptcy/insolvency is present). Holding on this thought tightly, in case firms require external financing, Islam enforces risk-sharing based partnership, which is realized through the engagement in equity and quasi-equity financing instruments (e.g., *Sukuk*). This further ensures to have implemented a model that itself is Shari'ah compliant by adhering to the essence of the *ayah* (*Qur'an* Surah Al-Baqarah, 2:275) and supports the notion of the Islamic financial system, as discussed and described in Section 3.4.

---

118 For more information see Ahmed (2007, pp. 17–19).

119 Muslims may disregard certain aspects or restriction of Shari'ah laws at times of dire necessity in order to save their lives or to preserve the Islamic community.

120 *Qard hassan* is only related to personal affairs.

121 See *Sahih Muslim, Book 13*. Retrieved from: https://sunnah.com/urn/1267490 (accessed July 30, 2020).

The proposed model assumes that a firm's objective is to maximize its Shari'ah compliance by following risk-sharing principles while minimizing financial risk exposure. In this order, firms tend to exhaust their internal funds first through retained earnings, which is not only the least costly but least risky option, i.e., no increase in financial distress and bankruptcy risk. The second option (equity financing) represents Islamic finance's fundamental notion of risk-sharing and profit-and-loss principles. The shareholders reap the profits and bear the costs of losses on the firm's overall performance. Furthermore, they possess the weakest claim on the distribution of a company's income, i.e., no or limited increase in financial distress. The third option (quasi-equity) is similar to equity financing but limited to *Sukuk*'s underlying assets. Specifically, there is no guarantee in returns, and the maximum claim is limited to the underlying asset and its cash flows, i.e., the overall risk is limited. The fourth and fifth financing options are an obligation, no matter interest-free or interest-based. Both the Islamic and conventional debt issuance increase the firm's overall riskiness, i.e., financial distress and bankruptcy risk increases. The former supports the Islamic financial system least, while the latter is only tolerable in *darurah*. A financial hierarchy is apparent, demonstrating the preferred financing sequence when firms face financial deficits as they go further down the financing order.

Note: During the hypotheses development in Section 4.3.2, we will be discussing the rationale behind the *Islamic Pecking Order* model in the context of the selected six debt determinants.

3.6 Conclusion

In this chapter, we have discussed the historical background of the newly implemented stocks screening procedure and showed the development of the Shari'ah screening methodology with its screening criterion set by DJIMI. Several authors have criticized the currently applied screening methodologies and highlighted the importance of harmonizing the screening criterion. In examining our research question, we found direct provision from the *Qur'an* that the most righteous and fair judgment is provided when "*endogenous factors*" are considered. In other words, only factors that are entirely within the control of each company, i.e., book values driven from their financial statements.

Furthermore, we have highlighted the importance of using a Shari'ah screening methodology that supports the main notion of Islamic finance/economics and emphasizes integrating equity-based rather than debt-based concept. We proposed a new screening solution that would allow companies to preserve higher equity in their capital structure. The solution offered is unique, and it exhibits a potential for harmonization of Shari'ah screening, which is the backbone of the Islamic capital markets.

A standardized solution encourages Muslim investors' participation by ensuring better awareness and confidence regarding Shari'ah compliance stock investments. Reflecting the proposed *RIEM* Shari'ah screening methodology to firms financing behavior, we have further proposed a financing hierarchy (i.e., *Islamic Pecking Order* model) that might support as a guideline for firms interested in operating under Islamic principles.

4 Establishing a Framework for Comparative Analysis

This chapter is designed to provide an in-depth understanding of the research methodology employed in this study. First, we show our comparative sample creation process step-by-step so the reader can follow, simulate, and apply these steps in any other similar research studies. Second, we provide a comprehensive discussion on the definition and the rationale of the dependent variables (book leverage and market leverage). Third, we offer a brief discussion about the independent variables (i.e., debt determinants) and consequently develop the hypothesis to answer RQ's 2–5. Fourth, we describe the model specifications and econometric techniques related to panel data analysis, namely, *static* and *dynamic* models using unbalanced panel datasets.[122] The models are designed based on theoretical and empirical considerations and are used to capture the relationship between capital structure determinants and firm leverage.

4.1 Data Selection Procedure/Data Sources and Classification of Datasets

The sample under study consists of SC and SNC firms from seven countries over 2004–2014. The selected countries are the United States (US), the United Kingdom (UK), Canada (CA), Japan (JP), Taiwan (TW), South Korea (SK), and India (IN). We focus only on non-Muslim countries because the firms operating in Muslim countries their capital structure might be affected by the existence of Islamic Capital Markets (as such case in Malaysia). These Islamic Capital Markets provide Islamic financing instruments that are debt-like and, at the same time, might not affect the leverage ratio of firms. Therefore, firms would prefer these instruments over conventional financing instruments to lead firms to be underleveraged (according to the applied Shari'ah screening). These countries could be categorized into two groups, market-based and bank-based economies. Demirgüç-Kunt and Levine (1999) These two groups almost coincide with the split between common law and code law countries, except for South Korea being a code law country. Table A.1 in Appendix A provides an overview of the panel data structure from a macro perspective.

The sample comprises all DJIMI SC firms with their SNC peers (traded on the sample countries' major stock exchanges).[123] Thus, we obtained the balance sheet, income

122 Our dataset is unbalanced due to missing observations of at least one-panel member (i.e., firm).
123 The reason for Dow Jones being selected is that it has launched the first global Shari'ah indices on the market based along with its applied Shari'ah screening methodology; back in 1999. See Section 3.2.

https://doi.org/10.1515/9783110713664-004

statement, and cash flow statement items for all samples included for their last 12 years of operations, i.e., 2003–2014.[124] Based on the above criteria, the focused industries are Oil and Gas (OILG), Basic Materials (BMAT), Industrials (IND), Consumer Goods (CGDS), Technology (TECH), Health Care (HCARE), and Consumer Services (CSRV).[125] The codes in the brackets are based on the Industry Classification Benchmark (ICB).[126]

We relied mainly on secondary data extracted from Thomson Reuters Eikon[127] and Thomson Reuters Datastream.[128] All macroeconomic data has been extracted from the World Development Indicator (WDI).[129] As our study is focused on the "global" perspective of the selected countries and industries, to overcome any possible inconsistencies, all financial data were annualized (on each company's fiscal year-ends) and standardized in US dollars and thousands. The selection criteria for the data sample are as follows:

1. Time series: between the years 2004 and 2014[130]
2. Firm type: non-financial corporations[131]
3. Firm size: market capitalization over USD 1 Billion[132]
4. Firm data: possess financial information for at least three years[133]
5. Compliance: firms must be throughout SC and SNC, respectively.[134]

---

124 Data of the year 2003 has been utilized to construct ratios (that require past data, e.g., change in debt ratio, sales growth, etc.) for the year 2004 and onward.

125 Due to the low number of data points (i.e., number of firms) in the sample countries for Telecommunications (6000–6999) and Utilities (7000–7999), these industries have been excluded.

126 ICB is an industry classification system created by the FTSE Group and Dow Jones Index in 2005. During this study, the ICB used a system of 10 industries, partitioned into 19 supersectors, which were further divided into 41 sectors, which then contained 114 subsectors. As of July 1, 2019, ICB policies, processes and structures have been enhanced. Details can be obtained at https://www.ftserussell.com/data/industry-classification-benchmark-icb, (accessed August 7, 2020).

127 Among others, Thomson Reuters Eikon is a research database for financial professionals to monitor and analyze financials, providing access to real-time market data, news, fundamental data, analytics, trading, and messaging tools.

128 Thomson Reuters Datastream is a research database, offering historical financial data on various financial instruments.

129 World Development Indicators (WDI) is the primary World Bank collection of development indicators, compiled from officially recognized international sources. It presents the most current and accurate global development data and includes national, regional, and global estimates. Data can be retrieved from http://databank.worldbank.org/, (accessed August 7, 2020).

130 Compared to other empirical studies, this time frame must be considered as rather sufficient.

131 Financial firms are generally required to adhere to the distinct regulatory financial requirements (e.g., Basel), these companies would bias the results. Moreover, in essence, the financial institution within these sample countries would not be SC.

132 Firms with more than USD 1 Billion market capitalization have been included in the sample. For more details, see Section 4.1.2.

133 This study uses *static* and *dynamic* models of estimation that require at least three consecutive annual observations. Firms with less than three years of financial information are excluded.

134 Section 4.1.2 describes the specific sample selection steps to identify SC and SNC firms. Furthermore, we classified each firm as either being SC or SNC throughout the time series.

4.1.1 The Motivation of the Selection Procedure

In this section, we elaborate on our approach to identifying SC firms and their SNC peers. We should keep in mind that this study's nature compares the financing behavior between both firm types. Therefore, it is of utmost importance to have "comparable" firm samples to avoid sampling bias. To begin with, this study requires having two major data: ***time series for the SC and SNC firms*** *(i.e., historical data)* and ***the consecutiveness of being SC and SNC,***[135] respectively. *How can we identify those firms' status, i.e., being SC or otherwise throughout the time series?* The DJIMI constituent list is dynamically changing due to the Dow Jones Shari'ah screening procedure applied regularly,[136] and firms' financial data are usually available annually. There are possible two ways to overcome this limitation:

- First, you obtain the DJIMI constituent list, including historical data (i.e., tracking list) that is only available for purchasing. This way, you overcome the issue that comes along with when DJIMI changes its screening calculation.[137] As a result, a company can be accepted as being SC for some years, but not in other years, even though the financial facts do not change (see Section 3.3).
- Second, you calculate the SC and SNC manually for all (sample) years by using the current financial screening ratios applied by Dow Jones (see Section 3.2). The manual calculation result is likely to be inconsistent with the Dow Jones screening methodology, i.e., current SC companies in the Dow Jones list likely become SNC in our calculation, and vice versa.[138] Being inconsistent with the results of Dow Jones does not necessarily mean that our results are not accurate. It's quite the opposite since we ensure firms' consecutiveness being SC and SNC throughout the time series.

---

135 Consecutiveness of being SC and SNC was required as it allowed us to scrutinize their financing behavior and conduct such a "comparative" analysis.

136 "*The Dow Jones Islamic Market Indices are reviewed quarterly. More frequent rebalancing presents the advantage of ensuring that non[-]compliant companies are removed[,] and newly compliant companies are added as quickly as possible.*" Orzano and Welling (2019). Retrieved from: https://www.spglobal.com/spdji/en/documents/methodologies/methodology-dj-islamic-market-indices.pdf (accessed July 30, 2020).

137 During our study period (time series) DJIMI has changed its screening calculation. Effective June 20, 2005, "*Dow Jones Indexes has revised one of the three financial screens that are used in selecting companies' stocks for the Dow Jones Islamic Market Indexes. The change addresses accounts receivable or the illiquid assets of [a] compliant company. The new screen is to eliminate companies whose accounts receivables divided by trailing 12-month average market capitalization is 33% or more. The previous screen limited accounts receivables to 45% of total assets.*" Retrieved from: http://www.mondovisione.com/news/dow-jones-indexes-announces-changes-to-dow-jones-islamic-market-indexes/, (accessed August 7, 2020).

138 There have been several debt-to-equity ratio calculation methods applied throughout the time series. For instance, the trailing methodology has changed throughout the time series, between 12, 24, and 36–months. The issue gets more complicated with the fact that various firms have different fiscal year start/end, and even these fiscal year start/end dates have been changed for some firms over time. Therefore it is not feasible to calculate this ratio for each company throughout the time series.

Unless money is not an issue, go for the first approach. In our case, we have decided on the second approach to identify each firm being SC and SNC manually.

4.1.2 Procedure to Identify SC and SNC Firms

As mentioned in Section 4.1.1, comparative analysis needs to have comparable firm samples with the required consecutiveness. Table 4.1. describes the sample selection procedure step-by-step to identify first the SC and then the SNC firm samples.

Our sample selection procedure provides consistent SC and SNC tracking history throughout the time series. However, it is important to note that we merely ensured that the filtered firms comply with the *quantitative* screening criteria. In other words, SC (SNC) firms consistently remained SC (SNC).[139] Our study's limitation is that we did not ensure that the SC firms always complied with the *qualitative* screening criteria, as described in Table 3.1. However, to reduce the deviation from all sets of criteria, we have chosen all SC firms listed in DJIMI as our investment universe. As for the SNC firms, the firms' universe was active stocks traded in the sample countries' main stock exchange.

By now, we have created our SC and SNC firms samples. Next, we will discuss all estimators and statistical tests applied to both firm samples.

Table 4.1: Identification of SC and SNC firms.

SC sample		
Steps		**# firms**
i.	DJIMI constituent list retrieved from Datastream as of March 2015.[1]	2616
ii.	Firms operating in the US, UK, CA, JP, SK, TW, and IN selected.[2]	1607
iii.	ICB Subsector assigned.[3]	
iv.	Cleansing activities applied.[4]	1322
v.	Minimum requirement of USD 1 Billion market capitalization applied.[5]	918
vi.	DJIMI financial criteria, with consecutiveness of a minimum of three years.[6]	812
vii.	Excluded firms with missing or error data.[7]	**791**
SNC sample		
viii.	Firms from the same countries as in Step b) selected.	21624
ix.	see step c)	
x.	see step d)[8]	17096
xi.	see step e)	1525
xii.	Leverage ratio > 33%, with consecutiveness of a minimum of three years.[9]	653
xiii.	see step g)	**615**

139 Table B.1 in Appendix B provides the participation pattern of all firms divided into SC and SNC, respectively. This table exhibits the pattern of consecutiveness.

Table 4.1 (continued)

Important notes
[1] Until Q1-2015, the DJIMI constituent list was freely available; however, with limitations showing only those who passed *the last Shari'ah screening cycle*, i.e., without the historical data (i.e., tracking list). Since Q2-2015, the proprietary DJIMI constituent list, maintained by S&P and Dow Jones, are no more publicly (i.e., free-of-charge) available.
[2] We scoped the countries based on two criteria: First, focus on countries with the highest number of SC firms (based on the constituent list of DJIMI as of March 2015), and second, focus only on non-Muslim countries.
[3] Step c) allowed us to identify the Industry Classification Benchmark (ICB) Subsector (level 4) in which each SC firm operates. This is later important in Step h) to determine their SNC peers. Note: This step is the closest way to ensure that SNC firms operate in the same ICB Subsector as SC firms and would potentially pass the *qualitative screens* of DJIMI (see Section 3.2).
[4] Cleansing activities for SC firms consist of: removal of all firms i) which were listed on foreign exchanges and foreign currency, ii) from industry Finance and Utilities, and Telecommunications and iii) with the age of four years and less as this study requires at least three consecutive annual observations and the first year of observation is needed for some calculations.
[5] During the sample creation, we faced having 1322 SC and 17096 SNC firms, which was not feasible to proceed with. To our discretion, we have applied a minimum floor size of US$1 Billion market capitalization value (as of the calendar (not fiscal) year 2014) to eliminate all firms with low market capitalization value. The number of firms dropped, as shown in step e) and k) for both firm types and allowed us to have a pool of comparable SC and SNC firms (in *quantity* and *size*).
[6] We calculated all screening ratios, i.e., Total Debt, Cash and Interest-Bearing Securities, and Accounts Receivables with the data taken from firms' financial statements (fiscal year) (see Table 3.1). We have divided each ratio by a *2–year average Market Capitalization* (fiscal year) for simplicity purposes.
[7] This is in line with Baker and Wurgler (2002) and other studies. First, we required a) book leverage between *zero* and *one*, b) market-to-book ratio between *zero* and *ten,* and c) all firms were excluded with incomplete data for relevant variables, e.g., total assets, total debt, total liability, total equity, market capitalization, etc. and to restrict the impact of outliers, we winsorized all financial variables at the 1% and 99% level.
Note to point a), since the market value cannot fall under zero, market leverage per se never exceeds one, implying that this limit extracts no effect on the market leverage samples.
[8] Like step d), we added two cleansing activities for SNC firms by removing all firms i) classified as being SC and ii), which operate outside of the ICB Subsector identified in step c).
[9] Since DJIMI requires that if one of the criteria (e.g., any financial ratio) is violated, it is sufficient to disqualify from being SC. Consequently, we only controlled for the leverage ratio.
Source: own contribution.

4.2 Estimator and Post–Estimation Tests

This study utilized panel data techniques due to the nature of the data that involves cross-*sections* and *time series* and is based on the number of firms from different countries and sectors across 11 years. Previous capital structure studies, such as D.E. Allen and Mizuno (1989) and Rajan and Zingales (1995), have conducted a cross-sectional analysis. More recent studies, such as Antoniou et al. (2008) and Faulkender and Petersen (2006), have utilized *panel data* to conduct their research. Panel data leads to more efficient estimates because it increases *the degree of freedom* and *reduces collinearity* among the explanatory variables. Antoniou et al. (2008) Additionally, the endogeneity problem will be reduced due to the consideration of specific industry and country effects, reverse causality, and measurement error (Sequeira and Nunes, 2008). Therefore, panel data models permit the investigation of problems that cannot be dealt with solely by cross-sections or time-series (Hsiao, 2003).

All these previous academic studies show and verify that panel data is superior to cross-section or time series, offering a high number of advantages, as stated in Baltagi (2005).[140] Among these advantages are:

i. Control for individual heterogeneity. In our case, panel data allows the firms to be heterogeneous, thus permitting this study to conclude why capital structure decisions differ amongst (SC and SNC) firms.
ii. Provide more informative data, more variability, less collinearity among the variables, more degrees of freedom, and more efficiency.
iii. Better able to study the dynamics of adjustment. Here it will be used to show how the debt determinants change over time and hence impact SC and SNC firms' financial decisions.
iv. Better justify and measure effects that are not detectable in pure cross-sections or pure time-series data.
v. Allow us to construct and test complicated behavioral models and avoid biases that result from the aggregation of firms or individuals.

As known, to every advantage, there is a corresponding disadvantage. The panel data method also poses some problems because it consists of both cross-section and time-series dimensions. Baltagi (2005) described the disadvantages of using panel data because most panel data deals with annual data, which covers only a short period. Consequently, asymptotic arguments rely on the number of individuals tending to infinity while the number of periods remains constant. Cross-sectional dependence also needs to be considered, as it may lead to misleading inference. Cross-sectional dependence is the possibility that the individual units, in our case firms, are inter-dependent in the panel. It also assumes that both slopes and intercepts are constant across countries. The *Fixed* and *Random Effects* models may help control for the intercept bias; however, there may be present slope biases that would be the case if the effects of a given independent variable are different for each country or industry.

In line with the objectives of this study, we used four main estimators: (i) pooled Ordinary Least Squares, (ii) Fixed Effects, and (iii) Random Effects (hereafter OLS,

---

140 See Baltagi (2005, pp. 3–6).

FE, and RE, respectively) for the *static* panel model, and (iv) Generalized Method of Moments (hereafter GMM) for the *dynamic* panel model. Next, we will elaborate on each of these estimators, and we have described them in an easy-to-read manner.

4.2.1 Static Panel Model – OLS, Fixed, and Random Effects Estimators

The sample created from Thomson Reuters (see Section 4.1) enabled the use of a panel data analysis. Even with this, complications do arise since the selection of *consistent* and *efficient estimators* is not without problems. First, let us consider a regression model of the following form[141]:

$$y_{it} = \alpha z_i + \beta x_{it} + \varepsilon_{it} \tag{1}$$

Where y_{it} indicates the dependent variable while x_{it} is the matrix of K explanatory variables that does not include a constant term and β is the vector of the estimated coefficients. z_i is the so-called *individual effect* (or individual heterogeneity effect) that contains a constant term and a set of individual (or group-specific) variables that may be observed (e.g., race, sex, location, etc.) or unobserved (e.g., skill or preferences, etc.). This *individual effect* and its potential correlation with x_{it}, which affect estimators' selection, are of interest. Next, we will elaborate on three general cases:

- First, z_i contains only a constant term and no unobserved effects. If this holds, then the "OLS" estimator is consistent and efficient and, therefore, should be used as if we had a time-series of the cross-sectional dataset. In other words, the assumption that a) the intercept and slope coefficients of the regression are constant across time and space and b) that ε_{it} (the error term) captures differences over time and individuals holds.
- Second, z_i contains unobserved effects and is correlated simultaneously with x_{it}. OLS is then biased and inconsistent due to an omitted variable, and the "fixed effects" estimator should be utilized. In FE, the individual effect is taken as a group-specific constant term in the regression model and thus treated as a parameter to be estimated for each cross-sectional observation *i*. If we take another look at equation (1), adopting fixed effects estimators would mean that $\alpha_i = \alpha z_i$ since this is now an estimable constant term, and thus, equation (1) is transformed into (2).

  More simply, this means that in (2), we assume that the slope coefficients are constant across individuals, in our case, firms, whereas we let the intercept vary for each company.

141 For more details, see Greene (2018, pp. 375–376).

$$y_{it} = \alpha_i + \beta x_{it} + \varepsilon_{it} \tag{2}$$

It should be noted that we cannot include time constant factors in x_{it}, because if z_i is correlated with each element of x_{it}, there is no way distinguishing the effects of the *time constant observables* from the *time constant unobservable* z_i. This could seem a big expense to bear, but it should also be considered that zero correlation between x_{it} and z_i doesn't need to be assumed, making the FE estimators an attractive choice. The only assumption required is that firm's individual effects are treated as fixed (i.e., do not vary over time) and estimable.

- Third, if the individual heterogeneity can be assumed to be uncorrelated with the independent variables, then equation (2) can be transformed into:

$$y_{it} = \alpha + \beta x_{it} + \mu_i + \varepsilon_{it} \tag{3}$$

Where α is the classic intercept term, and μ_i is a group-specific random element similar to ε_{it} except that, for each group, a single draw enters the regression identically for each period. Specifically, the individuals (N), i.e., firms, included in our sample are a drawing from a much larger universe, and that they have a common mean value for the intercept α. ε_{it} is the standard residual that has the usual properties: mean equal to zero, uncorrelated with itself, uncorrelated with x, uncorrelated with μ_i and homoskedastic, i.e., $\varepsilon_{it} \approx i.i.d.N(0,\sigma^2)$. This is the "random effects" estimator taking its name from the fact that μ_i is treated as a random variable rather than a constant term.[142]

Wooldridge (2002, p. 252) states that *"With a large number of random draws from the cross section, it almost always makes sense to treat the unobserved effects, c_i [μ_i], as random draws from the population, along with y_{it} and x_{it}"*. According to Wooldridge, the key point is whether or not the individual effect will be assumed to be correlated with the observable variables.

4.2.1.1 Econometric Tool and Derivation of Panel Data Estimator

In this study, we have utilized statistical software called Stata.[143] Stata has been a major tool for economics and finance researchers and is one of the most reliable statistical software programs in the market.

After discussing panel data estimators' theory, it would be useful to provide additional information regarding their derivation and the proper R^2 (R-squared) to be used when dealing with panel data. R^2 is, after all, a popular measure of how well the

142 For more details, see Greene (2018, pp. 375–383), Gujarati (2004, pp. 636–655), and Wooldridge (2002, pp. 247–278).

143 Stata is a general-purpose statistical software for data sciences. See http://www.stata.com.

sample regression line fits a set of data. As a measure of goodness of fit, researchers often attribute great significance to the values that R^2 receives. When FE or RE estimators are used, though, Stata reports three R^2's, namely, R_w^2 *(within)*, R_b^2 *(between)*, and R_o^2 *(overall)*.

What kind of information do these three different estimators provide, and which one should be selected as the most appropriate one? To provide an answer to this question, we should revisit equation (3):

$$y_{it} = \alpha + \beta x_{it} + \mu_i + \varepsilon_{it}$$

As mentioned before, x_{it} is the matrix of K explanatory variables, with β being the vector of the estimated coefficients. The unit-specific residual μ_i differs among units, and its value is constant for any specific individual (i.e., firms). The ε_{it} is the standard residual with the usual properties described above. By applying basic algebra calculations, if equation (3) holds, then so must the following equation[144]:

$$\bar{y}_i = \alpha + \beta \bar{x}_i + \mu_i + \bar{\varepsilon}_i \tag{4}$$

Where $\bar{y}_i$, $\bar{x}_i$ and $\bar{\varepsilon}_i$ *equals* $\sum_t y_{it}/T_i$, $\sum_t x_{it}/T_i$, *and* $\sum_t \varepsilon_{it}/T_i$, respectively. Furthermore, if we subtract (4) from (3), it must be equally valid that:

$$\left(y_{it} - \bar{y}_i\right) = \beta\left(x_{it} - \bar{x}_i\right) + \left(\varepsilon_{it} - \bar{\varepsilon}_i\right) \tag{5}$$

These three equations (3), (4), and (5) are the basis for estimating β. In other words, when the *"FE within"* estimator is utilized (Stata command *xtreg, fe*), OLS is used to estimate equation (5). The less known *"FE between"* estimator (Stata command *xtreg, be*) is utilized by performing OLS on equation (4). Finally, RE estimators are nothing more than a weighted average of the estimates produced by the *"within"* and *"between"* estimators and are equal to running the following model:

$$\left(y_{it} - \theta \bar{y}_i\right) = \left(1-\theta\right)\alpha + \beta\left(x_{it} - \theta \bar{x}_i\right) + \left\{\left(1-\theta\right)\mu_i + \left(\varepsilon_{it} - \theta \bar{\varepsilon}_i\right)\right\} \tag{6}$$

Where θ is a function of σ^2_μ and σ^2_ε. If $\sigma^2_\mu = 0$, then this means that $\mu_i = 0$ and $\theta = 0$ or, in other words, that individuals do not differ and therefore, we can estimate model (3) directly by OLS. In the case that $\sigma^2_\varepsilon = 0$, then we have $\varepsilon_{it} = 0$ and $\theta = 1$, this means that FE within estimators will return all the information available; thus, the regression will have an R^2 equal to unity. Nevertheless, it should be stated that both of these cases mentioned are rather extreme.

144 See Stata Longitudinal-Data/Panel Data Reference Manual Release 2013, *Remarks and examples*, pp. 366–367. Retrieved from: https://www.stata.com/manuals13/xt.pdf, (accessed August 8, 2020).

Let's go back to the original issue of R^2; the Stata command *xtreg* reports R^2's that correspond to the estimates of equations (3), (4), and (5) reported below.[145]

$$\hat{y}_{it} = \hat{\alpha} + \hat{\beta} x_{it} \tag{3'}$$

$$\widehat{\bar{y}}_{it} = \hat{\alpha} + \hat{\beta} \bar{x}_i \tag{4'}$$

$$\hat{y}_{it} - \widehat{\bar{y}}_{it} = \hat{\beta}\left(x_{it} - \bar{x}_i\right) \tag{5'}$$

As we already know from OLS, the ordinary properties of R^2 include it being equal to the fraction of variance in y explained by $\hat{y}$ as seen in (7) and also equal to the squared correlations between y and $\hat{y}$. When the Stata command *xtreg, be* is applied, the estimates are obtained by performing OLS on (4) and therefore, its R_b^2 is the ordinary R^2. Moreover, Stata command *xtreg, fe* performs OLS on (5) and thus, the reported R_w^2 is the ordinary R^2. As stated earlier, the Stata command *xtreg, re* applies OLS on (6), and thus none of the R^2 directly applies to it; in short, R_b^2 corresponds to (3′), R_w^2 to (4′) and R_w^2 to (5′). It can, therefore, be concluded that when FE estimators are utilized, the appropriate R^2 is the R_w^2. In the case of RE, none of the R^2 reported has the properties of the R^2 defined in equation (7). For instance, in Table D.2 in Appendix D, the R^2 values are not reported on the models estimated with RE.

$$r^2 = \frac{\sum\left(\hat{y}_i - \bar{y}\right)^2}{\sum\left(y_i - \bar{y}\right)^2} = \frac{ESS}{TSS} \tag{7}$$

4.2.1.2 Post Estimation Tests

The problem of choosing between OLS, FE, and RE remains. Fortunately, the Breusch and Pagan Lagrange Multiplier test (hereafter BPLM),[146] the Hausman test,[147] and finally, Wooldridge's test assure the use of efficient and consistent estimators.

The first test we ran is BPLM. This test helped us to detect the presence of an unobserved effect. As mentioned in Section 4.2.1, if unobserved effects are present, OLS is deemed inappropriate. The BPLM has a *chi-squared distribution* (denoted as) with one-degree freedom. If a p-value of under 0.05 (5%) for the chi-squared statistic is recorded, the hypothesis for no unobserved effects can be rejected.

If the BPLM test indicated OLS's rejection, we then proceeded with the Hausman test to help the choice between RE and FE. More specifically, as Wooldridge (2002,

145 See Stata Longitudinal-Data/Panel Data Reference Manual Release 2013, *Assessing goodness of fit*, p. 368. Retrieved from: https://www.stata.com/manuals13/xt.pdf, (accessed August 8, 2020).

146 See Breusch and Pagan (1980, pp. 239–253).

147 See Hausman (1978, pp. 1251–1271).

p. 288), *"Hausman (1978) proposed a test based on the difference between the random effects and fixed effects estimates."* Since FE is consistent when the individual effect and the observable variables are correlated, while RE is not, a statistical difference is interpreted as evidence against RE. The Hausman test has a and if p-values of over 0.05 (5%) are recorded, then the null hypothesis that the two estimates do not differ significantly cannot be rejected, and RE is preferred. It should be stated that if the model fitted on these data fails to meet the asymptotic assumptions, then the Hausman test fails.[148]

Furthermore, we also have utilized countermeasures for the existence of heteroskedasticity. Heteroskedasticity is likely to be present in a panel dataset with such a large number of individual cross-sectional observations. As suggested by Petersen (2009), to take heteroskedasticity into account, we have added the option "robust" (Stata command *vce (cluster code)*) in every regression to which was applicable.

To sum up, indeed, and from a purely practical point of view, it is difficult to make a real distinction between FE and RE models because each one has some technical and conceptual advantages, drawbacks, and the assumptions made by both. The RE assumption is that the individual effects are uncorrelated with the independent variables. The FE assumption is that the individual effect is correlated with the independent variables. If the RE assumption holds, the RE model is more efficient than the FE model. However, if this assumption does not hold, the RE model is not consistent.

Note, we applied all tests on each model to identify the appropriate estimator and conducted our regression accordingly. All test results can be found in Appendix B.

4.2.2 Dynamic Panel Model – Generalized Method of Moments (GMM) Estimator

As shown in Section 4.2.1, *static* panel models require pooled OLS, FE, or RE estimators. The regression models we have developed and used in the main empirical analysis (Sections 5.2 and 6.2) are *static* in nature as no lagged dependent variable is present. Therefore, these estimators are considered the appropriate choice and selected based on the relevant post–estimation test results. Nevertheless, the use of *dynamic* panel data models has its rewards since, as Roodman (2009)[149] reports, these models are specifically designed to deal with:

i. Panel datasets, with few periods (small T) and many individuals, i.e., firms (large N).
ii. A linear functional relationship.

148 It should be noted that other, more traditional tests (irrelevant to panel data) could be applied. For instance, autocorrelation can be detected by using the Wooldridge (2002, pp. 274–275) test with the Stata command *xtserial*. If the null hypothesis of no first-order autocorrelation cannot be rejected, then the Stata command *xtregar* can accommodate regression models in which first-order autocorrelation exists. See Stata Longitudinal-Data/Panel Data Reference Manual Release (2013, pp. 400–401).
149 See Roodman (2009, pp. 99–100).

iii. Some regressors may be endogenous.
iv. The inclusion of independent variables those are not strictly exogenous. In other words, independent variables that are correlated with the past and possibly current realizations of the error ε_{it}. The lagged dependent variable is an example.
v. Single left-hand side variable that is *dynamic*, i.e., depending on its (own) past realizations.
vi. Existence of heteroskedasticity and autocorrelation "within" individuals; but not "across" them.
vii. Presence of fixed individual effects.

The advantages of using *dynamic* panel data models on our dataset are evident. As shown in Tables A.2–A.4 in Appendix A, our dataset structure is such that the number of individuals is far higher than the number of years. The use of *dynamic* panel data models in cases such as this is advisable since, as reported by Bond (2002) and Sarafidis et al. (2006), they can control *dynamic* panel bias.

Furthermore, the regression models depicted in Section 6.1.1 have a *dynamic* nature as we have included the lagged dependent variable as an explanatory variable.[150] After deciding on incorporating *dynamic* panel data models, the next step would be to select the proper estimators that should be deployed. The inclusion of a lagged dependent variable on the right-hand side of a model (equation 8) automatically makes us reject both the FE and RE estimators. Due to the lagged dependent variable correlated with the compound disturbance, the same μ_i enters the equation for every observation in group *i* (Greene, 2018).[151]

$$y_{it} = \lambda y_{i,t-1} + \beta x_{it} + \mu_i + \varepsilon_{it} \tag{8}$$

Two main econometric problems exist when estimating the level equation (8). First, the possibility that some or all the explanatory variables are *endogenous*. Second, the correlation of unit-specific effect μi with some of the explanatory variables. It is possible to circumvent these two problems by first-differencing equation (8) into:

$$y_{it} - y_{i,t-1} = \alpha\left(y_{i,t-1} - y_{i,t-2}\right) + \beta\left(x_{it} - x_{i,t-1}\right) + \left(\varepsilon_{it} - \varepsilon_{i,t-1}\right) \tag{9}$$

As can be seen, due to its time-invariant nature, the unit-specific effect μ_i (i.e., $\mu_i - \mu_i = 0$) is now removed. If it is assumed that it ε_{it} is not serially correlated and that

150 Finally, the inclusion of a lag dependent variable on the right-hand side of the main regression models allowed us to examine whether our results hold when dynamic specifications are estimated. For all the reasons mentioned above, it was deemed useful to include and run *dynamic* panel data models in Section 6.1.1. These models will essentially operate as robustness tests and will complement and verify the main empirical analysis results. All various types of robustness tests are shown in Appendix E.
151 See Greene (2018, pp. 523–524).

the explanatory variables are weakly exogenous, then equation (9) can be estimated using the following moment conditions (Regression in Differences):

$$E\left[y_{i,t-s}\left(\varepsilon_{it}-\varepsilon_{it-1}\right)\right]=0 \quad for\ s \geq 2;\ t=3, \dots, T \tag{10}$$

$$E\left[x_{i,t-s}\left(\varepsilon_{it}-\varepsilon_{it-1}\right)\right]=0 \quad for\ s \geq 2;\ t=3, \dots, T$$

The GMM estimator based on these conditions is called the ***difference GMM*** estimator and can efficiently estimate *dynamic* panel data models (Levine et al., 2000).[152] Arellano and Bond (1991) developed this *difference GMM* estimator that uses all lagged values, i.e. $(y_{i,t-2}, y_{i,t-3}, \dots y_{i1})$ as *instruments* in the difference equation (9) for $\Delta y_{i,t-1}$. However, there are several conceptual and econometrical shortcomings with the *difference GMM* estimator, such as:

1. The pure cross-sectional dimension (e.g., firm characteristics) of the data will be eliminated by first-differencing.
2. Differencing may decrease the signal-to-noise ratio, thereby exacerbating measurement error biases Griliches and Hausman (1986).
3. Blundell and Bond (1998) show that if the lagged dependent and the explanatory variables are persistent over time, lagged levels of these variables are weak instruments for the "*regressions in differences*".
4. Too many instruments.

To overcome the shortcoming of *difference GMM* estimator in terms of weak instruments and finite sample bias, the Arellano and Bover (1995)/Blundell and Bond (1998) estimator, commonly known as **system GMM**, is the recommended choice. The *system GMM* estimator essentially combines the *regression in differences (equation (9))* with *regression in levels (equation (8))*. The instruments for the *regression in differences*, i.e., $(\Delta y_{i,t-1}, \Delta y_{i,t-2}, \dots \Delta y_{i1})$, are identical to those used in difference GMM. The instruments for the *regression in levels*, i.e., $(y_{i,t-1}, y_{i,t-2}, etc.)$, are the lagged differences of the corresponding variables, i.e., $(\Delta y_{i,t-2}, \Delta y_{i,t-3}, \dots \Delta y_{i2})$. The moment conditions (*regression in levels*) used are shown in equation (11). These are appropriate instruments as long as the assumption that the first differences of the "instrument variables" are uncorrelated with the unit-specific effect u_i holds (Levine et al., 2000).[153]

152 See Levine et al. (2000, pp. 51–52).
153 See Levine et al. (2000, pp. 51–52).

$$\mathrm{E}\left[\left(y_{i,t-s} - y_{i,t-s-1}\right)\left(\mu_i - \varepsilon_{it}\right)\right] = 0 \ \ for\ s = 1 \tag{11}$$

$$\mathrm{E}\left[\left(x_{i,t-s} - x_{i,t-s-1}\right)\left(\mu_i - \varepsilon_{it}\right)\right] = 0 \ \ for\ s = 1$$

Especially in unbalanced panels where some of the explanatory variables are expected to be endogenous, Flannery and Hankins (2013) find that *system GMM* estimator performs best. In the presence of heteroskedasticity and serial correlation, the *two-step system GMM* uses a consistent estimate of the weighting matrix, taking the residuals from the *one-step* estimate (Davidson and MacKinnon, 2004). Though asymptotically more efficient, the *two-step* GMM reports estimates of the standard errors that tend to be severely downward biased. However, it is possible to solve this problem using the finite sample correction to the *two-step* covariance matrix derived by Windmeijer bias-corrected (WC) robust VCE. The *two-step robust* GMM estimates become more efficient than the *one-step robust* GMM estimates, especially for *system GMM* (Roodman, 2009).

Nevertheless, it is important to note that under the following conditions, *difference GMM* tends to be more superior to *system GMM*:

1. As a rule of thumb, *difference GMM* is more appropriate if $T > N$ and the autoregressive parameter is low. *System GMM* is considered more appropriate if $N > T$ and the autoregressive parameter is high.
2. *"Difference GMM" outperforms "system GMM" when*
   - the autoregressive parameter is below 0.8,
   - the time series observations are relatively large, and
   - the autocorrelation requirements in the first-order (and not in the second-order) are fulfilled. (Blundell and Bond, 1998)
3. In the case of instrument proliferation, Roodman (2009) argued that there would be a greater likelihood of instrument proliferation resulting in biases of the coefficients in *system GMM* as compared to *difference GMM*.

As in the *static* panel data models, selecting the most appropriate method of estimation must be made. We have decided that using *system GMM* was more suitable for the reasons mentioned below:

1. *System GMM* generally provides more efficient and precise estimates and reduces the finite sample bias (Baltagi, 2005).[154]
2. The *difference GMM* performs when variables are close to a random walk poorly. Since our models and data include financial and economic variables, the presence of random walk variables is quite likely (Roodman, 2009).[155]

154 See Baltagi (2005 p. 148).

155 See Roodman, (2009, p. 114).

3. If *difference GMM* estimators are applied, then time-invariant regressors (e.g., dummy variables) will disappear due to the differencing of variables within groups (Roodman, 2009).[156]
4. In the case of an unbalanced dataset, it is better to avoid *difference GMM* because it has the weakness of magnifying gaps (Roodman, 2009).[157] As in our case, since our dataset is unbalanced, we preferred *system GMM* over *differenced GMM*.

4.2.2.1 Exogeneity vs. Endogeneity

The use of *system GMM* in Stata allows us to control one of the major shortcomings of the *static* panel estimator, namely, *endogeneity*. One of the assumptions required for all the discussed estimators is that the independent variables have to be *exogenous*, in other words, uncorrelated with the error term. Common reasons for *endogeneity* are i) the inclusion of lagged dependent variables, and ii) independent variables that are not *strictly exogenous*, followed by iii) omitted variables,[158] simultaneity,[159] and measurement error.[160] All these lead to the presence of *endogeneity*, which will result in biased estimates. One way to identify *endogeneity* is to regress the dependent variable onto the independent variables and the *leads* (i.e., one period ahead) of the same independent variables, as suggested by the authors Verbeek (2008) and Wooldridge (2002).[161]

We followed the suggestion made by Wooldridge (2002). We applied the *endogeneity test* (*strict exogeneity test*) by estimating an FE-/RE version[162] of equation (3) that includes future values (leads) of all firm-specific variables (see Table B.5 in Appendix B). We, therefore, can reject the assumption of *strict exogeneity* of such variables. In Flan-

156 See Roodman, (2009, p. 115).

157 See Roodman, (2009, p. 104).

158 Omitted variables appear when we would like to control for one or more additional variables, but usually, because of data unavailability, we cannot include them in a regression model. When an explanatory variable is correlated with the omitted variable (unobserved effect), the explanatory variable is endogenous. See Wooldridge (2002, pp. 50–51).

159 When an explanatory variable is determined "simultaneously" with the dependent variable (simultaneity), then the explanatory variable and the error term are generally correlated; hence the explanatory variable is endogenous. See Wooldridge (2002, p. 51).

160 Measurement error refers to the degree to which the variable is an accurate and consistent measure of the concept being studied. Endogeneity, especially in corporate finance, mostly arise from omitted variables and measurement error. Specifically, measurement error often occurs when proxies are used extensively in corporate finance, e.g., market-to-book value as a proxy for growth opportunities. In this example, the actual investment opportunities might not be represented by Tobin's q. See Erickson and Whited (2011, p. 2).

161 See, for instance, Wooldridge (2002, p. 285).

162 Depending on the estimator selection results from Table B.3 in Appendix B for each model applied in this study.

nery and Hankins (2013), the authors report that the validity of the system GMM method's estimates is intact despite endogeneity.

Therefore, in the *system GMM* estimation, we considered all "significant" lead variables as *endogenous* and the "insignificant" lead variables as *predetermined*. Macroeconomic variables such as GDP, Inflation, Interest Rate, etc. are exogenous by default.

4.2.2.2 Post Estimation Test

As in the *static* panel data models, a range of post estimation tests must be applied to verify the validity of the results. By default, the Stata command used to apply for *system GMM* estimator *xtabond2* reports the three most important post estimation tests: AR(1), AR(2), and the Sargan/Hansen test. In the Sargan test, which is a special form of the Hansen test, Baum et al. (2003), the hypothesis being tested is that the instruments as a group are exogenous; therefore, they are acceptable and healthy instruments. If the null hypothesis is not rejected (p-value higher than 0.05), the instruments pass the test (i.e., instruments satisfy the orthogonality conditions), and thus they are valid (i.e., exogenous).

The AR(1) and AR(2) Arellano and Bond (1991) tests have a null hypothesis of no autocorrelation and are applied to the differenced individuals. GMM estimator requires first-order autocorrelation AR(1), but no second-order autocorrelation AR(2). Arellano and Bond (1991). In our study, we initially set the instruments restricted to two lags, but if the serial correlation of the second-order, i.e., AR(2), was present, or if the Sargan/Hansen test failed, then lags of the third and higher-order was set.

4.3 Formulation of Variables

4.3.1 Dependent Variables

In Section 2.1, we have briefly defined the two types of leverage and highlighted financial leverage being the core element in this study. It is, therefore, important to define and apply a suitable leverage ratio.

As Rajan and Zingales (1995) state, the definition of capital structure is inconclusive and depends on the study's objective. Brealey et al. (2010) define the capital structure as the mix of "long-term debt and equity financing". However, the notion of capital structure relates to the way that companies finance their total assets. Therefore, it is not enough to consider only long-term debt and equity in the definition of capital as firms can obtain financing in the form of short-term debt or issue convertible bonds. The choice relates to firm preferences, as well as the nature of the asset to be financed. Furthermore, Welch (2011) challenges the use of only including financial debt (interest-bearing) and equity into the capital structure measure and strongly recommends a ratio, including total liabilities to total assets. Using this leverage ratio indicates that capital structure consists of all liabilities (i.e., interest-bearing and non-interest-bearing debt) and equity. Below is a list of different ratios/proxies of leverage and the corresponding pros and cons obtained from Rajan and Zingales (1995).

Table 4.2: Overview of different leverage measure.

#	Leverage Ratio/ Proxies	pros/ cons	Explanation
1	*Total Liability / Total Assets*	pro	The broadest definition of stock leverage is a proxy for what is left for shareholders in case of liquidation.
		con	Not a good indication of whether the firm is at risk of default in the near future. May overstate the amount of leverage since Total Liabilities include items like Accounts Payable, etc.
2	*Total Debt / Total Assets*	pro	Total Debt (=Short-Term Debt plus Long-Term Debt) does not include liabilities like Accounts Payable (used for transaction purposes), therefore more appropriate than (1) above.
		con	Fails to incorporate non-interest-bearing debt (e.g., Accounts Payables) that are used for assets financing.
3	*Total Debt / Net Assets*	pro	Net Assets (=Total Assets – Accounts Payable – Other Liabilities) not influenced by trade credit.
		con	It is still affected by factors that have nothing to do with financing, e.g., assets held against pension liabilities.
4	*Total Debt / Total Capital*	pro	Total Capital (=Total Debt + Total Equity) probably the best representation of past financing decisions.
		con	–
5	*EBIT / Interest Expense*	pro	Coverage Ratio measures the risk that equity holders will not make fixed payments and potentially have to give up control. An appropriate measure of investments – equal in magnitude to depreciation – needed to keep the firm a going concern.
		con	Based on the assumption that short-term liabilities like accounts payable and short-term debt will be rolled over. Very sensitive to income fluctuations.
6	*EBITDA / Interest Expense*	pro	see EBIT / Interest Expense. However, appropriate if no such investments as in (5) are needed.
		con	see con of EBIT / Interest Expense

Source: own contribution, in reference to Rajan and Zingales (1995, pp. 1428–1429).

In contrast to Welch's (2011) argument, Rajan and Zingales (1995) argue that total debt ratio definitions are considered more appropriate for financial leverage than total liabilities over total assets. The reason being that total debt ratio act as more accurate indicators of whether a company could be in default risk in the near future. Specific line items included in total liabilities, such as accounts payable, tend to be used for transaction purposes. As a result, any leverage ratio based on total liabilities would be exaggerated (see first leverage ratio in Table 4.2).

In the literature, two broad categories of leverage measures exist, the *book* and the *market* leverage. Book values are used primarily because using market values might yield doubtful results. For instance, if the market value of equity is used, a fall in stock prices implies an increase in leverage without increasing debt. The other way around, a rise in stock prices implies a decrease in leverage without decreasing debt. In Bowman's (1980) study, both book leverage and market leverage showed similar results with no essential differences. In Fama and French (2002), the authors find relatively large differences in the estimation results for book leverage and market leverage. Proponents of the market leverage argue against book leverage, as in Welch (2004). As highlighted in Section 3.4.1, market leverage proponents state that book leverage is past-oriented and influenced by the firm's choice of selecting an accounting method. They claim, market leverage is future-oriented and better reflect the intrinsic firm value. However, the Graham and Harvey (2001) survey study reports that the managers use book values to decide firms' capital structure.[163] A closer look at the leverage ratios itself used in the literature, it seems that the most important issue is choosing an appropriate leverage measure as the dependent variable.

We utilized both leverage measures as the dependent variable with book debt in the numerator, as shown in Table 4.3. Book debt is very close to total liabilities since the total amount of preferred stocks and deferred taxes is negligible. In the words of Welch (2011, p. 2), *"Convertible debt is, for all practical purposes, irrelevant in the average firm, as are minority interest, capitalized leases, income tax payable, and preferred stock."* As Rajan and Zingales (1995) stated (see Table 4.2), this broad definition of leverage is likely to overstate the financial leverage as it includes non-interest-bearing debt like accounts payable and other liabilities. However, for some firms, these non-interest-bearing items are a crucial part of the capital structure.

Table 4.3: Book and Market Value of Leverage (Dependent Variables).

Variables	Formula/Proxy	Abbreviation
Book Leverage	Book Debt[a] / Total Assets	BLEV
Market Leverage	Book Debt / (Total Assets – Book Equity[b] + Market Equity)	MLEV

[a] whereby, Book Debt = Total Assets – Book Equity.
[b] whereby, Book Equity = Total Assets – Total Liabilities – Preferred Stocks + Deferred Taxes
Source: own contribution.

163 According to Myers (1977), managers focus on book leverage because debt is better supported by assets-in-place than growth opportunities.

Credit rating agencies state that traditional measures focusing on long-term debt have lost much of their significance, and "*Pension and retiree obligations are similar to debt in many respects.*" (Standard & Poor's 2006, pp. 27–28) We followed past studies that have used the same or similar leverage proxies, such as Baker and Wurgler (2002), Fama and French (2002), R Huang and Ritter (2004), MacKay and Phillips (2005), Alti (2006), Kayhan and Titman (2007), Aggarwal and Zhao (2007), Mahajan and Tartaroglu (2008), Rongbing Huang and Ritter (2009), and P. F. P. Alves and Ferreira (2011).[164]

Important Note: As for the analysis of firms' capital structure and financing behavior, we relied on the accepted leverage ratios by the academia and capital structure theories (as described in previous paragraphs). As far as the DJIMI leverage ratio is concerned, we merely used it as a criterion for the sample creation in Section 4.1. The reason we did not use the DJIMI leverage ratio as a proxy for market leverage is two-fold: First, we could not find any source in the Body of Knowledge of Corporate Finance with such a definition. We cautiously state that this definition does not exist. Second, the DJ proxy (with 24–month trailing market capitalization value in the denominator) does not represent any rational meaning, such as from the Corporate Finance perspective.[165]

4.3.2 Independent Variables and Hypothesis Development

The past empirical research has shown that firm-specific and macroeconomic determinants greatly influence capital structure ratios. The leading capital structure theories use these determinants to explain the financing behavior of firms. In Section 2.5, we have briefly discussed the most relevant firm-specific and macroeconomic determinants and identified that nine out of 16 capital structure determinants have only predictions made by the Trade-Off Theory. The remaining seven have predictions made by both the Trade-Off Theory and Pecking Order Theory. To proceed with our comparative analysis, we focus on those determinants that have predictions made by both theories. We had to exclude research and development (R&D) expenses due to insufficient data availability and continued with the remaining six firm-specific and macroeconomic variables.

Next, we proceed with an in-depth empirical analysis and develop hypotheses for each independent variable based on the previous empirical results, from both the "conventional" capital structure theory's perspective. As far as SC firms are

164 Following past studies, we treated preferred stock as debt. The rationale is that considering the trade-off and pecking order effects, preferred stock, being a fixed claim, more closely resembles debt than equity.

165 This also strengthens the criticism that firms are not only judged (i.e., classified into SC and SNC) by an exogenous factor (see Section 3.4.1) but with a ratio that does not offer any rational interpretation.

concerned, it is of utmost importance to highlight that an Islamic capital structure theory, along with its hypotheses around “debt” or “equity” determinants, does not exist. Therefore, our discussion will remain in the realm of the Trade-Off Theory and Pecking Order Theory. This section will attempt to provide arguments on the selected six debt determinants from the Shari’ah perspective. If we believe that the mainstream results do not go along with our proposed *Islamic Pecking Order financing* model (see Figure 3.4), we will separately present hypotheses and apply them to SC firms. All created hypotheses are to provide an answer to the following research questions:

RQ 2. *What are the significant determinants of capital structure in the context of SC and SNC firms? (Hypothesis 1–6)*

RQ 3. *Are certain capital structure determinants only temporarily important in SC and SNC firms’ leverage decisions, or do they exhibit a consistent impact over time? (Hypothesis 7–12)*

RQ 4. *Are certain capital structure determinants, for SC and SNC firms, more important in some countries, yet unimportant elsewhere? (Hypothesis 13–18)*

RQ 5. *Are certain capital structure determinants, for SC and SNC firms, more important in some industries, yet unimportant elsewhere? (Hypothesis 19–24)*

Important Note: The discussions from the Shari’ah perspective serve as an exploratory consideration. It involves analogical reasoning to make the initial step developing the rationale of the proposed *Islamic Pecking Order* model, which needs an empirical confirmation of the proposed model.

4.3.2.1 Profitability

Profitability is one of the most tested leverage determinants in academic studies. Capital structure theories have different views on the relationship between leverage and *profitability*. According to the Trade-Off Theory (which argues two-sided), more profitable firms should use more debt because of the tax shield. This happens since they can shield more profit to get tax benefits associated with debt tax shields. A positive relationship can also be assumed because profitable companies incur a lower expected cost of financial distress, i.e., making debt financing less costly. Similarly, increased debt will serve as a disciplinary factor for managers when free-cash-flow likely increases together with increased profitability (Jensen, 1986). However, on the other side of the argument, Fama and French (2002), Frank and Goyal (2003), and other findings often show a negative relationship between leverage and *profitability*. For instance, Kayhan and Titman (2007) also find this negative relation in their analysis, but the effect is relatively weak. It is stated that in a dynamic environment of the Trade-Off Theory, the relationship between *profitability* and leverage is negatively related.[166] Furthermore, it is argued that profitable firms may choose to hold on to

166 See, for instance, Flannery and Rangan (2006), Gaud et al. (2005), and R. Huang and Ritter (2009).

their internal funds (retained earnings) to take advantage of future investment opportunities, resulting in lower leverage levels.[167]

According to Pecking Order Theory, retained earnings are the preferred financing option that stays in contrast to the predictions made by the Trade-Off Theory. As stated in Myers (1984), it is expected that profitable firms retain more earnings, which is the preferable source of funding. As such, the amount of leverage needed by the company should decrease. Thus, higher profits will, therefore, also be used to pay down debt, and the companies will achieve a low debt ratio over time.[168] From the Shari'ah perspective, we borrow the prediction made by Pecking Order Theory and complement that firms with excess cash (internal funds) are not permitted to invest in interest-bearing instruments (Thabet and Hanefah, 2014). Consequently, with a sufficient amount of idle cash, firms do not require to engage in any form of external financing. Since debt is highly discouraged by Shari'ah, SC firms are expected to decrease their debt level by debt settlement activities, which in return increases the overall equity ratio. We used EBITDA over total assets as a proxy for profitability.[169]

As predicted by the Pecking Order Theory, academic studies shown in Table 4.4 have found a consistently negative relationship between profitability and leverage. Based on the academic studies overview and the discussion from the Shari'ah perspective, our hypothesis is as follows:

Table 4.4: Academic Studies Overview – Leverage and Profitability.

Author	Year	Country Focus	Applied Methodology	Significant		
				positive	negative	non
Arif and Mai	2020	Indonesia	Cross-Section RE		✓	
Rahim et al.	2020	Malaysia	GMM		✓	
Halim, Sukor, and Bacha	2019	Malaysia	FE	✓		
Akinsomi et al.	2019	GCC	OLS, FE			✓
Alnori and Alqahtani	2019	Saudi Arabia	OLS, FE, GMM		✓	
Mai	2019	Indonesia	Cross-Section RE		✓	

167 See Hennessy and Whited (2005) and Strebulaev (2004).

168 Additionally, the more profitable companies are, the more cash they will carry. To mitigate such agency costs, debt should be more valuable (disciplinary effect on managers' actions). However, since the Pecking Order Theory suggest that internal funds (cash) should be utilized first, higher cash flows ceteris paribus reduce the necessity to issue debt. See Myers (1984).

169 In academic studies, the proxy for profitability differ as some use EBIT Fama and French (2002) and Flannery and Rangan (2006) while others use operating income Frank and Goyal (2003) and Titman and Wessels (1988). Since our sample consists of firms operating in various countries with different legal treatment of depreciation and amortization, EBITDA is believed to be a better measure than EBIT.

Table 4.4 (continued)

Author	Year	Country Focus	Applied Methodology	Significant positive	Significant negative	Significant non
Sahudin et al.	2019	Malaysia	OLS, FE, RE		✓	
Dang and Garrett	2015	USA	OLS		✓	
Ibrahim, Zulkafli, and Ying	2015	Malaysia	FE			✓
Andres et al.	2014	USA	OLS, Fama MacBeth		✓	
Dang, Kim, and Shin	2014	USA	Dynamic Threshold		✓	
Piaw and Jais	2014	Malaysia	OLS, FE, RE	✓		
Piaw and Jais	2014	Malaysia	GMM		✓	
Thabet and Hanefah	2014	Malaysia	OLS, FE, RE		✓	
Cekrezi	2013	Albania	OLS		✓	
Dang	2013	UK, France, Germany	GMM		✓	
McMillan and Camara	2012	USA	GMM, FEIV		✓	
Haron and Ibrahim	2012	Malaysia	GMM	✓	✓	
Fan, Titman, and Twite	2012	International	OLS		✓	
Guney, Li, and Fairchild	2011	China	OLS, FE, GMM		✓	
Hanousek and Shamshur	2011	Europe	OLS, FE, RE			✓
Haron, Ibrahim, and Ibrahim	2011	Asia	GMM		✓	
Kayo and Kimura	2011	International	FE, RE		✓	
Bas, Muradoglu, and Phylaktis	2009	International	OLS		✓	
Deesomsak, Paudyal, and Pescetto	2009	Asia	GMM	✓		
Frank and Goyal	2009	USA	OLS		✓	
Antoniou, Guney, and Paudyal	2008	G5	GMM		✓	
Ariff, Hassan, and Shamsher	2008	Malaysia	GMM, OLS		✓	
Byoun	2008	USA	OLS		✓	
De Jong, Kabir, and Nguyen	2008	International	OLS		✓	
Mahajan and Tartaroglu	2008	G7	OLS, Fama MacBeth		✓	
Cheng and Shiu	2007	International	FE, Tobit		✓	
Delcoure	2007	Europe	OLS, FE, RE	✓	✓	
Kayhan and Titman	2007	USA	Tobit		✓	
Flannery and Rangan	2006	USA	OLS, Fama MacBeth		✓	
Huang and Song	2006	China	OLS		✓	

Table 4.4 (continued)

Author	Year	Country Focus	Applied Methodology	Significant		
				positive	negative	non
Gajurel	2005	Nepal	OLS, GMM		✓	
Gaud et al.	2005	Swiss	OLS, Fama MacBeth, GMM		✓	
MacKay and Phillips	2005	USA	OLS, GMM		✓	
Deesomsak, Paudyal, and Pescetto	2004	Asia	FE		✓	
Dittmar	2004	USA	OLS			✓
Hovakimian, Hovakimian, and Tehranian	2004	USA	Multinomial Logistic		✓	
Frank and Goyal	2003	USA	OLS		✓	
Johnson	2003	International	OLS, FE		✓	
Antoniou, Guney, and Paudyal	2002	UK, France, Germany	GMM		✓	
Baker and Wurgler	2002	USA	OLS		✓	
Fama and French	2002	USA	OLS, Fama MacBeth		✓	
Booth et al.	2001	International	FE		✓	
Graham	2000	USA	Tobit	✓		
Kremp, Stöss, and Gerdesmeier	1999	Germany, French	OLS		✓	
Shyam-Sunder and Myers	1999	USA	OLS		✓	
Wald	1999	G5	OLS		✓	
Wiwattanakantang	1999	Thailand	-			✓
Rajan and Zingales	1995	G7	OLS		✓	
Titman and Wessels	1988	USA	OLS			✓
Kester	1986	USA, Japan	OLS		✓	
Long and Malitz	1985	USA	OLS			✓

Source: own contribution.

Hypothesis 1: *A significant negative relationship between profitability and leverage is expected among SC and SNC companies.*

4.3.2.2 Growth Opportunity

Companies with high growth rates tend to accept risky projects and seek to increase the shareholders' wealth. However, creditors are reluctant to borrow funds due to the higher risk and, accordingly, the cost of borrowing increases. Consequently, firms tend to avoid debt and turn into equity financing, which eventually leads to a negative relationship between *growth opportunity* and leverage. Barclay et al. (2006) state that the debt capacity for growth options is negative. Goyal et al. (2002)

find that when growth opportunities of defense companies decline, these firms increase their use of debt financing. With this consideration, the Trade-Off Theory suggests a negative relationship between *growth opportunity* and leverage (Titman and Wessels, 1988).

In contrast, the Pecking Order Theory predicts a positive relationship between *growth opportunity* and leverage. The rationale is that higher information asymmetries are involved as shareholders are not willing to expose much information about their investment opportunities. These investment opportunities require investment outlays, which leads to an increase in the companies financial deficit and thus causes the companies to issue external financing, preferably short-term debt financing (Gaud et al., 2005). Current and future growth must also arise from (real) investments, which should be financed with more debt according to the Pecking Order Theory. Thus, the negative relationship between *growth opportunity* and leverage is not consistent with the Pecking Order Theory. From the Shari'ah perspective, we disagree with the conventional Pecking Order Theory and call for the Trade-Off Theory's similar reasoning. Firms with investment opportunities are associated with increased financial distress and financial deficit. Even though external financing is required to close the gap, firms with outstanding debt may forgo potential investments (see Section 2.4.1), which eventually leads to a wealth transfer from shareholders to debtholders. Consequently, firms' financial leverage has to be kept low. With the debt restrictions imposed by Shari'ah, firms should utilize internal funds first then use equity and equity-like financing options. Following Frank and Goyal (2003) and many others, we used Market-To-Book (MTB) as a proxy for *growth opportunity*.

As predicted by the Trade-Off Theory, academic studies shown in Table 4.5 have found a consistently negative relationship between growth opportunity and leverage. Based on the academic studies overview and the discussion from the Shari'ah perspective, our hypothesis is as follows:

Table 4.5: Academic Studies Overview – Leverage and Growth Opportunity.

Author	Year	Country Focus	Applied Methodology	Significant		
				positive	negative	non
Rahim et al.	2020	Malaysia	GMM			✓
Akinsomi et al.	2019	GCC	OLS, FE	✓		
Alnori and Alqahtani	2019	Saudi Arabia	OLS, FE, GMM		✓	
Mai	2019	Indonesia	Cross-Section RE	✓	✓	
Sahudin et al.	2019	Malaysia	OLS, FE, RE			✓
Dang and Garrett	2015	USA	OLS		✓	
Ibrahim, Zulkafli, and Ying	2015	Malaysia	FE		✓	
Andres et al.	2014	USA	OLS, Fama MacBeth	✓		

Table 4.5 (continued)

Author	Year	Country Focus	Applied Methodology	Significant		
				positive	negative	non
Dang, Kim, and Shin	2014	USA	Dynamic Threshold	✓		
Piaw and Jais	2014	Malaysia	OLS, FE, RE			✓
Piaw and Jais	2014	Malaysia	GMM			✓
Dang	2013	UK, France, Germany	GMM		✓	
McMillan and Camara	2012	USA	GMM, FEIV		✓	
Haron and Ibrahim	2012	Malaysia	GMM			✓
Fan, Titman, and Twite	2012	International	OLS		✓	
Guney, Li, and Fairchild	2011	China	OLS, FE, GMM	✓		
Kayo and Kimura	2011	International	FE, RE		✓	
Chakraborty	2010	India	OLS, GMM	✓		
Chang, Lee, and Lee	2009	USA	MIMIC		✓	
Deesomsak, Paudyal, and Pescetto	2009	Asia	GMM			✓
Frank and Goyal	2009	USA	OLS		✓	
Antoniou, Guney, and Paudyal	2008	G5	GMM		✓	
Ariff, Hassan, and Shamsher	2008	Malaysia	GMM, OLS		✓	
Byoun	2008	USA	OLS		✓	
De Jong, Kabir, and Nguyen	2008	International	OLS		✓	
Cheng and Shiu	2007	International	FE, Tobit	✓		
Kayhan and Titman	2007	USA	Tobit		✓	
Flannery and Rangan	2006	USA	OLS, Fama MacBeth		✓	
Huang and Song	2006	China	OLS		✓	
Gajurel	2005	Nepal	OLS, GMM			✓
Gaud et al.	2005	Swiss	OLS, Fama MacBeth, GMM		✓	
Högfeldt and Oborenko	2005	Sweden	OLS		✓	
MacKay and Phillips	2005	USA	OLS, GMM		✓	
Deesomsak, Paudyal, and Pescetto	2004	Asia	FE		✓	
Dittmar	2004	USA	OLS			✓
Hovakimian, Hovakimian, and Tehranian	2004	USA	Multinomial Logistic		✓	
Frank and Goyal	2003	USA	OLS		✓	
Johnson	2003	International	OLS, FE		✓	

Table 4.5 (continued)

Author	Year	Country Focus	Applied Methodology	Significant		
				positive	negative	non
Antoniou, Guney, and Paudyal	2002	UK, France, Germany	GMM		✓	
Baker and Wurgler	2002	USA	OLS		✓	
Fama and French	2002	USA	OLS, Fama MacBeth		✓	
Booth et al.	2001	International	FE		✓	
Kremp, Stöss, and Gerdesmeier	1999	Germany, French	OLS	✓		
Shyam-Sunder and Myers	1999	USA	OLS		✓	
Wald	1999	G5	OLS		✓	
Rajan and Zingales	1995	G7	OLS		✓	
Titman and Wessels	1988	USA	OLS			✓
Long and Malitz	1985	USA	OLS		✓	

Source: own contribution.

Hypothesis 2: *A significant negative relationship between growth opportunity and leverage is expected among SC and SNC companies.*

4.3.2.3 Firm Size

Company *size* is one of those determinants, like *profitability* and *growth opportunity*, that provides consistent results in its relationship to leverage. The impact of the *size* effect on leverage depends on which capital structure theory to look at. According to the Trade-Off Theory, a positive relationship can be expected. It is argued that the bigger a company becomes, the less it will face bankruptcy risk. In order words, these companies are too big to fail. Furthermore, the larger a company, the less volatile the company's cash flows will be due to diversification effects that mostly materialize, the bigger a company is.[170]

However, according to the Pecking Order Theory, the situation changes because larger companies are exposed to more monitoring through the capital market, leading to lower information asymmetry. Accordingly, larger companies will be able to issue equity at lower costs, and it is assumed that larger companies have had an opportunity to retain earnings, Frank and Goyal (2009). From the Shari'ah perspective, similar to *profitability,* we borrow the predictions made by Pecking Order Theory.

---

170 Titman and Wessels (1988, p. 6) show *"that relatively large firms tend to be more diversified and less prone to bankruptcy."*

We argue that larger companies have access to both capital markets (i.e., debt and equity) assumingly to the same extent. Therefore, after utilizing their retained earnings, firms should engage primarily in the equity capital market and take the opportunity to issue at lower costs (due to the lower asymmetric information). Logarithm to either sales or total assets is commonly used as a proxy for *size*; thus, we applied the former alternative.

As predicted by the Trade-Off Theory, academic studies shown in Table 4.6 have found a consistently positive relationship between size and leverage. Based on the academic studies overview and the discussion from the Shari'ah perspective, our hypotheses are as follows:

Table 4.6: Academic Studies Overview – Leverage and Firm Size.

Author	Year	Country Focus	Applied Methodology	Significant		
				positive	negative	non
Arif and Mai	2020	Indonesia	Cross-Section RE		✓	
Rahim et al.	2020	Malaysia	GMM	✓		
Akinsomi et al.	2019	GCC	OLS, FE	✓		
Alnori and Alqahtani	2019	Saudi Arabia	OLS, FE, GMM	✓		
Mai	2019	Indonesia	Cross-Section RE	✓		✓
Sahudin et al.	2019	Malaysia	OLS, FE, RE		✓	
Dang and Garrett	2015	USA	OLS	✓		
Ibrahim, Zulkafli, and Ying	2015	Malaysia	FE	✓		
Andres et al.	2014	USA	OLS, Fama MacBeth	✓		
Dang, Kim, and Shin	2014	USA	Dynamic Threshold	✓		
Piaw and Jais	2014	Malaysia	OLS, FE, RE	✓		
Piaw and Jais	2014	Malaysia	GMM	✓		
Cekrezi	2013	Albania	OLS	✓		
Dang	2013	UK, France, Germany	GMM	✓		
McMillan and Camara	2012	USA	GMM, FEIV	✓		
Haron and Ibrahim	2012	Malaysia	GMM		✓	
Fan, Titman, and Twite	2012	International	OLS	✓		
Guney, Li, and Fairchild	2011	China	OLS, FE, GMM	✓		
Haron, Ibrahim, and Ibrahim	2011	Asia	GMM	✓		
Kayo and Kimura	2011	International	FE, RE	✓		
Chakraborty	2010	India	OLS, GMM		✓	
Bas, Muradoglu, and Phylaktis	2009	International	OLS	✓		
Deesomsak, Paudyal, and Pescetto	2009	Asia	GMM	✓		
Frank and Goyal	2009	USA	OLS	✓		
Antoniou, Guney, and Paudyal	2008	G5	GMM	✓		

Table 4.6 (continued)

Author	Year	Country Focus	Applied Methodology	Significant		
				positive	negative	non
Ariff, Hassan, and Shamsher	2008	Malaysia	GMM, OLS	✓		
Beck, Demirgüç-Kunt, and Maksimovic	2008	International	FE	✓		
De Jong, Kabir, and Nguyen	2008	International	OLS	✓		
Cheng and Shiu	2007	International	FE, Tobit	✓		
Delcoure	2007	Europe	OLS, FE, RE	✓		
Kayhan and Titman	2007	USA	Tobit	✓		
Flannery and Rangan	2006	USA	OLS, Fama MacBeth	✓		
Huang and Song	2006	China	OLS	✓		
Gajurel	2005	Nepal	OLS, GMM	✓		
Gaud et al.	2005	Swiss	OLS, Fama MacBeth, GMM	✓		
MacKay and Phillips	2005	USA	OLS, GMM	✓		
Deesomsak, Paudyal, and Pescetto	2004	Asia	FE	✓		
Dittmar	2004	USA	OLS	✓		
Hovakimian, Hovakimian, and Tehranian	2004	USA	Multinomial Logistic	✓		
Frank and Goyal	2003	USA	OLS	✓		
Johnson	2003	International	OLS, FE			✓
Antoniou, Guney, and Paudyal	2002	UK, France, Germany	GMM	✓		
Baker and Wurgler	2002	USA	OLS	✓		
Fama and French	2002	USA	OLS, Fama MacBeth	✓		
Booth et al.	2001	International	FE	✓		
Graham	2000	USA	Tobit	✓		
Wald	1999	G5	OLS	✓		
Rajan and Zingales	1995	G7	OLS	✓	✓	
Mackie-Mason	1990	USA	OLS	✓		
Fischer, Heinkel, and Zechner	1989	USA	OLS		✓	
Titman and Wessels	1988	USA	OLS		✓	
Kester	1986	USA, Japan	OLS		✓	
Marsh	1982	UK	Logit & Probit	✓		

Source: own contribution.

Hypothesis 3a: *A significant negative relationship between firm size and leverage is expected for SC companies.* ***Hypothesis 3b:*** *A significant positive relationship between firm size and leverage is expected for SNC companies.*

4.3.2.4 Tangibility

The quality of a firm's tangible assets directly measures the firm's security to the existing and potential investors. The Trade-Off Theory predicts that the company's leverage increases with *tangibility*. The reason is that fixed assets, being easier to value than intangibles, provide more security for potential investors as collateral. This will reduce the risk for debtholders and ultimately reduce the cost of debt for the companies. They will operate with higher leverage ratios without incurring higher financial distress costs (Titman and Wessels, 1988). Furthermore, collateralized debt makes it difficult for investors to conduct asset substitution as the debtholders have collateral in specific assets (Frank and Goyal, 2009). Therefore, agency costs should be lower between shareholders and debtholders, and companies should use more debt relative to the total amount of tangible assets they own.

The Pecking Order Theory argues in the opposite direction as it suggests that *tangibility* will generate fewer information asymmetries between potential investors and shareholders. Hence, the cost of issuing equity will fall, resulting in lower levels of debt (Frank and Goyal, 2009). So unless the cost of equity falls below the cost of debt (as predicted by Trade-Off Theory), the Pecking Order Theory implies that companies will use the cheapest sources of funding, debt would still be the preferred funding to equity, at least for moderate amounts of debt. However, Harris and Raviv (1991) state that it can be expected that companies with little tangible assets would have bigger asymmetric information problems. In this way, firms with few tangible assets will collect more debt over time and become more highly leveraged. Therefore, the prediction of the Pecking Order Theory might not be as explicit as some researchers argue. From the Shari'ah perspective, similar to *firm size, tangibility* generates fewer information asymmetries between potential investors and existing shareholders. Consequently, equity financing becomes cheaper than debt financing. Furthermore, firms can utilize their *tangible assets* as an underlying asset for issuing *Sukuk (plural for sakk)* through SPV (Special Purpose Vehicle).[171] The existence of a tangible underlying asset is obligatory in most forms of *Sukuk*. *Sukuk*, the most successful and most visible Islamic finance product today (worldwide), is a fund-raising Islamic finance product and has often been referred to as *Islamic bonds* (Bacha and Mirakhor, 2013). Unlike conventional bonds, *Sukuk* is not a debt but a quasi-*equity* (often called *hybrid*) financing instrument with both instruments' features.[172] Following Baker and Wurgler (2002) and Frank and Goyal (2009), we used property, plant, and equipment, net (PPE) over total assets as a proxy for *tangibility*.[173]

---

171 We disagree with the proponents who claim that Islamic firms could have their debt level as high as it does not exceed its tangible assets. Ahmed (2007) This way, we don't see any difference compared to the notion of Trade-Off Theory, which favors and emphasizes debt financing primarily.

172 For detailed information, see Bacha and Mirakhor (2013, pp. 171–176).

173 Measures of asset tangibility differ between the empirical papers. The measure taken for tangibility should be compared to the measure used for leverage. Suppose the leverage measure used is

As predicted by the Trade-Off Theory, academic studies shown in Table 4.7 have found a consistently positive relationship between tangibility and leverage. Based on the academic studies overview and the discussion from the Shari'ah perspective, our hypothesis is as follows:

Table 4.7: Academic Studies Overview – Leverage and Tangibility.

Author	Year	Country Focus	Applied Methodology	Significant		
				positive	negative	non
Arif and Mai	2020	Indonesia	CrossSection RE	✓		
Alnori and Alqahtani	2019	Saudi Arabia	OLS, FE, GMM	✓		
Mai	2019	Indonesia	CrossSection RE	✓		✓
Halim, Sukor, and Bacha	2019	Malaysia	FE			✓
Sahudin et al.	2019	Malaysia	OLS, FE, RE		✓	
Dang and Garrett	2015	USA	OLS	✓		
Ibrahim, Zulkafli, and Ying	2015	Malaysia	FE			✓
Andres et al.	2014	USA	OLS, Fama MacBeth	✓		
Dang, Kim, and Shin	2014	USA	Dynamic Threshold	✓		
Piaw and Jais	2014	Malaysia	OLS, FE, RE		✓	
Piaw and Jais	2014	Malaysia	GMM		✓	
Thabet and Hanefah	2014	Malaysia	OLS, FE, RE			✓
Cekrezi	2013	Albania	OLS	✓		
Dang	2013	UK, France, Germany	GMM	✓		
McMillan and Camara	2012	USA	GMM, FEIV	✓		
Haron and Ibrahim	2012	Malaysia	GMM	✓		
Fan, Titman, and Twite	2012	International	OLS	✓		
Guney, Li, and Fairchild	2011	China	OLS, FE, GMM	✓		
Hanousek and Shamshur	2011	Europe	OLS, FE, RE	✓		
Haron, Ibrahim, and Ibrahim	2011	Asia	GMM		✓	
Kayo and Kimura	2011	International	FE, RE	✓		
Chakraborty	2010	India	OLS, GMM	✓		
Bas, Muradoglu, and Phylaktis	2009	International	OLS		✓	
Deesomsak, Paudyal, and Pescetto	2009	Asia	GMM	✓		
Frank and Goyal	2009	USA	OLS	✓		

total liabilities to total assets. In that case, as Welch (2011) suggests, a broad measure of tangibility is likely needed to capture all factors that could serve as collateral, e.g., inventory, accounts receivables, etc. In studies using total debt to total assets as a proxy for leverage, fixed assets to total assets will be a suitable measure of asset tangibility.

Table 4.7 (continued)

Author	Year	Country Focus	Applied Methodology	Significant		
				positive	negative	non
Antoniou, Guney, and Paudyal	2008	G5	GMM	✓		
Ariff, Hassan, and Shamsher	2008	Malaysia	GMM, OLS	✓		
Byoun	2008	USA	OLS	✓		
De Jong, Kabir, and Nguyen	2008	International	OLS	✓		
Cheng and Shiu	2007	International	FE, Tobit		✓	
Delcoure	2007	Europe	OLS, FE, RE	✓		
Kayhan and Titman	2007	USA	Tobit	✓		
Flannery and Rangan	2006	USA	OLS, Fama MacBeth	✓		
Huang and Song	2006	China	OLS	✓		
Gajurel	2005	Nepal	OLS, GMM	✓		
Gaud et al.	2005	Swiss	OLS, Fama MacBeth, GMM	✓		
MacKay and Phillips	2005	USA	OLS, GMM	✓		
Deesomsak, Paudyal, and Pescetto	2004	Asia	FE	✓		
Dittmar	2004	USA	OLS	✓		
Frank and Goyal	2003	USA	OLS	✓		
Johnson	2003	International	OLS, FE	✓		
Antoniou, Guney, and Paudyal	2002	UK, France, Germany	GMM	✓		
Baker and Wurgler	2002	USA	OLS	✓		
Booth et al.	2001	International	FE		✓	
Graham	2000	USA	Tobit		✓	
Kremp, Stöss, and Gerdesmeier	1999	Germany, French	OLS	✓		
Shyam-Sunder and Myers	1999	USA	OLS	✓		
Wald	1999	G5	OLS	✓		
Wiwattanakantang	1999	Thailand		✓		
Rajan and Zingales	1995	G7	OLS	✓		
Mackie-Mason	1990	USA	OLS	✓		
Titman and Wessels	1988	USA	OLS	✓		
Long and Malitz	1985	USA	OLS	✓		
Bradley, Jarrell, and Kim	1984	USA	ANOVA	✓		
Marsh	1982	UK	Logit & Probit	✓		

Source: own contribution.

Hypothesis 4a: *A significant negative relationship between tangibility and leverage is expected for SC companies.* ***Hypothesis 4b:*** *A significant positive relationship between tangibility and leverage is expected for SNC companies.*

4.3.2.5 Business Risk (Earnings Volatility)

As the firm's earnings volatility increases, it increases the probability of default on its debt payment. This reduces creditors' confidence level to extend new loans to risky firms and ends up with a higher financial cost. Thus, according to the Trade-Off Theory, these firms need to lower their debt level to minimize their bankruptcy risk. Frank and Goyal (2009) state that volatility in earnings may limit the probability of fully utilizing the benefits from tax shields, leading to lower debt levels. DeAngelo and Masulis (1980) argue that the cost of debt will increase for firms with variability in their earnings since investors will not predict future earnings accurately based on the publicly available information. Bradley et al. (1984) argue further that the firm value variability is expected to negatively influence the debt ratio when financial distress costs are high. Consequently, this suggests a negative relationship between *business risk* and leverage.

On the contrary, the Pecking Order Theory predicts that higher risk leads to higher leverage. The rationale behind this is that volatility in earnings will lead investors to require a higher return rate, making it more expensive to issue equity (Rajan and Zingales, 1995). From the Shari'ah perspective, first, similar to *growth opportunity*, we disagree with the conventional Pecking Order Theory and are in line with the Trade-Off Theory's reasoning. Second, business risk and its positive association with reward/profit are essential from the Islamic perspective. Specifically, firms are exposed to business risk by default, and the legal maxim „*Al-Ghurm bi Al-Ghunm*"[174] forms the basis of Islamic economic transactions. It states that „*Liability [is an obligation that] accompanies gain*", and the notion of this maxim is that the benefits (*entitlement of gain*) and liabilities (*responsibility of loss*) go together. This maxim is usually used to propose the preference for profit-and-loss sharing financing instruments.[175] In other words, this legal maxim addresses the relationship between business risk and the capital (*mal*) provided by an individual or institution (*rab al-mal*) in the form of *Mudharabah/Musharakah* (equity financing). Consequently, firms with business risk are expected to engage in risk-sharing transactions such as equity and quasi-equity financing instruments (e.g., *Sukuk*). We used the most common measure for *business risk*, which is the standard deviation of EBIT (of the previous two years).

As predicted by the Trade-Off Theory, academic studies shown in Table 4.8 have found a predominantly negative relationship between business risk and leverage. Based on the academic studies overview and the discussion from the Shari'ah perspective, our hypothesis is as follows:

---

174 See Majallah Al-Ahkam Article 87. Retrieved from: http://legal.pipa.ps/files/server/ENG%20Ottoman%20Majalle%20(Civil%20Law).pdf (accessed August 1, 2020).

175 For more information, see ISRA (2016, p. 24).

Table 4.8: Academic Studies Overview – Leverage and Business Risk.

Author	Year	Country Focus	Applied Methodology	Significant		
				positive	negative	non
Rahim et al.	2020	Malaysia	GMM			✓
Mai	2019	Indonesia	CrossSection RE		✓	✓
Thabet and Hanefah	2014	Malaysia	OLS, FE, RE		✓	
Cekrezi	2013	Albania	OLS	✓		
Haron and Ibrahim	2012	Malaysia	GMM	✓		✓
Deesomsak, Paudyal, and Pescetto	2009	Asia	GMM		✓	
Frank and Goyal	2009	USA	OLS		✓	
Antoniou, Guney, and Paudyal	2008	G5	GMM			✓
Ariff, Hassan, and Shamsher	2008	Malaysia	GMM, OLS	✓		
De Jong, Kabir, and Nguyen	2008	International	OLS		✓	
Delcoure	2007	Europe	OLS, FE, RE		✓	
Huang and Song	2006	China	OLS		✓	
Gajurel	2005	Nepal	OLS, GMM	✓		
Gaud et al.	2005	Swiss	OLS, Fama MacBeth, GMM	✓		
Deesomsak, Paudyal, and Pescetto	2004	Asia	FE	✓		
Antoniou, Guney, and Paudyal	2002	UK, France, Germany	GMM			✓
Booth et al.	2001	International	FE		✓	
Kremp, Stöss, and Gerdesmeier	1999	Germany, French	OLS		✓	
Wald	1999	G5	OLS		✓	
Mackie-Mason	1990	USA	OLS		✓	
Titman and Wessels	1988	USA	OLS		✓	
Bradley, Jarrell, and Kim	1984	USA	ANOVA		✓	
Marsh	1982	UK	Logit & Probit		✓	

Source: own contribution.

Hypothesis 5: *A significant negative relationship between business risk and leverage is expected among SC and SNC companies.*

4.3.2.6 GDP Growth

Business activities usually go along with the economic growth of a country. Specifically, companies utilize opportunities to kick-off expansion and investment programs to generate more profits during peak times, thus enhancing the firm value. The Trade-Off Theory predicts that higher profits make debt financing due to larger tax shield benefits more attractive. De Jong et al. (2008) show that the higher the economic growth, the higher the firms' willingness to employ debts to finance their new investments. The Pecking Order Theory shares a similar notion that *GDP growth* is associated with higher profits for companies. However, contrary to the Trade-Off Theory, the Pecking Order Theory claims that firms can stack more internal capital, making debt financing less relevant. Following Beck et al. (2008), we used GDP growth (annual %) as a proxy for *economic growth.*

From the Shari'ah perspective, firms operating in countries with economic growth, their capital structure is affected two-fold: First, *ceteris paribus* remains as-is since firms usually generate more revenue and build up cash (internal funds). With the limitations imposed on them, as discussed in *profitability* in Section 4.3.2.1, they can utilize internal funds to finance their assets/investments. Second, firms' business spendings increase, including the addition of tangible assets, investment in new technologies, and the utilization of their investment opportunities (*growth opportunity*). In case internal funds are used up, and external financing is needed, when markets are at their peak, and stock prices are rising (bull market), the market sentiment becomes positive, which further leads to an increase in companies' confidence level investors. Consequently, firms are expected to go down the latter and issue equity or engage in quasi-equity financing (e.g., *Sukuk*).

Academic studies in Table 4.9 have found a rather mixed result of the relationship between *economic growth* and leverage. The results show a predominantly negative relationship that supports the prediction of the Pecking Order Theory. While Bas et al. (2009) and Hanousek and Shamshur (2011) find a positive relationship, other academics such as Ariff et al. (2008) and Haron and Ibrahim (2012) find a negative correlation between *economic growth* and leverage.

Based on the academic studies overview and the discussion from the Shari'ah perspective, our hypothesis is as follows:

Table 4.9: Academic Studies Overview – Leverage and GDP growth.

Author	Year	Country Focus	Applied Methodology	Significant		
				positive	negative	non
Arif and Mai	2020	Indonesia	Cross-Section RE			✓
Mai	2019	Indonesia	Cross-Section RE			✓
Halim, Sukor, and Bacha	2019	Malaysia	FE		✓	
Piaw and Jais	2014	Malaysia	GMM		✓	
Cekrezi	2013	Albania	OLS	✓		
Haron and Ibrahim	2012	Malaysia	GMM		✓	
Hanousek and Shamshur	2011	Europe	OLS, FE, RE	✓		
Haron, Ibrahim, and Ibrahim	2011	Asia	GMM	✓		
Kayo and Kimura	2011	International	FE, RE		✓	
Bas, Muradoglu, and Phylaktis	2009	International	OLS	✓		

Table 4.9 (continued)

Author	Year	Country Focus	Applied Methodology	Significant		
				positive	negative	non
Ariff, Hassan, and Shamsher	2008	Malaysia	GMM, OLS		✓	
Cheng and Shiu	2007	International	FE, Tobit		✓	
Gajurel	2005	Nepal	OLS, GMM		✓	

Source: own contribution.

Hypothesis 6: *A significant negative relationship between GDP growth and leverage is expected among SC and SNC companies.*

Table 4.10 summarizes the six firm-specific and macroeconomic variables and their proxy definition,[176] enhanced with the predictions made by the Trade-Off Theory and Pecking Order Theory (represented in Table 2.1), and the proposed Islamic version of the Pecking Order model.

Table 4.10: Firm-specific and macroeconomic determinants (Independent Variables).

Variables	Formula/Proxy	Description	Abbreviation	Predictions		
Firm-Specific				TOT	POT	IPOM
Profitability	EBITDA/Total Assets	Return on Assets (ROA)	PROF	+/[–]*	–	–
Growth Opportunity	Market Value Assets/ Book Value Assets	Market-to-Book	GROWTH	–	+	–
Size (Sales)	Logarithm of Total Sales	Firm Size	SIZE	+	–	–
Tangibility	Fixed (Tangible) Assets/ Total Assets	Fixed Assets	TANG	+	–	–
Business Risk	Std. Deviation of EBIT	Earnings Volatility	RISK	–	+	–
Macroeconomic						
GDP	GDP Growth	GDP growth (annual %)	GDP	+	–	–

* Dynamic Trade-Off Theory.
IPOM = Islamic Pecking Order Model.

Source: own contribution.

176 We have applied a various number of other proxies for each of the firm-specific variables such as ROE (for *profitability*), the natural logarithm of assets (*firm size*), accounts receivable (*tangibility*), etc. However, due to multicollinearity and Variance Inflation Factor (VIF) results, we have removed those variables that were highly correlated with other variables. Table A.6 in Appendix A provides an overview of all of the financial items and its description used to construct all firm-specific and macroeconomic variables in this study.

Until this point, we developed our hypotheses to evaluate the impact of debt determinants on SC and SNC firms' leverage decisions, in general. We were also interested in finding out whether these capital structure determinants lose their significance over time. We controlled that certain determinants that seem important in our *overall (pooled)* sample analysis might fail to have a permanent and consistent impact on the capital structure over time. Accordingly, based on this rationale, we developed and represented ***Hypothesis 7–12*** in Table 4.11 under Research Question 3. Furthermore, to identify the cross-sectional differences, we also analyzed the importance of these determinants in each *country* and each business *industry*. Hence, we developed the subsequent hypotheses, ***Hypothesis 13–18*** and ***Hypothesis 19–23*** and represented in Table 4.11 under Research Questions 4 and 5, respectively.

4.4 Model Specification and Testing Model

4.4.1 Regression Model Specification

In Section 4.3, we described the dataset, the dependent variables, and explanatory (independent) variables. Now, we move on to a formal depiction of the regression models that are utilized. The general form of the *static* models is:

$$y_{it} = \alpha + \beta x_{i,t-1} + \mu_i + \mu_t + \varepsilon_{it} \tag{12}$$

Where $x_{i,t-1}$ is the vector of 1–year lagged firm-specific and macroeconomic control independent variables, α is the constant term, μ_i the individual error, μ_t a time-specific component of the error term (in other words, we have added time dummies to account for global financial crisis effects) and ε_{it} the classical error term. The independent variable vector includes proxies for firm-specific variables such as profitability (*prof*), growth opportunity (*growth*), firm size (*size*), tangibility (*tang*), volatility (*risk*), and macroeconomic variable GDP growth (*gdp*). After replacing the vector $x_{i,t-1}$ with the firm-specific and macroeconomic determinants, the *static* regression model (12) became:

$$\begin{aligned} blev_{it} = \alpha &+ \beta_1 prof_{i,t-1} + \beta_2 growth_{i,t-1} + \beta_3 size_{i,t-1} \\ &+ \beta_4 tang_{i,t-1} + \beta_5 risk_{i,t-1} + \beta_6 gdp_{i,t-1} + \mu_i + \mu_t + \varepsilon_{it} \end{aligned} \tag{13}$$

$$\begin{aligned} mlev_{it} = \alpha &+ \beta_1 prof_{i,t-1} + \beta_2 growth_{i,t-1} + \beta_3 size_{i,t-1} \\ &+ \beta_4 tang_{i,t-1} + \beta_5 risk_{i,t-1} + \beta_6 gdp_{i,t-1} + \mu_i + \mu_t + \varepsilon_{it} \end{aligned} \tag{14}$$

Where *blev* and *mlev* are the book and market leverage for firm *i* in year *t*, respectively, with the respective determinants. The μ_i denotes the time-invariant unobserv-

Table 4.11: Overview of Hypotheses.

Research Question 2:		**What are the significant determinants of capital structure in the context of SC and SNC firms?**
Determinants	**ID**	**Hypothesis**
Profitability	H.1	A significant negative relationship between profitability and leverage is expected among SC and SNC companies.
Growth Opportunity	H.2	A significant negative relationship between growth opportunity and leverage is expected among SC and SNC companies.
Firm Size	H.3a	A significant positive relationship between firm size and leverage is expected among SC and SNC companies.
	H.3b	A significant negative relationship between firm size and leverage is expected for SC companies.
Tangibility	H.4a	A significant positive relationship between tangibility and leverage is expected among SC and SNC companies.
	H.4b	A significant negative relationship between tangibility and leverage is expected for SC companies.
Business Risk	H.5	A significant negative relationship between business risk and leverage is expected among SC and SNC companies.
GDP growth	H.6	A significant negative relationship between GDP growth and leverage is expected among SC and SNC companies.
Research Question 3:		**Are certain capital structure determinants only temporarily important in SC and SNC firms' leverage decisions, or do they exhibit a consistent impact over time?**
Determinants	**ID**	**Hypothesis**
Profitability	H.7	The positive/negative impact of profitability on SC and SNC company's capital structure remains the same over time.
Growth Opportunity	H.8	The positive/negative impact of growth opportunity on SC and SNC company's capital structure remains the same over time.
Firm Size	H.9	The positive/negative impact of firm size on SC and SNC company's capital structure remains the same over time.
Tangibility	H.10	The positive/negative impact of tangibility on SC and SNC company's capital structure remains the same over time.
Business Risk	H.11	The positive/negative impact of business risk on SC and SNC company's capital structure remains the same over time.
GDP growth	H.12	The positive/negative impact of GDP growth on SC and SNC company's capital structure remains the same over time.

Research Question 4:		**Are certain capital structure determinants, for SC and SNC firms, more important in some *countries*, yet unimportant elsewhere?**
Determinants	**ID**	**Hypothesis**
Profitability	H.13	The effect of profitability on SC and SNC company's capital structure differs among *countries*.
Growth Opportunity	H.14	The growth opportunity effect on SC and SNC company's capital structure differs among *countries*.
Firm Size	H.15	The firm size effect on SC and SNC company's capital structure differs among *countries*.
Tangibility	H.16	The effect of the tangibility on SC and SNC company's capital structure differs among *countries*.
Business Risk	H.17	The risk effect on SC and SNC company's capital structure differs among *countries*.
GDP growth	H.18	The effect of GDP growth on SC and SNC company's capital structure differs among *countries*.
Research Question 5:		**Are certain capital structure determinants, for SC and SNC firms, more important in some *industries*, yet unimportant elsewhere?**
Determinants	**ID**	**Hypothesis**
Profitability	H.19	The effect of profitability on SC and SNC company's capital structure differs among *industries*.
Growth Opportunity	H.20	The growth opportunity effect on SC and SNC company's capital structure differs among *industries*.
Firm Size	H.21	The firm size effect on SC and SNC company's capital structure differs among *industries*.
Tangibility	H.22	The effect of the tangibility on SC and SNC company's capital structure differs among *industries*.
Business Risk	H.23	The risk effect on SC and SNC company's capital structure differs among *industries*.
GDP growth	H.24	The effect of GDP growth on SC and SNC company's capital structure differs among *industries*.

Source: own contribution.

able firm-specific fixed effects (e.g., management performance, reputation, capital intensity, etc.). The μ_t represents the firm-invariant time-specific fixed effects (e.g., stagflation, interest rates, inflation rates, demand shocks, etc.), common to all firms but change through time. The disturbance term is denoted as ε_{it} and is assumed to be mean equal to zero, uncorrelated with itself, uncorrelated with x, uncorrelated with μ_i and homoskedastic, i.e., $\varepsilon_{it} \approx i.i.d.N(0,\sigma^2)$.

We made use of 1–year lagged explanatory variables for two reasons. First, to mitigate the endogeneity problem (see Section 4.2.2) and second, it is believed that the impact of the debt determinants (especially firm-specific determinants) have their impact on the firm's leverage decision at least one year later. The notion behind this is that firm managers need a certain "buffer time" to oversee and evaluate the firm's internal position before making such a strategic financing decision. The survey of Graham and Harvey (2001) supports the notion and report that managers use book values (which indicates past values) to decide the firm's capital structure.

4.4.2 Testing Models

4.4.2.1 Testing Approach I

We conducted our analysis from three perspectives, namely *overall (pooled)*, *country*, and *industry*, respectively. As pointed out in Myers (2002), certain financing characteristics might vary among firms operating under certain circumstances; hence the reason for differentiating between various countries and industries in our sample is to detect possible cross-sectional variations in the effect of certain debt determinants. The equations (13) and (14) supported us in answering the RQ's 2, 3, 4, and 5.

4.4.2.2 Testing Approach II

We followed a similar testing approach used in Öztekin (2013) and Weigl (2011)[177] to answer RQ 6. Specifically, to determine the explanatory power of both capital structure theories, including the proposed *Islamic Pecking Order* model, we assessed whether the sign (positive/negative) of each determinant is consistent with the predictions made by Trade-Off Theory and Pecking Order Theory. It should be noted that we did

177 In Weigl (2011), the author applied a similar testing approach with the focus on the US market only; however, analyzing the capital structure determinants of 11 industries over the period from 1990 to 2008. Similarly, Öztekin (2013) examined the explanation power of capital structure theories and investigates the international determinants of capital structure using a large sample of firms from 37 countries over the period from 1991 to 2006.

not define any focus variable nor applied any weight on the debt determinants. In other words, we treated all variables equally.

As for the *overall (pooled)* approach, we estimated the regression models (13) and (14) as a pooled model. All SC and SNC firms are combined individually to estimate the *overall (pooled)* sample's capital structure determinants (a single *β's*), using both leverage measures. If a determinant was statistically significant at the 90% or higher confidence level, we assumed that it is a reliable factor across all firms around the sample countries, respectively sample industries, hence assigned to it a score of 1 (one). Alternatively, we assigned a 0 (zero) score if the capital structure determinants had an insignificant coefficient estimate. We required a score of 1 (one) to consider a debt factor to be reliable.

As for the cross-section approach, for instance, in the *country* perspective, we estimated the regression models (13) and (14) separately for each country to obtain an estimate of each country's capital structure determinants (*β*'s), using both leverage measures. We then summed up the number of countries (out of seven) separately where each determinant showed the same sign (positive/negative) and was statistically significant at the 90% or higher confidence level. If the correlations consistently hold for the sample countries, we concluded that the debt determinant in question is a reliable factor for the financing decision cross-*country*. As a rule of thumb, we required a capital structure determinant to be significant with a consistent sign in at least 50% of the time, thus in at least 4 (four) countries. The *industry* perspective approach resembled the same testing procedure as the *country* approach.

4.4.2.3 Testing Approach III

We strengthened our analysis by applying a direct measure of each dominant capital structure theory. First, we tested the *dynamic* version of the Trade-Off Theory, which allowed us to identify whether firms under study follow an optimal capital structure (see Section 2.3). In this case (i.e., the *dynamic* regression models), both equations (13) and (14) remained the same with the differences that we a) incorporated the lagged dependent variable on the right side of the models and b) classified all independent variables into *endogenous*, *predetermined* and *exogenous*, as described in Section 4.2.2. The higher the speed of adjustment value (i.e., the estimated coefficient (*β*) of the lagged dependent variable) suggests that firms actively pursue their target capital structure.

Second, we regressed the firms' financial deficit against their *debt issues* and *equity issues* as predicted by the Pecking Order Theory. We analyzed and compared the magnitude of the estimated coefficients (*β*) of the financial deficit on both issues. The higher the estimated coefficients on the former (*debt issues*) than the latter (*equity issues*), the more Pecking Order Theory exhibits its dominance. This analysis will support us in answering RQ 7 for SC firms.

4.4.2.4 Testing Approach IV

Last, to answer the same RQ 7, however, for SC *(RIEM)* firms, we compared the financing behavior of the SC/SNC *(RIEM)* firm sample identified based on the proposed *RIEM 66 Index* represented in Table 3.8. We aim to determine whether the proposed lenient-type equity ratio yields a better SC firm sample than the firms identified by the Shari'ah screening criterion of DJIMI. The empirical results will help determine whether these firms follow a financing order closer to the postulated *Islamic Pecking Order* financing hierarchy represented in Figure 3.4.

4.4.2.5 Robustness Tests

Any proper research has robustness tests integrated to validate the estimation results. This study identified and incorporated three robustness tests to validate the results obtained for RQ 2–6.

4.5 Conclusion

The appropriateness of a research method's determination is a crucial task in research. A systematic procedure is essential to carry out valid research. This depends on the data sources, formulation of the dependent and independent variables, and the modeling specifications and selected estimators. This study focused primarily on SC and SNC listed firms, identified by Dow Jones (DJ), operating in seven countries and seven industries. Furthermore, we captured country-/industry-specific behavior (the relationship between capital structure determinants and leverage) with the support of the most advanced econometric tools and techniques using an unbalanced dataset. In general, we utilized panel data analysis (with *static* and *dynamic* regression models) to test the hypotheses, as all the models are designed and based on theoretical and empirical considerations.

5 Cross-Country and Cross-Industry Determinants

This chapter presents and discusses the empirical results of various data analysis carried out in this study. The progress of this chapter resembles the structure of the developed hypotheses summarized in Table 4.11. Before examining the impact of the selected debt determinants on firm leverage for the *overall (pooled)*, cross-*country*, and cross-*industry* firm samples, we also present the descriptive statistics that show the range of data and its dispersion from its central tendency. The correlation analysis offers the examination of the bivariate relationship of the variables used in this study. This chapter also provides the time-breakdown analysis applied to the *overall (pooled)* sample and investigates the explanatory power of both capital structure theories discussed in Sections 2.3 and 2.4, respectively. RQ's 2–6 will be answered systematically throughout the sections, and this chapter ends with Section 5.3 robustness tests and Section 5.4 conclusion. Appendices A through F provide supplementary information on the results and regressions presented in Chapter 5 and Chapter 6.

5.1 Descriptive Summary and Correlation Matrix Analysis

As mentioned in Section 4.1, only non-financial companies have been included in our study, totaling a sample of 1406 firms. A total of 791 and 615 firms were classified as being SC and SNC, respectively. Figure 5.1 represents the sample breakdown, and the number of SC firms almost double compared to SNC firms in four out of seven countries. These companies operate in different industries, and similarly, the number of SC firms exceeds the number of SNC firms (Figure 5.2) in four out of seven industries. The largest number of SC firms under study is from the United States and Japan, and the industries' point of view, Industrials, Consumer Goods and Technology, respectively.[178]

In selected countries and industries, the real number of SC firms is much less than SNC firms. Our sample is affected by applying the strict selection criteria, especially the *three years of consecutiveness* criteria, as described in Section 4.1. However, it should be noted that the number of SC and SNC firms and their number of observations are sufficient enough to proceed with and conduct our comparative analysis among both firm types.[179]

178 Table A.2 in Appendix A provides a detailed overview of all companies under study, classified in countries, industries, and in SC and SNC, respectively.

179 Tables A.3–A.5 in Appendix A provide the structure of panel data used in this study.

https://doi.org/10.1515/9783110713664-005

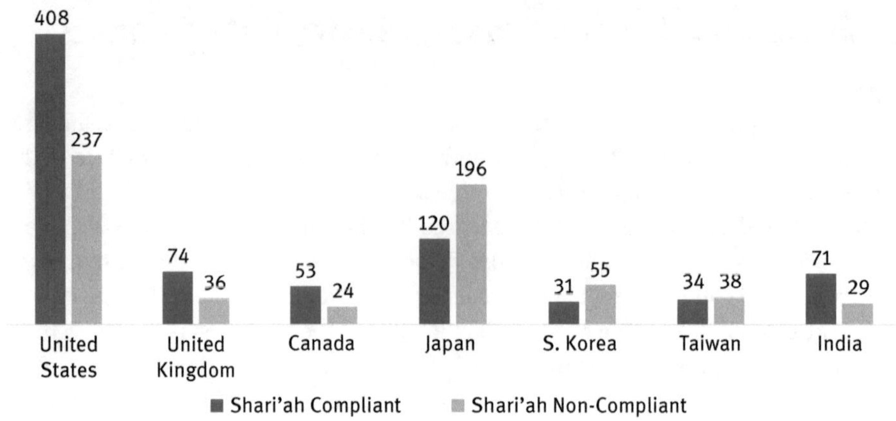

Figure 5.1: *Country* Breakdown (Number of Firms).
Source: own contribution.

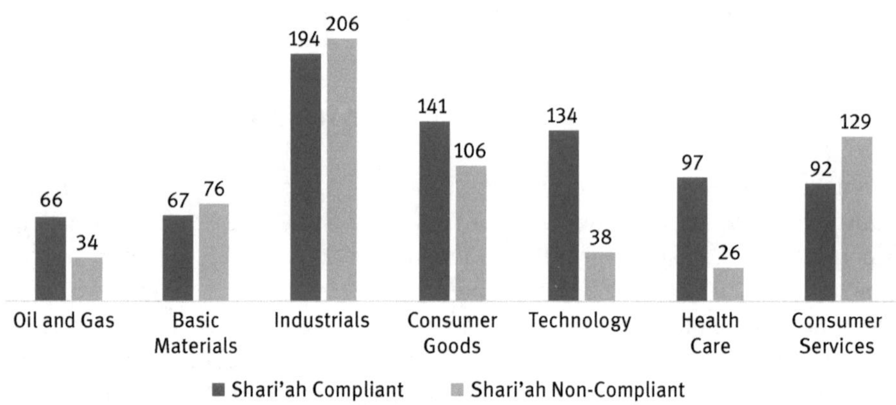

Figure 5.2: *Industry* Breakdown (Number of Firms).
Source: own contribution.

5.1.1 Descriptive Analysis

The following section deals with the capital structure of the sample. The sample firms were determined according to the Dow Jones Shari'ah screening methodologies (i.e., DJIMI), with a debt-to-equity ratio of 33% (maximum threshold) (see Section 4.1). Firms with a leverage ratio below the Shari'ah threshold were considered to be SC, otherwise SNC. Tables 5.1 and 5.2 provide an overview of both leverage proxies for the sample under study, differentiating in *overall (pooled)*, SC and SNC, and in each year, respectively. The main reason to divide this study into each year is to detect possible diverging results within the given time frame.

Table 5.1 describes the mean, standard deviation, minimum, maximum, and the number of observations of both leverage proxies based on the unbalanced overall

Table 5.1: Summary Statistics of Leverage.

Sample	Leverage	Mean	SD	Min	Max	Obs
Overall (Pooled)	Book	0.51	0.20	0.08	0.92	11551
	Market	0.37	0.24	0.02	0.88	11551
Shari'ah Compliant	Book	0.40	0.17	0.08	0.92	6618
	Market	0.19	0.11	0.02	0.70	6618
Shari'ah Non-Compliant	Book	0.66	0.13	0.22	0.92	4933
	Market	0.60	0.14	0.22	0.88	4933

Source: own contribution.

(pooled) sample. The definitions of book leverage and market leverage are provided in Table 4.3 (see Section 4.3.1). All variables are winsorized at the 1% and 99% level. The descriptive statistics reveal that the mean book leverage for all SC firms is 40%,[180] which is much less than that of SNC, which reports a mean of 66%, indicating that SC firms borrow less than their non-compliant peers. It can be observed that SCs leverage ratio for maximum percentiles reaches 92% as high as their non-compliant peers, which indicates that SC firms on the higher percentile are on the same level of indebtedness. This result is surprising, but it confirms the issue raised in Section 3.4.3 that some SC firms potentially keep their interest-bearing debt level low and rely heavily on non-interest-bearing debt (which is not prohibited but discouraged by Islam).

In Table 5.2, it is interesting to note that the book leverage of SC firms follows a rather steady pattern throughout the whole sample period, although with a minor upward trend. Marginal increases can be seen between 2007–2008, implying that leverage increased during the GFC. In contrast, the SC firms' market leverage is exposed to slight changes throughout observation time. Especially starting from as low as 17% in 2005, a steady increase is observed until it peaked at 23% in 2008. Post-crisis, the market leverage recovered and decreased back to 18% in 2014 as it was in 2004. A similar pattern is shown for the SNC firms throughout the years. However, both leverage proxies show a downward trend, although the financial crisis showed its (temporarily) impact on both, especially with an increase of 2%-points on book leverage and 9%-points on market leverage.

Since the market leverage proxy has the market value of equity in the denominator, a change of the market leverage can be "ceteris paribus" caused by the fall of the stock prices during the financial crisis, unless the amount of debt is also increased accordingly. Table C.1 in Appendix C provides an overview of the mean book debt size and the mean stock price for the sample under study, differentiating overall (pooled), SC and SNC, and each year, respectively. It is interesting to observe that the mean

180 See Important Note in Section 4.3.1.

Table 5.2: Summary Statistics of Leverage – Divided by Years.[181]

Sample	Leverage	2004–2014	2004	2005	2006	2007	2008	2009	2010	2011	2012	2013	2014	Trend
Overall (pooled)	Book	0.51	0.50	0.50	0.50	0.51	0.53	0.51	0.51	0.52	0.51	0.50	0.51	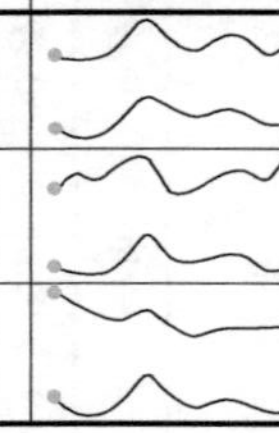
	Market	0.37	0.34	0.31	0.32	0.36	0.44	0.38	0.37	0.39	0.38	0.35	0.34	
Shari'ah Compliant	Book	0.40	0.39	0.40	0.40	0.40	0.41	0.39	0.39	0.40	0.40	0.39	0.40	
	Market	0.19	0.18	0.17	0.17	0.19	0.23	0.19	0.19	0.20	0.20	0.18	0.18	
Shari'ah Non-Compliant	Book	0.66	0.69	0.68	0.67	0.66	0.68	0.65	0.64	0.65	0.66	0.65	0.66	
	Market	0.60	0.61	0.56	0.56	0.59	0.68	0.61	0.59	0.61	0.60	0.57	0.57	

Source: own contribution.

181 For a detailed overview of the descriptive statistics of the leverage proxies and the corresponding *country* and *industry* breakdown (along with the trend over the sample period), see Table C.2 and Table C.3 in Appendix C, respectively.

debt follows an increasing pattern throughout the whole sample period at a steady rate. However, during the years 2007–09, the book debt remained constant (for SC firms) and decreased (for SNC firms), indicating that the security issuance by firms and lending by financial institutions was greatly reduced or rather not available. As for the SC, the mean debt size trend, especially during 2008–09, does not show any major differences. The sudden increase in market leverage of 4–5% cannot be count on the level of debt firms issue.

Similar to book debt, the mean stock price follows an increasing trend throughout the whole sample period. Specifically, SC firms' stock price shows an increase of approximately 250% from 2004–2014 (USD 24.96 to USD 68.70), and SNC firms' stock price exhibit an increase of approximately 100% (USD 17.71 to USD 35.87). However, the financial crisis showed a major impact on the financial markets, especially in 2008. The mean stock price shows a fall from USD 27.65 to USD 20.21 (approximately. 27%). As for the SC and SNC firms, both experienced a fall of about 19% and 38%, respectively. The sudden increase in market leverage of 8–9% during the financial crisis, as discussed, can be accounted for the sudden price falls in the stock markets, even though SNC firms marginally decreased their book debt level.

As mentioned earlier, the leverage ratios vary among different countries and different industries. The mean values of the entire sample period (2004–2014) from Table C.4 in Appendix C are represented in Figures 5.3 and 5.4 for SC and SNC, respectively. Figure 5.3 shows that both leverage proxies of SC firms vary among the countries and the industries. Specifically, the sample mean values for book leverage show that SC firms in the United States, United Kingdom, and India are overleveraged, with the United Kingdom representing the highest book leverage of 46%. The relatively high leverage ratio shows that SC firms in the United Kingdom tend to borrow more than SC firms in other countries. This is surprising because the United Kingdom's capital market is more developed than other countries, and firms should rely on it to utilize more through equity financing rather than debt financing.

In contrast, Canada, Japan, S. Korea, and Taiwan are underleveraged, with Canada showing the lowest mean value of 32%. SC firms operating in industries such as Industrials, Consumer Goods, and Consumer Services are overleveraged, with Industrials representing the highest book leverage of 44%. Other industries are underleveraged, with Basic Materials and Technology showing the lowest mean value of 35%. This result explains the low financial leverage of SC firms operating in Technology industries. This indicates that SC firms within Basic Materials and Technology have an increased level of fixed costs, which leads to increased operating leverage (i.e., increased business risk).[182] Firms with higher operating leverage usually keep

182 Industries such as Oil and Gas, Basic Materials, Industrials, Consumer Goods, and Technology fall under the Manufacturing sector, whereby Health Care and Consumer Services fall under the Services Sector. It is generally believed that firms operating in the former sector are usually exposed to higher fixed and lower variable costs, which leads to a higher level of operational leverage (i.e.,

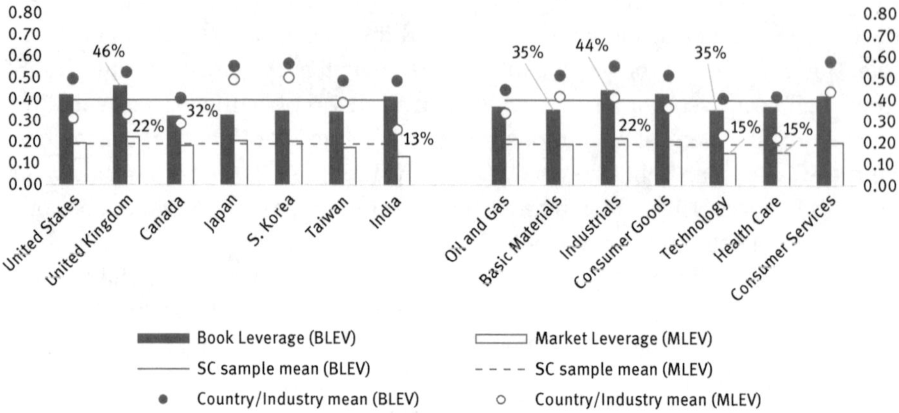

Figure 5.3: Leverage ratio of SC firms, *Country* and *Industry* Breakdown (2014–2014). Source: own contribution.

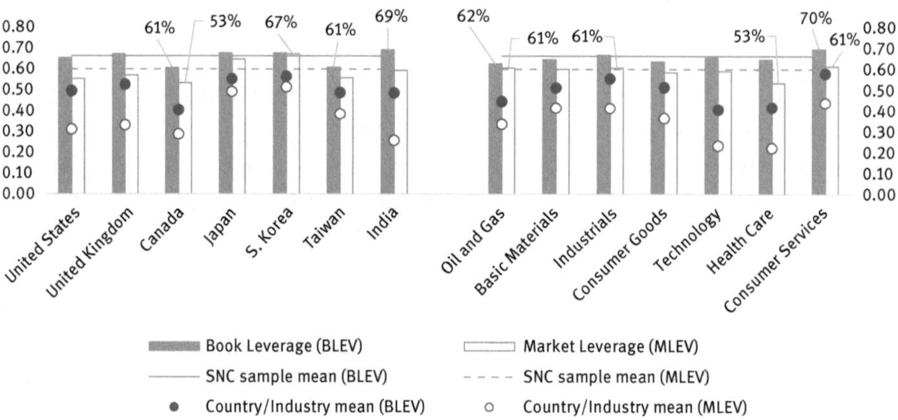

Figure 5.4: Leverage ratio of SNC firms, *Country* and *Industry* Breakdown (2014–2014). Source: own contribution.

their financial leverage level low to decrease the total risk (which equals business risk plus financial risk, see Section 2.1) of the firm and operate successfully in the competitive market. In contrast, it is interesting to observe that SC firms within Industrials keep their financial leverage level relatively high compared to the other industries within the Manufacturing sector even though they are, on average, exposed to high operating leverage.

increased business risk). An overview of all sample firms and their affiliation to different sectors and industries are shown in Table A.2 in Appendix A.

As for the market leverage, SC firms in the United Kingdom, Japan, and S. Korea are overleveraged (above sample mean value), with the United Kingdom showing the highest market leverage of 22%. Other countries are underleveraged, with India representing the lowest mean value of 13%. SC firms operating in industries such as Oil and Gas, Industrials, Consumer Goods, and Consumer Services are all overleveraged, with Industrials showing the highest market leverage of 22%. Technology and Health Care are underleveraged, with both representing the lowest mean value of 15%. As far as the country and industry average value is concerned, SC firms are underleveraged throughout the sample countries and industries, respectively. This can be explained by the strict sample creation criteria set on firms to pass the Shari'ah screening (see Section 3.2).

Figure 5.4 reveals that both leverage proxies of SNC firms vary slightly and further show a similar indebtedness level among the countries and industries. Specifically, the sample mean values for book leverage show that SNC firms in the United Kingdom, Japan, S. Korea, and India are overleveraged. India represents the highest book leverage of 69%. In contrast, the United States, Canada, and Taiwan are underleveraged (below mean value), with both Canada and Taiwan representing the lowest mean value of 61%. SNC firms operating in industries such as Industrials and Consumer Services are overleveraged, with Consumer Services representing the highest book leverage of 70%. Other industries are underleveraged, with Oil and Gas representing the lowest mean value of 62%. This result supports the notion that firms operating in the services sector (e.g., Consumer Services) are exposed to lower operational leverage, thus keep their financial leverage relatively high.

As for the market leverage, SNC firms in Japan and S. Korea are overleveraged, with S. Korea representing the highest market leverage of 67%. The remaining countries are underleveraged, with Canada representing the lowest mean value of 53%. SNC firms operating in industries such as Oil and Gas, Industrials, and Consumer Services are overleveraged, with each showing the highest market leverage of 61%. In contrast, Consumer Goods, Technology, and Health Care are underleveraged, with Health Care representing the lowest mean value of 53%. As far as the country and industry average value is concerned, SNC firms are overleveraged throughout the sample countries and industries, respectively. Compared to the SC firms, there are no restrictions imposed on them, and these firms can utilize the benefits that come with debt financing (e.g., tax shield, prevention of ownership dilution, etc.) to its maximum.

Additionally, we want to highlight briefly the equity ratios of SC and SNC firms identified by DJIMI. Like the leverage level, the same also applies to the equity level among different countries and industries. The mean values of the entire sample period (2004–2014) from Table C.5 in Appendix C are represented in Figure 5.5 for SC and SNC firms. Figure 5.5 shows that SC firms' equity ratio varies more than SNC firms in different countries and industries. Specifically, the mean values for equity ratio show a range from as high as 68% and as low as 54% in Canada and the United Kingdom, respectively. The relatively high equity ratio indicates that SC firms in Canada prefer equity financ-

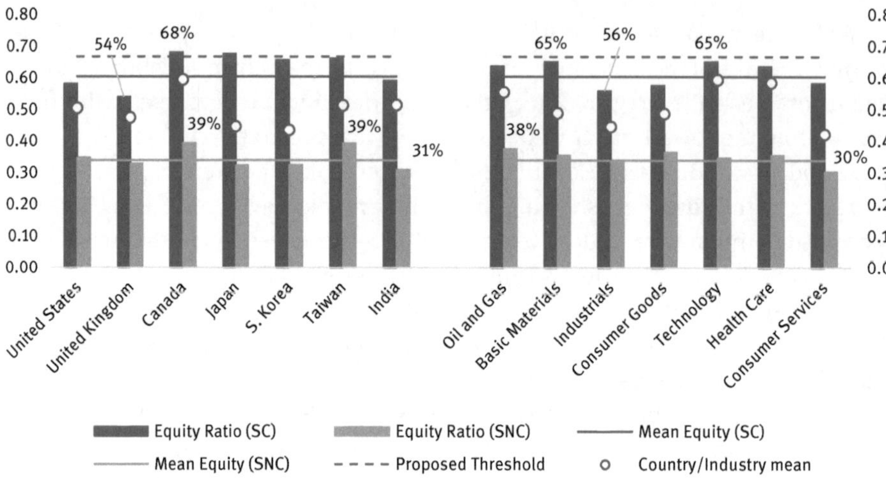

Figure 5.5: Equity Ratio of SC and SNC firms, *Country* and *Industry* Breakdown (2014–2014). Source: own contribution.

ing over debt financing. It is interesting to observe that Canada, with 68%, followed by Japan, with 67%, would even fulfill the equity criterion of a minimum of 66.67% of the proposed Shari'ah screening, as discussed in Section 3.4 (see dotted line in Figure 5.5). This preliminary result is especially surprising for Japan since the market is strongly bank-based. Firms in bank-based financial systems usually have traditionally built a close relationship with banks and tend to utilize more debt financing. SC firms operating in industries such as Basic Materials and Technology tend to have the highest mean value of 65% of equity ratio and with Industrials showing the lowest mean value of 56%.

As for the SNC firms, Figure 5.5 reveals less variation in the equity ratio among different countries and industries, ranging from as high as 39% and as low as 30%. Specifically, SNC firms in Canada and Taiwan both show the highest equity ratio of 39%, whereby India shows the lowest mean value of 31%. SNC firms operating in industries such as Oil and Gas show the highest equity ratio of 38%. Other industries are moderately on the same level, with Consumer Services representing a mean value of 30%.

In Section 4.3.2, six variables have been selected as potential determinants of capital structure. While Table 5.3 provides the mean, standard deviation, minimum, maximum, and the number of observations of the proxies for firm-specific and macroeconomic determinants, Table 5.4 reports the mean values of these capital structure determinants of the sample countries and industries separately.

The descriptive statistics reveal that the mean firm's *profitability*, measured by EBITDA, among SC and SNC firms is 17.8% and 9.6%, respectively. This result signifies that SC firms are among the highly profitable firms compared to SNC firms, which comprise less profitable firms. Table 5.4 reveals that each *country* and *industry* consist of a mixture of performing and underperforming firms. However, SC firms consistently overperform their non-compliant peers.

Table 5.3: Overall Means of Leverage Determinants.

Sample	Determinants	Mean	SD	Min	Max	Obs
Overall (Pooled)	Profitability	0.143	0.080	−0.034	0.398	11517
	Growth Opportunity	1.960	1.273	0.752	7.295	11551
	Firm Size	14.931	1.446	11.334	18.390	11541
	Tangibility	0.304	0.215	0.008	0.886	11551
	Business Risk	0.019	0.023	0.000	0.130	11543
	GDP growth	2.007	2.704	−5.527	10.260	10964
Shari'ah Compliant	Profitability	0.178	0.080	−0.034	0.398	6593
	Growth Opportunity	2.572	1.381	0.752	7.295	6618
	Firm Size	14.552	1.462	11.334	18.390	6608
	Tangibility	0.261	0.206	0.008	0.886	6618
	Business Risk	0.022	0.025	0.000	0.130	6614
	GDP growth	2.231	2.681	−5.527	10.260	6355
Shari'ah Non-Compliant	Profitability	0.096	0.048	−0.034	0.376	4924
	Growth Opportunity	1.140	0.254	0.752	3.093	4933
	Firm Size	15.438	1.256	11.334	18.390	4933
	Tangibility	0.361	0.213	0.008	0.886	4933
	Business Risk	0.015	0.019	0.000	0.130	4929
	GDP growth	1.699	2.706	−5.527	10.260	4609

Source: own contribution.

Market-to-book proxy that measures the *growth opportunity* varies among SC and SNC firms substantially, 2.57 and 1.14, respectively. The table also shows that variations also persist in the maximum growth percentage rate with 7.29 and 3.09, for both firm types, respectively. This may reflect that for the SC firms, the increase in stock prices during the study period made the market value of equity (market cap) higher than its book value. Additionally, individual countries and industries for both firm type show a sharp fluctuation (especially a decrease) in firms' growth opportunities during the financial crisis years due to the dramatic decreases in stock price changes (see Table C.6 in Appendix C).

In terms of *firm size*, measured by the natural logarithm of sales, the mean values show that SC and SNC are among firms that are of similar size. The average firm size for SC is 14.55, while SNC shows a slightly higher value of 15.43, but both with identical range percentile. From Table 5.4, we observed that SNC firms are somewhat larger in terms of revenue (sales) generation in all countries and all industries compared to SC firms.

Regarding *tangibility*, which represents the proxy for the firm's collateral value, Table 5.3 reports the average ratio of 26% for SC firms compared to 36% for SNC firms, indicating that SNC can offer more of its assets as collateral for debt financing. However, SC firms in Canada (52.7%) and in industries such as Oil and Gas (57.8%) and Basic Materials (42.4%), the mean value of *tangibility* is greater compared to SNC firms.

Table 5.4: Means of Leverage Proxies and Determinants per *Country* and *Industry*.[183]

Sample	Shari'ah Compliant Firms								Shari'ah Non-Compliant Firms							
	BLEV	MLEV	PROF	GRWTH	SIZE	TANG	RISK	GDP	BLEV	MLEV	PROF	GRWTH	SIZE	TANG	RISK	GDP
Overall (pooled)	0.397	0.191	0.178	2.572	14.552	0.261	0.022	2.231	0.661	0.599	0.096	1.140	15.438	0.361	0.015	1.699
SD	0.168	0.108	0.080	1.381	1.462	0.206	0.025	2.681	0.132	0.142	0.048	0.254	1.256	0.213	0.019	2.706
United States	0.419	0.193	0.182	2.648	14.865	0.233	0.022	1.697	0.652	0.553	0.108	1.221	15.226	0.316	0.016	1.528
SD	0.170	0.107	0.079	1.310	1.440	0.201	0.025	1.769	0.139	0.139	0.048	0.282	1.228	0.234	0.020	1.778
United Kingdom	0.461	0.224	0.193	2.471	14.566	0.216	0.021	1.443	0.672	0.570	0.129	1.226	15.017	0.426	0.010	1.117
SD	0.177	0.111	0.085	1.197	1.546	0.189	0.024	1.943	0.114	0.131	0.052	0.297	1.103	0.270	0.012	2.183
Canada	0.321	0.183	0.155	2.037	13.862	0.527	0.028	2.013	0.606	0.534	0.119	1.163	14.860	0.418	0.015	1.820
SD	0.148	0.102	0.081	0.952	1.506	0.306	0.030	1.605	0.153	0.148	0.045	0.219	1.297	0.220	0.019	1.823
Japan	0.326	0.206	0.152	1.913	14.634	0.251	0.016	0.792	0.677	0.647	0.080	1.063	15.875	0.372	0.012	0.638
SD	0.126	0.109	0.068	1.146	1.065	0.129	0.019	2.442	0.121	0.122	0.036	0.184	1.097	0.186	0.016	2.642
S. Korea	0.344	0.202	0.161	2.170	14.433	0.320	0.023	3.593	0.676	0.671	0.086	1.028	15.699	0.375	0.018	3.668
SD	0.127	0.105	0.080	1.279	1.581	0.126	0.025	1.576	0.148	0.143	0.051	0.205	1.258	0.172	0.021	1.616
Taiwan	0.340	0.175	0.170	2.409	13.872	0.285	0.025	–	0.608	0.557	0.086	1.120	14.936	0.410	0.022	–
SD	0.156	0.105	0.091	1.192	1.431	0.168	0.025		0.128	0.127	0.053	0.228	1.061	0.192	0.027	
India	0.410	0.132	0.211	3.774	13.493	0.264	0.025	7.679	0.691	0.593	0.103	1.226	14.920	0.399	0.020	7.580
SD	0.169	0.088	0.076	1.692	1.166	0.146	0.024	1.935	0.102	0.150	0.052	0.313	1.680	0.193	0.020	1.972

183 For more details, Table C.6 in Appendix C provides the trend (time series) of the leverage determinants.

Table 5.4 (continued)

Oil and Gas	0.364	0.212	0.191	1.908	14.822	0.578	0.030	–	0.625	0.606	0.099	1.061	16.037	0.542	0.022	–
SD	0.139	0.096	0.080	0.819	1.806	0.271	0.029		0.168	0.170	0.053	0.240	1.569	0.194	0.023	
Basic Materials	0.350	0.191	0.163	2.232	14.372	0.424	0.027	–	0.646	0.599	0.101	1.114	15.507	0.394	0.017	–
SD	0.173	0.113	0.094	1.209	1.528	0.203	0.029		0.119	0.139	0.037	0.236	1.033	0.134	0.019	
Industrials	0.442	0.217	0.174	2.398	14.503	0.231	0.018	–	0.667	0.605	0.091	1.141	15.377	0.312	0.014	–
SD	0.168	0.111	0.067	1.099	1.227	0.177	0.020		0.133	0.148	0.051	0.261	1.245	0.206	0.017	
Cons. Goods	0.424	0.203	0.183	2.668	14.717	0.231	0.020	–	0.635	0.584	0.095	1.112	15.513	0.294	0.017	–
SD	0.167	0.110	0.082	1.575	1.403	0.121	0.022		0.123	0.124	0.045	0.228	1.324	0.150	0.020	
Technologies	0.349	0.150	0.169	2.926	14.331	0.148	0.027	–	0.654	0.590	0.106	1.148	15.522	0.321	0.026	–
SD	0.162	0.098	0.082	1.530	1.475	0.136	0.029		0.123	0.135	0.064	0.269	1.292	0.216	0.030	
Health Care	0.365	0.153	0.166	2.881	14.210	0.186	0.022	–	0.645	0.533	0.114	1.269	14.509	0.276	0.014	–
SD	0.167	0.086	0.076	1.451	1.511	0.112	0.027		0.138	0.153	0.045	0.316	1.171	0.204	0.016	
Cons. Services	0.417	0.199	0.210	2.666	15.044	0.280	0.019	–	0.697	0.613	0.095	1.170	15.436	0.455	0.010	–
SD	0.154	0.109	0.084	1.472	1.436	0.189	0.022		0.128	0.134	0.042	0.249	1.156	0.249	0.014	

Source: own contribution.

Business risk (earnings volatility) is measured by using the standard deviation of EBIT. This business risk measure indicates a slightly higher variability and spread in returns for SC (2.2%) than SNC firms (1.5%).

In terms of economic development, measured by GDP annual growth rate, the mean values in Table 5.4 indicate India as the fastest growing country among the sample emerging countries with an increase of 767%, followed by S. Korea with 359% (cumulative growth). In contrast to the emerging countries, all developed countries show a much slower pace in economic growth, with Canada being the fastest and Japan the least growing markets, both showing a mean value of 201% and 79%, respectively.

We have conducted an additional test to verify the significance of the differences between the sample means of both dependent and independent variables for SC and SNC firms. According to the paired z-test shown in Table C.7 in Appendix C, the results suggest that firm type (i.e., being SC or SNC) affects the values of all variables under study. The test results show their means are significantly different from each other in all perspectives, i.e., the *overall (pooled)*, *country*, and *industry* sample. An exception is observed in *business risk* (for the country of Taiwan and Technology industries) and *GDP* growth (for most country samples). As for the latter, the means are expected to be similar since *GDP growth* is a macroeconomic aggregated variable that applies to all firms in a particular country. However, the significant mean difference in GDP for SC and SNC firms operating in the US and UK is probably due to our unbalanced sample data. These test results indicated that our analysis in the previous paragraphs is statistically supported and justified.

5.1.2 Pairwise Correlation Analysis

Table 5.5 presents the results of a pair-wise correlation matrix for all dependent and independent variables used in the regression analysis. Observations for all variables in the correlation matrix show that all of the coefficients are below 80%. A correlation coefficient of more than 80% indicates a serious multicollinearity problem.[184] As expected, the correlation between book leverage (BLEV) and market leverage (MLEV) is high due to their very similar definitions. The same applies to the high correlation between *growth opportunity* (GROWTH) and market leverage (MLEV) since both variables have the same market value of equity in their ratio. The maximum correlation among the independent variables is recorded at 59% between *profitability* (PROF) and *growth opportunity* (GROWTH). As such, it can be concluded that multicollinearity is not detrimental to our regression analysis results.

184 See Brooks (2014, p. 218).

Table 5.5: Pairwise Correlation Matrix.[185]

		BLev	MLev	Prof	Growth	Size	Tang	Risk	GDP
	a								
BLev	b	1							
	c								
	a	0.7904*							
MLev	b	0.6134*	1						
	c	0.6194*							
	a	−0.3476*	−0.5919*						
Prof	b	0.0205	−0.3430*	1					
	c	−0.1426*	−0.4135*						
	a	−0.3434*	−0.6824*	0.5953*					
Growth	b	0.007	−0.6301*	0.4637*	1				
	c	0.2470*	−0.5751*	0.3697*					
	a	0.3945*	0.4289*	−0.1469*	−0.3393*				
Size	b	0.2855*	0.3774*	0.0698*	−0.2536*	1			
	c	0.2483*	0.3182*	−0.1358*	−0.1542*				
	a	0.0890*	0.2184*	−0.0196*	−0.2506*	0.0514*			
Tang	b	−0.0979*	0.0652*	0.0900*	−0.1955*	0.0529*	1		
	c	−0.0536*	0.0264	0.1906*	−0.0808*	−0.1287*			
	a	−0.1430*	−0.1759*	0.1335*	0.1814*	−0.1721*	−0.0024		
Risk	b	−0.0641*	−0.1318*	0.0851*	0.1393*	−0.1708*	0.0383*	1	
	c	−0.0404*	−0.0298*	0.0024	0.0128	−0.0568*	0.0288*		
	a	−0.0431*	−0.1553*	0.1560*	0.2348*	−0.1561*	−0.0006	−0.0068	
GDP	b	0.0283*	−0.1856*	0.1298*	0.2711*	−0.1728*	0.024	−0.0253*	1
	c	0.0236	−0.0948*	0.1240*	0.1506*	−0.0724*	0.0183	−0.0200	

Source: own contribution.

Another method to test the existence of multicollinearity is by calculating the Variance Inflation Factor (*VIF*) for each independent variable. *VIF* can be calculated through the equation $VIF = 1/(1-R^2)$. Under this test, a *VIF* value greater than 10 indicates a multicollinearity problem.[186] From the results shown in Table C.8 in Appendix C, it can be confirmed that multicollinearity is not an issue since the *VIF* values are far below the cut-off point. Hence, our results from the pairwise correlation matrix can be confirmed, and no multicollinearity is evident in the model.

185 This table shows the coefficient correlations between dependent and independent variables for the overall (pooled), SC and SNC sample firms. Note: [a] Denoted for the overall pooled sample. [b] Denoted for SC firms. [c] Denoted for SNC firms. * Indicates that the coefficient is significant at 5% level.
186 For more details, see Chapter 10 in Gujarati (2004, pp. 341–386).

Concerning the SC firms, Table 5.5 reports mixed positive and negative correlations between book leverage (BLEV) and market leverage (MLEV) with firm-specific and macroeconomic variables. As for the book leverage (BLEV), *firm size* (SIZE), and *GDP growth* (GDP), correlations are positively significant, and *tangibility* (TANG) and *business risk* (RISK) correlations are negatively significant at 5% level. These results suggest, for instance, that an increase (decrease) in *firm size* (*tangibility*) might increase the firm's book leverage (BLEV) and vice-versa.

As for the market leverage (MLEV), *firm size* (SIZE), and *tangibility* (TANG), correlations are positively significant, and *profitability* (PROF), *growth opportunity* (GROWTH), *business risk* (RISK), and *GDP growth* (GDP) correlations are negatively significant at 5% level. These results suggest an increase in *firm size* and *tangibility* might increase market leverage (MLEV) and vice versa. On the other hand, a decrease in *profitability* (PROF) and *business risk* (RISK) might increase the firm's market leverage (MLEV) and vice versa. When examining the relationship between the independent variables, the highest correlation coefficient can be observed between *growth opportunity* (GROWTH) and *profitability* (PROF) at a 5% significant level. This result indicates that an increase in SC firm's *growth opportunity* might increase *profitability* by about 47%.

As for SNC firms, Table 5.5 reports results similar to that of SC firms, mixed positive and negative correlations between book leverage (BLEV) and market leverage (MLEV) with firm-specific and macroeconomic variables. As for the book leverage (BLEV), *growth opportunity* (GROWTH) and *firms size* (SIZE) correlations are positively significant, and *profitability* (PROF) and *tangibility* (TANG) correlations are negatively significant at the 5% level. These results suggest that an increase (decrease) in the growth opportunities (performance) might increase the firm's book leverage (BLEV) and vice-versa.

As for the market leverage (MLEV), only the *firm size* (SIZE) correlation is positively significant, and *profitability* (PROF), *growth opportunity* (GROWTH), *business risk* (RISK), and *GDP growth* (GDP) correlations are negatively significant at 5% level. These results suggest that an increase in *firm size* might increase market leverage (MLEV) and vice versa. On the other hand, a decrease in *profitability* (PROF) and *growth opportunity* (GROWTH) might increase the firm's market leverage (MLEV) and vice versa. When examining the relationship between the independent variables, the highest correlation coefficient can be observed between *growth opportunity* (GROWTH) and *profitability* (PROF) at a 5% significant level, similar to SC firms' finding. This result indicates that an increase in the SNC firm's *growth opportunity* could increase *profitability* by about 37%. To summarize the above discussion, the following points are salient:

i. The *firm size* (SIZE) variable is positive and significantly correlated with both book leverage (BLEV) and market leverage (MLEV) under both SC and SNC firms.
ii. The *tangibility* (TANG) and *business risk* (RISK) variables are negative and significantly correlated with book leverage (BLEV) under both SC and SNC firms.
iii. The *profitability* (PROF), *growth opportunity* (GROWTH), *business risk* (RISK), and *GDP growth* (GDP) are negative and significantly correlated with market leverage (MLEV) under both SC and SNC firms.

iv. There are positive and significant correlations among independent variables such as between GROWTH-PROF, TANG-PROF, GDP-PROF, and GDP-GROWTH under both SC and SNC firms.
v. There are negative and significant correlations among independent variables such as between SIZE-GROWTH, TANG-GROWTH, RISK-SIZE, and GDP-SIZE under both SC and SNC firms.
vi. There are positive and significant correlations among independent variables between RISK-TANG and GDP-GROWTH under SC and SNC firms.

As mentioned above, both the Pairwise Correlation Matrix and the VIF do not report high correlations among the independent variables; hence, multicollinearity is not a concern. Next, we will proceed with our empirical analysis using the most advanced econometric tools and techniques.

5.2 Empirical Results and Analysis

The following sections deal with the empirical findings of our regression analysis. While Section 5.2.1 provides comments and annotations to the empirical tests in general, Section 5.2.2 provides the *overall (pooled)* sample analysis, including the time-breakdown results to answer the RQ 2 and RQ 3, respectively. Section 5.2.3 shows that cross-*country* and cross-*industry* sample results are included, dealing with RQ 4 and RQ 5, respectively. Finally, Section 5.2.4 consolidates the empirical results and attempts to answer RQ 6.

5.2.1 Annotations to the Results and Approach

In Section 4.2, we highlighted that selecting the proper estimators when analyzing panel data is of great importance. To correctly identify the best linear unbiased estimator (BLUE), we conducted several post-estimation tests.[187] Even though Section 4.2 presented the methodology in general, we provide several statistical comments on the application of that methodology in this section.

Initially, we ran the BPLM test on each model separately, i.e., on the *overall (pooled)* and each *country* and *industry*. If the p-value obtained by the BPLM was below 0.05 (5%), then the null hypothesis of no unobserved effects was rejected. Therefore, the use of OLS was deemed inappropriate. Considering the restrictive assumptions that should hold for OLS when using panel data (i.e., not being biased and inconsistent), it should

187 Specifically, we performed *linearity*, *normality*, *heteroskedasticity*, *autocorrelation*, and *multicollinearity* tests of the estimation models. Figures B.2 and B.3 in Appendix B provide the tests of linearity and normality, respectively.

not be a surprise that in most of our regressions, the BPLM recorded the rejection of OLS. Hence, the use of the FE and RE approach was inevitable. (see Table B.3, Panel B)

Next, to choose between FE and RE estimator, we ran the Hausman test. If the p-value estimation was below 0.05 (5%), we chose the FE estimator, otherwise the RE estimator. Remember, the assumption holds that the RE model is more efficient than the FE model. (see Section 4.2.1)

Last, we have checked the presence of heteroskedasticity and auto-/serial correlation and applied the "robust" option where applicable. All tests have been applied for the reason, as described in Section 4.2. Tables B.3 and B.4 in Appendix B report the results of the estimator selection procedure (which includes BPLM, Hausman, and heteroskedasticity tests) and auto-/serial correlation test, respectively, applied to each regression model in this section.

As mentioned in Section 4.3.2 (hypothesis development), the aim of differentiating between various countries and industries in our sample is to detect possible cross-sectional variations in the effect of certain debt factors. All analysis is based on the numerical results shown in Tables D.2 and D.3 in Appendix D., respectively.

Important Note: It is quite a challenge to conduct a study considering multiple dimensions, i.e., ***overall (pooled)***, ***country***, and ***industry***, ***Shari'ah compliance (SC)*** and ***non-compliance (SNC)***, and ***book*** and ***market leverage measures***. For this reason, to provide and maintain a more structured approach, we split our analysis in Sections 5.2.2 until 5.2.4 into "SC firms" followed by "SNC firms" and have highlighted and differentiated between the *material significance* (sign and value of the coefficient) and the *statistical significance* (econometrical).

Limitations: We did not explore the estimation results of the determinants per ***sub-period*** or ***country/industry***, nor did we provide reasons for an "insignificant" result. Our analysis remained at a superficial level but sufficient to reach the objective of this study. Specifically, a detailed discussion, in Section 5.2.3, on the differences between both firm types, would have required to dive into *country* and *industry* level, that in turn would result mathematically in 98 different dimensions, i.e., two firm types (SC/SNC), seven countries and seven industries (2×7×7). Discussion on that level would change the objective of this study and would require independent research.

5.2.2 *Overall (pooled)* Analysis

To start with and to ensure reliable results, we have incorporated all six independent variables into the static regression models (13) and (14) to determine the most important and relevant debt factors. Table 5.6 provides the overall (pooled) sample results in which all debt determinants are lagged one year and are regressed on the dependent variables book leverage (BLEV) and market leverage (MLEV), respectively. The definitions of the dependent and independent variables are provided in Tables

Table 5.6: Determinants of Leverage – *Overall (pooled)* regression.

Overall Regression	Book Leverage		Market Leverage	
Determinants	SC (1)	SNC (2)	SC (3)	SNC (4)
Profitability $_{t-1}$	−0.124***	−0.422***	−0.182***	−0.554***
	[0.037]	[0.055]	[0.026]	[0.067]
Growth Opportunity $_{t-1}$	−0.004	0.056***	−0.016***	−0.116***
	[0.002]	[0.010]	[0.001]	[0.012]
Firm Size $_{t-1}$	−0.008	0.036***	0.024***	0.055***
	[0.008]	[0.007]	[0.005]	[0.007]
Tangibility $_{t-1}$	0.066	0.085**	0.070***	0.088**
	[0.045]	[0.043]	[0.026]	[0.043]
Business Risk $_{t-1}$	0.179***	0.029	−0.040	−0.194*
	[0.068]	[0.083]	[0.042]	[0.100]
GDP growth $_{t-1}$	0.002	−0.002**	−0.000	−0.008***
	[0.001]	[0.001]	[0.001]	[0.001]
Constant	0.509***	0.071	−0.125*	−0.103
	[0.106]	[0.113]	[0.065]	[0.107]
R^2	0.029	0.102	0.207	0.344
Adjusted R^2	0.027	0.098	0.205	0.341
Firms	756	577	756	577
Observations	5562	4021	5562	4021
Time Effects	yes	yes	yes	yes
Estimator	FE	FE	FE	FE

Source: own contribution.

4.3 and 4.10, respectively. Regressions are run for the entire period 2004–2014, divided into SC and SNC firms, respectively. Book leverage and market leverage results for SC and SNC firms are represented in models (1) and (2) and models (3) and (4), respectively. At first glance, all debt determinants show statistical significance indicating the impact on firms' leverage decisions. These data show a positive or negative significant coefficient at the 90% or higher confidence level; however, even insignificant results are also reported.

As far as the time-breakdown results are concerned, Table D.1 in Appendix D shows the parameter estimates of the *overall (pooled)* sample results, differentiated between three time periods, namely *pre-crisis* (2004–07), *crisis* (2008–09), and *post-crisis* (2010–14). We split into different periods to find out whether or not certain capital structure determinants have changed over the years regarding their importance and impact on the leverage decision of SC and SNC firms. In other words, the results show that the importance and the impact of the capital structure determinants diverge over the different periods. The estimated coefficient results are represented in Figures 5.6 until 5.11 for both leverage measures, divided into the periods mentioned above. These figures provide a graphical representation of the development of the six capital structure determinants of the *overall (pooled)* sample.

All model regressions contain time fixed effects (time dummies), and the econometric estimators applied to each model are shown in the last row. Company cluster robust standard errors are reported in the brackets. *, **, and *** denote significance at 10%, 5%, and 1% levels, respectively. All variables are winsorized at the 1% and 99% level. The following sub-section elaborates on the econometric estimator results obtained from the *overall (pooled)* regression.

5.2.2.1 Profitability

The results show that the *profitability* is highly significant and negatively related to leverage for both leverage measures and both SC and SNC firms. As mentioned earlier in the hypothesis development in Section 4.3.2, the negative relationship between *profitability* and leverage is among the most consistent findings in capital structure research, e.g., in Ariff et al. (2008), Cekrezi (2013), and Rajan and Zingales (1995). The negative relationship is consistent with the conventional Pecking Order Theory predictions and the proposed *Islamic Pecking Order* model. Both posit that higher profitability should enable the company to retain more earnings, which are the preferable funding; hence, its debt should decrease (Myers, 1984). Furthermore, the negative relationship indicates that SC firms utilize their extra cash to pay back their debt, a financing behavior highly appreciated from the Shari'ah perspective. (see Section 3.4.2)

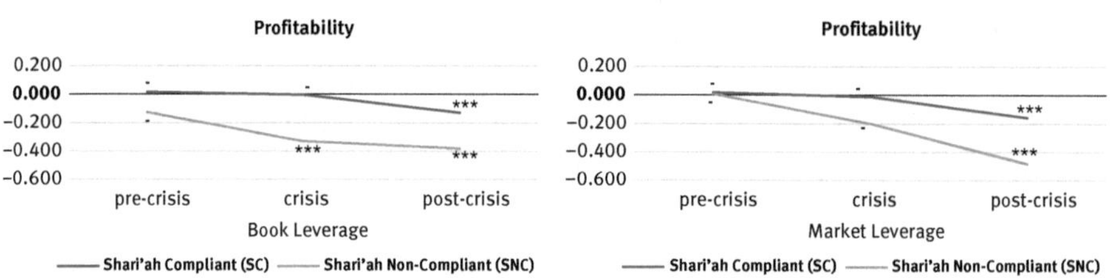

Figure 5.6: Coefficient Estimates[188] of Profitability, Time Breakdown.
Source: own contribution.

Even though the negative relationship is often considered a contradiction of the Trade-Off Theory Frank and Goyal (2009), possible explanations for this negative relationship are offered by the *dynamic* version of the Trade-Off Theory. For instance, the existence of adjustment costs (higher transaction costs) can lead firms to utilize

188 The y-axis represents the coefficient estimates of the FE estimator, and the symbol "-" illustrates insignificant coefficient results, while *, **, and *** denote the significance of coefficient estimates at 10%, 5%, and 1% levels, respectively.

internal funds (retained earnings) to take advantage of future investment opportunities. This is consistent with the survey results of Graham and Harvey (2001), which states that firms are willing to hold on to their cash availability to preserve financial flexibility.

Studies on Shari'ah compliant firms: Similar results were reported in Haron and Ibrahim (2012) and Thabet and Hanefah (2014), in which the authors exhibited a negative relationship between *profitability* and leverage for SC firms in Malaysia. The authors suggested that profitable SC firms operating in the Malaysian context prefer internal funds to finance their investment activities, which align with Pecking Order Theory. Other studies with firm samples outside of Malaysia, such as Alnori and Alqahtani (2019), Arif and Mai (2020), and Mai (2019), all reported a negative relationship between *profitability* and leverage, strengthening the unique position of this debt determinant. According to the results in Table 5.6 and the explanation mentioned above, we confirmed **Hypothesis H.1** for book leverage and market leverage for both SC and SNC firms, respectively.

The material significance in Figure 5.6 reveals that the impact of *profitability* on both leverages has been exposed to substantial changes. Specifically, for the pre-crisis period, *profitability* exhibits a positive coefficient, implying that SC firms actively engaged in debt financing. However, since then, the results show an inverse relationship, demonstrating that profitable SC firms were associated with less debt for both leverage measures during and post-crisis, suggesting no consistent impact throughout the years. The statistical significance shows that *profitability* even gained in importance in recent years for both leverage measures. Overall it can be argued that the profitability effect is one of the most important debt factors.

As far as the SNC firms are concerned, the material significance shows that the negative correlation between *profitability* and leverage remained the same throughout the years for book leverage, although with some turbulence during the financial crisis. Similar to SC firms, the *profitability* effect is one of the most important debt factors post-crisis for both leverages; however, the strong significant result during the crisis time indicates that SNC firms relied less on debt financing. Earlier, in the descriptive analysis in Section 5.1.1, we found that SNC firms sharply decreased their book debt level during the financial crisis compared to the SC firms. (see Table C.1 in Appendix C) According to the results in Table D.1 in Appendix D, for not showing a consistent impact over the sample years, we rejected **Hypothesis H.7** for SC firms for both leverage measures and SNC firms for market leverage. As for the SNC book leverage measure, we have confirmed **Hypothesis H.7**.

5.2.2.2 Growth Opportunity

It has been predicted that higher firm valuation (market-to-book) exploits a negative impact on firms' leverage decisions. The coefficients of the *growth* variable do show mixed results on both leverage measures. The market-to-book ratio (*growth opportunity*) is significant and negative with market leverage on both SC and SNC firms, as predicted by the Trade-Off Theory. It is consistent with our expectations and with most academic findings studies such as Ariff et al. (2008), Booth et al. (2001), and Rajan and Zingales (1995). Higher market-to-book ratios arise from higher expected future cash flows. The inverse relation supports the view that the cost of financial distress of high growth firms is relatively high, thus, leading to an increase in agency cost of debt. Because of the high cost of debt, capital providers demand higher interest; hence managers would be discouraged from raising debt capital, causing a lower leverage ratio.[189] Furthermore, this finding further indicates that companies refuse to take leverage when their valuation tends to be relatively high.[190] Finally, from the Shari'ah perspective, investment opportunities are associated with increased financial distress and financial deficit, which calls for external financing. The significant negative estimation result with leverage indicates that SC firms were engaged in equity financing to close the deficit. This is in line with the proposed *Islamic Pecking Order* model.

However, contrary to our expectations, *growth* is positively related and significant for SNC firms' book leverage. These results can be explained by the arguments made by Welch (2011) who found, that if companies use book measures to determine their optimal capital structure, that market-to-book ratio might be a poor proxy for *growth opportunity* for book debt. The significant positive result for SNC firms supports the Pecking Order Theory notion, with the rationale that higher information asymmetries lead shareholders not willing to expose much information about their investment, i.e., growth opportunities. Consequently, investment opportunities increase financial deficits that further cause companies to raise external financing, preferable short-term (Gaud et al., 2005). As for SC firms, the market-to-book ratio exhibits no statistical significance for book leverage measure, indicating that future growth opportunities do not significantly influence their capital structure decision.

Studies on Shari'ah compliant firms: Like our results, Haron and Ibrahim (2012), Rahim et al. (2020), and Sahudin et al. (2019) exhibited no significant effects in both leverage measures for SC firms operating in Malaysian. Based on the results in Table 5.6, the *growth opportunity* exhibit for market leverage a negative impact on the

189 For instance, Baker and Wurgler (2002, p. 2) used the market-to-book ratio to measure the market timing opportunities realized by managers and state "*[...] low leverage firms are those that raised funds when their market valuations were high, as measured by the market-to-book ratio, while high leverage firms are those that raised funds when their market valuations were low.*" In this case, high market-to-book ratios may reduce managers' motivation to issue debt, and internal equity remains preferable to both managers and shareholders of high growth firms.

190 This finding mirrors the notion of the capital structure theory called "Market-Timing", which states that firms issue equity when their firm value is overvalued (higher stock price valuation, i.e., higher market-to-book ratio).

financial decision of both SC and SNC firms. Hence, we confirmed **Hypothesis H.2** for market leverage. As for the book leverage measure, it showed that *growth* exhibits a positive impact on the financing decision of SNC firms only. Thus, we rejected **Hypothesis H.2.** in the context of book leverage. Although *growth* shows a negative sign for book leverage, the insignificant result led to a non-confirmation of the **Hypothesis H.2** for SC firms.

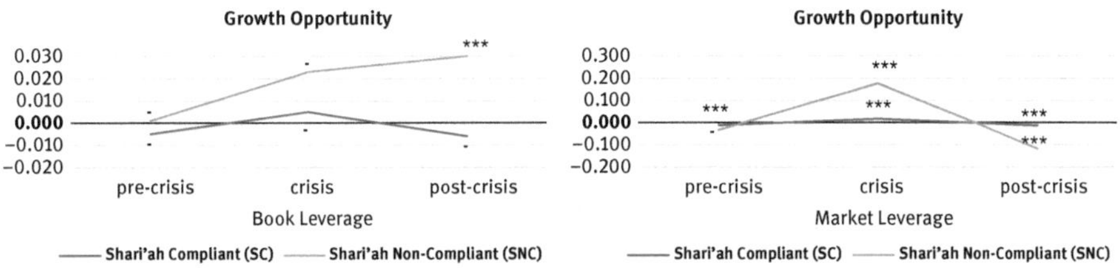

Figure 5.7: Coefficient Estimates of Growth Opportunity, Time Breakdown.
Source: own contribution.

In Figure 5.7, the impact of *growth opportunity* continues to be mixed. The material significance reveals that despite the *overall (pooled)* regression results, which showed negative (insignificant) and positive (significant) results for book leverage, the effect of *growth opportunity* has changed throughout the years. As for the book leverage, the coefficient result changed from negative to positive, indicating that SC firms utilized debt financing, especially during the financial crisis. This positive correlation between the *growth* determinant and leverage showed a temporary effect since the material significance changed back to be negative during the post-crisis years. However, even though *growth* gained in importance during the post-crisis period, it did not affect the book leverage's insignificant estimation results. As for market leverage, the *growth opportunity* is one of SC firms' most important debt factors throughout the years. The significant positive correlation observed in the crisis period reflects the increase in debt level during 2007 and 2008 (see Table C.1 in Appendix C), suggesting that SC firms relied on debt financing to finance their growth investment opportunities.

For SNC firms, the material significance of the positive correlation between *growth opportunity* and book leverage remained the same throughout the years, with an upward trend. However, as for the market leverage, the effect of *growth opportunity* seems to have changed drastically over time. During the crisis period, a strong positive relationship was reported, which drastically changed to become negative during the post-crisis period; however, the strong significance level remained the same. The former can be attributed to the rapid fall in the stock price in 2008, which caused the mean market leverage value to reach its peak. The latter exhibits that *growth* diminished over time, and the significant negative relationship is in line with the *overall (pooled)* regression results. Based on the estimated results, similar to *profitability*, we rejected **Hypothesis H.8** for SC firms for both leverage measures and SNC firms for market leverage. As for the SNC book leverage measure, we have confirmed **Hypothesis H.8**.

5.2.2.3 Firm Size

As mentioned in Section 4.3.2, company *size* is one of those determinants that provide consistent results in its relationship to leverage. While market leverage results show positive and significant for both SC and SNC firms, *firm size* (measured by log sales) shows a positive relationship on book leverage only for SNC firms. All these results are in line with the notion of the Trade-Off Theory, suggesting that the bigger a firm becomes, the less it is exposed to bankruptcy risk (see Section 2.3), and consequently, the more leverage the company tends to hold. Additionally, this result can be explained because bigger firms are well-diversified and have a lower risk of bankruptcy costs. Likewise, they have greater access to the credit market, which enhances their debt capacity. While this variable features strong statistical significance (99% confidence level), we concluded that the effect of *size* on the capital structure decision of especially SNC firms (for both leverage measures) and SC firms (for market leverage) is straightforward. Specifically, the more sales revenue these companies generate, the more debt they carry and become indebted. The Trade-Off Theory has been confirmed concerning *firm size* for SNC firms for both leverage measures. As for the SC firms, the positive relationship runs against the proposed *Islamic Pecking Order* model. Especially with greater access to the capital market, SC firms are expected to engage in the equity capital market (rather than in the debt capital market) to take the opportunity to issue equity at lower costs, as discussed in Section 4.3.2.3.

The *firm size* coefficient on book leverage for SC firms exhibits insignificant results. This finding is comparable to those reported by Alves and Ferreira (2011), Chung (1993), De Jong et al. (2008), W. S. Kim and Sorensen (1986), and Titman and Wessels (1988), who also found insignificant results for *firm size*. These SC firms' size might not affect book leverage because they rely on bank lending (especially in bank-based countries such as Japan, Taiwan, and India). The long-term relationships between banking institutions and companies, and the less asymmetric information associated with bank financing, cause even important factors such as *firm size* to be less important.[191] Frank and Goyal (2009, p. 7) stated, "*If we had been focusing on a*

191 The correlation among variables could be another reason for a variable to be insignificant. For instance, business risk has been mentioned to be correlated with size, with the rationale that as larger (or more diversified) the less risky a company becomes (Gaud et al., 2007). We conducted an *alternative model specification* test to verify whether this is the case, by leaving out one or more of the "independent variables" that showed no significance. (see Table B.2 in Appendix B) This test revealed that the results obtained in Tables 5.6 are robust to alternative model specifications.

book-based definition of leverage, the market-to-book ratio, firm size[,] and expected inflation would all have been excluded from the core model." In other words, *firm size* (and *growth opportunity*, as discussed in Sections 5.2.2.1 and 5.2.2.2) is a more reliable factor for market leverage rather than book leverage measure.

Studies on Shari'ah compliant firms: Haron and Ibrahim (2012) found the *firm size* proxy (calculated by the natural logarithm of total assets) to be negative and significant for SC firms in Malaysia both leverage measures. The authors argued that larger firms tend to generate higher profit, thus have higher retained earnings (internal funds available) to support their future investment. Based on the results in Table 5.6 and the rationale mentioned above, we rejected **Hypothesis H.3a** for SC firms for market leverage and fully confirmed **Hypothesis H.3b** for SNC firms for both leverage measures. The insignificant result of book leverage led to a non-confirmation of the **Hypothesis H.3a** for SC firms.

In Table 5.6, we have shown mixed outcomes on the relationship between *firm size* and leverage decisions for SC firms but consistent results for SNC firms for both leverage measures. Our time breakdown results, represented in Figure 5.8, align with the *overall (pooled)* regression results. The material significance reveals that despite the *overall (pooled)* regression results, which showed the negative insignificance for book leverage only, the effect of *firm size* went through different changes for both leverage measures. Hence, the *firm size* variable fails to have a consistent pattern throughout the years. During the pre-crisis, SC firms employed less debt financing. This trend changed slightly, reaching a marginally positive relationship during the crisis period and onwards; however, it remained insignificant throughout the years. As for the market leverage, the material importance has increased especially since the crisis years, which indicates that the *firm size* effect becomes materially more important over time, and SC firms increase their debt level the bigger they are (in terms of revenue generation).

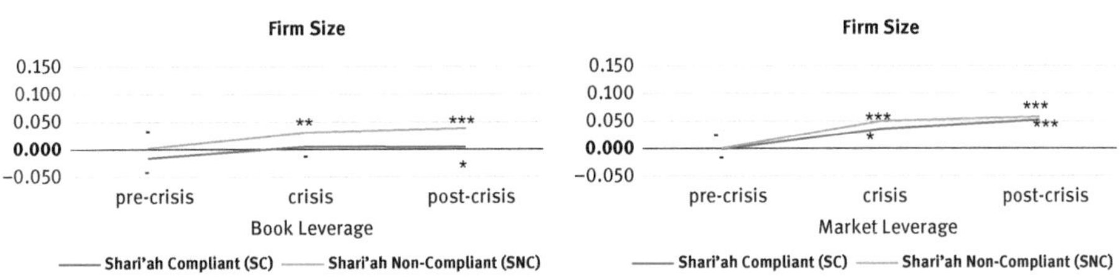

Figure 5.8: Coefficient Estimates of Firm Size, Time Breakdown.
Source: own contribution.

As for the SNC firms, the material significance reveals that *firm size* gained more importance and remained the same throughout the years. These results show a consistent pattern, indicating that these firms employed debt financing whenever external financing was required, especially during and post-crisis. The outcome of the regression estimates of *firm size* determinant allowed us to reject and confirm **Hypothesis H.9** for SC and SNC firms for both leverage measures, respectively.

5.2.2.4 Tangibility

Similar to *firm size*, the firm's tangible assets are determinants that show consistent results in its relationship to leverage. Except for book leverage for SC firms, all other models in Table 5.6 exhibit a positive relationship with debt financing. Similar results can be found in academic studies with an international focus.[192] In general, it is predicted that the firm's *tangibility* leads to an increase in leverage due to the collateral characteristic. Specifically, tangible assets (opposite to intangible assets) provide more security as collateral for potential investors. For this reason, Titman and Wessels (1988) stated, tangible assets reduce the risk for debt holders and consequently reduce the cost of debt for the companies. Therefore, companies will be able to operate with higher leverage ratios without incurring higher financial distress costs. This is in line with the notion of the Trade-Off Theory. The positive relationship between tangibility and leverage also confirms the role of tangible assets in reducing the agency costs for outside investors, which raises firm leverage.

Studies on Shari'ah compliant firms: Haron and Ibrahim (2012) and Mai (2019) found a positive relationship between *tangibility* and market leverage (insignificant for book leverage), thus supports the notion of the Trade-Off Theory. The authors argued with the statements made by Ahmed (2007) that debt must be asset-backed, which means Islamic firms cannot have debt exceeding tangible assets. This further implies that firms with more tangible assets will have higher debt levels, and the other way around, a firm with less tangible assets will consequently have a lower debt level (see Section 2.6). On the contrary, Ibrahim et al. (2015), Mai (2019), and Thabet and Hanefah (2014) found the insignificant relationship of *tangibility* on book leverage, which indicates that there is no evidence that SC firms consider their fixed assets when financing decision activities occur. Thabet and Hanefah (2014) argued their finding by referring to Al-Ajmi et al. (2009), who stated that firms with more tangible assets prefer to use equity financing over debt financing.

Like *firm size*, the positive relationship runs against the proposed *Islamic Pecking Order* model, positing a negative relationship between *tangibility* and leverage for firms operating under Shari'ah principles. Since high tangible assets generate less asymmetric information between existing shareholders and investors, equity financing becomes cheaper than debt financing. In case SC firms prefer not to dilute their earnings-per-share (EPS) by issuing additional equity, they have the opportunity to engage in quasi-equity financing instruments such as *Sukuk*. (see Section 4.3.2.4)

---

192 See J. P. H. Fan et al. (2012), Johnson (2003), and Kayo and Kimura (2011).

However, the estimation results suggest that SC firm follow their non-compliant peers by collateralizing their tangible assets. According to the results in Table 5.6, similar to the *firm size* hypothesis, we rejected **Hypothesis H.4a** for SC firms for market leverage and fully confirmed **Hypothesis H.4b** for SNC firms for both leverage measures. The insignificant result of book leverage led to a non-confirmation of the **Hypothesis H.4a** for SC firms.

Our time breakdown results in Figure 5.9 reveal that the significant impact of the *tangibility* variable on leverage is contrary to the *overall (pooled)* regression results, which showed that the amount of fixed assets is associated with the larger amount of leverage. The material significance reveals that the *tangibility* effect went through changes for the book leverage measure for both SC and SNC firms, respectively. Therefore, it fails to have a consistent pattern throughout the years. The positive relationship reached its peak during the crisis period for book leverage. However, both firm types employed debt financing, and this trend changed slightly during the post-crisis period, reaching a marginally negative relationship. It is interesting to observe that the effect of *tangibility* became only (but strongly) significant in both materially and statistically, during the crisis. These results indicate that these firms utilized their fixed assets as collateral in debt financing during the financial crisis. As for the market leverage, *tangibility* constantly exhibits a positive relation for SC firms only. Although *overall (pooled)* reported a significant positive relationship, the results obtained for all periods exhibit throughout insignificance. As for SNC firms, tangibility's material significance has changed in the post-crisis period; however, it remained insignificant. We rejected Hypothesis H.10 for SC firms for book leverage and SNC firms for both leverages based on the estimated results. As for the SC market leverage measure, we have confirmed **Hypothesis H.10**.

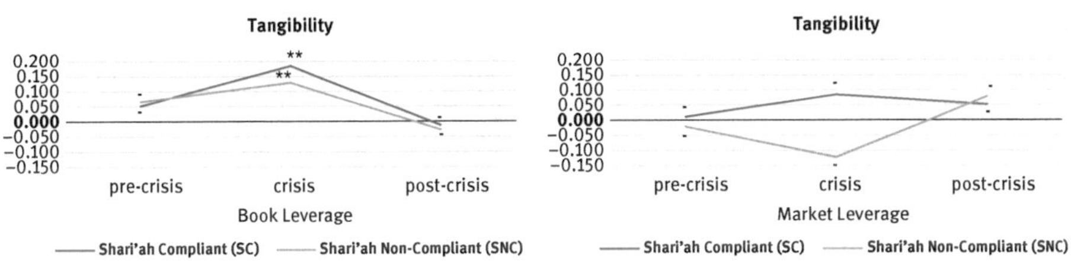

Figure 5.9: Coefficient Estimates of Tangibility, Time Breakdown.
Source: own contribution.

5.2.2.5 Business Risk (Earnings Volatility)

The results of the *business risk* determinant in Table 5.6 stays in contrast to the predominantly negative relationship of previous academic studies. Like the *growth opportunity* variable, the sign and coefficient of *business risk* (volatility) show mixed results on both book leverage and market leverage. Contrary to our hypothesized relationship and the proposed *Islamic Pecking Order* model, the book leverage results show a significant positive relationship for SC firms. A similar finding is found in Ariff et al. (2008), Cekrezi (2013), and Gaud et al. (2005). This supports the Pecking Order Theory's notion that earnings volatility will lead investors to require a higher return (information asymmetry), hence, the cost of issuing equity will increase. As long as the cost of equity is higher than the cost of debt, the Pecking Order Theory implies that companies will use the cheapest funding sources. Consequently, debt would be the preferred external funding to equity. Table C.1 in Appendix C shows that SC firms increased their debt level by approximately 45 % in the post-crisis period.

As for the market leverage, *business risk* exhibits a negative relationship with SNC firms. As *earnings volatility* increases, the probability of default on debt payment increases. This leads to a higher financial cost, as discussed in Section 4.3.2. Therefore, according to the Trade-Off Theory, firms with high-risk exposure need to lower their debt level to minimize their bankruptcy risk.

Studies on Shari'ah compliant firms: The limited number of academic studies on SC firms shows contrary results and contrary explanation on the relationship between *earnings volatility* and leverage. For instance, while Mai (2019) and Thabet and Hanefah (2014) found an inverse relationship, Haron and Ibrahim (2012) reported a positive relationship. They argued and referred to Obaidullah (2007, p. 14), who stated, "*The association between business risk and return is central to Islamic Finance. The legal maxim "Al-Kharaj bi Al-Daman"*[193] *[(The right to) profit (from something) goes with liability (for it)] underlies all forms of financial contracting in Islamic jurisprudence.*"[194] In other words, this maxim requires that liabilities (risk) and benefits (returns) go together, indicating the higher the risk, the higher the return.[195] However, we disagree with this argumentation postulated by Haron and Ibrahim (2012) in the context of leveraging (debt financing). The rationale of this maxim is related to the profit earned/lost due to the *operational risk* inherent to any business, not due to the increased (financial) risk raised by leveraging. According to the results in Table 5.6 and the explanation mentioned above, we rejected **Hypothesis H.5** for the book leverage of the SC firms and confirmed market leverage for SNC firms. The insignificant result of book leverage and market leverage led to a non-confirmation of the **Hypothesis H.5** for SNC and SC firms, respectively.

The results from the *overall (pooled)* estimations continue to be a mix. A look into the time breakdown estimation results reveals that the *business risk* variable's impact on both leverage measures is in line with the *overall (pooled)* regression results. The

193 See Majallah Al-Ahkam Article 85. Retrieved from: http://legal.pipa.ps/files/server/ENG%20Ottoman%20Majalle%20(Civil%20Law).pdf (accessed August 1, 2020).

194 For more information, see https://www.investment-and-finance.net/islamic-finance/a/al-kharaj-bil-dhaman.html (accessed August 26, 2020).

195 For more information, see ISRA (2016, p. 24).

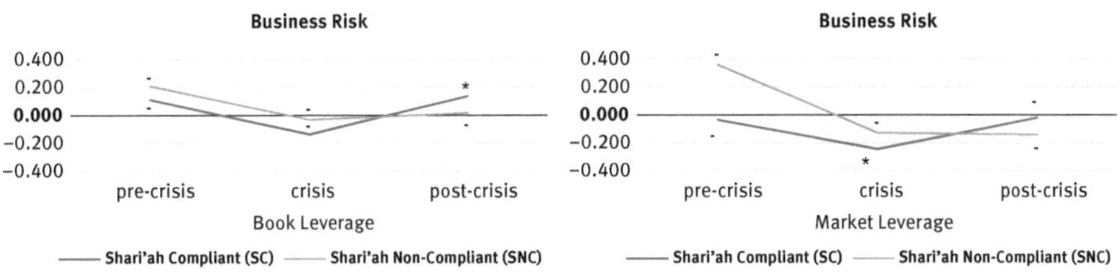

Figure 5.10: Coefficient Estimates of Business Risk, Time Breakdown.
Source: own contribution.

material significance reveals that despite the *overall (pooled)* regression results, which showed a positive and negative (significant) result for book leverage and market leverage, respectively, the effect of earnings volatility has changed throughout the years, especially for book leverage. (see Figure 5.10) The coefficient result changed from positive to negative, indicating that SC firms decreased their debt financing during the financial crisis. However, this negative correlation showed a temporary effect. The material significance gained importance during the post-crisis and changed back to be positive, confirming the observed increase in firms' debt level (see Table C.1 in Appendix C). The effect on market leverage remained negative throughout the years showing its statistical significance during the crisis only.

The results for SNC firms show that *earnings volatility* determinant changed throughout the years for both leverage measures. However, although the *overall (pooled)* regression result reported significance for market leverage, the effect of *business risk* on both leverage measures seems to be insignificant in all periods. Like *tangibility,* we rejected **Hypothesis H.11** for SC firms for book leverage and SNC firms for both leverages. As for the SC market leverage measure, we have confirmed **Hypothesis H.11**.

5.2.2.6 GDP Growth

The only macroeconomic variable we have tested in the leverage decision of firms is the *GDP growth* rate. In line with the Pecking Order Theory, the results in Table 5.6 show for both leverage measures that an increase in *GDP growth* rate is associated with a decrease in debt financing (negative relationship), however only for SNC firms. These findings suggest that SNC firms issue more equity in times when the economy grows. In other words, internal funds do not have an impact on the debt financing decision. This financing behavior leads to a decrease in firm leverage. Studies such as Ariff et al. (2008), Bokpin (2009), Dincergok and Yalciner (2011), and Rajan and Zingales (1995) also found a significant negative influence of *GDP growth* on leverage. The coefficient of *GDP growth* determinant on both leverage measures for SC firms is insignificant, which indicates that there is no evidence that SC firms consider the country's economic growth when financing decision activities occur.

Studies on Shari'ah compliant firms: In contrast to our insignificant result, Haron et al. (2011) reported a significant positive relationship between *economic growth* and financing decisions of SC firms in the Malaysian and Indonesian context, respectively. This suggests that SC firms, especially in Malaysia, prefer debt financing to utilize business opportunities by implementing expansionary and investment programs during higher economic growth. Similar to our result Arif and Mai (2020) and Mai (2019) exhibit insignificant *GDP growth* results. According to the results in Table 5.6 and the explanation mentioned above, we have confirmed **Hypothesis H.6** for SNC firms only. The insignificant results led to a non-confirmation of the **Hypothesis H.6** for SC firms.

Earlier, the test results in Section 5.2.2 have shown insignificant results between the *GDP growth* variable and both leverage measures for SC firms and significant negative results for SNC firms for both leverage measures. The GDP growth variable's impact on both leverage measures for SC firms does not reflect the *overall (pooled)* regression results. Even though a positive (insignificant) result is shown, the effect of *GDP growth* on book leverage changed throughout the years in both material and statistical significance. Consequently, they failed to have a consistent pattern throughout the years. During pre-crisis, the *GDP growth* rate was associated with a decrease in SC firms' leverage decisions. This trend changed slightly, reaching a marginally positive relationship post-crisis. However, both periods are reported with significant results. The results indicate that SC firms tend to increase their debt financing together with economic growth. A consistent positive relationship is reported throughout the years for market leverage, which contradicts the negative correlation reported in the *overall (pooled)* regression.

The material significance reveals that the effect of *GDP growth* on leverage decreased throughout the three periods, and its coefficient still changed from positive to negative for book leverage. Figure 5.11 reveals that the coefficient result for market leverage has reached its peak during the crisis period, indicating that SNC firms increased their debt financing, especially during the financial crisis. However, this significant positive effect sharply decreased and changed to become negative, but remained important during the post-crisis. As mentioned in the *overall (pooled)* part, this result suggests that SNC firms tend to issue equity to finance their operation and are less involved in debt financing with economic growth. According to the results in Table D.1 in Appendix D, similar to *business risk*, we rejected **Hypothesis H.12** for SC firms for book leverage and SNC firms for both leverages. As for the SC market leverage measure, we have confirmed **Hypothesis H.12.**

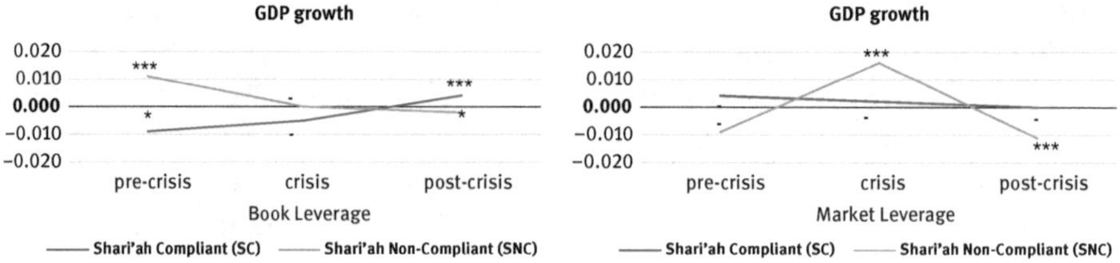

Figure 5.11: Coefficient Estimates of GDP Growth, Time Breakdown.
Source: own contribution.

Similar to the "significance of the differences" test (discussed in the last paragraph in Section 5.1.1), we have conducted additional analysis to test the differences between SC and SNC firm samples' coefficients. According to the z-test shown in Table C.9 in Appendix C,[196] the beta coefficient test results, derived from the *overall (pooled)* estimations, suggest that some independent variables have the same effect on the leverage of both firm types, while others differ. Specifically, as for the book value measure, *profitability* significantly differs between both firm types. This result suggests that, although SC firms are more profitable (see Table 5.3), they cannot retain to the same extent as their counterpart. SNC firms can retain more, which further leads to a decrease in firms' leverage since firms can utilize more internal financing.

The z-test results show mixed results (similar to book value measure) for the market value measure. Specifically, the determinants *profitability*, *growth opportunity*, and *firm size* exhibit a significant difference for both SC and SNC firms. It means that these determinants affect both firm types differently from a global perspective, i.e., regardless of the *country* and *industry* they are operating in. Furthermore, in Table 5.6, *tangibility* reported significant results for both firm types for market leverage. The z-test outcome reveals insignificant results for both leverage measures, indicating that both firm types do not differ. In other words, being low (SC) or high leveraged (SNC), firms operating under the same macroeconomic environment (i.e., *country* and *industry*) securitize their fixed assets as collateral for debt financing to the same extend. It confirms our findings in Section 5.2.3.4 that SC firm follow their non-compliant peers by collateralizing their tangible assets.

5.2.2.7 Summary

The analysis in this sub-section has shown the debt determinants that impact the financing decision of both SC and SNC firms. In essence, most of the debt factors do exhibit different effects among SC and SNC firms. However, depending on the definition of the leverage ratio, the effect of different independent variables on firms' capital structure varies. Some exhibit strong statistical significance, while others show less statistical significance or even insignificant results in both/either one of the leverage measures. However, a uniform effect from the *overall (pooled)* perspective can be exerted for debt determinant *profitability* (significantly negatively correlated) for both leverage measures and *growth opportunity* (significantly negatively correlated), *firm size*, and *tangibility* (both significantly positively correlated) for market leverage. Hence, the RQ 2 must be affirmed. Table 5.7 provides a summary of the tested hypotheses.

Furthermore, we dealt with the time breakdown analysis. In essence, the results in Table D.1 in Appendix D have shown that certain debt factors exhibit a consistent effect (coefficient sign) over time. However, depending on the leverage definition, the

---

196 This table also includes the z-test results for the cross-section samples, i.e., *country* and *industry*.

Table 5.7: Overview Tested Hypotheses – Research Question 2.

RQ 2		**What are the significant determinants of capital structure in the context of SC and SNC firms?**	**BLEV**		**MLEV**	
			SC	***SNC***	***SC***	***SNC***
Determinants	**ID**	**Hypothesis**	*Statistically Significant*			
Profitability	H.1	A significant negative relationship between profitability and leverage is expected among SC and SNC companies.	✓ (–)	✓ (–)	✓ (–)	✓ (–)
Growth Opportunity	H.2	A significant negative relationship between growth opportunity and leverage is expected among SC and SNC companies.	– (–)	× (+)	✓ (–)	✓ (–)
Firm Size	H.3a	A significant negative relationship between firm size and leverage is expected for SC companies.	– (–)	✓ (+)	× (+)	✓ (+)
	H.3b	A significant positive relationship between firm size and leverage is expected for SNC companies.				
Tangibility	H.4a	A significant negative relationship between tangibility and leverage is expected for SC companies.	– (+)	✓ (+)	× (+)	✓ (+)
	H.4b	A significant positive relationship between tangibility and leverage is expected for SNC companies.				
Business Risk	H.5	A significant negative relationship between business risk and leverage is expected among SC and SNC companies.	× (+)	– (+)	– (–)	✓ (–)
GDP growth	H.6	A significant negative relationship between GDP growth and leverage is expected among SC and SNC companies.	– (–)	✓ (–)	– (–)	✓ (–)
	✓	Hypothesis confirmed				
	×	Hypothesis rejected				
	–	Regression result: insignificant				
	(–/+)	Uniformity (coefficient sign and significance)				

Source: own contribution.

impact (significance) of different independent variables on firms' capital structure varies throughout different periods. Hence, the RQ 3 must be affirmed. Table 5.8 provides a summary of the tested hypotheses.

5.2.3 Cross-*Country* and Cross-*Industry* Analysis

This sub-section provides a cross-sectional analysis and shows that the importance of various debt determinants diverges from different *countries* and *industries*. With the material significance (i.e., sign and value of the coefficient), obtained from Tables D.2

Table 5.8: Overview Tested Hypotheses – Research Question 3.

RQ 3		**Are certain capital structure determinants only temporarily important in SC and SNC firms' leverage decisions, or do they exhibit a consistent impact over time?**	**BLEV**		**MLEV**	
			SC	*SNC*	*SC*	*SNC*
Determinants	**ID**	**Hypothesis**	*Statistically Significant*			
Profitability	H.7	The positive/negative impact of profitability on SC and SNC company's capital structure remains the same over time.	×	✓	×	×
Growth Opportunity	H.8	The positive/negative impact of growth opportunity on SC and SNC company's capital structure remains the same over time.	×	✓	×	×
Firm Size	H.9	The positive/negative impact of firm size on SC and SNC company's capital structure remains the same over time.	×	✓	×	✓
Tangibility	H.10	The positive/negative impact of tangibility on SC and SNC company's capital structure remains the same over time.	×	×	✓	×
Business Risk	H.11	The positive/negative impact of business risk on SC and SNC company's capital structure remains the same over time.	×	×	✓	×
GDP growth	H.12	The positive/negative impact of GDP growth on SC and SNC company's capital structure remains the same over time.	×	×	✓	×
	✓	Hypothesis confirmed				
	×	Hypothesis rejected				
	–	Regression result: insignificant				

Source: own contribution.

and D.3 in Appendix D, we compared the estimated signs of the *countries* and *industries* and required at least 50% of each (i.e., four out of seven) to have a capital structure determinant in the same direction. Based on the predictions made by each capital structure theory (see Tables 2.1 and 4.10), we provided a "sub-conclusion" in which we suggested that either the Trade-Off Theory or Pecking Order Theory could best explain the financing behavior of the SC or SNC firms. For completeness, we also have incorporated our proposed *Islamic Pecking Order* model into the sub-conclusions. However, the statistical conclusion will be provided in Section 5.2.4.

All model regressions contain time fixed effects (time dummies) and, where applicable, the country fixed (country dummies) respectively industry fixed (industry dummies) effect. The econometric estimators applied to each model are shown in the last row.

Company cluster robust standard errors are reported in the brackets. *, **, and *** denote significance at 10%, 5%, and 1% levels, respectively. All variables are winsorized at the 1% and 99% level. We elaborate on the econometric estimator results obtained from the cross-*country* and cross-*industry* regression in the following sub-section.

5.2.3.1 Profitability

Figure 5.12 shows how *profitability* behaves within the seven different countries. As can be seen, *profitability* constantly exhibits a negative relationship with both leverage measures for all countries. Hence, *profitability* ultimately leads to a decrease in debt financing, similar to our *overall (pooled)* regression results. The results show that profitable SC firms tend to employ less leverage in all countries, except in the United Kingdom. This finding indicates that SC firms in the United Kingdom increase their financial leverage when they are profitable. Strong material significance can be found especially in Japan, for both leverage measures. Referring to the estimated results, except for S. Korea, *profitability* exhibits strong statistical significance in all countries for market leverage. As for the book leverage, the results are statistically significant for the United States, Canada, Japan, and India.

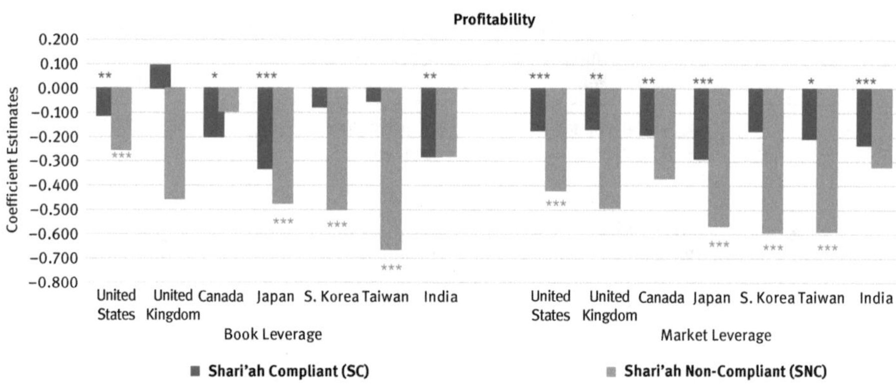

Figure 5.12: Coefficient Estimates of Profitability, *Country* Breakdown.
Source: own contribution.

Similar to SC firms' findings, profitable SNC firms tend to employ less leverage in all countries. This negative relationship indicates that the amount of debt needed decreases as the firms become more profitable. Strong material significance can be found in Taiwan, followed by S. Korea and Japan in both leverage measures. Referring to the estimated results, we see the same results for both leverage measures. *Profitability* exhibits only statistical significance in the United States, Japan, S. Korea, and Taiwan. Sub-conclusion: The material significance suggests that SC and SNC firms financing behavior seems to be best explained by the Pecking Order Theory and the proposed *Islamic Pecking Order* model for both leverage measures. According to the results in Tables D.2 and D.3 in Appendix D, we fully rejected **Hypothesis H.13** for SC and SNC firms for both leverage measures.

As mentioned earlier, *profitability* is one of the determinants that provide consistent results. Figure 5.13 shows that *profitability* constantly exhibits a negative relationship with both leverage measures for all industries. The *industry* perspective supports our *overall (pooled)* regression results, represented in Table 5.6. Specifically, both leverage measures show that profitable SC firms tend to employ less leverage in all industries. We found strong material significance in Consumer Goods for both leverage measures and in Health Care for book leverage measures. Referring to the estimated results, except for Health Care and Consumer Services, *profitability* exhibits strong statistical significance in all industries for market leverage. The book leverage, the results are statistically significant and similar to market leverage, except in Industrials, Technology, and Consumer Services. Sub-conclusion: Like the country results, the results' material significance suggests that SC firms' financing behavior seems to be best explained by the Pecking Order Theory for both leverage measures.

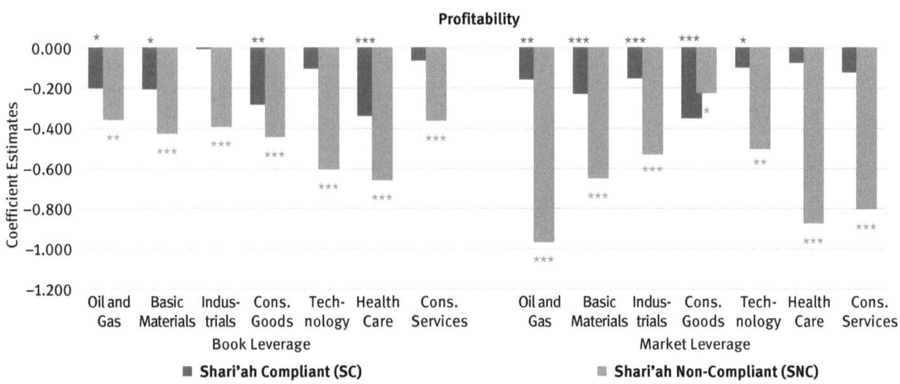

Figure 5.13: Coefficient Estimates of Profitability, *Industry* Breakdown.
Source: own contribution.

Similar to SC firms' findings, profitable SNC firms tend to employ less leverage in all industries. This negative relationship between profitability and leverage indicates that the amount of debt needed decreases as the firms become more profitable. The results show strong material significance in Oil and Gas for market leverage and Health Care industries for both leverage measures. The magnitude of the coefficient estimates of SNC firms overall outrages the coefficient estimates of their SC counterparts. Referring to the estimated results, strong statistical significance, for both book leverage and market leverage, is exhibited in all industries for *profitability*. Sub-conclusion: The material significance suggests, similar to the *country* perspective, that SC and SNC firms financing behavior seems to be best explained by the Pecking Order Theory and the proposed *Islamic Pecking Order* model for both leverage measures. According to the results in Tables D.2 and D.3 in Appendix D, we fully rejected **Hypothesis H.19** for SC and SNC firms for both leverage measures.

5.2.3.2 Growth Opportunity

Figure 5.14 shows different results for various. Similar to the findings in our *overall (pooled)* analysis, the results show rather mix results for both leverage measures. The majority of the countries show the positive impact of *growth opportunity* on book leverage for both SC and SNC firms, however insignificant for the former. Additionally, we noted that the material significance of SNC firms in all countries outrages the coefficient estimates of SC firms in both book and market leverage. Regarding the market leverage, the sign of the *growth opportunity* coefficient constantly shows a negative relationship in all countries (except SNC firms in Canada), with a similar high gap between SC and SNC firms' material significance. We concluded that the market-to-book ratio seems to be rather marginally relevant for SC firms due to its relatively low coefficient value.

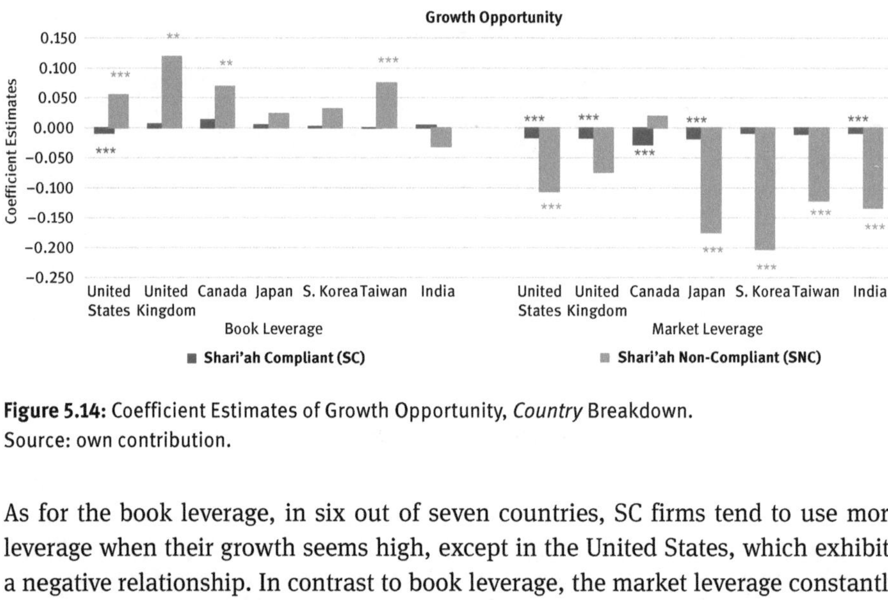

Figure 5.14: Coefficient Estimates of Growth Opportunity, *Country* Breakdown.
Source: own contribution.

As for the book leverage, in six out of seven countries, SC firms tend to use more leverage when their growth seems high, except in the United States, which exhibits a negative relationship. In contrast to book leverage, the market leverage constantly exhibits a negative relationship with *growth opportunity* in all sample countries. This negative relationship is consistent with earlier academic findings (see Table 4.5 in Section 4.3.2). As mentioned above, SC firms' material significance in all countries for both leverage measures is very low compared to their non-compliant counterpart. Referring to the estimated results, the United States (for both leverage measures) and the United Kingdom, Canada, Japan, and India (for market leverage) exhibit strong statistical significance, with a 99% significance level, for *growth opportunity*. Sub-conclusion: The material significance of the results shown in Figure 5.14 suggests that SC firms financing behavior seems to be best explained by the Pecking Order Theory for book leverage and the Trade-Off Theory and the proposed *Islamic Pecking Order* model for the market leverage.

Like SC firms, book leverage results in six out of seven countries show that SNC firms tend to increase their debt level when their market value is higher than their book value. In contrast, the market leverage shows a negative relationship with *growth opportunity* and SNC firms' market leverage ratio, except for Canada. Strong material significance can be found in S. Korea and Japan, followed by India and Taiwan for market leverage and in the United Kingdom for book leverage. Referring to the estimated results, except the United Kingdom and Canada (for market leverage) and Japan, S. Korea, and India (for book leverage), strong statistical significance for *growth opportunity* is shown in all countries for both leverage measures. Sub-conclusion: The material significance of the results shown in Figure 5.14 suggests that SNC firms' financing behavior seems to be best explained by the Pecking Order Theory for book leverage and the Trade-Off Theory and the proposed *Islamic Pecking Order* model for market leverage. According to the results in Tables D.2 and D.3 in Appendix D, we rejected **Hypothesis H.14** for SC firms for market leverage and SNC firms for both leverage measures. As for the SC book leverage measure, we confirmed **Hypothesis H.14**.

Like the country results, Figure 5.15 shows different results for various industries. Similar to the mix of findings from the *country* perspectives. The majority of the industries show the positive impact of *growth opportunity* on book leverage for both SC and SNC firms. Additionally, we noted that the material significance of SNC firms overall outrages the coefficient estimates of SC firms in both leverages with minor exceptions for market leverage (i.e., Oil and Gas and Health Care). The relatively low coefficient value of the market-to-book ratio suggests this debt determinant be rather marginally relevant for SC firms. Referring to the estimated results, Health Care (for book leverage) and all industries exhibit strong statistical significance for *growth opportunity* (for market leverage). As for the book leverage, in four out of seven industries, SC firms

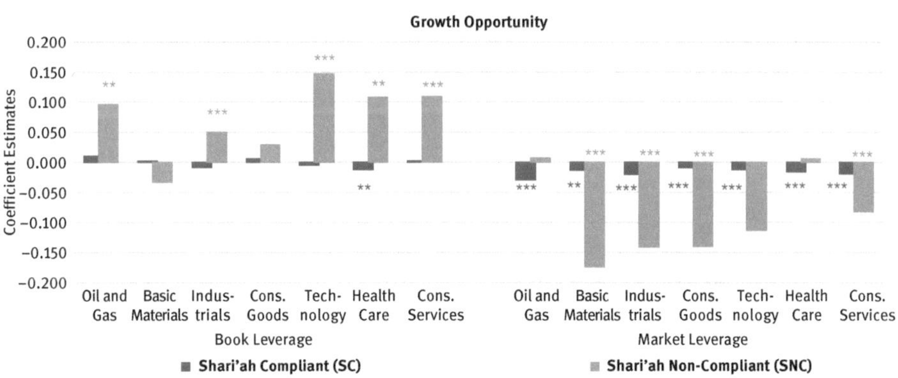

Figure 5.15: Coefficient Estimates of Growth Opportunity, *Industry* Breakdown.
Source: own contribution.

tend to use more leverage when their growth seems high. In contrast, the market leverage constantly exhibits a negative relationship with *growth opportunity* determinant in all sample industries. This negative relationship is consistent with earlier academic findings (see Table 4.5 in Section 4.3.2). Sub-conclusion: The material significance of the results shown in Figure 5.15 resembles the *country* perspective for SC firms.

The book leverage results show that SNC firms engage in debt financing in six out of seven industries when their market value is higher than their book value. In contrast, the market leverage shows in all industries a negative relationship with *growth opportunity* and SNC firms leverage ratio, except for Oil and Gas and Health Care industries. Strong material significance can be found in Technology, followed by Health Care and Consumer Services for book leverage and in Basic Materials, followed by Industrials and Consumer Goods for market leverage. Referring to the estimated results, except Basic Materials and Consumer Goods (for book leverage) and Oil and Gas, Technology, and Health Care (for market leverage), strong statistical significance for *growth opportunity*, is shown in all countries for both leverage measures. Sub-conclusion: Similarly, the material significance of the results shown in Figure 5.15 resembles the *country* perspective for SNC firms. Consequently, we rejected **Hypothesis H.20** for SC firms for market leverage and SNC firms for both leverage measures. As for the SC book leverage measure, we have confirmed **Hypothesis H.20**.

5.2.3.3 Firm Size

Figure 5.16 shows how *firm size*, measured by total revenue (log of sales), relates to leverage within the seven different countries. The results show that *firm size* constantly exhibits a positive relationship with market leverage measures for both firm types in all countries. Hence, *firm size* does ultimately lead to an increase in debt financing, especially for market leverage. For book leverage measures, especially for SC firms, we detected different results.

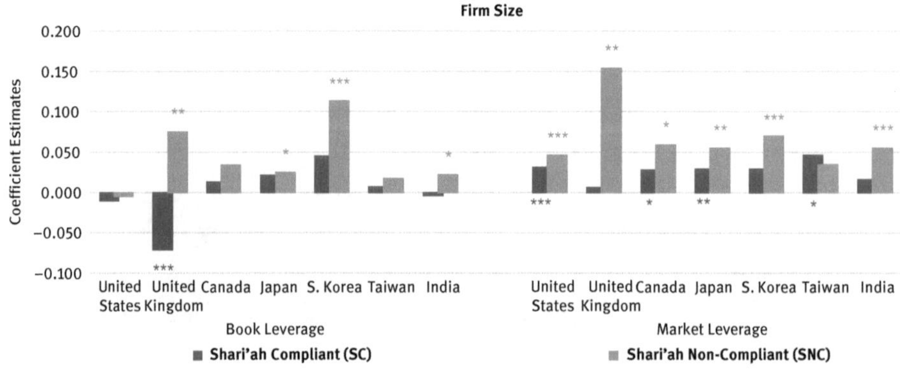

Figure 5.16: Coefficient Estimates of Firm Size, *Country* Breakdown.
Source: own contribution.

SC firms in all countries tend to employ more leverage, the bigger they are for market leverage, with Taiwan reporting the highest material significance. On the contrary, book leverage results report that only in four out of seven countries *firm size* plays a positive role in debt financing. However, in the case of the United Kingdom, the financing behavior changes drastically. Specifically, a significant negative relationship with the *firm size* is detected, leading to SC firms decreasing their leverage ratio the bigger they are. Interestingly, even though most countries exhibit a positive correlation, the strongest material significance is shown in the United Kingdom. Referring to the estimated results, the United Kingdom (for book leverage) and the United States, Canada, Japan, and Taiwan (for market leverage) show statistical significance for *firm size*. Hence, SC firms' size does not lead ultimately to an increase in debt financing, especially for book leverage. Our *overall (pooled)* sample reported similar results.

The *firm size* exhibits a positive relationship for both leverage measures in all countries (except in the United States for book leverage), indicating that SNC firms tend to employ more leverage the bigger they are. The *firm size* variable shows the strongest material significance for SNC firms in the United Kingdom for market leverage and S. Korea for book leverage. Referring to the estimated results, except for Taiwan, *firm size* shows statistical significance in all countries for market leverage. The United Kingdom, Japan, S. Korea, and India exhibit statistical significance for book leverage. In contrast to SC firms, SNC firms' *firm size* for SNC leads to increased debt financing. Sub-conclusion: The material significance of the results shown in Figure 5.16 suggests that SNC firms financing behavior seems to be best explained by the Trade-Off Theory for both leverage measures. According to the results in Tables D.2 and D.3 in Appendix D, similar to the *growth opportunity* determinant, we rejected **Hypothesis H.15** for SC firms for market leverage and SNC firms for both leverage measures. As for the SC book leverage measure, we have confirmed **Hypothesis H.15**.

Figure 5.17 shows how *firm size* relates to leverage from the *industry* perspective. The results indicate a constant positive relationship with both leverage measures for

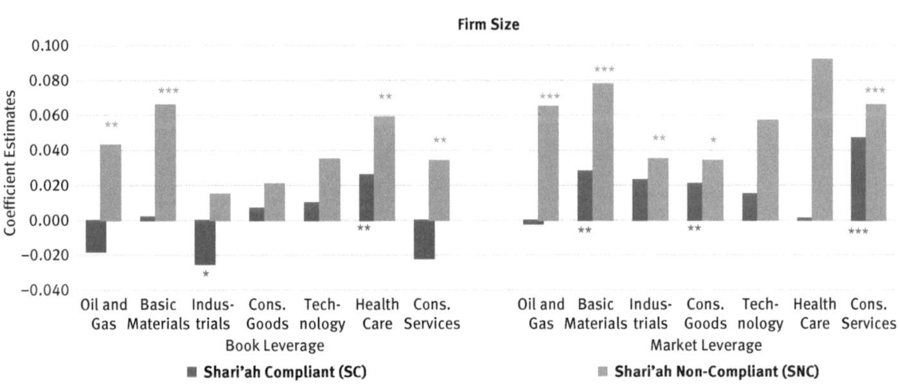

Figure 5.17: Coefficient Estimates of Firm Size, *Industry* Breakdown.
Source: own contribution.

SNC firms in all industries. Hence, *firm size* does ultimately lead to an increase in debt financing. For book leverage, especially for SC firms, we detected different results. For instance, the results for book leverage are rather mixed. Three out of seven industries play a negative role in leverage, leading to SC firms decreasing their leverage ratio the bigger they are. On the contrary, except in Oil and Gas, SC firms tend to employ more leverage. The bigger they are as for market leverage, with Health Care reporting the highest material significance. Referring to the estimated results, except for Industrial and Health Care, firm size shows insignificant results in all remaining industries for book leverage. The former exhibits a negative the latter a positive correlation. Market leverage results do not show much difference, with Basic Materials, Consumer Goods, and Consumer Services only reporting a significant positive outcome, with Consumer Services exhibiting the highest materials significance. Sub-conclusion: The material significance of the results shown in Figure 5.17 suggests that SC firms financing behavior seems to be best explained by the Trade-Off Theory for both leverage measures.

As mentioned above, the results for SNC firms are straightforward – positive relationship for both leverage measures in all industries. These results indicate that these firms tend to employ more leverage the bigger they are. The *size* variable shows the strongest material significance in Health Care for market leverage and Basic Materials for book leverage measures. Referring to the estimated results, except Industrials, Consumer Goods, and Technology (for book leverage) and Technology and Health Care (for market leverage), statistical significance for firm size, is shown in all industries for both leverage measure. In contrast to SC firms, SNC firms' *size* ultimately leads to an increase in debt financing. Sub-conclusion: The material significance of the results shown in Figure 5.17 suggests that SNC firms financing behavior seems to be best explained by the Trade-Off Theory for both leverage measures. According to the results in Tables D.2 and D.3 in Appendix D, we rejected **Hypothesis H.21** for SNC firms for both leverage measures. As for the SC firms, we confirm **Hypothesis H.21.**

5.2.3.4 Tangibility

The *overall (pooled)* regression reported that *tangibility* (fixed assets) leads to increased leverages. As far SC firms are concerned, *tangibility* is positively related to leverage in all countries except for India in book leverage and except in S. Korea and India for market leverage. This finding indicates that SC firms tend to employ more leverage the more fixed assets they possess, which eventually serves as collateral for debt financing. In the United States, SC firms show the highest material significance for book leverage and in Japan for market leverage measures. Referring to the estimated results, only the United States exhibit significant positive result for both leverage measures. The significant positive result in the *overall (pooled)* regression for market leverage can be accounted for by SC firms from the United States only. Sub-conclusion: The material significance of the results shown in Figure 5.18 suggests that SC firms financing behavior seems to be best explained by the Trade-Off Theory for both leverage measures.

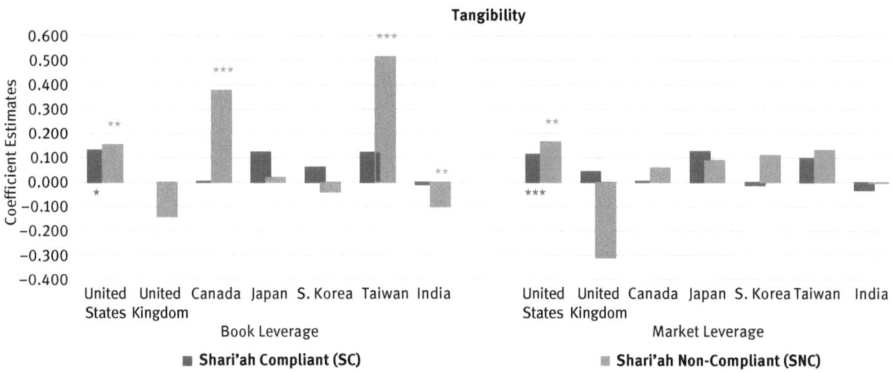

Figure 5.18: Coefficient Estimates of Tangibility, *Country* Breakdown.
Source: own contribution.

In the context of SNC firms, *tangibility* seems to be positively related in the United States, Canada, Japan, and Taiwan, with Taiwan showing the highest material significance for book leverage. This finding indicates that SNC firms tend to increase their debt level by providing their fixed assets as security for debt financing. Contrary to SC firms, both leverage measures report the highest negative material significance in the United Kingdom. Strong statistical significance can only be found in the United States, followed by Canada, Taiwan, and India for book leverage, with India showing a negative relationship to leverage. As for the market leverage, only the United States has the highest positive material and, at the same time, statistical significance. Similar to SC firms, the significant positive result for both leverages in the *overall (pooled)* regression can be account for by the SNC firms operating in the United States (market leverage) and the United States, Canada, and Taiwan (book leverage) only. Sub-conclusion: The material significance shown in Figure 5.18 suggests, similar to SC firms, that SNC firms financing behavior seems to be best explained by the Trade-Off Theory for both leverage measures. According to the results in Tables D.2 and D.3 in Appendix D, the mixed cross-*country* results of *tangibility* led us to confirm **Hypothesis H.16** for SC and SNC firms for both leverage measures. Thus, the *tangibility* determinant does not seem to be consistent across countries.

At first glance, the *industry* perspective seems to support the *overall* regression (pooled analysis) results. More specifically, Figure 5.19 reveals that *tangibility* is positively related to leverage in all industries under study except for Oil and Gas in book leverage and except in Consumer Goods and Health Care industries for market leverage. This finding indicates that SC firms tend to employ more leverage the more fixed assets they possess, which serves as collateral for debt financing. SC firms in Health Care show the highest material significance for book leverage, followed by Consumer Services and Technology in both leverage measures. Referring to the estimated results, Oil and Gas shows a significant negative result, while Technology, Health Care, and Consumer Services exhibit strong significant positive outcomes for

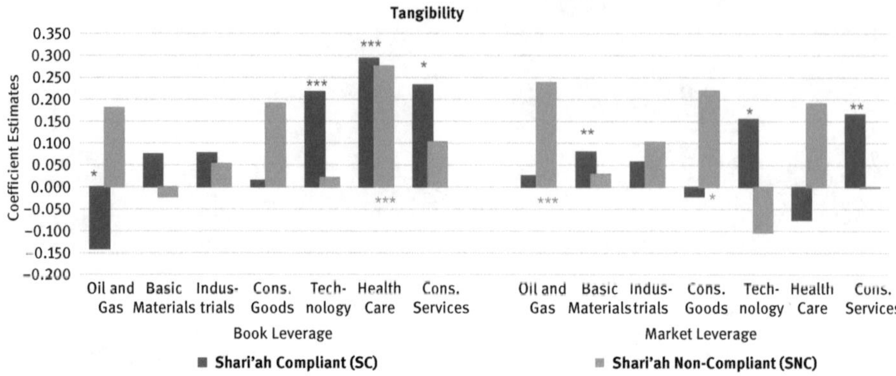

Figure 5.19: Coefficient Estimates of Tangibility, *Industry* Breakdown.
Source: own contribution.

book leverage. The significant positive result in the *overall (pooled)* regression for market leverage can be accounted for by SC firms from Basic Materials, Technology, and Consumer Services. Sub-conclusion: The material significance suggests that SC firms financing behavior seems to be best explained by the Trade-Off Theory for both leverage measures.

Tangibility seems to be positively related in all industries, except in Basic Materials, with Health Care showing the highest material significance for book leverage. These results indicate that SNC firms tend to increase their debt level by providing their fixed assets as security for debt financing. Contrary to SC firms, the highest negative material significance is Technology, where market leverage is concerned. Referring to statistical significance, only Health Care shows of statistical importance for book leverage. Oil and Gas and Consumer Goods represent the highest positive material and statistical significance for the market leverage. Like SC firms, the consistent positive significant result in the *overall (pooled)* regression for both leverage measures can be accounted for by SNC firms from Health Care, Oil and Gas, and Consumer Goods. Sub-conclusion: The material significance of the results shown in Figure 5.19 suggests, similar to SC firms, that SNC firms financing behavior seems to be best explained by the Trade-Off Theory for both leverage measures. According to Tables D.2 and D.3 in Appendix D, the results of *tangibility* led us to confirm **Hypothesis H.22** for SC and SNC firms for both leverage measures. Similar to the *country* perspective, the *tangibility* determinant does not seem to be consistent across industries.

5.2.3.5 Business Risk (Earnings Volatility)

Figure 5.20 shows how the impact of *business risk* on firms' leverage decisions varies among the sample countries. Similar to the *tangibility* determinant, the results shown for both SC and SNC firms are rather mixed. SC firms in the United States, Canada, and India tend to have more leverage when their *earnings volatility* seems rather high

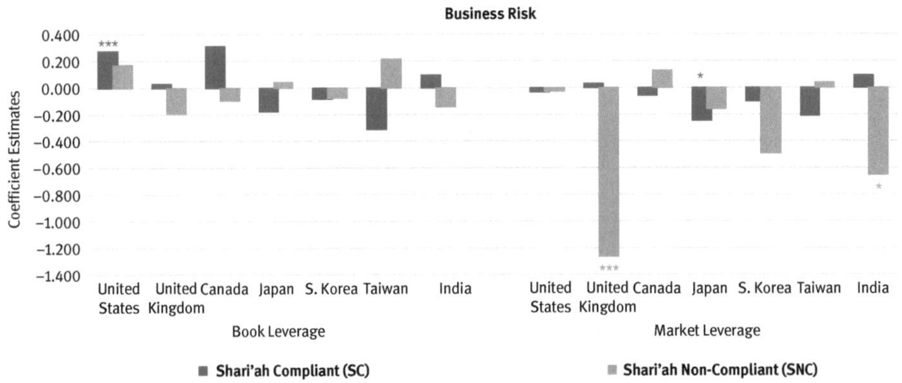

Figure 5.20: Coefficient Estimates of Business Risk, *Country* Breakdown.
Source: own contribution.

for the book leverage. Canada shows the highest positive material significance. In Japan and Taiwan, SC firms with high *earnings volatility* tend to have less leverage for both leverage measures. In contrast, Taiwan shows the highest material significance for book leverage. Referring to the estimated results, only the United States and Japan exhibit significant results for book and market leverage, respectively. Interestingly, the significant positive result in the *overall (pooled)* regression for book leverage can be accounted for by SC firms from the United States only. Sub-conclusion: The material significance shown in Figure 5.20 suggests that SC firms financing behavior seems to be best explained by the Pecking Order Theory for book leverage and the Trade-Off Theory, and the proposed *Islamic Pecking Order* model for market leverage.

SNC firms in the United Kingdom, Japan, S. Korea, and India seem to have less leverage for both leverage measures. The material significance for all the four countries is higher on market leverage, with United Kingdom exhibit the highest material significance. It outnumbers by far all other SNC firms (including SC firms) in all other sample countries. Results for the United States, Japan, and Taiwan show that SNC firms are characterized by possessing more leverage when the *business risk* determinant increases. Referring to the estimated results, while all countries show insignificant results for book leverage, market leverage exhibits only significant results for SNC firms in the United Kingdom and India. Sub-conclusion: The material significance suggests that SNC firms financing behavior seems to be best explained by the Trade-Off Theory and proposed the *Islamic Pecking Order* model for both leverage measures. According to the results in Tables D.2 and D.3 in Appendix D, similar to the *tangibility* determinant, the mixed cross-*country* results of *business risk* led us to confirm **Hypothesis H.17** for SC and SNC firms for both leverage measures. However, we could not validate **Hypothesis H.17** for SNC firms' book leverage since all results were insignificant. Thus, the impact of *earnings volatility* on leverage does not seem to be consistent across countries.

Figure 5.21 exhibits similar to Figure 5.20 rather mixed results. Specifically, SC firms in Basic Materials and Health Care tend to have more leverage when their

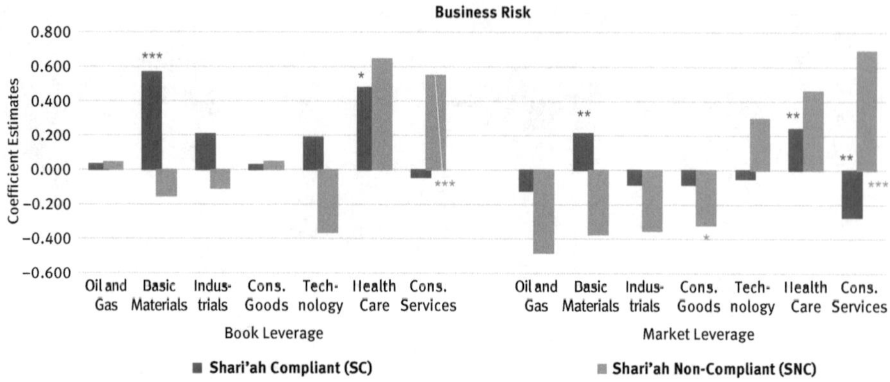

Figure 5.21: Coefficient Estimates of Business Risk, *Industry* Breakdown.
Source: own contribution.

standard deviation of EBIT seems relatively high for the book leverage. Both industries show the highest positive material significance. SC firms operating in Consumer Services tend to engage less in debt financing, considering both leverage measures when facing high *earnings volatility*; market leverage shows the highest material and statistical significance. Similarly, Basic Materials and Health Care exhibit statistically significant results for both leverage measures. From the industry perspective, the significant positive result obtained from the *overall (pooled)* regression for book leverage can be account for by the SC firms operating in Basic Materials. Sub-conclusion: The material significance of the results shown in Figure 5.21 suggests that SC firms financing behavior seems to be best explained by the Pecking Order Theory for book leverage and the Trade-Off Theory, and the proposed *Islamic Pecking Order* model for market leverage.

SNC firms operating in Health Care and Consumer Services tend to increase their debt level when their standards deviation of EBIT seems to be relatively high for both leverage measures. The highest material significance is reported for market leverage in Consumer Services. In contrast, SNC firms in Oil and Gas, Basic Materials, Industrials, and Consumer Goods seems to decrease their debt level when the business risk determinant increases. Similar findings are shown for SNC firms in Basic Materials, Industrials, and Technology industries for book leverage. Referring to the statistical significance, only Consumer Services shows strong statistical significance for both leverage measures, while Consumer Goods exhibit a negative statistical significance only for market leverage. Sub-conclusion: The material significance of the results shown in Figure 5.21 suggests that SNC firms financing behavior seems to be best explained by the Pecking Order Theory for book leverage and the Trade-Off Theory, and the proposed *Islamic Pecking Order* model for market leverage.

According to Tables D.2 and D.3 in Appendix D, the mixed cross-*industry* results led us to confirm **Hypothesis H.23** for SC and SNC firms for both leverage measures. Thus, the effect of *business risk* seems also not to be consistent across industries.

5.2.3.6 GDP Growth

The only variable we have incorporated to test the macroeconomic impact on SC and SNC firms' leverage decision is *GDP growth*. *Overall (pooled)* regression estimates have shown both positive and negative results, but insignificant for SC firms, while significant negative results for SNC firms for both leverage measures. When economic growth is anticipated, SC firms operating in Canada and Japan seem to utilize the peak times to increase their debt financing. Canada shows the highest positive material significance for both leverage measures. United States, S. Korea, and India exhibit a negative relationship for both leverage measures, indicating that SC firms in these countries prefer equity financing over debt financing during economic peaks. The United States shows the strongest negative material significance for both leverage measures. It outnumbers the impact of GDP growth determinant on firms' leverage of all other countries in the study. Where statistical significance is concerned, the United States, Canada, Japan, and India exhibits the significant impact of GDP growth on SC firms leverage decision; however, in both directions (i.e., positive and negative). Sub-conclusion: The material significance of the results shown in Figure 5.22 suggests that SC firms' financing behavior seems inconclusive for both leverage measures. In other words, neither the Pecking Order, Trade-Off Order, nor the proposed *Islamic Pecking Order* model can dominantly explain the financing decision of SC firms.

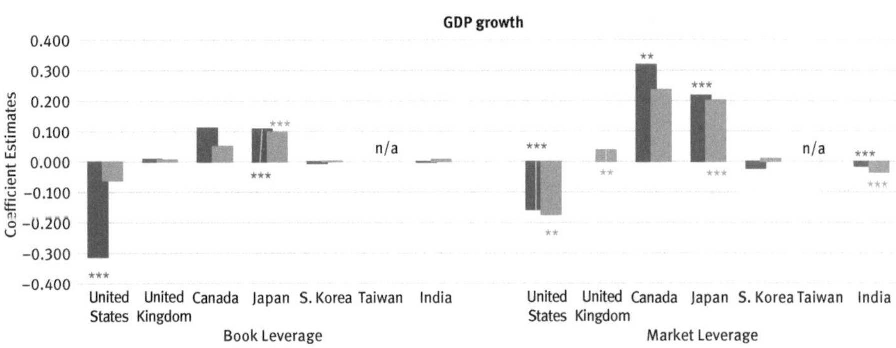

Figure 5.22: Coefficient Estimates of GDP Growth, *Country* Breakdown.[197]
Source: own contribution.

Economic growth shows its positive impact on SNC firms' leverage decisions in the United Kingdom, Canada, Japan, and S. Korea for both leverage measures, with Japan and Canada showing the highest material significance in book and market leverage measures, respectively. Referring to statistical significance, only Japan exhibits significant results for book leverage. As for the market leverage measures, the United

197 Due to data availability, Taiwan's GDP has been excluded.

States, United Kingdom, Japan, and India exhibit the significant impact of *GDP growth* on SNC firms' leverage decisions; however, similar to SC firms, in both directions (i.e., positive and negative). Sub-conclusion: The material significance of the results shown in Figure 5.22 suggests that SNC firms financing behavior seems to be best explained by the Trade-Off Theory for both leverage measures. According to the results in Tables D.2 and D.3 in Appendix D, the mixed cross-*country* results of *GDP growth* led us to confirm **Hypothesis H.18** for SC and SNC firms for both leverage measures.

Figure 5.23 reveals that SC firms operating only in Basic Materials and Consumer Goods utilize the economic peak times with debt financing, with Basic Materials showing the highest positive material significance for book leverage. The opposite results can be detected for SC firms operating in Consumer Services and Oil and Gas industries. The results exhibit a negative relationship between economic *growth* and leverage, indicating that SC firms in these industries prefer equity financing over debt financing during economic peaks. Referring to statistical significance, Consumer Goods and Consumer Services exhibit the significant impact of *GDP growth* on SC firms' leverage decision for book leverage and only shows statistical significance in Oil and Gas for market leverage. Sub-conclusion: The material significance of the results shown in Figure 5.23 suggests that SC firms financing behavior seems to be best explained by the Pecking Order Theory and the proposed *Islamic Pecking Order* model for book leverage and Trade-Off Theory for market leverage.

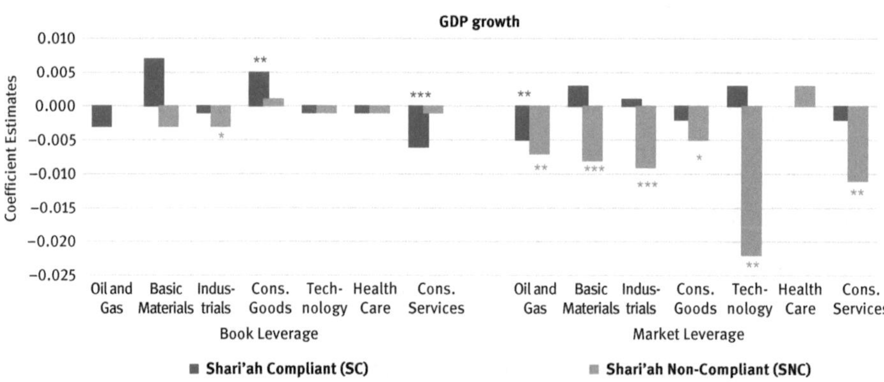

Figure 5.23: Coefficient Estimates of GDP Growth, *Industry* Breakdown.
Source: own contribution.

Economic *growth* shows its negative impact on SNC firms' leverage decision in six out of seven industries for market leverage, with Technology showing the highest material significance. This negative correlation between *GDP growth* determinant and firm leverage implies that SNC firms utilized equity financing as an external funding instrument. Statistically, *GDP growth* exhibits statistical importance in all industries for market leverage (except for Health Care). It only shows statistical importance in

Industrials for book leverage, which also seems to account for the significant negative result in the *overall (pooled)* regression. Sub-conclusion: The material significance of the results shown in Figure 5.23 suggests that SNC firms financing behavior seems to be best explained by the Pecking Order Theory and the proposed *Islamic Pecking Order* model for both leverage measures. According to the results in Tables D.2 and D.3 in Appendix D, we confirmed **Hypothesis H.24** for SC firms for both leverage measures and SNC firms for book leverage. As for the SNC market leverage measure, we rejected **Hypothesis H.24**.

5.2.3.7 Summary

This sub-section dealt with the cross-sectional analysis to identify the important debt determinants in each *country* and *industry*. While the *overall (pooled)* regression results provided a consolidated view of both the SC and SNC samples, this section allowed us to investigate the cross-sectional differences among both firm types operating in each sample *country* and *industry*, respectively. Depending on the definition of the leverage ratio, the effect of different independent variables

Table 5.9: Overview Tested Hypotheses – Research Question 4.

RQ 4		**Are certain capital structure determinants, for SC and SNC firms, more important in some *countries* yet unimportant elsewhere?**	**BLEV**		**MLEV**	
			SC	***SNC***	***SC***	***SNC***
Determinants	**ID**	**Hypothesis**	*Statistically Significant*			
Profitability	H.13	The effect of profitability on SC and SNC company's capital structure differs among *countries*.	×	×	×	×
Growth Opportunity	H.14	The growth opportunity effect on SC and SNC company's capital structure differs among *countries*.	✓	×	×	×
Firm Size	H.15	The firm size effect on SC and SNC company's capital structure differs among *countries*.	✓	×	×	×
Tangibility	H.16	The effect of the tangibility on SC and SNC company's capital structure differs among *countries*.	✓	✓	✓	✓
Business Risk	H.17	The risk effect on SC and SNC company's capital structure differs among *countries*.	✓	–	✓	✓
GDP growth	H.18	The effect of GDP growth on SC and SNC company's capital structure differs among *countries*.	✓	✓	✓	✓
	✓	Hypothesis confirmed				
	×	Hypothesis rejected				
	–	Regression result: insignificant				

Source: own contribution.

Table 5.10: Overview Tested Hypotheses – Research Question 5.

RQ 5		**Are certain capital structure determinants, for SC and SNC firms, more important in some *industries* yet unimportant elsewhere?**	**BLEV**		**MLEV**	
			SC	*SNC*	*SC*	*SNC*
Determinants	**ID**	**Hypothesis**	*Statistically Significant*			
Profitability	H.19	The effect of profitability on SC and SNC company's capital structure differs among *industries*.	×	×	×	×
Growth Opportunity	H.20	The growth opportunity effect on SC and SNC company's capital structure differs among *industries*.	✓	×	×	×
Firm Size	H.21	The firm size effect on SC and SNC company's capital structure differs among *industries*.	✓	×	✓	×
Tangibility	H.22	The effect of the tangibility on SC and SNC company's capital structure differs among *industries*.	✓	✓	✓	✓
Business Risk	H.23	The risk effect on SC and SNC company's capital structure differs among *industries*.	✓	✓	✓	✓
GDP growth	H.24	The effect of GDP growth on SC and SNC company's capital structure differs among *industries*.	✓	✓	✓	×
	✓	Hypothesis confirmed				
	×	Hypothesis rejected				
	–	Regression result: insignificant				

Source: own contribution.

varied. Similar to the *overall (pooled)* analysis, a uniform effect can be exerted as follows:

- *profitability* for both leverage measures and *growth opportunity* and *firm size* for market leverage (cross-*country*)
- *profitability* for both leverage measures and *growth opportunity* for market leverage (cross-*industry*)

Nevertheless, the results in Tables D.2 and D.3 in Appendix D have shown that certain debt factors are dominant in some countries and industries while unimportant elsewhere. Hence, RQ 4 and RQ 5 must be affirmed. Tables 5.9 and 5.10 provide a summary of the tested hypotheses.

5.2.4 Explanatory Power of Capital Structure Theories

With the objective to identify the most reliable leverage determinants, this subsection makes the initial attempt to investigate the relative power of the Trade-Off and

Pecking Order Theories and the proposed *Islamic Pecking Order* model in explaining the financing decision of SC and SNC firms. As highlighted in Section 2.7, compared to the conventional studies, the capital structure studies applied to SC firms per se are limited in number and scope. Recap, Haron et al. (2011) and Haron and Ibrahim (2012) use a data set of SC firms only operating in Malaysia and find support for the *dynamic* version of the Trade-Off Theory. Similarly, Ramli and Haron (2017b) find that SC firms in Malaysia opt for adjusting towards an optimal capital structure, supporting the Trade-Off Theory. On the contrary, Thabet and Hanefah (2014) find support for the Pecking Order Theory of SC firms operating in Malaysia. Akinsomi et al. (2019) enhanced the scope by conducting a comparative analysis among property firms operating in the GCC countries. The authors conclude that the Pecking Order Theory may explain the capital structure of SC property firms.

The inconclusive results derived from the previous studies demonstrate the importance of capital structure studies by utilizing the SC firm dataset. We highlighted in Section 1.1 that diversified studies are required to substantiate the financing behavior of firms operating under the Islamic principles. Ahmed (2007) suggests that Islamic firms should follow a slightly revised version of the Pecking Order Theory to seek the least costly financing alternative. This is in line with Obaidullah (2007), a proponent of a pecking order financing. However, the author advocates that the Trade-Off Theory is irrelevant for the firms operating under Shari'ah principles due to the non-existence of a tax shield on interest from an Islamic perspective.[198]

5.2.4.1 Capital Structure Determinants and its Dominance

This section combined the regression results obtained from Section 5.2.2 and Section 5.2.3 to evaluate each capital structure theory's explanatory power. We established the relevance and importance of the capital structure determinants by comparing their significant signs (see Section 4.4.2) with the predictions of capital structure theories. This approach led us to answer RQ 6 as to whether the Trade-Off Theory, Pecking Order Theory, or the proposed *Islamic Pecking Order* model dominate in explaining the financing behavior of, especially, SC firms.

We start by reporting an overview of the firm-specific and macroeconomic determinants under study and their correlation with both leverage measures, namely book leverage (BLEV) and market leverage (MLEV), for both SC and SNC firms by using *overall (pooled)*, *country*, and *industry* sample in Table 5.11. The columns (1)–(2), (5)–(6) and (9)–(10) summarize the *overall (pooled)*, *country*, and *industry* results retrieved from the models (1) and (3) in Table 5.6 and Panel A and C from Tables D.2 and D.3 in Appendix D, respectively, representing SC firms. Similarly, the columns (3)–(4), (7)–(8) and (11)–(12) summarize the results retrieved from

198 See (Obaidullah, 2007), p. 76.

Table 5.11: Explanatory Power of Capital Structure Theories.

Determinants	Book Leverage (BLEV)												Market Leverage (MLEV)											
	Overall (pooled)				*Country*				*Industry*				*Overall (pooled)*				*Country*				*Industry*			
	SC		SNC		SC		SNC		SC		SNC		SC		SNC		SC		SNC		SC		SNC	
	(1)	(2)	(3)	(4)	(5)	(6)	(7)	(8)	(9)	(10)	(11)	(12)	(13)	(14)	(15)	(16)	(17)	(18)	(19)	(20)	(21)	(22)	(23)	(24)
	+	–	+	–	+	–	+	–	+	–	+	–	+	–	+	–	+	–	+	–	+	–	+	–
Part A	*Panel A: Number of Significant Correlations*																							
Profitability	0	**1**	0	**1**	0	**4**	0	**4**	0	**4**	0	**7**	0	**1**	0	**1**	0	**6**	0	**4**	0	**5**	0	**7**
Growth Opportunity	0	0	**1**	0	0	1	**4**	0	0	1	**5**	0	0	**1**	0	**1**	0	**5**	0	**5**	0	**7**	0	**4**
Firm Size	0	0	**1**	0	0	1	**4**	0	1	1	**4**	0	**1**	0	**1**	0	**4**	0	**6**	0	3	0	**5**	0
Tangibility	0	0	**1**	0	1	0	3	1	3	1	1	0	**1**	0	**1**	0	1	0	1	0	3	0	2	0
Business Risk	**1**	0	0	0	1	0	0	0	2	0	1	0	0	0	0	**1**	0	1	0	2	2	1	1	1
GDP growth	0	0	0	**1**	1	1	1	0	1	1	0	1	0	0	0	**1**	2	2	2	2	0	1	0	**6**
	Panel B: Reliable(Core) Leverage Determinants																							
Profitability		✓		✓		✓		✓		✓		✓		✓		✓		✓		✓		✓		✓
Growth Opportunity			✓				✓				✓			✓		✓		✓		✓		✓		✓
Firm Size			✓				✓				✓		✓		✓		✓		✓				✓	
Tangibility			✓										✓		✓									
Business Risk	✓															✓								
GDP growth				✓												✓								✓
	Panel C: Empirical Results (Consolidated)																							
Profitability	–		–		–		–		–		–		–		–		–		–		–		–	
Growth Opportunity			+				+				+		–		–		–		–		–		–	
Firm Size			+				+				+		+		+		+		+				+	
Tangibility			+										+		+									
Business Risk	+														–									
GDP Growth			–												–								–	

Part B		Panel D: Consolidated Results (by Capital Structure Theory/Model)											
		(1)	(2)	(3)	(4)	(5)	(6)	(7)	(8)	(9)	(10)	(11)	(12)
Profitability		P,T*,IP	P,T*,IP	P,T*,IP	P,T*,IP	P,T*,IP	P,T*,IP	P,T*,IP	P,T*,IP	P,T*,IP	P,T*,IP	P,T*,IP	P,T*,IP
Growth Opportunity			P		P		P	T,IP	T,IP	T,IP	T,IP	T,IP	T,IP
Firm Size			T		T		T	T	T	T	T		T
Tangibility			T					T	T				
Business Risk		P							T,IP				
GDP Growth			P,IP						P,IP				P,IP
		Panel E: Number of Matching Capital Structure Theories/Model											
Trade-Off Theory	(T)	1	3	1	2	1	2	4	5	3	3	2	3
Pecking Order Theory	(P)	2	3	1	2	1	2	1	2	1	1	1	2
Pecking Order Model (Islamic)	(IP)	1	2	1	1	1	1	2	4	2	2	2	3
		Panel F: Explanatory Power of the Capital Structure Theories/Model											
Trade-Off Theory	(T)	25%	38%	33%	40%	33%	40%	57%	45%	50%	50%	40%	38%
Pecking Order Theory	(P)	50%	38%	33%	40%	33%	40%	14%	18%	17%	17%	20%	25%
Pecking Order Model (Islamic)	(IP)	25%	25%	33%	20%	33%	20%	29%	36%	33%	33%	40%	38%

T* = Dynamic Trade-Off Theory.

the models (2) and (4) in Table 5.6 and Panel B and D from Tables D.2 and D.3 in Appendix D, respectively, representing SNC firms; both for book and market leverage measures.

In **Part A**, Panel A summarizes the consistency of the relationship between the six determinants and both leverage measures, each divided into SC and SNC firms. We reported the number of instances, i.e., number one (1) for *overall (pooled)* and any number out of total seven for *country* and *industry* sample, respectively, if the given leverage determinant had a positive or negative significant coefficient at the 90% or higher confidence level; and reported zero (0) otherwise. Positive[+]/negative[–] coefficient results are documented in odd/even-numbered columns, respectively. In Panel B, we evaluated whether the debt determinants are reliable and assigned a "✓" by using the score of one (1) for the *overall (pooled)* sample. As far as the *country* and *industry* samples are concerned, we assigned a "✓" and applied a simple rule of thumb requiring a minimum score of four (out of max. seven) for each determinant. Then in Panel C, we consolidated the direction of the empirically observed relationships and assigned a + (positive) or – (negative) sign if the determinant is previously assigned in with a "✓".

At first sight, Table 5.11 reveals that from both sample perspectives, i.e., *country* and *industry*, the results are mostly identical for both firm types and both leverage measures. However, looking closer to all six determinants from all three sample perspectives and within each leverage measure, different relationship results can be detected for SC firms and SNC firms, individually. Consequently, these results distinguish SC firms from SNC firms. We retrieved the following outcome from the *overall (pooled)* results:

- As for the BLEV measure, only *profitability* is found to be consistent among SC and SNC firms. The remaining determinants distinguish between SC and SNC firms with *growth opportunity*, *firm size*, *tangibility*, and *GDP growth* only show its dominance for SNC firms, while the *business risk* for SC firms only.
- As for the MLEV measure, most of the determinants exhibit consistency among both firm types, for instance, *profitability*, *growth opportunity*, *firm size*, and *tangibility*. *Business risk* and *GDP growth* exhibit its dominance for SNC firms only.

As mentioned earlier, the aim of differentiating our sample between various countries and industries was to identify possible cross-sectional differences in the effect of certain debt factors. This provided a more accurate and realistic view of the relationship between leverage and its determinants. We retrieved the following outcome from the *country* and *industry* results:

- As for BLEV measure, only *profitability* is found to be consistent among SC and SNC firms. *Growth opportunity* and *firm size* only show its dominance for SNC firms, while *tangibility*, *business risk*, and *GDP growth* exhibit insignificant results for both SC and SNC firms.

- As for the MLEV measure, three out of six determinants exhibit consistency among SC and SNC firms, namely, *profitability* and *growth opportunity* for both cross-sections and *firm size* for the *country* only. Similarly, with insignificant results for *tangibility*, *business risk*, and *GDP growth*, no differences can be detected for both firm types (except *industry* results showing the dominance of *firm size* and *GDP growth* for SNC firms only).

We can conclude that depending on the leverage measurement (book or market), various capital structure determinants show different effects among SC and SNC firms. The regression results show that *profitability* is negatively related to firms' capital structure uniform across both the firm types and leverage measures. This finding supports the Pecking Order Theory's basic notion and the proposed *Islamic Pecking Order* model, which postulate that retained earnings (internal financing) are the preferred financing option. It is argued that profitable firms may choose to hold on to their internal funds to take advantage of future investment opportunities, resulting in lower leverage levels, see Hennessy and Whited (2005), Ramli and Haron (2017b), and Strebulaev (2004). Our finding is consistent with others Cekrezi (2013), Fama and French (2002), Frank and Goyal (2003), Haron and Ibrahim (2012), and Rajan and Zingales (1995). As for the SC firms, the negative relationship can be explained by these firms' inability to invest their idle cash in interest-based instruments. SC firms can utilize their idle cash to finance their activities internally instead of borrowing from outside (debt/equity financing). This rationale stays clearly in contrast to the predictions made by Trade-Off Theory, which posits a positive relationship between *profitability* and leverage. It is argued that profitable firms can utilize the tax benefits by engaging in massive debt financing (through increased debt tax shield) as they are exposed to less financial distress. However, in the *dynamic* version of the Trade-Off Theory, the relationship is expected to be negative between *profitability* and leverage, see Flannery and Rangan (2006), Gaud et al. (2005), and R. Huang and Ritter (2009). In the context of SC firms operating in Malaysia, Rahim et al. (2020) and Sahudin et al. (2019) both found an inverse relationship between *profitability* and leverage. While Rahim et al. (2020) investigated the *dynamic* aspects of capital structure and found support for the Trade-Off Theory, Sahudin et al. (2019) concluded that the Pecking Order Theory dominates over the Trade-Off Theory.

We observed a uniform relationship between the market-to-book ratio (*growth opportunity*) and MLEV among both firm types. The negative relationship supports the notion of the Trade-Off Theory and is consistent with most academic studies such as Ariff et al. (2008), Booth et al. (2001), Dang and Garrett (2015), and Rajan and Zingales (1995). This prediction stays in contrast to the Pecking Order Theory's basic idea, which states that firms with growth opportunities should utilize external financing in the form of debt (not equity). Although it is expected that the Pecking Order Theory to explain the financing behavior of those firms following the Shari'ah principles, this rationale and prediction postulated around *growth opportunity* is clearly on the contrary. However, this prediction runs against the proposed Islamic version of the Pecking Order, which states that firms with investment opportunities face financial distress and financial deficit, which calls for external financing in the form of equity and quasi-equity, but not debt.

Firm size and *tangibility* are determinants, similar to *profitability* and *growth opportunity*, that provide consistent results in its relationship to leverage. Our findings support the Trade-Off Theory, which predicts a positive relationship between both determinants and leverage for both determinants. As for the *firm size*, it is argued that the bigger a company becomes, the less it will face bankruptcy risk, or in other words, these companies are too big to fail. Furthermore, the larger a company, the less volatile the company's cash flows will be due to diversification effects that mostly materialize, the bigger a company is. The positive relationship of *tangibility* with leverage is commonly referred to that fixed assets serve as collateral for debt financing. As far as SC firms are concerned, we expected a negative relationship for both determinants with the rationale and predictions discussed in Sections 4.3.2.3 and 4.3.2.4. The Pecking Order Theory and the proposed *Islamic Pecking Order* model argue that larger and mature firms and firms with high fixed assets are exposed to more monitoring. As a result, asymmetric information between potential investors and shareholders decreases, and firms can issue equity at a lower cost, among others, Arif and Mai (2020), Chakraborty (2010), J. J. Chen (2004), Cheng and Shiu (2007), Graham (2000), Haron and Ibrahim (2012), Jung et al. (1996), Piaw and Jais (2014b), Rajan and Zingales (1995), and Sahudin et al. (2019).

Part A in Table 5.11 shows overall mixed estimation results in almost all capital structure determinants (except for *profitability*). Consequently, determinants such as *tangibility*, *business risk*, and *GDP growth* are found to be not reliable. This finding suggests further investigation of capital structure and its determinants, particularly on firms classified as Shari'ah compliant (SC). It seems that other determinants (e.g., equity and quasi-equity) might play a more significant role in SC firms' financing decisions.

5.2.4.2 Capital Structure Theory and its Empirical Relevance

In Table 5.11 **Part B**, Panel D matches and assigns the capital structure theories to the respective determinants based on the comparison between the empirically observed results (Part A – Panel C) and its theoretical predictions listed in Table 4.10, respectively. Panel E adds-up the numbers of the assigned capital structure theories in Panel D. Finally, to identify the explanatory power of the theories in Panel F, we compare the number of determinants that favor one theory over the number of the determinants which favor the other theory. This provides each theory's power in explaining the financing behavior of SC and SNC firms in both leverage measures separately. The results reveal the followings for SC firms:

- The BLEV measure shows for the *overall (pooled)* level that the Pecking Order Theory dominates the Trade-Off Theory and the Islamic version of the Pecking

Order model, with 25%–50%–25%, respectively. As mentioned above, the cross-sectional results do provide a more accurate and realistic view. In this line of thought, the cross-section results report 33%–33%–33%, indicating that the explanatory power of both capital structure theories and the *Islamic Pecking Order* model is the same.
- As for the MLEV measure, the results reported in *overall (pooled)*, *country*, and *industry* show 57%–14%–29%, 50%–17%–33%, and 40%–20–40%, respectively. These results show a clear tendency towards Trade-Off Theory in explaining the financing behavior of SC firms.

The results reveal the followings for SNC firms:
- The BLEV measure exhibits that both capital structure theories' explanatory power is throughout the same, i.e., 38%–38%–25% for *overall (pooled)* and 40%–40%–20% for *country* and *industry* level, respectively. Both conventional theories dominate the *Islamic Pecking Order* model from all three perspectives.
- As for the MLEV measure, the explanatory power of the Trade-Off Theory is higher than the explanatory power of the Pecking Order Theory and the *Islamic Pecking Order* model, which shows 45%–18%–36%, 50%–17%–33%, and 38%–25%–38% for *overall (pooled)*, *country*, and *industry* level, respectively. Similar to SC firms, this result indicates that the Trade-Off Theory better explains the financing behavior of SNC firms.

To sum up, **Part B** in Table 5.11 shows how prediction meets empirical results. In essence, it is a challenge to conclude with certainty which of the well-established capital structure theories has better explanatory power in the context of SC and SNC firms. With the book leverage measure, the results are somewhat inconclusive. This finding can perfectly be addressed by Fama and French (2005, pp. 580–581) citation "*Perhaps it is best to regard the two models as stable[-]mates, with each having elements of truth that help explain some aspects of financing decisions.*" As for the market leverage, contrary to the expected dominance of the Pecking Order Theory, our findings indicate and show the importance of the Trade-Off Theory in explaining the financing behavior of both firm types. Whether the Pecking Order Theory dominates over Trade-Off Theory in explaining SC firms' financing behavior per se, as postulated by Ahmed (2007) and Obaidullah (2007), cannot be confirmed. Hence, the RQ 6 can be affirmed for market leverage measure, but not for book leverage.

Comparing the explanatory power of the conventional Pecking Order Theory with the proposed *Islamic Pecking Order* model, as far as SC firms are concerned, they ranked equally for book leverage. However, for the market leverage measure, the latter outperformed the former. This suggests that market leverage proxy might be a better descriptor of the proposed *Islamic Pecking Order* model in the context of SC firms' capital structure.

5.3 Robustness Tests

Referring back to the overview of the different leverage measures presented in Table 4.2, Rajan and Zingales (1995) state that Total Debt over Total Capital (sum of Total Debt plus Total Equity) probably represents best the past financing decision of firms. Taking this into consideration, we have employed and extended our research approach with robustness checks, that can comprise various forms in the academic world (not limited to), which we briefly explain next:

i. using different proxies for given variables (such in the above case), or
ii. applying other econometric estimators; or
iii. using a different model specification.

In Rajan and Zingales (1995, p. 1429), the authors have scrutinized and discussed the pros/cons of a wide range of leverage definitions. They highlighted and suggested that "*the effect of past financing decisions is probably best represented by the ratio of total debt to total capital.*". (see Table 4.2) We have followed this suggestion and replaced both dependent variables with book leverage 2 (BLEV2) and market leverage 2 (MLEV2), as defined in Table E.1 in Appendix E. The estimated regression results, from models (13a) and (14a), are shown in Appendix E in Tables E.2–E.4, and the final Explanatory Power of the Capital Structure Theories are represented in Table E.5.[199]

For the reasons mentioned in Section 4.2.2, it was deemed useful to run *dynamic* panel data models in Robustness Test II. Section 6.1 deals with the direct measure of the Trade-Off Theory for which we have applied system GMM on the models (18) and (19). Although the focus was merely the incorporated lagged dependent variable (details in Section 6.2.1), we utilized the regression estimates to identify the most important debt determinants and the explanatory power of both theories, respectively. The former is represented in Tables D.5–D.6 in Appendix D and the latter in Table E.6 in Appendix E.

Finally, in Robustness Test III, we have modified our *dynamic* estimation models into (18a) and (19a) by replacing the lagged (*t–1*) explanatory variables with the current year (*t*). All robustness test results are provided in Appendix E.7–E.9.

Overall, the estimation results from the alternative leverage measures (Robustness Test I) do support our earlier findings. Specifically, both capital structure theories' explanatory power cannot be concluded with certainty for book leverage, although a trend is visible towards the Trade-Off Theory. For market leverage measure, the Trade-Off Theory dominates the Pecking Order Theory for both firm types.

---

199 Similar to the model estimation in Section 5.2, we conducted post estimation tests (i.e. BPLM, Hausman, Heteroskedasticity, and auto-/serial correlation) for both estimation models (13a) and (14a) and represented in Panel B, Table B.3 in Appendix B, respectively.

As far as the Robustness Tests II and III are concerned, even though some estimation results were not available, the results led us to conclude that the Trade-Off Theory is a better descriptor of both firm types' financing decisions.

5.4 Conclusion

In this chapter, we aimed to identify the most reliable (significant) debt determinants that influence the financing decision and, ultimately, SC and SNC firms' capital structure. We found out that all debt factors play an important role with positive and negative effects on firms' leverage ratio. Depending on the firm type and leverage measure, the results varied between statistical significance and insignificance. Certain debt factors exhibited their dominance in any circumstances. Specifically, independent of being SC or SNC and book or market leverage, *profitability* reported consistent results from all three perspectives: *overall (pooled)*, *country*, and *industry*. A uniform effect could also be exerted for *growth opportunity*, *firm size*, and *tangibility* in the *overall (pooled)* sample, limited to the market leverage measure. The results obtained from the cross-sectional analysis only confirmed the uniformity for both *growth opportunity* and *firm size*. As far as *tangibility* is concerned, it seems to vary among the cross-section.

Most of the debt determinants did not show a consistent effect throughout the sample years (2004–2014), indicating a dynamic role, depending on the country's/industry's economic circumstances. Even though *profitability* and *growth opportunity* are reported to have a uniform effect, these determinants' importance seems to have only increased during the post-crisis period. The remaining determinants exhibit mixed or partial consistent results. For instance, *tangibility*, *business risk*, and *GDP growth* determinants seem to have a consistent effect (over the period) on the market leverage of SC firms only regardless of the mixed significance results obtained from the regression estimates.

Due to the mixed empirical results retrieved from the *overall (pooled)*, *country*, and *industry* samples, the question of which theory offers a better explanation of SC and SNC firms' capital structure remains uncertain; however, with a clear trend towards the Trade-Off Theory. These results are contrary to Islamic finance literature, suggesting the Pecking Order Theory among these two conventional theories.

6 Direct Measures of Capital Structure Theories

This chapter is designed to provide a direct measure analysis. Specifically, to determine the relevance of both capital structure theories, specifications based on both the dynamic Trade-Off model and the Pecking Order model are used. This section aims not to provide full-fledged research of both theories; it is merely intended to support the findings from Section 5.2 and strengthen those results with a direct measure of each dominant capital structure theory.

6.1 Partial Adjustment Model (Speed of Adjustment)

In this section, we want to examine the Partial Adjustment Model (Speed of Adjustment) in providing a plausible explanation of firms' financing behavior. According to the Trade-Off Theory, the companies are constantly striving to achieve an optimal capital structure. This optimum is achieved by reaching a target debt level. As a result of the economy's cyclical nature, this level is influenced by disturbances, which cause firms distraction from reaching this optimum. If being distracted, the firm would have to return to the target debt level Frank and Goyal (2008). Having a stable point of optimal debt would, therefore, result in a mean-reverting behavior. (see Figure 2.2)

In the *dynamic* version of the classic Trade-Off Theory, the firm's optimal leverage can be time-varying. Specifically, the theory states that when firms deviate from their "optimum", there will be a correction towards the "optimum" target. The most important objective of a capital structure study using dynamic partial adjustment models is to estimate the adjustment speed (also called speed of adjustment).

6.1.1 Model Specification

Earlier in Section 4.4, we assumed that the capital structure of SC and SNC firms are *static* in nature and specified the optimal leverage ratio as follows:

$$y_{it}^{*} = \alpha + \beta x_{i,t-1} + \mu_i + \mu_t + \varepsilon_{it} \tag{15}$$

Where y_{it}^{*} is the target debt ratio for firm *i* in year *t*, which is explained by $x_{i,t-1}$ the vector of 1–year lagged firm-specific and macroeconomic control independent variables. α is the constant term, μ_i the individual error, μ_t a time-specific component of the error term, and ε_{it} the classical error term, which is assumed to be mean equal to zero, uncorrelated with itself, uncorrelated with x, uncorrelated with μ_i and homoskedastic, i.e., $\varepsilon_{it} \approx i.i.d.N(0,\sigma^2)$.

The regression model (15) refers to the basic notion of static Trade-Off Theory and MM's extreme assumption (i.e., the perfect world, frictionless with no adjustment

https://doi.org/10.1515/9783110713664-006

costs). Firms are expected to respond to a variation in the explanatory variables by changing their existing leverage to equal its optimal leverage target, i.e., a complete adjustment. This implies that a firms leverage ratio equals its optimal leverage at any point in time, $y_{it} = y_{it}^*$. Consequently, any change in leverage equals the change needed for the firm to be at its optimal leverage, i.e., $y_{it} - y_{i,t-1} = y_{it}^* - y_{i,t-1}$.

As discussed in Chapter 2.4.2, firms operate in dynamic settings with imperfect knowledge, information, and adjustment costs. Therefore, analyzing firms' capital structure would require a framework that considers such *dynamic* aspects. The process of adjusting firms' capital structure has its associated "transaction" costs, and therefore, it is likely that firms adjust their capital structures only gradually or partially. This can be represented as below:

$$y_{it} - y_{i,t-1} = \lambda\left(y_{it}^* - y_{i,t-1}\right) \tag{16}$$

Where $0 < \lambda < 1$, y_{it} is the current leverage ratio and y_{it}^* the target leverage ratio of firm *i* at time *t*. $\left(y_{it}^* - y_{i,t-1}\right)$ is the target change while only a portion of λ of the target change is achieved, which is equal to $y_{it} - y_{i,t-1}$. The coefficient (λ) represents the magnitude of the desired adjustment between two subsequent periods (years) or the rate of convergence (i.e., speed of adjustment). The combination of model (15) and (16) produces the following:

$$y_{it} = (1-\lambda)y_{i,t-1} + x_{i,t-1} + \mu_i + \mu_t + \varepsilon_{it} \tag{17}$$

Replacing the vector $x_{i,t-1}$ with the firm-specific and macroeconomic determinants, the *dynamic* regression model (17) became:

$$\begin{aligned} blev_{it} &= \alpha + (1-\lambda)blev_{i,t-1} + \beta_1 prof_{i,t-1} + \beta_2 growth_{i,t-1} \\ &\quad + \beta_3 size_{i,t-1} + \beta_4 tang_{i,t-1} + \beta_5 risk_{i,t-1} + \beta_6 gdp_{i,t-1} + \mu_i + \mu_t + \varepsilon_{it} \end{aligned} \tag{18}$$

$$\begin{aligned} mlev_{it} &= \alpha + (1-\lambda)mlev_{i,t-1} + \beta_1 prof_{i,t-1} + \beta_2 growth_{i,t-1} \\ &\quad + \beta_3 size_{i,t-1} + \beta_4 tang_{i,t-1} + \beta_5 risk_{i,t-1} + \beta_6 gdp_{i,t-1} + \mu_i + \mu_t + \varepsilon_{it} \end{aligned} \tag{19}$$

Where *blev* and *mlev* is the book and market leverage for firm *i* in year *t* with the *lagged book* and *lagged market* leverage and the six debt determinants, respectively. This analysis assesses the factors that are associated with a firm's leverage. The μ_i and μ_t represent unobserved firm-specific and time-specific effects, and the classical disturbance is denoted as ε_{it}.

Based on these regression models (18) and (19), if $\lambda = 1$, the actual change in leverage is equal to the desired change, and the adjustment is free of any transaction cost. The entire adjustment is made within one period, and the firm is consistently at its optimal debt level. If $\lambda = 0$, there is no adjustment in leverage and, therefore, firms set their current debt ratio to the past leverage. In most cases, the value of λ or the convergence rate varies between zero to one due to the adjustment process. If the λ value is greater than one, it implies that the firm makes more adjustments than necessary and is eventually unable to achieve its optimal debt level.

Both regression models (18) and (19) include the lagged dependent variable, which converts any model from its *static* nature into *dynamic* nature. With all the reasons discussed in Section 4.2.2 and with the given data structure (see Tables A.2–A.4 in Appendix A), the advantages of applying *dynamic* panel data estimators are evident. In short, the *dynamic* model used to estimate these models involves regressing the leverage ratio in year *t* on a set of explanatory variables, including the leverage ratio in year *t–1*. The fact that the lagged dependent variable is now a part of explanatory variables, the strict exogeneity assumption required by the previously applied estimators (*static* estimators) is not satisfied. It is well documented and accepted that applying OLS and FE estimation to the *dynamic* panel model in (18) and (19) will generate biased coefficients Flannery and Hankins (2013). Specifically, OLS (FE) will generate an upward (downward) bias to the coefficient of the lagged leverage resulting in a downward (upward) bias in the estimated speed of adjustment λ.

Based on simulation data from a standard capital structure panel, in unbalanced panels and endogeneity (arising from measurement error and missing data), the Blundell-Bond system-GMM estimator suffers less bias than other alternative estimators (Flannery and Hankins, 2013). Following Flannery and Hankins (2013) findings, we employ the system GMM estimator Blundell and Bond (1998) to combine the *regression in differences* with *regression in levels*. (see Section 4.2.2) The instrument variables for the *differences* are the lagged levels, while for the *levels*, they are the lagged difference of the corresponding variables. The system GMM estimator is more efficient as it addresses *weak instruments* for the regression equation in differences (Blundell and Bond, 1998). This is due to the assumption that the lagged values of the dependent variable and the other explanatory variables are valid instruments with no serial correlation in the error terms. We have conducted two standard tests validating these assumptions; first, the *Sargan/Hansen* test for overidentifying restrictions. Second, the *Arellano-Bond* test for zero autocorrelation in first-differenced errors.

6.1.2 Empirical Results

The following discussion will focus on the speed of adjustment of SC and SNC firms. But beforehand, to determine whether these firms have been over-/ or underleveraged in the sample period, the target leverage ratios are compared to the observed (actual) leverage ratios. Figures 6.1 and 6.2 represent the target and actual leverage ratios obtained from Table D.4 in Appendix D for SC and SNC firms, respectively. At first sight, the deviations between target and actual leverage ratios are smaller for market

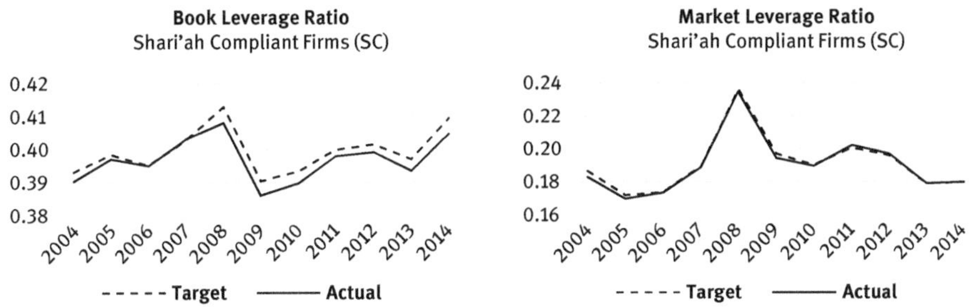

Figure 6.1: Target versus Actual Leverage Ratio (SC).
Source: own contribution.

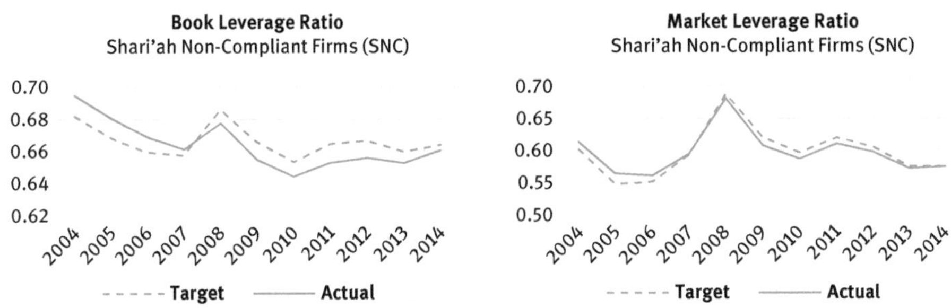

Figure 6.2: Target versus Actual Leverage Ratio (SNC).
Source: own contribution.

leverage than for book measures, which appears inconsistent with the notion that firms use book measures when deciding upon their capital structures (Welch, 2011). It is interesting to observe that SC firms matched their capital structure to their target based on the market leverage measure over a long period, namely 2005–2009.

As for the book leverage measure, the deviations between target and actual leverage ratios show mixed results over the sample period. Figure 6.1 shows that SC firms were underleveraged throughout the time series, except being sharply or closely on their target leverage right before the crisis started. The results suggest that, on average, these firms appeared to have a robust capital structure. This further indicates that SC firms are within the "acceptable range" as discussed in Section 2.3.2 and hence will not adjust to its target leverage (optimum debt level) as the cost of adjustment is higher than the potential tax savings (tax shield). Similar findings can be observed for SNC firms, starting from the crisis period. Specifically, pre-crisis, they were highly leveraged, and with the crisis, they changed their position and consistently remained below target. Remaining long-term below target can be explained by the existing high cost of adjustment and the firm's willingness to preserve financial flexibility. Figure 6.2 also exhibits that SNC firms lately in 2014 follow their target leverage ratio more closely, suggesting that these companies have increased their focus on being at their target capital structure compared to the SC firms. The developments in leverage ratios shown in Figures 6.1 and 6.2 suggest that companies adjust towards their target capital structure, which is in accordance with the Trade-Off Theory. Next, we further discuss the speed of this adjustment.

Section 5.2 shows evidence and support for the Trade-Off Theory concerning the relationship between the selected debt determinants and leverage. Next, we attempted to identify the speed of adjustment by which the firms adjust from their actual towards their target capital structure. In other words, we wanted to identify whether SC and SNC firms do follow a target or not. The speed of adjustment λ will provide us with two information, first, the time a firm requires to revert to its mean and second, that these firms follow a target, which by default would support the notion of the Trade-Off Theory.

We report the estimated regression results consolidated in Table 6.1. Panel A represents the equation model (18), and similarly, Panel B depicts the coefficient estimates of the equation model (19) for SC and SNC firms, respectively. The dynamic Trade-Off models are applied to the *overall (pooled)*, *country,* and *industry* perspectives separately, using system GMM estimator, considering the respective *endogenous*, *predetermined,* and *exogenous* variables (see Table B.5 in Appendix B), as discussed in Section 4.2.2.1. Table 6.1 provides us with the coefficient estimates and the speed of adjustment λ and the leverage *half-life*. Leverage half-life is defined as the time a firm requires (in years) to adjust back to the target leverage after a one-unit shock to ε, $ln(0.5)/ln(1\text{-}\lambda)$. All data are retrieved from the Tables D.5–D.7 in Appendix D.

Panel A in Table 6.1 shows that the average speed of adjustment for SC firms is 0.191 (5.24 years). This means that, on average, 19.10% of the target deviation spread is covered in one year; this is equivalent to approximately 5.24 years $(1/\lambda)$ to reach the target fully. The half-life is 3.27 years on average, indicating that it takes 3.27 years to close the gap between the actual and the target leverage ratio by 50% provided that the firms maintain the same adjustment speed. As for SNC firms, the results exhibit a faster adjustment of 26.5% (approximately four years) towards its target with a half-life of 2.25 years, indicating that it takes about 2 years and 3 months to close the gap between the actual and target leverage ratio by 50% provided that the firms maintain the same adjustment speed. Similar findings are reported in Fama and French (2002) and R. Huang and Ritter (2009) with up to 17% and 21% adjustment speed, respectively. Haron and Ibrahim (2012) investigate the *dynamic* aspects of the capital structure, looking particularly for the existence of target capital structure and the speed of adjustment of SC firms in Malaysia. They report an adjustment speed of 60,13%, equivalent to 1.66 years, much faster than the SC firms in our sample study. The high adjustment speed of the SC firms might be motivated by the fact that these firms have a low debt ratio by default. Consequently, an adjustment towards the target is probably less challenging than firms with high debt ratios, assuming there are no debt capacity issues. This finding confirms the existence of the dynamic Trade-Off Theory and that firms seek a target capital structure. In case the firm's actual leverage varies

Table 6.1: Speed of Adjustment (Dynamic TOT) – *Overall (pooled)*, *Country* and *Industry*.

This table provides the results estimates retrieved from Table D.5, Table D.6, and Table D.7 in Appendix D. The lagged book leverage ($blev_{i,t-1}$) is incorporated as an independent variable. All firm-specific and macroeconomic debt determinants used in the equation model (18) and (19) are lagged one year and regressed separately for SC and SNC firms for the overall (pooled), country, and industry samples for the entire period 2004–2014. SC and SNC firms are determined based on DJIMI (see Table 4.1). Tables 4.3 and 4.10 provide the definitions of all variables. Panel A and Panel B represent the regression results for book leverage and market leverage for SC and SNC firms, respectively. Models 1–15 represent the estimated coefficients for *overall (pooled)*, *country*, and *industry* samples for the entire period 2004–2014. Coefficients estimates are shown by β. The speed of adjustment is shown by λ along with the Hansen test for overidentifying restrictions. Leverage half-life is defined as the time a firm requires (in years) to adjust back to the target leverage after a one-unit shock to ε, $ln(0.5)/ln(1-\lambda)$. First and second level attempts are shown in the last column. *, ** and *** denote significance at 10%, 5% and 1% levels, respectively. All variables are winsorized at the 1% and 99% level. Model specifications are provided in Section 6.1.1.

Panel A: Speed of Adjustment (Book Leverage)											
Book Leverage		**SC**				**SNC**				**Attempts**	
Sample		**β**	**λ**	**Hansen Test**	**Half-Life**	**β**	**λ**	**Hansen Test**	**Half-Life**	**1st Attempts**	**2nd Attempts**
Overall (pooled)	Model 1	0.809***	0.191	0.058	3.27	0.735***	0.265	0.072	2.25	✓	
United States	Model 2	0.662***	0.338	0.113	1.68	0.809***	0.191	0.089	3.27	✓	
United Kingdom	Model 3	0.772***	0.228	0.223	2.68	0.882***	0.118	0.361	5.52	✓	
Canada	Model 4	0.649***	0.351	0.240	1.60	0.555*	0.445	0.240	1.18	✗[1]	✓✓
Japan	Model 5	0.836***	0.164	0.359	3.87	0.888***	0.112	0.130	5.84	✓	
South Korea	Model 6	0.667***	0.333	0.206	1.71	0.778***	0.222	0.236	2.76	✓	
Taiwan	Model 7	0.820***	0.180	0.661	3.49	0.571***	0.429	0.128	1.24	✓	
India	Model 8	0.959***	0.041	0.346	16.56	0.840*	0.160	0.175	3.98	✓	
Oil and Gas	Model 9	0.638***	0.362	0.243	1.54	0.700***	0.300	0.480	1.94	✓	
Basic Materials	Model 10	0.616***	0.384	0.163	1.43	0.762***	0.238	0.094	2.55	✓	
Industrials	Model 11	0.701***	0.299	0.285	1.95	0.869***	0.131	0.063	4.94	✓	
Consumer Goods	Model 12	0.656***	0.344	0.314	1.64	0.885***	0.115	0.193	5.67	✓	
Technology	Model 13	0.866***	0.134	0.408	4.82	0.748***	0.252	0.408	2.39	✗[2]	✓✓
Health Care	Model 14	0.827***	0.173	0.394	3.65	0.559**	0.441	0.394	1.19	✗[3]	✓✓
Consumer Services	Model 15	0.656***	0.344	0.410	1.64	0.831***	0.169	0.184	3.74	✓	

(continued)

Table 6.1 (continued)

Panel B: Speed of Adjustment (Market Leverage)											
Market Leverage		**SC**				**SNC**				**Remedy**	
Sample		**β**	**λ**	**Hansen Test**	**Half-Life**	**β**	**λ**	**Hansen Test**	**Half-Life**	**1st**	**2nd**
										Attempts	
Overall (pooled)	Model 1	0.806**	0.194	0.622	3.21					×[4]	××
United States	Model 2	0.644***	0.356	0.087	1.58	0.626***	0.374	0.669	1.48	✓	
United Kingdom	Model 3	0.485***	0.515	0.423	0.96	0.946***	0.054	0.191	12.49	✓	
Canada	Model 4	0.551***	0.449	0.291	1.16	0.569**	0.431	0.291	1.23	×[5]	✓✓
Japan	Model 5	0.784***	0.216	0.140	2.85	0.742***	0.258	0.245	2.32	✓	
South Korea	Model 6	0.763***	0.237	0.159	2.56	0.598***	0.402	0.079	1.35	✓	
Taiwan	Model 7	0.572***	0.428	0.695	1.24	0.434**	0.566	0.195	0.83	✓	
India	Model 8	0.335***	0.665	0.209	0.63	0.515	0.485	0.079	1.04	✓	
Oil and Gas	Model 9	0.327**	0.673	0.394	0.62	0.842***	0.158	0.256	4.03	✓	
Basic Materials	Model 10	0.697***	0.303	0.174	1.92	0.359***	0.641	0.367	0.68	✓	
Industrials	Model 11	0.475***	0.525	0.215	0.93	0.752***	0.248	0.438	2.43	✓	
Consumer Goods	Model 12	0.519***	0.481	0.253	1.06	0.762***	0.238	0.067	2.55	✓	
Technology	Model 13	0.877***	0.123	0.134	5.28	0.223*	0.777	0.134	0.46	×[6]	✓✓
Health Care	Model 14	0.869***	0.131	0.114	4.94	0.349***	0.651	0.114	0.66	×[7]	✓✓
Consumer Services	Model 15	0.491***	0.509	0.106	0.97	0.946***	0.054	0.238	12.49	✓	

× unsuccessful 1st attempt. ×× unsuccessful 2nd attempt. ✓✓ *successful remedy.*

Source: Own contribution.

from the target (see Figures 6.1 and 6.2), firms initiate some adjustment activities to rebalance to their target leverage. Fischer et al. (1989) highlight that firms may not adjust instantaneously to their aimed leverage level due to capital market imperfection. The firms under study exhibit coefficient estimate significantly greater than zero but less than one *($0 < \lambda < 1$)*, indicating that these firms do not adjust sufficiently (i.e., under-adjust) to reach their target capital structure as the Trade-Off Theory emphasizes it.

A clearer picture can be observed in the country and industry sample. Panel A in Table 6.1 shows, the speed of adjustment varies among countries from as low as 4.10% (India) and 35.10% (Canada) and among industries from 13.40% (Technology) and 38.40% (Basic Materials). In four out of seven countries (United States, United Kingdom, Japan, and South Korea), and similarly in five out of seven industries (except Technology and Health Care), SC firms adjust towards their target faster than their non-compliant peers. This finding highlights that SC firms do follow the basic idea of the Trade-Off Theory, which we have shown above in Figure 6.1 that SC firms are closer to their target leverage than SNC firms over the sample period.

While the *industry* sample shows relatively the same range of adjustment speed, the *country* sample exhibits a much bigger range. For instance, India (SC firms) exhibit a slow speed of adjustment (approximately 16.5 years), and the United Kingdom and Japan (SNC firms) a relatively slow speed of adjustment; around 5–6 years. The interpretation of the speed of adjustment is crucial and requires proper interpretation. For instance, while the speed of adjustment of 100% would fully support the notion of the static Trade-Off Theory, the speed of adjustment of 0% only indicates that firms have placed importance on other factors rather than to target capital structure. Slow adjustment speeds as those reported in academic studies such as in Fama and French (2002) and Hovakimian and Li (2011) have often been interpreted against the Trade-Off Theory's basic notion, implying that target capital structure was not a part of firms' main priority. This way of interpretation relaxed, for instance, by DeAngelo et al. (2011) and Strebulaev and Whited (2012), in which the authors explain that slow adjustment speed is not necessarily against the *dynamic* version of the Trade-Off Theory, but simply a result of firm's willingness to hold and maintain such financial flexibility.

Panel B in Table 6.1 shows that the average speed of adjustment for SC firms is 0.194 (5.15 years). Specifically, the speed of adjustment can also be converted in 5.15 years *($1/\lambda$)* and 3.21 years [*$ln(0.5)/ln(1\text{-}\lambda)$*], respectively. This concludes that SC firms close the gap between current and target leverage by 19.40% within one year. This is equivalent to 5.15 years to fully reach the target or 3.21 years to reach 50% of the target from the current debt level. The *country* and *industry* further exhibit that the coefficients are significantly greater than zero but less than one *($0 < \lambda < 1$)*. However, according to the market leverage measure, SC firms adjust faster to their target leverage than the book leverage measure in both *country* and *industry* samples.

A direct comparison among SC and SNC firms for market leverage is not feasible at this stage because of unsuccessful econometrical attempts on the *overall (pooled)* sample. As shown in Table 6.1, the results for SNC firms are incomplete due to the econometrical issues we faced during our analysis. Due to the available data structure (dataset) and dynamic estimators' requirements, it was not always feasible to obtain a regression estimate for all sub-samples, e.g., due to a low number of SC or SNC firms in selected countries and industries. (see Table A.2 in Appendix A) We have applied a 2-level attempt in which we regressed models (18) and (19) in *overall (pooled), country,* and *industry* samples separately for SC and SNC firms. In case we could not obtain an acceptable result in one of the samples (denoted with ×), we have combined the samples within each section (e.g., SC and SNC firms of Canada, Technology and Health Care in book leverage measure) and included an *interactive dummy* ($dsc * blev_{i,t-1}$) in the second attempt. Either we could obtain an acceptable result (denoted with ✓✓), or the second attempt failed (denoted with ××). As shown in Table 6.1, we successfully passed the second attempt and obtained estimation results for all models (denoted with ×), except for the *overall (pooled)* sample for market leverage. Table D.7 in Appendix D provides a consolidated view of all models undergone such remedy procedure.

In light of these findings (despite the limitation as describe above), the dynamic Trade-Off Analysis in this section provide us with the following results:

1. The comparison of the speed of adjustment, documented with λ, yields consistent support to the dynamic Trade-Off Theory for both SC and SNC firms for both leverage measures.
2. For both leverage measures, all coefficient estimates β for SC and SNC firms show strong statistical significance in *overall (pooled), country,* and *industry* samples.
3. SC firms exhibit a much faster adjustment than their non-compliant counterparts in most countries and industries for both leverage measures. For instance, in five out of seven countries, namely the United States, the United Kingdom, Japan, and S. Korea (for book leverage).
4. SC firms exhibit a much faster speed of adjustment for market leverage than book leverage in both *country* and *industry* perspectives. For instance, in four out of seven industries, namely Oil and Gas, Basic Materials, Industrials, and Consumer Services.

We concluded that our investigation of the dynamic Trade-Off model confirms the adjustment speeds for SC and SNC firms, similar to the results reported by Haron and Ibrahim (2012). Other studies, such as Alnori and Alqahtani (2019) and Rahim et al. (2020), also confirmed the existence of speed adjustments in the context of SC firms. The fact that SC firms rebalance their optimal capital structure at a significantly higher speed than their non-compliant peers indicates and supports the existence of dynamic Trade-Off Theory. These results suggest that SC firms actively utilize, among others, interest-bearing debt as an instrument to increase firm value.

6.2 Pecking Order Model

In this section, we want to examine the Pecking Order Theory's relevance in providing a plausible explanation of firms' financing behavior. Although implicitly, the firm's financing suggests convergence to some targets, we cannot ignore certain financing hierarchy evidence. For instance, Claggett (1991), Fama and French (2002), Ghosh and Cai (1999), Jensen and Meckling (1976), Myers and Majluf (1984), and Shyam-Sunder and Myers (1999) found strong evidence for Pecking Order Theory.

As mentioned in Section 2.4, Shyam-Sunder and Myers (1999) state that the Pecking Order Theory assumes that every capital-outflow creates by the same amount a financial deficit in firms' accounting books. In general, there are three sources of funding available to firms, namely, retained earnings, debt, and equity. From an investors' perspective, with the asymmetric information (see Section 2.2), equity is riskier than debt. Therefore, an outside investor will require a higher rate of return on equity than on debt. On the other hand, (from the firms' perspective) retained earnings (internal cash availability) are better than debt Frank and Goyal (2003). Consequently, if firms face a financial deficit, it will tend to finance (ceteris paribus) all upcoming projects with internal funds first, followed by the use of safe debt and, as a last resort, use riskier equity financing. A financial hierarchy is apparent, demonstrating that when firms face financial deficits (insufficient internal funds), they tend to go further down the pecking order (as shown in Figure 2.3). Thus, all financial deficits should match the firms' debt issues under normal business operations, and room for equity issues will only be considered a last resort.

6.2.1 Model Specification

The Pecking Order Theory can be tested by constructing a financial deficit (DEF) variable from the balance sheet items.[200]

200 Alternatively, these variables can also be calculated from the cash flow statements. Specifically, for debt issuance, either net debt issues or gross debt issues are applied in the literature. *Net debt issues* equal to long-term debt issuance minus long-term debt reduction – or – *gross debt issues* equal to total debt issuance minus total debt reduction. *Net equity issues* equal to the sale of common and preferred stock minus the purchase of common and preferred stock. An alternative proxy for the *financial deficit* (external financing) used in the academics is the combination of the following cash flow items: *cash dividend payments* plus *net investment* plus *change in working capital* less *operating cash flows* (after interest and taxes). See Shyam-Sunder and Myers (1999) and Frank and Goyal (2003) for a detailed discussion of the components, especially of the financial deficit variable for different format codes in the cash flow statement. Variables constructed from cash flow statements have missing data (e.g., dividend payments), leading to fewer datapoints available for empirical analysis. Following, among others, Baker and Wurgler (2002) and R. Huang and Ritter (2004), we use the balance sheet items for calculating net debt issues and net equity issues. Consequently, the financial deficit is the sum of equity and debt issues.

$$DEF_{it} = \Delta Debt_{it} + \Delta Equity_{it} \tag{20}$$

Both debt and equity issues are identified by tracking changes in balance sheet figures. The debt issue is the residual change in assets (change in total assets minus change in equity). The equity issue is defined as the change in book equity net of retained earnings (change in equity minus change in retained earnings). These variables are scaled by total assets,[201] and their components are presented in Table 6.2.

Table 6.2: Definitions of Debt Issues, Equity Issues, and Financial Deficit.

Variables	Formula/Description	Abbreviation
Debt Issues	*(ΔTotal Assets$_t$ / Total Assets$_t$) – Equity Issues$_t$ – Newly Retained Earnings$_t$*	*ΔDebt*
Equity Issues	*(ΔBook Equity$_t$ – ΔRetained Earnings$_t$) / Total Assets$_t$*	*ΔEquity*
Financial Deficit	*Debt Issues + Equity Issues*	*DEF*

* *whereby, Book Equity = Total Assets – Total Liabilities – Preferred Stocks + Deferred Taxes*
***whereby, New Retained Earnings = ΔRetained Earnings$_t$ / Total Assets$_t$*
Source: Own contribution.

We started with the simple model of Shyam-Sunder and Myers (1999) and Frank and Goyal (2003) to analyze how the pecking order model performs over time. In our first step, we included only the financial deficit, as follows:

$$\Delta DebtIssues_{it} = \alpha + \beta_1 DEF_{it} + \mu_i + \mu_t + \varepsilon_{it} \tag{21}$$

Where ΔDebt is the amount of debt issued for firm *i* in year *t* and DEF is the firms' financial deficit. α is the constant term, μ_i the individual error, μ_t a time-specific component of the error term, and *ε* it the classical error term.

Suppose the equation model (21) is correct in describing the SC and SNC firms' financing decisions. In that case, the constant term should equal zero *(α = 0)*, and the coefficient of DEF should equal one *(β = 1)* in the simple pecking order theory (also called strong-form pecking order). This implies that debt issues are directly propor-

201 Notes on scaling methodology: We were following the standard practice and scaled all variables and components, i.e., we scaled the absolute values of firm *i* by firms' total assets at *t*. For instance, a firm with a higher amount of assets will generally need more financing than a firm with fewer assets, therefore there it is important to interpret this data relative to each other instead of in absolute values. There has been a consensus among researchers in this area that scaling is the best method: For instance, in previous academic studies such as of Seifert and Gonenc (2008) and Shyam-Sunder and Myers (1999), and many more, the authors scaled the debt issues and equity issues relative to firms' total assets. This allows controlling for asset size or differences in financing requirements due to the nature of the firm's operation.

tional to the deficit of funds; consequently, there is no space for equity issues. Since the theory also accommodates some equity issues (in a broader view of the hypothesis), we also tested the so-called the semi-strong assumption of the Pecking Order Model, embraced by Chirinko and Singha (2000), by running a regression between equity issues and financial deficit variable as in equation (22).[202]

$$\Delta EquityIssues_{it} = \alpha + \beta_1 DEF_{it} + \mu_i + \mu_t + \varepsilon_{it} \tag{22}$$

Where ΔEquity is the amount of equity issued for firm *i* in year *t* and DEF is the firms' financial deficit. α is the constant term, *μi* the individual error, *μt* a time-specific component of the error term, and *εit* the classical error term. We performed both regression models (21) and (22) for the *overall (pooled)* sample and for all seven countries and seven industries separately.

In this section, we examined the financing behavior of SC and SNC firms in direct comparison. Thus, we introduced an *interaction term* to analyze the comparative differences between both firm types effectively. Specifically, using the dummy variable *dsc* (dummy Shari'ah Compliant) and interacting with the DEF variable (dsc*DEF), we analyzed the debt issues and equity issues of SC and SNC firms together in a single model. The interactive dummy variable's coefficient is the calculated difference in slope between both firm types. However, we were also interested in finding out the coefficient estimates that represent SC firms individually. The Stata command *lincom* computes point estimates, standard errors, *t* or *z statistics*, p-values, and confidence intervals for linear combinations of coefficients after any estimation command.[203] Such an approach will allow us to retrieve first, the coefficient estimates for SNC firms (separately), second, the coefficient estimates that represents the comparative differences, i.e., (the slope of) SC *compared to* (the slope of) SNC firms, and last, the coefficient estimates for SC firms (separately).[204] The following equations explain the Pecking Order Model regression with interaction term:

$$\Delta DebtIssues_{it} = \alpha + \beta_1 DEF_{it} + \beta_2 dsc * DEF_{it} + dsc + \mu_i + \mu_t + \varepsilon_{it} \tag{23}$$

$$\Delta EquityIssues_{it} = \alpha + \beta_1 DEF_{it} + \beta_2 dsc * DEF_{it} + dsc + \mu_i + \mu_t + \varepsilon_{it} \tag{24}$$

---

202 The strong-form pecking order view is too restricted in practicality, as defined by Shyam-Sunder and Myers (1999). Therefore, we assume the semi-strong form of the pecking order as defined by Chirinko and Singha (2000), which allows for the possible issuance of equity in firms' financing hierarchy. This approach is used, among others, by D.-H. Chen et al. (2013) and R. Huang and Ritter (2004).

203 See Stata Base Reference Manual, Release 13, p. 1029.

204 For a similar test application, see Beck et al. (2013, p. 444). Important note: In an interesting publication by Brambor et al. (2006), the authors provide a simple checklist of dos and don'ts when using interaction models. They further state that only 10% of the academic research and publications they surveyed followed such a checklist. We believe in to have applied the necessary actions by applying the Stata command *lincom* to overcome the concerns these authors raised.

Where *dsc* is a categorical dummy variable that equals one (1) if the company is SC, and zero (0) if SNC. Next, we will examine the results and the development of the estimated coefficients.

6.2.2 Empirical Results

Table 6.3 describes the mean, standard deviation, minimum, maximum, and the number of observations of debt issues, equity issues, and financial deficit of SC and SNC firms in the *overall (pooled)* sample and the entire sample period.[205] The descriptive statistics reveal that all SC firms' mean debt issues are 3.1%, which is slightly higher than that of SNC firms, which report a mean of 2.8%. This indicates that SC firms issue more debt when facing financial deficits compared to their non-compliant peers. Reporting identical range percentile indicates that SC and SNC firms show the same debt financing behavior on the extreme percentiles. Specifically, both firm types issue (retire) the same amount of debt in maximum (minimum) percentile when facing financial deficit (financial surplus).

As for the equity issues, differences can be observed between SC and SNC firms. The mean value for SC firms exhibits 1.2%, while for SNC firms, 0.7% indicating that SC firms do consider equity financing more when facing financial deficit compared to the SNC firms. However, similar to debt issues, both firm types show the same equity financing behavior on extreme percentiles.

Table 6.3: Overall Means of Debt Issues, Equity Issues, and Financial Deficit.

The table below shows the mean, standard deviation, minimum, maximum, and the number of observations of debt issues (ΔDebt), equity issues (ΔEquity), and financial deficit (DEF) for the entire period 2004–2014. Table 6.2 provides the definitions of all the variables. SC and SNC firms are determined based on DJIMI (see Table 4.1). All variables are winsorized at the 1% and 99% level.

Variables	Firm Type	Mean	SD	Min	Max	Obs
Debt Issues	SC	0.031	0.087	−0.250	0.365	6615
Equity Issues	SC	0.012	0.087	−0.208	0.410	6615
Financial Deficit	SC	0.044	0.125	−0.458	0.775	6615
Debt Issues	SNC	0.028	0.109	−0.250	0.365	4929
Equity Issues	SNC	0.007	0.056	−0.208	0.410	4929
Financial Deficit	SNC	0.035	0.129	−0.458	0.775	4929

Source: Own contribution.

205 For pairwise correlations between these variables and summary statistics by year, see Tables D.8 and D.9 in Appendix D, respectively.

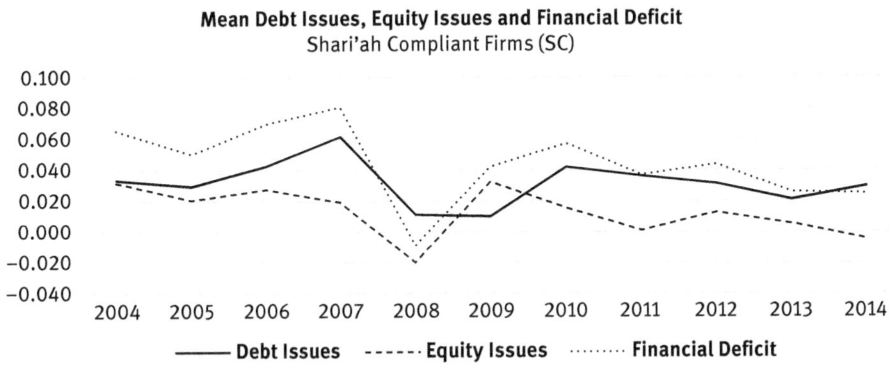

Figure 6.3: Debt Issues, Equity Issues, and Financial Deficit (SC).
Source: Own contribution.

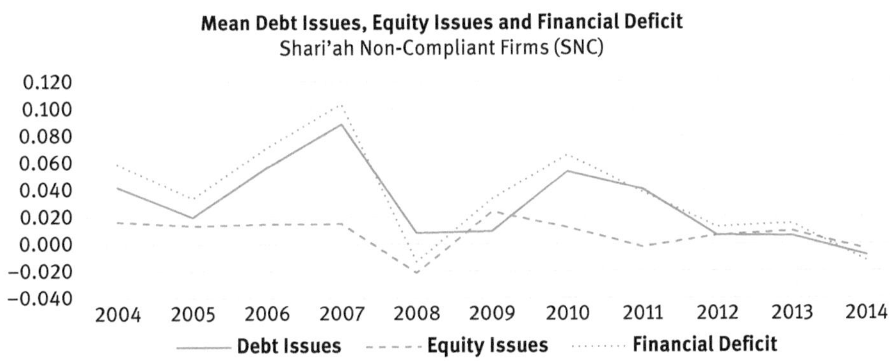

Figure 6.4: Debt Issues, Equity Issues, and Financial Deficit (SNC).
Source: Own contribution.

Figures 6.3 and 6.4 represent the mean values per year obtained from Table D.9 in Appendix D for SC and SNC firms, respectively. The figures illustrate the development in average debt issues, equity issues, and financial deficits for the entire sample period. Debt has been the most common form of external financing for both firm types.[206] The trend indicates that the financing behavior tracks more debt issues than equity issues throughout the sample years, except for the crisis period. Specifically, the pre-crisis (2004–2007) and post-crisis (2010–2013) periods show that SC and SNC firms have issued debt and equity to cover their financial deficit, however, preferably with debt. Furthermore, both firm types issued debt even though facing financing surplus and retiring equity during the crisis period (especially in 2008).

206 The accounting identity restricts that the financial deficit is tracked by the sum of debt- and equity issues. If the Pecking Order Theory holds, we expect that the debt issues would track the financial deficit much more closely than equity issues.

This behavior suggests that these firms might have been involved in timing the market and retired equity while the stock prices were under-priced (see Table C.1 in Appendix C). However, it is interesting to observe that starting from 2013, SC firms issue more debt than their financial deficit and additionally retire equity, while SNC firms retire both debt and equity while facing financing surplus. From these initial findings, it doesn't seem that SC and SNC firms are following the Pecking Order Theory. Using equity issues to retire debt (SNC firms during 2013–2014) or issuing equity more than debt (SC firms in 2009) is clearly against the main notion of the Pecking Order Theory. Looking from a different angle, except in 2009, SC firms (identified by DJIMI) do not actively engage in equity and quasi-equity financing activities as expected throughout the sample period. This is surprising and contrary to the expected financing hierarchy proposed in the *Islamic Pecking Order* model.

We report the regression results with equations (23) and (24) consolidated in Table 6.4 in Panel A, Columns (1)–(3) represent the coefficient estimates of the equation model (23) for debt issues and similarly, in Panel B columns (4)–(6) represent the coefficient estimates of the equation model (24) for equity issues. We applied both Pecking Order models on the *overall (pooled)*, *country*, and *industry* separately, using the proper estimator represented for each sample.[207] As described above, our approach provides us with the coefficient estimates for SC firms (columns 1 and 4), the difference in slope between both firm groups (interactive dummy represented in columns 2 and 5), and for SNC firms (columns 3 and 6). All regression results are available in Table D.10 in Appendix D.

Panel A in Table 6.4 shows the estimated coefficients throughout the samples in columns 1 and 3 for SC and SNC firms, respectively, which are all significantly greater than zero (less than one). The estimated coefficients in column (2) show that SC firms' debt issues are significantly lower (negative) throughout all sample perspectives *compared to* the SNC firms.[208] As for the debt issues, the estimated coefficients vary among countries from 41.70% (Canada) and 77.60% (India) and among industries from 42.20% (Basic Materials) and 69.60% (Consumer Goods). These results are somewhat similar to other studies' conclusions, especially Shyam-Sunder and Myers (1999), in which the authors found high financial deficit coefficients. If the Pecking Order Theory holds, then external funding is dominated by debt issues. The simple Pecking Order Theory implies that if financial distress costs are ignored, the firm will finance investment by issuing debt, which is not supported by our test results. Our coefficients in columns (1) and (3) for SC and SNC firms, respectively, are all sig-

---

207 Similar to the model estimation in Section 5.2, we conducted post estimation tests (i.e., BPLM, Hausman, Heteroskedasticity, and auto-/serial correlation) for both estimation models (23) and (24), and represented in Panel C, in Table B.3 in Appendix B, respectively.

208 Except for the United Kingdom, Taiwan, and India, the interactive Dummy variable exhibit a negative but insignificant coefficient, indicating that the effect of financial deficit on debt issuance for both firm types operating in these countries is the same.

Table 6.4: Pecking Order Estimation Results (Consolidated).

This table provides the results estimates retrieved from Table D.10 in Appendix D. The financial deficit (DEF) and its interactive dummy variable (dsc*DEF) are used in the equation models (23) and (24) and regressed on the dependent variables debt issues (ΔDebt) and equity issues (ΔEquity), respectively. The definitions of the variables in the regressions are provided in Table 6.2. SC and SNC firms are determined based on DJIMI (see Table 4.1). Models 1–15 represent the estimated coefficients for *overall (pooled)*, *country*, and *industry* samples for the entire period 2004–2014. Econometric estimators applied to each model are shown in the last column. All regressions were applied with the respective estimator, as identified by the model estimation procedure described in Panel C in Table B.3 in Appendix B. *, **, and *** denote significance at 10%, 5%, and 1% levels, respectively. All variables are winsorized at the 1% and 99% level. Model specifications are provided in Section 6.2.1.

		Panel A: Debt Issues			*Panel B: Equity Issues*			
Financial Deficit$_t$		**SC**	**SC compared to SNC**	**SNC**	**SC**	**SC compared to SNC**	**SNC**	
Sample		(1)	(2)	(3)	(4)	(5)	(6)	***Estimator***
Overall (pooled)	Model 1	0.560***	−0.204***	0.765***	0.440***	0.204***	0.235***	FE
United States	Model 2	0.510***	−0.209***	0.719***	0.490***	0.209***	0.281***	FE
United Kingdom	Model 3	0.669***	−0.034	0.698***	0.331***	0.034	0.302***	OLS
Canada	Model 4	0.417***	−0.245***	0.663***	0.583***	0.245***	0.337***	FE
Japan	Model 5	0.662***	−0.150***	0.811***	0.338***	0.150***	0.189***	OLS
South Korea	Model 6	0.550***	−0.261***	0.815***	0.450***	0.261***	0.185***	OLS
Taiwan	Model 7	0.612***	−0.099	0.707***	0.388***	0.099	0.293***	OLS
India	Model 8	0.776***	−0.069	0.852***	0.224***	0.069	0.148***	OLS
Oil and Gas	Model 9	0.450***	−0.337***	0.788***	0.550***	0.338***	0.212***	FE
Basic Materials	Model 10	0.422***	−0.363***	0.785***	0.578***	0.363***	0.215***	FE
Industrials	Model 11	0.632***	−0.131***	0.760***	0.368***	0.131***	0.240***	RE
Consumer Goods	Model 12	0.696***	−0.115***	0.810***	0.304***	0.115***	0.190***	FE
Technology	Model 13	0.475***	−0.234***	0.707***	0.525***	0.234***	0.293***	RE
Health Care	Model 14	0.567***	−0.181**	0.749***	0.433***	0.181**	0.251***	FE
Consumer Services	Model 15	0.543***	−0.209***	0.752***	0.457***	0.209***	0.248***	FE

Source: own contribution.

nificantly less than the simple strong-form of Pecking Order prediction of 1. Specifically, these coefficients of less than one ($0 < \beta$DEF < 1) weakens the assumption of the strong-form Pecking Order model.[209]

Panel B in Table 6.4 reveals that SC firms issue throughout the samples more equity (column 4) than their non-compliant counterpart (column 6). The estimated coefficients in column (5) show that SC firms' equity issues are significantly higher (positive) throughout all sample perspectives *compared to* the SNC firms.[210] As for the equity issues, the estimated coefficients vary among countries from 22.40% (India) and 58.30% (Canada) and among industries from 30.40% (Consumer Goods) and 57.80% (Basic Materials). These results indicate that SC firms facing financial deficits prefer equity financing as a source of external capital more than SNC firms. However, as mentioned earlier, the Pecking Order Theory's broader view accommodates some equity issues next to debt issues. Yet, the equity component is much less important than the debt issues. The results for the semi-strong assumption of Pecking Order Theory, as embraced by Chirinko and Singha (2000), reveal that the equity issues (column 4) compared to debt issues (column 1) of SC firms are all at significantly lower levels in all samples.[211] These results further indicate that firms may cover part of their financial deficit by issuing equity as external capital in addition to debt issues. The semi-strong form of the Pecking Order Theory, suggested by Chirinko and Singha (2000), is shown to be workable in describing SC and SNC firms financing behavior throughout the sample, i.e., *overall (pooled)*, *country*, and *industry*. Hence, (complement to the findings in debt issues), the Pecking Order Theory's strong-form is rejected.

In light of these findings, the positive debt and equity issuance might be a result of the following two scenarios:

1. Either, SC and SNC firms seek debt and equity issue with the rationale to reach optimal capital structure; as Myers (1984, p. 577) states, *"The firm is supposed to substitute debt for equity, or equity for debt, until the value of the firm, is maximized"*; or
2. SC and SNC firms seek equity issues in the case when debt cannot fully cover their financial deficit (inferring the semi-strong form of financing behavior).

How to differentiate between both scenarios when both external capital sources are the driving force in the firms' debt policy? The following suggestions can be made in the

209 The constant term α in Table D.10 in Appendix D show near zero in most of the samples, indicating that firms which do not experience any financial deficit will almost no issue any debt, respectively equity.
210 Except for the United Kingdom, Taiwan, and India, the interactive Dummy variable exhibit a positive but insignificant coefficient, indicating that the effect of financial deficit on equity issuance for both firm types operating in these countries is the same.
211 With the exception in Canada (*country*) and Oil and Gas, Basic Materials, and Technology (*industry*) for book leverage.

first scenario: DEF's estimated coefficients (financial deficit) for both debt issues and equity issues should be somehow "comparable" in magnitude. The second scenario is a little tricky since we don't know the sample firms' debt capacity. Bulan and Yan (2009, p. 14) state that "*They [*referring to Agca and Mozumdar (2004) and Lemmon and Zender (2010)*] point out that debt-capacity constraint is particularly binding for smaller, less-established firms.*" With the assumption that our firm samples are not small in size (see Step v. in Table 4.1), we further assume these firms have access to the debt market and utilize their debt-capacity to the fullest to cover their financial deficit. If the financial deficit is greater than the debt-capacity, firms have no other choice but to issue equity to close the gap. Therefore, we expect that the estimated coefficients of debt issues should always be greater than the estimated coefficients of equity issues.

The results in Table 6.4 exhibit for SC firms that the coefficients of DEF for debt issues (column 1) are mostly greater but "comparable" with the coefficients of DEF for equity issues (column 4) throughout the sample. Thus, the first scenario applies and suggests that SC firms somehow follow the notion of firm value maximization (i.e., Trade-Off Theory), as stated by Myers (1984). As for the SNC firms, the results show that DEF's coefficients for debt issues (column 3) are always significantly greater in magnitude than the coefficients of DEF for equity issues (column 6) throughout the sample. As highlighted in the second scenario, these results suggest that SNC firms issue equity as a last resort when debt issues cannot fully cover their financial deficit.

Notice, the Pecking Order regression models (23) and (24) correspond to Shyam-Sunder and Myers (1999) definition of the *contemporaneous deficit*. In other words, the firm's financial deficit at the end of year *t* is estimated when sudden and unanticipated cash in-/outflows occur. These changes could result during the fiscal year (beginning, middle, or end of the year). This type of deficit Shyam-Sunder and Myers (1999, p. 233) "*has more to do with short-term adjustments than planned financing.*" As mentioned in Section 4.4.1, managers need a certain "buffer time" to oversee and evaluate the firms' internal position before making such a strategic decision (i.e., financing decision). Thus we also regressed models (23a) and (24a) with the lagged deficit on year (DEF_{t-1}). The results are shown in Tables D.11 and D.12 in Appendix D.

$$\Delta DebtIssues_{it} = \alpha + \beta_1 DEF_{i,t-1} + \beta_2 dsc * DEF_{i,t-1} + dsc + \mu_i + \mu_t + \varepsilon_{it} \tag{23a}$$

$$\Delta EquityIssues_{it} = \alpha + \beta_1 DEF_{i,t-1} + \beta_2 dsc * DEF_{i,t-1} + dsc + \mu_i + \mu_t + \varepsilon_{it} \tag{24a}$$

For the test with the lagged deficit *(t–1)*, there seems to be much less "pecking order-like" behavior than when the deficit in the same year *(t)* is used. For instance, the highest (negative) significant coefficient for SC firms is shown with 0.128 for the United States, and the highest (positive) significant coefficient is shown with 0.124 for Taiwan. These results indicate that US managers with given buffer time to plan financing activities consider a retiring debt of about 12.80%. On the other hand, in Taiwan, managers consider additional debt issues of approximately 12.40% next to the short-term adjustments. However, these coefficient estimates are still very low compared to the predicted Pecking Order hypothesis, which expects a coefficient of (near) 1. Most of the *country* and *industry* samples exhibit insignificant coefficients, suggesting that, taken lagged deficit into account (i.e., long-term planning), Pecking Order Theory does not explain best the financing behavior of SC and SNC firms. Consequently, we relied on the estimation results shown in Table 6.4 with the contemporaneous-approach (i.e., short-term planning) as suggested and applied by Frank and Goyal (2003), Shyam-Sunder and Myers (1999), and other researchers.

6.3 Financing Behavior of SC *(RIEM)* Firms

Let's refer back to the results we have obtained so far. The debt determinants analysis (in Section 5.2), the dynamic Trade-Off model (in Section 6.1), as well as the Pecking Order model (in Section 6.2) all suggest that the capital structure and financing behavior, particularly of the SC firms (identified by Dow Jones), represent the notion of the Trade-Off Theory closely. Even if the results would have favored the Pecking Order model, in essence, similar to the Trade-Off Theory, debt is preferred over equity (last resort). In a nutshell, it's all about debt financing. Since we are dealing with SC firms, their capital structure and financing behavior should reflect more the principles of Shari'ah, and Islam enforces risk-sharing based partnerships such as the issuance of equity. (see Section 3.5)

Due to these unexpected results, we have questioned and re-considered the critical elements required to conduct this research. These are the i) firm sample identified by Dow Jones), ii) the collected firm-level/macroeconomic data, and iii) the applied statistical methodologies (including the regression estimator). After scrutinizing the second and third elements, we gave special attention to the first element, i.e., firm sample. Similarly, we found no issues in our firm sample neither in our sample selection procedure in Section 4.1.2. However, we started questioning whether the DJIMI Shari'ah screening methodology truly yields firms to be considered SC (e.g., among other characteristics, following a financing behavior compliant with Shari'ah principles). Therefore, in this section, we dealt with an additional regression on a new SC and SNC firm sample. Specifically, we have taken the proposed *RIEM 66 Index* (see Table 3.8) and created a new sample; call it "SC/SNC *(RIEM)* firms". We analyzed these firms' financing behavior, with special attention given to the SC *(RIEM)* firms, and compared them with the results mainly obtained in Section 6.2. Specifically, we tested whether "SC *(RIEM)* firms" engage more in equity financing compared to "SC firms" when financial deficit (insufficient internal funds) occurs. Even though we will keep this section brief, it will help us answer RQ 7.

6.3.1 Procedure to Identify the SC *(RIEM 66 Index)* Firms

Similar to the previous sample selection in Section 4.1, we applied the manual calculation to identify each firm being SC or SNC based on the *RIEM 66 Index*, proposed in Table 3.8. First, we have taken the pool with 719 SC firms and directly applied the equity ratio with the 66.67% minimum threshold. As shown in Table 6.5, the number of SC *(RIEM)* firms reduced to 267 as expected, since our criterion is more strict than the debt ratio criteria currently embedded in all Shari'ah screening methodologies (see Table 3.4). We then added the remaining "non-compliant" firms to the SNC firm pool applied similarly to identify the SNC *(RIEM)* firms, as shown in Table 6.5. Utilizing the SC and SNC samples as a basis ensured that SC/SNC *(RIEM)* firms are compliant with the Dow Jones business line screens (*qualitative screens*). (see Section 3.4)

Table 6.5: Identification of SC/SNC *(RIEM)* sample.

SC *(RIEM)* sample		
Steps		**# firms**
i.	SC firm sample	791
ii.	Equity ratio ≥ 66.67% with a minimum of 3 years of consecutiveness applied	267
SNC *(RIEM)* sample		
iii.	Remaining non-compliant firms (791–267 = 524) + SNC firm sample 615	1139
iv.	Equity ratio < 66.67% with a minimum of 3 years of consecutiveness applied	1124

6.3.2 Empirical Results

Table 6.6 describes the mean of debt issues, equity issues, and financial deficit of SC/SNC *(RIEM)* firms in the *overall (pooled)* sample and the entire sample period. First, the mean debt issues of 1.2% are significantly less than the 3.1% reported in Table 6.3. This shows that our new SC *(RIEM)* firms issue much less debt and consequently rely more on equity issues when facing financial deficits. Second, significant differences can be observed in equity issues between both SC firm types. A mean value of 2.6% indicates that SC *(RIEM)* firms engaged more in equity financing to cover their financing needs. The mean values for SNC *(RIEM)* firms are similar to those reported in Table 6.3, indicating heavy reliance on debt issuance when financial deficit rises.

Figure 6.5 represents the development of debt issues, equity issues, and financial deficits for the entire sample period, obtained from Table F.2 in Appendix F. We can immediately see that equity has been the most common form of external financing. The trend indicates that the financing behavior tracks more equity issues than debt issues throughout the sample years, except for 2011. However, compared to the SC firms

Table 6.6: Means of Debt/Equity Issues and Financial Deficit – SC/SNC *(RIEM)*.

The table below shows the mean, standard deviation, minimum, maximum, and the number of observations of debt issues (ΔDebt), equities issues (ΔEquity), and financial deficit (DEF) for the entire period 2004–2014. Table 6.2 provides the definitions of the variables. SC/SNC *(RIEM)* firms are determined based on the proposed *RIEM 66 Index* (see Tables 3.8 and 6.5). All variables are winsorized at the 1% and 99% level.

Sample	Firm Type	Mean	SD	Min	Max	Obs
Debt Issues	SC *(RIEM)*	0.012	0.055	−0.250	0.237	1752
Equity Issues	SC *(RIEM)*	0.026	0.097	−0.208	0.410	1752
Financial Deficit	SC *(RIEM)*	0.038	0.114	−0.360	0.583	1752
Debt Issues	SNC *(RIEM)*	0.032	0.102	−0.250	0.365	8733
Equity Issues	SNC *(RIEM)*	0.005	0.065	−0.208	0.410	8733
Financial Deficit	SNC *(RIEM)*	0.037	0.125	−0.458	0.775	8733

Source: Own contribution.

(Figure 6.3), during the crisis period, SC *(RIEM)* firms were not involved in debt financing; instead, they used their financial surplus to retire both equity and debt (see the year 2008 in Table F.2 in Appendix F). This is quite interesting since "*Freedom from liability [retiring debt] is a fundamental principle.*" is one of the essential values Shari'ah promotes (see Section 3.4.2). Similarly, Islam discourages debt as discussed in Sections 3.4.2 and 3.5, and as a result, it is expected that firms classified as Shari'ah compliant suppose to keep their leverage ratios as low as possible. Table F.3 in Appendix F shows the mean leverage for both SC/SNC *(RIEM)* firms. The low standard deviation for book leverage indicates that SC *(RIEM)* firms remain in the first tertile throughout the sample year and reach a maximum percentile of 33.20% compared to the maximum percentile value of 92% reported for SC firms (see Tables 5.1 and C.2 in Appendix C). Similarly, significant differences in *country* and *industry* sample can be observed in Tables F.4 and F.5 in Appendix F. Specifically, SC *(RIEM)* firms operating in our sample countries and industries exhibit a mean leverage value ranging from as low as 15.36% (Canada) to a maximum of 23.16% (Consumer Services), while their non-compliant peers report 49.82% (Oil and Gas) and 63.45% (Japan), respectively. As far as equity ratio is concerned, SC *(RIEM)* firms hold on average 30% more equity than the mean reported for each *country* and *industry* they are operating. From these initial findings, it seems that SC *(RIEM)* firms follow a financing pattern that resembles the proposed *Islamic Pecking Order* hierarchy model introduced in Section 3.5 (see Figure 3.4).

Similar to Table 6.4, we report the regression results of equations (23) and (24)[212] using the SC/SNC *(RIEM)* firm sample in Table 6.7.[213] In short, the *overall (pooled)*

212 We have employed all preliminary tests for SC/SNC *(RIEM)* firm sample. All results can be found in Tables F.6 and F.7 in Appendix F.

213 All results are available in Table F.8 in Appendix F.

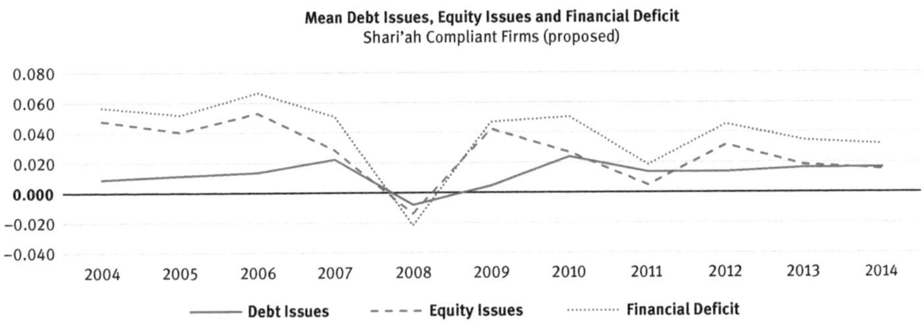

Figure 6.5: Debt Issues, Equity Issues, and Financial Deficit – SC *(RIEM)*.
Source: Own contribution.[214]

sample results show that SC *(RIEM)* firms are materially more engaged in equity financing, with an estimated coefficient of 0.694. This result indicates that SC *(RIEM)* firms cover their financial deficit on average by approximately 70%. Market-based countries such as the United States, United Kingdom, and Canada seem to have utilized their access to their well-developed equity market, reporting an estimation coefficient up to 78.6%. Basic Materials, Technology, and Consumer Services are among those industries which report estimated values above the *overall (pooled)* results, with Consumer Services even up to 82.7%.

As expected and confirming the results in Section 6.2, SNC *(RIEM)* firms follow the basic notion of the Pecking Order Theory, which is based on the least costly option of financing and move down in the sequence from the lowest to highest, and cover their financial deficit mainly through debt issues. The results in columns (3) and (6) indicate that SNC *(RIEM)* firms issue equity (as a last resort) when debt issues reach debt-capacity and cannot fully cover their financial deficit.

As far as SC *(RIEM)* firms are concerned, it is interesting to observe that these firms with a high equity ratio are still engaged in equity financing when facing a financial deficit. It seems that the debt component, on average, is much less important, as shown in column (1), compared to column (4). *What could be the reason these firms do engage mainly in equity financing?* Since the benefits that come with debt financing are well-known (see Section 2.1), the question arises: *Why do SC (RIEM) firms not max-out their debt level and utilize debt to the same extent as their non-compliant peers?* One possible explanation could be provided by analyzing each sample country's macroeconomic factors or analyzing the industry-specific characteristics these firms are operating in. However, we believe neither the country's financial system (market- or bank-based) nor the industry-specific characteristics (e.g., capital-intensive/less-intensive) can

214 In this section, since our focus lies on SC *(RIEM)* firms, the same figure for SNC *(RIEM)* is provided in Figure F.1 in Appendix F.

Table 6.7: Pecking Order Estimation (Consolidated) – SC *(RIEM)*.

This table provides the results estimates retrieved from Table F.8 in Appendix F. The financial deficit (DEF) and its interactive dummy variable *(dsc*DEF)* are used in the equation models (23) and (24) and regressed on the dependent variables debt issues (ΔDebt) and equity issues (ΔEquity), respectively. The definitions of the variables in the regressions are provided in Table 6.2. SC/SNC (*RIEM*) firms are determined based on the proposed *RIEM 66 Index* (see Tables 3.8 and 6.5). Models 1–15 represent the estimated coefficients for *overall (pooled)*, *country*, and *industry* samples for the entire period 2004–2014. Econometric estimators applied to each model are shown in the last column. All regressions were applied with the respective estimator, as identified by the model estimation procedure described in Table F.6 in Appendix F. *, ** and *** denote significance at 10%, 5%, and 1% levels, respectively. All variables are winsorized at the 1% and 99% level. Model specifications are provided in Section 6.2.1.

		Panel A: Debt Issues			*Panel B: Equity Issues*			
Financial Deficit$_t$		**SC**	**SC compared to SNC**	**SNC**	**SC**	**SC compared to SNC**	**SNC**	
Sample		(1)	(2)	(3)	(4)	(5)	(6)	***Estimator***
Overall (pooled)	Model 1	0.306**	−0.415***	0.721***	0.694**	0.415***	0.279***	FE
United States	Model 2	0.214**	−0.442***	0.656***	0.786**	0.442***	0.344***	FE
United Kingdom	Model 3	0.228*	−0.504***	0.732***	0.772*	0.504***	0.268***	OLS
Canada	Model 4	0.268**	−0.377***	0.644***	0.732**	0.377***	0.356***	FE
Japan	Model 5	0.479*	−0.325***	0.804***	0.521*	0.325***	0.196***	OLS
South Korea	Model 6	0.438*	−0.347***	0.786***	0.562*	0.347***	0.214***	OLS
Taiwan	Model 7	0.420*	−0.296***	0.717***	0.580*	0.296***	0.283***	OLS
India	Model 8	0.540*	−0.297***	0.838***	0.460*	0.298***	0.162***	OLS
Oil and Gas	Model 9	0.319*	−0.334***	0.653***	0.681*	0.334***	0.347***	FE
Basic Materials	Model 10	0.281*	−0.467***	0.748***	0.719*	0.467***	0.252***	FE
Industrials	Model 11	0.344*	−0.387***	0.731***	0.656*	0.387***	0.269***	RE
Consumer Goods	Model 12	0.539*	−0.237***	0.777***	0.461*	0.238***	0.223***	FE
Technology	Model 13	0.233**	−0.403***	0.636***	0.767**	0.403***	0.364***	RE
Health Care	Model 14	0.335*	−0.345***	0.680***	0.665*	0.345***	0.320***	FE
Consumer Services	Model 15	0.173*	−0.549***	0.722***	0.827*	0.549***	0.278***	FE

Source: own contribution.

be the factors to explain the significant differences compared to their non-compliant counterpart. The reason is that all firms under study, i.e., SC/SNC *(RIEM)* firms, are exposed to the same macroeconomic environment and same industry-specific characteristics. Another and more likely explanation could be found by analyzing the debt capacity of these firms. If SC *(RIEM)* firms suffer from low debt capacity, these firms would have no other choice but to issue equity as the primary funding source. Debt financing would then become secondary, covering only a (small) portion of the firms' financial deficit. However, in this case, the debt-constraint (i.e., low debt capacity) scenario would favor the financing behavior as postulated by Shari'ah.

As mentioned earlier and illustrated in Figure 3.4 in Section 3.5, the broader view of our proposed *Islamic Pecking Order* hierarchy accommodates next to equity issues some debt issues as a last resort. In light of these findings, SC *(RIEM)* firms tend to exhaust their internal funds first through retained earnings and cover their financial deficit mainly by equity and debt financing as a last resort. Consequently, and intuitively, we believe that both SC/SNC *(RIEM)* firms' financing behavior is characterized by the firms' financing preference/policy. About the SC *(RIEM)* firms, we cannot claim with certainty that these firms follow our proposed *Islamic Pecking Order* model. However, the above-estimated results indicate that these firms implicitly follow such a financing order that resembles our proposed pecking order financing hierarchy. In either way, this financing pattern supports the notion of the Islamic financial system and adheres to the essence of the *ayah* (*Qur'an* Surah Al-Baqarah, 2:275), as described in Section 3.4.2. Hence, the RQ 7 cannot be affirmed for SC firms. As for SC *(RIEM)* firms, RQ 7 must be affirmed.

6.4 Conclusion

This chapter aimed to strengthen the outcome of Chapter 5 by applying a direct measure of the Trade-Off Theory and the Pecking Order Theory. The investigation of the *dynamic* version of the Trade-Off model confirmed the existence of a target (i.e., optimal capital structure) to which both firm types actively aim for. The fact that SC firms significantly rebalance towards their target indicates that they actively utilize the tax benefits that come with debt financing (see Section 2.3).

Under normal circumstances, firms engage in external financing when they face a financial deficit. We found a behavior that resembled pecking-order-like financing. Overall, the results showed that both SC and SNC firms closed their financial deficit, mainly with debt followed by equity. A deeper look at SC firms' financing behavior per se exhibits that these firms do not follow the principles of Shari'ah, as discussed in Section 3.5. For this reason, we created a new SC firm sample based on our proposed *RIEM 66 Index*. We conducted a direct measure for the Pecking Order Theory. In the case of financial deficit arises, SC *(RIEM)* firms cover their financing needs mainly through equity issues, whereas the SC firms (identified by DJIMI Shari'ah screening methodology) with both debt and equity to the same extent (with slightly more reliance on debt financing). These results tend to claim that *RIEM* methodology with its *RIEM 66 Index* (i.e., lenient-type equity ratio) yields a sample of firms that comply more with the main notion of Islamic principles than the sample of firms filtered through DJIMI.

7 Overall Conclusion and Future Research

In this chapter, we conclude our study by consolidating our major findings and its limitation. Furthermore, this study's implications and the contribution will be highlighted and finalized by providing recommendations and suggestions for further research.

7.1 Overview and Key Findings

In this study, we conducted a comprehensive comparative analysis among Shari'ah compliant (SC) firms and their Shari'ah non-compliant (SNC) peers during the 2004–2014 period. Throughout the course, we analyzed both sample firms from three perspectives: *overall (pooled)*, to detect possible cross-sectional variations, cross-*country*, and cross-*industry*. According to the Shari'ah screening methodologies applied in the Dow Jones Islamic Market Index (DJIMI), we determined firm samples. We classified firms who passed both *qualitative* and *quantitative* screenings successfully as SC, otherwise as SNC.

Capital structure, which is the mixture of debt, equity, or hybrid capital of a company, is very important since the decisions taken by the management are crucial to the survival of the firms, and it is related to the ability of the firm to fulfill the needs of its stakeholders. Chapter two discussed the main competing theories, which attempt to understand how firm management's financing decisions have emerged and developed over the last decades, namely, the Trade-Off Theory and the Pecking Order Theory. The notion of the Trade-Off Theory predicts that firms should balance the benefits against the costs of debt. Both factors, benefit vs. the cost of debt, eventually led to the belief that firms should have an optimal capital structure. In contrast, the Pecking Order Theory does not imply that the notion of optimal capital structure drives firms financing decisions. It is based on the idea of the "least costly option". It implies a straightforward financing hierarchy in which firms use internal financing (retained earnings) first, followed by any form of external financing (preferably debt over equity). Over the last decades, academics have also identified key debt determinants (firm-specific and macroeconomic variables), supporting and driving firm management when making financing decisions. We discussed all key determinants and focused in our study only on six commonly used determinants, those who have predictions made by both theories (see Section 2.5). The literature revealed a gap in empirical research in capital structure and its determinants, especially on firms operating under the principles of Shari'ah (i.e., SC firms), supporting the need for this research study.

Chapter three discussed the historical background and the development of the newly implemented stock screening procedure, called *Shari'ah screening methodology*,

https://doi.org/10.1515/9783110713664-007

with its criterion set by the Dow Jones Islamic Market Index (DJIMI). Several authors have criticized the currently applied screening methodologies and highlighted the importance of harmonizing the screening criterion. In examining RQ 1, we broadly identified three key findings. First, we found strong evidence from the *Qur'an* that most righteous and fair judgments exist when "endogenous factors" are considered in the screening criterion. In other words, only factors that are entirely in the control of each company, i.e., book values driven from their financial statements. Second, we have highlighted the importance of implementing a tool (i.e., Shari'ah screening methodology) that supports the notion of Islamic finance and emphasized the integration of equity-based rather than debt-based concept. The *ahadith* Sahih Muslim, Book 13 *Kitab Al-Wasiyya* No: 3991, 3996, and 3997, also known as "*one-third is big*" *ahadith*, allowed us to derive a financial ratio with all its components (i.e., *numerator, denominator, relational operator,* and *threshold*) (see Section 3.4.2). The screening solution offered is unique, and it exhibits a potential for standardization. Last, using an exploratory approach, we introduced an *Islamic Pecking Order* model, a financing hierarchy that provides useful insights to firms interested in operating under the Islamic principles (see Section 3.5). It suggests that firms with a financial deficit (after utilizing internal funds) opt first for equity and quasi-equity instruments to finance their assets/investments before engaging in debt financing, including the instruments provided by the Islamic financial institutions. This financing behavior would ensure firms a) to preserve higher equity in their capital structure, b) to follow a model that itself is Shari'ah compliant, and c) to support the notion of the Islamic financial system by adhering to the essence of the *ayah* (*Qur'an* Surah Al-Baqarah, 2:275).

Chapter four discussed the foundation and the theoretical framework for this study, including the *firm sample creation* and *hypotheses development*. We introduced a step-by-step approach to identify SC and SNC firm samples based on the *Shari'ah screening criterion* set by DJIMI. Our sample selection procedure (see Section 4.1) provided *consistent* tracking history and ensured the *consecutiveness* of being SC and SNC throughout the time series. Relying on the past empirical studies, we developed all hypotheses around the six selected debt determinants considering the Trade-Off Theory and Pecking Order Theory predictions. In the context of SC firms, we enhanced and complemented the hypotheses with the predictions proposed by the *Islamic Pecking Order* model (see Table 4.10). Intending to address RQ2–RQ7, we discussed the deployment of advanced and appropriate econometric methods that estimate firms' static and dynamic financing behavior. Following early studies, we use *OLS, Fixed Effects*, and *Random Effects* estimators on all of our defined *static* models and using a two-step estimation procedure, namely, *System-GMM estimator*, to the partial adjustment (*dynamic*) models.

In chapter five, we elaborated on the empirical data used in testing the theoretical framework and hypotheses. We identified the most reliable (significant) debt determinants that influence the financing decision and, ultimately, SC and SNC firms' capital structure. The estimation results revealed that all debt determinants play an important role with positive and negative effects on firms' leverage ratio. Depending on the firm type (i.e., SC and SNC) and leverage measure (book and market), the results varied between statistical significance and insignificance. Certain debt factors exhibited their dominance in any circumstances. Specifically, independent of being SC or SNC and book or market leverage, debt determinant *profitability* reported consistent results from all three perspectives: *overall (pooled)*, *country*, and *industry*. Determinants such as *growth opportunity*, *firm size*, and *tangibility* reported uniform effect in the *overall (pooled)* sample, limited to the market leverage measure. However, the cross-sectional analysis only confirmed the uniformity of *growth opportunity* and *firm size*. The remaining determinants revealed either insignificant or contradictory results.

As far as SC firms are concerned, the results obtained for *profitability* and *growth opportunity* align with the *Islamic Pecking Order* model. The results indicate that profitable SC firms generated sufficient internal funds and retained more earnings. Since the Shari'ah does not permit investment activities in interest-bearing instruments, SC firms utilized their excess cash (internal funds) in activities such as debt settlements. Depending on the investment projects, when internal funds became insufficient and financial deficit occurred, the negative relation with leverage indicates that these firms were engaged in equity financing to close the gap required for their investment opportunities. Regarding the other determinants, the results showed, especially for book leverage measure of SC firms, that almost all capital structure determinants under study cannot be considered reliable. This further indicates that the market leverage might be a better proxy to analyze SC firms' capital structure.

Our time-breakdown analysis revealed most of the debt determinants did not show a consistent effect throughout the sample years (2004–2014), indicating a dynamic role, depending on the country's or industry's economic circumstances. Even though *profitability* and *growth opportunity* reported to have a uniform effect, these determinants' importance seems to have been raised during the post-crisis period (2010–2014). The remaining determinants exhibit mixed or partial consistent results in both leverage measures.

We consolidated all empirical results (i.e., coefficient signs) observed in the *overall (pooled)*, *country*, and *industry* sample and compared them with the theoretical predictions made by both capital structure theories. These determinants' coefficient signs give support for both capital structure theories. In terms of both theories' explanatory power, our findings are inconclusive for the book leverage measure. Specifically, both capital structure theories describe both firm types' financing behavior somewhat to the same extent. As far as market leverage measure is concerned, contrary to Islamic finance literature, the Trade-Off Theory tends to dominate the Pecking Order Theory. However, comparing the explanatory power of the conventional Pecking Order Theory with the proposed *Islamic Pecking Order* model, as far as SC firms are concerned, they ranked equally for book leverage. However, for the market leverage measure, the latter outperformed the former.

Chapter six validated and strengthened our findings and conducted a direct measure of each capital structure theory. The regression results revealed that SC and SNC firms are actively and frequently engaged in debt adjustment behavior. Comparing both firm types, we reported that SC firms exhibit a much faster adjustment speed than their non-compliant counterparts in most countries and industries for both leverage measures (see Section 6.1.2). The fact that SC firms rebalance towards their optimal capital structure supports the existence of dynamic Trade-Off Theory. We confirmed our previous findings and concluded that SC firms actively utilize, among others, interest-bearing debt as an instrument to increase firm value.

Furthermore, we investigated SC and SNC firms' financing behavior and found evidence of the semi-strong form of the Pecking Order Theory (see Section 6.2.2). The results indicated that both firm types cover their financing needs with debt and equity issues, whereas the SNC firms predominantly finance debt issues. As far as SC firms are concerned, the results revealed that these firms close their financing gap by issuing debt and equity somewhat equally in magnitude. That, in turn, suggests that SC firms somehow follow the notion of firm value maximization, an indication of Trade-Off Theory. From these results, we conclude that there is no difference in SC firms' financing behavior than SNC firms.

The results obtained from the debt determinant analysis, the dynamic Trade-Off model, and the Pecking Order model reveal the Trade-Off Theory's dominance over the Pecking Order Theory. In other words, a closer look at the financing behavior of SC firms shows that these firms do not follow the principles of Shari'ah. These results, especially for SC firms, contradict the suggestions made by Ahmed (2007) and Obaidullah (2007). Both authors suggested that the Pecking Order Theory better explain firms' capital structure decisions under Shari'ah principles. Obaidullah (2007) went even further and advocates that the Trade-Off Theory, with its "debt tax shield" concept, is irrelevant from an Islamic perspective. From our results, we can derive the following indications: First, other determinants potentially play a more significant role in SC firms' capital structure decisions. Second, it confirms that an Islamic capital structure theory and its determinants that would explain the financing behavior of firms operating under Shari'ah principles have not been developed yet (Yildirim et al., 2018). Last, it raises the critical question, whether the existing applied screening methodologies provide a sample of firms operating under Shari'ah principles as claimed by the proprietary owners of the current *Shari'ah screening methodologies* (e.g., Dow Jones).

We have extended our direct measure analysis by conducting an additional test on a new firm sample identified based on our proposed *RIEM 66 Index*. We employed the direct measure of the Pecking Order Theory, which postulates firms financing behavior by engaging in external financing when a financial deficit occurs. The results show that in the case of financial deficit arises, SC *(RIEM)* firms cover their financing needs mainly through equity issues. The broader view of the *Islamic Pecking Order* model accommodates some debt issues next to equity issues. Yet, the debt component is much less important than the equity issues (see Table 6.7). As part of the proposed *RIEM* methodology, we claim that the lenient-type equity ratio (*RIEM 66 Index*) is simple and practical, and foremost, in itself, Shari'ah compliant. Furthermore, it yields a sample of firms their financing behavior complies more with the notion of the Islamic financial system and adheres to the essence of the *ayah* (*Qur'an* Surah Al-Baqarah, 2:275).

7.2 Implications of the Study

In the last decades, starting with the MM Irrelevance Theory, many studies attempt to discuss the capital structure and its effects on firms' value. Nevertheless, it is unlikely to explain firms' financing behavior with certainty due to the drastic financial changes and innovations in the business and financing worlds. Given these changes, we are still able to offer practical advice to policymakers. Given different economic and financial orientations, we will discuss the implications of this study to these respective parties in global markets under the following headings:

- Implications for Policymakers
- Implications of Risk-Sharing Instruments on Capital Structure Theories.

7.2.1 Implications for Policymakers

In the efforts to further transform Islamic financial stock markets into a market in which the activities are entirely in compliance with Islamic Shari'ah as determined by Sheikh Yaqoubi in Gamaleldin (2015), policymakers should provide instruments and solutions to encourage participation in this market. Islamic law strictly bans interest-bearing debt. It is advantageous to finance the needed capital (financial deficit) as many countries' tax-shelter provision attracts debt financing as a cheap financing option. The less risk and high return projects are generally financed through debt since it prevents ownership dilution effects. Otherwise, the expected return has to be shared with new shareholders, which does not benefit the current shareholders.

Therefore, to provide fairness to the Islamic financial system and minimize the interest-bearing debt financing behavior of firms and investors, policymakers must first introduce a tax incentive mechanism that favors equity financing. As one of the policy instruments, the tax system should fully offset corporate debt's tax incentive by giving tax incentives to corporate dividend payments. Second, as practiced in Malaysia, policymakers could lift off the tax payment on investors' dividend income. Finally, since preferring debt may lead to high leverage, which increases the firm's riskiness (bankruptcy risk), risk-sharing instruments, which are entirely in line with the Islamic financial system's spirit, should be supported by the policymakers. These instruments should not only serve the *Maqasid Al-Shari'ah* but must be competitive and feasible at the same time. Therefore, these risk-sharing instruments should eliminate the drawbacks of debt and equity financing and provide benefits that render them competitive. Even though equity issuance is a fully Shari'ah compliant option (in contrast to debt financing), it causes an ownership dilution effect not preferred by the shareholders. Furthermore, issuing shares is generally costlier than borrowing. Therefore, as Bacha et al. (2015) suggested, risk-sharing instruments, having underlying contracts based on *musharakah* and *mudharabah*, can be promoted and introduced as a competitive Shari'ah compliant financing. These instruments are project-specific, hence do not entitle the new shareholders as the owner of the entire firm. This prevents the ownership dilution effect. Since these instruments are not treated as debt instruments, this will not increase the firms' leverage ratio. Hence, the riskiness will not be as high as in the case debt financing is preferred. Therefore, policymakers must promote risk-sharing instruments (e.g., *mudharabah* and *musharakah*-based *sukuk*) instead of Shari'ah compliant debt-like instruments (e.g., *murabahah, ijarah, salam, and istisna*). The latter instruments would increase firms' financial leverage and riskiness, similar to the conventional debt instruments.

Our suggested policy recommendations can help financial managers of SC firms go for external financing that does not harm the competitiveness from the least costly financing perspective and, at the same time, align with the Shari'ah principles.

7.2.2 Implications of Risk-Sharing Instruments on Capital Structure Theories

As mentioned earlier, in Section 1.1, various capital structure theories exist, explaining companies' debt-/equity choice. While the Trade-Off Theory shows the benefit of debt in the form of a tax shield for income, the Pecking Order Theory applies the asymmetric information and signaling framework. Both theories promote and favor debt financing and attempt to find suitable justification and explanation for leveraging. Graham and Harvey (2001) conducted a questionnaire survey to determine which debt- and equity factors matter *in practice*.[215] Surprisingly, factors such as bankruptcy costs or the corporate tax advantage, which play a crucial role in the theoretical capital structure literature, exhibit relatively minor importance in firms' debt decisions. In contrast, ***financial flexibility***, which has almost completely been neglected in capital structure theories, seems to be the most crucial debt factor. Furthermore, CFOs regard

215 Graham and Harvey (2001) are one of the first to determine which factors are reliably important in the mix by providing a comprehensive interview survey to chief financial executives (CFOs) in US companies. They sent a survey to each CFO in the 1998 Fortune 500 list and 4400 publicly traded US companies, a member of the "Financial Executive Institute (FEI)". With a response rate close to 9%, the authors surveyed 392 CFOs about their firms' capital structure decisions. Almost 59% of the respondents regard financial flexibility, and 68% regard earnings dilution as the most important factor in issuing debt and equity, respectively.

earnings dilution as the most critical equity factor. The concern for earnings dilution is even more severe for large and dividend-paying companies.

Both concerns, i.e., financial flexibility and earnings dilution, can be addressed with risk-sharing contracts such as *mudharabah* and *musharakah*. Especially, *Mudharabah* is a hybrid financing and risk-sharing instrument with features of both debt and equity without the disadvantages of both. This allows more flexibility in a firm's capital structure. Specifically, comparing risk-sharing finance relative to debt, *mudharabah* and *musharakah sukuk* returns are based on profits and losses, i.e., without profits, nothing to share (similar to dividend payments). Additionally, there will be no increase in firms' leverage with fixed charges, hence decreases the firm's financial distress (bankruptcy costs). On the other hand, comparing risk-sharing finance relative to equity, with *mudharabah* and *musharakah sukuk*, the right of claim is only on the profits generated by the new project(s), i.e., it has a restrictive earnings dilution effect. Furthermore, ownership dilution is not perpetual (compared to new shares issued) and is only limited to the new project/asset being financed.

As mentioned in Section 7.2.1, policymakers must introduce and support tax incentive mechanisms that favor equity and hybrid financing. Next, we want to highlight the potential impact of tax incentives on dividend payments (similar to interest payments) on the established capital structure theories. Table 7.1 shows the attractiveness level of debt, equity, and hybrid financing from the established and proposed capital structure theories perspective based on their rationale. Scenarios 1, 3, and 5 refer to the status quo, the tax incentives regulations in most countries worldwide. If regulatory bodies would introduce tax incentives programs to corporate dividend payments, as discussed in Section 7.2.1, its potential impact is highlighted in scenarios 2, 4, and 6.

Table 7.1: Impact of (Debt-/Dividend) Tax Shield on Capital Structure Theories.

Capital Structure		Scen.	Tax Incentives		Attractiveness		
Theories/Model	**Rationale**		**Interest**	**Dividend**	**Debt**	**Equity**	**Hybrid**
MM Irrelevance	perfect-market condition	0	*taxes not recognized*		*irrelevant*		
Trade-Off	firm value maximization (optimal capital structure exists)	1	✓	×	more	less	**most**
		2	✓	✓	less	more	**most**
Pecking Order	least cost perspective (optimal capital structure does not exist)	3	✓	×	most	less	**more**
		4	✓	✓	most	less	**more**
Islamic Pecking Order	least financial risk exposure (risk-sharing principle)	5	✓	×	less	**most**	more
		6	✓	✓	less	**most**	more

Source: Own contribution.

The MM theorem is purely theoretical and applies arbitrage arguments and illustrates that, due to the restrictive assumptions, the impact of a firm's capital structure decision on firm value becomes irrelevant. The theorem rationale is based on perfect-market conditions with strict assumptions of, for instance, no recognition of any taxes (see Section 2.2). Consequently, the introduction of hybrid financing as a financing option would remain irrelevant.

With the current government tax treatment (scenario one), debt financing is more attractive than equity financing, as argued and justified by the Trade-Off Theory with its rationale of firm value maximization. The hybrid financing option would relax debt's attractiveness since it mitigates two main intrinsic issues with debt financing. First, excessive leverage increases firms' financial distress and bankruptcy risk. Second, firms might max out their debt capacity and compromise their financial flexibility (see CFOs concern highlighted in previous paragraphs). Given these arguments, hybrid financing is the most attractive financing option for firms.

Suppose the government would provide the same tax incentives for dividend payments (scenario two), then the equity financing would yield more attractiveness. Since the tax incentives for both interest and dividend payments would balance off, the equity issues come with two benefits. First, it reduces the chances of bankruptcy, therefore decreases the cost of financial distress. Second, it keeps firms' leverage low and assures financial flexibility (argued by the *dynamic* version of Trade-Off Theory). However, since new shares issues raise the concern of ownership and earnings dilution, hybrid financing mitigates the long-term ownership dilution effect as it is not perpetual. Given these arguments, hybrid financing is considered the most attractive financing option for firms under scenario 2.

In contrast to Trade-Off Theory, Pecking Order Theory does not imply that optimal capital structure drives firms' capital structure decisions. Rather, the underlying assumption is that the firm minimizes the total cost of financing when choosing among the available alternatives. Consequently, firms rely on internal financing (retained earnings) over external financing (debt and equity), and if external financing is required, the firm issues debt over equity. As mentioned in Section 2.1, in general, debt financing is more attractive than equity financing due to the following arguments:

i. The pre-tax rate of interest is consistently lower than the return required by shareholders.
ii. The interest paid on debt is used as a tax-shield, thus leads to a tax advantage.
iii. The costs involved in the administration and debt issuance are usually not as high as for equity issuance.

With the current government tax treatment (scenario 3) and if the government would provide the same tax incentives for dividend payments (scenario 4), debt financing is more attractive than equity financing, even in the latter scenario. While in scenario 3, all three arguments apply, in scenario 4, only the statement (ii) would balance off. The statements (i) and (iii) still need to be considered. The benefits that come along with hybrid financing (as mentioned above) is not the concern of the Pecking Order Theory per se. Consequently, the attractiveness of hybrid financing in scenarios three and four would depend on the total cost of hybrid financing compared to debt financing. However, under normal conditions, the cost of hybrid financing should be less than the cost of equity, making hybrid financing the next available funding source (after debt) following the hierarchical latter.

In contrast to Trade-Off Theory, Pecking Order Theory does not imply that optimal capital structure drives firms' capital structure decisions. Rather, the underlying assumption is that the firm minimizes the total cost of financing when choosing among the available alternatives. Consequently, firms rely on internal financing (retained earnings) over external financing (debt and equity), and if external financing is required, the firm issues debt over equity.

As far as the *Islamic Pecking Order* model is concerned, its fundamental notion is that firms maximize their Shari'ah compliance by following risk-sharing principles while minimizing financial risk exposure. Therefore, internal financing is given the highest priority over external financing. If a financial deficit exists, these firms close the gap by engaging in equity and quasi-equity financing over debt financing.

In the current government tax treatment (scenario five), equity financing is most attractive since it represents the basic notion of profit-and-loss sharing, as postulated by Shari'ah. Furthermore, it mitigates bankruptcy risk, therefore, decreases the cost of financial distress. Last, it keeps firms' leverage low and assures financial flexibility if debt financing becomes necessary. Since hybrid financing providers have the right and claim to the underlying assets, the financial risk exposure is more than equity. Consequently, consideration is given only after equity financing.

If regulators introduced tax incentives for dividend payments (scenario six), equity financing would become even more attractive without affecting the attractiveness of hybrid financing. In either scenario, debt financing remains less attractive.

7.3 Contribution of the Study

This study's main contribution to the academic world is two-fold:

First, from the corporate finance/capital structure perspective, it is the first full-fledged comparative study in the literature of SC and SNC firms. It contributes to the limited amount of capital structure literature, especially by analyzing the debt determinants and the financing behavior of an SC firm sample defined by DJIMI. For the first time, the two main capital structure theories were put on a scale to show how well these different theories fit the data and trying to shed more light on the debate as to whether the Trade-Off or Pecking Order Theory has greater explanatory power.

Second, from the Shari'ah perspective, this study provides for the first time a solution to the long-lasting criticism of the Shari'ah screening methodologies applied by Dow Jones and other providers. The proposed solution has the potential for the standardization that Shari'ah scholars and academicians are striving for. For the first time, it offers an in-depth understanding and evaluation of the Islamic sources (i.e., *Qur'an* and *Sunnah*) with a limited scope around Shari'ah screens. Furthermore, this study introduces a new corporate financing framework for firms interested in operating in alignment with Shari'ah principles.

Note: We suggest Islamic finance regulators, such as the AAOIFI, IFSB, and BNM, to consider including the proposed screening solution(s) (see Table 3.8) in their Shari'ah standards. Islamic index providers may also look into this screening criterion and consider it complementary, or as a substitution, to their currently applied screening methodology.

These contributions will ultimately support Islamic finance's growth, which depends on diversified academic studies.

7.4 Limitations of the Study

Like other capital structure studies, this research depends on data based on financial statements and its financial items that may not represent all factors influencing the financing decisions. For instance, regarding financing decisions, the management may be affected by human characteristics, such as belief, attitudes, experience, and knowledge. Therefore, capital structure studies may need to conduct a survey analysis to investigate the impacts of management characteristics on financing decisions. In the same line of thought, such a survey could have been used to identify whether firms classified as SC are intentionally SC and not only based on some pre-defined screening ratios. Such research would have been much better had it been able to encompass such information.

Second, data availability is another limitation in studies that require SC firm samples. This study required historical data that is not available publicly. The sample selection procedure to identify SC and SNC firms employed in this research may subject to possible human error.

Finally, limitations might arise due to the definitions of the dependent and explanatory variables used in this study. Even though we followed common definitions applied in the capital structure literature, other proxies might have yielded different results. Therefore, it is difficult to expect that such a study finds perfect proxies. Therefore, as mentioned above, the results of this study have to be interpreted with caution.

7.5 Suggestions for Future Research

Potential researchers may consider the following recommendations for further studies:

First, the empirical findings of the capital structure determinants are from a global perspective. Even though we have included cross-*country* and cross-*industry* views, the notion of this analysis remained global (superficial). Hence, it offers to study whether the observed financing effects and leverage determinants show significant differences in individual countries or industries analysis. Furthermore, future researches could focus on potential equity determinants and regress it against the equity ratios.

Second, future studies could split the full sample into subsamples (e.g., over-/under leveraged or in small-/medium/-large) to provide more precise results about the firms' financing behavior. For instance, underleveraged firms opt to adjust faster to their target capital structure when taxes are high (unless financial flexibility is given more priority). Similarly, overleveraged firms would also adjust faster when financial distress costs are high and potentially could raise penalties. Furthermore, it is well-known that firm financing behavior varies among firms of different sizes. Future studies can focus on whether significant differences in the firm's financing pattern exist in small, medium, and large firm samples.

Third, the Market-Timing Theory might provide an additional explanation of the financing behavior of SC firms. Especially when firms' valuation is high, the notion of *Market-Timing of Equity* suggests that firms should issue equity to benefit from their stock price's overvaluation. Another string of this theory is the *Market-Timing of Debt* that indicates that companies utilize debt issuance when the interest rate is relatively low. Since financing hierarchy is a concern especially for the SC firms, future studies could provide insight on which effect is stronger when analyzing both equity-timing and debt-timing simultaneously. Specifically, if interest rates are relatively low and the market-to-book ratio is relatively high, do SC firms still engage in equity financing over debt financing.

Fourth, we strongly recommend future studies using a firm sample based on the proposed *RIEM* methodologies, i.e., *RIEM 75*, *66-33*, and *66 Index*. Over time, future studies might shed more light on the SC *(RIEM)* firms' characteristics, generate more authentic results, and change the current perception and impression that *"there is no difference between SC and SNC firms"* among the academic world.

Last, the discussions from the Shari'ah perspective serve as an exploratory consideration. It involves analogical reasoning to make the initial step developing the rationale of the proposed *Islamic Pecking Order* model, which needs an empirical confirmation of the proposed model. This can be considered the beginning of a journey to establish an Islamic capital structure theory.

References

Adam, N. L., & Bakar, N. A. (2014). Shariah Screening Process in Malaysia. *Procedia – Social and Behavioral Sciences*, *121*, 113–123. https://doi.org/10.1016/j.sbspro.2014.01.1113

Adedeji, A. (2002). *A Cross-Sectional Test of Pecking Order Hypothesis against Static Trade-Off Theory on UK Data* (Working Paper). https://doi.org/http://dx.doi.org/10.2139/ssrn.302827

Agarwal, S., & Mohtadi, H. (2004). Financial Markets and the Financing Choice of Firms: Evidence from Developing Countries. *Global Finance Journal*, *15*, 57–70.

Agca, S., & Mozumdar, A. (2004). Firm Size, Debt Capacity, and Corporate Financing Choices. *SSRN Electronic Journal*. https://doi.org/10.2139/ssrn.687369

Aggarwal, R., & Zhao, X. (2007). The leverage–value relationship puzzle: An industry effects resolution. *Journal of Economics and Business*, *59*(4), 286–297. https://doi.org/10.1016/j.jeconbus.2006.07.001

Aggarwal, R., & Zong, S. (2006). The cash flow–investment relationship: International evidence of limited access to external finance. *Journal of Multinational Financial Management*, *16*(1), 89–104. https://doi.org/10.1016/j.mulfin.2005.04.009

Ahmed, H. (2007). Issues in Islamic Corporate Finance – Capital Structure in Firms. *IRTI Research Paper Series*, 1–70.

Akerlof, G. A. (1970). Market for "Lemons": Quality Uncertainty and the Market Mechanism. *The Quarterly Journal of Economics*, *84*(3), 488–500.

Akinsomi, O., Ong, S. E., Ibrahim, M. F., & Newell, G. (2019). Does Being Islamic or Shariah-Compliant Affect Capital Structure? Evidence from Real-estate Firms in the Gulf Cooperation Council States. *SSRN Electronic Journal*, 1–27. https://doi.org/10.2139/ssrn.3346456

Al-Ajmi, J., Abo Hussain, H., & Al-Saleh, N. (2009). Decisions on capital structure in a Zakat environment with prohibition of riba: The case of Saudi Arabia. *Journal of Risk Finance*, *10*(5), 460–476. https://doi.org/10.1108/15265940911001376

Alhabshi, S. J. (2008). Stock Screening Process. *Islamic Finance Bulletin*, (20), 24–30.

Allen, D. E. (1993). The pecking order hypothesis: Australian evidence. *Applied Financial Economics*, *3*(2), 101–112. https://doi.org/10.1080/758532828

Allen, D. E., & Mizuno, H. (1989). The determinants of corporate capital structure: Japanese evidence. *Applied Economics*, *21*(5), 569–585. https://doi.org/10.1080/758524891

Allen, F., & Rajan, R. G. (2008). The Contributions of Stewart Myers to the Theory and Practice of Corporate Finance. *Journal of Applied Corporate Finance*, *20*(4), 8–19. https://doi.org/10.1017/CBO9781107415324.004

Alnori, F., & Alqahtani, F. (2019). Capital structure and speed of adjustment in non-financial firms: Does sharia compliance matter? Evidence from Saudi Arabia. *Emerging Markets Review*, *39* (August 2018), 50–67. https://doi.org/10.1016/j.ememar.2019.03.008

Alti, A. (2006). How Persistent Is the Impact of Market Timing on Capital Structure? *The Journal of Finance*, *61*(4), 1681–1710. https://doi.org/doi:10.1111/j.1540-6261.2006.00886.x

Alves, P. F. P., & Ferreira, M. A. (2011). Capital structure and law around the world. *Journal of Multinational Financial Management*, *21*(3), 119–150. https://doi.org/10.1016/j.mulfin.2011.02.001

Alves, P. F. P., & Francisco, P. (2013). *The Impact of Institutional Environment in Firms' Capital Structure during the Recent Financial Crisis* (Working Paper). http://mpra.ub.uni-muenchen.de/51300/

Andres, C., Cumming, D., Karabiber, T., & Schweizer, D. (2014). Do markets anticipate capital structure decisions? – Feedback effects in equity liquidity. *Journal of Corporate Finance*, *27*, 133–156. https://doi.org/10.1016/j.jcorpfin.2014.02.006

Antoniou, A., Guney, Y., & Paudyal, K. (2002). *Determinants of Corporate Capital Structure: Evidence from European Countries* (Working Paper).

https://doi.org/10.1515/9783110713664-008

Antoniou, A., Guney, Y., & Paudyal, K. (2008). The Determinants of Capital Structure: Capital Market-Oriented versus Bank-Oriented Institutions. *Journal of Financial and Quantitative Analysis, 43*(01), 59–92. https://doi.org/10.1017/S0022109000002751

Arellano, M., & Bond, S. (1991). Some tests of specification for panel data: Monte Carlo evidence and an application to employment equations. *The Review of Economic Studies, 58*(2), 277–297.

Arellano, M., & Bover, O. (1995). Another look at the instrumental variable estimation of error-components models. *Journal of Econometrics, 68*(1), 29–51. https://doi.org/10.1016/0304-4076(94)01642-D

Arif, I. A. I., & Mai, M. U. (2020). The Determinants of Capital Structure: A Comparative Study between Sharia and Non-Sharia Manufacturing Companies in Indonesia Stock Exchange (IDX). *International Journal of Applied Business Research, 2*(01), 73–85. https://doi.org/10.35313/ijabr.v0i0.67

Ariff, M., Hassan, T., & Shamsher, M. (2008). How Capital Structure Adjusts Dynamically During Financial Crises. *Corporate Finance Review, 13*(3), 11–24.

Askari, H., Iqbal, Z., Mirakhor, A., & Krichene, N. (2012). *Risk Sharing in Finance: The Islamic Finance Alternative*. Wiley.

Autore, D. M., & Kovacs, T. (2010). Equity issues and temporal variation in information asymmetry. *Journal of Banking and Finance, 34*(1), 12–23. https://doi.org/10.1016/j.jbankfin.2009.06.016

Bacha, O. I., & Mirakhor, A. (2013). *Islamic Capital Markets – A Comparative Approach*. John Wiley & Sons, Ltd.

Bacha, O. I., Mirakhor, A., & Askari, H. (2015). Risk sharing in corporate and public finance: the contribution of Islamic finance. *PSL Quarterly Review, 68*(274), 187–213.

Baker, M., & Wurgler, J. (2002). Market Timing and Capital Structure. *Journal of Finance, 57*, 1–48.

Baltagi, B. H. (2005). *Econometric Analysis of Panel Data*. John Wiley & Sons Ltd. https://doi.org/10.1017/CBO9781107415324.004

Barclay, M. J., Smith, C. W., & Morellec, E. (2006). On the debt capacity of growth options. *Journal of Business, 79*(1), 37–59. https://doi.org/10.1086/497404

Barry, C. B., Mann, S. C., Mihov, V. T., & Rodríguez, M. (2008). Corporate Debt Issuance and the Historical Level of Interest Rates. *Financial Management, 37*(3), 413–430. https://doi.org/10. 1111/j.1755-053X.2008.00019.x

Bartoloni, E. (2013). Capital structure and innovation: causality and determinants. *Empirica, 40*(1), 111–151. https://doi.org/10.1007/s10663-011-9179-y

Bas, T., Muradoglu, G., & Phylaktis, K. (2009). *Determinants of Capital Structure in Developing Countries* (Working Paper).

Baskin, J. (1989). An Empirical Investigation of the Pecking Order Hypothesis. *Financial Management, 18*(1), 26–35.

Baum, C. F., Schaffer, M. E., & Stillman, S. (2003). Instrumental variables and GMM: Estimation and testing. *The Stata Journal, 3*(1), 1–31. https://doi.org/The Stata Journal

Baxter, N. D. (1967). Leverage, Risk of Ruin and the Cost of Capital. *The Journal of Finance, 22*(3), 395–403. https://doi.org/10.2307/2978892

Beattie, V., Goodacre, A., & Thomson, S. J. (2006). Corporate Financing Decisions: UK Survey Evidence. *Journal of Business Finance and Accounting, 33*(9–10), 1402–1434. https://doi.org/10.1111/j.1468-5957.2006.00640.x

Beck, T., Demirgüç-Kunt, A., & Maksimovic, V. (2002). Financing patterns around the world: Are small firms different? *Journal of Financial Economics, 89*(3), 467–487. https://doi.org/10.1016/j.jfineco.2007.10.005

Beck, T., Demirgüç-Kunt, A., & Maksimovic, V. (2008). Financing patterns around the world: Are small firms different? *Journal of Financial Economics, 89*(3), 467–487. https://doi.org/10.1016/j.jfineco.2007.10.005

Beck, T., Demirgüç-Kunt, A., & Merrouche, O. (2013). Islamic vs. conventional banking: Business model, efficiency and stability. *Journal of Banking & Finance*, *37*(2), 433–447. https://doi.org/10.1016/j.jbankfin.2012.09.016

Berk, J., & DeMarzo, P. (2014). *Corporate Finance* (3rd ed.). Pearson.

Blundell, R., & Bond, S. (1998). Initial conditions and moment restrictions in dynamic panel data models. *Journal of Econometrics*, *87*(1), 115–143. https://doi.org/10.1016/S0304-4076(98)00009-8

Bokpin, G. A. (2009). Macroeconomic development and capital structure decisions of firms: Evidence from emerging market economies. *Studies in Economics and Finance*, *26*(2), 129–142. https://doi.org/10.1108/10867370910963055

Bond, S. (2002). Dynamic Panel Data Models: A Guide to Micro Data Methods and Practice. *Portuguese Economic Journal*, *1*, 141–162. https://doi.org/10.1007/s10258-002-0009-9

Bontempi, M. E. (2002). The dynamic specification of the modified pecking order theory: its relevance to Italy. *Empirical Economics*, *27*(1), 1–22.

Booth, L., Aivazian, V., Demirgüç-Kunt, A., & Maksimovic, V. (2001). Capital Structures in Developing Countries. *Journal of Finance*, *56*(1), 87–130.

Bowman, R. G. (1980). The Importance of a Market-Value Measurement of Debt in Assessing Leverage. *Journal of Accounting Research*, *18*(1), 242–254. https://doi.org/10.2307/2490400

Bradley, M., Jarrell, G. A., & Kim, E. H. (1984). On the Existence of an Optimal Capital Structure: Theory and Evidence. *Journal of Finance*, *39*, 857–878.

Brambor, T., Clark, W. R., & Golder, M. (2006). Understanding Interaction Models: Improving Empirical Analyses. *Political Analysis*, *14*, 63–82. https://doi.org/10.1093/pan/mpi014

Braudel, F. (1982). Civilization and Capitalism. In *The Wheels of Commerce, William Collins Sons & Co Ltd London* (Harpe & Ro). University of California Press. https://doi.org/10.1023/A:1024404620759

Brealey, R. A., Myers, S. C., & Allen, F. (2010). Principles of Corporate Finance. In *Book*. The McGraw-Hill Companies. https://doi.org/10.1016/0378-4266(82)90040-1

Brennan, M., & Kraus, A. (1987). Efficient Financing under Asymmetric Information. *The Journal of Finance*, *42*(5), 1225–1243. https://doi.org/10.1111/j.1540-6261.1987.tb04363.x

Brennan, M., & Schwartz, E. S. (1984). Optimal Financial Policy and Firm Valuation. *The Journal of Finance*, *39*(3), 593–607. https://doi.org/10.1111/j.1540-6261.1984.tb03647.x

Breusch, T. S., & Pagan, A. R. (1980). The Lagrange Multiplier Test and its Applications to Model Specification in Econometrics. *The Review of Economic Studies*, *47*(1), 239–253. https://doi.org/10.2307/2297111

Brooks, C. (2014). *Introductory Econometrics for Finance* (3rd ed.). Cambridge University Press.

Bulan, L., & Yan, Z. (2009). The Pecking Order of Financing in the Firm's Life Cycle. *Banking and Finance Letter*, *1*(3), 1–42.

Byoun, S. (2008). How and when do firms adjust their capital structures toward targets? *Journal of Finance*, *63*(6), 3069–3096. https://doi.org/10.1111/j.1540-6261.2008.01421.x

Cekrezi, A. (2013). The Determinants of Capital Structure: Evidence from Albania. *Academic Journal of Interdisciplinary Studies*, *2*(9), 370–376. https://doi.org/10.5901/ajis.2013.v2n9p370

Chakraborty, I. (2010). Capital structure in an emerging stock market: The case of India. *Research in International Business and Finance*, *24*(3), 295–314. https://doi.org/10.1016/j.ribaf.2010.02.001

Chang, C., Lee, A. C., & Lee, C.-F. (2009). Determinants of capital structure choice: A structural equation modeling approach. *The Quarterly Review of Economics and Finance*, *49*(2), 197–213. https://doi.org/10.1016/j.qref.2008.03.004

Chaplinsky, S., & Niehaus, G. (1993). Do inside Ownership and Leverage Share Common Determinants? *Quarterly Journal of Business and Economics*, *32*(4), 51–65.

Chen, D.-H., Chen, C.-D., Chen, J., & Huang, Y.-F. (2013). Panel data analyses of the pecking order theory and the market timing theory of capital structure in Taiwan. *International Review of Economics & Finance*, *27*, 1–13. https://doi.org/10.1016/j.iref.2012.09.011

Chen, J. J. (2004). Determinants of capital structure of Chinese-listed companies. *Journal of Business Research*, *57*(12), 1341–1351. https://doi.org/10.1016/S0148-2963(03)00070-5

Chen, L., & Zhao, X. (2005). *Profitability, Mean Reversion of Leverage Ratios, and Capital Structure Choices*. https://doi.org/https://dx.doi.org/10.2139/ssrn.666992

Cheng, S.-R., & Shiu, C.-Y. (2007). Investor protection and capital structure: International evidence. *Journal of Multinational Financial Management*, *17*(1), 30–44. https://doi.org/10.1016/j.mulfin.2006.03.002

Chirinko, R. S., & Singha, A. R. (2000). Testing static tradeoff against pecking order models of capital structure: A critical comment. *Journal of Financial Economics*, *58*(3), 417–425. https://doi.org/10.1016/S0304-405X(00)00078-7

Chung, K. H. (1993). Asset Characteristics And Corporate Debt Policy: An Empirical Test. *Journal of Business Finance & Accounting*, *20*(1), 83–98. https://doi.org/10.1111/j.1468-5957.1993.tb00251.x

Claggett, E. T. (1991). Capital structure: convergent and pecking order evidence. *Review of Financial Economics*, *1*(1), 35.

Copeland, T. E., Weston, J. F., & Shastri, K. (2005). *Financial Theory and Corporate Policy* (4th ed.). Pearson Addison Wesley. https://doi.org/10.1016/0378-4266(81)90050-9

Correa, C. A., Fernando, L. C. B., & Nakamura, T. W. (2005). *What Determines The Capital Structure of the Largest Brazilian Firms? An Empirical Analysis Using Panel Data* (Issue 1984).

Cotei, C., & Farhat, J. (2013). *The Trade-Off Theory and The Pecking Order Theory: Are They Mutually Exclusive?* http://ssrn.com/abstract=1404576

D'Mello, R., & Ferris, S. P. (2000). The Information Effects of Analyst Activity at the Announcement of New Equity Issues. *Financial Management*, *29*(1), 78–95. https://doi.org/10.2307/3666363

Dang, V. A. (2013). Testing capital structure theories using error correction models: evidence from the UK, France and Germany. *Applied Economics*, *45*(2), 171–190. https://doi.org/10.1080/00036846.2011.597724

Dang, V. A., & Garrett, I. (2015). On corporate capital structure adjustments. *Finance Research Letters*, *14*, 56–63. https://doi.org/10.1016/j.frl.2015.05.016

Dang, V. A., Kim, M., & Shin, Y. (2014). Asymmetric adjustment toward optimal capital structure: Evidence from a crisis. *International Review of Financial Analysis*, *33*, 226–242. https://doi.org/10.1016/j.irfa.2014.02.013

Daude, C., & Fratzscher, M. (2006). *The Pecking Order of Cross-Border Investment* (Working Paper). http://ssrn.com/abstract_id=885321

Davidson, R., & MacKinnon, J. G. (2004). Instructor's Manual to Accompany Econometric Theory and Methods. In *Oxford University Press*.

De Jong, A., Kabir, R., & Nguyen, T. T. (2008). Capital structure around the world: The roles of firm- and country-specific determinants. *Journal of Banking & Finance*, *32*(9), 1954–1969. https://doi.org/10.1016/j.jbankfin.2007.12.034

De Jong, A., Verbeek, M., & Verwijmeren, P. (2007). Testing the Pecking Order Theory: The Impact of Financing Surpluses and Large Financing Deficits. *Financial Management*, *39*(2), 733–756. https://doi.org/10.1111/j.1755-053X.2010.01090.x

De Miguel, A., & Pindado, J. (2001). Determinants of capital structure: new evidence from Spanish panel data. *Journal of Corporate Finance*, *7*(1), 77–99. https://doi.org/10.1016/S0929-1199(00)00020-1

DeAngelo, H., DeAngelo, L., & Whited, T. M. (2011). Capital structure dynamics and transitory debt. *Journal of Financial Economics*, *99*(2), 235–261. https://doi.org/10.1016/j.jfineco.2010.09.005

DeAngelo, H., & Masulis, R. W. (1980). Optimal Capital Structure under Corporate and Personal Taxation. *Journal of Financial Economics*, *8*, 3–29.
Deesomsak, R., Paudyal, K., & Pescetto, G. (2004). The Determinants of Capital Structure: Evidence from the Asia Pacific Region. *Journal of Multinational Financial Management*, *14*(4–5), 387–405. https://doi.org/10.1016/j.mulfin.2004.03.001
Deesomsak, R., Paudyal, K., & Pescetto, G. (2009). Debt maturity structure and the 1997 Asian financial crisis. *Journal of Multinational Financial Management*, *19*(1), 26–42. https://doi.org/10.1016/j.mulfin.2008.03.001
Delcoure, N. (2007). The determinants of capital structure in transitional economies. *International Review of Economics & Finance*, *16*(3), 400–415. https://doi.org/10.1016/j.iref.2005.03.005
Demirgüç-Kunt, A., & Levine, R. (1999). *Bank-Based and Market-Based Financial Systems: Cross Country Comparisons* (Working Paper).
Demirgüç-Kunt, A., & Maksimovic, V. (1999). Institutions, financial markets, and firm debt maturity. *Journal of Financial Economics*, *54*(3), 295–336. https://doi.org/10.1016/S0304-405X(99)00039-2
Derigs, U., & Marzban, S. (2008). Review and analysis of current Shariah compliant equity screening practices. *International Journal of Islamic and Middle Eastern Finance and Management*, *1*(4), 285–303. https://doi.org/10.1108/17538390810919600
Dincergok, B., & Yalciner, K. (2011). Capital structure decisions of manufacturing firms' in developing countries. *Middle Eastern Finance and Economics*, *4*(12), 86–100.
Dittmar, A. (2004). Capital Structure in Corporate Spin-Offs. *The Journal of Business*, *77*(1), 9–41.
Drobetz, W., & Fix, R. (2005). What Are the Determinants of the Capital Structure? Evidence from Switzerland. *Swiss Journal of Economics and Statistics*, *141* (I),71–113. http://www.sjes.ch/papers/2005-I-3.pdf
Drukker, D. M. (2003). Testing for serial correlation in linear panel-data models. *Stata Journal*, *3*(2), 168–177. http://econpapers.repec.org/RePEc:tsj:stataj:v:3:y:2003:i:2:p:168-177
Dybvig, P. H., & Zender, J. F. (1991). Capital Structure and Dividend Irrelevance with Asymmetric Information. *The Review of Financial Studies*, *4*(1), 201–219. https://doi.org/10.1093/rfs/4.1.201
Eldomiaty, T. I., & Ismail, M. A. (2009). Modeling capital structure decisions in a transition market: Empirical analysis of firms in Egypt. *Review of Quantitative Finance and Accounting*, *32*(3), 211–233. https://doi.org/10.1007/s11156-008-0091-x
Erickson, T., & Whited, T. M. (2011). *Treating Measurement Error in Tobin's q* (Working Paper). https://doi.org/10.1093/rfs/hhr120
Fama, E. F., & French, K. R. (2002). Testing Tradeoff and Pecking Order Predictions About Dividends and Debt. *The Review of Financial Studies*, *15*(1), 1–33.
Fama, E. F., & French, K. R. (2005). Financing decisions: who issues stock? *Journal of Financial Economics*, *76*(3), 549–582. https://doi.org/10.1016/j.jfineco.2004.10.003
Fama, E. F., & Miller, M. H. (1972). *The Theory of Finance*. Holt Rinehart & Winston.
Fan, H., & Sundaresan, S. M. (2000). Debt Valuation, Renegotiation, and Optimal Dividend Policy. *The Review of Financial Studies*, *13*(4), 1057–1099. https://doi.org/10.1007/BF02809469
Fan, J. P. H., Titman, S., & Twite, G. (2012). An International Comparison of Capital Structure and Debt Maturity Choices. *The Journal of Financial and Quantitative Analysis*, *47*(1), 23–56.
Faulkender, M., & Petersen, M. A. (2006). Does the source of capital affect capital structure? *Review of Financial Studies*, *19*, 45–79. https://doi.org/10.1093/rfs/hhj003
Feidakis, A., & Rovolis, A. (2007). Capital structure choice in European Union: evidence from the construction industry. *Applied Financial Economics*, *17*(12), 989–1002. https://doi.org/10.1080/09603100600749311
Fischer, E. O., Heinkel, R., & Zechner, J. (1989). Dynamic Capital Structure Choice: Theory and Tests. *Journal of Finance*, *44*(1), 19–40. https://doi.org/10.2307/2328273

Flannery, M. J., & Hankins, K. W. (2013). Estimating dynamic panel models in corporate finance. *Journal of Corporate Finance*, *19*(1), 1–19. https://doi.org/10.1016/j.jcorpfin.2012.09.004

Flannery, M. J., & Rangan, K. P. (2006). Partial adjustment toward target capital structures. *Journal of Financial Economics*, *79*(3), 469–506. https://doi.org/10.1016/j.jfineco.2005.03.004

Forte, G., & Miglietta, F. (2007). Islamic mutual funds as faith-based funds in a socially responsible context. *SSRN Electronic Journal*, 1–27. https://doi.org/10.2139/ssrn.1012813

Frank, M. Z., & Goyal, V. K. (2003). Testing the pecking order theory of capital structure. *Journal of Financial Economics*, *67*(2), 217–248. https://doi.org/10.1016/S0304-405X(02)00252-0

Frank, M. Z., & Goyal, V. K. (2008). Trade-Off and Pecking Order Theories of Debt. In *Handbook of Empirical Corporate Finance* (pp. 135–202). https://doi.org/10.1016/B978-0-444-53265-7.50004-4

Frank, M. Z., & Goyal, V. K. (2009). Capital Structure Decisions: Which Factors are Reliably Important? *Financial Management*, 1–37.

Gajurel, D. P. (2005). Capital Structure Management in Nepalese Enterprises. *SSRN Electronic Journal*, *2005*, 0–108. https://doi.org/10.2139/ssrn.778106

Gamaleldin, F. M. (2015). Shariah-Compliant Stocks Screening and Purification. *Research Gate, October*, 1–44. https://doi.org/10.13140/RG.2.1.3063.0249

Gaud, P., Hoesli, M., & Bender, A. (2007). Debt-equity choice in Europe. *International Review of Financial Analysis*, *16*(3), 201–222. https://doi.org/10.1016/j.irfa.2006.08.003

Gaud, P., Jani, E., Hoesli, M., & Bender, A. (2005). The Capital Structure of Swiss Companies: an Empirical Analysis Using Dynamic Panel Data. *European Financial Management*, *11*(1), 51–69. https://doi.org/10.1111/j.1354-7798.2005.00275.x

Ghosh, A., & Cai, F. (1999). Capital structure: New evidence of optimality and pecking order theory. *American Business Review*, *28*, 32–38.

González, V. M., & González, F. (2014). Banking liberalization and firms' debt structure: International evidence. *International Review of Economics & Finance*, *29*, 466–482. https://doi.org/10.1016/j.iref.2013.07.008

Goyal, V. K., Lehn, K., & Racic, S. (2002). Growth opportunities and corporate debt policy: the case of the U.S. defense industry. *Journal of Financial Economics*, *64*(1), 35–59. https://doi.org/10.1016/S0304-405X(02)00070-3

Graham, J. R. (1996). Debt and the marginal tax rate. *Journal of Financial Economics*, *41*(1), 41–73. https://doi.org/http://dx.doi.org/10.1016/0304-405X(95)00857-B

Graham, J. R. (2000). How Big Are the Tax Benefits of Debt? *The Journal of Finance, LV*(5), 1901–1942.

Graham, J. R., & Harvey, C. R. (2001). The theory and practice of corporate finance: evidence from the field. *Journal of Financial Economics*, *60*(2–3), 187–243. https://doi.org/10.1016/S0304-405X(01)00044-7

Grais, W., & Pellegrini, M. (2006). Corporate Governance And Shariah Compliance In Institutions Offering Islamic Financial Services. In *Policy Research Working Papers* (Working Paper). The World Bank. https://doi.org/10.1596/1813-9450-4054

Greene, W. H. (2018). *Econometric Analysis* (Eighth ed.). Pearson.

Griliches, Z., & Hausman, J. A. (1986). Errors in variables in panel data. *Journal of Econometrics*, *31*(1), 93–118. https://doi.org/10.1016/0304-4076(86)90058-8

Gujarati, D. N. (2004). *Basic Econometrics (4th Edition)* (4th ed.). The McGraw-Hill Companies.

Guney, Y., Li, L., & Fairchild, R. (2011). The relationship between product market competition and capital structure in Chinese listed firms. *International Review of Financial Analysis*, *20*(1), 41–51. https://doi.org/10.1016/j.irfa.2010.10.003

Gungoraydinoglu, A., & Öztekin, Ö. (2011). Firm- and country-level determinants of corporate leverage: Some new international evidence. *Journal of Corporate Finance*, *17*(5), 1457–1474. https://doi.org/10.1016/j.jcorpfin.2011.08.004

Habib, F., & Ahmad, A. U. F. (2017). Revisiting the AAOIFI Shariah standards' stock screening criteria. *International Journal of Business and Society*, *18*, 151–166.

Hackbarth, D., Hennessy, C. A., & Leland, H. E. (2007). Can the Trade-off Theory Explain Debt Structure? *The Review of Financial Studies*, *20*(5), 1389–1428. https://doi.org/10.1093/rfs/hhl047

Halim, A. A., Sukor, M. E. A., & Bacha, O. I. (2019). Capital Structure and Shari'ah Compliance Firms: Malaysian Evidence. In M. Zulkhibri & T. A. Abdul Manap (Eds.), *Islamic Finance, Risk-Sharing and Macroeconomic Stability* (pp. 63–79). Springer International Publishing. https://doi.org/10.1007/978-3-030-05225-6_4

Hanousek, J., & Shamshur, A. (2011). A stubborn persistence: Is the stability of leverage ratios determined by the stability of the economy? *Journal of Corporate Finance*, *17*(5), 1360–1376. https://doi.org/10.1016/j.jcorpfin.2011.07.004

Haron, R. (2017). *Ownership structure of family-owned firms and debt financing. evidence on Shari'ah-compliant firms in Malaysia. November*, 139–163.

Haron, R., & Ibrahim, K. (2012). Target Capital Structure and Speed of Adjustment: Panel Data Evidence on Malaysia Shariah Compliant Securities. *International Journal of Economics, Management and Accounting*, *2*(2), 87–107.

Haron, R., Ibrahim, K., & Ibrahim, I. (2011). Determinants of Target Capital Structure: Evidence on South East Asia Countries. *Journal of Business and Policy Research*, *6*(3), 39–61.

Harris, M., & Raviv, A. (1991). The Theory of Capital Structure. *Journal of Finance*, *46*(1), 297–355.

Hart, O., & Moore, J. (1995). Debt and Seniority: An Analysis of the Role of Hard Claims in Constraining Management. *The American Economic Review*, *85*(3), 567–585.

Hatfield, G. B., Cheng, L. T. W., & Davidson, W. N. (1994). The determination of optimal capital structure: The effect of firm and industry debt ratios on market value. *Journal of Financial and Strategy Decisions*, *7*(3), 1–14.

Hatzinikolaou, D., Katsimbris, G. M., & Noulas, A. G. (2002). Inflation uncertainty and capital structure. *International Review of Economics & Finance*, *11*(1), 45–55. https://doi.org/10.1016/S1059-0560(01)00085-5

Haugen, R. A., & Senbet, L. W. (1978). The Insignificance of Bankruptcy Cost to the Theory of Optimal Capial Structure. *The Journal of Finance*, *33*(2), 383–393. https://doi.org/10.1111/j.1540-6261.1978.tb04855.x

Hausman, J. A. (1978). Specification Tests in Econometrics. *The Econometric Society*, *46*(6), 1251–1271. https://doi.org/10.1017/CBO9781107415324.004

Helwege, J., & Liang, N. (1996). Is there a pecking order? Evidence from a panel of IPO firms. *Journal of Financial Economics*, *40*(3), 429–458. https://doi.org/10.1016/0304-405X(95)00851-5

Hennessy, C. A., & Whited, T. M. (2005). Debt Dynamics. *The Journal of Finance*, *60*(3), 1129–1165. https://doi.org/10.1111/j.1540-6261.2005.00758.x

Ho, C. S. F. (2015). International comparison of Shari'ah compliance screening standards. *International Journal of Islamic and Middle Eastern Finance and Management*, *8*(2), 222–245. https://doi.org/10.1108/IMEFM-07-2014-0065

Högfeldt, P., & Oborenko, A. (2005). Does Market Timing or Enhanced Pecking Order Determine Capital Structure? In *SSRN Electronic Journal*. https://doi.org/10.2139/ssrn.592501

Hovakimian, A., Hovakimian, G., & Tehranian, H. (2004). Determinants of target capital structure: The case of dual debt and equity issues. *Journal of Financial Economics*, *71*(3), 517–540. https://doi.org/10.1016/S0304-405X(03)00181-8

Hovakimian, A., & Li, G. (2011). In search of conclusive evidence: How to test for adjustment to target capital structure. *Journal of Corporate Finance*, *17*(1), 33–44. https://doi.org/10.1016/j.jcorpfin.2010.07.004

Hovakimian, A., Opler, T., & Titman, S. (2001). The Debt-Equity Choice. *The Journal of Financial and Quantitative Analysis*, *36*(1), 1–24. https://doi.org/10.2307/2676195

Hsiao, C. (2003). *Analysis of Panel Data (Second Edition)*. Cambridge University Press.

Htay, S. N. N., Abedeen, Z., & Salman, S. A. (2013). Towards Standardization of Shari'ah Screening Norms and Practices. *International Journal of Humanities and Social Science Invention*, *2*(11), 23–30.

Huang, G., & Song, F. M. (2006). The determinants of capital structure: Evidence from China. *China Economic Review*, *17*(1), 14–36. https://doi.org/10.1016/j.chieco.2005.02.007

Huang, R., & Ritter, J. R. (2004). *Testing the market timing theory of capital structure*.

Huang, R., & Ritter, J. R. (2009). Testing Theories of Capital Structure and Estimating the Speed of Adjustment. *Journal of Financial and Quantitative Analysis*, *44*(2), 237–271. https://doi.org/10.1017/S0022109009090152

Ibrahim, H., Zulkafli, A. H., & Ying, T. H. (2015). Capital Structure of Shariah-Compliant Companies in Malaysia. *Advanced Science Letters*, *21*, 937–941.

Ibrahimo, M. V., & Barros, C. P. (2009). Relevance or irrelevance of capital structure? *Economic Modelling*, *26*(2), 473–479. https://doi.org/10.1016/j.econmod.2008.10.003

ISRA. (2016). *Islamic Financial System: Principles & Operation*. International Shari'ah Research Academy for Islamic Finance (ISRA).

Jensen, M. C. (1986). Agency Costs of Free Cash Flow, Corporate Finance, and Takeovers Agency Costs of Free Cash Flow, Corporate Finance, and Takeovers. *American Economic Review*, *76*(2), 323–329. https://doi.org/10.2139/ssrn.99580

Jensen, M. C., & Meckling, W. H. (1976). Theory of the firm: Managerial Behavior, Agency Costs and Ownership Structure. *Journal of Financial Economics*, *3*(4), 305–360. https://doi.org/10.1016/0304-405X(76)90026-X

Johnson, S. a. (2003). Debt Maturity and the Effects of Growth Opportunities and Liquidity Risk on Leverage. *Review of Financial Studies*, *16*(1), 209–236. https://doi.org/10.1093/rfs/16.1.209

Jung, K., Kim, Y.-C., & Stulz, R. M. (1996). Timing, investment opportunities, managerial discretion, and the security issue decision. *Journal of Financial Economics*, *42*(2), 159–186. https://doi.org/10.1016/0304-405X(96)00881-1

Kane, A., Marcus, A. J., & McDonald, R. L. (1984). *How Big is the Tax Advantage to Debt?* (Working Paper). https://doi.org/10.3386/w1286

Kayhan, A., & Titman, S. (2007). Firms' histories and their capital structures. *Journal of Financial Economics*, *83*(1), 1–32. https://doi.org/10.1016/j.jfineco.2005.10.007

Kayo, E. K., & Kimura, H. (2011). Hierarchical determinants of capital structure. *Journal of Banking & Finance*, *35*(2), 358–371. https://doi.org/10.1016/j.jbankfin.2010.08.015

Kester, C. W. (1986). Capital and Ownership Structure- A Comparison of United Studies and Japanese Manufacturing Corporations. *Financial Management*, *15*, 5–16.

Khatkhatay, M. H., & Nisar, S. (2007a). Investment in Stocks: A Critical Review of Dow Jones Shariah Screening Norms. *International Conference on Islamic Capital Markets*.

Khatkhatay, M. H., & Nisar, S. (2007b). Shariah Compliant Equity Investments: an Assessment of Current Screening Norms. *Islamic Economic Studies*, *15*(1), 47–76.

Kim, E. H. (1978). A Mean Variance Theory of Optimal Capital Structure and Corporate Debit Capacity. *The Journal of Finance*, *33*(1), 45–63. https://doi.org/10.1111/j.1540-6261.1978.tb03388.x

Kim, W. S., & Sorensen, E. H. (1986). Evidence on the Impact of the Agency Costs of Debt on Corporate Debt Policy. *The Journal of Financial and Quantitative Analysis*, *21*(2), 131–144. https://doi.org/10.2307/2330733

Kraus, A., & Litzenberger, R. H. (1973). A State-Preference Model of Optimal Financial Leverage. *The Journal of Finance*, *28*(4), 911–922. https://doi.org/10.1111/j.1540-6261.1973.tb01415.x

Kremp, E., Stöss, E., & Gerdesmeier, D. (1999). *Estimation of a debt function: evidence from French and German firm panel data* (Working Paper).

Leland, H. E. (1994). Corporate Debt Value, Bond Covenants, and Optimal Capital Structure. *The Journal of Finance*, *49*(4), 1213–1252. https://doi.org/10.1111/j.1540-6261.1994.tb02452.x

Leland, H. E., & Pyle, D. H. (1977). Informational Asymmetries, Financial Structure, and Financial Intermediation. *The Journal of Finance*, *32*(2), 371–387.

Lemmon, M. L., & Zender, J. F. (2010). Debt Capacity and Tests of Capital Structure Theories. *Journal of Financial and Quantitative Analysis*, *45*(5), 1161–1187. https://doi.org/10.1017/S0022109010000499

Levine, R., Loayza, N., & Beck, T. (2000). Financial Intermediation and Growth: Causality and Causes Additional Tables and Figures. *Journal of Monetary Economics*, *46*(August), 31–77.

Lin, Y. H., Hu, S. Y., & Chen, M. S. (2008). Testing pecking order prediction from the viewpoint of managerial optimism: Some empirical evidence from Taiwan. *Pacific Basin Finance Journal*, *16*(1–2), 160–181. https://doi.org/10.1016/j.pacfin.2007.04.007

Long, M. S., & Malitz, I. B. (1985). Investment patterns and financial leverage. *Corporate Capital Structures in the United States, I*, 325–352. https://doi.org/10.2307/2328856

López-Gracia, J., & Sogorb-Mira, F. (2008). Testing trade-off and pecking order theories financing SMEs. *Small Business Economics*, *31*(2), 117–136. http://www.jstor.org/stable/40650934

Lucas, D. J., & McDonald, R. L. (1990). Equity Issues and Stock Price Dynamics. *The Journal of Finance*, *45*(4), 1019–1043.

MacKay, P., & Phillips, G. M. (2005). How Does Industry Affect Firm Financial Structure? *Review of Financial Studies*, *18*(4), 1433–1466. https://doi.org/10.1093/rfs/hhi032

Mackie-Mason, J. K. (1990). Do Taxes affect Corporate Financing Decisions. *Journal of Finance*, *45*, 1417–1493.

Mahajan, A., & Tartaroglu, S. (2008). Equity market timing and capital structure: International evidence. *Journal of Banking & Finance*, *32*(5), 754–766. https://doi.org/10.1016/j.jbankfin.2007.05.007

Mahfooz, S. bin, & Ahmed, H. (2014). Sharīah investment screening criteria: A critical review. *Journal of King Abdulaziz University, Islamic Economics*, *27*(1), 111–145. https://doi.org/10.4197/Islec.27-1.1

Mai, M. U. (2019). Determinants of capital structure in Sharia criteria manufacturing firms on the Indonesia Stock Exchange. *Jurnal Keuangan Dan Perbankan*, *23*(3), 418–429. https://doi.org/10.26905/jkdp.v23i3.1860

Marsh, P. (1982). The Choice Between Equity and Debt: An Empirical Study. *Journal of Finance*, *37*(1), 121–144.

Matlay, H. (2005). The Impact of Resources on SMEs: Critical Perspectives. *Journal of Small Business and Enterprise Development*, *12*, 155–290.

McDaniel, W. R., Madura, J., & Akhigbe, A. (1994). The Valuation Effects of Frequent Common Stock Issuance. *The Journal of Financial Research, XVII*(3), 417–426.

McMillan, D. G., & Camara, O. (2012). Dynamic capital structure adjustment: US MNCs & DCs. *Journal of Multinational Financial Management*, *22*(5), 278–301. https://doi.org/10.1016/j.mulfin.2012.10.001

Mella-Barral, P. (1999). The dynamics of default and debt reorganization. *Review of Financial Studies*, *12*(3), 535–578. https://doi.org/10.1093/rfs/12.3.535

Mian, K. M. (2014). Sharia screening and Islamic equity indexes. In *Islamic Finance: A Practical Guide* (pp. 1–200).

Michaelas, N., Chittenden, F., & Poutziouris, P. (1999). Financial Policy and Capital Structure Choice in U.K. SMEs: Empirical Evidence from Company Panel Data. *Small Business Economics*, *12*(2), 113–130. https://doi.org/10.1023/A:1008010724051

Miller, M. H. (1977). Debt and Taxes. *Journal of Finance*, *32*, 261–275.

Mitton, T. (2008). Why have debt ratios increased for firms in emerging markets? *European Financial Management*, *14*(1), 127–151. https://doi.org/10.1111/j.1468-036X.2007.00430.x

Modigliani, F., & Miller, M. H. (1958). The Cost of Capital, Corporation Finance, and the Theory of Investment. *American Economic Review*, *48*(6), 261–297.

Modigliani, F., & Miller, M. H. (1963). Corporate Income Taxes and the Cost of Capital – A Correction. *American Economic Review*, *53*(3), 433–443.

Mohd-Sanusi, Z., Ismail, R., Hudayati, A., & Harjito, D. A. (2015). Screening process of Shariah-compliant companies: The relevance of financial risk management. *International Journal of Economics and Management*, *9*(1), 177–195.

Myers, S. C. (1977). Determinants of corporate borrowing. *Journal of Financial Economics*, *5*(2), 147–175. https://doi.org/10.1016/0304-405X(77)90015-0

Myers, S. C. (1984). The Capital Structure Puzzle. *The Journal of Finance*, *39*(3), 574–592. https://doi.org/10.1111/j.1540-6261.1984.tb03646.x

Myers, S. C. (1993). Still Searching for Optimal Capital Structure? *Journal of Applied Corporate Finance*, *6*(1), 80–105. https://doi.org/10.1111/j.1745-6622.1993.tb00369.x

Myers, S. C. (2001). Capital structure. *The Journal of Economic Perspectives*, *15*(2), 81–102.

Myers, S. C. (2002). Financing of Corporations. *Handbook of the Economics of Finance*, *2001*, 1–41.

Myers, S. C., & Majluf, N. S. (1984). Corporate financing and investment decisions when firms have information that investors do not have. *Journal of Financial Economics*, *13*(2), 187–221. https://doi.org/10.1016/0304-405X(84)90023-0

Najib, N. H. B., Hamid, I. R. B., Nasarudin, S. N. B., & Saiti, B. (2014). The comparison of Shariah screening methodology for stocks between Malaysia Security Commission criteria and Dow Jones method: A critical assessment. *Unikl Business School Management and Entrepreneurship Conference, December*, 1–12.

Ni, J., & Yu, M. (2008). Testing the Pecking-Order Theory: Evidence from Chinese Listed Companies. *The Chinese Economy*, *41*(1), 97–113. https://doi.org/10.2753/CES1097-1475410105

Obaidullah, M. (2007). *Teaching Corporate Finance from an Islamic Perspective*. Islamic Economics Research Centre.

Ozkan, A. (2001). Determinants of Capital Structure and Adjustment to Long Run Target: Evidence From UK Company Panel Data. *Journal of Business Finance & Accounting*, *28*(1–2), 175–198. https://doi.org/10.1111/1468-5957.00370

Öztekin, Ö. (2013). Capital structure decisions around the world: Which factors are reliably important? *Journal of Financial and Quantitative Analysis*, *50*(3), 301–323. https://doi.org/10.2139/ssrn.1464471

Pandey, I. M. (2002). Capital Structure and Market Power Interaction: Evidence from Malaysia. *Capital Market Review*, *10*(1), 23–40.

Pao, H.-T. (2008). A comparison of neural network and multiple regression analysis in modeling capital structure. *Expert Systems with Applications*, *35*(3), 720–727. https://doi.org/10.1016/j.eswa.2007.07.018

Petersen, M. A. (2009). Estimating Standard Errors in Finance Panel Data Sets: Comparing Approaches. *Review of Financial Studies*, *22*(1), 435–480. https://doi.org/10.1093/rfs/hhn053

Piaw, L. L. T., & Jais, M. (2014a). How do firms in country with dual-financial system determine their Capital Structure – Evidence from Malaysia. *Journal of Global Management*, *8*(7), 55–67. https://doi.org/10.1016/S0140-3664(14)00351-X

Piaw, L. L. T., & Jais, M. (2014b). The Capital Structure of Malaysian Firms in the Aftermath of Asian Financial Crisis 1997. *Journal of Global Business and Economics*, *8*(1), 24–41.

Raghibi, A., & Oubdi, L. (2020). Shari'ah-compliant Stock Screening: A Financial Perspective. In *MPRA Munich Personal RePEc Archive* (Issue 101845).

Rahim, N., Mat Nor, F., Ramli, N., & Marzuki, A. (2020). Determinants of Capital Structure for Malaysian Shariah-Compliant Firms: The Impact of Revised Screening Methodology. *International Journal of Banking and Finance*, *14*(1), 45–74. https://doi.org/10.32890/ijbf2019.14.0.9911

Rajan, R. G., & Zingales, L. (1995). What do we know about Capital Structure? Some evidence from International Data.pdf. *Journal of Finance*, *50*(5), 1421–1460.

Ramli, N. E., & Haron, R. (2017a). Debt Determinants of Shari'ah Approved Firms: Empirical Evidence from Malaysia. *Journal of Islamic Finance (Special Issue)*, *6*(1), 188–204. https://doi.org/10.12816/0047349

Ramli, N. E., & Haron, R. (2017b). Target Capital Structure and Speed of Adjustment: A Dynamic Evidence From Shariah Approved Firms in Malaysia. *The Journal of Muamalat and Islamic Finance Research*, *14*(2), 65–91.

Ronn, E. I., & Senbet, L. W. (1995). Debt and market incompleteness. *Journal of Banking & Finance*, *19*(8), 1379–1400.

Roodman, D. (2009). How to xtabond2: An introduction to difference and system GMM in Stata. *Stata Journal*, *9*(1), 86–136.

Ross, S. A. (1977). The Determination of Financial Structure: The Incentive-Signalling Approach. *Bell Journal of Economics*, *8*(1), 23–40.

Ross, S. A. (1985). Debt and Taxes and Uncertainty. *The Journal of Finance*, *40*(3), 637–657. https://doi.org/10.2307/2327786

Sabiwalsky, R. (2010). Nonlinear modelling of target leverage with latent determinant variables – new evidence on the trade-off theory. *Review of Financial Economics*, *19*(4), 137–150. https://doi.org/10.1016/j.rfe.2010.06.001

Sahudin, Z., Ismail, Z., Sulaiman, S., Rahman, H. A., & Jaafar, M. N. (2019). Capital Structure Determinants of Shariah-compliant Firms. *Journal of Emerging Economies and Islamic Research*, *7*(1), 65. https://doi.org/10.24191/jeeir.v7i1.7256

Saiti, B., & Ahmad, K. (2017). Fundamentals, Universe Creation and Appraisal Of Major Shari'ah-Compliant Stocks Screening Methodologies. *Journal of Islamic Thought and Civilization*, *53*(9), 1689–1699.

Sakai, K. (2009). Financing Behavior of Japanese Firms. *Japanese Economy*, *36*(4), 3–30. https://doi.org/10.2753/JES1097-203X360401

Sani, N., & Othman, R. (2013). Revision of Shari'ah screening methodology: The status of Shari'ah compliant companies in Malaysia. *International Conference On Management*.

Sarafidis, V., Yamagata, T., & Robertson, R. (2006). A Test of Cross-Section Dependence for a Linear Dynamic Panel Model with Regressors. *Faculty of Economics, University of Cambridge*, 1–29.

Scott, J. H. (1976). A Theory of Optimal Capital Structure. *The Bell Journal of Economics*, *7*(1), 33–54. https://doi.org/10.2307/3003189

Seifert, B., & Gonenc, H. (2008). The international evidence on the pecking order hypothesis. *Journal of Multinational Financial Management*, *18*(3), 244–260. https://doi.org/10.1016/j.mulfin.2007.10.002

Sequeira, T. N., & Nunes, P. M. (2008). Does Country Risk Influence International Tourism? A Dynamic Panel Data Analysis. *Economic Record*, *84*(265), 223–236. https://doi.org/10.1111/j.1475-4932.2008.00464.x

Shyam-Sunder, L., & Myers, S. C. (1999). Testing static tradeoff against pecking order models of capital structure. *Journal of Financial Economics*, *51*(2), 219–244. https://doi.org/10.1016/S0304-405X(98)00051-8

Standard & Poor's. (2006). *Corporate Ratings Criteria. 1*, 1–128.

Standard & Poor's. (2020). *Dow Jones Islamic Market Indices Methodology. January*, 1–42.

Stöter, A. (2013). *Capital Structure Decisions and the Use of Factoring* [Universität zu Köln]. http://kups.ub.uni-koeln.de/5165/1/Dissertation_08.06.2013_Alwin_Stoeter.pdf

Strebulaev, I. A. (2004). *Do Tests of Capital Structure Theory Mean What They Say?* (Working Paper).

Strebulaev, I. A., & Whited, T. M. (2012). Dynamic models and structural estimation in corporate finance. *Foundations and Trends in Finance, June*, 1–160. https://doi.org/10.2139/ssrn.2091854

Stulz, R. M. (1990). Managerial discretion and optimal financing policies. *Journal of Financial Economics*, *26*(1), 3–27. https://doi.org/10.1016/0304-405X(90)90011-N

Sun, J. (2013). *Research on Capital Structure and Financing Decision: Evidence from the UK*. Durham University.

Taggart, R. A. (1977). A Model of Corporate Financing Decisions. *The Journal of Finance*, *32*(5), 1467–1484. https://doi.org/10.2307/2326804

Thabet, O. Bin, & Hanefah, M. M. (2014). Capital Structure in Islamic Capital Markets: Evidences From Bursa Malaysia. *Journal of Developing Areas*, *2014*(2001).

Thabet, O. Bin, Shawtari, F. A., Ayedh, A. M., & Ali, F. (2017). Capital structure of Malaysian Shari'ah-compliant firms. *Journal of King Abdulaziz University, Islamic Economics*, *30*(1), 105–116. https://doi.org/10.4197/Islec.30-1.10

Titman, S., & Tsyplakov, S. (2006). A Dynamic Model of Optimal Capital Structure. *McCombs Research Paper Series, May*. https://doi.org/10.1093/rof/rfm017

Titman, S., & Wessels, R. (1988). The Determinants of Capital Structure Choice. *Journal of Finance*, *43*(1), 1–19.

Tong, G., & Green, C. J. (2005). Pecking order or trade-off hypothesis? Evidence on the capital structure of Chinese companies. *Applied Economics*, *37*(19), 2179–2189. https://doi.org/10.1080/00036840500319873

Trezevant, R. (1992). Debt Financing and Tax Status: Tests of the Substitution Effect and the Tax Exhaustion Hypothesis Using Firms' Responses to the Economic Recovery Tax Act of 1981. *The Journal of Finance*, *47*(4), 1557–1568.

Tsuji, C. (2011). An International Survey of the Evidence of the Pecking Order Theory of Corporate Financing. *Business and Economic Research*, *1*(1), 1–13. https://doi.org/10.5296/ber.v1i1.952

Tversky, A., & Kahneman, D. (1981). The framing of decisions and the psychology of choice. *Science*, *211* (4481),453 LP – 458. https://doi.org/10.1126/science.7455683

Vasiliou, D., & Daskalakis, N. (2009). Behavioral Capital Structure: Is the Neoclassical Paradigm Threatened? Evidence from the Field. *Journal of Behavioral Finance*, *10*(1), 19–32. https://doi.org/10.1080/15427560902719802

Verbeek, M. (2008). *A Guide to Modern Econometrics* (2nd ed.). John Wiley & Sons Ltd. https://doi.org/10.1017/CBO9781107415324.004

Wald, J. K. (1999). How Firm Characteristics Affect Capital Structure: An International Comparison. *Journal of Financial Research*, *12*(2), 161–187.

Weigl, J. (2011). *Market-Timing of Capital Structure and Factors Influencing the Leverage Decision of Firms*. University of Chemnitz.

Welch, I. (2004). Capital Structure and Stock Returns. *Journal of Political Economy*, *112*(1), 106–132. https://doi.org/10.1086/379933

Welch, I. (2011). Two Common Problems in Capital Structure Research: The Financial-Debt-To-Asset Ratio and Issuing Activity Versus Leverage Changes. *International Review of Finance*, *11*(1), 1–17. https://doi.org/10.1111/j.1468-2443.2010.01125.x

Williamson, O. E. (1988). Corporate Finance and Corporate Governance. *The Journal of Finance*, *43*(3), 567–591. https://doi.org/10.1111/j.1540-6261.1988.tb04592.x

Wiwattanakantang, Y. (1999). An empirical study on the determinants of the capital structure of Thai firms. *Pacific-Basin Finance Journal*, *7*(3–4), 371–403. https://doi.org/10.1016/S0927-538X(99)00007-4

Wooldridge, J. M. (2002). *Econometric Analysis of Cross Section and Panel Data*. The MIT Press. https://doi.org/10.1515/humr.2003.021

Wooldridge, J. M. (2010). *Econometric Analysis of Cross Section and Panel Data* (2nd ed.). The MIT Press.

Yildirim, R., & Ilhan, B. (2018). Shari'ah Screening Methodology – New Shari'ah Compliant Approach. *Journal of Islamic Economics, Banking and Finance*, *14*(1), 168–191. http://ibtra.com/pdf/journal/v14_n1_article8.pdf

Yildirim, R., Masih, M., & Bacha, O. I. (2018). Determinants of capital structure: evidence from Shari'ah compliant and non-compliant firms. *Pacific Basin Finance Journal*, *51*, 198–219. https://doi.org/10.1016/j.pacfin.2018.06.008

Zandi, G., Razak, D. A., & Hussin, N. H. (2014). Stock market screening: An analogical study on conventional and shariah-compliant stock markets. *Asian Social Science*, *10*(22), 270–279. https://doi.org/10.5539/ass.v10n22p270

Appendices

Appendix A

Table A.1: Structure of Panel Data (macro perspective).

Countries	Legal System	Economic Dev.	Financial System
United States	common law	developed	market-based
United Kingdom	common law	developed	market-based
Canada	common law	developed	market-based
Japan	code/mix law	developed	bank-based
South Korea	code/mix law	developing	market-based
Taiwan	code/mix law	developing	bank-based
India	common law	developing	bank-based

Source: own contribution, in reference to Demirguc-Kunt and Levine (1999) and Demirguc-Kunt and Maksimovic (2002).

https://doi.org/10.1515/9783110713664-009

Table A.2: Panel Data – No. of firms per country and industry.

Sector		Manufacturing					Services		Sample		
Industry ICB (Level 1)		Oil and Gas	Basic Materials	Industrials	Consumer Goods	Technology	Health Care	Consumer Services	all	SC	SNC
Country	US	57	45	180	84	97	70	112	**645**	408	237
	UK	6	11	39	16	7	6	25	**110**	74	36
	CA	21	19	17	5	4	1	10	**77**	53	24
	JP	4	39	88	72	25	28	60	**316**	120	196
	SK	4	12	29	26	6	3	6	**86**	31	55
	TW	1	6	17	17	26		5	**72**	34	38
	IN	7	11	30	27	7	15	3	**100**	71	29
Sample	**all**	**100**	**143**	**400**	**247**	**172**	**123**	**221**	**1406**	**791**	**615**
	SC	66	67	194	141	134	97	92	**791**		
	SNC	34	76	206	106	38	26	129	**615**		
% of	**all**	**7.1%**	**10.2%**	**28.4%**	**17.6%**	**12.2%**	**8.7%**	**15.7%**	**100%**	**57%**	**43%**
	SC	4.7%	4.8%	13.8%	10.0%	9.5%	6.9%	6.5%	**57%**		
	SNC	2.4%	5.4%	14.7%	7.5%	2.7%	1.8%	9.2%	**43%**		

Source: own contribution.

Table A.3: Panel Data – No. of observation per country and industry.

Sector		Manufacturing					Services		Sample		
Industry ICB (Level 1)		Oil and Gas	Basic Materials	Industrials	Consumer Goods	Technology	Health Care	Consumer Services	all	SC	SNC
Country	US	441	337	1531	669	752	606	912	**5248**	3518	1730
	UK	48	86	310	123	63	58	190	**878**	606	272
	CA	173	157	141	48	29	4	77	**629**	441	188
	JP	35	335	788	574	201	223	516	**2672**	931	1741
	SK	39	97	206	204	36	27	45	**654**	217	437
	TW	10	58	138	139	193		49	**587**	263	324
	IN	66	94	249	240	70	141	23	**883**	642	241
Sample	**all**	**812**	**1164**	**3363**	**1997**	**1344**	**1059**	**1812**	**11551**	**6618**	**4933**
	SC	556	527	1668	1150	1089	867	761	**6618**		
	SNC	256	637	1695	847	255	192	1051	**4933**		

Source: own contribution.

Table A.4: Panel Data – No. of observation per year and industry.

Sector		Manufacturing					Services		Sample		
Industry ICB (Level 1)		Oil and Gas	Basic Materials	Industrials	Consumer Goods	Technology	Health Care	Consumer Services	all	SC	SNC
Years	2004	50	72	225	142	87	73	113	**762**	481	281
	2005	58	82	252	158	95	82	125	**852**	541	311
	2006	62	93	271	169	110	90	145	**940**	584	356
	2007	68	98	297	186	123	98	163	**1033**	603	430
	2008	77	112	318	198	133	102	180	**1120**	615	505
	2009	76	116	322	207	132	104	186	**1143**	616	527
	2010	86	125	341	206	146	107	197	**1208**	659	549
	2011	92	125	353	203	143	106	198	**1220**	658	562
	2012	86	122	346	195	135	104	190	**1178**	647	531
	2013	83	117	328	173	127	101	175	**1104**	635	469
	2014	74	102	310	160	113	92	140	**991**	579	412
Sample	**all**	**812**	**1164**	**3363**	**1997**	**1344**	**1059**	**1812**	**11551**	**6618**	**4933**
	SC	556	527	1668	1150	1089	867	761	**6618**		
	SNC	256	637	1695	847	255	192	1051	**4933**		

Source: own contribution.

Table A.5: Panel Data – No. of observation per dependent and independent variable.

Shari'ah Compliant								
Sample	**BLEV**	**MLEV**	**PROF**	**GRWTH**	**SIZE**	**TANG**	**RISK**	**GDP**
Overall (pooled)	6618	6618	6593	6618	6608	6618	6614	6355
United States	3518	3518	3502	3518	3514	3518	3517	3518
United Kingdom	606	606	603	606	605	606	606	606
Canada	441	441	437	441	436	441	441	441
Japan	931	931	930	931	931	931	930	931
S. Korea	217	217	217	217	217	217	216	217
Taiwan	263	263	263	263	263	263	263	–
India	642	642	641	642	642	642	641	642
Oil and Gas	556	556	550	556	551	556	556	–
Basic Materials	527	527	526	527	522	527	526	–
Industrials	1668	1668	1665	1668	1668	1668	1668	–
Cons. Goods	1150	1150	1146	1150	1150	1150	1149	–
Technologies	1089	1089	1086	1089	1089	1089	1088	–
Health Care	867	867	862	867	867	867	867	–
Cons. Services	761	761	758	761	761	761	760	–
Shari'ah Non-Compliant								
Sample	**BLEV**	**MLEV**	**PROF**	**GRWTH**	**SIZE**	**TANG**	**RISK**	**GDP**
Overall (pooled)	4933	4933	4924	4933	4933	4933	4929	4609
United States	1730	1730	1721	1730	1730	1730	1730	1730
United Kingdom	272	272	272	272	272	272	272	272
Canada	188	188	188	188	188	188	188	188
Japan	1741	1741	1741	1741	1741	1741	1739	1741
S. Korea	437	437	437	437	437	437	436	437
Taiwan	324	324	324	324	324	324	324	–
India	241	241	241	241	241	241	240	241
Oil and Gas	256	256	256	256	256	256	255	–
Basic Materials	637	637	637	637	637	637	636	–
Industrials	1695	1695	1691	1695	1695	1695	1695	–
Cons. Goods	847	847	842	847	847	847	847	–
Technologies	255	255	255	255	255	255	254	–
Health Care	192	192	192	192	192	192	191	–
Cons. Services	1051	1051	1051	1051	1051	1051	1051	–

Source: own contribution.

Table A.6: Data Types.

The table shows all the data types and their definition (used in this study) imported from Thomson Reuters (TR) Eikon, Datastream (DS) database, and World Development Indicators (WDI), (as of 2020).

Part A: Financial Items Description	
Financial Items [TR Eikon/DS DataType/Code]	**Description**
Market Capitalization [TR: *TR.CompanyMarketCap*] [DS: *WC08002*]	The Company Market Capitalization represents the sum of market value for all relevant issue level share types. The issue level market value is calculated by multiplying the requested shares type by latest close price. This item supports Default, Free Float and Outstanding shares types. The default shares type is the most widely reported outstanding shares for a market and it is most commonly Issued, Outstanding, or Listed shares.
Equity [TR: *TR.TotalEquity*]	Consists of the equity value of preferred shareholders, general and limited partners, and common shareholders, but does not include minority shareholders' interest.
Assets [TR: *TR.TotalAssetsReported*]	Represents the total assets of a company.
Fixed Assets [TR: *TR.PropertyPlantEquipmentTotalNet*]	Normally represents Property/Plant/Equipment, Total & Gross reduced by Accumulated Depreciation, Total. However, when a company reports its fixed assets net of accumulated depreciation, fixed assets are compiled using Property/Plant/Equipment, Total & Net.
Debt [TR: *TR.TotalDebtOutstanding*]	Total Debt represents total interest-bearing debt outstanding, which includes Notes/Payable/Short-Term Debt, Current Portion of Long-Term Debt/Capital Leases and Total Long-Term Debt. (It is the sum of long- and short-term debt)
Liabilities [TR: *TR.TotalLiabilities*]	Represents the sum of: Total Current Liabilities, Total Long-Term Debt, Deferred Income Tax, Minority Interest and Other Liabilities, Total.
Deferred Tax [TR: *TR.DeferredIncomeTaxLTLiability*]	Represents the sum of Defereed Income Tax – Long Term Liability [LBDT]
Preferred Stock [TR: *TR.RedeemablePreferredTtl*]	Represents the sum of Redeemable Preferred Stock and Redeemable Convertible Preferred Stock.
Retained Earnings [TR: *TR.RetainedEarnings*]	Represents residual earnings from operations, not distributed to shareholders. It may represent accumulated deficit when a company incurs losses over time.

Sales/Revenue [TR: *TR.TotalRevenue*]	Represents revenue from all of a company's operating activities after deducting any sales adjustments and their equivalents.
EBIT [TR: *TR.NormalizedEbit*]	Represents sum of: Operating Income, Unusual Expense (Income), Total of Non-Recurring Items and Total Interest Expense (Income), Net-Operating.
EBITDA [TR: *TR.NormalizedEbitda*]	Represents the sum of: Operating Income; Interest Expense (Income), Net Operating, Unusual Expense (Income), Loss (Gain) on Sale of Assets & Operating; Depreciation, Supplemental; Amortization of Acquisition Costs, Supplemental and Amortization of Intangibles, Supplemental.
GDP growth [WDI: *NY.GDP.MKTP.KD.ZG*]	Annual percentage growth rate of GDP at market prices based on constant local currency. Aggregates are based on constant 2010 U.S. dollars. GDP is the sum of gross value added by all resident producers in the economy plus any product taxes and minus any subsidies not included in the value of the products. It is calculated without making deductions for depreciation of fabricated assets or for depletion and degradation of natural resources.

Part B: Firm-specific and macroeconomic variables (Description and Formula)

Variables	Mnemonic	Formula/Description	References (not limited to)
Shari'ah Compliance	*sc*	$TotalDebt_t/([MarketCap_t + MarketCap_{(t-1)}]/2) < 33\%$	Dow Jones Islamic Index
	RIEM 66 Index	$TotalEquity_t/TotalAssets_t \geq 66.67\%$	Yildirim and Ilhan (2018)
Market Equity	*mcap*	Market capitalization (*Common Shares Outstanding * Stock Price*)	Baker and Wurgler (2002), Fama and French (2002), and R. Huang and Ritter (2004)
Book Equity	*bequity*	$TotalAssets_t - TotalLiability_t - PreferredStock_t + DeferredTaxes_t$	Baker and Wurgler (2002), Fama and French (2002), and R. Huang and Ritter (2004)
Book Debt	*bdebt*	$TotalAssets_t - bequity_t$	Baker and Wurgler (2002), Fama and French (2002), and R. Huang and Ritter (2004)
Book Leverage	*blev1*	$bdebt_t/TotalAssets_t$	Baker and Wurgler (2002), De Miguel and Pindado (2001), Fama and French (2002), R. Huang and Ritter (2004), Kayhan and Titman (2007), and Titman and Wessels (1988)
	blev2	$TotalDebt_t/(TotalDebt_t + bequity_t)$	
Market Leverage	*mlev1*	$bdebt_t/(TotalAssets_t - bequity_t + mcap_t)$	
	mlev2	$TotalDebt_t/(TotalDebt_t + mcap_t)$	

(continued)

Table A.6 (continued)

Part B: Firm-specific and macroeconomic variables (Description and Formula)			
Variables	**Mnemonic**	**Formula/Description**	**References (not limited to)**
Newly Retained Earnings	*newretearn*	$\Delta Retained\ Earnings_t / TotalAssets_t$	Baker and Wurgler (2002), and R. Huang and Ritter (2004)
Equity Issues	*equityissues*	$(\Delta bequity_t - \Delta RetainedEarnings_t)/TotalAssets_t$	Baker and Wurgler (2002), Fama and French (2002), and R. Huang and Ritter (2004)
Debt Issues	*debtissues*	$(\Delta TotalAssets_t/TotalAssets_t) - equityissues_t - newretearn_t)$	Baker and Wurgler (2002), and R. Huang and Ritter (2004)
Profitability (ROA)	*prof*	$EBITDA_t/TotalAssets_t$	Antoniou et al. (2008), Booth et al. (2001), Correa et al. (2005), Frank and Goyal (2009), Gungoraydinoglu and Öztekin (2011), Hovakimian et al. (2001), MacKay and Phillips (2005), and Titman and Wessels (1988)
Growth Opportunity (Tobin's Q)	*growth*	$(TotalAssets_t - bequity_t + mcap_t)/TotalAssets_t$	Antoniou et al. (2008), Baker and Wurgler (2002), Booth et al. (2001), J. J. Chen (2004), Correa et al. (2005), Demirgüç-Kunt and Maksimovic (1999), Frank and Goyal (2009), Gungoraydinoglu and Öztekin (2011), Hovakimian et al. (2001), MacKay and Phillips (2005), and Rajan and Zingales (1995)
Firm Size	*size*	*Natural Logarithm of* $TotalRevenue_t$	Antoniou et al. (2008); Baker and Wurgler (2002); Booth et al. (2001), J. J. Chen (2004), Correa et al. (2005), Frank and Goyal (2009), Gaud et al. (2005), Gungoraydinoglu and Öztekin (2011), MacKay and Phillips (2005), Ozkan (2001), Pandey (2002), Rajan and Zingales (1995), Titman and Wessels (1988), and Wiwattanakantang (1999)
Tangibility	*tang*	*Plant, Property and Equipment* $(Net)_t/TotalAssets_t)$	Antoniou et al. (2008), Baker and Wurgler (2002), Booth et al. (2001), J. J. Chen (2004), Feidakis and Rovolis (2007), Frank and Goyal (2009), Gaud et al. (2005), and Kayo and Kimura (2011)
Business Risk	*risk*	*Std. Deviation of EBIT, up to the previous two years of data for a given firm-year observation*	Antoniou et al. (2008), Correa et al. (2005), De Jong et al. (2008), Gungoraydinoglu and Öztekin (2011), and Pao (2008)

GDP growth	*gdp*	*GDP growth (annual %)*	Ariff et al. (2008), Bokpin (2009), Booth et al. (2001), Dincergok and Yalciner (2011), Feidakis and Rovolis (2007), Frank and Goyal (2009), Gajurel (2005), Gungoraydinoglu and Öztekin (2011), Hanousek and Shamshur (2011), Kayo and Kimura (2011), and McMillan and Camara (2012)
Financial Deficit	*def*	$debtissues_t + equityissues_t$	Baker and Wurgler (2002), R. Huang and Ritter (2009), and Mahajan and Tartaroglu (2008)
Non-Financial Debt (non-interest-bearing debt)	*nibd*	$(TotalLiabilities_t - TotalDebt_t)/\mathrm{TotalAssets}_t$	n/a
Dummy Shari'ah Compliance	*dsc*	*A categorical dummy variable that equals one (1) if the company is classified as Shari'ah Compliant (SC) and zero (0) if it is Shari'ah non-compliant (SNC).*	n/a

Appendix B

https://doi.org/10.1515/9783110713664-010

Table B.1: Participation Pattern of Panel Data.

Panel A and Panel B in this table describe the participation pattern of panel data for SC and SNC firms, respectively. We have 719 SC and 615 SNC firms in the sample. The minimum and the maximum number of years over which any SC (SNC) firm is observed is 3 and 11 (4 and 11), respectively. The most common pattern is participation in a full time-frame of 11 years (340 or 42.98% are observed in this pattern for SC, while 193 or 31.38% are observed for SNC).

The bottom line of this table gives the totals for participation patterns not observed.

Panel A: Shari'ah Compliant Sample (SC)				Panel B: Shari'ah Non-Compliant Sample (SNC)			
Code: 1, 2, … , 791		Year: 2004, 2005, … , 2014		Code: 792, 793, … , 1406		Year: 2004, 2005, … , 2014	
Frequency	**Percentage**	**Cumulative**	**Pattern**	**Frequency**	**Percentage**	**Cumulative**	**Pattern**
340	42.98	42.98	11111111111	193	31.38	31.38	11111111111
63	7.96	50.95	11111	56	9.11	40.49	1111111
40	5.06	56.01	111111111	36	5.85	46.34	11111111
32	4.05	60.05	1111111111	31	5.04	51.38	1111
29	3.67	63.72	111111	31	5.04	56.42	11111
28	3.54	67.26	1111	25	4.07	60.49	111111111
25	3.16	70.42	11111	23	3.74	64.23	111111
23	2.91	73.32	111111111	22	3.58	67.80	111111111
22	2.78	76.11	1111111	21	3.41	71.22	1111111111
189	23.89	100.00	(other patterns)	177	28.78	100.00	(other patterns)
791	**100 .00**		XXXXXXXXXXX	**615**	**100.00**		XXXXXXXXXXX

Source: own contribution.

Table B.2: Alternative Model Specification.

The table below tests alternative model specifications, as some determinants showed to be insignificant (in bold). As the table shows, the results presented in this study are robust to alternative model specifications. Column (I) and (III) are the full model specification of the book and market leverage, respectively. As for the book leverage, columns (II) exclude *growth opportunity* (reason: insignificant). For market leverage, columns (IV) and (V) exclude *GDP growth* and *business risk*, respectively. Columns (VI) exclude both insignificant variables, such as *GDP growth* and *business risk* (volatility). Company cluster robust standard errors are reported in the brackets. *, ** and *** denote significance at 10%, 5% and 1% levels, respectively. All variables are winsorized at the 1% and 99% level.

	Book Leverage		**Market Leverage**			
	(I)	**(II)**	**(III)**	**(IV)**	**(V)**	**(VI)**
Profitability	−0.196***	−0.196***	−0.227***	−0.226***	−0.227***	−0.227***
	[0.029]	[0.028]	0.027]	[0.026]	[0.027]	[0.026]
Growth	−0.000		−0.018***	−0.018***	−0.018***	−0.018***
Opportunity	[0.002]		[0.001]	[0.001]	[0.001]	[0.001]
Firm Size	0.012***	0.012***	0.030***	0.030***	0.030***	0.030***
	[0.004]	[0.004]	[0.003]	[0.003]	[0.003]	[0.003]
Tangibility	0.057*	0.057*	0.075***	0.077***	0.073***	0.076***
	[0.031]	[0.031]	[0.025]	[0.024]	[0.025]	[0.024]
Business Risk	0.140**	0.139**	−0.007	−0.003		
	[0.054]	[0.054]	[0.044]	[0.042]		
GDP growth	0.002***	0.002***	0.000		0.000	
	[0.000]	[0.000]	[0.000]		[0.000]	
Constant	0.335***	0.335***	−0.044	−0.045	−0.043	−0.043
	[0.068]	[0.067]	[0.050]	[0.049]	[0.050]	[0.049]
R^2	0.019	0.019	0.068	0.067	0.068	0.067
Adj. R^2	0.018	0.018	0.068	0.067	0.068	0.067
Firms	1333	1333	1333	1405	1333	1405
Observations	9583	9583	9583	10098	9591	10106
Estimator	FE	FE	FE	FE	FE	FE

Standard errors in brackets, * p<0.10, ** p<0.05, *** p<0.01.
Source: own contribution.

Table B.3: Estimator Selection (*Overall (pooled)*, *Country*, and *Industry*).

This table presents the post-estimation tests conducted on different estimation models for the *overall (pooled)*, *country,* and *industry* samples separately. Panel A represents the leverage regression model with book and market leverage measure, as defined in Table 4.3. Panel B represents the leverage regression model with the alternative leverage proxy defined in Table E.1 in Appendix E (Robustness Test I), and Panel C represents the pecking order model with debt and equity issue as defined in Table 6.2 (direct measure). The test is recommended by Baltagi (2005) and Wooldridge (2010). All test results have been reported for each sample. The corresponding p-value estimates of each test, namely, BPLM, Hausman, and Heteroskedasticity, are presented in the column "Results". Column "Estimator" reflects the final estimator selection.

- The BPLM test has been conducted to identify the appropriateness of using the Fixed-/Random Effects vs. OLS estimator. The BPLM test for unobservable effects tests the null hypothesis of equal variances across companies; H_0: $Var(\alpha_i) = 0$.
- The Hausman test has been applied to identify the RE estimation's consistency and efficiency vs. the FE estimation. The Hausman test examines whether the estimated coefficients from the FE estimation and the RE estimation is statistically significant; H_0: $\hat{\beta}_{RE} = \hat{\beta}_{FE}$. The rejection (p-value<0.05 (5%)) of the test is commonly interpreted as a rejection of the RE model estimation, although Wooldridge (2010) lists some potential drawbacks of this interpretation.
- The presence of heteroskedasticity or serial (auto-)correlation leads to incorrect standard errors. A modified Wald test is used to test for the presence of heteroskedasticity. A simple test of the first-order autocorrelation consists of regressing the residuals from the model estimation onto their lagged counterparts; H_0: $\hat{e}_{it} = p\hat{e}_{i,t} + \varepsilon_{it}$ (Verbeek, 2008). It tests the null hypothesis that the variances are equal across all firms.

Result Interpretation (examples)

- *Overall (pooled):* All three test results show that the null hypothesis is rejected (p-value 0.000) in Panel A, B, and C. We concluded that unobservable effects are present (rejection of OLS), and the test results favored FE over RE as the appropriate estimator. In all models, the Wald test results (i.e., homoskedasticity test) are rejected, which means that heteroskedasticity is present. Consequently, we applied the "robust" option, as discussed in Sections 4.2.1.2 and 5.2.1.
- *United Kingdom:* The BPLM test in Panel C revealed a p-value of 0.102; hence, it cannot be rejected. A non-rejection indicates that there are no unobservable effects, and consequently, OLS is deemed appropriate.
- *Technology:* The BPLM test in Panel A is rejected with a p-value 0.000. The Hausman test result with a p-value of 0.080 cannot be rejected; consequently, RE is the appropriate estimator.

Sample	Post Estimation Test		Panel A: Leverage Regression (Determinants)				Panel B: Robustness Test I				Panel C: Pecking Order (Direct Measure)			
			Book Leverage		Market Leverage		Book Leverage 2		Market Leverage 2		Debt Issue		Equity Issue	
			Results	Estimator	Results	Estimator	Results	Estimator	Results	Estimator	Results	Estimator	Results	Estimator
Overall (pooled)	BPLM	RE	0.000		0.000		0.000		0.000		0.000		0.000	
	Hausman	RE	0.000	**FE**	0.000	**FE**	0.000	**FE**	0.000	**FE**	0.000	**FE**	0.000	**FE**
	Heteroskedasticity	FE	0.000		0.000		0.000		0.000		0.000		0.000	
United States	BPLM	RE	0.000		0.000		0.000		0.000		0.000		0.000	
	Hausman	RE	0.000	**FE**	0.000	**FE**	0.000	**FE**	0.000	**FE**	0.000	**FE**	0.000	**FE**
	Heteroskedasticity	FE	0.000		0.000		0.000		0.000		0.000		0.000	
United Kingdom	BPLM	RE	0.000		0.000		0.000		0.000		0.102		0.102	
	Hausman	RE	0.000	**FE**	0.000	**FE**	0.000	**FE**	0.000	**FE**	–	**OLS**	–	**OLS**
	Heteroskedasticity	FE	0.000		0.000		0.000		0.000		–		–	
Canada	BPLM	RE	0.000		0.000		0.000		0.000		0.002		0.002	
	Hausman	RE	0.000	**FE**	0.000	**FE**	0.000	**FE**	0.000	**FE**	0.000	**FE**	0.000	**FE**
	Heteroskedasticity	FE	0.000		0.000		0.000		0.000		0.000		0.000	
Japan	BPLM	RE	0.000		0.000		0.000		0.000		1.000		1.000	
	Hausman	RE	0.000	**FE**	0.000	**FE**	0.000	**FE**	0.023	**FE**	–	**OLS**	–	**OLS**
	Heteroskedasticity	FE	0.000		0.000		0.000		0.000		–		–	
S. Korea	BPLM	RE	0.000		0.000		0.000		0.000		1.000		1.000	
	Hausman	RE	0.016	**FE**	0.000	**FE**	0.016	**FE**	0.000	**FE**	–	**OLS**	–	**OLS**
	Heteroskedasticity	FE	0.000		0.000		0.000		0.000		–		–	
Taiwan	BPLM	RE	0.000		0.000		0.000		0.000		0.073		0.073	
	Hausman	RE	0.000	**FE**	0.000	**FE**	0.006	**FE**	0.000	**FE**	–	**OLS**	–	**OLS**
	Heteroskedasticity	FE	0.000		0.000		0.000		0.000		–		–	
India	BPLM	RE	0.000		0.000		0.000		0.000		0.382		0.382	
	Hausman	RE	0.000	**FE**	0.000	**FE**	0.000	**FE**	0.000	**FE**	–	**OLS**	–	**OLS**
	Heteroskedasticity	FE	0.000		0.000		0.000		0.000		–		–	

(continued)

Table B.3 (continued)

Sample	Post Estimation Test		Panel A: Leverage Regression (Determinants)				Panel B: Robustness Test I				Panel C: Pecking Order (Direct Measure)			
			Book Leverage		Market Leverage		Book Leverage 2		Market Leverage 2		Debt Issue		Equity Issue	
			Results	Selection	Results	Selection	Results	Selection	Results	Selection	Results	Selection	Results	Selection
Oil and Gas	BPLM	RE	0.000		0.000		0.000		0.000		0.002		0.002	
	Hausman	RE	0.000	FE	0.000	FE	0.000	FE	0.000	FE	0.000	FE	0.000	FE
	Heteroskedasticity	FE	0.000		0.000		0.000		0.000		0.000		0.000	
Basic Materials	BPLM	RE	0.000		0.000		0.000		0.000		0.000		0.000	
	Hausman	RE	0.000	FE	0.000	FE	0.002	FE	0.000	FE	0.000	FE	0.000	FE
	Heteroskedasticity	FE	0.000		0.000		0.000		0.000		0.000		0.000	
Industrials	BPLM	RE	0.000		0.000		0.000		0.000		0.000		0.000	
	Hausman	RE	0.000	FE	0.000	FE	0.000	FE	0.000	FE	0.605	RE	0.605	RE
	Heteroskedasticity	FE	0.000		0.000		0.000		0.000		–		–	
Cons. Goods	BPLM	RE	0.000		0.000		0.000		0.000		0.000		0.000	
	Hausman	RE	0.044	FE	0.000	FE	0.016	FE	0.000	FE	0.000	FE	0.000	FE
	Heteroskedasticity	FE	0.000		0.000		0.000		0.000		0.000		0.000	
Technology	BPLM	RE	0.000		0.000		0.000		0.000		0.000		0.000	
	Hausman	RE	0.080	RE	0.000	FE	0.004	FE	0.000	FE	0.184	RE	0.183	RE
	Heteroskedasticity	FE	–		0.000		0.000		0.000		–		–	
Health Care	BPLM	RE	0.000		0.000		0.000		0.000		0.000		0.000	
	Hausman	RE	0.051	RE	0.000	FE	0.298	RE	0.000	FE	0.000	FE	0.000	FE
	Heteroskedasticity	FE	–		0.000		–		0.000		0.000		0.000	
Cons. Services	BPLM	RE	0.000		0.000		0.000		0.000		0.000		0.000	
	Hausman	RE	0.000	FE	0.000	FE	0.000	FE	0.000	FE	0.000	FE	0.000	FE
	Heteroskedasticity	FE	0.000		0.000		0.000		0.000		0.000		0.000	

Source: own contribution.

Table B.4: Auto–Serial Correlation Test.

This table presents the auto-serial correlation tests conducted on different estimation models for the *overall (pooled)*, *country,* and *industry* samples separately. Panel A represents the leverage regression model with book and market leverage measure, as defined in Table 4.3. Panel B represents the leverage regression model with the alternative leverage proxy defined in Table E.1 in Appendix E (Robustness Test I), and Panel C represents the pecking order model with debt and equity issue as defined in Table 6.2 (direct measure). The model tested is $\hat{e}_{it} = p\hat{e}_{i,t-1} + \varepsilon_{it}$. The null hypothesis is that p=0, i.e., no first-order autocorrelation. Similar to the consequences of heteroskedasticity, the presence of autocorrelation leads to incorrect standard errors. This test is proposed and suggested by Wooldridge (2002). This test involves regression of the residuals from the estimation upon its lag. If the coefficient of the lagged residuals is significant, the first-order autocorrelation is present, and the standard errors need to be adjusted. The test is conducted using the *xtserial* function in Stata, which equals the test proposed by Drukker (2003). The results show that all estimated models in the study suffer from first-order serial correlation in Panel A and Panel B. Therefore, we applied standard errors robust to serial correlation. Petersen (2009) discusses several robust standard errors and recommends using cluster robust standard error in finance panels. Even though selected samples in Panel C exhibit a non-rejection (e.g., Canada with p-value 0.8256), we followed the recommendation by Petersen (2009). We applied the "robust" option in all model estimations in this study. (see Section 4.2.1)

	Panel A: Leverage Regression (Determinants)				Panel B: Robustness Test I				Panel C: Pecking Order (Direct Measure)			
	Book Leverage		Market Leverage		Book Leverage2		Market Leverage2		Debt Issue		Equity Issue	
Overall	F(1, 1329)	728.012***	F(1, 1329)	706.483***	F(1, 1329)	676.721***	F(1, 1329)	532.916***	F(1, 1405)	15.694***	F(1, 1405)	15.690***
(pooled)	*Prob.*	*0.000*	*Prob.*	*0.000*	*Prob.*	*0.000*	*Prob.*	*0.000*	*Prob.*	*0.0001*	*Prob.*	*0.0001*
United	F(1, 641)	292.511***	F(1, 641)	338.068***	F(1, 641)	270.049***	F(1, 641)	240.011***	F(1, 644)	5.951**	F(1, 644)	5.950**
States	*Prob.*	*0.000*	*Prob.*	*0.000*	*Prob.*	*0.000*	*Prob.*	*0.000*	*Prob.*	*0.015*	*Prob.*	*0.015*
United	F(1, 109)	162.909***	F(1, 109)	95.708***	F(1, 109)	72.314***	F(1, 109)	94.797***	F(1, 109)	5.118**	F(1, 109)	5.113**
Kingdom	*Prob.*	*0.000*	*Prob.*	*0.000*	*Prob.*	*0.000*	*Prob.*	*0.000*	*Prob.*	*0.0257*	*Prob.*	*0.0257*
Canada	F(1, 75)	82.936***	F(1, 75)	31.088***	F(1, 75)	83.933***	F(1, 75)	34.711***	F(1, 76)	0.049	F(1, 76)	0.048
	Prob.	*0.000*	*Prob.*	*0.000*	*Prob.*	*0.000*	*Prob.*	*0.000*	*Prob.*	*0.8256*	*Prob.*	*0.8268*
Japan	F(1, 315)	323.599***	F(1, 315)	278.301***	F(1, 315)	286.094***	F(1, 315)	225.941***	F(1, 315)	3.902**	F(1, 315)	3.904**
	Prob.	*0.000*	*Prob.*	*0.000*	*Prob.*	*0.000*	*Prob.*	*0.000*	*Prob.*	*0.0491*	*Prob.*	*0.049*
S. Korea	F(1, 85)	136.32***	F(1, 85)	22.64***	F(1, 85)	107.302***	F(1, 85)	16.087***	F(1, 85)	1.017	F(1, 85)	1.019
	Prob.	*0.000*	*Prob.*	*0.000*	*Prob.*	*0.000*	*Prob.*	*0.000*	*Prob.*	*0.3162*	*Prob.*	*0.3157*

(continued)

Table B.4 (continued)

	Panel A: Leverage Regression (Determinants)				Panel B: Robustness Test I				Panel C: Pecking Order (Direct Measure)			
	Book Leverage		Market Leverage		Book Leverage2		Market Leverage2		Debt Issue		Equity Issue	
Taiwan	F(1, 71)	124.412***	F(1, 71)	23.529***	F(1, 71)	84.201***	F(1, 71)	17.952***	F(1, 71)	3.68*	F(1, 71)	3.688*
	Prob.	*0.000*	*Prob.*	*0.000*	*Prob.*	*0.000*	*Prob.*	*0.000*	*Prob.*	*0.0591*	*Prob.*	*0.0588*
India	F(1, 99)	102.48***	F(1, 99)	31.957***	F(1, 99)	75.584***	F(1, 99)	16.343***	F(1, 99)	4.502**	F(1, 99)	4.507**
	Prob.	*0.000*	*Prob.*	*0.000*	*Prob.*	*0.000*	*Prob.*	*0.000*	*Prob.*	*0.0364*	*Prob.*	*0.0362*
Oil and Gas	F(1, 96)	61.086***	F(1, 96)	55.281***	F(1, 96)	84.207***	F(1, 96)	58.029***	F(1, 99)	5.575**	F(1, 99)	5.585**
	Prob.	*0.000*	*Prob.*	*0.000*	*Prob.*	*0.000*	*Prob.*	*0.000*	*Prob.*	*0.0202*	*Prob.*	*0.0201*
Basic Materials	F(1, 136)	120.426***	F(1, 136)	65.924***	F(1, 136)	98.613***	F(1, 136)	41.389***	F(1, 142)	3.569*	F(1, 142)	3.57*
	Prob.	*0.000*	*Prob.*	*0.000*	*Prob.*	*0.000*	*Prob.*	*0.000*	*Prob.*	*0.0609*	*Prob.*	*0.0609*
Industrials	F(1, 381)	366.569***	F(1, 381)	341.107***	F(1, 381)	367.885***	F(1, 381)	300.109***	F(1, 399)	4.283**	F(1, 399)	4.276**
	Prob.	*0.000*	*Prob.*	*0.000*	*Prob.*	*0.000*	*Prob.*	*0.000*	*Prob.*	*0.0391*	*Prob.*	*0.0393*
Cons. Goods	F(1, 228)	201.648***	F(1, 228)	122.019***	F(1, 228)	158.006***	F(1, 228)	73.971***	F(1, 246)	0.435	F(1, 246)	0.435
	Prob.	*0.000*	*Prob.*	*0.000*	*Prob.*	*0.000*	*Prob.*	*0.000*	*Prob.*	*0.5102*	*Prob.*	*0.51*
Technology	F(1, 145)	47.906***	F(1, 145)	17.411***	F(1, 145)	80.993***	F(1, 145)	8.564***	F(1, 171)	3.138*	F(1, 171)	3.139*
	Prob.	*0.000*	*Prob.*	*0.000*	*Prob.*	*0.000*	*Prob.*	*0.004*	*Prob.*	*0.0783*	*Prob.*	*0.0782*
Health Care	F(1, 122)	67.112***	F(1, 122)	97.561***	F(1, 122)	28.929***	F(1, 122)	77.255***	F(1, 122)	3.047*	F(1, 122)	3.048*
	Prob.	*0.000*	*Prob.*	*0.000*	*Prob.*	*0.000*	*Prob.*	*0.000*	*Prob.*	*0.0834*	*Prob.*	*0.0833*
Cons. Services	F(1, 215)	165.199***	F(1, 215)	166.142***	F(1, 215)	146.197***	F(1, 215)	123.598***	F(1, 220)	19.325***	F(1, 220)	19.335***
	Prob.	*0.000*	*Prob.*	*0.000*	*Prob.*	*0.000*	*Prob.*	*0.000*	*Prob.*	*0.000*	*Prob.*	*0.000*

Source: Own contribution.

Table B.5: Endogeneity Test.

This table presents the endogeneity tests conducted on the leverage regression model for the overall (pooled), country, and industry samples separately. The test is recommended by Wooldridge (2002). The test involves regressing the dependent variable (BLEV and MLEV) against the independent variables, i.e., profitability, growth opportunity, firm size, tangibility, and risk and the leads (one period ahead) of the same independent variables. If the lead independent variable (t+1) is significant, the hypothesis states that the variable might be endogenous. Note: We did not add GDP growth since it is an exogenous variable by default. The results show that some of the lead variables are significant, while others are insignificant. Accordingly, as Wooldridge (2010) recommended, significant lead variables are considered endogenous, while the insignificant variables are predetermined.

The endogeneity test was applied to the respective estimator, as identified by the model estimation procedure described in Table B.3 in Appendix B.

	Overall (pooled)		United States		United Kingdom		Canada		Japan		S. Korea		Taiwan		India	
	Book	Market	Book	Market	Book	Market	Book	Market	Book	Market	Book	Market	Book	Market	Book	Market
$Profitability_t$	-0.251***	-0.400***	-0.185***	-0.310***	-0.020	-0.248**	-0.000	-0.151*	-0.337***	-0.814***	-0.451***	-0.518***	-0.509***	-0.826***	-0.301***	-0.315***
	-0.033	-0.030	-0.046	-0.039	-0.120	-0.098	-0.093	-0.077	-0.057	-0.086	-0.115	-0.114	-0.114	-0.146	-0.092	-0.073
$Growth_t$	-0.002	-0.044***	-0.007***	-0.042***	-0.000	-0.054***	0.011	-0.053***	0.004	-0.049***	0.026**	-0.063***	0.005	-0.035***	0.001	-0.037***
	-0.002	-0.002	-0.003	-0.003	-0.007	-0.010	-0.013	-0.008	-0.005	-0.009	-0.010	-0.016	-0.008	-0.009	-0.004	-0.004
$Firm\ Size_t$	0.031***	0.085***	0.020*	0.105***	-0.007	0.052**	0.016	0.031**	0.024***	0.121***	0.115***	0.082***	0.061***	0.102***	0.014	0.051***
	-0.006	-0.006	-0.011	-0.011	-0.020	-0.024	-0.020	-0.014	-0.008	-0.012	-0.017	-0.016	-0.021	-0.028	-0.012	-0.015
$Tangibility_t$	0.074**	0.131***	0.142***	0.157***	-0.020	0.003	0.023	-0.075*	-0.051	0.218***	0.012	0.288**	0.365***	0.311***	-0.152*	-0.097
	-0.031	-0.029	-0.051	-0.050	-0.071	-0.100	-0.077	-0.043	-0.068	-0.070	-0.124	-0.118	-0.079	-0.102	-0.080	-0.066
$Risk_t$	0.251***	0.218***	0.448***	0.266***	0.053	-0.016	-0.011	-0.053	0.053	0.289***	-0.192	-0.260	-0.008	0.048	0.269*	0.298***
	-0.059	-0.041	-0.093	-0.060	-0.157	-0.120	-0.154	-0.116	-0.100	-0.107	-0.269	-0.307	-0.166	-0.145	-0.141	-0.105
$Profitability_{t+1}$	**0.205***	**0.120***	**0.125***	**0.084**	**0.409***	**0.234**	0.015	0.063	**0.323***	0.071	**0.693***	**0.521***	**0.181**	**0.389**	**0.231***	**0.133**
	-0.031	-0.025	-0.043	-0.033	-0.131	-0.104	-0.105	-0.074	-0.061	-0.078	-0.106	-0.121	-0.122	-0.173	-0.072	-0.057
$Growth_{t+1}$	0.001	**0.002*	0.001	0.002	-0.011	-0.002	**0.017*	0.002	-0.001	**0.007*	0.004	**-0.021**	-0.003	-0.002	-0.001	0.003
	-0.002	-0.001	-0.003	-0.002	-0.007	-0.009	-0.009	-0.005	-0.006	-0.004	-0.009	-0.009	-0.007	-0.006	-0.004	-0.003
$Firm\ Size_{t+1}$	**-0.024***	**-0.077***	**-0.016*	**-0.108***	-0.031	**-0.051**	0.005	**-0.029*	**-0.025***	**-0.070***	**-0.057***	**-0.048***	-0.026	**-0.124***	-0.005	**-0.031**
	-0.006	-0.006	-0.009	-0.011	-0.020	-0.023	-0.021	-0.017	-0.009	-0.011	-0.012	-0.011	-0.020	-0.030	-0.013	-0.013

(continued)

Table B.5 (continued)

	Overall (pooled)		United States		United Kingdom		Canada		Japan		S. Korea		Taiwan		India	
	Book	**Market**	**Book**	**Market**	**Book**	**Market**	**Book**	**Market**	**Book**	**Market**	**Book**	**Market**	**Book**	**Market**	**Book**	**Market**
$Tangibility_{t+1}$	−0.000	0.008	−0.040	−0.002	0.060	−0.029	−0.036	0.053	−0.006	0.046	**0.222*****	0.099	−0.066	**−0.174****	**0.159****	0.104
	−0.025	−0.024	−0.042	−0.037	−0.121	−0.071	−0.070	−0.050	−0.056	−0.053	−0.078	−0.088	−0.063	−0.081	−0.073	−0.077
$Risk_{t+1}$	**0.051**	**0.143*****	**0.203****	**0.170*****	−0.138	−0.057	−0.145	0.041	−0.067	0.095	0.020	−0.024	−0.133	−0.000	0.000	0.143
	−0.052	−0.042	−0.080	−0.060	−0.181	−0.182	−0.212	−0.131	−0.099	−0.113	−0.230	−0.204	−0.106	−0.148	−0.169	−0.122
Constant	0.391***	0.318***	0.405***	0.442***	1.026***	0.446*	0.069	0.382***	0.595***	−0.253	−0.459	−0.007	−0.077	0.793***	0.365**	0.106
	−0.078	−0.059	−0.125	−0.084	−0.292	−0.245	−0.180	−0.129	−0.165	−0.164	−0.355	−0.315	−0.207	−0.222	−0.159	−0.104
R^2	0.029	0.276	0.039	0.318	0.057	0.262	0.049	0.244	0.045	0.350	0.249	0.294	0.235	0.369	0.051	0.269
Adjusted R^2	0.028	0.275	0.037	0.317	0.044	0.252	0.031	0.230	0.040	0.347	0.236	0.281	0.220	0.356	0.039	0.259
Firms	1404	1404	644	644	110	110	76	76	316	316	86	86	72	72	100	100
Observations	10081	10081	4565	4565	762	762	543	543	2351	2351	566	566	515	515	779	779
Estimator	*FE*	*FE*	*FE*	*FE*	*FE*	*FE*	*FE*	*FE*	*FE*	*FE*	*FE*	*FE*	*FE*	*FE*	*FE*	*FE*

	Oil and Gas		Basic Materials		Industrials		Consumer Goods		Technologies		Health Care		Consumer Services	
	Book	**Market**	**Book**	**Market**	**Book**	**Market**	**Book**	**Market**	**Book**	**Market**	**Book**	**Market**	**Book**	**Market**
$Profitability_t$	−0.093	−0.164**	−0.237**	−0.538***	−0.266***	−0.471***	−0.345***	−0.483***	−0.259***	−0.324***	−0.495***	−0.295***	−0.118	−0.367***
	−0.093	−0.070	−0.096	−0.095	−0.071	−0.060	−0.076	−0.070	−0.082	−0.077	−0.095	−0.079	−0.076	−0.101
$Growth_t$	0.010	−0.075***	0.003	−0.049***	−0.007	−0.070***	0.000	−0.045***	−0.001	−0.025***	−0.006	−0.034***	0.001	−0.053***
	−0.013	−0.009	−0.007	−0.009	−0.005	−0.007	−0.004	−0.005	−0.003	−0.002	−0.005	−0.004	−0.005	−0.006
Firm $Size_t$	0.028	0.074***	0.040**	0.101***	0.037***	0.100***	0.040***	0.065***	0.049**	0.087***	0.005	0.043**	0.010	0.083***
	−0.019	−0.014	−0.015	−0.018	−0.013	−0.011	−0.012	−0.013	−0.020	−0.019	−0.023	−0.020	−0.018	−0.021
$Tangibility_t$	−0.007	0.013	0.044	0.011	0.038	0.192***	0.079	0.169**	0.292***	0.293***	0.198	0.061	0.144*	0.109
	−0.102	−0.085	−0.073	−0.078	−0.053	−0.055	−0.092	−0.070	−0.087	−0.097	−0.121	−0.088	−0.083	−0.097

$Risk_t$	−0.012	−0.133	0.142	0.166	0.178	0.095	0.120	0.317***	0.250*	0.128	0.724***	0.314***	0.467***	0.620***
	−0.140	−0.096	−0.141	−0.140	−0.123	−0.091	−0.101	−0.088	−0.142	−0.083	−0.236	−0.097	−0.133	−0.143
$Profitability_{t+1}$	**0.160****	**0.130*****	**0.182***	**0.147***	**0.271*****	**0.167*****	**0.259*****	0.011	**0.163****	**0.150****	0.067	**0.123***	0.101	0.094
	−0.079	−0.048	−0.106	−0.078	−0.064	−0.053	−0.067	−0.064	−0.072	−0.066	−0.114	−0.063	−0.075	−0.079
$Growth_{t+1}$	0.015	**0.014***	−0.000	**0.009***	−0.001	0.004	−0.005	−0.000	0.003	**0.004***	0.000	−0.003	−0.003	−0.001
	−0.010	−0.007	−0.008	−0.005	−0.004	−0.003	−0.004	−0.003	−0.003	−0.002	−0.006	−0.003	−0.005	−0.003
$Firm\ Size_{t+1}$	−0.011	**−0.057*****	**−0.044*****	**−0.087*****	**−0.042*****	**−0.101*****	−0.019	**−0.053*****	−0.020	**−0.084*****	0.022	**−0.023***	0.004	**−0.064*****
	−0.017	−0.011	−0.015	−0.018	−0.011	−0.011	−0.012	−0.015	−0.019	−0.019	−0.019	−0.013	−0.017	−0.022
$Tangibility_{t+1}$	0.009	0.057	−0.048	−0.006	−0.042	−0.047	0.045	0.072	−0.077	**−0.154***	0.178	0.057	−0.006	**0.139****
	−0.063	−0.052	−0.058	−0.059	−0.043	−0.050	−0.068	−0.054	−0.073	−0.087	−0.132	−0.079	−0.063	−0.068
$Risk_{t+1}$	−0.060	−0.111	−0.120	0.201	0.033	−0.000	−0.085	**0.360*****	−0.061	−0.054	**0.479****	0.091	0.173	0.222
	−0.138	−0.103	−0.112	−0.123	−0.113	−0.088	−0.106	−0.109	−0.107	−0.081	−0.232	−0.097	−0.124	−0.154
Constant	0.132	0.151	0.587***	0.325	0.645***	0.555***	0.183	0.271*	−0.031	0.258**	0.012	0.036	0.309	0.186
	−0.240	−0.200	−0.190	−0.198	−0.156	−0.115	−0.186	−0.145	−0.127	−0.101	−0.163	−0.177	−0.235	−0.184
R^2	0.050	0.385	0.033	0.257	0.034	0.334	0.051	0.326		0.308		0.246	0.030	0.307
Adjusted R^2	0.037	0.376	0.024	0.250	0.031	0.332	0.046	0.322		0.302		0.238	0.024	0.303
Firms	98	98	143	143	400	400	247	247	172	172	123	123	221	221
Observations	699	699	1012	1012	2955	2955	1737	1737	1166	1166	927	927	1585	1585
Estimator	*FE*	*FE*	*FE*	*FE*	*FE*	*FE*	*FE*	*FE*	*RE*	*FE*	*RE*	*FE*	*FE*	*FE*

Standard errors in parentheses, * p<0.10, ** p<0.05, *** p<0.01.
Source: own contribution.

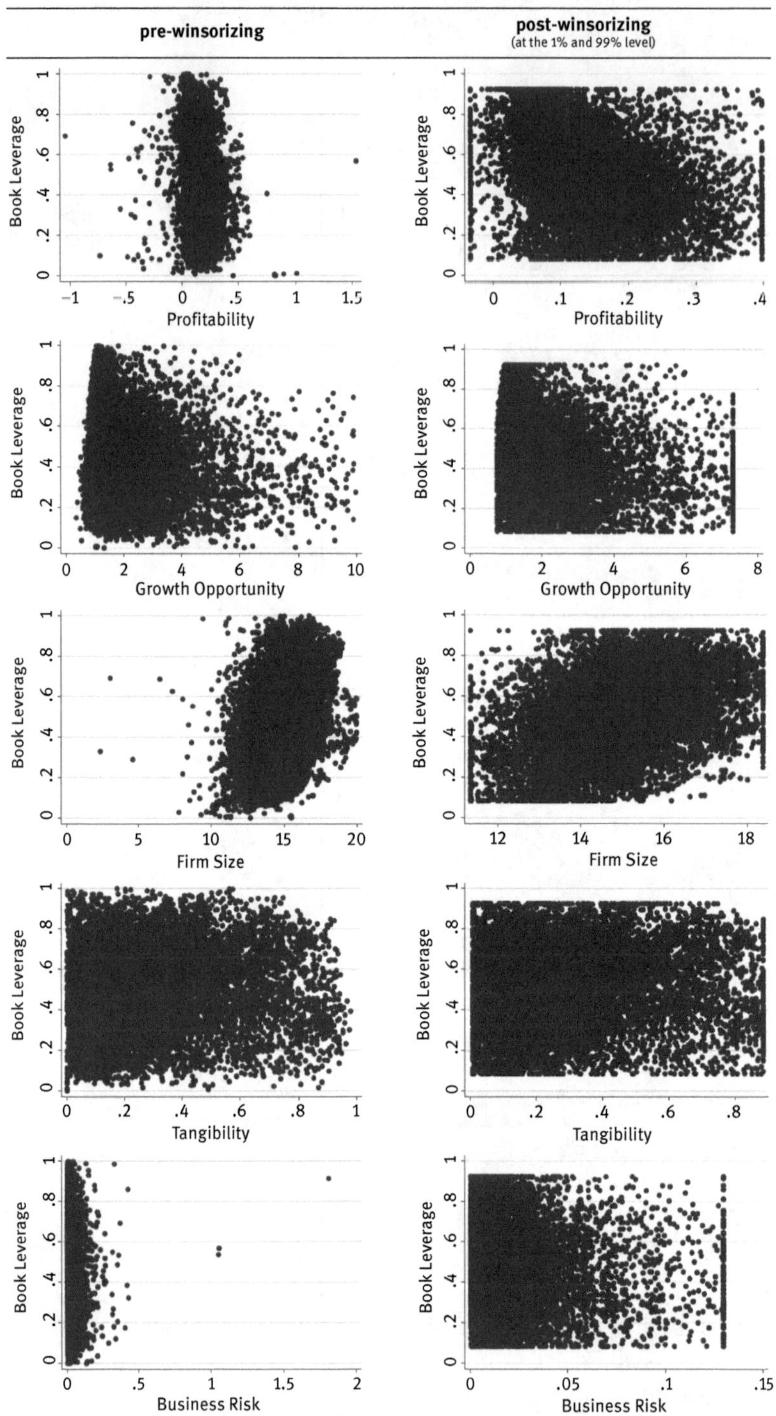

Figure B.1: Effects of winsorizing of variables.

Figure B.1 (continued)
The figures on the left and right show the impact of winsorizing on the individual variables. They are regressed against book leverage by the use of scatterplot (Stata command *scatter)*. Hence, the "before" figures illustrate if the variables suffered from outliers.
Source: own contribution

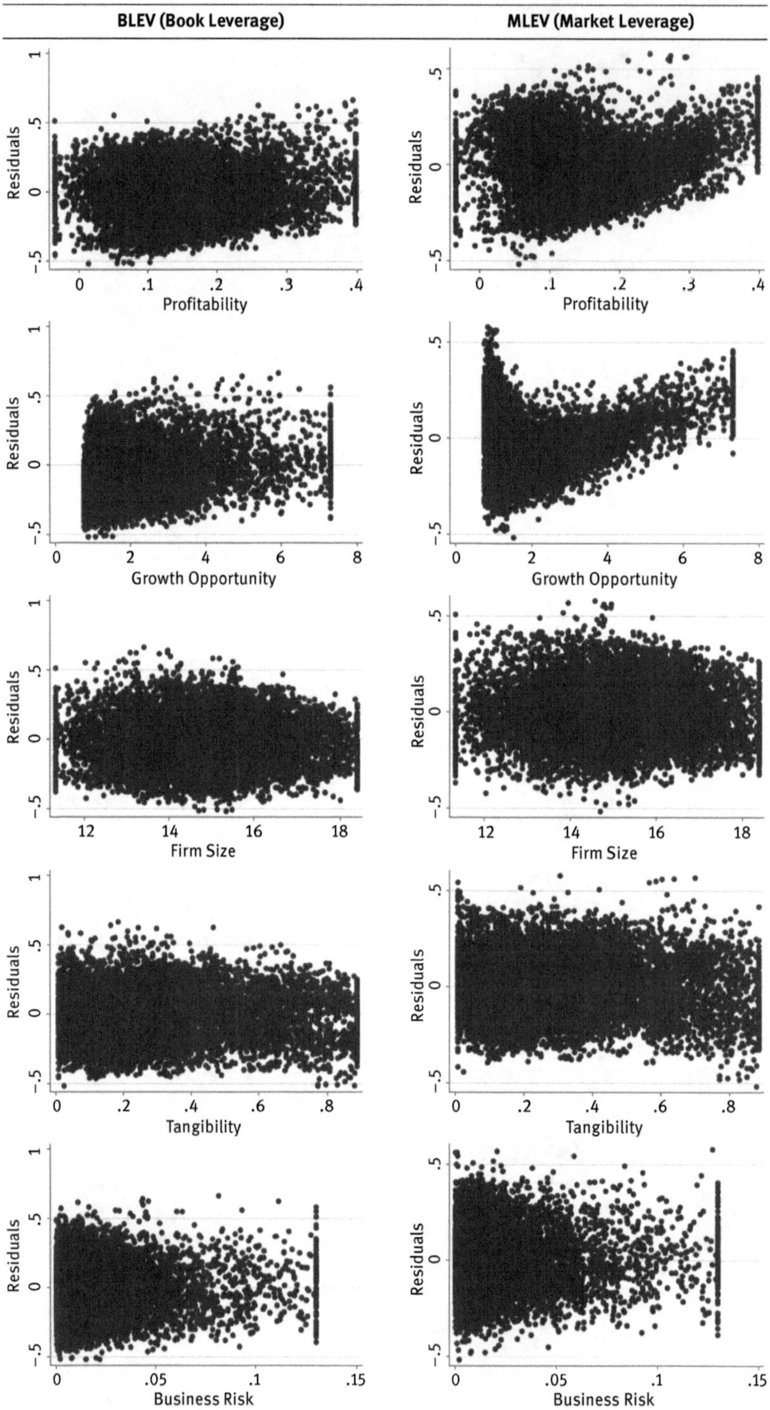

Figure B.2: Linearity Test.

Figure B.2 (continued)

The most frequently used method to test the assumption of linearity is to create a plot showing *residuals versus fitted values*. In general, the estimation model assumes that the relationship between the dependent and independent variables is linear. If a linear regression model is fitted to variables that do not have a linear relationship with the dependent variable, the results can be flawed. Perfect linearity is rarely existent in empirical research, but non-linearity should be examined and detected as it can indicate that variables should have a different functional form.

The left (right) side figures provide a scatterplot of the variables against the residuals derived from the estimation model with book leverage (market leverage) as the dependent variable. If the residuals are plotted randomly around a horizontal line from 0 on the y-axis, then the assumption of linearity is reasonable. Some outliers are detected in the linear relationships, but as a whole, the variables provide a satisfactory degree of linearity. All variables are winsorized at the 1% and 99% level.

Source: own contribution

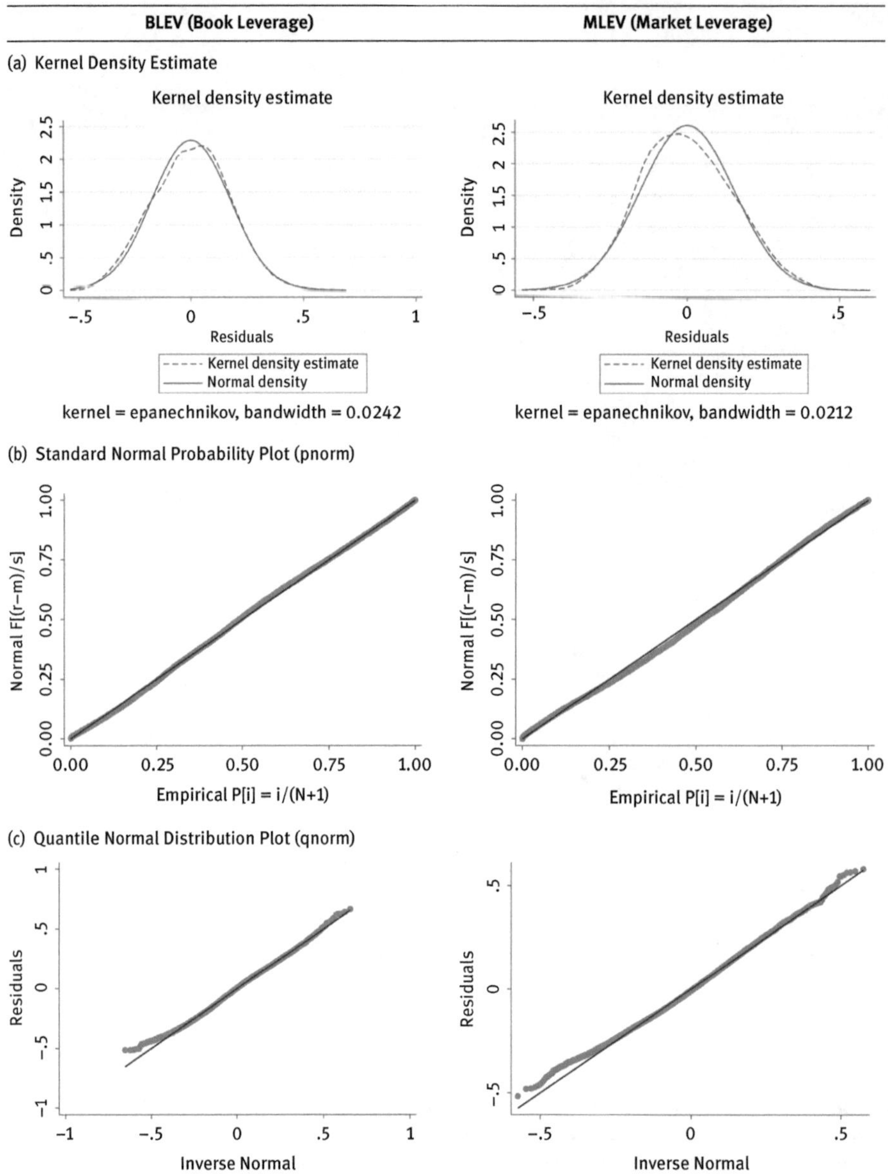

Figure B.3: Normality Test.
Normality in the residuals is necessary to conduct valid hypothesis testing because it assures that the p-values for the t-statistics and the F-test are reliable. The two most common ways to test the assumption of normality is by conducting either a Skewness/Kurtosis test or running a Kernel Density Estimate followed by *pnorm* and *qnorm* plots. The former test is numerical, while the latter test illustrates the issue graphically. Note: The left(right) side figures provide the results derived from the estimation model with book leverage (market leverage) as the dependent variable.

The skewness/kurtosis test (Stata command *sktest*) measures the skewness and excess kurtosis for normality. The null hypothesis states that there is no significant deviation from normality

Figure B.3 (continued)
in the data. However, the Kernel Density Estimate is used to test the assumption of normality in the models. This tests the error term in the regression models. Figures in B.3a show the kernel density estimate with the blue line representing the residuals and the black (straight line) line representing the normal distribution. The figures illustrate that the residuals are close to normally distributed. Hence the assumption of normality holds. However, in addition to the kernel density estimate, as mentioned above, a standardized normal probability plot (Stata command *pnorm*) and a plot showing the quantiles of a variable against the quantiles of normal distribution (Stata command *qnorm*) is created to examine the normality assumption further.

For *pnorm*, the data is plotted against a straight line of normal distribution. The data points are then plotted around this line. If the data deviates from the straight line, this indicates a violation of the normality assumption. The figures in B.3b exhibit no/or slight deviation from the normality line. However, *pnorm* is very sensitive to non-normality in the middle range of the data. Overall it can be concluded that the observations satisfy the assumption of normality.

Qnorm is sensitive to non-normality near the tails. Figures in B.3c exhibit some deviations from normality in both the upper and lower tail; thus, it can (or might) be considered a (slight) discrepancy. However, overall we concluded that the residuals are close to a normal distribution.
All variables are winsorized at the 1% and 99% level.
Source: own contribution

Appendix C

https://doi.org/10.1515/9783110713664-011

Table C.1: Descriptive – *Overall (pooled)* Book Debt and Stock Price (time series).

This table shows the mean for book debt and stock price for all firms in the *overall (pooled)* sample separated in SC and SNC firms for the entire period 2004–2014. Table 4.3 provides the definitions of Book Debt, and the Stock Price represents the closing price (fiscal year). SC and SNC firms are determined based on DJIMI (see Table 4.1). Book debt is winsorized at the 1% and 99% level.

Sample		2004–2014	2004	2005	2006	2007	2008	2009	2010	2011	2012	2013	2014	Trend
Overall (pooled)	Book Debt	6526.28	5550.95	5199.83	5428.68	6079.03	6157.59	6156.35	6578.07	6962.54	7277.10	7617.56	8058.88	
	Stock Price	34.16	22.28	25.00	27.32	27.65	20.21	27.98	34.97	34.88	42.38	52.72	55.04	
Shari'ah Compliant	Book Debt	3806.18	3011.63	2969.07	3080.50	3471.93	3564.99	3434.33	3958.36	4086.35	4359.94	4625.57	4971.23	
	Stock Price	40.24	24.96	27.23	29.17	30.40	24.64	34.43	40.74	42.35	51.10	63.47	68.70	
Shari'ah Non-Compliant	Book Debt	10175.50	9897.61	9080.35	9280.74	9735.03	9314.91	9338.07	9722.67	10330.03	10831.52	11668.55	12398.08	
	Stock Price	26.01	17.71	21.12	24.28	23.81	14.81	20.46	28.05	26.13	31.76	38.16	35.87	

Source: own contribution

Table C.2: Descriptive – *Overall (pooled)* Firm Leverage (time series).

This table shows the mean, standard deviation, minimum, maximum, and the number of observations of the book- and market leverage proxies for all firms in the *overall (pooled)* sample and separated in SC and SNC firms for the entire period 2004–2014 and each year. Table 4.3 provides the definitions of both leverage proxies. SC and SNC firms are determined based on DJIMI (see Table 4.1). All variables are winsorized at the 1% and 99% level.

Sample	Leverage	Stats	2004–2014	2004	2005	2006	2007	2008	2009	2010	2011	2012	2013	2014
Pooled	Book	Mean	0.51	0.50	0.50	0.50	0.51	0.53	0.51	0.51	0.52	0.51	0.50	0.51
		SD	0.20	0.21	0.21	0.20	0.20	0.21	0.21	0.20	0.20	0.20	0.19	0.20
		Min	0.08	0.08	0.08	0.08	0.08	0.08	0.08	0.08	0.08	0.08	0.08	0.08
		Max	0.92	0.92	0.92	0.92	0.92	0.92	0.92	0.92	0.92	0.92	0.92	0.92
		Obs	11551	762	852	940	1033	1120	1143	1208	1220	1178	1104	991
	Market	Mean	0.37	0.34	0.31	0.32	0.36	0.44	0.38	0.37	0.39	0.38	0.35	0.34
		SD	0.24	0.24	0.22	0.22	0.23	0.26	0.24	0.23	0.24	0.23	0.23	0.23
		Min	0.02	0.02	0.02	0.02	0.02	0.02	0.02	0.02	0.02	0.02	0.02	0.02
		Max	0.88	0.88	0.88	0.88	0.88	0.88	0.88	0.88	0.88	0.88	0.88	0.88
		Obs	11551	762	852	940	1033	1120	1143	1208	1220	1178	1104	991
Shari'ah Compliant	Book	Mean	0.40	0.39	0.40	0.40	0.40	0.41	0.39	0.39	0.40	0.40	0.39	0.40
		SD	0.17	0.17	0.17	0.17	0.17	0.18	0.17	0.17	0.17	0.16	0.16	0.17
		Min	0.08	0.08	0.08	0.08	0.08	0.08	0.08	0.08	0.08	0.08	0.08	0.08
		Max	0.92	0.92	0.92	0.92	0.92	0.92	0.92	0.92	0.87	0.88	0.87	0.92
		Obs	6618	481	541	584	603	615	616	659	658	647	635	579
	Market	Mean	0.19	0.18	0.17	0.17	0.19	0.23	0.19	0.19	0.20	0.20	0.18	0.18
		SD	0.11	0.11	0.10	0.10	0.11	0.13	0.11	0.10	0.11	0.11	0.10	0.10
		Min	0.02	0.02	0.02	0.02	0.02	0.02	0.02	0.02	0.02	0.02	0.02	0.02
		Max	0.70	0.50	0.47	0.49	0.62	0.70	0.55	0.58	0.61	0.54	0.49	0.56
		Obs	6618	481	541	584	603	615	616	659	658	647	635	579

(continued)

Table C.2 (continued)

Sample	Leverage	Stats	2004–2014	2004	2005	2006	2007	2008	2009	2010	2011	2012	2013	2014
		Mean	0.66	0.69	0.68	0.67	0.66	0.68	0.65	0.64	0.65	0.66	0.65	0.66
		SD	0.13	0.13	0.13	0.13	0.13	0.14	0.14	0.13	0.13	0.13	0.13	0.13
	Book	Min	0.22	0.33	0.30	0.34	0.31	0.36	0.22	0.29	0.31	0.29	0.31	0.32
		Max	0.92	0.92	0.92	0.92	0.92	0.92	0.92	0.92	0.92	0.92	0.92	0.92
Shari'ah		Obs	4933	281	311	356	430	505	527	549	562	531	469	412
Non-Compliant		Mean	0.60	0.61	0.56	0.56	0.59	0.68	0.61	0.59	0.61	0.60	0.57	0.57
		SD	0.14	0.14	0.13	0.14	0.14	0.13	0.14	0.13	0.14	0.14	0.15	0.14
	Market	Min	0.22	0.28	0.28	0.27	0.22	0.30	0.28	0.26	0.23	0.29	0.24	0.24
		Max	0.88	0.88	0.88	0.88	0.88	0.88	0.88	0.88	0.88	0.88	0.88	0.88
		Obs	4933	281	311	356	430	505	527	549	562	531	469	412

Source: own contribution.

Table C.3: Descriptive – *Country* and *Industry* Firm Leverage (time series).

This table shows the mean values of the book- and market leverage proxies for all firms in the *overall (pooled)* sample and separated in each *country* and *industry*, for the entire period 2004–2014 and each year separately. Table 4.3 provides the definitions of both leverage proxies. The trend column includes sparklines representing the trend of the period 2004 to 2014. SC and SNC firms are determined based on DJIMI (see Table 4.1). All variables are winsorized at the 1% and 99% level.

Leverage	Sample	*Panel A: Shari'ah Compliant (SC)*													*Panel B: Shari'ah Non-Compliant (SNC)*												
		2004–2014	2004	2005	2006	2007	2008	2009	2010	2011	2012	2013	2014	Trend	2004–2014	2004	2005	2006	2007	2008	2009	2010	2011	2012	2013	2014	Trend
	Overall (pooled)	0.40	0.39	0.40	0.40	0.40	0.41	0.39	0.39	0.40	0.40	0.39	0.40		0.66	0.69	0.68	0.67	0.66	0.68	0.65	0.64	0.65	0.66	0.65	0.66	
	United States	0.42	0.40	0.41	0.41	0.43	0.44	0.41	0.41	0.42	0.42	0.42	0.45		0.65	0.66	0.66	0.65	0.64	0.67	0.64	0.64	0.65	0.66	0.65	0.66	
	United Kingdom	0.46	0.46	0.47	0.47	0.48	0.49	0.45	0.45	0.46	0.46	0.44	0.45		0.67	0.66	0.66	0.65	0.67	0.70	0.68	0.65	0.65	0.67	0.70	0.73	
	Canada	0.32	0.29	0.32	0.30	0.31	0.32	0.29	0.33	0.33	0.33	0.34	0.35		0.61	0.65	0.62	0.61	0.62	0.59	0.57	0.56	0.59	0.62	0.65	0.66	
	Japan	0.33	0.35	0.35	0.35	0.33	0.31	0.31	0.32	0.33	0.32	0.31	0.29		0.68	0.75	0.72	0.70	0.68	0.68	0.67	0.66	0.66	0.66	0.65	0.64	
	S. Korea	0.34	0.33	0.38	0.35	0.34	0.39	0.36	0.32	0.34	0.34	0.34	0.33		0.68	0.71	0.71	0.73	0.73	0.75	0.69	0.62	0.64	0.64	0.65	0.67	
	Taiwan	0.34	0.32	0.30	0.28	0.29	0.29	0.34	0.36	0.37	0.38	0.38	0.37		0.61	0.60	0.60	0.58	0.58	0.62	0.61	0.61	0.63	0.62	0.62	0.61	
Book	India	0.41	0.43	0.45	0.43	0.42	0.42	0.39	0.42	0.40	0.39	0.38	0.38		0.69	0.62	0.64	0.66	0.69	0.70	0.68	0.68	0.71	0.70	0.73	0.75	
	Oil and Gas	0.36	0.37	0.40	0.40	0.37	0.37	0.33	0.34	0.35	0.37	0.37	0.36		0.62	0.64	0.67	0.65	0.64	0.61	0.60	0.60	0.62	0.62	0.63	0.64	
	Basic Materials	0.35	0.35	0.36	0.35	0.36	0.37	0.35	0.37	0.35	0.34	0.34	0.34		0.65	0.68	0.66	0.66	0.67	0.69	0.66	0.64	0.62	0.63	0.61	0.61	
	Industrials	0.44	0.43	0.44	0.43	0.44	0.46	0.43	0.43	0.45	0.45	0.43	0.45		0.67	0.71	0.69	0.67	0.66	0.68	0.66	0.65	0.66	0.66	0.66	0.67	
	Cons. Goods	0.42	0.42	0.41	0.42	0.43	0.44	0.42	0.43	0.43	0.43	0.42	0.42		0.63	0.64	0.65	0.64	0.63	0.65	0.64	0.62	0.63	0.63	0.63	0.63	
	Technology	0.35	0.32	0.33	0.34	0.35	0.36	0.35	0.35	0.36	0.36	0.36	0.37		0.65	0.69	0.69	0.65	0.63	0.66	0.64	0.64	0.68	0.67	0.64	0.64	
	Health Care	0.37	0.37	0.38	0.37	0.38	0.38	0.35	0.34	0.36	0.36	0.35	0.38		0.65	0.65	0.65	0.63	0.63	0.65	0.62	0.62	0.65	0.66	0.66	0.69	
	Cons. Services	0.42	0.42	0.41	0.41	0.42	0.42	0.41	0.41	0.41	0.42	0.42	0.44		0.70	0.73	0.72	0.70	0.70	0.71	0.68	0.68	0.68	0.69	0.69	0.70	

(continued)

Table C.3 (continued)

Leverage	Sample	Panel A: Shari'ah Compliant (SC)												Panel B: Shari'ah Non-Compliant (SNC)											
		2004–2014	2004	2005	2006	2007	2008	2009	2010	2011	2012	2013	2014	Trend	2004–2014	2004	2005	2006	2007	2008	2009	2010	2011	2012	2013	2014	Trend
Market	*Overall (pooled)*	0.19	0.18	0.17	0.17	0.19	0.23	0.19	0.19	0.20	0.20	0.18	0.18		0.60	0.61	0.56	0.56	0.59	0.68	0.61	0.59	0.61	0.60	0.57	0.57	
	United States	0.19	0.18	0.17	0.18	0.19	0.24	0.20	0.19	0.20	0.20	0.17	0.19		0.55	0.54	0.53	0.52	0.55	0.66	0.58	0.54	0.58	0.55	0.49	0.51	
	United Kingdom	0.22	0.21	0.19	0.20	0.22	0.26	0.24	0.22	0.25	0.23	0.21	0.21		0.57	0.54	0.49	0.48	0.56	0.68	0.60	0.54	0.59	0.56	0.55	0.59	
	Canada	0.18	0.15	0.15	0.14	0.17	0.21	0.18	0.18	0.19	0.20	0.20	0.22		0.53	0.58	0.54	0.50	0.54	0.60	0.56	0.50	0.53	0.51	0.48	0.52	
	Japan	0.21	0.21	0.19	0.19	0.23	0.23	0.20	0.22	0.23	0.21	0.20	0.17		0.65	0.67	0.59	0.60	0.66	0.70	0.65	0.66	0.66	0.65	0.63	0.61	
	S. Korea	0.20	0.24	0.17	0.18	0.16	0.20	0.23	0.18	0.20	0.23	0.21	0.20		0.67	0.77	0.70	0.70	0.65	0.75	0.70	0.59	0.63	0.65	0.66	0.69	
	Taiwan	0.17	0.19	0.15	0.14	0.14	0.21	0.18	0.18	0.20	0.19	0.16	0.16		0.56	0.54	0.56	0.51	0.50	0.65	0.52	0.52	0.58	0.59	0.57	0.56	
	India	0.13	0.15	0.12	0.13	0.13	0.20	0.13	0.13	0.13	0.12	0.12	0.10		0.59	0.51	0.50	0.56	0.54	0.72	0.54	0.56	0.62	0.64	0.65	0.60	
	Oil and Gas	0.21	0.21	0.19	0.20	0.18	0.26	0.19	0.19	0.22	0.23	0.21	0.26		0.61	0.61	0.61	0.63	0.58	0.68	0.61	0.57	0.58	0.61	0.59	0.62	
	Basic Materials	0.19	0.18	0.18	0.17	0.18	0.22	0.19	0.18	0.19	0.20	0.20	0.20		0.60	0.62	0.54	0.56	0.59	0.71	0.60	0.58	0.60	0.60	0.58	0.59	
	Industrials	0.22	0.21	0.19	0.19	0.21	0.28	0.23	0.22	0.24	0.23	0.20	0.20		0.61	0.63	0.57	0.56	0.58	0.68	0.62	0.59	0.62	0.61	0.58	0.58	
	Cons. Goods	0.20	0.22	0.19	0.19	0.21	0.24	0.21	0.21	0.21	0.20	0.18	0.17		0.58	0.57	0.55	0.56	0.59	0.67	0.60	0.58	0.59	0.56	0.55	0.56	
	Technology	0.15	0.13	0.13	0.13	0.15	0.20	0.15	0.15	0.16	0.16	0.14	0.14		0.59	0.57	0.56	0.53	0.56	0.68	0.54	0.57	0.64	0.63	0.56	0.57	
	Health Care	0.15	0.15	0.14	0.14	0.15	0.18	0.16	0.15	0.16	0.16	0.14	0.14		0.53	0.47	0.48	0.48	0.54	0.66	0.53	0.52	0.55	0.53	0.49	0.54	
	Cons. Services	0.20	0.17	0.16	0.18	0.25	0.24	0.21	0.21	0.20	0.20	0.18	0.19		0.61	0.64	0.58	0.57	0.64	0.68	0.64	0.61	0.61	0.60	0.58	0.56	

Source: own contribution.

Table C.4: Descriptive – *Country* and *Industry* Leverage Ratio.

This table shows the mean and industry-mean values of the book- and market leverage proxies for all firms in the *overall (pooled)* sample and separated in each *country* and *industry*, for the entire period 2004–2014. Table 4.3 provides the definitions of both leverage proxies. SC and SNC firms are determined based on DJIMI (see Table 4.1). All variables are winsorized at the 1% and 99% level.

Sample	**Shari'ah Compliant**		**Shari'ah Non-Compliant**		*Country/ Industry mean (BLEV)*	*Country/ Industry mean (MLEV)*	***Overall (pooled)***			
	Book Leverage (BLEV)	***Market Leverage (MLEV)***	***Book Leverage (BLEV)***	***Market Leverage (MLEV)***			***SC sample mean (BLEV)***	***SC sample mean (MLEV)***	***SNC sample mean (BLEV)***	***SNC sample mean (MLEV)***
United States	41.93%	19.28%	65.23%	55.29%	49.61%	31.15%				
United Kingdom	46.09%	22.37%	67.23%	56.95%	52.64%	33.09%				
Canada	32.06%	18.34%	60.64%	53.39%	40.60%	28.82%				
Japan	32.58%	20.64%	67.68%	64.66%	55.45%	49.32%				
S. Korea	34.45%	20.20%	67.62%	67.15%	56.61%	51.57%				
Taiwan	33.97%	17.46%	60.83%	55.71%	48.80%	38.58%				
India	40.98%	13.22%	69.14%	59.34%	48.67%	25.81%	39.69%	19.06%	66.15%	59.89%
Oil and Gas	36.36%	21.24%	62.49%	60.62%	44.60%	33.65%				
Basic Materials	35.01%	19.09%	64.59%	59.91%	51.20%	41.43%				
Industrials	44.20%	21.69%	66.71%	60.53%	55.54%	41.27%				
Consumer Goods	42.44%	20.29%	63.49%	58.42%	51.37%	36.46%				
Technology	34.93%	15.05%	65.38%	58.99%	40.71%	23.38%				
Health Care	36.52%	15.27%	64.53%	53.32%	41.60%	22.17%				
Consumer Services	41.71%	19.91%	69.69%	61.29%	57.94%	43.91%				

Source: own contribution.

Table C.5: Descriptive – *Country* and *Industry* Equity Ratio.

This table shows the mean and industry-mean values of the book equity ratio for all firms in the *overall (pooled)* sample and separated in each *country* and *industry*, for the entire period 2004–2014. The book equity ratio is calculated by book equity over total assets, whereas book equity equals total assets minus total liabilities and preferred stocks plus deferred taxes. SC and SNC firms are determined based on DJIMI (see Table 4.1). All variables are winsorized at the 1% and 99% level.

Sample	***Equity Ratio (SC)***	***Equity Ratio (SNC)***	***Country/ Industry mean***	***Overall (pooled)***		***Proposed Threshold***
				Mean Equity (SC)	***Mean Equity (SNC)***	
United States	58.07%	34.77%	50.39%	60.31%	33.85%	66.67%
United Kingdom	53.91%	32.77%	47.36%			
Canada	67.94%	39.36%	59.40%			
Japan	67.42%	32.32%	44.55%			
S. Korea	65.55%	32.38%	43.39%			
Taiwan	66.03%	39.17%	51.20%			
India	59.02%	30.86%	51.33%			
Oil and Gas	63.64%	37.51%	55.40%			
Basic Materials	64.99%	35.41%	48.80%			
Industrials	55.80%	33.29%	44.46%			
Consumer Goods	57.56%	36.51%	48.63%			
Technology	65.07%	34.62%	59.29%			
Health Care	63.48%	35.47%	58.40%			
Consumer Services	58.29%	30.31%	42.06%			

Source: own contribution.

Table C.6: Descriptive – Overall Determinants (time series).

This table shows the mean values of the firm-specific and macroeconomic debt determinants for all firms in the overall (pooled) sample and separated in each country and industry, for the entire period 2004–2014 and each year separately. Table 4.10 provides the definitions of all debt determinants. Panel A and Panel B represent the mean values for SC and SNC firms, respectively. The trend column includes sparklines representing the trend of the period 2004 to 2014. SC and SNC firms are determined based on DJIMI (see Table 4.1). All variables are winsorized at the 1% and 99% level.

		Panel A: Shari'ah Compliant												
Sample	**Determinants**	**2004–2014**	**2004**	**2005**	**2006**	**2007**	**2008**	**2009**	**2010**	**2011**	**2012**	**2013**	**2014**	**Trend**
Overall (pooled)	Profitability	0.18	0.18	0.18	0.18	0.19	0.18	0.17	0.18	0.18	0.18	0.17	0.17	
	Growth Opportunity	2.57	2.62	2.86	2.76	2.64	2.10	2.41	2.52	2.45	2.49	2.71	2.81	
	Firm Size	14.55	14.21	14.26	14.37	14.49	14.48	14.41	14.58	14.68	14.76	14.84	14.87	
	Tangibility	0.26	0.27	0.27	0.26	0.26	0.27	0.26	0.25	0.26	0.26	0.26	0.25	
	Business Risk	0.02	0.02	0.02	0.02	0.02	0.03	0.03	0.03	0.02	0.02	0.02	0.02	
	GDP growth	2.23	3.82	3.54	3.22	2.83	0.18	−1.96	3.70	2.08	2.36	2.62	2.65	
United States	Profitability	0.18	0.17	0.19	0.18	0.18	0.19	0.16	0.18	0.19	0.18	0.18	0.18	
	Growth Opportunity	2.65	2.84	2.88	2.78	2.73	2.16	2.44	2.59	2.50	2.59	2.89	2.84	
	Firm Size	14.87	14.57	14.64	14.70	14.76	14.82	14.71	14.85	14.98	15.07	15.16	15.22	
	Tangibility	0.23	0.24	0.23	0.23	0.23	0.24	0.23	0.23	0.23	0.23	0.24	0.23	
	Business Risk	0.02	0.02	0.02	0.02	0.02	0.02	0.03	0.03	0.02	0.02	0.02	0.02	
	GDP growth	1.70	3.79	3.35	2.67	1.78	−0.29	−2.78	2.53	1.60	2.32	2.22	2.39	
United Kingdom	Profitability	0.19	0.20	0.20	0.21	0.20	0.19	0.19	0.19	0.20	0.19	0.19	0.18	
	Growth Opportunity	2.47	2.37	2.78	2.71	2.58	2.16	2.29	2.51	2.33	2.42	2.56	2.54	
	Firm Size	14.57	14.14	14.20	14.41	14.59	14.32	14.38	14.50	14.66	14.81	14.90	14.86	
	Tangibility	0.22	0.23	0.22	0.21	0.21	0.21	0.22	0.22	0.21	0.21	0.22	0.22	
	Business Risk	0.02	0.03	0.02	0.02	0.02	0.02	0.03	0.03	0.02	0.02	0.02	0.01	
	GDP growth	1.44	2.49	3.00	2.66	2.59	−0.47	−4.19	1.54	1.97	1.18	2.16	2.94	

(continued)

Table C.6 (continued)

Sample	Determinants	Panel A: Shari'ah Compliant												
Sample	**Determinants**	**2004–2014**	**2004**	**2005**	**2006**	**2007**	**2008**	**2009**	**2010**	**2011**	**2012**	**2013**	**2014**	**Trend**
Canada	Profitability	0.16	0.15	0.16	0.17	0.17	0.18	0.12	0.14	0.16	0.15	0.15	0.15	
	Growth Opportunity	2.04	2.23	2.49	2.44	2.24	1.81	1.71	2.05	1.95	1.86	1.93	1.89	
	Firm Size	13.86	13.22	13.44	13.63	13.88	13.83	13.57	13.88	14.06	14.08	14.24	14.31	
	Tangibility	0.53	0.51	0.55	0.53	0.55	0.54	0.53	0.50	0.52	0.52	0.53	0.52	
	Business Risk	0.03	0.03	0.03	0.02	0.02	0.04	0.05	0.04	0.03	0.02	0.02	0.02	
	GDP growth	2.01	3.14	3.16	2.62	2.01	1.18	−2.71	3.37	2.96	1.92	2.00	2.44	
Japan	Profitability	0.15	0.15	0.14	0.15	0.17	0.15	0.14	0.16	0.16	0.15	0.14	0.14	
	Growth Opportunity	1.91	1.94	2.22	2.13	1.80	1.61	1.91	1.71	1.78	1.88	1.87	2.18	
	Firm Size	14.63	14.52	14.46	14.49	14.60	14.53	14.52	14.74	14.83	14.77	14.82	14.73	
	Tangibility	0.25	0.28	0.26	0.26	0.27	0.28	0.25	0.24	0.23	0.23	0.23	0.22	
	Business Risk	0.02	0.01	0.01	0.01	0.01	0.02	0.02	0.02	0.01	0.01	0.02	0.02	
	GDP growth	0.79	2.36	1.30	1.69	2.19	−1.04	−5.53	4.65	−0.45	1.75	1.61	−0.10	
S. Korea	Profitability	0.16	0.20	0.19	0.17	0.17	0.17	0.18	0.18	0.15	0.15	0.14	0.15	
	Growth Opportunity	2.17	1.86	2.45	2.09	2.53	2.66	2.08	2.26	2.15	1.86	1.93	2.32	
	Firm Size	14.43	13.81	13.84	14.00	14.14	14.07	14.27	14.42	14.46	14.69	14.75	14.84	
	Tangibility	0.32	0.37	0.35	0.35	0.36	0.37	0.35	0.30	0.29	0.31	0.31	0.30	
	Business Risk	0.02	0.03	0.03	0.02	0.02	0.02	0.03	0.02	0.02	0.02	0.02	0.02	
	GDP growth	3.59	4.90	3.92	5.18	5.46	2.83	0.71	6.50	3.68	2.29	2.90	3.31	
Taiwan	Profitability	0.17	0.22	0.20	0.20	0.19	0.16	0.15	0.17	0.15	0.14	0.16	0.15	
	Growth Opportunity	2.41	2.11	2.88	2.79	2.52	1.54	2.27	2.20	2.09	2.23	2.87	2.86	
	Firm Size	13.87	13.08	13.31	13.59	13.85	13.92	13.83	14.02	14.01	14.12	14.16	14.15	
	Tangibility	0.28	0.33	0.33	0.31	0.30	0.33	0.27	0.27	0.27	0.26	0.27	0.25	
	Business Risk	0.03	0.03	0.02	0.03	0.02	0.04	0.03	0.03	0.02	0.02	0.02	0.02	
	GDP growth													

India	Profitability	0.21	0.22	0.21	0.23	0.22	0.22	0.22	0.21	0.21	0.20	0.20	0.19	
	Growth Opportunity	3.77	3.23	4.25	4.09	3.78	2.71	3.56	3.77	3.82	3.75	3.82	4.75	
	Firm Size	13.49	12.75	12.87	13.11	13.35	13.29	13.47	13.73	13.76	13.84	13.90	14.03	
	Tangibility	0.26	0.28	0.28	0.27	0.27	0.27	0.26	0.25	0.25	0.26	0.26	0.26	
	Business Risk	0.03	0.02	0.03	0.03	0.02	0.03	0.03	0.03	0.02	0.02	0.02	0.02	
	GDP growth	7.68	7.92	9.28	9.26	9.80	3.89	8.48	10.26	6.64	5.08	6.90	7.29	
Oil and Gas	Profitability	0.19	0.19	0.22	0.24	0.23	0.25	0.16	0.16	0.17	0.16	0.17	0.17	
	Growth Opportunity	1.91	1.91	2.35	2.16	2.35	1.61	1.88	1.97	1.72	1.68	1.88	1.54	
	Firm Size	14.82	14.27	14.53	14.75	14.89	14.83	14.52	14.79	14.92	14.98	15.12	15.29	
	Tangibility	0.58	0.57	0.56	0.57	0.59	0.59	0.59	0.55	0.58	0.58	0.58	0.58	
	Business Risk	0.03	0.02	0.04	0.03	0.03	0.04	0.07	0.03	0.03	0.02	0.02	0.02	
	GDP growth	1.98	3.58	3.39	2.79	2.23	0.31	−2.41	2.95	2.23	2.18	2.32	2.67	
Basic Materials	Profitability	0.16	0.15	0.16	0.17	0.17	0.18	0.15	0.17	0.19	0.16	0.15	0.15	
	Growth Opportunity	2.23	2.32	2.47	2.41	2.41	2.06	2.31	2.51	2.19	2.08	1.89	2.05	
	Firm Size	14.37	13.79	13.85	14.16	14.32	14.30	14.13	14.44	14.59	14.63	14.70	14.71	
	Tangibility	0.42	0.39	0.42	0.41	0.43	0.43	0.44	0.41	0.43	0.43	0.44	0.43	
	Business Risk	0.03	0.04	0.02	0.03	0.02	0.03	0.04	0.04	0.03	0.03	0.02	0.01	
	GDP growth	2.20	3.61	3.45	3.03	2.61	0.56	−1.91	3.58	2.47	2.11	2.39	2.55	
Industrials	Profitability	0.17	0.17	0.18	0.19	0.19	0.18	0.16	0.17	0.17	0.17	0.17	0.17	
	Growth Opportunity	2.40	2.44	2.72	2.61	2.51	1.87	2.11	2.35	2.21	2.30	2.54	2.72	
	Firm Size	14.50	14.12	14.17	14.29	14.43	14.43	14.37	14.53	14.67	14.74	14.79	14.85	
	Tangibility	0.23	0.24	0.23	0.23	0.23	0.23	0.22	0.23	0.23	0.24	0.24	0.24	
	Business Risk	0.02	0.02	0.02	0.02	0.02	0.02	0.03	0.03	0.02	0.02	0.01	0.01	
	GDP growth	2.32	3.74	3.64	3.25	2.91	0.16	−1.82	3.70	2.12	2.38	2.71	2.79	

(continued)

Table C.6 (continued)

Sample	Determinants	Panel A: Shari'ah Compliant											Trend
		2004–2014	2004	2005	2006	2007	2008	2009	2010	2011	2012	2013	2014	
Cons. Goods	Profitability	0.18	0.19	0.18	0.19	0.19	0.18	0.17	0.19	0.18	0.18	0.19	0.18	
	Growth Opportunity	2.67	2.34	2.77	2.74	2.63	2.19	2.41	2.56	2.71	2.71	3.02	3.23	
	Firm Size	14.72	14.50	14.50	14.54	14.65	14.62	14.57	14.71	14.79	14.88	15.00	15.05	
	Tangibility	0.23	0.27	0.25	0.25	0.25	0.25	0.23	0.21	0.21	0.21	0.21	0.21	
	Business Risk	0.02	0.02	0.02	0.02	0.02	0.02	0.03	0.03	0.02	0.02	0.02	0.02	
	GDP growth	2.74	4.16	3.88	3.83	3.67	0.52	−1.05	4.73	2.43	2.58	3.03	2.91	
Technology	Profitability	0.17	0.17	0.18	0.17	0.17	0.17	0.15	0.18	0.17	0.16	0.16	0.17	
	Growth Opportunity	2.93	3.12	3.32	3.29	2.94	2.19	2.84	2.87	2.67	2.87	3.11	3.18	
	Firm Size	14.33	14.05	14.13	14.20	14.32	14.27	14.21	14.30	14.36	14.48	14.57	14.70	
	Tangibility	0.15	0.16	0.16	0.14	0.15	0.16	0.14	0.14	0.14	0.14	0.15	0.15	
	Business Risk	0.03	0.03	0.02	0.03	0.02	0.03	0.03	0.03	0.03	0.02	0.02	0.02	
	GDP growth	2.04	3.77	3.37	3.02	2.52	0.02	−2.26	3.39	1.91	2.39	2.53	2.63	
Health Care	Profitability	0.17	0.16	0.16	0.17	0.16	0.17	0.17	0.18	0.17	0.17	0.16	0.15	
	Growth Opportunity	2.88	2.99	3.12	3.07	3.07	2.50	2.70	2.68	2.73	2.75	2.96	3.22	
	Firm Size	14.21	13.83	13.87	13.94	14.08	14.14	14.13	14.30	14.40	14.45	14.53	14.57	
	Tangibility	0.19	0.20	0.20	0.20	0.19	0.19	0.19	0.18	0.18	0.18	0.18	0.17	
	Business Risk	0.02	0.03	0.02	0.03	0.02	0.02	0.02	0.02	0.02	0.02	0.02	0.02	
	GDP growth	2.38	4.07	3.65	3.45	3.10	0.16	−1.70	4.19	2.04	2.53	2.81	2.64	
Cons. Services	Profitability	0.21	0.21	0.20	0.20	0.21	0.20	0.20	0.21	0.23	0.23	0.22	0.19	
	Growth Opportunity	2.67	3.00	2.99	2.68	2.33	2.25	2.46	2.55	2.68	2.67	2.98	2.88	
	Firm Size	15.04	14.90	14.89	14.90	14.91	14.94	14.99	15.10	15.15	15.21	15.28	15.03	
	Tangibility	0.28	0.35	0.32	0.31	0.29	0.30	0.27	0.26	0.25	0.26	0.26	0.24	
	Business Risk	0.02	0.02	0.01	0.02	0.02	0.02	0.02	0.02	0.02	0.02	0.02	0.02	
	GDP growth	1.58	3.50	3.00	2.62	2.04	−0.34	−3.21	2.88	1.47	2.13	2.17	1.97	

Table C.6 (continued)

		Panel B: Shari'ah Non-Compliant												
Sample	**Determinants**	**2004–2014**	**2004**	**2005**	**2006**	**2007**	**2008**	**2009**	**2010**	**2011**	**2012**	**2013**	**2014**	**Trend**
Overall (pooled)	Profitability	0.10	0.10	0.10	0.10	0.10	0.09	0.09	0.10	0.10	0.09	0.09	0.09	
	Growth Opportunity	1.14	1.16	1.24	1.23	1.15	1.01	1.10	1.13	1.10	1.13	1.20	1.20	
	Firm Size	15.44	15.21	15.21	15.27	15.38	15.39	15.33	15.46	15.51	15.56	15.63	15.67	
	Tangibility	0.36	0.39	0.37	0.37	0.36	0.37	0.37	0.35	0.35	0.35	0.35	0.36	
	Business Risk	0.02	0.01	0.01	0.01	0.01	0.02	0.02	0.02	0.01	0.01	0.01	0.01	
	GDP growth	1.70	3.36	2.85	2.86	2.71	−0.09	−3.03	4.04	1.42	2.18	2.31	1.88	
United States	Profitability	0.11	0.11	0.11	0.11	0.11	0.11	0.10	0.10	0.11	0.11	0.11	0.11	
	Growth Opportunity	1.22	1.27	1.28	1.29	1.20	1.03	1.14	1.20	1.16	1.25	1.37	1.36	
	Firm Size	15.23	15.11	15.12	15.18	15.16	15.27	15.08	15.16	15.23	15.29	15.36	15.45	
	Tangibility	0.32	0.32	0.29	0.31	0.30	0.32	0.32	0.31	0.32	0.32	0.33	0.32	
	Business Risk	0.02	0.01	0.02	0.01	0.02	0.02	0.03	0.02	0.01	0.01	0.01	0.01	
	GDP growth	1.53	3.79	3.35	2.67	1.78	−0.29	−2.78	2.53	1.60	2.32	2.22	2.39	
United Kingdom	Profitability	0.13	0.14	0.13	0.13	0.13	0.12	0.12	0.13	0.13	0.13	0.13	0.12	
	Growth Opportunity	1.23	1.24	1.36	1.38	1.22	1.05	1.16	1.24	1.13	1.24	1.35	1.32	
	Firm Size	15.02	14.41	14.52	14.67	14.90	15.05	15.08	15.13	15.17	15.24	15.36	15.28	
	Tangibility	0.43	0.52	0.47	0.42	0.38	0.40	0.40	0.39	0.42	0.43	0.47	0.47	
	Business Risk	0.01	0.01	0.01	0.01	0.01	0.01	0.01	0.01	0.01	0.01	0.01	0.01	
	GDP growth	1.12	2.49	3.00	2.66	2.59	−0.47	−4.19	1.54	1.97	1.18	2.16	2.94	
Canada	Profitability	0.12	0.11	0.12	0.13	0.12	0.11	0.10	0.12	0.13	0.14	0.12	0.12	
	Growth Opportunity	1.16	1.14	1.17	1.25	1.17	1.03	1.04	1.14	1.13	1.24	1.40	1.31	
	Firm Size	14.86	14.88	14.84	14.93	15.03	14.77	14.78	14.62	14.78	14.93	15.09	15.11	
	Tangibility	0.42	0.41	0.42	0.45	0.41	0.44	0.44	0.42	0.41	0.42	0.36	0.36	
	Business Risk	0.01	0.01	0.01	0.02	0.01	0.02	0.01	0.02	0.01	0.01	0.01	0.01	
	GDP growth	1.82	3.14	3.16	2.62	2.01	1.18	−2.71	3.37	2.96	1.92	2.00	2.44	

(continued)

Table C.6 (continued)

		Panel B: Shari'ah Non-Compliant												
Sample	**Determinants**	**2004–2014**	**2004**	**2005**	**2006**	**2007**	**2008**	**2009**	**2010**	**2011**	**2012**	**2013**	**2014**	**Trend**
Japan	Profitability	0.08	0.09	0.09	0.08	0.09	0.07	0.07	0.09	0.08	0.07	0.08	0.07	
	Growth Opportunity	1.06	1.13	1.26	1.19	1.04	0.99	1.04	1.01	1.02	1.02	1.05	1.07	
	Firm Size	15.88	15.70	15.65	15.71	15.88	15.82	15.81	15.99	16.03	15.98	15.97	15.93	
	Tangibility	0.37	0.40	0.38	0.38	0.37	0.38	0.37	0.37	0.36	0.36	0.36	0.37	
	Business Risk	0.01	0.01	0.01	0.01	0.01	0.02	0.02	0.02	0.01	0.01	0.01	0.01	
	GDP growth	0.64	2.36	1.30	1.69	2.19	−1.04	−5.53	4.65	−0.45	1.75	1.61	−0.10	
S. Korea	Profitability	0.09	0.11	0.10	0.09	0.10	0.08	0.09	0.10	0.09	0.08	0.07	0.07	
	Growth Opportunity	1.03	0.92	1.04	1.06	1.16	1.01	1.00	1.07	1.04	1.01	1.01	0.99	
	Firm Size	15.70	15.37	15.53	15.58	15.72	15.50	15.52	15.53	15.69	15.89	15.93	16.06	
	Tangibility	0.38	0.44	0.44	0.41	0.42	0.38	0.40	0.35	0.34	0.35	0.34	0.36	
	Business Risk	0.02	0.01	0.01	0.01	0.01	0.02	0.02	0.03	0.02	0.02	0.01	0.01	
	GDP growth	3.67	4.90	3.92	5.18	5.46	2.83	0.71	6.50	3.68	2.29	2.90	3.31	
Taiwan	Profitability	0.09	0.10	0.09	0.09	0.09	0.07	0.08	0.11	0.08	0.08	0.09	0.08	
	Growth Opportunity	1.12	1.13	1.08	1.17	1.18	0.97	1.19	1.19	1.11	1.09	1.12	1.10	
	Firm Size	14.94	14.21	14.43	14.52	14.61	14.79	14.83	15.30	15.18	15.24	15.29	15.32	
	Tangibility	0.41	0.42	0.43	0.43	0.43	0.45	0.44	0.42	0.39	0.39	0.37	0.36	
	Business Risk	0.02	0.01	0.02	0.02	0.02	0.02	0.03	0.03	0.03	0.01	0.02	0.01	
	GDP growth													
India	Profitability	0.10	0.11	0.10	0.12	0.12	0.10	0.11	0.11	0.10	0.10	0.10	0.08	
	Growth Opportunity	1.23	1.22	1.34	1.20	1.37	0.98	1.32	1.26	1.17	1.13	1.20	1.36	
	Firm Size	14.92	13.96	14.24	14.40	14.60	14.65	14.87	15.05	15.13	15.34	15.52	15.64	
	Tangibility	0.40	0.42	0.42	0.40	0.41	0.42	0.41	0.37	0.39	0.38	0.38	0.41	
	Business Risk	0.02	0.02	0.02	0.02	0.02	0.03	0.02	0.02	0.02	0.02	0.02	0.01	
	GDP growth	7.58	7.92	9.28	9.26	9.80	3.89	8.48	10.26	6.64	5.08	6.90	7.29	

Oil and Gas	Profitability	0.10	0.11	0.10	0.11	0.10	0.11	0.08	0.09	0.12	0.10	0.09	0.09	
	Growth Opportunity	1.06	1.07	1.12	1.05	1.17	0.90	1.00	1.08	1.10	1.05	1.11	1.05	
	Firm Size	16.04	15.41	15.80	16.00	16.04	16.10	15.89	16.06	16.04	16.18	16.15	16.18	
	Tangibility	0.54	0.54	0.51	0.51	0.50	0.57	0.57	0.53	0.54	0.54	0.55	0.56	
	Business Risk	0.02	0.02	0.02	0.02	0.02	0.03	0.04	0.02	0.02	0.02	0.02	0.02	
	GDP growth	2.85	4.86	4.99	4.95	4.24	0.89	−0.82	4.54	2.41	2.68	3.03	3.02	
Basic Materials	Profitability	0.10	0.11	0.11	0.11	0.11	0.10	0.09	0.11	0.10	0.09	0.09	0.09	
	Growth Opportunity	1.11	1.13	1.27	1.22	1.19	0.99	1.12	1.13	1.06	1.08	1.11	1.07	
	Firm Size	15.51	15.12	15.04	15.17	15.41	15.48	15.31	15.63	15.73	15.67	15.77	15.91	
	Tangibility	0.39	0.42	0.40	0.39	0.39	0.40	0.41	0.39	0.38	0.39	0.38	0.40	
	Business Risk	0.02	0.01	0.01	0.01	0.02	0.03	0.03	0.03	0.01	0.01	0.01	0.01	
	GDP growth	1.95	3.64	3.16	3.38	3.35	0.11	−2.67	4.52	1.36	2.24	2.40	1.64	
Industrials	Profitability	0.09	0.09	0.10	0.10	0.10	0.09	0.08	0.10	0.09	0.09	0.09	0.09	
	Growth Opportunity	1.14	1.16	1.23	1.24	1.17	1.01	1.10	1.13	1.08	1.12	1.19	1.21	
	Firm Size	15.38	15.34	15.32	15.39	15.39	15.32	15.23	15.31	15.36	15.43	15.53	15.53	
	Tangibility	0.31	0.33	0.32	0.32	0.31	0.32	0.32	0.31	0.31	0.31	0.30	0.30	
	Business Risk	0.01	0.01	0.01	0.01	0.01	0.02	0.02	0.02	0.02	0.01	0.01	0.01	
	GDP growth	1.66	3.16	2.61	2.52	2.42	−0.13	−2.99	4.02	1.51	2.20	2.36	2.01	
Cons. Goods	Profitability	0.09	0.11	0.11	0.10	0.11	0.09	0.09	0.10	0.09	0.09	0.09	0.09	
	Growth Opportunity	1.11	1.15	1.21	1.18	1.09	0.99	1.08	1.08	1.08	1.14	1.17	1.16	
	Firm Size	15.51	15.13	15.13	15.25	15.48	15.45	15.46	15.60	15.69	15.74	15.75	15.80	
	Tangibility	0.29	0.33	0.32	0.32	0.30	0.31	0.30	0.29	0.27	0.27	0.27	0.26	
	Business Risk	0.02	0.01	0.01	0.02	0.02	0.02	0.02	0.02	0.01	0.01	0.01	0.01	
	GDP growth	1.73	3.65	3.07	3.16	2.90	−0.04	−3.15	4.40	1.26	2.17	2.21	1.62	

(continued)

Table C.6 (continued)

		Panel B: Shari'ah Non-Compliant											
Sample	**Determinants**	**2004–2014**	**2004**	**2005**	**2006**	**2007**	**2008**	**2009**	**2010**	**2011**	**2012**	**2013**	**2014**	**Trend**
Technology	Profitability	0.11	0.12	0.10	0.12	0.11	0.09	0.09	0.12	0.09	0.10	0.12	0.11	
	Growth Opportunity	1.15	1.26	1.25	1.26	1.16	0.99	1.23	1.17	1.09	1.11	1.19	1.13	
	Firm Size	15.52	15.51	15.52	15.30	15.41	15.42	15.30	15.64	15.54	15.51	15.71	15.72	
	Tangibility	0.32	0.30	0.33	0.35	0.34	0.35	0.35	0.32	0.32	0.32	0.28	0.28	
	Business Risk	0.03	0.02	0.03	0.03	0.03	0.04	0.03	0.03	0.03	0.02	0.02	0.01	
	GDP growth	1.10	2.84	1.98	2.02	2.32	−0.64	−4.42	4.12	0.76	2.02	1.90	1.34	
Health Care	Profitability	0.11	0.10	0.10	0.10	0.10	0.11	0.13	0.12	0.12	0.12	0.12	0.10	
	Growth Opportunity	1.27	1.45	1.42	1.36	1.20	1.03	1.20	1.21	1.22	1.29	1.48	1.33	
	Firm Size	14.51	14.52	14.37	14.00	14.16	14.25	14.23	14.38	14.54	14.74	14.97	15.27	
	Tangibility	0.28	0.31	0.27	0.31	0.29	0.30	0.31	0.27	0.26	0.25	0.25	0.25	
	Business Risk	0.01	0.02	0.02	0.01	0.01	0.02	0.01	0.01	0.01	0.01	0.01	0.01	
	GDP growth	1.96	3.97	3.55	3.46	2.81	0.00	−2.24	3.52	1.74	2.30	2.35	2.22	
Cons. Services	Profitability	0.09	0.09	0.09	0.09	0.09	0.09	0.09	0.10	0.10	0.10	0.10	0.10	
	Growth Opportunity	1.17	1.17	1.26	1.25	1.12	1.07	1.09	1.13	1.13	1.19	1.26	1.31	
	Firm Size	15.44	15.12	15.14	15.27	15.35	15.43	15.47	15.51	15.52	15.58	15.60	15.54	
	Tangibility	0.45	0.52	0.48	0.46	0.45	0.45	0.45	0.44	0.44	0.45	0.45	0.47	
	Business Risk	0.01	0.01	0.01	0.01	0.01	0.02	0.01	0.01	0.01	0.01	0.01	0.01	
	GDP growth	1.33	2.96	2.40	2.37	2.33	−0.36	−3.64	3.50	1.19	2.00	2.07	1.58	

Source: own contribution.

Table C.7: Paired z-test for Sample Means.

This table provides the mean and variance test of all variables (dependent and independent) for both firm samples, i.e., SC and SNC firms, in the *overall (pooled)* sample and separated in each *country* and *industry*. SC and SNC firms are determined based on DJIMI (see Table 4.1). The z-test results show whether both sample means are significantly different from each other. The test statistic is assumed to have a normal distribution. Referring to Figure B.3 in Appendix B, the normality test suggests and concludes that the residuals are close to a normal distribution.

$$Z = \frac{\overline{X}1 - \overline{X}2}{\sqrt{SE_{x1}^2 + SE_{x2}^2}}, \text{ where } SE = \frac{\sigma}{\sqrt{n}}$$

Z-values > 1.96 represent significantly difference, whereas Z-values < 1.96 represent insignificance. All means (x) and their respective standard deviations (σ) are retrieved from Table 5.4, and the respective number of observations (n) is retrieved from Table A.5 in Appendix A.

Determinants	BLEV	MLEV	Prof	Growth	Size	Tang	Risk	GDP
Overall (pooled)	94.78	169.12	68.88	82.50	34.92	25.15	17.49	10.20
United States	53.02	94.70	41.89	61.73	9.43	12.62	9.94	3.23
United Kingdom	21.18	37.95	13.77	24.02	4.92	11.55	9.18	2.12
Canada	21.63	29.56	7.17	18.18	8.39	5.05	6.89	1.25
Japan	69.68	95.45	30.04	22.47	28.41	19.55	4.81	1.51
S. Korea	29.76	47.37	12.58	13.07	10.29	4.66	2.74	0.57
Taiwan	22.46	39.94	13.29	17.29	10.03	8.42	1.71	–
India	30.14	44.81	23.85	36.53	12.14	9.87	3.38	0.67
Oil and Gas	21.71	34.60	19.37	22.40	9.75	2.15	3.86	–
Basic Materials	33.29	55.26	14.31	20.89	14.49	2.96	6.89	–
Industrials	43.09	86.25	40.03	45.50	20.51	12.31	6.62	–
Cons. Goods	32.41	71.08	30.68	33.05	12.94	10.07	3.15	–
Technologies	33.24	48.96	13.39	36.05	12.88	12.24	0.34	–
Health Care	24.50	33.25	12.53	29.68	3.03	5.90	5.60	–
Cons. Services	40.89	72.34	34.79	27.74	6.20	17.03	10.16	–

Source: own contribution.

Table C.8: Variance Inflation Factors.

The following table shows the VIF for all independent variables. VIF is determined as $1/(1–R^2)$.			
Variables		**VIF**	**1/VIF**
Profitability	a	1.62	0.62
	b	1.42	0.70
	c	1.25	0.80
Growth Opportunity	a	1.97	0.51
	b	1.64	0.61
	c	1.24	0.81
Firm Size	a	1.17	0.85
	b	1.18	0.85
	c	1.06	0.94
Tangibility	a	1.11	0.90
	b	1.11	0.90
	c	1.09	0.92
Risk	a	1.06	0.94
	b	1.06	0.95
	c	1.00	1.00
GDP growth	a	1.07	0.93
	b	1.11	0.90
	c	1.03	0.97
Mean	a	1.33	
	b	1.25	
	c	1.11	

Note: [a] Denoted for the overall pooled sample.
[b] Denoted for SC firms.
[c] Denoted for SNC firms. SC and SNC firms are determined based on DJIMI (see Table 4.1).
Source: own contribution.

Table C.9: Beta Coefficient Test.

This table provides an overview of the beta coefficients of the estimation results for both firm samples, i.e., SC and SNC firms, in the *overall (pooled)* sample and separated in each *country* and *industry*. SC and SNC firms are determined based on DJIMI (see Table 4.1). Results are shown with a dash-sign "–" represent either data, not available or not applicable. The test statistic is assumed to have a normal distribution. Referring to Figure B.3 in Appendix B, the normality test suggests and concludes that the residuals are close to a normal distribution.

$$Z = \frac{\beta_1 - \beta_2}{\sqrt{SE_{\beta_1}^2 + SE_{\beta_2}^2}}, \text{ where } SE = \frac{\sigma}{\sqrt{n}}$$

Z-values > 1.96 represent significantly difference, whereas Z-values < 1.96 represent insignificance. All coefficient results (β) and their respective standard errors are retrieved from Table 5.6 and Tables D.2–D.3 in Appendix D for *overall (pooled)*, *country*, and *industry*, respectively.

Leverage			**BLEV**						**MLEV**			
Determinants	**Prof**	**Growth**	**Size**	**Tang**	**Risk**	**GDP**	**Prof**	**Growth**	**Size**	**Tang**	**Risk**	**GDP**
Overall	4.50	5.88	4.14	0.31	1.40	2.83	5.18	8.30	3.60	0.36	1.42	5.66
United States	1.48	3.93	0.27	0.23	0.68	3.20	2.39	4.97	0.91	0.63	0.03	2.53
United Kingdom	1.61	2.41	3.27	0.57	0.41	0.50	1.07	1.20	2.36	1.45	3.08	0.06
Canada	0.41	1.65	0.78	2.77	0.91	0.06	0.63	0.69	0.89	0.40	0.39	1.98
Japan	0.88	0.93	0.16	0.78	1.17	0.23	1.76	6.20	1.11	0.30	0.43	1.51
S. Korea	1.98	0.87	2.02	0.66	0.02	0.35	2.16	5.96	1.27	0.92	0.96	0.17
Taiwan	3.66	2.77	0.26	2.36	1.69	–	1.96	3.23	0.30	0.27	0.86	–
India	0.01	1.32	1.14	0.69	0.83	1.85	0.37	3.09	2.04	0.23	2.07	0.51
Oil and Gas	0.84	2.19	2.31	1.62	0.04	0.83	4.26	0.95	4.05	2.05	1.16	0.55
Basic Materials	1.52	1.24	2.99	1.03	2.69	1.58	2.41	4.20	2.25	0.45	2.36	2.20
Industrials	2.99	3.06	1.82	0.23	1.37	0.71	2.88	6.93	0.57	0.52	1.19	4.47
Cons. Goods	0.93	0.97	0.55	0.97	0.08	1.41	0.86	5.42	0.59	1.74	1.09	0.95
Technologies	2.90	3.55	0.81	1.73	1.90	0.19	1.73	1.38	1.08	1.68	1.10	3.03
Health Care	1.53	2.41	1.18	0.23	0.29	0.00	2.77	0.43	1.51	0.83	0.44	0.49
Cons. Services	1.52	4.50	1.83	0.84	2.44	1.77	2.97	2.23	0.86	1.36	3.94	3.18

Source: own contribution.

Appendix D

https://doi.org/10.1515/9783110713664-012

Table D.1: *Overall (pooled)* Regression – Time Breakdown.

This table provides the coefficients of panel regressions with book leverage and market leverage as the dependent variables. All independent variables used in the equation model (13) and (14) are lagged one year and regressed separately for SC and SNC firms for the *overall (pooled)* sample divided into the pre-crisis, crisis, and post-crisis period. Tables 4.3 and 4.10 provide the definitions of all variables. SC and SNC firms are determined based on DJIMI (see Table 4.1). Models (1)–(3) and (4)–(6) represent the regression results for book leverage for SC and SNC firms, respectively. Model (7)–(9) and (10–12) represent the regression results for market leverage for SC and SNC firms, respectively. Models (1), (4), (7), and (10) show the results for the period 2004–2007, whereas Model (2), (5), (8), and (11) show the results for the period 2008–2009, representing the financial crisis (GFC). Finally, Model (3), (6), (9), and (12) show the results for the period 2010–2014. The regressions in all models contain *time fixed effects* (time dummies). Econometric estimators applied to each model are shown in the last row. Company cluster robust standard errors are reported in the brackets. *, ** and *** denote significance at 10%, 5% and 1% levels, respectively. All variables are winsorized at the 1% and 99% level. Model specifications are provided in Section 4.4.1.

$$blev_{it} = \alpha + \beta_1 prof_{i,t-1} + \beta_2 growth_{i,t-1} + \beta_3 size_{i,t-1} + \beta_4 tang_{i,t-1} + \beta_5 risk_{i,t-1} + \beta_6 gdp_{i,t-1} + \mu_i + \mu_t + \varepsilon_{it} \quad (13)$$

$$mlev_{it} = \alpha + \beta_1 prof_{i,t-1} + \beta_2 growth_{i,t-1} + \beta_3 size_{i,t-1} + \beta_4 tang_{i,t-1} + \beta_5 risk_{i,t-1} + \beta_6 gdp_{i,t-1} + \mu_i + \mu_t + \varepsilon_{it} \quad (14)$$

Overall (pooled)	Book Leverage						Market Leverage					
	Shari'ah Compliant			Shari'ah Non-Compliant			Shari'ah Compliant			Shari'ah Non-Compliant		
Determinants	2004–2007 pre (1)	2008–2009 crisis (2)	2010–2014 post (3)	2004–2007 pre (4)	2008–2009 crisis (5)	2010–2014 post (6)	2004–2007 pre (7)	2008–2009 crisis (8)	2010–2014 post (9)	2004–2007 pre (10)	2008–2009 crisis (11)	2010–2014 post (12)
Profitability $_{t-1}$	0.015	−0.004	−0.130**	−0.126	−0.331***	−0.381***	0.019	−0.013	−0.158***	0.007	−0.202	−0.482***
	[0.071]	[0.068]	[0.056]	[0.124]	[0.082]	[0.064]	[0.046]	[0.081]	[0.041]	[0.186]	[0.138]	[0.081]
Growth Opportunity $_{t-1}$	−0.005	0.005	−0.006*	0.001	0.023	0.030**	−0.011***	0.017***	−0.013***	−0.033	0.176***	−0.118***
	[0.005]	[0.003]	[0.003]	[0.016]	[0.016]	[0.014]	[0.003]	[0.003]	[0.002]	[0.029]	[0.023]	[0.016]
Firm Size $_{t-1}$	−0.016	0.005	0.004	0.003	0.031**	0.038***	−0.001	0.035*	0.052***	0.001	0.050***	0.058***
	[0.017]	[0.030]	[0.012]	[0.015]	[0.013]	[0.010]	[0.009]	[0.019]	[0.010]	[0.027]	[0.014]	[0.013]
Tangibility $_{t-1}$	0.052	0.184**	−0.012	0.066	0.129**	−0.027	0.012	0.085	0.053	−0.020	−0.123	0.079
	[0.074]	[0.073]	[0.054]	[0.072]	[0.052]	[0.055]	[0.042]	[0.113]	[0.041]	[0.142]	[0.093]	[0.080]

Business	0.112	−0.137	0.136*	0.209	−0.031	0.018	−0.034	−0.246*	−0.019	0.361	−0.127	−0.139
$Risk_{t-1}$	[0.141]	[0.104]	[0.074]	[0.189]	[0.125]	[0.100]	[0.064]	[0.130]	[0.050]	[0.316]	[0.158]	[0.122]
GDP $growth_{t-1}$	−0.009*	−0.005	0.004***	0.011***	0.000	−0.002**	0.004	0.002	0.000	−0.009	0.016***	−0.011***
	[0.005]	[0.003]	[0.001]	[0.003]	[0.003]	[0.001]	[0.003]	[0.003]	[0.001]	[0.009]	[0.006]	[0.001]
Constant	0.648***	0.295	0.373**	0.581***	0.179	0.076	0.186	−0.335	−0.518***	0.625	−0.258	−0.174
	[0.244]	[0.430]	[0.170]	[0.218]	[0.208]	[0.157]	[0.130]	[0.273]	[0.134]	[0.427]	[0.233]	[0.211]
R^2	0.018	0.143	0.035	0.032	0.228	0.062	0.104	0.251	0.123	0.184	0.513	0.286
Adjusted R^2	0.013	0.137	0.031	0.023	0.222	0.057	0.099	0.247	0.120	0.176	0.509	0.283
Firms	560	589	669	328	471	544	560	589	669	328	471	544
Observations	1521	1115	2926	875	854	2292	1521	1115	2926	875	854	2292
Time Effects	yes	yes	yes	yes	yes	yes	yes	yes	yes	yes	yes	yes
Estimator	FE	FE	FE	FE	FE	FE	FE	FE	FE	FE	FE	FE

Source: own contribution.

Table D.2: *Country* and *Industry* Regression (Book Leverage).

This table provides the coefficients of panel regressions with book leverage as the dependent variables. All independent variables used in the equation model (13) are lagged one year and regressed separately for SC and SNC firms for the *country and industry* samples for the entire period 2004–2014. Table 4.3 and Table 4.10 provide the definitions of all variables. SC and SNC firms are determined based on DJIMI (see Table 4.1). US, UK, CA, JP, SK, TW, and IN denote countries such as United States, United Kingdom, Canada, Japan, South Korea, Taiwan, and India. OILG, BMAT, IND, CGDS, TECH, HCARE, and CSRV denote industries such as Oil and Gas, Basic Materials, Industrials, Consumer Goods, Technology, Health Care, and Consumer Services. Panel A and B represent the regression results for book leverage for SC and SNC firms, respectively. Results are shown with a dash–sign "–" represent either data, not available or not applicable. The regressions in all models contain *time fixed effects* (time dummies), *country* and *industry fixed effects* (i.e., dummies), while the *country* samples contain industry dummies, the *industry* samples contain country dummies (where applicable). Econometric estimators applied to each model are shown in the last row. All regressions were applied with the respective estimator, as identified by the model estimation procedure described in Panel A in Table B.3 in Appendix B. Company cluster robust standard errors are reported in the brackets. *, ** and *** denote significance at 10%, 5% and 1% levels, respectively. All variables are winsorized at the 1% and 99% level. Model specifications are provided in Section 4.4.1.

$$blev_{it} = \alpha + \beta_1 prof_{i,t-1} + \beta_2 growth_{i,t-1} + \beta_3 size_{i,t-1} + \beta_4 tang_{i,t-1} + \beta_5 risk_{i,t-1} + \beta_6 gdp_{i,t-1} + \mu_i + \mu_t + \varepsilon_{it} \quad (13)$$

	Panel A: Shari'ah Compliant (SC)													
	Country							*Industry*						
	US	UK	CA	JP	SK	TW	IN	OILG	BMAT	IND	CGDS	TECH	HCARE	CSRV
	(1)	(2)	(3)	(4)	(5)	(6)	(7)	(8)	(9)	(10)	(11)	(12)	(13)	(14)
Determinants	Book Leverage													
Profitability$_{t-1}$	−0.112**	0.093	−0.199*	−0.332***	−0.077	−0.053	−0.281**	−0.196*	−0.202*	−0.001	−0.279**	−0.100	−0.333***	−0.058
	[0.046]	[0.132]	[0.108]	[0.127]	[0.178]	[0.105]	[0.113]	[0.106]	[0.106]	[0.073]	[0.126]	[0.072]	[0.092]	[0.100]
Growth Opportunity$_{t-1}$	−0.009***	0.006	0.013	0.005	0.002	−0.001	0.004	0.010	0.002	−0.008	0.006	−0.005	−0.012**	0.002
	[0.003]	[0.009]	[0.011]	[0.007]	[0.009]	[0.005]	[0.005]	[0.013]	[0.008]	[0.006]	[0.006]	[0.004]	[0.006]	[0.006]
Firm Size$_{t-1}$	−0.010	−0.071***	0.013	0.021	0.045	0.007	−0.004	−0.018	0.002	−0.025*	0.007	0.010	0.026**	−0.022
	[0.012]	[0.025]	[0.018]	[0.020]	[0.027]	[0.033]	[0.020]	[0.021]	[0.017]	[0.015]	[0.020]	[0.010]	[0.011]	[0.026]

$Tangibility_{t-1}$	0.131*	0.000	0.004	0.122	0.061	0.121	−0.010	−0.140*	0.075	0.077	0.015	0.218***	0.294***	0.233*
	[0.076]	[0.128]	[0.083]	[0.110]	[0.124]	[0.130]	[0.125]	[0.079]	[0.069]	[0.083]	[0.108]	[0.077]	[0.112]	[0.130]
Business $Risk_{t-1}$	0.275***	0.030	0.311	−0.176	−0.082	−0.312	0.096	0.032	0.567***	0.208	0.028	0.189	0.479*	−0.044
	[0.101]	[0.180]	[0.213]	[0.150]	[0.210]	[0.251]	[0.118]	[0.114]	[0.197]	[0.142]	[0.131]	[0.140]	[0.258]	[0.150]
GDP $growth_{t-1}$	−0.312***	0.008	0.111	0.108***	−0.005	–	−0.002	−0.003	0.007	−0.001	0.005**	−0.001	−0.001	−0.006***
	[0.048]	[0.006]	[0.145]	[0.036]	[0.015]		[0.005]	[0.003]	[0.006]	[0.002]	[0.002]	[0.002]	[0.003]	[0.002]
Constant	1.306***	1.442***	−0.060	−0.177	−0.331	0.232	0.504*	0.746**	0.284	0.806***	0.347	0.252*	0.084	0.736*
	[0.235]	[0.361]	[0.355]	[0.278]	[0.356]	[0.470]	[0.275]	[0.321]	[0.240]	[0.213]	[0.303]	[0.151]	[0.160]	[0.399]
R^2	0.076	0.097	0.077	0.091	0.134	0.085	0.056	0.116	0.087	0.042	0.061			0.054
Adjusted R^2	0.072	0.073	0.042	0.075	0.063	0.025	0.032	0.087	0.053	0.032	0.046			0.032
Firms	407	74	53	120	31	34	71	64	63	188	132	121	97	91
Observations	3091	528	380	809	185	229	569	472	417	1430	949	869	765	660
Time Effects	yes	yes	yes	yes	yes	yes	yes	yes	yes	yes	yes	yes	yes	yes
Country Effects	–	–	–	–	–	–	–	–	–	–	–	yes	yes	–
Industry Effects	–	–	–	–	–	–	–	–	–	–	–	–	–	–
Estimator	FE	FE	FE	FE	FE	FE	FE	FE	FE	FE	FE	RE	RE	FE

(continued)

Table D.2 (continued)

	Panel B: Shari'ah Non-Compliant (SNC)													
	Country							*Industry*						
	US	UK	CA	JP	SK	TW	IN	OILG	BMAT	IND	CGDS	TECH	HCARE	CSRV
	(1)	(2)	(3)	(4)	(5)	(6)	(7)	(8)	(9)	(10)	(11)	(12)	(13)	(14)
Determinants	Book Leverage													
$Profitability_{t-1}$	−0.254***	−0.456	−0.095	−0.474***	−0.499***	−0.664***	−0.279	−0.355**	−0.423***	−0.388***	−0.439***	−0.600***	−0.654***	−0.360**
	[0.084]	[0.314]	[0.228]	[0.101]	[0.117]	[0.130]	[0.192]	[0.157]	[0.100]	[0.107]	[0.116]	[0.159]	[0.238]	[0.172]
Growth $Opportunity_{t-1}$	0.055***	0.119**	0.069**	0.023	0.031	0.075***	−0.031	0.096**	−0.033	0.050***	0.029	0.147***	0.108**	0.109***
	[0.016]	[0.046]	[0.032]	[0.018]	[0.032]	[0.027]	[0.026]	[0.037]	[0.027]	[0.018]	[0.023]	[0.045]	[0.048]	[0.023]
Firm $Size_{t-1}$	−0.005	0.075**	0.034	0.025*	0.113***	0.017	0.022*	0.043**	0.066***	0.015	0.021	0.035	0.059**	0.034**
	[0.014]	[0.037]	[0.020]	[0.014]	[0.020]	[0.019]	[0.011]	[0.016]	[0.013]	[0.016]	[0.016]	[0.023]	[0.025]	[0.016]
$Tangibility_{t-1}$	0.154**	−0.141	0.377***	0.019	−0.040	0.514***	−0.101**	0.181	−0.022	0.053	0.191	0.021	0.276***	0.103
	[0.062]	[0.210]	[0.106]	[0.073]	[0.088]	[0.104]	[0.042]	[0.182]	[0.064]	[0.061]	[0.145]	[0.114]	[0.070]	[0.083]
Business $Risk_{t-1}$	0.172	−0.190	−0.095	0.041	−0.075	0.214	−0.143	0.042	−0.153	−0.109	0.047	−0.363	0.644	0.549***
	[0.114]	[0.503]	[0.393]	[0.109]	[0.292]	[0.184]	[0.261]	[0.248]	[0.181]	[0.182]	[0.195]	[0.267]	[0.431]	[0.191]
GDP $growth_{t-1}$	−0.061	0.006	0.050	0.099***	0.002	–	0.007	0.000	−0.003	−0.003*	0.001	−0.001	−0.001	−0.001
	[0.046]	[0.017]	[0.328]	[0.020]	[0.012]		[0.005]	[0.002]	[0.002]	[0.002]	[0.002]	[0.005]	[0.003]	[0.002]
Constant	0.772***	−0.491	−0.216	0.081	−1.113***	0.126	0.451**	−0.217	−0.321	0.394	0.246	−0.005	−0.357	0.010
	[0.261]	[0.505]	[0.701]	[0.229]	[0.307]	[0.308]	[0.181]	[0.356]	[0.194]	[0.241]	[0.254]	[0.361]	[0.357]	[0.253]
R^2	0.089	0.198	0.265	0.238	0.340	0.503	0.264	0.187	0.290	0.082	0.136			0.138
Adjusted R^2	0.080	0.147	0.196	0.231	0.315	0.478	0.212	0.127	0.270	0.072	0.116			0.124
Firms	237	36	24	196	55	38	29	34	74	195	98	25	26	125
Observations	1486	236	164	1543	381	286	211	221	544	1406	670	132	165	883

Time Effects	yes	yes	yes	yes	yes	yes	yes	yes	yes	yes	yes	yes	yes	yes
Country Effects	–	–	–	–	–	–	–	–	–	–	–	yes	yes	–
Industry Effects	–	–	–	–	–	–	–	–	–	–	–	–	–	–
Estimator	FE	FE	FE	FE	FE	FE	FE	FE	FE	FE	FE	RE	RE	FE

Source: own contribution.

Table D.3: *Country* and *Industry* Regression (Market Leverage).

This table provides the coefficients of panel regressions with market leverage as the dependent variables. All independent variables used in the equation model (14) are lagged one year and regressed separately for SC and SNC firms for the *country and industry* samples for the entire period 2004–2014. Tables 4.3 and 4.10 provide the definitions of all variables. SC and SNC firms are determined based on DJIMI (see Table 4.1). US, UK, CA, JP, SK, TW, and IN denote countries such as United States, United Kingdom, Canada, Japan, South Korea, Taiwan, and India. OILG, BMAT, IND, CGDS, TECH, HCARE, and CSRV denote industries such as Oil and Gas, Basic Materials, Industrials, Consumer Goods, Technology, Health Care, and Consumer Services. Panel A and B represent the regression results for market leverage for SC and SNC firms, respectively. Results are shown with a dash-sign "-" represent either data, not available or not applicable. The regressions in all models contain *time fixed effects* (time dummies), *country* and *industry fixed effects* (i.e., dummies), while the *country* samples contain industry dummies, the *industry* samples contain country dummies (where applicable). Econometric estimators applied to each model are shown in the last row. All regressions were applied with the respective estimator, as identified by the model estimation procedure described in Panel A in Table B.3 in Appendix B. Company cluster robust standard errors are reported in the brackets. *, ** and *** denote significance at 10%, 5% and 1% levels, respectively. All variables are winsorized at the 1% and 99% level. Model specifications are provided in Section 4.4.1.

$$mlev_{it} = \alpha + \beta_1 prof_{i,t-1} + \beta_2 growth_{i,t-1} + \beta_3 size_{i,t-1} + \beta_4 tang_{i,t-1} + \beta_5 risk_{i,t-1} + \beta_6 gdp_{i,t-1} + \mu_i + \mu_t + \varepsilon_{it} \quad (14)$$

Determinants	Panel A: Shari'ah Compliant (SC)													
	Country							*Industry*						
	US	UK	CA	JP	SK	TW	IN	OILG	BMAT	IND	CGDS	TECH	HCARE	CSRV
	(1)	(2)	(3)	(4)	(5)	(6)	(7)	(8)	(9)	(10)	(11)	(12)	(13)	(14)
	Market Leverage													
$Profitability_{t-1}$	−0.171***	−0.167**	−0.189**	−0.287***	−0.173	−0.205*	−0.231***	−0.154**	−0.226***	−0.149***	−0.347***	−0.094*	−0.070	−0.119
	[0.033]	[0.081]	[0.080]	[0.086]	[0.123]	[0.109]	[0.083]	[0.076]	[0.082]	[0.052]	[0.089]	[0.053]	[0.060]	[0.077]
$Growth\ Opportunity_{t-1}$	−0.016***	−0.017***	−0.028***	−0.018***	−0.009	−0.010	−0.009***	−0.029***	−0.013**	−0.020***	−0.009***	−0.012***	−0.016***	−0.019***
	[0.002]	[0.006]	[0.007]	[0.004]	[0.006]	[0.007]	[0.003]	[0.008]	[0.005]	[0.004]	[0.003]	[0.002]	[0.003]	[0.004]

Firm Size $_{t-1}$	0.031***	0.006	0.028*	0.029**	0.029	0.046*	0.016	−0.002	0.028**	0.023	0.021**	0.015	0.001	0.047***
	[0.007]	[0.015]	[0.016]	[0.012]	[0.026]	[0.024]	[0.014]	[0.015]	[0.013]	[0.015]	[0.009]	[0.012]	[0.012]	[0.014]
Tangibility $_{t-1}$	0.114***	0.042	0.003	0.126	−0.012	0.098	−0.033	0.026	0.080**	0.057	−0.021	0.155*	−0.074	0.166**
	[0.040]	[0.092]	[0.048]	[0.084]	[0.092]	[0.082]	[0.076]	[0.066]	[0.038]	[0.054]	[0.073]	[0.081]	[0.073]	[0.083]
Business Risk $_{t-1}$	−0.033	0.030	−0.059	−0.246*	−0.101	−0.211	0.091	−0.120	0.213**	−0.085	−0.084	−0.049	0.242**	−0.273**
	[0.061]	[0.125]	[0.127]	[0.129]	[0.269]	[0.152]	[0.086]	[0.092]	[0.090]	[0.072]	[0.115]	[0.118]	[0.102]	[0.124]
GDP growth $_{t-1}$	−0.157***	0.000	0.319**	0.218***	−0.023	–	−0.015***	−0.005**	0.003	0.001	−0.002	0.003	0.000	−0.002
	[0.030]	[0.005]	[0.152]	[0.030]	[0.019]		[0.003]	[0.002]	[0.004]	[0.001]	[0.001]	[0.002]	[0.001]	[0.002]
Constant	0.126	0.171	−0.730**	−0.575***	−0.126	−0.468	0.055	0.369	−0.191	−0.093	−0.043	−0.049	0.197	−0.491**
	[0.141]	[0.207]	[0.345]	[0.185]	[0.366]	[0.339]	[0.190]	[0.240]	[0.183]	[0.222]	[0.127]	[0.171]	[0.176]	[0.209]
R^2	0.236	0.265	0.251	0.336	0.139	0.326	0.290	0.342	0.203	0.284	0.264	0.251	0.185	0.269
Adjusted R^2	0.233	0.245	0.222	0.324	0.069	0.282	0.272	0.320	0.174	0.276	0.252	0.238	0.169	0.252
Firms	407	74	53	120	31	34	71	64	63	188	132	121	97	91
Observations	3091	528	380	809	185	229	569	472	417	1430	949	869	765	660
Time Effects	yes	yes	yes	yes	yes	yes	yes	yes	yes	yes	yes	yes	yes	yes
Country Effects	–	–	–	–	–	–	–	–	–	–	–	–	–	–
Industry Effects	–	–	–	–	–	–	–	–	–	–	–	–	–	–
Estimator	FE	FE	FE	FE	FE	FE	FE	FE	FE	FE	FE	FE	FE	FE

(continued)

Table D.3 (continued)

Determinants	Panel B: Shari'ah Non-Compliant (SNC)													
	Country							*Industry*						
	US	UK	CA	JP	SK	TW	IN	OILG	BMAT	IND	CGDS	TECH	HCARE	CSRV
	(1)	(2)	(3)	(4)	(5)	(6)	(7)	(8)	(9)	(10)	(11)	(12)	(13)	(14)
	Market Leverage													
$Profitability_{t-1}$	−0.420***	−0.491	−0.370	−0.565***	−0.592***	−0.588***	−0.321	−0.963***	−0.646***	−0.528***	−0.223*	−0.500**	−0.870***	−0.800***
	[0.099]	[0.291]	[0.277]	[0.133]	[0.150]	[0.162]	[0.232]	[0.174]	[0.154]	[0.121]	[0.114]	[0.229]	[0.283]	[0.216]
$Growth\ Opportunity_{t-1}$	−0.106***	−0.074	0.019	−0.175***	−0.203***	−0.122***	−0.133***	0.007	−0.174***	−0.141***	−0.140***	−0.113	0.006	−0.082***
	[0.018]	[0.047]	[0.068]	[0.025]	[0.032]	[0.034]	[0.040]	[0.037]	[0.038]	[0.017]	[0.024]	[0.073]	[0.051]	[0.028]
$Firm\ Size_{t-1}$	0.046***	0.154**	0.059*	0.055***	0.070***	0.035	0.055***	0.065***	0.078***	0.035**	0.034*	0.057	0.092	0.066***
	[0.015]	[0.061]	[0.031]	[0.020]	[0.019]	[0.027]	[0.013]	[0.007]	[0.018]	[0.015]	[0.020]	[0.037]	[0.059]	[0.017]
$Tangibility_{t-1}$	0.165**	−0.310	0.059	0.089	0.110	0.131	−0.004	0.239***	0.030	0.102	0.220*	−0.103	0.191	−0.002
	[0.071]	[0.225]	[0.131]	[0.089]	[0.096]	[0.093]	[0.098]	[0.080]	[0.104]	[0.068]	[0.118]	[0.130]	[0.311]	[0.092]
Business	−0.028	−1.262***	0.127	−0.159	−0.493	0.038	−0.655*	−0.480	−0.371	−0.353	−0.318*	0.301	0.458	0.692***
$Risk_{t-1}$	[0.146]	[0.401]	[0.454]	[0.157]	[0.308]	[0.248]	[0.350]	[0.295]	[0.230]	[0.214]	[0.181]	[0.297]	[0.476]	[0.211]
$GDP\ growth_{t-1}$	−0.174**	0.037**	0.236	0.201***	0.009	–	−0.035***	−0.007**	−0.008***	−0.009***	−0.005*	−0.022**	0.003	−0.011***
	[0.072]	[0.016]	[0.353]	[0.041]	[0.024]		[0.010]	[0.003]	[0.003]	[0.002]	[0.003]	[0.008]	[0.006]	[0.002]
Constant	0.304	−1.547*	−0.871	−0.404	−0.239	0.144	0.164	−0.440***	−0.383	0.226	0.136	−0.117	−0.832	−0.276
	[0.314]	[0.889]	[0.781]	[0.321]	[0.278]	[0.415]	[0.236]	[0.125]	[0.293]	[0.222]	[0.312]	[0.572]	[0.883]	[0.255]
R^2	0.397	0.562	0.243	0.436	0.360	0.403	0.454	0.379	0.454	0.352	0.369	0.531	0.441	0.385
Adjusted R^2	0.392	0.535	0.171	0.431	0.336	0.373	0.415	0.333	0.438	0.345	0.355	0.470	0.385	0.374
Firms	237	36	24	196	55	38	29	34	74	195	98	25	26	125
Observations	1486	236	164	1543	381	286	211	221	544	1406	670	132	165	883

Time Effects	yes	yes	yes	yes	yes	yes	yes	yes	yes	yes	yes	yes	yes	yes
Country Effects	–	–	–	–	–	–	–	–	–	–	–	–	–	–
Industry Effects	–	–	–	–	–	–	–	–	–	–	–	–	–	–
Estimator	FE	FE	FE	FE	FE	FE	FE	FE	FE	FE	FE	FE	FE	FE

Source: own contribution.

Table D.4: Target vs. Actual Leverage.

This table shows the target leverage and actual leverage ratios of SC and SNC firms obtained from the *overall (pooled)* sample for each year during 2004–2014. Table 4.3 provides the definitions of book and market leverage variables. The target leverage ratios are determined using the Stata command *predict, xb*. This command calculates the linear prediction from the fitted model applied to each model shown below. Actual leverage (observed) values are retrieved from the descriptive statistics represented in Table 5.2 in Section 5.1.1. SC and SNC firms are determined based on DJIMI (see Table 4.1). All variables are winsorized at the 1% and 99% level.

$$blev_{it} = \alpha + \beta_1 prof_{it} + \beta_2 growth_{it} + \beta_3 size_{it} + \beta_4 tang_{it} + \beta_5 risk_{it} + \beta_6 gdp_{it} + \mu_i + \mu_t + \varepsilon_{it} \quad (13)$$

$$mlev_{it} = \alpha + \beta_1 prof_{it} + \beta_2 growth_{it} + \beta_3 size_{it} + \beta_4 tang_{it} + \beta_5 risk_{it} + \beta_6 gdp_{it} + \mu_i + \mu_t + \varepsilon_{it} \quad (14)$$

Leverage	Sample	Values	2004	2005	2006	2007	2008	2009	2010	2011	2012	2013	2014
Book	SC	Target	0.3932	0.3984	0.3951	0.4028	0.4130	0.3904	0.3934	0.3999	0.4015	0.3970	0.4094
	SC	Actual	0.3904	0.3970	0.3950	0.4032	0.4082	0.3861	0.3898	0.3980	0.3991	0.3935	0.4048
Market	SC	Target	0.1865	0.1719	0.1738	0.1891	0.2363	0.1971	0.1901	0.2006	0.1958	0.1789	0.1796
	SC	Actual	0.1828	0.1698	0.1733	0.1887	0.2349	0.1941	0.1897	0.2020	0.1967	0.1788	0.1798
Book	SNC	Target	0.6818	0.6681	0.6593	0.6573	0.6860	0.6655	0.6531	0.6644	0.6662	0.6594	0.6636
	SNC	Actual	0.6947	0.6808	0.6687	0.6611	0.6776	0.6545	0.6441	0.6527	0.6556	0.6525	0.6603
Market	SNC	Target	0.6016	0.5477	0.5511	0.5933	0.6882	0.6202	0.5964	0.6200	0.6050	0.5754	0.5748
	SNC	Actual	0.6131	0.5637	0.5607	0.5947	0.6812	0.6073	0.5867	0.6101	0.5978	0.5723	0.5745

Source: own contribution.

Table D.5: Dynamic Trade-Off, Speed of Adjustment (SOA) – Book Leverage.

This table provides the results from estimating the partial adjustment model (SOA) with book leverage as the dependent variables. The lagged book leverage ($blev_{i,t-1}$) is incorporated as an independent variable. All firm-specific and macroeconomic debt determinants used in the equation model (18) are lagged one year and regressed separately for SC and SNC firms for the *overall (pooled), country, and industry* samples for the entire period 2004–2014. Tables 4.3 and 4.10 provide the definitions of all variables. SC and SNC firms are determined based on DJIMI (see Table 4.1). US, UK, CA, JP, SK, TW, and IN denote countries such as United States, United Kingdom, Canada, Japan, South Korea, Taiwan, and India. OILG, BMAT, IND, CGDS, TECH, HCARE, and CSRV denote industries such as Oil and Gas, Basic Materials, Industrials, Consumer Goods, Technology, Health Care, and Consumer Services. Panel A and B represent the regression results for book leverage for SC and SNC firms, respectively. Results are shown with a dash-sign "-" represent either data, not available or not applicable. The regressions in all models contain time fixed effects (time dummies). The *overall (pooled)* sample contains country and industry fixed effects (country and industry dummy), the *country* sample contains industry fixed effects, the *industry* sample contains country fixed effects – (where applicable). AR (1) and AR (2) are the first- and second-order autocorrelations of residuals under the null of no serial correlation. The Hansen test provides the over-identifying restrictions under the null of the instruments' validity. SOA is one minus the coefficient on lagged book leverage. Leverage half-life is defined as the time a firm requires (in years) to adjust back to the target leverage after a one-unit shock to ε, *ln(0.5)/ln(1-λ)*. The estimation results are shown in the row "Successful Results" after passing the AR(1), AR(2), and the Sargan/Hansen tests successfully. (see Section 4.2.2) ✓ denotes acceptable result, ✗ unsuccessful econometrical attempt – 1st level. The econometric estimator applied to each model is shown in the last row. Company cluster robust standard errors are reported in the brackets. *, ** and *** denote significance at 10%, 5% and 1% levels, respectively. All variables are winsorized at the 1% and 99% level. Model specifications are provided in Section 6.1.1.

$$blev_{it} = \alpha + (1-\lambda) blev_{i,t-1} + \beta_1 prof_{i,t-1} + \beta_2 growth_{i,t-1} + \beta_3 size_{i,t-1} + \beta_4 tang_{i,t-1} + \beta_5 risk_{i,t-1} + \beta_6 gdp_{i,t-1} + \mu_i + \mu_t + \varepsilon_{it} \quad (18)$$

Dynamic Trade-Off	*Overall (pooled)*	*Country*							*Industry*						
		US	UK	CA	JP	SK	TW	IN	OILG	BMAT	IND	CGDS	TECH	HCARE	CSRV
Determinants	(1)	(2)	(3)	(4)	(5)	(6)	(7)	(8)	(9)	(10)	(11)	(12)	(13)	(14)	(15)
Panel A: Shari'ah Compliant (SC)															
Book Leverage $_{t-1}$	0.809***	0.662***	0.772***	0.568***	0.836***	0.667***	0.820***	0.959***	0.638***	0.616***	0.701***	0.656***	0.561***	0.742***	0.656***
	[0.041]	[0.071]	[0.081]	[0.113]	[0.070]	[0.114]	[0.237]	[0.139]	[0.106]	[0.146]	[0.066]	[0.076]	[0.104]	[0.059]	[0.095]
Profitability $_{t-1}$	−0.128**	−0.154	−0.062	−0.220***	−0.136**	0.043	−0.397	0.080	−0.172*	−0.143**	−0.091	−0.052	−0.101	−0.024	−0.020
	[0.060]	[0.104]	[0.102]	[0.084]	[0.057]	[0.106]	[0.558]	[0.147]	[0.091]	[0.064]	[0.056]	[0.059]	[0.074]	[0.073]	[0.054]

(continued)

Table D.5 (continued)

Dynamic Trade-Off	*Overall (pooled)*	*Country*							*Industry*						
		US	UK	CA	JP	SK	TW	IN	OILG	BMAT	IND	CGDS	TECH	HCARE	CSRV
Determinants	(1)	(2)	(3)	(4)	(5)	(6)	(7)	(8)	(9)	(10)	(11)	(12)	(13)	(14)	(15)
								Panel A: Shari'ah Compliant (SC)							
Growth Opportunity $_{t-1}$	0.006*	0.007	0.004	0.016*	0.013***	0.004	0.015	0.001	0.006	0.006	0.003	0.006*	−0.001	−0.001	0.001
	[0.003]	[0.007]	[0.006]	[0.009]	[0.005]	[0.009]	[0.022]	[0.009]	[0.010]	[0.006]	[0.004]	[0.003]	[0.004]	[0.004]	[0.004]
Firm Size $_{t-1}$	0.014**	0.009	0.012**	0.020***	0.005	0.007	0.005	−0.022	0.009	0.024***	0.018***	0.011**	0.007	0.012***	0.015**
	[0.006]	[0.007]	[0.005]	[0.007]	[0.004]	[0.006]	[0.006]	[0.027]	[0.009]	[0.009]	[0.005]	[0.005]	[0.007]	[0.005]	[0.006]
Tangibility $_{t-1}$	0.078*	0.047	0.009	−0.060*	0.024	0.004	0.111	−0.049	−0.056	−0.077*	−0.056***	0.085*	−0.032	0.051	0.008
	[0.044]	[0.112]	[0.043]	[0.031]	[0.024]	[0.115]	[0.096]	[0.191]	[0.041]	[0.044]	[0.020]	[0.047]	[0.062]	[0.039]	[0.022]
Business Risk $_{t-1}$	0.033	−0.152	0.000	0.220	−0.104	−0.096	−0.556	−0.240*	0.061	0.286	−0.089	−0.210*	−0.105	−0.069	−0.309**
	[0.066]	[0.143]	[0.115]	[0.215]	[0.084]	[1.675]	[0.602]	[0.141]	[0.150]	[0.178]	[0.087]	[0.119]	[0.125]	[0.141]	[0.153]
GDP growth $_{t-1}$	0.001	−0.001	–	−0.006**	–	0.001	–	–	0.074*	−0.007	−0.001	0.003	−0.004*	0.003	0.000
	[0.001]	[0.001]		[0.003]		[0.024]			[0.042]	[0.005]	[0.001]	[0.002]	[0.002]	[0.002]	[0.003]
Constant	−0.206**	−0.036	−0.083	−0.082	−0.033	0.000	0.000	0.000	0.000	−0.100	0.000	−0.045	0.000	−0.074	0.000
	[0.102]	[0.144]	[0.055]	[0.071]	[0.051]	[.]	[.]	[.]	[.]	[0.070]	[.]	[0.067]	[.]	[0.061]	[.]
Observations	5562	3091	528	380	809	185	229	569	472	417	1430	949	869	765	660
Time Effects	yes	yes	yes	yes	yes	yes	yes	yes	yes	yes	yes	yes	yes	yes	yes
Country Effects	yes	no	no	no	no	no	no	no	yes	yes	yes	yes	yes	yes	yes
Industry Effects	yes	yes	yes	yes	yes	yes	yes	yes	no	no	no	no	no	no	no
# Instruments	237	69	31	30	74	30	31	41	39	31	75	75	75	74	74
# Groups/Firms	756	407	74	53	120	31	34	71	64	63	188	132	121	97	91
AR (1)	0.000	0.000	0.000	0.001	0.000	0.016	0.006	0.000	0.000	0.003	0.000	0.000	0.002	0.000	0.002
AR (2)	0.713	0.107	0.280	0.123	0.756	0.054	0.794	0.054	0.595	0.202	0.773	0.156	0.477	0.127	0.504

SOA	0.191	0.338	0.228	0.432	0.164	0.333	0.180	0.041	0.362	0.384	0.299	0.344	0.439	0.258	0.344
Hansen Test	0.052	0.065	0.066	0.063	0.225	0.132	0.554	0.185	0.190	0.106	0.253	0.280	0.096	0.194	0.371
Half-Life	3.27	1.68	2.68	1.23	3.87	1.71	3.49	16.56	1.54	1.43	1.95	1.64	1.20	2.32	1.64
Successful Results	✓	✓	✓	✓	✓	✓	✓	✓	✓	✓	✓	✓	✓	✓	✓
Estimator	Blundell-Bond 2-Step System GMM														

✘ unsuccessful 1st attempt

Dynamic Trade-Off	*Overall (pooled)*	*Country*							*Industry*						
		US	UK	CA	JP	SK	TW	IN	OILG	BMAT	IND	CGDS	TECH	HCARE	CSRV
Determinants	(1)	(2)	(3)	(4)	(5)	(6)	(7)	(8)	(9)	(10)	(11)	(12)	(13)	(14)	(15)
Panel B: Shari'ah Non-Compliant (SNC)															
Book Leverage $_{t-1}$	0.735***	0.809***	0.882***	0.202	0.888***	0.778***	0.571***	0.840*	0.700***	0.762***	0.869***	0.885***	1.109***	0.703	0.831***
	[0.085]	[0.043]	[0.300]	[0.344]	[0.035]	[0.087]	[0.148]	[0.463]	[0.121]	[0.115]	[0.040]	[0.078]	[0.429]	[0.661]	[0.092]
Profitability $_{t-1}$	−0.224*	−0.209**	0.260	−0.703	−0.169**	−0.102	−0.338	−0.307	−0.114	−0.02	−0.158	−0.065	−0.003	0.083	−0.287**
	[0.135]	[0.084]	[0.682]	[0.622]	[0.076]	[0.137]	[0.210]	[0.439]	[0.137]	[0.165]	[0.122]	[0.057]	[0.399]	[0.485]	[0.140]
Growth Opportunity $_{t-1}$	0.068***	0.020	−0.017	0.001	−0.010	−0.006	0.076**	0.219	0.044	−0.034	0.010	−0.026	−0.078	0.012	0.023
	[0.025]	[0.013]	[0.079]	[0.107]	[0.014]	[0.030]	[0.030]	[0.181]	[0.059]	[0.029]	[0.014]	[0.023]	[0.107]	[0.110]	[0.022]
Firm Size $_{t-1}$	0.010**	0.007***	−0.012	0.036**	0.004*	0.004	0.026***	0.007	0.004	0.006*	0.004*	0.002	0.008	−0.039	0.002
	[0.005]	[0.002]	[0.063]	[0.014]	[0.002]	[0.006]	[0.009]	[0.010]	[0.013]	[0.004]	[0.002]	[0.002]	[0.040]	[0.036]	[0.004]
Tangibility $_{t-1}$	0.082*	0.026*	−0.078	0.004	0.000	0.046	0.045	−0.051	0.007	−0.006	−0.004	0.022	0.106	0.222	0.012
	[0.043]	[0.016]	[0.229]	[0.067]	[0.019]	[0.036]	[0.042]	[0.092]	[0.067]	[0.022]	[0.015]	[0.030]	[0.193]	[0.212]	[0.030]
Business Risk $_{t-1}$	−0.16	−0.029	−0.259	0.394	0.111	−0.024	0.226	0.134	−0.310	0.084	0.022	0.010	0.122	−0.327	−0.164
	[0.142]	[0.101]	[1.003]	[0.996]	[0.104]	[0.143]	[0.151]	[0.322]	[0.218]	[0.187]	[0.160]	[0.097]	[0.630]	[0.834]	[0.181]
GDP growth $_{t-1}$	−0.001	–	0.003	0.000	0.001***	0.017	–	−0.024	−0.002	−0.003*	−0.001	−0.001	−0.007	−0.002	0.003
	[0.001]		[0.005]	[0.003]	[0.000]	[0.014]		[0.040]	[0.003]	[0.002]	[0.001]	[0.003]	[0.019]	[0.005]	[0.004]

(continued)

Table D.5 (continued)

Dynamic Trade-Off	*Overall (pooled)*	*Country*							*Industry*						
		US	UK	CA	JP	SK	TW	IN	OILG	BMAT	IND	CGDS	TECH	HCARE	CSRV
Determinants	**(1)**	**(2)**	**(3)**	**(4)**	**(5)**	**(6)**	**(7)**	**(8)**	**(9)**	**(10)**	**(11)**	**(12)**	**(13)**	**(14)**	**(15)**
Constant	−0.079	−0.018	0.000	0.234	0.109	0.000	0.000	0.000	0.062	0.000	0.011	0.000	0.000	0.000	0.078
	[0.111]	[0.031]	[.]	[0.452]	[0.080]	[.]	[.]	[.]	[0.253]	[.]	[0.030]	[.]	[.]	[.]	[0.089]
Observations	4021	1486	236	164	1543	381	286	211	221	544	1406	670	132	165	883
Time Effects	yes	yes	yes	yes	yes	yes	yes	yes	yes	yes	yes	yes	yes	yes	yes
Country Effects	yes	no	no	no	no	no	no	no	yes	yes	yes	yes	yes	yes	yes
Industry Effects	yes	yes	yes	yes	yes	yes	yes	yes	no	no	no	no	no	no	no
# Instruments	119	128	34	**30**	175	39	38	29	30	31	128	75	**26**	**30**	123
# Groups/Firms	577	237	36	24	196	55	38	29	34	74	195	98	25	26	125
AR (1)	0.000	0.000	0.049	**0.191**	0.000	0.002	0.006	0.016	0.018	0.000	0.000	0.000	0.045	**0.543**	0.000
AR (2)	0.114	0.352	0.412	0.555	0.450	0.411	0.149	0.194	0.059	0.064	0.367	0.322	0.536	0.211	0.100
SOA	0.265	0.191	0.118	0.798	0.112	0.222	0.429	0.160	0.300	0.238	0.131	0.115	−0.109	0.297	0.169
Hansen Test	0.063	0.061	0.279	0.719	0.098	0.184	0.094	0.104	0.356	0.057	0.055	0.168	**0.007**	0.834	0.166
Half-Life	2.25	3.27	5.52	0.43	5.84	2.76	1.24	3.98	1.94	2.55	4.94	5.67	−6.70	1.97	3.74
Successful Results	✓	✓	✓	✗[1]	✓	✓	✓	✓	✓	✓	✓	✓	✗[2]	✗[3]	✓
Estimator	Blundell-Bond 2-Step System GMM														

✗ unsuccessful 1st attempt

Table D.6: Dynamic Trade-Off, Speed of Adjustment (SOA) – Market Leverage.

This table provides the results from estimating the partial adjustment model (SOA) with market leverage as the dependent variables. The lagged market leverage ($mlev_{i,t-1}$) is incorporated as an independent variable. All firm-specific and macroeconomic debt determinants used in the equation model (19) are lagged one year and regressed separately for SC and SNC firms for the *overall (pooled), country, and industry* samples for the entire period 2004–2014. Tables 4.3 and 4.10 provide the definitions of all variables. SC and SNC firms are determined based on DJIMI (see Table 4.1). US, UK, CA, JP, SK, TW, and IN denote countries such as United States, United Kingdom, Canada, Japan, South Korea, Taiwan, and India. OILG, BMAT, IND, CGDS, TECH, HCARE, and CSRV denote industries such as Oil and Gas, Basic Materials, Industrials, Consumer Goods, Technology, Health Care, and Consumer Services. Panel A and B represent the regression results for market leverage for SC and SNC firms, respectively. Results are shown with a dash-sign "-" represent either data, not available or not applicable. The regressions in all models contain time fixed effects (time dummies). The *overall (pooled)* sample contains country and industry fixed effects (country and industry dummy), the *country* sample contains industry fixed effects, the *industry* sample contains country fixed effects – (where applicable). AR (1) and AR (2) are the first- and second-order autocorrelations of residuals under the null of no serial correlation. The Hansen test provides the over-identifying restrictions under the null of the instruments' validity. SOA is one minus the coefficient on lagged book leverage. Leverage half-life is defined as the time a firm requires (in years) to adjust back to the target leverage after a one-unit shock to ε, $ln(0.5)/ln(1-\lambda)$. The estimation results are shown in the row "Successful Results" after passing the AR(1), AR(2), and the Sargan/Hansen tests successfully. (see Section 4.2.2) ✓ denotes acceptable result, ✗ unsuccessful econometrical attempt – 1st level. The econometric estimator applied to each model is shown in the last row. Company cluster robust standard errors are reported in the brackets. *, ** and *** denote significance at 10%, 5% and 1% levels, respectively. All variables are winsorized at the 1% and 99% level. Model specifications are provided in Section 6.1.1.

$$mlev_{it} = \alpha + (1-\lambda) mlev_{i,t-1} + \beta_1 prof_{i,t-1} + \beta_2 growth_{i,t-1} + \beta_3 size_{i,t-1} + \beta_4 tang_{i,t-1} + \beta_5 risk_{i,t-1} + \beta_6 gdp_{i,t-1} + \mu_i + \mu_t + \varepsilon_{it} \quad (19)$$

Dynamic Trade-Off	*Overall (pooled)*	*Country*							*Industry*						
		US	UK	CA	JP	SK	TW	IN	OILG	BMAT	IND	CGDS	TECH	HCARE	CSRV
Determinants	(1)	(2)	(3)	(4)	(5)	(6)	(7)	(8)	(9)	(10)	(11)	(12)	(13)	(14)	(15)
								Panel A: Shari'ah Compliant (SC)							
Market	0.806**	0.644***	0.485***	0.381***	0.784***	0.763***	0.572**	0.335*	0.327**	0.697***	0.475***	0.519***	0.375**	0.721***	0.491***
Leverage$_{t-1}$	[0.403]	[0.057]	[0.102]	[0.116]	[0.085]	[0.176]	[0.256]	[0.196]	[0.139]	[0.126]	[0.059]	[0.084]	[0.159]	[0.114]	[0.112]

(continued)

Table D.6 (continued)

Dynamic Trade-Off	*Overall (pooled)*	*Country*							*Industry*						
		US	UK	CA	JP	SK	TW	IN	OILG	BMAT	IND	CGDS	TECH	HCARE	CSRV
Determinants	(1)	(2)	(3)	(4)	(5)	(6)	(7)	(8)	(9)	(10)	(11)	(12)	(13)	(14)	(15)
								Panel A: Shari'ah Compliant (SC)							
$\text{Profitability}_{t-1}$	−0.102	−0.155***	−0.103	−0.133**	−0.009	−0.146**	−0.085	−0.226*	−0.198*	0.018	−0.242***	−0.195***	−0.078	0.006	−0.145*
	[0.627]	[0.058]	[0.195]	[0.058]	[0.070]	[0.063]	[0.087]	[0.132]	[0.114]	[0.244]	[0.084]	[0.042]	[0.048]	[0.033]	[0.084]
Growth	−0.014	−0.004	−0.003	−0.018***	0.000	0.004	−0.002	−0.005	0.004	−0.004	0.002	0.002	−0.007	0.005	−0.004
Opportunity_{t-1}	[0.016]	[0.003]	[0.015]	[0.006]	[0.005]	[0.010]	[0.009]	[0.007]	[0.013]	[0.009]	[0.005]	[0.004]	[0.005]	[0.004]	[0.005]
Firm Size_{t-1}	0.017	0.022***	0.048**	0.014***	0.011	0.013**	0.010	0.010	0.037*	0.011	0.021***	0.015***	0.011**	0.010***	0.012***
	[0.026]	[0.005]	[0.024]	[0.004]	[0.008]	[0.005]	[0.017]	[0.011]	[0.021]	[0.009]	[0.004]	[0.003]	[0.004]	[0.003]	[0.004]
Tangibility_{t-1}	0.345	−0.036	−0.023	−0.002	0.017	−0.068	0.038	0.013	0.038	0.004	−0.006	0.013	0.005	0.042	−0.004
	[0.265]	[0.037]	[0.221]	[0.018]	[0.024]	[0.042]	[0.060]	[0.048]	[0.061]	[0.030]	[0.017]	[0.029]	[0.040]	[0.029]	[0.025]
$\text{Business Risk}_{t-1}$	4.110*	−0.054	−0.074	−0.041	−0.224	−0.065	−0.127	0.015	0.070	−0.02	−0.230***	−0.295***	−0.219**	−0.089	−0.337**
	[2.405]	[0.055]	[0.114]	[0.096]	[0.177]	[0.275]	[0.152]	[0.098]	[0.133]	[0.147]	[0.088]	[0.107]	[0.095]	[0.087]	[0.136]
GDP growth_{t-1}	−0.037*	–	0.010***	0.001	−0.002**	−0.014	–	–	0.001	−0.001	0.000	−0.002	0.001	0.001	0.000
	[0.020]		[0.003]	[0.002]	[0.001]	[0.016]			[0.018]	[0.005]	[0.002]	[0.001]	[0.003]	[0.001]	[0.006]
Constant	−0.339	−0.201***	−0.287	−0.020	0.000	0.000	−0.029	0.000	−0.353	−0.097	0.000	−0.048	0.000	0.000	0.005
	[0.372]	[0.074]	[0.522]	[0.053]	[.]	[.]	[0.337]	[.]	[0.327]	[0.085]	[.]	[0.042]	[.]	[.]	[0.053]
Observations	5562	3091	528	380	809	185	229	569	472	417	1430	949	869	765	660
Time Effects	yes	yes	yes	yes	yes	yes	yes	yes	yes	yes	yes	yes	yes	yes	yes
Country Effects	yes	no	no	no	no	no	no	no	yes	yes	yes	yes	yes	yes	yes
Industry Effects	yes	yes	yes	yes	yes	yes	yes	yes	no	no	no	no	no	no	no
# Instruments	38	237	60	30	108	31	30	49	53	55	128	75	75	74	74
# Groups/Firms	756	407	74	53	120	31	34	71	64	63	188	132	121	97	91
AR (1)	0.025	0.000	0.000	0.001	0.000	0.007	0.017	0.010	0.001	0.002	0.000	0.000	0.000	0.000	0.002
AR (2)	0.449	0.741	0.057	0.756	0.173	0.196	0.404	0.805	0.063	0.052	0.750	0.121	0.882	0.382	0.072

SOA	0.194	0.356	0.515	0.619	0.216	0.237	0.428	0.665	0.673	0.303	0.525	0.481	0.625	0.279	0.509
Hansen Test	0.514	0.067	0.293	0.289	0.084	0.103	0.581	0.112	0.344	0.144	0.195	0.223	0.050	0.391	0.089
Half-Life	3.21	1.58	0.96	0.72	2.85	2.56	1.24	0.63	0.62	1.92	0.93	1.06	0.71	2.12	0.97
Successful Results	✓	✓	✓	✓	✓	✓	✓	✓	✓	✓	✓	✓	✓	✓	✓
Estimator	Blundell-Bond 2-Step System GMM														

Panel B: Shari'ah Non-Compliant (SNC)															
Market	0.643***	0.626***	0.946***	0.019	0.742***	0.598***	0.434**	0.515	0.842***	0.359***	0.752***	0.762***	−0.632	0.842	0.946***
$Leverage_{t-1}$	[0.099]	[0.049]	[0.214]	[0.894]	[0.088]	[0.157]	[0.193]	[0.747]	[0.317]	[0.135]	[0.087]	[0.113]	[1.419]	[0.667]	[0.071]
$Profitability_{t-1}$	−0.317**	−0.163*	0.723	−0.789	0.063	−0.045	−0.049	−0.033	−0.216	−0.025	−0.184	0.013	−0.953	−0.262	−0.344***
	[0.157]	[0.090]	[0.766]	[1.350]	[0.306]	[0.202]	[0.206]	[0.736]	[0.380]	[0.173]	[0.216]	[0.139]	[0.940]	[0.734]	[0.117]
Growth	0.060*	0.002	0.157	−0.243	0.087**	−0.03	−0.083	−0.061	0.064	−0.07	0.093*	0.107*	−0.26	0.114	0.104***
$Opportunity_{t-1}$	[0.031]	[0.022]	[0.095]	[0.560]	[0.035]	[0.061]	[0.078]	[0.273]	[0.066]	[0.085]	[0.052]	[0.065]	[0.359]	[0.224]	[0.024]
$Firm\ Size_{t-1}$	0.016**	0.011***	0.008	0.042	0.036***	0.021***	0.030**	0.009	−0.016	0.077***	0.005	0.032*	0.058	−0.051	0.014
	[0.007]	[0.003]	[0.029]	[0.084]	[0.012]	[0.007]	[0.012]	[0.020]	[0.030]	[0.025]	[0.010]	[0.018]	[0.049]	[0.035]	[0.010]
$Tangibility_{t-1}$	0.127*	0.140***	0.399**	−0.225	0.077	0.054	0.023	−0.073	0.32	−0.056	0.06	−0.003	0.266	0.208	0.008
	[0.077]	[0.038]	[0.190]	[0.488]	[0.062]	[0.041]	[0.056]	[0.370]	[0.197]	[0.090]	[0.055]	[0.048]	[0.349]	[0.208]	[0.049]
$Business\ Risk_{t-1}$	−0.252*	−0.138	−2.899	−1.734	−0.51	−0.166	−0.101	−0.183	0.141	−0.292	−0.970*	−0.392**	−0.199	−0.648	−0.189
	[0.152]	[0.114]	[1.854]	[4.578]	[0.336]	[0.256]	[0.278]	[0.729]	[0.626]	[0.245]	[0.530]	[0.163]	[1.319]	[0.901]	[0.240]
$GDP\ growth_{t-1}$	−0.015***	–	−0.004	0.007	–	−0.012	–	0.048	−0.003	−0.008*	−0.017***	−0.008**	−0.022**	0.008	−0.010***
	[0.003]		[0.006]	[0.016]		[0.021]		[0.095]	[0.013]	[0.005]	[0.003]	[0.003]	[0.011]	[0.009]	[0.003]
Constant	0.000	−0.085	0.000	0.677	−0.515**	0.000	0.000	0.000	0.000	−0.768*	−0.026	−0.434	0.468	0.000	−0.289*
	[.]	[0.059]	[.]	[2.311]	[0.219]	[.]	[.]	[.]	[.]	[0.434]	[0.195]	[0.344]	[0.867]	[.]	[0.153]
Observations	4021	1486	236	164	1543	381	286	211	221	544	1406	670	132	165	883
Time Effects	yes	yes	yes	yes	yes	yes	yes	yes	yes	yes	yes	yes	yes	yes	yes
Country Effects	yes	no	no	no	no	no	no	no	yes	yes	yes	yes	yes	yes	yes

(continued)

Table D.6 (continued)

Dynamic Trade-Off	***Overall (pooled)***				*Country*							*Industry*			
		US	**UK**	**CA**	**JP**	**SK**	**TW**	**IN**	**OILG**	**BMAT**	**IND**	**CGDS**	**TECH**	**HCARE**	**CSRV**
Determinants	**(1)**	**(2)**	**(3)**	**(4)**	**(5)**	**(6)**	**(7)**	**(8)**	**(9)**	**(10)**	**(11)**	**(12)**	**(13)**	**(14)**	**(15)**
Industry Effects	yes	yes	yes	yes	yes	yes	yes	yes	no	no	no	no	no	no	no
# Instruments	143	234	36	24	156	39	38	29	32	53	173	58	**28**	**30**	123
# Groups/Firms	577	237	36	24	196	55	38	29	34	74	195	98	25	26	125
AR (1)	0.000	0.000	0.003	**0.429**	0.000	0.000	0.000	0.008	0.009	0.000	0.000	0.000	**0.875**	**0.164**	0.000
AR (2)	0.111	0.339	0.143	0.141	0.074	0.719	0.146	0.205	0.776	0.170	0.069	0.261	0.234	0.274	0.055
SOA	0.357	0.374	0.054	0.981	0.258	0.402	0.566	0.485	0.158	0.641	0.248	0.238	1.632	0.158	0.054
Hansen Test	**0.000**	0.614	0.141	.	0.192	0.057	0.149	**0.042**	0.181	0.319	0.415	0.053	**0.017**	0.631	0.217
Half-Life	1.57	1.48	12.49	–	2.32	1.35	0.83	1.04	4.03	0.68	2.43	2.55	#NUM!	4.03	12.49
Successful Results	✗[4]	✓	✓	✗[5]	✓	✓	✓	✓	✓	✓	✓	✓	✗[6]	✗[7]	✓
Estimator	Blundell-Bond 2-Step System GMM														

Source: own contribution.

Table D.7: Alternative Approach For Unsuccessful Econometrical Results.

This table is an extension of Table D.5 and Table D.6. All regression models with unsuccessful results are denoted with ×. In our second attempt, we pooled SC and SNC firms and executed using equation model (18) for ×¹ – ×³ with an interactive dummy (dsc* $blev_{i,t-1}$) included and (19) for ×⁴ – ×⁷ with an interactive dummy (dsc* $mlev_{i,t-1}$) included. Since we are also interested in finding out the coefficient estimates of SC firms per se, we have employed the Stata command lincom. The lincom command computes point estimates, standard errors, t or z statistics, p-values, and confidence intervals for linear combinations of coefficients after any estimation command. Coefficient results for SNC are obtained from the variable $blev_{i,t-1}$ or $mlev_{i,t-1}$, respectively, and the row "Test for SC" represents the coefficient results for SC firms (output from lincom). The overall (pooled) sample contains country and industry fixed effects (country and industry dummy), the country sample contains industry fixed effects, the industry sample contains country fixed effects - (where applicable). AR (1) and AR (2) are the first- and second-order autocorrelations of residuals under the null of no serial correlation. The Hansen test provides the over-identifying restrictions under the null of the instruments' validity. SOA is one minus the coefficient on lagged book leverage. Leverage half-life is defined as the time a firm requires (in years) to adjust back to the target leverage after a one-unit shock to ε, ln(0.5)/ln(1-λ). Results are shown with a dash-sign "-" represent either data, not available or not applicable. The estimation results are shown in the row "Successful Results" after passing the AR(1), AR(2), and the Sargan/Hansen tests successfully. (see Section 4.2.2) ✓✓ denotes acceptable result/successful remedy, ×(××)unsuccessful econometrical attempt – 1st(2nd) level. The econometric estimator applied to each model is shown in the last row. Company cluster robust standard errors are reported in the brackets. *, ** and *** denote significance at 10%, 5% and 1% levels, respectively. All variables are winsorized at the 1% and 99% level. Model specifications are provided in Section 6.1.1.

$$blev_{it} = \alpha + (1-\lambda)blev_{i,t-1} + dsc * blev_{i,t-1} + \beta_1 prof_{i,t-1} + \beta_2 growth_{i,t-1} + \beta_3 size_{i,t-1} + \beta_4 tang_{i,t-1} + \beta_5 risk_{i,t-1} + \beta_6 gdp_{i,t-1} + dsc + \mu_i + \mu_t + \varepsilon_{it} \quad (18)$$

$$mlev_{it} = \alpha + (1-\lambda)mlev_{i,t-1} + dsc * mlev_{i,t-1} + \beta_1 prof_{i,t-1} + \beta_2 growth_{i,t-1} + \beta_3 size_{i,t-1} + \beta_4 tang_{i,t-1} + \beta_5 risk_{i,t-1} + \beta_6 gdp_{i,t-1} + dsc + \mu_i + \mu_t + \varepsilon_{it} \quad (19)$$

		Book Leverage			Market Leverage			
Dynamic Trade-Off (SOA - Speed of Adjustment)		**CA**	**TECH**	**HCARE**	***Overall (pooled)***	**CA**	**TECH**	**HCARE**
Determinants		×¹	×²	×³	×⁴	×⁵	×⁶	×⁷
Book Leverage$_{t-1}$	(a)	0.555* [0.324]	0.748*** [0.185]	0.559** [0.218]				

(continued)

Table D.7 (continued)

		Book Leverage				Market Leverage			
Dynamic Trade-Off (SOA - Speed of Adjustment)		**CA**	**TECH**	**HCARE**		***Overall (pooled)***	**CA**	**TECH**	**HCARE**
Determinants		x^1	x^2	x^3		x^4	x^5	x^6	x^7
Interactive $BLev_{t-1}$	(b)	0.095	0.119	0.268					
		[0.367]	[0.207]	[0.221]					
Market $Leverage_{t-1}$					(c)	0.542***	0.569**	0.223*	0.349***
						[0.066]	[0.243]	[0.124]	[0.096]
Interactive $MLev_{t-1}$					(d)	0.119	−0.018	0.653***	0.520**
						[0.105]	[0.317]	[0.137]	[0.255]
$Profitability_{t-1}$		−0.179*	−0.056	0.025		−0.121**	−0.279**	−0.049	−0.126
		[0.099]	[0.099]	[0.081]		[0.060]	[0.138]	[0.073]	[0.079]
Growth $Opportunity_{t-1}$		0.002	−0.004	−0.001		0.010**	−0.009	−0.001	0.000
		[0.014]	[0.005]	[0.006]		[0.005]	[0.011]	[0.005]	[0.010]
Firm $Size_{t-1}$		0.017*	0.01	0.012**		0.064***	0.020**	0.013**	0.013*
		[0.010]	[0.008]	[0.005]		[0.011]	[0.010]	[0.007]	[0.008]
$Tangibility_{t-1}$		−0.052	0.008	0.079		0.059	−0.047	0.013	0.054
		[0.044]	[0.027]	[0.059]		[0.037]	[0.047]	[0.029]	[0.072]
Business $Risk_{t-1}$		0.089	−0.122	−0.096		−0.03	−0.071	−0.054	−0.057
		[0.205]	[0.093]	[0.156]		[0.087]	[0.151]	[0.094]	[0.142]
GDP $growth_{t-1}$		–	−0.001	0.004**		−0.002	–	0.000	−0.013
			[0.002]	[0.002]		[0.001]		[0.003]	[0.010]
Dummy SC		−0.066	−0.085	−0.21		−0.104**	−0.129	−0.362***	−0.253***
		[0.154]	[0.129]	[0.147]		[0.047]	[0.154]	[0.080]	[0.074]
Constant		0.021	0.044	0.000		−0.832***	0.052	0.199*	0.000
		[0.107]	[0.160]	[.]		[0.177]	[0.176]	[0.118]	[.]

Observations	544	1001	930	1333	544	1001	930
Time Effects	yes	yes	yes	yes	yes	yes	yes
Country Effects	no	yes	yes	yes	no	yes	yes
Industry Effects	yes	no	no	yes	yes	no	no
# Instruments	75	110	75	185	68	110	70
# Groups/Firms	77	146	123	1333	77	146	123
AR (1)	0.000	0.000	0.000	0.000	0.001	0.000	0.000
AR (2)	0.148	0.604	0.175	**0.001**	0.166	0.729	0.649
SOA (SNC)	0.445	0.252	0.441	0.458	0.431	0.777	0.651
Hansen Test	0.240	0.408	0.394	**0.000**	0.291	0.134	0.114
Half-Life – SNC	1.18	2.39	1.19	1.13	1.23	0.46	0.66
Test p-values for SC:	0.649***	0.866***	0.827***				
(a) + (b) = 0	[0.090]	[0.067]	[0.087]				
SOA (SC)	0.351	0.134	0.173				
Half-Life – SC	1.60	4.82	3.65				
Test p-values for SC:				0.662***	0.551***	0.877***	0.869***
(c) + (d) = 0				[0.116]	[0.157]	[0.113]	[0.234]
SOA (SC)				0.338	0.449	0.123	0.131
Half-Life – SC				1.68	1.16	5.28	4.94
Successful Results (Remedy)	✓✓	✓✓	✓✓	✗✗	✓✓	✓✓	✓✓
Estimator	BB-2Step GMM						

✗ unsuccessful 1st attempt ✗✗ unsuccessful 2nd attempt ✓✓ *successful remedy*

Source: own contribution.

Table D.8: Pairwise Correlation Matrix – Pecking Order Theory.

This table, Pairwise Correlation Matrix, shows the coefficient correlations between dependent and independent variables for the *overall (pooled)*, Shari'ah compliant (SC), and Shari'ah non-compliant (SNC) sample firms.

		Debt Issues	Equity Issues	Financial Deficit
Debt Issues	a			
	b	1		
	c			
Equity Issues	a	0.0583*		
	b	0.0162	1	
	c	0.1368*		
Financial Deficit	a	0.1040*	0.0941*	
	b	0.0268*	0.1359*	1
	c	0.2233*	0.0208	

[a] Denoted for *overall (pooled)* sample.
[b] Denoted for Shari'ah compliant (SC) firms.
[c] Denoted for Shari'ah non-compliant (SNC) firms.
* Indicates that the coefficient is significant at 5% level.
Source: own contribution.

Table D.9: Descriptive – *Overall (pooled)* Debt Issues, Equity Issues, and Financial Deficit.

This table shows the mean values of the debt issues, equity issues, and financial deficit for all firms in the *overall (pooled)* sample separated in SC and SNC firms for the entire period 2004–2014 and each year. Table 6.2 provides the definitions of debt issues, equity issues, and financial deficit variables. SC and SNC firms are determined based on DJIMI (see Table 4.1). All variables are winsorized at the 1% and 99% level.

Variables	Firm Type	2004	2005	2006	2007	2008	2009	2010	2011	2012	2013	2014
Debt Issues	SC	0.034	0.030	0.043	0.061	0.011	0.010	0.042	0.036	0.031	0.021	0.029
Equity Issues	SC	0.032	0.021	0.027	0.019	−0.020	0.032	0.015	0.001	0.012	0.005	−0.005
Financial Deficit	SC	0.066	0.050	0.070	0.081	−0.009	0.042	0.057	0.037	0.043	0.026	0.025
Debt Issues	SNC	0.042	0.020	0.057	0.089	0.008	0.009	0.054	0.040	0.006	0.006	−0.008
Equity Issues	SNC	0.017	0.014	0.015	0.015	−0.021	0.024	0.012	−0.002	0.006	0.009	−0.004
Financial Deficit	SNC	0.059	0.034	0.071	0.104	−0.013	0.033	0.066	0.038	0.013	0.015	−0.013

Source: own contribution.

Table D.10: Pecking Order Estimation Results.

This table provides the coefficients of panel regressions with debt issues (ΔDebt) and equity issues (ΔEquity) as the dependent variables. The single variable financial deficit (DEF) and its interactive dummy variable *(dsc*DEF)* are used in the equation model (23) and (24) and regressed for the *overall (pooled), country, and industry* samples for the entire period 2004–2014. Table 6.2 provides the definitions of all variables. SC and SNC firms are determined based on DJIMI (see Table 4.1). US, UK, CA, JP, SK, TW, and IN denote countries such as United States, United Kingdom, Canada, Japan, South Korea, Taiwan, and India. OILG, BMAT, IND, CGDS, TECH, HCARE, and CSRV denote industries such as Oil and Gas, Basic Materials, Industrials, Consumer Goods, Technology, Health Care, and Consumer Services. Since we are interested in examining the financing behavior of SC and SNC firms in direct comparison, we have incorporated an interactive dummy ($dsc * DEF_{it}$) and also employed the Stata command *lincom*. The *lincom* command computes point estimates, standard errors, t or z statistics, p-values, and confidence intervals for linear combinations of coefficients after any estimation command. Coefficient results for SNC are obtained from the variable "Financial Deficit" and the row "Test for SC" represents the coefficient results for SC firms (output from *lincom*). Panel A and B represent the regression results for debt issues and equity issues for SC and SNC firms, respectively. The *overall (pooled)* sample contains country and industry fixed effects (country and industry dummy), the *country* sample contains industry fixed effects, the *industry* sample contains country fixed effects – (where applicable). Econometric estimators applied to each model are shown in the last row. Results are shown with a dash-sign "-" represent either data, not available or not applicable. All regressions were applied with the respective estimator, as identified by the model estimation procedure described in Panel C in Table B.3 in Appendix B. Company cluster robust standard errors are reported in the brackets. *, ** and *** denote significance at 10%, 5% and 1% levels, respectively. All variables are winsorized at the 1% and 99% level. Model specifications are provided in Section 6.2.2.

$$\Delta DebtIssues_{it} = \alpha + \beta_1 DEF_{it} + \beta_2 dsc * DEF_{it} + dsc + \mu_i + \mu_t + \varepsilon_{it} \tag{23}$$

$$\Delta EquityIssues_{it} = \alpha + \beta_1 DEF_{it} + \beta_2 dsc * DEF_{it} + dsc + \mu_i + \mu_t + \varepsilon_{it} \tag{24}$$

Determinants		*Overall (pooled)*	*Country*						*Industry*								
			US	UK	CA	JP	SK	TW	IN	OILG	BMAT	IND	CGDS	TECH	HCARE	CSRV
		(1)	(2)	(3)	(4)	(5)	(6)	(7)	(8)	(9)	(10)	(11)	(12)	(13)	(14)	(15)
									Panel A: Debt Issues							
Financial	(a)	0.765***	0.719***	0.698***	0.663***	0.811***	0.815***	0.707***	0.852***	0.788***	0.785***	0.760***	0.810***	0.707***	0.749***	0.752***
Deficit $_t$		[0.012]	[0.019]	[0.037]	[0.076]	[0.018]	[0.026]	[0.073]	[0.033]	[0.043]	[0.032]	[0.019]	[0.027]	[0.051]	[0.060]	[0.028]
interactive-	(b)	−0.204***	−0.209***	−0.034	−0.245***	−0.150***	−0.261***	−0.099	−0.069	−0.337***	−0.363***	−0.131***	−0.115***	−0.234***	−0.181**	−0.209***
Def $_t$		[0.019]	[0.028]	[0.056]	[0.083]	[0.039]	[0.080]	[0.080]	[0.050]	[0.055]	[0.060]	[0.035]	[0.043]	[0.057]	[0.070]	[0.060]
Dummy SC		–	–	−0.005	–	0.005***	0.001	−0.005	−0.005	–	–	0.007***	–	0.004	–	–
				[0.004]		[0.001]	[0.005]	[0.005]	[0.004]			[0.002]		[0.004]		
Constant		−0.006***	−0.007**	0.027**	−0.018**	−0.003	0.005	0.000	0.010	−0.003	−0.013**	−0.006*	−0.003	−0.015**	−0.004	0.005
		[0.002]	[0.003]	[0.013]	[0.009]	[0.003]	[0.007]	[0.009]	[0.008]	[0.007]	[0.006]	[0.003]	[0.004]	[0.008]	[0.007]	[0.006]
R^2		0.688	0.621	0.744	0.587	0.845	0.825	0.738	0.855	0.691	0.696		0.750		0.669	0.684
Adjusted R^2		0.688	0.621	0.738	0.579	0.844	0.819	0.729	0.851	0.686	0.693		0.749		0.665	0.682
Firms		1406	645		77					100	143	400	247	172	123	221
Observations		11544	5247	878	629	2669	652	587	882	811	1162	3363	1996	1343	1058	1811
Test for SC:		0.560***	0.510***	0.669***	0.417***	0.662***	0.550***	0.612***	0.776***	0.450***	0.422***	0.632***	0.696***	0.475***	0.567***	0.543***
(a) + (b) = 0																
Standard Error		[0.016]	[0.021]	[0.046]	[0.04]	[0.037]	[0.072]	[0.035]	[0.044]	[0.035]	[0.052]	[0.03]	[0.035]	[0.028]	[0.037]	[0.054]
Time Effects		yes	yes	yes	yes	yes	yes	yes	yes	yes	yes	yes	yes	yes	yes	yes
Country Effects		–	–	–	–	–	–	–	–	–	–	yes	–	yes	–	–
Industry Effects		–	–	yes	–	yes	yes	yes	yes	–	–	–	–	–	–	–
Estimator		FE	FE	OLS	FE	OLS	OLS	OLS	OLS	FE	FE	RE	FE	RE	FE	FE

(continued)

Table D.10 (continued)

Determinants		Overall (pooled)	Country						Industry							
			US	UK	CA	JP	SK	TW	IN	OILG	BMAT	IND	CGDS	TECH	HCARE	CSRV
		(1)	(2)	(3)	(4)	(5)	(6)	(7)	(8)	(9)	(10)	(11)	(12)	(13)	(14)	(15)
Panel B: Equity Issues																
Financial Deficit $_t$	(a)	0.235***	0.281***	0.302***	0.337***	0.189***	0.185***	0.293***	0.148***	0.212***	0.215***	0.240***	0.190***	0.293***	0.251***	0.248***
		[0.012]	[0.019]	[0.037]	[0.076]	[0.018]	[0.026]	[0.073]	[0.033]	[0.043]	[0.032]	[0.019]	[0.027]	[0.051]	[0.060]	[0.028]
interactive-Def $_t$	(b)	0.204***	0.209***	0.034	0.245***	0.150***	0.261***	0.099	0.069	0.338***	0.363***	0.131***	0.115***	0.234***	0.181**	0.209***
		[0.019]	[0.028]	[0.056]	[0.083]	[0.039]	[0.080]	[0.080]	[0.050]	[0.055]	[0.060]	[0.035]	[0.043]	[0.057]	[0.070]	[0.060]
Dummy SC		–	–	0.005	–	−0.005***	−0.001	0.005	0.005	–	–	−0.007***	–	−0.004	–	–
				[0.004]		[0.001]	[0.005]	[0.005]	[0.004]			[0.002]		[0.004]		
Constant		0.006***	0.007**	−0.027**	0.018**	0.003	−0.005	0.000	−0.01	0.003	0.013**	0.006*	0.003	0.015**	0.004	−0.005
		[0.002]	[0.003]	[0.013]	[0.009]	[0.003]	[0.007]	[0.009]	[0.008]	[0.007]	[0.006]	[0.003]	[0.004]	[0.008]	[0.007]	[0.006]
R^2		0.408	0.449	0.373	0.627	0.366	0.445	0.477	0.321	0.548	0.530		0.307		0.467	0.334
Adjusted R^2		0.408	0.447	0.359	0.620	0.361	0.429	0.461	0.306	0.541	0.525		0.303		0.461	0.330
Firms		1406	645		77					100	143	400	247	172	123	221
Observations		11544	5247	878	629	2669	652	587	882	811	1162	3363	1996	1343	1058	1811
Test for SC: (a) + (b) = 0		0.440***	0.490***	0.331***	0.583***	0.338***	0.450***	0.388***	0.224***	0.550***	0.578***	0.368***	0.304***	0.525***	0.433***	0.457***
Standard Error		[0.016]	[0.021]	[0.046]	[0.04]	[0.037]	[0.072]	[0.035]	[0.044]	[0.035]	[0.052]	[0.03]	[0.035]	[0.028]	[0.037]	[0.054]
Time Effects		yes	yes	yes	yes	yes	yes	yes	yes	yes	yes	yes	yes	yes	yes	yes
Country Effects		–	–	–	–	–	–	–	–	–	–	yes	–	yes	–	–
Industry Effects		–	–	yes	–	yes	yes	yes	yes	–	–	–	–	–	–	–
Estimator		FE	FE	OLS	FE	OLS	OLS	OLS	OLS	FE	FE	RE	FE	RE	FE	FE

Source: own contribution.

Table D.11: Pecking Order Estimation Results (lagged).

This table provides the coefficients of panel regressions with debt issues (ΔDebt) and equity issues (ΔEquity) as the dependent variables. The single variable financial deficit (DEF) and its interactive dummy variable *(dsc*DEF)* are used in the equation model (23a) and (24a) and regressed for the *overall (pooled), country, and industry* samples for the entire period 2004–2014. Table 6.2 provides the definitions of all variables. SC and SNC firms are determined based on DJIMI (see Table 4.1). US, UK, CA, JP, SK, TW, and IN denote countries such as United States, United Kingdom, Canada, Japan, South Korea, Taiwan, and India. OILG, BMAT, IND, CGDS, TECH, HCARE, and CSRV denote industries such as Oil and Gas, Basic Materials, Industrials, Consumer Goods, Technology, Health Care, and Consumer Services. Since we are interested in examining the financing behavior of SC and SNC firms in direct comparison, we have incorporated an interactive dummy ($dsc*DEF_{it}$) and also employed the Stata command *lincom*. The *lincom* command computes point estimates, standard errors, *t* or *z* statistics, p-values, and confidence intervals for linear combinations of coefficients after any estimation command. Coefficient results for SNC are obtained from the variable "Financial Deficit" and the row "Test for SC" represents the coefficient results for SC firms (output from *lincom*). Panel A and B represent the regression results for debt issues and equity issues for SC and SNC firms, respectively. The *overall (pooled)* sample contains country and industry fixed effects (country and industry dummy), the *country* sample contains industry fixed effects, the *industry* sample contains country fixed effects – (where applicable). Econometric estimators applied to each model are shown in the last row. Results are shown with a dash-sign "-" represent either data, not available or not applicable. All regressions were applied with the respective estimator, as identified by the model estimation procedure described in Panel C in Table B.3 in Appendix B. Company cluster robust standard errors are reported in the brackets. *, ** and *** denote significance at 10%, 5% and 1% levels, respectively. All variables are winsorized at the 1% and 99% level. Model specifications are provided in Section 6.2.2.

$$\Delta DebtIssues_{it} = \alpha + \beta_1 DEF_{i,t-1} + \beta_2 dsc*DEF_{i,t-1} + dsc + \mu_i + \mu_t + \varepsilon_{it} \quad (23a)$$

$$\Delta EquityIssues_{it} = \alpha + \beta_1 DEF_{i,t-1} + \beta_2 dsc*DEF_{i,t-1} + dsc + \mu_i + \mu_t + \varepsilon_{it} \quad (24a)$$

Table D.11 (continued)

Determinants		*Overall* (*pooled*)	*Country*						*Industry*								
			US	UK	CA	JP	SK	TW	IN	OILG	BMAT	IND	CGDS	TECH	HCARE	CSRV
		(1)	(2)	(3)	(4)	(5)	(6)	(7)	(8)	(9)	(10)	(11)	(12)	(13)	(14)	(15)
Panel A: Debt Issues																
Financial	(a)	−0.007	−0.042*	0.033	−0.121***	0.116***	0.084**	0.167***	0.127*	−0.033	−0.117***	0.088***	0.006	0.170***	0.011	0.068**
$Deficit_{t-1}$		[0.015]	[0.022]	[0.052]	[0.045]	[0.032]	[0.036]	[0.043]	[0.068]	[0.065]	[0.040]	[0.028]	[0.040]	[0.053]	[0.035]	[0.030]
interactive-	(b)	−0.092***	−0.086***	−0.079	0.090*	−0.087**	−0.116*	−0.061	−0.072	−0.018	0.042	−0.082**	−0.093*	−0.152***	−0.127***	−0.145***
Def_{t-1}		[0.019]	[0.027]	[0.064]	[0.053]	[0.040]	[0.064]	[0.059]	[0.075]	[0.071]	[0.050]	[0.038]	[0.050]	[0.058]	[0.047]	[0.046]
Dummy SC		–	–	0.018*	–	0.012***	0.001	0.002	−0.042***	–	–	0.006	–	0.020**	–	–
				[0.009]		[0.003]	[0.010]	[0.009]	[0.011]			[0.004]		[0.009]		
Constant		0.013***	0.056***	0.033*	0.029*	0.013**	0.059***	0.009	0.108***	0.016	−0.016**	0.004	0.004	0.026**	0.072***	0.002
		[0.003]	[0.004]	[0.019]	[0.015]	[0.005]	[0.022]	[0.019]	[0.018]	[0.012]	[0.007]	[0.006]	[0.006]	[0.013]	[0.010]	[0.008]
R^2		0.058	0.072	0.129	0.107	0.290	0.091	0.128	0.234	0.081	0.107		0.070		0.061	0.053
Adjusted R^2		0.057	0.070	0.108	0.088	0.285	0.061	0.098	0.216	0.067	0.097		0.064		0.050	0.046
Firms		1406	645		77					100	143	400	247	172	123	221
Observations		10138	4602	768	552	2353	566	515	782	711	1019	2963	1749	1171	935	1590
Test for SC: (a) + (b) = 0		−0.099***	−0.128***	−0.034	−0.031	0.035	−0.027	0.124***	0.058	−0.051*	−0.075**	0.02	−0.087**	0.037	−0.116***	−0.077**
Standard Error		0.012	0.017	0.038	0.031	0.029	0.053	0.044	0.041	0.028	0.034	0.028	0.033	0.028	0.034	0.035
Time Effects		yes	yes	yes	yes	yes	yes	yes	yes	yes	yes	yes	yes	yes	yes	yes
Country Effects		–	–	–	–	–	–	–	–	–	–	yes	–	yes	–	–
Industry Effects		–	–	yes	–	yes	yes	yes	yes	–	–	–	–	–	–	–
Estimator		FE	FE	OLS	FE	OLS	OLS	OLS	OLS	FE	FE	RE	FE	RE	FE	FE

		Panel B: Equity Issues														
Financial	(a)	−0.019**	−0.018	−0.006	−0.054	0.009	−0.006	0.036	0.009	0.017	−0.012	0.004	−0.025	0.064*	−0.037	−0.016
$Deficit_{t-1}$		[0.008]	[0.015]	[0.023]	[0.044]	[0.010]	[0.019]	[0.040]	[0.027]	[0.029]	[0.020]	[0.013]	[0.016]	[0.034]	[0.044]	[0.017]
interactive-	(b)	0.010	0.025	0.018	0.000	−0.002	0.022	0.083	0.035	−0.085	0.055	0.077***	−0.003	0.095**	0.027	0.005
Def_{t-1}		[0.016]	[0.023]	[0.036]	[0.083]	[0.022]	[0.040]	[0.064]	[0.034]	[0.066]	[0.069]	[0.022]	[0.026]	[0.048]	[0.053]	[0.038]
Dummy SC		–	–	0.006	–	−0.001	0.002	0.006	−0.007	–	–	−0.009***	–	0.002	–	–
				[0.005]		[0.002]	[0.005]	[0.005]	[0.005]			[0.003]		[0.005]		
Constant		−0.005**	−0.018***	−0.006	0.026**	0.002	−0.006	0.024**	0.025***	0.004	−0.003	−0.012**	−0.005	0.008	0.003	−0.017***
		[0.002]	[0.004]	[0.010]	[0.012]	[0.003]	[0.010]	[0.010]	[0.009]	[0.008]	[0.006]	[0.005]	[0.005]	[0.011]	[0.007]	[0.004]
R^2		0.053	0.043	0.052	0.111	0.135	0.109	0.175	0.149	0.063	0.121		0.092		0.051	0.027
Adjusted R^2		0.052	0.040	0.030	0.093	0.128	0.079	0.146	0.129	0.048	0.111		0.086		0.040	0.020
Firms		1406	645		77					100	143	400	247	172	123	221
Observations		10138	4602	768	552	2353	566	515	782	711	1019	2963	1749	1171	935	1590
Test for SC: (a) + (b) = 0		−0.009	0.007	0.016	−0.054	0.008	0.037	0.126**	0.047**	−0.068	0.043	0.078***	−0.028	0.166***	−0.01	−0.011
Standard Error		0.014	0.017	0.026	0.070	0.020	0.033	0.053	0.023	0.059	0.067	0.019	0.022	0.034	0.029	0.035
Time Effects		yes	yes	yes	yes	yes	yes	yes	yes	yes	yes	yes	yes	yes	yes	yes
Country Effects		–	–	–	–	–	–	–	–	–	–	yes	–	yes	-	-
Industry Effects		–	–	yes	–	yes	yes	yes	yes	–	–	–	–	–	-	-
Estimator		FE	FE	OLS	FE	OLS	OLS	OLS	OLS	FE	FE	RE	FE	RE	FE	FE

Source: own contribution.

Table D.12: Pecking Order Estimation Results (lagged) – Consolidated.

This table provides the results estimates retrieved from Table D.11 in Appendix D. The financial deficit (DEF) and its interactive dummy variable *(dsc*DEF)* are used in the equation models (23a) and (24a) and regressed on the dependent variables debt issues (ΔDebt) and equity issues (ΔEquity), respectively. The definitions of the variables in the regressions are provided in Table 6.2. SC and SNC firms are determined based on DJIMI (see Table 4.1). Models 1–15 represent the estimated coefficients for *overall (pooled)*, *country*, and *industry* samples for the entire period 2004–2014. Econometric estimators applied to each model are shown in the last column. All regressions were applied with the respective estimator, as identified by the model estimation procedure described in Panel C in Table B.3 in Appendix B. *, **, and *** denote significance at 10%, 5%, and 1% levels, respectively. All variables are winsorized at the 1% and 99% level. Model specifications are provided in Section 6.2.2.

$$\Delta DebtIssues_{it} = \alpha + \beta_1 DEF_{i,t-1} + \beta_2 dsc * DEF_{i,t-1} + dsc + \mu_i + \mu_t + \varepsilon_{it} \quad (23a)$$

$$\Delta EquityIssues_{it} = \alpha + \beta_1 DEF_{i,t-1} + \beta_2 dsc * DEF_{i,t-1} + dsc + \mu_i + \mu_t + \varepsilon_{it} \quad (24a)$$

		Panel A: Debt Issues			Panel B: Equity Issues			
Financial Deficit$_{t-1}$		**SC**	**SC vs. SNC**	**SNC**	**SC**	**SC vs. SNC**	**SNC**	
Sample		**(1)**	**(2)**	**(3)**	**(4)**	**(5)**	**(6)**	***Estimator***
Overall (pooled)	Model 1	−0.099***	−0.092***	−0.007	−0.009	0.010	−0.019**	FE
United States	Model 2	−0.128***	−0.086***	−0.042*	0.007	0.025	−0.018	FE
United Kingdom	Model 3	−0.034	−0.079	0.033	0.016	0.018	−0.006	OLS
Canada	Model 4	−0.031	0.090*	−0.121***	−0.054	0.000	−0.054	FE
Japan	Model 5	0.035	−0.087**	0.116***	0.008	−0.002	0.009	OLS
South Korea	Model 6	−0.027	−0.116*	0.084**	0.037	0.022	−0.006	OLS
Taiwan	Model 7	0.124***	−0.061	0.167***	0.126**	0.083	0.036	OLS
India	Model 8	0.058	−0.072	0.127*	0.047**	0.035	0.009	OLS

Oil and Gas	Model 9	−0.051*	−0.018	−0.033	−0.068	−0.085	0.017	FE
Basic Materials	Model 10	−0.075**	0.042	−0.117***	0.043	0.055	−0.012	FE
Industrials	Model 11	0.02	−0.082**	0.088***	0.078***	0.077***	0.004	RE
Consumer Goods	Model 12	−0.087**	−0.093*	0.006	−0.028	−0.003	−0.025	FE
Technology	Model 13	0.037	−0.152***	0.170***	0.166***	0.095**	0.064*	RE
Health Care	Model 14	−0.116***	−0.127***	0.011	−0.01	0.027	−0.037	FE
Consumer Services	Model 15	−0.077**	−0.145***	0.068**	−0.011	0.005	−0.016	FE

Source: own contribution.

Appendix E (Robustness Tests)

Robustness I: Different Proxy (leverage)

Table E.1: Dependent Variables Book and Market Value of Leverage.

Variables	Formula/Description	Abbreviation
Book Leverage 2	Total Debt / (Total Debt + Book Equity[a])	BLEV2
Market Leverage 2	Total Debt / (Total Debt + Market Equity)	MLEV2

[a] whereby, Book Equity = Total Assets – Total Liabilities – Preferred Stocks + Deferred Taxes

Table E.2: Determinants of Leverage, *Overall (pooled)* regression.

This table provides the coefficients of panel regressions with book leverage 2 (blev2) and market leverage 2 (mlev2) as the dependent variables. All independent variables used in the equation model (13a) and (14a) are lagged one year and regressed separately for SC and SNC firms for the *overall (pooled)* sample for the entire period 2004–2014. Table E.1 and Table 4.10 provide the definitions of all variables. Book leverage and market leverage results for SC and SNC firms are represented in models (1) and (2) and models (3) and (4), respectively. SC and SNC firms are determined based on DJIMI (see Table 4.1). The regressions in all models contain time fixed effects (time dummies). Econometric estimators applied to each model are shown in the last row. All regressions were applied with the respective estimator, as identified by the model estimation procedure described in Panel B in Table B.3 in Appendix B. Company cluster robust standard errors are reported in the brackets. *, ** and *** denote significance at 1%, 5% and 10% levels, respectively. All variables are winsorized at the 1% and 99% level. Model specifications are provided in Section 4.4.1.

$$\begin{aligned} blev2_{it} = {} & \alpha + \beta_1 prof_{i,t-1} + \beta_2 growth_{i,t-1} + \beta_3 size_{i,t-1} \\ & + \beta_4 tang_{i,t-1} + \beta_5 risk_{i,t-1} + \beta_6 gdp_{i,t-1} + \mu_i + \mu_t + \varepsilon_{it} \end{aligned} \tag{13a}$$

$$\begin{aligned} mlev2_{it} = {} & \alpha + \beta_1 prof_{i,t-1} + \beta_2 growth_{i,t-1} + \beta_3 size_{i,t-1} \\ & + \beta_4 tang_{i,t-1} + \beta_5 risk_{i,t-1} + \beta_6 gdp_{i,t-1} + \mu_i + \mu_t + \varepsilon_{it} \end{aligned} \tag{14a}$$

Overall Regression	Book Leverage 2		Market Leverage 2	
	SC	SNC	SC	SNC
Determinants	(1)	(2)	(3)	(4)
Profitability $_{t-1}$	−0.143***	−0.540***	−0.118***	−0.658***
	[0.044]	[0.067]	[0.020]	[0.076]
Growth Opportunity $_{t-1}$	−0.010***	0.069***	−0.008***	−0.108***
	[0.003]	[0.013]	[0.001]	[0.013]
Firm Size $_{t-1}$	−0.004	0.037***	0.014***	0.055***
	[0.011]	[0.009]	[0.004]	[0.009]
Tangibility $_{t-1}$	0.114**	0.151***	0.072***	0.162***
	[0.054]	[0.049]	[0.023]	[0.048]

https://doi.org/10.1515/9783110713664-013

Table E.2 (continued)

Overall Regression	**Book Leverage 2**		**Market Leverage 2**	
	SC	**SNC**	**SC**	**SNC**
Determinants	**(1)**	**(2)**	**(3)**	**(4)**
Business Risk$_{t-1}$	0.115 [0.079]	0.017 [0.105]	−0.027 [0.030]	−0.243** [0.116]
GDP growth$_{t-1}$	0.004*** [0.001]	−0.001 [0.001]	0.001* [0.001]	−0.008*** [0.001]
Constant	0.267* [0.160]	−0.138 [0.144]	−0.115* [0.061]	−0.293** [0.133]
R^2	0.047	0.11	0.117	0.324
Adjusted R^2	0.044	0.107	0.114	0.322
Firms	756	577	756	577
Observations	5562	4021	5562	4021
Time Effects	yes	yes	yes	yes
Estimator	FE	FE	FE	FE

Source: own contribution.

Table E.3: *Country* and *Industry* Regression (Book Leverage 2).

This table provides the coefficients of panel regressions with book leverage 2 (blev2) as the dependent variables. All independent variables used in the equation model (13a) are lagged one year and regressed separately for SC and SNC firms for the *country and industry* samples for the entire period 2004–2014. Table E.1 Appendix E and Table 4.10 provide the definitions of all variables. SC and SNC firms are determined based on DJIMI (see Table 4.1). US, UK, CA, JP, SK, TW, and IN denote countries such as United States, United Kingdom, Canada, Japan, South Korea, Taiwan, and India. OILG, BMAT, IND, CGDS, TECH, HCARE, and CSRV denote industries such as Oil and Gas, Basic Materials, Industrials, Consumer Goods, Technology, Health Care, and Consumer Services. Panel A and B represent the regression results for book leverage 2 (blev2) for SC and SNC firms, respectively. Results are shown with a dash-sign "-" represent either data, not available or not applicable. The regressions in all models contain *time fixed effects* (time dummies), *country* and *industry fixed effects* (i.e., dummies), while the *country* samples contain industry dummies, the *industry* samples contain country dummies (where applicable). Econometric estimators applied to each model are shown in the last row. All regressions were applied with the respective estimator, as identified by the model estimation procedure described in Panel B in Table B.3 in Appendix B. Company cluster robust standard errors are reported in the brackets. *, ** and *** denote significance at 10%, 5% and 1% levels, respectively. All variables are winsorized at the 1% and 99% level. Section 4.4.1 provides the specification of the model (13) from whom Model (13a) is derived.

$$blev2_{it} = \alpha + \beta_1 prof_{i,t-1} + \beta_2 growth_{i,t-1} + \beta_3 size_{i,t-1} + \beta_4 tang_{i,t-1} + \beta_5 risk_{i,t-1} + \beta_6 gdp_{i,t-1} + \mu_i + \mu_t + \varepsilon_{it} \quad (13a)$$

	Panel A: Shari'ah Compliant (SC)													
	Country							*Industry*						
	US	UK	CA	JP	SK	TW	IN	OILG	BMAT	IND	CGDS	TECH	HCARE	CSRV
	(1)	(2)	(3)	(4)	(5)	(6)	(7)	(8)	(9)	(10)	(11)	(12)	(13)	(14)
Determinants	Book Leverage 2													
Profitability $_{t-1}$	−0.143**	−0.114	−0.185	−0.259**	−0.201	−0.346***	−0.333***	−0.323***	−0.250**	−0.010	−0.185	−0.118	−0.303***	−0.064
	[0.061]	[0.151]	[0.130]	[0.119]	[0.152]	[0.117]	[0.121]	[0.115]	[0.114]	[0.089]	[0.126]	[0.114]	[0.099]	[0.122]
Growth	−0.013***	0.003	0.012	0.003	0.006	0.006	−0.012**	0.013	−0.009	−0.017**	−0.005	−0.009	−0.019***	−0.003
Opportunity $_{t-1}$	[0.004]	[0.010]	[0.014]	[0.006]	[0.010]	[0.006]	[0.005]	[0.015]	[0.009]	[0.009]	[0.005]	[0.006]	[0.006]	[0.006]
	0.002	−0.037	0.016	0.024*	0.111**	0.014	−0.019	−0.017	−0.007	0.029	−0.006	0.011	0.021*	−0.010
Firm Size $_{t-1}$	[0.019]	[0.031]	[0.021]	[0.013]	[0.050]	[0.015]	[0.023]	[0.023]	[0.014]	[0.031]	[0.024]	[0.026]	[0.011]	[0.029]

(continued)

Table E.3 (continued)

	Panel A: Shari'ah Compliant (SC)													
	Country							*Industry*						
	US	UK	CA	JP	SK	TW	IN	OILG	BMAT	IND	CGDS	TECH	HCARE	CSRV
	(1)	(2)	(3)	(4)	(5)	(6)	(7)	(8)	(9)	(10)	(11)	(12)	(13)	(14)
Determinants	Book Leverage 2													
Tangibility $_{t-1}$	0.175*	−0.046	0.098	−0.013	0.031	0.210	0.220*	−0.047	0.054	0.100	0.070	0.373**	0.365***	0.370***
	[0.092]	[0.142]	[0.076]	[0.112]	[0.135]	[0.134]	[0.120]	[0.089]	[0.067]	[0.100]	[0.134]	[0.153]	[0.117]	[0.133]
Business Risk $_{t-1}$	0.217*	−0.166	0.327	−0.025	−0.146	−0.168	−0.016	−0.160	0.597***	0.027	−0.087	0.081	0.528*	0.021
	[0.116]	[0.227]	[0.234]	[0.175]	[0.168]	[0.187]	[0.130]	[0.125]	[0.202]	[0.200]	[0.126]	[0.149]	[0.287]	[0.170]
GDP growth $_{t-1}$	−0.403***	0.007	0.087	0.074**	−0.015	–	−0.005	−0.008	0.008	0.001	0.007***	0.005*	0.001	−0.001
	[0.068]	[0.010]	[0.166]	[0.036]	[0.018]		[0.005]	[0.006]	[0.005]	[0.002]	[0.003]	[0.003]	[0.003]	[0.003]
Constant	1.138***	0.779*	−0.227	−0.358*	−1.443*	−0.044	0.451	0.573	0.309	−0.198	0.304	−0.015	0.004	0.273
	[0.379]	[0.436]	[0.409]	[0.190]	[0.742]	[0.212]	[0.312]	[0.346]	[0.203]	[0.462]	[0.354]	[0.386]	[0.173]	[0.440]
R^2	0.094	0.052	0.092	0.033	0.135	0.139	0.153	0.135	0.119	0.054	0.045	0.094		0.073
Adjusted R^2	0.090	0.027	0.057	0.016	0.064	0.082	0.132	0.106	0.086	0.044	0.030	0.079		0.051
Firms	407	74	53	120	31	34	71	64	63	188	132	121	97	91
Observations	3091	528	380	809	185	229	569	472	417	1430	949	869	765	660
Time Effects	yes	yes	yes	yes	yes	yes	yes	yes	yes	yes	yes	yes	yes	yes
Country Effects	–	–	–	–	–	–	–	–	–	–	–	–	yes	–
Industry Effects	–	–	–	–	–	–	–	–	–	–	–	–	–	–
Estimator	FE	FE	FE	FE	FE	FE	FE	FE	FE	FE	FE	FE	RE	FE

	Panel B: Shari'ah Non-Compliant (SNC)													
	Country							*Industry*						
	US	UK	CA	JP	SK	TW	IN	OILG	BMAT	IND	CGDS	TECH	HCARE	CSRV
	(1)	(2)	(3)	(4)	(5)	(6)	(7)	(8)	(9)	(10)	(11)	(12)	(13)	(14)
Determinants	Book Leverage 2													
$Profitability_{t-1}$	−0.307***	−0.381	−0.128	−0.725***	−0.495***	−0.842***	−0.307	−0.309	−0.496***	−0.548***	−0.537***	−0.786**	−0.691**	−0.526**
	[0.111]	[0.418]	[0.277]	[0.128]	[0.171]	[0.145]	[0.253]	[0.234]	[0.127]	[0.122]	[0.131]	[0.294]	[0.275]	[0.249]
Growth	0.061***	0.133**	0.101**	0.014	0.051	0.088***	−0.033	0.100**	−0.042	0.064***	0.028	0.105	0.132**	0.140***
$Opportunity_{t-1}$	[0.021]	[0.062]	[0.048]	[0.026]	[0.039]	[0.031]	[0.035]	[0.040]	[0.034]	[0.021]	[0.032]	[0.079]	[0.054]	[0.030]
$Firm\ Size_{t-1}$	−0.020	0.103**	0.025	0.035*	0.109***	0.019	0.025	0.033*	0.078***	0.026	0.008	0.145**	0.052*	0.026
	[0.019]	[0.043]	[0.031]	[0.020]	[0.018]	[0.025]	[0.016]	[0.017]	[0.016]	[0.019]	[0.023]	[0.063]	[0.028]	[0.021]
$Tangibility_{t-1}$	0.219***	0.078	0.518***	0.089	−0.009	0.495***	−0.035	0.127	0.031	0.132*	0.317*	−0.398***	0.261***	0.235**
	[0.079]	[0.246]	[0.181]	[0.094]	[0.124]	[0.085]	[0.063]	[0.157]	[0.079]	[0.070]	[0.179]	[0.132]	[0.083]	[0.116]
$Business\ Risk_{t-1}$	0.091	0.287	0.086	0.041	−0.177	0.352	−0.378	−0.129	−0.173	−0.092	−0.018	−0.396	0.745	0.703**
	[0.143]	[0.957]	[0.445]	[0.156]	[0.299]	[0.236]	[0.385]	[0.287]	[0.202]	[0.210]	[0.253]	[0.283]	[0.539]	[0.313]
$GDP\ growth_{t-1}$	−0.064	0.013	0.044	0.098***	−0.006	–	0.002	−0.001	−0.002	−0.004	0.002	−0.010	−0.002	0.000
	[0.055]	[0.023]	[0.395]	[0.028]	[0.015]		[0.008]	[0.003]	[0.002]	[0.002]	[0.003]	[0.008]	[0.004]	[0.003]
Constant	0.879**	−1.187*	−0.271	−0.237	−1.183***	−0.023	0.292	−0.168	−0.648**	0.047	0.274	−1.717*	−0.339	−0.063
	[0.355]	[0.588]	[0.935]	[0.322]	[0.272]	[0.378]	[0.258]	[0.339]	[0.259]	[0.302]	[0.374]	[0.983]	[0.396]	[0.330]
R^2	0.095	0.200	0.277	0.236	0.289	0.452	0.182	0.133	0.296	0.098	0.155	0.318		0.153
Adjusted R^2	0.087	0.149	0.209	0.229	0.262	0.424	0.123	0.070	0.276	0.089	0.135	0.230		0.138
Firms	237	36	24	196	55	38	29	34	74	195	98	25	26	125
Observations	1486	236	164	1543	381	286	211	221	544	1406	670	132	165	883
Time Effects	yes	yes	yes	yes	yes	yes	yes	yes	yes	yes	yes	yes	yes	yes
Country Effects	–	–	–	–	–	–	–	–	–	–	–	–	yes	–
Industry Effects	–	–	–	–	–	–	–	–	–	–	–	–	–	–
Estimator	FE	FE	FE	FE	FE	FE	FE	FE	FE	FE	FE	FE	RE	FE

Source: own contribution.

Table E.4: *Country* and *Industry* Regression (Market Leverage 2).

This table provides the coefficients of panel regressions with market leverage 2 (mlev2) as the dependent variables. All independent variables used in the equation model (14a) are lagged one year and regressed separately for SC and SNC firms for the *country and industry* samples for the entire period 2004–2014. Table E.1 Appendix E and Table 4.10 provide the definitions of all variables. SC and SNC firms are determined based on DJIMI (see Table 4.1). US, UK, CA, JP, SK, TW, and IN denote countries such as United States, United Kingdom, Canada, Japan, South Korea, Taiwan, and India. OILG, BMAT, IND, CGDS, TECH, HCARE, and CSRV denote industries such as Oil and Gas, Basic Materials, Industrials, Consumer Goods, Technology, Health Care, and Consumer Services. Panel A and B represent the regression results for market leverage 2 (mlev2) for SC and SNC firms, respectively. Results are shown with a dash-sign "-" represent either data, not available or not applicable. The regressions in all models contain *time fixed effects* (time dummies), *country* and *industry fixed effects* (i.e., dummies), while the *country* samples contain industry dummies, the *industry* samples contain country dummies (where applicable). Econometric estimators applied to each model are shown in the last row. All regressions were applied with the respective estimator, as identified by the model estimation procedure described in Panel B in Table B.3 in Appendix B. Company cluster robust standard errors are reported in the brackets. *, ** and *** denote significance at 10%, 5% and 1% levels, respectively. All variables are winsorized at the 1% and 99% level. Section 4.4.1 provides the specification of the model (14) from whom Model (14a) is derived.

$$mlev2_{it} = \alpha + \beta_1 prof_{i,t-1} + \beta_2 growth_{i,t-1} + \beta_3 size_{i,t-1} + \beta_4 tang_{i,t-1} + \beta_5 risk_{i,t-1} + \beta_6 gdp_{i,t-1} + \mu_i + \mu_t + \varepsilon_{i}, \tag{14a}$$

	Panel A: Shari'ah Compliant (SC)													
	Country							*Industry*						
	US	UK	CA	JP	SK	TW	IN	OILG	BMAT	IND	CGDS	TECH	HCARE	CSRV
	(1)	(2)	(3)	(4)	(5)	(6)	(7)	(8)	(9)	(10)	(11)	(12)	(13)	(14)
Determinants	Market Leverage 2													
Profitability $_{t-1}$	−0.134***	−0.149**	−0.118*	−0.111*	−0.139	−0.222***	−0.112***	−0.191***	−0.178**	−0.064*	−0.123**	−0.083	−0.051	−0.038
	[0.030]	[0.066]	[0.068]	[0.066]	[0.097]	[0.073]	[0.034]	[0.062]	[0.080]	[0.033]	[0.048]	[0.050]	[0.049]	[0.065]
Growth Opportunity $_{t-1}$	−0.008***	−0.006	−0.016***	−0.006*	−0.004	0.000	−0.006***	−0.016**	−0.008**	−0.013***	−0.006**	−0.005***	−0.010***	−0.007***
	[0.001]	[0.004]	[0.006]	[0.003]	[0.004]	[0.004]	[0.002]	[0.007]	[0.004]	[0.002]	[0.003]	[0.002]	[0.003]	[0.003]
Firm Size $_{t-1}$	0.022***	0.008	0.019	0.012	0.048*	0.030*	−0.013*	−0.008	0.012	0.034***	0.014*	0.009	−0.002	0.010
	[0.006]	[0.014]	[0.013]	[0.009]	[0.027]	[0.015]	[0.008]	[0.013]	[0.010]	[0.011]	[0.008]	[0.009]	[0.009]	[0.012]
Tangibility $_{t-1}$	0.106***	0.014	0.037	0.039	0.011	0.090	0.030	0.055	0.059*	0.017	0.022	0.157*	−0.011	0.152**
	[0.038]	[0.071]	[0.041]	[0.075]	[0.082]	[0.066]	[0.042]	[0.054]	[0.031]	[0.041]	[0.055]	[0.090]	[0.066]	[0.060]

Business Risk $_{t-1}$	−0.018	−0.010	−0.049	−0.039	−0.078	−0.085	0.027	−0.236***	0.157**	−0.067	−0.064	−0.005	0.142**	−0.018
	[0.041]	[0.087]	[0.112]	[0.106]	[0.153]	[0.119]	[0.059]	[0.080]	[0.065]	[0.056]	[0.075]	[0.081]	[0.069]	[0.070]
GDP growth $_{t-1}$	−0.125***	0.000	0.243**	0.086***	−0.008	–	−0.003**	−0.006	0.002	0.001	0.000	0.002*	0.001	0.001
	[0.025]	[0.004]	[0.120]	[0.022]	[0.013]		[0.001]	[0.004]	[0.002]	[0.001]	[0.001]	[0.001]	[0.001]	[0.002]
Constant	0.055	−0.007	−0.592**	−0.256**	−0.583	−0.349	0.263**	0.321	−0.051	−0.381**	−0.114	−0.081	0.132	−0.109
	[0.127]	[0.199]	[0.268]	[0.127]	[0.375]	[0.214]	[0.110]	[0.214]	[0.145]	[0.159]	[0.124]	[0.134]	[0.135]	[0.176]
R^2	0.150	0.136	0.220	0.108	0.117	0.182	0.203	0.333	0.223	0.156	0.126	0.111	0.120	0.116
Adjusted R^2	0.146	0.112	0.190	0.092	0.044	0.129	0.182	0.311	0.194	0.148	0.112	0.096	0.102	0.095
Firms	407	74	53	120	31	34	71	64	63	188	132	121	97	91
Observations	3091	528	380	809	185	229	569	472	417	1430	949	869	765	660
Time Effects	yes	yes	yes	yes	yes	yes	yes	yes	yes	yes	yes	yes	yes	yes
Country Effects	–	–	–	–	–	–	–	–	–	–	–	–	–	–
Industry Effects	–	–	–	–	–	–	–	–	–	–	–	–	–	–
Estimator	FE	FE	FE	FE	FE	FE	FE	FE	FE	FE	FE	FE	FE	FE

	Panel B: Shari'ah Non-Compliant (SNC)													
	Country							*Industry*						
	US	UK	CA	JP	SK	TW	IN	OILG	BMAT	IND	CGDS	TECH	HCARE	CSRV
Determinants	**(1)**	**(2)**	**(3)**	**(4)**	**(5)**	**(6)**	**(7)**	**(8)**	**(9)**	**(10)**	**(11)**	**(12)**	**(13)**	**(14)**
	Market Leverage 2													
Profitability $_{t-1}$	−0.437***	−0.674**	−0.364	−0.812***	−0.570**	−0.763***	−0.330	−0.961***	−0.742***	−0.660***	−0.291**	−0.535*	−0.824**	−0.937***
	[0.109]	[0.304]	[0.325]	[0.163]	[0.219]	[0.172]	[0.246]	[0.202]	[0.197]	[0.139]	[0.115]	[0.279]	[0.322]	[0.265]
Growth Opportunity $_{t-1}$	−0.103***	−0.069	0.050	−0.192***	−0.210***	−0.111***	−0.133***	0.000	−0.172***	−0.138***	−0.142***	−0.152	0.016	−0.057*
	[0.021]	[0.058]	[0.074]	[0.033]	[0.041]	[0.037]	[0.040]	[0.046]	[0.041]	[0.019]	[0.031]	[0.090]	[0.056]	[0.032]
Firm Size $_{t-1}$	0.032*	0.180**	0.048	0.066**	0.069***	0.044	0.054***	0.049***	0.088***	0.050***	0.021	0.088	0.069	0.054**
	[0.018]	[0.078]	[0.031]	[0.028]	[0.020]	[0.036]	[0.016]	[0.010]	[0.019]	[0.018]	[0.024]	[0.055]	[0.073]	[0.024]

Table E.4 (continued)

	Panel B: Shari'ah Non-Compliant (SNC)													
	Country							*Industry*						
	US	UK	CA	JP	SK	TW	IN	OILG	BMAT	IND	CGDS	TECH	HCARE	CSRV
Determinants	(1)	(2)	(3)	(4)	(5)	(6)	(7)	(8)	(9)	(10)	(11)	(12)	(13)	(14)
	Market Leverage 2													
$Tangibility_{t-1}$	0.213**	−0.052	0.153	0.177	0.203	0.063	0.099	0.229**	0.117	0.189**	0.324**	−0.272	0.091	0.125
	[0.082]	[0.249]	[0.172]	[0.109]	[0.126]	[0.126]	[0.124]	[0.100]	[0.133]	[0.077]	[0.129]	[0.167]	[0.359]	[0.114]
$Business\ Risk_{t-1}$	−0.106	−1.268***	0.348	−0.261	−0.517	0.063	−0.964**	−0.541	−0.454*	−0.285	−0.443**	0.349	0.546	0.638**
	[0.169]	[0.423]	[0.501]	[0.187]	[0.345]	[0.296]	[0.400]	[0.388]	[0.248]	[0.253]	[0.215]	[0.281]	[0.546]	[0.249]
$GDP\ growth_{t-1}$	−0.146*	0.033**	0.229	0.192***	0.011	–	−0.045***	−0.009**	−0.007**	−0.010***	−0.004	−0.028**	0.003	−0.010***
	[0.074]	[0.016]	[0.362]	[0.047]	[0.028]		[0.011]	[0.004]	[0.003]	[0.003]	[0.003]	[0.010]	[0.006]	[0.003]
Constant	0.330	−2.191*	−0.895	−0.725	−0.379	−0.098	0.092	−0.288*	−0.712**	−0.177	0.174	−0.666	−0.546	−0.306
	[0.380]	[1.162]	[0.810]	[0.456]	[0.288]	[0.548]	[0.282]	[0.152]	[0.315]	[0.285]	[0.382]	[0.830]	[1.080]	[0.370]
R^2	0.344	0.528	0.225	0.422	0.323	0.383	0.438	0.344	0.472	0.337	0.352	0.535	0.363	0.342
Adjusted R^2	0.338	0.498	0.152	0.416	0.297	0.352	0.398	0.296	0.457	0.330	0.338	0.474	0.299	0.330
Firms	237	36	24	196	55	38	29	34	74	195	98	25	26	125
Observations	1486	236	164	1543	381	286	211	221	544	1406	670	132	165	883
Time Effects	yes	yes	yes	yes	yes	yes	yes	yes	yes	yes	yes	yes	yes	yes
Country Effects	–	–	–	–	–	–	–	–	–	–	–	–	–	–
Industry Effects	–	–	–	–	–	–	–	–	–	–	–	–	–	–
Estimator	FE	FE	FE	FE	FE	FE	FE	FE	FE	FE	FE	FE	FE	FE

Source: own contribution.

Table E.5: Explanatory Power of Capital Structure Theories (Robustness Test I).

Determinants	**Book Leverage 2 (BLEV2)**												**Market Leverage 2 (MLEV2)**											
	Overall (pooled)				***Country***				***Industry***				***Overall (pooled)***				***Country***				***Industry***			
	SC		**SNC**		**SC**		**SNC**		**SC**		**SNC**		**SC**		**SNC**		**SC**		**SNC**		**SC**		**SNC**	
	(1)	**(2)**	**(3)**	**(4)**	**(5)**	**(6)**	**(7)**	**(8)**	**(9)**	**(10)**	**(11)**	**(12)**	**(13)**	**(14)**	**(15)**	**(16)**	**(17)**	**(18)**	**(19)**	**(20)**	**(21)**	**(22)**	**(23)**	**(24)**
	+	**−**	**+**	**−**	**+**	**−**	**+**	**−**	**+**	**−**	**+**	**−**	**+**	**−**	**+**	**−**	**+**	**−**	**+**	**−**	**+**	**−**	**+**	**−**
Part A	*Panel A: Number of Significant Correlations*																							
Profitability	0	1	0	1	0	4	0	4	0	3	0	6	0	1	0	1	0	6	0	5	0	4	0	7
Growth Opportunity	0	1	1	0	0	2	4	0	0	2	4	0	0	1	0	1	0	4	0	5	0	7	0	4
Firm Size	0	0	1	0	2	0	3	0	1	0	4	0	1	0	1	0	3	1	5	0	2	0	4	0
Tangibility	1	0	1	0	2	0	3	0	3	0	4	1	1	0	1	0	1	0	1	0	3	0	3	0
Business Risk	0	0	0	0	1	0	0	0	2	0	0	0	0	0	0	1	0	0	0	2	2	1	1	2
GDP growth	1	0	0	0	1	1	1	0	2	0	0	0	1	0	0	1	2	2	2	2	1	0	0	5
	Panel B: Reliable(Core) Leverage Determinants																							
Profitability		✓		✓		✓		✓				✓		✓		✓		✓		✓		✓		✓
Growth Opportunity		✓	✓				✓				✓			✓		✓		✓		✓		✓		✓
Firm Size			✓								✓		✓		✓				✓				✓	
Tangibility	✓		✓								✓		✓		✓									
Business Risk																✓								
GDP growth	✓												✓			✓								✓
	Panel C: Empirical Results (Consolidated)																							
Profitability	−		−		−		−				−		−		−		−		−		−		−	
Growth Opportunity	−		+				+				+		−		−		−		−		−		−	
Firm Size			+								+		+		+				+				+	
Tangibility	+		+								+		+		+									
Business Risk															−									
GDP Growth	+												+		−								−	

(continued)

Table E.5 (continued)

Determinants		Book Leverage 2 (BLEV2)						Market Leverage 2 (MLEV2)					
		Overall (pooled)		*Country*		*Industry*		*Overall (pooled)*		*Country*		*Industry*	
		SC	SNC	SC	SNC	SC	SNC	SC	SNC	SC	SNC	SC	SNC
		(1) (2)	(3) (4)	(5) (6)	(7) (8)	(9) (10)	(11) (12)	(13) (14)	(15) (16)	(17) (18)	(19) (20)	(21) (22)	(23) (24)
		+ –	+ –	+ –	+ –	+ –	+ –	+ –	+ –	+ –	+ –	+ –	+ –
Part B		*Panel D: Consolidated Results (by Capital Structure Theory/Model)*											
		(1)	(2)	(3)	(4)	(5)	(6)	(7)	(8)	(9)	(10)	(11)	(12)
Profitability		P,T*,IP	P,T*,IP	P,T*,IP	P,T*,IP		P,T*,IP	P,T*,IP	P,T*,IP	P,T*,IP	P,T*,IP	P,T*,IP	P,T*,IP
Growth Opportunity		T,IP	P		P		P	T,IP	T,IP	T,IP	T,IP	T,IP	T,IP
Firm Size			T				T	T	T		T		T
Tangibility		T	T				T	T	T				
Business Risk									T,IP				
GDP Growth		T						T	P,IP				P,IP
		Panel E: Number of Matching Capital Structure Theories/Model											
Trade–Off Theory	(T)	4	3	1	1	–	3	5	5	2	3	2	3
Pecking Order Theory	(P)	1	2	1	2	–	2	1	2	1	1	1	2
Pecking Order Model (Islamic)	(IP)	2	1	1	1	–	1	2	4	2	2	2	3
		Panel F: Explanatory Power of the Capital Structure Theories/Model											
Trade–Off Theory	(T)	57%	50%	33%	25%	–	50%	63%	45%	40%	50%	40%	38%
Pecking Order Theory	(P)	14%	33%	33%	50%	–	33%	13%	18%	20%	17%	20%	25%
Pecking Order Model (Islamic)	(IP)	29%	17%	33%	25%	–	17%	25%	36%	40%	33%	40%	38%

T* = Dynamic Trade-Off Theory

Robustness II: Different Estimator on Lagged Determinants (t–1), using GMM

Table E.6: Explanatory Power of Capital Structure Theories (Robustness Test II).

Determinants	Book Leverage (BLEV)												Market Leverage (MLEV)											
	Overall (pooled)				*Country*				*Industry*				*Overall (pooled)*				*Country*				*Industry*			
	SC		SNC		SC		SNC		SC		SNC		SC		SNC		SC		SNC		SC		SNC	
	(1)	(2)	(3)	(4)	(5)	(6)	(7)	(8)	(9)	(10)	(11)	(12)	(13)	(14)	(15)	(16)	(17)	(18)	(19)	(20)	(21)	(22)	(23)	(24)
	+	–	+	–	+	–	+	–	+	–	+	–	+	–	+	–	+	–	+	–	+	–	+	–
Part A	*Panel A: Number of Significant Correlations*																							
Profitability	0	**1**	0	**1**	0	2	0	2	0	2	0	1	0	0			0	**4**	0	2	0	**4**	0	1
Growth Opportunity	**1**	0	**1**	0	2	0	1	0	1	0	0	0	0	0			1	0	1	0	0	0	3	0
Firm Size	**1**	0	**1**	0	2	0	**4**	0	**5**	0	3	0	0	0			**4**	0	**5**	0	**6**	0	**4**	0
Tangibility	**1**	0	**1**	0	0	1	1	0	1	2	0	0	0	0	n/a		0	0	2	0	0	0	0	0
Business Risk	0	0	0	0	0	1	0	0	0	2	0	0	**1**	0			0	0	0	0	0	**4**	0	2
GDP growth	0	0	0	0	0	1	1	0	1	1	1	1	0	**1**			2	1	1	1	0	0	0	**4**
	Panel B: Reliable(Core) Leverage Determinants																							
Profitability		✓		✓														✓				✓		
Growth Opportunity	✓		✓																					
Firm Size	✓		✓				✓		✓								✓		✓		✓		✓	
Tangibility	✓		✓												n/a									
Business Risk													✓									✓		
GDP growth														✓										✓

(continued)

Panel C: Empirical Results (Consolidated)													
Profitability		–	–							–		–	
Growth Opportunity		+	+										
Firm Size		+	+		+	+			n/a	+	+	+	+
Tangibility		+	+										
Business Risk								+				–	
GDP Growth								–					–
Part B	*Panel D: Consolidated Results (by Capital Structure Theory/Model)*												
		(1)	(2)	(3)	(4)	(5)	(6)	(7)	(8)	(9)	(10)	(11)	(12)
Profitability		P,T*,IP	P,T*,IP							P,T*,IP		P,T*,IP	
Growth Opportunity		P	P										
Firm Size		T	T		T	T			n/a	T	T	T	T
Tangibility		T	T										
Business Risk								P				T,IP	
GDP Growth								P,IP					P,IP
Panel E: Number of Matching Capital Structure Theories/Model													
Trade–Off Theory	(T)	3	3	–	1	1	–	0		2	1	3	1
Pecking Order Theory	(P)	2	2	–	0	0	–	2	n/a	1	0	1	1
Pecking Order Model (Islamic)	(IP)	1	1	–	0	0	–	1		1	0	2	1
Panel F: Explanatory Power of the Capital Structure Theories/Model													
Trade–Off Theory	(T)	50%	50%	–	100%	100%	–	0%		50%	100%	50%	33%
Pecking Order Theory	(P)	33%	33%	–	0%	0%	–	67%	n/a	25%	0%	17%	33%
Pecking Order Model (Islamic)	(IP)	17%	17%	–	0%	0%	–	33%		25%	0%	33%	33%

T* = Dynamic Trade-Off Theory

Robustness III: Different Model Specification

Table E.7: Dynamic Trade-Off, Speed of Adjustment (SOA) – Book Leverage (Robustness Test III).

This table provides the results from estimating the partial adjustment model (SOA) with book leverage as the dependent variables. The lagged book leverage ($blev_{i,t\ 1}$ is incorporated as an independent variable. All firm-specific and macroeconomic debt determinants used in the equation model (18a) are regressed separately for SC and SNC firms for the *overall (pooled), country, and industry* samples for the entire period 2004–2014. Tables 4.3 and 4.10 provide the definitions of all variables. SC and SNC firms are determined based on DJIMI (see Table 4.1). US, UK, CA, JP, SK, TW, and IN denote countries such as United States, United Kingdom, Canada, Japan, South Korea, Taiwan, and India. OILG, BMAT, IND, CGDS, TECH, HCARE, and CSRV denote industries such as Oil and Gas, Basic Materials, Industrials, Consumer Goods, Technology, Health Care, and Consumer Services. Panel A and B represent the regression results for book leverage for SC and SNC firms, respectively. Results are shown with a dash-sign "-" represent either data, not available or not applicable. The regressions in all models contain time fixed effects (time dummies). The *overall (pooled)* sample contains country and industry fixed effects (country and industry dummy), the *country* sample contains industry fixed effects, the *industry* sample contains country fixed effects – (where applicable). AR (1) and AR (2) are the first- and second-order autocorrelations of residuals under the null of no serial correlation. The Hansen test provides the over-identifying restrictions under the null of the instruments' validity. SOA is one minus the coefficient on lagged book leverage. Leverage half-life is defined as the time a firm requires (in years) to adjust back to the target leverage after a one-unit shock to ε, *ln(0.5)/ ln(1-λ)*. The estimation results are shown in the row "Successful Results" after passing the AR(1), AR(2), and the Sargan/Hansen tests successfully. (see Section 4.2.2) ✓ denotes acceptable result, ✗ unsuccessful econometrical attempt – 1st level. The econometric estimator applied to each model is shown in the last row. Company cluster robust standard errors are reported in the brackets. *, ** and *** denote significance at 10%, 5% and 1% levels, respectively. All variables are winsorized at the 1% and 99% level. Section 6.1.1 provides the specification of the model (18) from whom model (18a) is derived.

$$blev_{it} = \alpha + (1-\lambda) blev_{it-1} + \beta_1 prof_{it} + \beta_2 growth_{it} + \beta_3 size_{it} + \beta_4 tang_{it} + \beta_5 risk_{it} + \beta_6 gdp_{it} + \mu_i + \mu_t + \varepsilon_{it} \quad (18a)$$

(continued)

Table E.7 (continued)

Dynamic Trade-Off	*Overall (pooled)*	*Country*							*Industry*						
		US	UK	CA	JP	SK	TW	IN	OILG	BMAT	IND	CGDS	TECH	HCARE	CSRV
Determinants	(1)	(2)	(3)	(4)	(5)	(6)	(7)	(8)	(9)	(10)	(11)	(12)	(13)	(14)	(15)
								Panel A: Shari'ah Compliant (SC)							
Book Leverage $_{t-1}$	0.849***	0.854***	0.893***	0.584***	0.736***	1.127***	0.766***	0.779***	0.766***	0.757***	0.896***	0.779***	0.702***	0.752***	0.661***
	[0.031]	[0.050]	[0.104]	[0.067]	[0.078]	[0.340]	[0.028]	[0.082]	[0.072]	[0.155]	[0.085]	[0.112]	[0.132]	[0.085]	[0.092]
Profitability $_t$	−0.143**	−0.060	−0.533***	−0.233**	−0.191	0.161	−0.476	−0.349**	−0.401**	0.783*	−0.052	0.028	0.120	−0.208***	0.032
	[0.062]	[0.131]	[0.205]	[0.110]	[0.151]	[0.231]	[0.462]	[0.144]	[0.203]	[0.429]	[0.141]	[0.194]	[0.181]	[0.074]	[0.101]
Growth Opportunity $_t$	0.004	0.005	0.022**	0.026	0.013	−0.028*	0.023	0.004	0.023**	−0.038**	0.000	0.000	−0.006	0.002	0.001
	[0.004]	[0.005]	[0.010]	[0.017]	[0.009]	[0.014]	[0.025]	[0.005]	[0.012]	[0.017]	[0.006]	[0.007]	[0.006]	[0.004]	[0.006]
Firm Size $_t$	0.020***	0.022**	0.013**	0.015**	0.005	−0.012	0.045	0.017*	0.006*	−0.043	0.004	0.009*	0.003	0.012***	0.017***
	[0.007]	[0.009]	[0.006]	[0.007]	[0.012]	[0.011]	[.]	[0.010]	[0.004]	[0.036]	[0.013]	[0.006]	[0.006]	[0.004]	[0.006]
Tangibility $_t$	−0.016	−0.009	0.064*	−0.048*	−0.019	−0.076	0.136	−0.107	0.001	0.031	−0.030	0.014	−0.044	0.071*	0.000
	[0.011]	[0.015]	[0.035]	[0.025]	[0.036]	[0.079]	[0.087]	[0.123]	[0.026]	[0.104]	[0.029]	[0.038]	[0.054]	[0.042]	[0.018]
Business Risk $_t$	0.023	−0.635**	0.243	0.001	−0.102	0.298	0.764	0.300	0.094	0.121	0.187	0.017	0.132	−0.833	−0.067
	[0.163]	[0.284]	[0.197]	[0.185]	[0.157]	[0.378]	[0.530]	[0.197]	[0.252]	[0.374]	[0.116]	[0.201]	[0.180]	[0.575]	[0.152]
GDP growth $_t$	0.000	0.001	0.002	0.005**	0.000	0.019	–	–	0.006	0.001	0.003	0.000	0.001	−0.003	−0.006
	[0.001]	[0.002]	[0.002]	[0.003]	[0.001]	[0.022]			[0.004]	[0.006]	[0.002]	[0.003]	[0.003]	[0.002]	[0.007]
Constant	−0.225**	−0.277**	−0.144**	−0.051	0.030	0.000	−0.997***	−0.147	0.000	0.000	−0.006	0.000	0.053	−0.039	−0.107*
	[0.106]	[0.123]	[0.069]	[0.098]	[0.193]	[.]	[0.339]	[0.214]	[.]	[.]	[0.175]	[.]	[0.094]	[0.047]	[0.063]
Observations	5567	3091	529	381	810	186	229	570	471	420	1431	950	869	765	661
Time Effects	yes	yes	yes	yes	yes	yes	yes	yes	yes	yes	yes	yes	yes	yes	yes
Country Effects	yes	no	no	no	no	no	no	no	yes	yes	yes	yes	yes	yes	yes
Industry Effects	yes	yes	yes	yes	yes	yes	yes	yes	no	no	no	no	no	no	no
# Instruments	243	82	52	51	66	30	27	67	50	28	67	52	78	51	36
# Groups/Firms	755	407	74	52	120	31	34	71	63	63	188	132	121	97	91

Dynamic Trade-Off	*Overall (pooled)*	*Country*							*Industry*						
		US	**UK**	**CA**	**JP**	**SK**	**TW**	**IN**	**OILG**	**BMAT**	**IND**	**CGDS**	**TECH**	**HCARE**	**CSRV**
Determinants	**(1)**	**(2)**	**(3)**	**(4)**	**(5)**	**(6)**	**(7)**	**(8)**	**(9)**	**(10)**	**(11)**	**(12)**	**(13)**	**(14)**	**(15)**
Panel A: Shari'ah Compliant (SC)															
AR (1)	0.000	0.000	0.000	0.000	0.000	0.037	0.003	0.000	0.000	0.002	0.000	0.000	0.002	0.000	0.005
AR (2)	0.636	0.141	0.249	0.332	0.641	0.048	0.182	0.152	0.524	0.099	0.786	0.327	0.485	0.259	0.545
SOA	0.151	0.146	0.107	0.416	0.264	−0.127	0.234	0.221	0.234	0.243	0.104	0.221	0.298	0.248	0.339
Hansen Test	0.069	0.171	0.387	0.261	0.142	0.285	0.478	0.400	0.122	0.694	0.092	0.174	0.158	0.196	0.532
Half-Life	4.23	4.39	6.12	1.29	2.26	–	2.60	2.78	2.60	2.49	6.31	2.78	1.96	2.43	1.67
Successful Results	✓	✓	✓	✓	✓	✗[1]	✓	✓	✓	✓	✓	✓	✓	✓	✓
Estimator	Blundell-Bond 2-Step System GMM														

✗ unsuccessful attempt

(continued)

Table E.7 (continued)

Dynamic Trade-Off	*Overall (pooled)*	*Country*							*Industry*						
		US	UK	CA	JP	SK	TW	IN	OILG	BMAT	IND	CGDS	TECH	HCARE	CSRV
Determinants	(1)	(2)	(3)	(4)	(5)	(6)	(7)	(8)	(9)	(10)	(11)	(12)	(13)	(14)	(15)
Panel B: Shari'ah Non-Compliant (SNC)															
Book Leverage $_{t-1}$	0.831***	0.830***	0.945***	0.587*	0.893***	0.782***	0.767***	0.978***	0.637***	0.808***	0.835***	0.865***	0.806**	0.938***	0.801***
	[0.073]	[0.051]	[0.126]	[0.318]	[0.035]	[0.146]	[0.160]	[0.273]	[0.241]	[0.062]	[0.069]	[0.050]	[0.369]	[0.191]	[0.053]
Profitability $_t$	−0.488***	−0.646***	−0.161	−0.889	−0.345*	−0.183	−0.982***	−0.722***	−0.794*	−0.428	−0.430**	−0.743***	−0.678***	−0.506***	−0.311***
	[0.167]	[0.146]	[0.283]	[0.837]	[0.188]	[0.476]	[0.373]	[0.179]	[0.407]	[0.356]	[0.184]	[0.214]	[0.262]	[0.166]	[0.073]
Growth Opportunity $_t$	0.061***	0.080***	0.027	0.173	0.034	0.066	0.098**	−0.004	0.174	0.031	0.048**	0.071***	0.089	−0.018	0.065***
	[0.021]	[0.017]	[0.037]	[0.167]	[0.024]	[0.063]	[0.046]	[0.018]	[0.132]	[0.031]	[0.019]	[0.023]	[0.066]	[0.035]	[0.013]
Firm Size $_t$	0.030***	0.022***	0.012	0.001	0.011	0.031	0.018	−0.001	0.026	0.005	0.009	0.003**	0.003	0.005	0.006**
	[0.010]	[0.008]	[0.008]	[0.025]	[0.007]	[0.024]	[0.011]	[0.006]	[0.019]	[0.008]	[0.012]	[0.002]	[0.014]	[0.011]	[0.002]
Tangibility $_t$	0.052***	0.059***	0.034	−0.151	0.031	0.114	0.101**	0.011	0.083	0.010	0.028	0.113***	0.144	0.028	0.039***
	[0.018]	[0.019]	[0.031]	[0.163]	[0.019]	[0.124]	[0.045]	[0.062]	[0.071]	[0.027]	[0.036]	[0.036]	[0.141]	[0.034]	[0.013]
Business Risk $_t$	−0.026	−0.038	0.558	−0.477	0.189*	0.527**	−0.190	0.565	1.192**	−0.175	−0.065	0.002	−1.589	1.093	0.444***
	[0.508]	[0.392]	[0.553]	[0.779]	[0.098]	[0.263]	[0.261]	[0.398]	[0.552]	[0.182]	[0.140]	[0.089]	[1.791]	[0.715]	[0.168]
GDP growth $_t$	0.001	0.002*	0.005	0.006	–	−0.081	–	0.008	−0.001	0.000	0.002**	0.003	0.010	0.002	0.002
	[0.001]	[0.001]	[0.004]	[0.005]		[0.072]		[0.020]	[0.003]	[0.002]	[0.001]	[0.002]	[0.011]	[0.004]	[0.001]
Constant	−0.419***	−0.302**	0.000	0.317	−0.151	0.000	−0.153	0.000	−0.380	0.000	0.000	−0.015	0.000	0.044	0.000
	[0.157]	[0.124]	[.]	[0.702]	[0.128]	[.]	[0.123]	[.]	[0.364]	[.]	[.]	[0.031]	[.]	[0.095]	[.]
Observations	4024	1485	236	164	1545	382	286	212	222	545	1406	669	133	166	883
Time Effects	yes	yes	yes	yes	yes	yes	yes	yes	yes	yes	yes	yes	yes	yes	yes
Country Effects	yes	no	no	no	no	no	no	no	yes	yes	yes	yes	yes	yes	yes
Industry Effects	yes	yes	yes	yes	yes	yes	yes	yes	no	no	no	no	no	no	no
# Instruments	92	110	36	26	67	49	34	29	31	67	88	52	29	31	55
# Groups/Firms	577	237	36	24	196	55	38	29	34	74	195	98	25	26	125

Dynamic Trade-Off	*Overall (pooled)*	*Country*							*Industry*						
		US	UK	CA	JP	SK	TW	IN	OILG	BMAT	IND	CGDS	TECH	HCARE	CSRV
Determinants	**(1)**	**(2)**	**(3)**	**(4)**	**(5)**	**(6)**	**(7)**	**(8)**	**(9)**	**(10)**	**(11)**	**(12)**	**(13)**	**(14)**	**(15)**
Panel B: Shari'ah Non-Compliant (SNC)															
AR (1)	0.000	0.000	0.002	0.027	0.000	0.007	0.009	0.006	0.009	0.000	0.000	0.000	0.030	0.047	0.000
AR (2)	0.085	0.257	0.412	0.076	0.661	0.726	0.442	0.308	0.251	0.101	0.340	0.260	0.539	0.118	0.312
SOA	0.169	0.170	0.055	0.413	0.107	0.218	0.233	0.022	0.363	0.192	0.165	0.135	0.194	0.062	0.199
Hansen Test	0.172	0.152	0.167	0.043	0.657	0.574	0.414	0.414	0.364	0.235	0.232	0.865	0.824	0.998	0.087
Half-Life	3.74	3.72	12.25	1.30	6.12	2.82	2.61	31.16	1.54	3.25	3.84	4.78	3.21	10.83	3.12
Successful Results	✓	✓	✓	✗[2]	✓	✓	✓	✓	✓	✓	✓	✓	✗[3]	✗[4]	✓
Estimator	Blundell-Bond 2-Step System GMM														

✗ unsuccessful attempt
Source: own contribution.

Table E.8: Dynamic Trade-Off, Speed of Adjustment (SOA) – Market Leverage (Robustness Test III).

This table provides the results from estimating the partial adjustment model (SOA) with market leverage as the dependent variables. The lagged book leverage ($mlev_{i,t-1}$) is incorporated as an independent variable. All firm-specific and macroeconomic debt determinants used in the equation model (19a) are regressed separately for SC and SNC firms for the *overall (pooled), country, and industry* samples for the entire period 2004–2014. Tables 4.3 and 4.10 provide the definitions of all variables. SC and SNC firms are determined based on DJIMI (see Table 4.1). US, UK, CA, JP, SK, TW, and IN denote countries such as United States, United Kingdom, Canada, Japan, South Korea, Taiwan, and India. OILG, BMAT, IND, CGDS, TECH, HCARE, and CSRV denote industries such as Oil and Gas, Basic Materials, Industrials, Consumer Goods, Technology, Health Care, and Consumer Services. Panel A and B represent the regression results for market leverage for SC and SNC firms, respectively. Results are shown with a dash-sign "-" represent either data, not available or not applicable. The regressions in all models contain time fixed effects (time dummies). The *overall (pooled)* sample contains country and industry fixed effects (country and industry dummy), the *country* sample contains industry fixed effects, the *industry* sample contains country fixed effects – (where applicable). AR (1) and AR (2) are the first- and second-order autocorrelations of residuals under the null of no serial correlation. The Hansen test provides the over-identifying restrictions under the null of the instruments' validity. SOA is one minus the coefficient on lagged market leverage. Leverage half-life is defined as the time a firm requires (in years) to adjust back to the target leverage after a one-unit shock to *ε, ln(0.5)/ln(1-λ)*. The estimation results are shown in the row "Successful Results" after passing the AR(1), AR(2), and the Sargan/Hansen tests successfully. (see Section 4.2.2) ✓ denotes acceptable result, ✗ unsuccessful econometrical attempt – 1st level. The econometric estimator applied to each model is shown in the last row. Company cluster robust standard errors are reported in the brackets. *, ** and *** denote significance at 10%, 5% and 1% levels, respectively. All variables are winsorized at the 1% and 99% level. Section 6.1.1 provides the specification of the model (19) from whom model (19a) is derived.

$$mlev_{it} = \alpha + (1-\lambda) mlev_{it-1} + \beta_1 prof_{it} + \beta_2 growth_{it} + \beta_3 size_{it} + \beta_4 tang_{it} + \beta_5 risk_{it} + \beta_6 gdp_{it} + \mu_i + \mu_t + \varepsilon_{it} \tag{19a}$$

Dynamic Trade-Off	Overall (pooled)	Country							Industry						
		US	UK	CA	JP	SK	TW	IN	OILG	BMAT	IND	CGDS	TECH	HCARE	CSRV
Determinants	(1)	(2)	(3)	(4)	(5)	(6)	(7)	(8)	(9)	(10)	(11)	(12)	(13)	(14)	(15)
Panel A: Shari'ah Compliant (SC)															
Market Leverage $_{t-1}$	0.659***	0.517***	0.473***	0.272**	0.772***	0.587**	0.739***	0.297***	0.451**	0.642***	0.468***	0.650***	0.588***	0.709***	0.562***
	[0.042]	[0.109]	[0.131]	[0.136]	[0.068]	[0.243]	[0.197]	[0.080]	[0.194]	[0.199]	[0.070]	[0.083]	[0.084]	[0.076]	[0.094]
Profitability $_t$	−0.141**	−0.014	0.141	−0.112	−0.105*	0.007	−0.312	−0.328**	−0.578***	−0.109	−0.242**	−0.075	−0.197**	−0.025	0.128*
	[0.060]	[0.181]	[0.142]	[0.101]	[0.059]	[0.359]	[0.291]	[0.142]	[0.190]	[0.274]	[0.113]	[0.062]	[0.095]	[0.094]	[0.075]
Growth Opportunity $_t$	−0.019***	−0.031***	−0.035**	−0.049***	−0.007*	−0.031***	0.000	−0.016***	−0.006	−0.044***	−0.032***	−0.018***	−0.020***	−0.014***	−0.026***
	[0.005]	[0.008]	[0.016]	[0.009]	[0.004]	[0.009]	[0.019]	[0.004]	[0.020]	[0.017]	[0.009]	[0.005]	[0.006]	[0.004]	[0.006]
Firm Size $_t$	0.007	0.002	0.014**	0.002	0.001	0.012	0.038	−0.004	0.023	0.008	0.026***	0.002	0.015	0.007	0.013**
	[0.006]	[0.009]	[0.006]	[0.008]	[0.008]	[0.013]	[0.040]	[0.009]	[0.020]	[0.012]	[0.010]	[0.013]	[0.013]	[0.007]	[0.006]
Tangibility $_t$	−0.008	−0.017	−0.038	−0.027	0.005	0.017	0.082	0.016	0.020	0.041	−0.041*	0.018	0.088*	0.040	−0.147***
	[0.009]	[0.015]	[0.035]	[0.025]	[0.026]	[0.098]	[0.197]	[0.052]	[0.031]	[0.219]	[0.023]	[0.038]	[0.053]	[0.027]	[0.049]
Business Risk $_t$	0.116**	0.914***	−0.081	0.057	0.096	0.682	0.664**	0.181*	0.231	0.279	0.185*	0.455	0.047	0.161	0.038
	[0.053]	[0.352]	[0.128]	[0.177]	[0.110]	[1.109]	[0.319]	[0.103]	[0.239]	[0.333]	[0.106]	[0.364]	[0.094]	[0.119]	[0.131]
GDP growth $_t$	0.000	0.004***	−0.004	0.003	0.004***	−0.016	–	–	−0.004	0.006	0.001	0.004**	0.002	−0.002	−0.001
	[0.001]	[0.001]	[0.002]	[0.002]	[0.001]	[0.030]			[0.005]	[0.006]	[0.002]	[0.002]	[0.003]	[0.001]	[0.003]
Constant	0.042	0.100	−0.034	0.233*	0.065	0.000	0.000	0.236	−0.027	0.000	0.000	0.084	−0.086	0.000	0.000
	[0.089]	[0.138]	[0.074]	[0.119]	[0.113]	[.]	[.]	[0.175]	[0.314]	[.]	[.]	[0.198]	[0.180]	[.]	[.]
Observations	5567	3091	529	381	810	186	229	570	471	420	1431	950	869	765	661
Time Effects	yes	yes	yes	yes	yes	yes	yes	yes	yes	yes	yes	yes	yes	yes	yes
Country Effects	yes	no	no	no	no	no	no	no	yes	yes	yes	yes	yes	yes	yes
Industry Effects	yes	yes	yes	yes	yes	yes	yes	yes	no	no	no	no	no	no	no
# Instruments	164	50	61	51	105	29	33	67	48	52	134	67	97	66	66
# Groups/Firms	755	407	74	52	120	31	34	71	63	63	188	132	121	97	91

(continued)

Table E.8 (continued)

Dynamic Trade-Off	*Overall (pooled)*	*Country*							*Industry*						
		US	**UK**	**CA**	**JP**	**SK**	**TW**	**IN**	**OILG**	**BMAT**	**IND**	**CGDS**	**TECH**	**HCARE**	**CSRV**
Determinants	**(1)**	**(2)**	**(3)**	**(4)**	**(5)**	**(6)**	**(7)**	**(8)**	**(9)**	**(10)**	**(11)**	**(12)**	**(13)**	**(14)**	**(15)**
Panel A: Shari'ah Compliant (SC)															
AR (1)	0.000	0.000	0.002	0.048	0.000	0.048	0.003	0.011	0.005	0.035	0.000	0.000	0.000	0.000	0.002
AR (2)	0.510	0.490	0.051	0.389	0.173	0.137	0.494	0.660	0.117	0.103	0.351	0.230	0.653	0.587	0.095
SOA	0.341	0.483	0.527	0.728	0.228	0.413	0.261	0.703	0.549	0.358	0.532	0.350	0.412	0.291	0.438
Hansen Test	0.000	0.214	0.197	0.126	0.361	0.487	0.569	0.365	0.269	0.413	0.081	0.150	0.289	0.256	0.206
Half-Life	1.66	1.05	0.93	0.53	2.68	1.30	2.29	0.57	0.87	1.56	0.91	1.61	1.31	2.02	1.20
Successful Results	×[1]	✓	✓	✓	✓	✓	✓	✓	✓	✓	✓	✓	✓	✓	✓
Estimator	Blundell-Bond 2-Step System GMM														

× unsuccessful attempt

Dynamic Trade-Off	*Overall (pooled)*	*Country*							*Industry*							
		US	**UK**	**CA**	**JP**	**SK**	**TW**	**IN**	**OILG**	**BMAT**	**IND**	**CGDS**	**TECH**	**HCARE**	**CSRV**
Determinants	**(1)**	**(2)**	**(3)**	**(4)**	**(5)**	**(6)**	**(7)**	**(8)**	**(9)**	**(10)**	**(11)**	**(12)**	**(13)**	**(14)**	**(15)**
	Panel B: Shari'ah Non-Compliant (SNC)														
Market Leverage $_{t-1}$	0.411***	0.556***	0.837***	0.674	0.702***	0.634***	0.348**	1.007***	0.491*	0.293*	0.490***	0.558***	−0.245	0.624***	0.525***
	[0.046]	[0.072]	[0.204]	[0.426]	[0.041]	[0.168]	[0.137]	[0.361]	[0.279]	[0.152]	[0.060]	[0.111]	[.]	[0.078]	[0.067]
Profitability $_t$	−0.387***	−0.168	−0.051	0.845*	−0.348**	−1.045	−0.741***	−0.211	−0.093	−0.498**	−0.229	−0.326**	−0.981***	0.193	−0.415***
	[0.121]	[0.157]	[1.167]	[0.479]	[0.145]	[0.816]	[0.253]	[0.316]	[0.527]	[0.244]	[0.196]	[0.160]	[0.284]	[.]	[0.143]
Growth Opportunity $_t$	−0.247***	−0.141***	−0.115	−0.455**	−0.169***	−0.270***	−0.170***	−0.156**	−0.116	−0.385***	−0.271***	−0.172***	−0.176***	−0.251***	−0.166***
	[0.023]	[0.021]	[0.121]	[0.191]	[0.027]	[0.074]	[0.021]	[0.068]	[0.091]	[0.079]	[0.026]	[0.041]	[0.048]	[0.077]	[0.028]
Firm Size $_t$	0.018**	0.027***	−0.005	0.094	0.024***	0.064**	0.035***	0.011	0.018	0.018**	0.011	0.002	0.035***	−0.034	−0.014
	[0.009]	[0.009]	[0.074]	[0.063]	[0.007]	[0.028]	[0.013]	[0.016]	[0.023]	[0.009]	[0.009]	[0.009]	[0.005]	[.]	[0.011]
Tangibility $_t$	0.014	0.050*	−0.014	0.222**	0.027	0.074	0.129***	−0.012	0.138	−0.035	−0.050	0.086*	0.324***	0.271	0.145***
	[0.020]	[0.026]	[0.047]	[0.110]	[0.026]	[0.063]	[0.049]	[0.055]	[0.119]	[0.063]	[0.031]	[0.052]	[0.034]	[.]	[0.048]
Business Risk $_t$	−0.519*	−0.232	0.269	−1.350	0.018	0.868**	−0.043	−0.118	0.442	−0.134	−0.074	−0.175	−1.517*	0.825	0.746***
	[0.292]	[0.406]	[1.123]	[1.871]	[0.127]	[0.430]	[0.250]	[0.343]	[0.591]	[0.223]	[0.217]	[0.542]	[0.871]	[2.826]	[0.285]
GDP growth $_t$	0.004***	0.003	0.011*	0.006	–	−0.087	–	0.003	0.001	0.002	0.004*	0.004	0.022***	−0.008	0.009***
	[0.001]	[0.002]	[0.006]	[0.008]		[0.078]		[0.037]	[0.004]	[0.004]	[0.002]	[0.003]	[0.003]	[0.005]	[0.002]
Constant	0.367**	−0.083	0.000	−1.016	−0.046	0.000	0.000	0.000	0.077	0.635***	0.463***	0.000	0.000	1.001	0.000
	[0.154]	[0.144]	[.]	[0.871]	[0.117]	[.]	[.]	[.]	[0.372]	[0.198]	[0.152]	[.]	[.]	[.]	[.]
Observations	4024	1485	236	164	1545	382	286	212	222	545	1406	669	133	166	883
Time Effects	yes	yes	yes	yes	yes	yes	yes	yes	yes	yes	yes	yes	yes	yes	yes
Country Effects	yes	no	no	no	no	no	no	no	yes	yes	yes	yes	yes	yes	yes
Industry Effects	yes	yes	yes	yes	yes	yes	yes	yes	no	no	no	no	no	no	no
# Instruments	243	110	35	29	194	49	35	27	31	42	158	67	27	27	121
# Groups/Firms	577	237	36	24	196	55	38	29	34	74	195	98	25	26	125

(continued)

Table E.8 (continued)

Dynamic Trade-Off	*Overall (pooled)*	*Country*							*Industry*							
		US	**UK**	**CA**	**JP**	**SK**	**TW**	**IN**	**OILG**	**BMAT**	**IND**	**CGDS**	**TECH**	**HCARE**	**CSRV**
Determinants	**(1)**	**(2)**	**(3)**	**(4)**	**(5)**	**(6)**	**(7)**	**(8)**	**(9)**	**(10)**	**(11)**	**(12)**	**(13)**	**(14)**	**(15)**
								Panel B: Shari'ah Non-Compliant (SNC)							
AR (1)	0.000	0.000	0.002	0.130	0.000	0.006	0.011	0.028	0.050	0.032	0.000	0.000	0.069	0.025	0.000
AR (2)	0.016	0.711	0.123	0.588	0.086	0.333	0.796	0.149	0.986	0.070	0.069	0.595	0.925	0.050	0.218
SOA	0.589	0.444	0.163	0.326	0.298	0.366	0.652	−0.007	0.509	0.707	0.510	0.442	1.245	0.376	0.475
Hansen Test	0.000	0.278	0.212	0.742	0.249	0.450	0.308	0.305	0.289	0.101	0.163	0.118	0.486	0.292	0.160
Half-Life	0.78	1.18	3.90	1.76	1.96	1.52	0.66	–	0.97	0.56	0.97	1.19	–	1.47	1.08
Successful Results	×[2]	✓	✓	✓[3]	✓	✓	✓	✓	✓[4]	✓	✓	✓	✓[5]	✓[6]	✓
Estimator									Blundell-Bond 2-Step System GMM						

× unsuccessful attempt

Source: own contribution.

Table E.9: Explanatory Power of Capital Structure Theories (Robustness Test III).

Determinants	Book Leverage (BLEV)												Market Leverage (MLEV)											
	Overall (pooled)				*Country*				*Industry*				*Overall (pooled)*				*Country*				*Industry*			
	SC		SNC		SC		SNC		SC		SNC		SC		SNC		SC		SNC		SC		SNC	
	(1)	(2)	(3)	(4)	(5)	(6)	(7)	(8)	(9)	(10)	(11)	(12)	(13)	(14)	(15)	(16)	(17)	(18)	(19)	(20)	(21)	(22)	(23)	(24)
	+	–	+	–	+	–	+	–	+	–	+	–	+	–	+	–	+	–	+	–	+	–	+	–
Part A	*Panel A: Number of Significant Correlations*																							
Profitability	0	**1**	0	**1**	0	3	0	**4**	1	2	0	**4**					0	2	0	2	3	1	0	3
Growth Opportunity	0	0	**1**	0	1	0	2	0	1	1	3	0					0	**6**	0	**5**	0	**6**	0	**4**
Firm Size	**1**	0	**1**	0	**4**	0	1	0	**4**	0	2	0					1	0	**4**	0	2	0	1	0
Tangibility	0	0	**1**	0	1	1	2	0	1	0	2	0	n/a		n/a		0	0	2	0	1	2	2	0
Business Risk	0	0	0	0	0	1	2	0	0	0	2	0					3	0	1	0	1	0	1	0
GDP growth	0	0	0	0	1	0	1	0	0	0	1	0					2	0	1	0	1	0	2	0
	Panel B: Reliable(Core) Leverage Determinants																							
Profitability		✓		✓				✓				✓												
Growth Opportunity			✓															✓		✓		✓		✓
Firm Size	✓		✓		✓				✓										✓					
Tangibility			✓										n/a		n/a									
Business Risk																								
GDP growth																								

(continued)

Table E.9 (continued)

		Panel C: Empirical Results (Consolidated)											
Profitability		–	–		–		–						
Growth Opportunity			+							–	–	–	–
Firm Size		+	+	+		+					+		
Tangibility			+					n/a	n/a				
Business Risk													
GDP Growth													
Part B		*Panel D: Consolidated Results (by Capital Structure Theory/Model)*											
Profitability		P,T*,IP	P,T*,IP		P,T*,IP		P,T*,IP						
Growth Opportunity			P							T,IP	T,IP	T,IP	T,IP
Firm Size		T	T	T		T					T		
Tangibility			T					n/a	n/a				
Business Risk													
GDP Growth													
		Panel E: Number of Matching Capital Structure Theories/Model											
Trade-Off Theory	(T)	2	3	1	1	1	1			1	2	1	1
Pecking Order Theory	(P)	1	2	0	1	0	1			0	0	0	0
Pecking Order Model (Islamic)	(IP)	1	1	0	1	0	1	n/a	n/a	1	1	1	1
		Panel F: Explanatory Power of the Capital Structure Theories/Model											
Trade-Off Theory	(T)	50%	50%	100%	33%	100%	33%			50%	67%	50%	50%
Pecking Order Theory	(P)	25%	33%	0%	33%	0%	33%			0%	0%	0%	0%
Pecking Order Model (Islamic)	(IP)	25%	17%	0%	33%	0%	33%	n/a	n/a	50%	33%	50%	50%

T* = Dynamic Trade-Off Theory

Appendix F (SC/SNC *(RIEM)* Firms)

https://doi.org/10.1515/9783110713664-014

Table F.1: Participation Pattern of Panel Data – SC/SNC *(RIEM)* Firms.

Panel A and Panel B in this table describe the participation pattern of panel data for SC and SNC *(RIEM)* firms, respectively. We have 267 SC and 1124 SNC firms in the sample. The minimum and the maximum number of years over which any SC and SNC firm is observed is 3 and 11, respectively. The most common pattern is participation in a full time-frame of 11 years (46 or 17.23% are observed in this pattern for SC, while 334 or 29.72% are observed for SNC).

The bottom line of this table gives the totals for participation patterns not observed.

Panel A: Shari'ah Compliant (proposed) Sample (SC)				**Panel B: Shari'ah Non-Compliant (proposed) Sample (SNC)**			
Code: 1, 2, ..., 267		***Year: 2004, 2005, ..., 2014***		***Code: 268, 269, ..., 1391***		***Year: 2004, 2005, ..., 2014***	
Frequency	**Percentage**	**Cumulative**	**Pattern**	**Frequency**	**Percentage**	**Cumulative**	**Pattern**
46	17.23	17.23	11111111111	334	29.72	29.72	11111111111
16	5.99	23.22	111	78	6.94	36.65	11111
16	5.99	29.21	1111111	66	5.87	42.53	1111111
14	5.24	34.46	11111	55	4.89	47.42	1111
13	4.87	39.33	11111111	48	4.27	51.69	1111111111
12	4.49	43.82	1111111	47	4.18	55.87	11111111
10	3.75	47.57	111	44	3.91	59.79	111111111
10	3.75	51.31	1111	42	3.74	63.52	111111
9	3.37	54.68	111111	42	3.74	67.26	1111111111
121	45.32	100.00	(other patterns)	368	32.74	100.00	(other patterns)
267	**100.00**		XXXXXXXXXXX	**1124**	**100.00**		XXXXXXXXXXX

Source: own contribution.

Table F.2: Descriptive – *Overall (pooled)* Debt Issues, Equity Issues, and Financial Deficit – SC/SNC *(RIEM)* Firms.

This table shows the mean values of the debt issues, equity issues, and financial deficit for all firms in the *overall (pooled)* sample separated in SC/SNC *(RIEM)* firms for the entire period 2004–2014 and each year. Table 6.2 provides the definitions of debt issues, equity issues, and financial deficit variables. SC/SNC *(RIEM)* firms are determined based on the proposed *RIEM 66 Index* (see Table 3.8 and Table 6.5). All variables are winsorized at the 1% and 99% level.

Variables	**Firm Type**	**2004**	**2005**	**2006**	**2007**	**2008**	**2009**	**2010**	**2011**	**2012**	**2013**	**2014**
Debt Issue	SC *(RIEM)*	0.009	0.011	0.014	0.022	−0.008	0.005	0.024	0.013	0.014	0.016	0.017
Equity Issue	SC *(RIEM)*	0.048	0.041	0.053	0.028	−0.014	0.042	0.027	0.005	0.032	0.018	0.015
Financial Deficit	SC *(RIEM)*	0.057	0.052	0.067	0.051	−0.022	0.047	0.050	0.018	0.045	0.034	0.032
Debt Issue	SNC *(RIEM)*	0.044	0.030	0.055	0.083	0.012	0.011	0.052	0.040	0.018	0.012	0.006
Equity Issue	SNC *(RIEM)*	0.018	0.009	0.011	0.012	−0.022	0.023	0.011	−0.004	0.004	0.005	−0.010
Financial Deficit	SNC *(RIEM)*	0.061	0.039	0.066	0.094	−0.010	0.033	0.063	0.037	0.022	0.018	−0.004

Source: own contribution.

Table F.3: Descriptive – *Overall (pooled)* Firm Leverage by Year – SC/SNC *(RIEM)* Firms.

This table shows the mean, standard deviation, minimum, maximum, and the number of observations of the book- and market leverage proxies for all firms in the *overall (pooled)* sample and separated in SC/SNC *(RIEM)* firms for the entire period 2004–2014 and each year. Table 4.3 provides the definitions of both leverage proxies. SC/SNC *(RIEM)* firms are determined based on the proposed *RIEM 66 Index* (see Table 3.8 and Table 6.5). All variables are winsorized at the 1% and 99% level.

Sample	Leverage	Stats	2004–2014	2004	2005	2006	2007	2008	2009	2010	2011	2012	2013	2014
Shari'ah Compliant *(RIEM)*	Book	Mean	0.205	0.202	0.206	0.204	0.208	0.207	0.200	0.203	0.209	0.209	0.209	0.205
		SD	0.069	0.073	0.067	0.070	0.067	0.068	0.067	0.068	0.073	0.072	0.070	0.067
		Min	0.085	0.085	0.085	0.085	0.085	0.085	0.085	0.085	0.085	0.085	0.085	0.085
		Max	0.332	0.329	0.332	0.327	0.329	0.327	0.331	0.330	0.330	0.330	0.332	0.326
		Obs	1753	119	137	161	168	178	183	185	172	166	156	128
	Market	Mean	0.100	0.087	0.081	0.083	0.102	0.123	0.099	0.102	0.107	0.108	0.101	0.094
		SD	0.069	0.061	0.049	0.051	0.073	0.079	0.066	0.076	0.075	0.070	0.065	0.066
		Min	0.024	0.024	0.024	0.024	0.024	0.024	0.024	0.024	0.024	0.024	0.024	0.024
		Max	0.591	0.282	0.216	0.297	0.460	0.591	0.518	0.564	0.467	0.348	0.297	0.308
		Obs	1753	119	137	161	168	178	183	185	172	166	156	128
Shari'ah Non-Compliant *(RIEM)*	Book	Mean	0.590	0.602	0.591	0.582	0.589	0.611	0.589	0.580	0.588	0.587	0.581	0.593
		SD	0.153	0.160	0.156	0.154	0.150	0.160	0.156	0.149	0.151	0.151	0.150	0.153
		Min	0.153	0.162	0.207	0.193	0.153	0.183	0.216	0.197	0.247	0.228	0.225	0.244
		Max	0.923	0.923	0.923	0.923	0.923	0.923	0.923	0.923	0.923	0.923	0.923	0.923
		Obs	8739	537	615	700	785	859	879	939	953	916	830	726
	Market	Mean	0.442	0.434	0.393	0.393	0.432	0.522	0.463	0.442	0.462	0.447	0.418	0.423
		SD	0.218	0.223	0.205	0.205	0.218	0.228	0.215	0.208	0.215	0.217	0.217	0.211
		Min	0.035	0.048	0.052	0.041	0.043	0.049	0.052	0.045	0.050	0.036	0.035	0.043
		Max	0.884	0.884	0.884	0.884	0.884	0.884	0.884	0.884	0.884	0.884	0.884	0.884
		Obs	8739	537	615	700	785	859	879	939	953	916	830	726

Source: own contribution.

Table F.4: Descriptive – *Country* and *Industry* Leverage Ratio – SC/SNC *(RIEM)* Firms.

This table shows the mean and industry-mean values of the book- and market leverage proxies for all firms in the *overall (pooled)* sample and separated in each *country* and *industry*, for the entire period 2004–2014. Table 4.3 provides the definitions of both leverage proxies. SC/SNC *(RIEM)* firms are determined based on the proposed *RIEM 66 Index* (see Table 3.8 and Table 6.5). All variables are winsorized at the 1% and 99% level.

Sample	**Shari'ah Compliant (*RIEM*)**		**Shari'ah Non-Compliant (*RIEM*)**		***Country/ Industry* mean (BLEV)**	***Country/ Industry* mean (MLEV)**	***Overall (pooled)***			
	Book Leverage (BLEV)	***Market Leverage (MLEV)***	***Book Leverage (BLEV)***	***Market Leverage (MLEV)***			***SC sample mean (BLEV)***	***SC sample mean (MLEV)***	***SNC sample mean (BLEV)***	***SNC sample mean (MLEV)***
United States	20.69%	8.41%	56.92%	37.52%	51.08%	32.82%	20.55%	9.97%	52.55%	38.49%
United Kingdom	19.04%	10.70%	58.30%	37.49%	54.13%	34.64%				
Canada	15.36%	9.33%	50.35%	37.07%	42.44%	30.79%				
Japan	21.21%	13.90%	63.45%	58.12%	56.73%	51.08%				
S. Korea	21.97%	14.38%	63.41%	59.17%	58.37%	53.73%				
Taiwan	20.18%	9.43%	58.76%	49.25%	50.20%	40.41%				
India	22.23%	6.65%	59.71%	35.11%	50.31%	27.98%				
Oil and Gas	16.20%	9.06%	49.82%	38.52%	46.33%	35.46%				
Basic Materials	16.94%	10.36%	59.74%	49.72%	52.91%	43.44%				
Industrials	20.59%	10.47%	60.66%	46.26%	56.77%	42.79%				
Consumer Goods	22.04%	12.38%	57.90%	42.37%	52.84%	38.14%				
Technology	20.63%	8.40%	55.69%	35.86%	41.52%	24.76%				
Health Care	20.83%	9.01%	55.25%	32.71%	42.05%	23.62%				
Consumer Services	23.16%	11.47%	63.00%	48.96%	59.25%	45.44%				

Source: own contribution.

Table F.5: Descriptive – *Country* and *Industry* Equity Ratio – SC/SNC *(RIEM)* Firms.

This table shows the mean and industry-mean values of the book equity ratio for all firms in the *overall (pooled)* sample and separated in each *country* and *industry*, for the entire period 2004–2014. The book equity ratio is calculated by book equity over total assets, whereas book equity equals total assets minus total liabilities and preferred stocks plus deferred taxes. SC/SNC *(RIEM)* firms are determined based on the proposed *RIEM 66 Index* (see Tables 3.8 and 6.5). All variables are winsorized at the 1% and 99% level.

Sample	***Equity Ratio (SC)***	***Equity Ratio (SNC)***	***Country/ Industry mean***	***Overall (pooled)***		***Proposed Threshold***
				Mean Equity (SC)	***Mean Equity (SNC)***	
United States	79.31%	43.08%	48.92%	79.45%	41.03%	66.67%
United Kingdom	80.96%	41.70%	45.87%			
Canada	84.64%	49.65%	57.56%			
Japan	78.79%	36.55%	43.27%			
S. Korea	78.03%	36.59%	41.63%			
Taiwan	79.82%	41.24%	49.80%			
India	77.77%	40.29%	49.69%			
Oil and Gas	83.80%	50.18%	53.67%			
Basic Materials	83.06%	40.26%	47.09%			
Industrials	79.41%	39.34%	43.23%			
Consumer Goods	77.96%	42.10%	47.16%			
Technology	79.37%	44.31%	58.48%			
Health Care	79.17%	44.75%	57.95%			
Consumer Services	76.84%	37.00%	40.75%			

Source: own contribution.

Table F.6: Estimator Selection (*Overall (pooled)*, *Country* and *Industry*) – SC/SNC *(RIEM)* Firms.

This table presents the post-estimation tests conducted on the pecking order model, with debt and equity issues defined in Table 6.2 (direct measure), for the *overall (pooled)*, *country,* and *industry* samples separately. The test is recommended by Baltagi (2005) and Wooldridge (2010). All test results have been reported for each sample. The corresponding p-value estimates of each test, namely, BPLM, Hausman, and Heteroskedasticity, are presented in the column "Results". Column "Estimator" reflects the final estimator selection.

- The BPLM test has been conducted to identify the appropriateness of using the Fixed-/Random Effects vs. OLS estimator. The BPLM test for unobservable effects tests the null hypothesis of equal variances across companies; $H_0: Var(\alpha_i) = 0$.
- The Hausman test has been applied to identify the RE estimation's consistency and efficiency vs. the FE estimation. The Hausman test examines whether the estimated coefficients from the FE estimation and the RE estimation is statistically significant; $H_0: \hat{\beta}_{RE} = \hat{\beta}_{FE}$. The rejection (p-value < 0.05 (5%)) of the test is commonly interpreted as a rejection of the RE model estimation, although Wooldridge (2010) lists some potential drawbacks of this interpretation.

Table F.6 (continued)

- The presence of heteroskedasticity or serial (auto-)correlation leads to incorrect standard errors. A modified Wald test is used to test for the presence of heteroskedasticity. A simple test of the first-order autocorrelation consists of regressing the residuals from the model estimation onto their lagged counterparts; $H_0: \hat{e}_{it} = p\hat{e}_{i,t-1} + \varepsilon_{it}$(Verbeek, 2008). It tests the null hypothesis that the variances are equal across all firms.

Result Interpretation (examples)

- *Overall (pooled):* All three test results show that the null hypothesis is rejected (p-value 0.000). We concluded that unobservable effects are present (rejection of OLS), and the test results favored FE over RE as the appropriate estimator. In all models, the Wald test results (i.e., homoskedasticity test) are rejected, which means that heteroskedasticity is present. Consequently, we applied the "robust" option, as discussed in Sections 4.2.1.2 and 5.2.1.
- *Taiwan:* The BPLM test revealed a p-value of 0.174; hence, it cannot be rejected. A non-rejection indicates that there are no unobservable effects, and consequently, OLS is deemed appropriate.
- *Industrials:* The BPLM test is rejected with a p-value 0.000. The Hausman test result with a p-value of 0.947 cannot be rejected; consequently, RE is the appropriate estimator.

Sample	Post Estimation Test		Pecking Order (Direct Measure)			
			Debt Issue		Equity Issue	
			Test Results	Selection	Test Results	Selection
	BPLM	RE	0.000		0.000	
Overall (pooled)	Hausman	RE	0.000	FE	0.000	FE
	Heteroskedasticity	FE	0.000		0.000	
	BPLM	RE	0.000		0.000	
United States	Hausman	RE	0.000	FE	0.000	FE
	Heteroskedasticity	FE	0.000		0.000	
	BPLM	RE	0.412		0.412	
United Kingdom	Hausman	RE	–	OLS	–	OLS
	Heteroskedasticity	FE	–		–	
	BPLM	RE	0.000		0.000	
Canada	Hausman	RE	0.000	FE	0.000	FE
	Heteroskedasticity	FE	0.000		0.000	
	BPLM	RE	1.000		1.000	
Japan	Hausman	RE	–	OLS	–	OLS
	Heteroskedasticity	FE	–		–	
	BPLM	RE	0.064		0.064	
S. Korea	Hausman	RE	–	OLS	–	OLS
	Heteroskedasticity	FE	–		–	
	BPLM	RE	0.174		0.175	
Taiwan	Hausman	RE	–	OLS	–	OLS
	Heteroskedasticity	FE	–		–	

Table F.6 (continued)

Sample	Post Estimation Test		Pecking Order (Direct Measure)			
			Debt Issue		Equity Issue	
			Test Results	Selection	Test Results	Selection
India	BPLM	RE	0.419		0.420	
	Hausman	RE	–	OLS	–	OLS
	Heteroskedasticity	FE	–		–	
Oil and Gas	BPLM	RE	0.005		0.005	
	Hausman	RE	0.000	FE	0.000	FE
	Heteroskedasticity	FE	0.000		0.000	
Basic Materials	BPLM	RE	0.000		0.000	
	Hausman	RE	0.000	FE	0.000	FE
	Heteroskedasticity	FE	0.000		0.000	
Industrials	BPLM	RE	0.000		0.000	
	Hausman	RE	0.947	RE	0.947	RE
	Heteroskedasticity	FE	–		–	
Cons. Goods	BPLM	RE	0.001		0.001	
	Hausman	RE	0.000	FE	0.000	FE
	Heteroskedasticity	FE	–		–	
Technology	BPLM	RE	0.000		0.000	
	Hausman	RE	0.060	RE	0.060	RE
	Heteroskedasticity	FE	–		–	
Health Care	BPLM	RE	0.000		0.000	
	Hausman	RE	0.000	FE	0.000	FE
	Heteroskedasticity	FE	0.000		0.000	
Cons. Services	BPLM	RE	0.031		0.031	
	Hausman	RE	0.008	FE	0.008	FE
	Heteroskedasticity	FE	0.000		0.000	

Source: own contribution.

Table F.7: Auto–Serial Correlation Test – SC/SNC *(RIEM)* Firms.

This table presents the auto-serial correlation tests conducted on the pecking order model, with debt and equity issues defined in Table 6.2 (direct measure), for the *overall (pooled)*, *country*, and *industry* samples separately. The model tested is $\hat{e}_{it} = p\hat{e}_{i,t-1} + \varepsilon_{it}$. The null hypothesis is that p = 0, i.e., no first-order autocorrelation. Similar to the consequences of heteroskedasticity, the presence of autocorrelation leads to incorrect standard errors. This test is proposed and suggested by Wooldridge (2002). This test involves regression of the residuals from the estimation upon its lag. If the coefficient of the lagged residuals is significant, the first-order autocorrelation is present, and the standard errors need to be adjusted. The test is conducted using the *xtserial* function in Stata, which equals the test proposed by Drukker (2003). The results show that most estimated models in the study suffer from first-order serial correlation. Therefore, we applied standard errors robust to serial correlation. Petersen (2009) discusses several robust standard errors and recommends using cluster robust standard error in finance panels. Even though selected samples exhibit a non-rejection (e.g., India with p-value 0.306), we followed the recommendation by Petersen (2009). We applied the "robust" option in all model estimations in this study. (see Section 4.2.1)

	Pecking Order (Direct Measure)			
	Debt Issue		**Equity Issue**	
Overall (pooled)	F(1, 1390)	24.726***	F(1, 1390)	24.716***
	Prob.	*0.000*	*Prob.*	*0.000*
United States	F(1, 637)	9.502***	F(1, 637)	9.497***
	Prob.	*0.002*	*Prob.*	*0.002*
United Kingdom	F(1, 108)	5.251**	F(1, 108)	5.246**
	Prob.	*0.024*	*Prob.*	*0.024*
Canada	F(1, 73)	0.139	F(1, 73)	0.137
	Prob.	*0.711*	*Prob.*	*0.712*
Japan	F(1, 314)	5.686**	F(1, 314)	5.69**
	Prob.	*0.018*	*Prob.*	*0.018*
S. Korea	F(1, 84)	0.119	F(1, 84)	0.119
	Prob.	*0.731*	*Prob.*	*0.731*
Taiwan	F(1, 69)	7.687***	F(1, 69)	7.697***
	Prob.	*0.007*	*Prob.*	*0.007*
India	F(1, 99)	1.057	F(1, 99)	1.059
	Prob.	*0.306*	*Prob.*	*0.306*
Oil and Gas	F(1, 98)	3.979**	F(1, 98)	3.989**
	Prob.	*0.049*	*Prob.*	*0.049*
Basic Materials	F(1, 141)	1.652	F(1, 141)	1.653
	Prob.	*0.201*	*Prob.*	*0.201*
Industrials	F(1, 396)	5.55**	F(1, 396)	5.543**
	Prob.	*0.019*	*Prob.*	*0.019*
Cons. Goods	F(1, 246)	1.672	F(1, 246)	1.672
	Prob.	*0.197*	*Prob.*	*0.197*

Table F.7 (continued)

Technology	F(1, 163)	8.765***	F(1, 163)	8.764***
	Prob.	*0.004*	*Prob.*	*0.004*
Health Care	F(1, 121)	2.259	F(1, 121)	2.258
	Prob.	*0.136*	*Prob.*	*0.136*
Cons. Services	F(1, 219)	21.421***	F(1, 219)	21.434***
	Prob.	*0.000*	*Prob.*	*0.000*

Source: Own contribution.

Table F.8: Pecking Order Estimation Results – SC/SNC *(RIEM)* Firms.

This table provides the coefficients of panel regressions with debt issues (ΔDebt) and equity issues (ΔEquity) as the dependent variables. The single variable financial deficit (DEF) and its interactive dummy variable *(dsc*DEF)* are used in the equation model (23) and (24) and regressed for the *overall (pooled), country, and industry* samples for the entire period 2004–2014. Table 6.2 provides the definitions of all variables. SC/SNC *(RIEM)* firms are determined based on the proposed *RIEM 66 Index* (see Tables 3.8 and 6.5). US, UK, CA, JP, SK, TW, and IN denote countries such as United States, United Kingdom, Canada, Japan, South Korea, Taiwan, and India. OILG, BMAT, IND, CGDS, TECH, HCARE, and CSRV denote industries such as Oil and Gas, Basic Materials, Industrials, Consumer Goods, Technology, Health Care, and Consumer Services. Since we are interested in examining the financing behavior of SC/SNC *(RIEM)* firms in direct comparison, we have incorporated an interactive dummy ($dsc * DEF_{it}$) and employed the Stata command *lincom*. The *lincom* command computes point estimates, standard errors, *t* or *z* statistics, p-values, and confidence intervals for linear combinations of coefficients after any estimation command. Coefficient results for SNC are obtained from the variable "Financial Deficit" and the row "Test for SC" represents the coefficient results for SC *(RIEM)* firms (output from *lincom*). Panel A and B represent the regression results for debt issues and equity issues for SC *(RIEM)* and SNC *(RIEM)* firms, respectively. The *overall (pooled)* sample contains country and industry fixed effects (country and industry dummy), the *country* sample contains industry fixed effects, the *industry* sample contains country fixed effects – (where applicable). Econometric estimators applied to each model are shown in the last row. Results are shown with a dash-sign "-" represent either data, not available or not applicable. All regressions were applied with the respective estimator, as identified by the model estimation procedure described in Table F.6 in Appendix F. Company cluster robust standard errors are reported in the brackets. *, ** and *** denote significance at 10%, 5% and 1% levels, respectively. All variables are winsorized at the 1% and 99% level. Model specifications are provided in Section 6.2.2.

$$\Delta DebtIssues_{it} = \alpha + \beta_1 DEF_{it} + \beta_2 dsc * DEF_{it} + dsc + \mu_i + \mu_t + \varepsilon_{it} \quad (23)$$

$$\Delta EquityIssues_{it} = \alpha + \beta_1 DEF_{it} + \beta_2 dsc * DEF_{it} + dsc + \mu_i + \mu_t + \varepsilon_{it} \quad (24)$$

Table F.8 (continued)

Determinants		*Overall (pooled)*	*Country*							*Industry*						
			US	UK	CA	JP	SK	TW	IN	OILG	BMAT	IND	CGDS	TECH	HCARE	CSRV
		(1)	(2)	(3)	(4)	(5)	(6)	(7)	(8)	(9)	(10)	(11)	(12)	(13)	(14)	(15)
Panel A: Debt Issues																
Financial Deficit $_t$	(a)	0.721***	0.656***	0.732***	0.644***	0.804***	0.786***	0.717***	0.838***	0.653***	0.748***	0.731***	0.777***	0.636***	0.680***	0.722***
		[0.011]	[0.016]	[0.026]	[0.045]	[0.018]	[0.033]	[0.059]	[0.028]	[0.038]	[0.034]	[0.018]	[0.026]	[0.033]	[0.038]	[0.025]
interactive-Financial Deficit $_t$	(b)	−0.415***	−0.442***	−0.504***	−0.377***	−0.325***	−0.347***	−0.296***	−0.297***	−0.334***	−0.467***	−0.387***	−0.237***	−0.403***	−0.345***	−0.549***
		[0.025]	[0.033]	[0.100]	[0.057]	[0.062]	[0.071]	[0.092]	[0.082]	[0.075]	[0.059]	[0.060]	[0.060]	[0.044]	[0.069]	[0.076]
Dummy SC		–	–	−0.010*	–	0.002	−0.013**	−0.004	0.003	–	–	−0.006**	–	−0.001	–	–
				[0.006]		[0.002]	[0.006]	[0.005]	[0.004]			[0.003]		[0.005]		
Constant		−0.005**	−0.004	0.015	−0.011	−0.005	0.006	−0.006	0.009	−0.005	−0.010*	0.000	−0.003	−0.004	−0.007	0.008
		[0.002]	[0.003]	[0.013]	[0.008]	[0.003]	[0.008]	[0.007]	[0.007]	[0.009]	[0.006]	[0.003]	[0.004]	[0.008]	[0.006]	[0.005]
R^2		0.722	0.648	0.776	0.700	0.858	0.841	0.773	0.881	0.696	0.752		0.765		0.698	0.702
Adjusted R^2		0.722	0.647	0.770	0.693	0.857	0.836	0.765	0.878	0.690	0.749		0.764		0.693	0.700
Firms		1391	638		74					99	142	397	247	164	122	220
Observations		10485	4733	810	535	2516	607	527	757	721	1069	3175	1837	1105	865	1713
Test for SC: (a) + (b) = 0		0.306**	0.214**	0.228*	0.268**	0.479*	0.438*	0.42*	0.54*	0.319*	0.281*	0.344*	0.539*	0.233**	0.335*	0.173*
Standard Error		[0.023]	[0.029]	[0.097]	[0.039]	[0.06]	[0.064]	[0.073]	[0.079]	[0.063]	[0.051]	[0.057]	[0.056]	[0.032]	[0.059]	[0.072]
Time Effects		yes	yes	yes	yes	yes	yes	yes	yes	yes	yes	yes	yes	yes	yes	yes
Country Effects		–	–	–	–	–	–	–	–	–	–	yes	–	yes	–	–
Industry Effects		–	–	yes	–	yes	yes	yes	yes	–	–	–	–	–	–	–
Estimator		FE	FE	OLS	FE	OLS	OLS	OLS	OLS	FE	FE	RE	FE	RE	FE	FE

Panel B: Equity Issues																
Financial $Deficit_t$	(a)	0.279***	0.344***	0.268***	0.356***	0.196***	0.214***	0.283***	0.162***	0.347***	0.252***	0.269***	0.223***	0.364***	0.320***	0.278***
		[0.011]	[0.016]	[0.026]	[0.045]	[0.018]	[0.033]	[0.059]	[0.028]	[0.038]	[0.034]	[0.018]	[0.026]	[0.033]	[0.038]	[0.025]
interactive-Financial $Deficit_t$	(b)	0.415***	0.442***	0.504***	0.377***	0.325***	0.347***	0.296***	0.298***	0.334***	0.467***	0.387***	0.238***	0.403***	0.345***	0.549***
		[0.025]	[0.033]	[0.100]	[0.057]	[0.062]	[0.071]	[0.092]	[0.082]	[0.075]	[0.059]	[0.060]	[0.060]	[0.044]	[0.069]	[0.076]
Dummy SC		–	–	0.010*	–	−0.002	0.013**	0.004	−0.003	–	–	0.006**	–	0.001	–	–
				[0.006]		[0.002]	[0.006]	[0.005]	[0.004]			[0.003]		[0.005]		
Constant		0.005**	0.004	−0.015	0.011	0.005	−0.006	0.006	−0.009	0.005	0.010*	0.000	0.003	0.004	0.007	−0.008
		[0.002]	[0.003]	[0.013]	[0.008]	[0.003]	[0.008]	[0.007]	[0.007]	[0.009]	[0.006]	[0.003]	[0.004]	[0.008]	[0.006]	[0.005]
R^2		0.425	0.460	0.436	0.693	0.387	0.432	0.492	0.374	0.482	0.565		0.297		0.502	0.371
Adjusted R^2		0.424	0.459	0.423	0.686	0.382	0.414	0.474	0.358	0.473	0.561		0.293		0.495	0.367
Firms		1391	638		74					99	142	397	247	164	122	220
Observations		10485	4733	810	535	2516	607	527	757	721	1069	3175	1837	1105	865	1713
Test for SC: (a) + (b) = 0		0.694**	0.786**	0.772*	0.732**	0.521*	0.562*	0.58*	0.46*	0.681*	0.719*	0.656*	0.461*	0.767**	0.665*	0.827*
Standard Error		[0.023]	[0.029]	[0.097]	[0.039]	[0.06]	[0.064]	[0.073]	[0.079]	[0.063]	[0.051]	[0.057]	[0.056]	[0.032]	[0.059]	[0.072]
Time Effects		yes	yes	yes	yes	yes	yes	yes	yes	yes	yes	yes	yes	yes	yes	yes
Country Effects		–	–	–	–	–	–	–	–	–	–	yes	–	yes	–	–
Industry Effects		–	–	yes	–	yes	yes	yes	yes		–	–	–	–	–	–
Estimator		FE	FE	OLS	FE	OLS	OLS	OLS	OLS	FE	FE	RE	FE	RE	FE	FE

Source: own contribution.

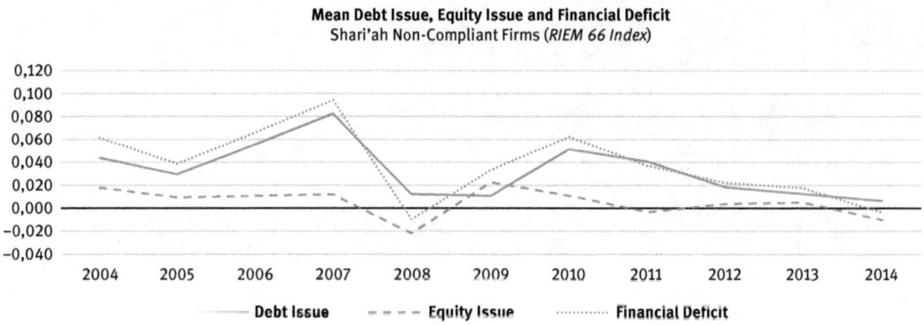

Figure F.1: Debt Issue, Equity Issue, and Financial Deficit – SNC *(RIEM)* Firms.
This figure represents the mean values per year obtained from Table F.2 in Appendix F for SNC *(RIEM)* firms. The figure illustrates the development in average debt issues, equity issues, and financial deficits for the entire sample period.
Source: own contribution.

Appendix G (Stata *<commands>*)

In this Appendix, we provide an excerpt of all the Stata commands we used to conduct this study. Most of the tables below explain what we have done in Stata and offer real examples from our study to better understand. The reader can use these Stata commands and use them as a template for any other research.

https://doi.org/10.1515/9783110713664-015

Table G.1: Participation Pattern of Panel Data.

Reference(s)	**Table B.1 in Appendix B and Table F.1 in Appendix F**	**Notes/Comments**
Pre-Set	***set more off, permanently***	/*Tell Stata not to pause or display the – more – message.
Command	***xtdes if dsc==1*** ***xtdes if dsc==0***	/*for SC sample /*for SNC sample

Table G.2: Effects of winsorizing of variables.

Reference(s)	**Figure B.1 in Appendix B**	**Notes/Comments**
Pre-Set	***set more off, permanently***	/*Tell Stata not to pause or display the – more – message.
Command	Run BEFORE winsorizing.	
	scatter blev1 prof	/*for *profitability*
	scatter blev1 growth	/*for *growth opportunity*
	scatter blev1 size	/*for *firm size*
	scatter blev1 tang	/*for *tangibility*
	scatter blev1 risk	/*for *business risk*
To-Do	Repeat the same procedure AFTER winsorizing.	

Table G.3: OLS Assumption – Linearity Test.

Reference(s)	**Figure B.2 in Appendix B**	**Notes/Comments**
Pre-Set	***set more off, permanently***	/*Tell Stata not to pause or display the – more – message.
	xtset code year, yearly	/*Declare data set as a panel data, whereby *code* represents "firms" and *year* represents "time series".
Command	Book Leverage	
	Step 1: Run the regression model.	/*Use the model (13) in the current form (not in the lag form).
	reg blev1 prof growth size tang risk	
	Step 2: Plot for each independent variable (debt determinant).	/*for each independent variable
	rvpplot prof	/*e.g., for *profitability*
	rvpplot growth	/*e.g., for *growth opportunity*
To-Do	Market Leverage	/*Model (14) and run Step 1 and Step 2.

Table G.4: OLS Assumption – Normality Test.

Reference(s)	**Figure B.3 in Appendix B**	**Notes/Comments**
Pre-Set	***set more off, permanently*** ***xtset code year, yearly***	/*Tell Stata not to pause or display the – more – message. /*Declare data set as a panel data, whereby *code* represents "firms" and *year* represents "time series".
Command	Book Leverage	
	Step 1: Run the regression model. ***reg blev1 prof growth size tang risk*** Step 2: Predict residuals after regressing and follow the following commands. ***predict <anyname>, resid*** ***sktest XYZ*** ***kdensity XYZ, normal***	/*Use the model (13) in the current form (not in the lag form). /*e.g., predict XYZ, resid.
	In addition to the Kernel density estimate, a standardized normal probability plot *(pnorm)* and a plot showing the quantiles or a variable against the quantiles of normal distribution (*qnorm*) can be created to further examine the normality assumption.	
	pnorm XYZ ***qnorm XYZ***	
To-Do	Market Leverage	/*Use the model (14) and re-run Step 1 and Step 2.

Table G.5: Alternative Model Specification.

Reference(s)	**Table B.2 in Appendix B**	**Notes/Comments**
Pre-Set	***log using "<working directory>\<file name>.log", replace***	/*Tell Stata to protocol the log-file; provide path and file name.
	set more off, permanently	/*Tell Stata not to pause or display the – more – message.
	xtset code year, yearly	/*Declare data set as a panel data, whereby *code* represents "firms" and *year* represents "time series".
Command	Book Leverage	
	Step 1: Run the regression model. ***eststo fe1: xtreg blev1 l.prof l.growth l.size l.tang l.risk l.gdp, fe vce (cluster code)***	/*Use the model (13)
	Step 2: Check for insignificant variables. ***eststo fe2: xtreg blev1 l.prof l.size l.tang l.risk l.gdp, fe vce (cluster code)***	/*remove growth (insignificant)
	Market Leverage	
	Step 1: Run the regression model. ***eststo fe3: xtreg mlev1 l.prof l.growth l.size l.tang l.risk l.gdp, fe vce (cluster code)***	/*Use the model (14)
	Step 2: Check for insignificant variables. ***eststo fe4: xtreg mlev1 l.prof l.growth l.size l.tang l.risk, fe vce (cluster code)***	/*remove first *l.gdp* (insignificant) only, then
	eststo fe5: xtreg mlev1 l.prof l.growth l.size l.tang l.gdp, fe vce (cluster code)	/*remove risk *l.risk* (insignificant) only, then
	eststo fe6: xtreg mlev1 l.prof l.growth l.size l.tang, fe vce (cluster code)	/*remove both *l.gdp* and *l.risk*.

Output	***esttab fe1 fe2 fe3 fe4 fe5 fe6 using*** ///	/*Tell Stata to produce publication-style table(s) that display(s) the estimation results.
	log using "<working directory>\<file name>.rtf" ///	/*Output in .rtf file format; provide path and file name.
	replace b(3) se(3) r2(3) ar2(3) scalars(N_g) obslast nogap title ("<any name>") ///	/*(*title*) Title of the table; provide any name.
	mtitle("Model (BLEV)" "II" "Model (MLEV)" "IV" "V" "VI") label starlevels(* 0.10 ** 0.05 *** 0.01) compress varwidth(20) brackets nonum page	/*(*mtitle*) Title(s) of each model(s), provide any name.
	log close	/*Tell Stata to close the log-file.
	estimates clear	/*Tell Stata to drop all stored estimation results.

Table G.6: Estimator Selection – BPLM, Hausman, and Heteroskedasticity Tests.

Reference(s)	**Table B.3 in Appendix B (Leverage Regression) and Table F.6 in Appendix F (POT Regression)**	**Notes/Comments**
Pre-Set	***log using "<working directory>\<file name>.log", replace*** ***set more off, permanently*** ***xtset code year, yearly***	/*Tell Stata to protocol the log-file; provide path and file name. /*Tell Stata not to pause or display the – more – message. /*Declare data set as a panel data, whereby *code* represents "firms" and *year* represents "time series".
Command	Book Leverage	Example: *overall (pooled)* sample
	Step 1: Run the regression model => Example: *overall (pooled)* sample ***eststo re1: xtreg blev1 l.prof l.growth l.size l.tang l.risk l.gdp, re*** ***xttest0*** ***estadd scalar bplm = r(p)*** ***eststo bplm1***	/*Use the model (13) using Random Effects. /**BPLM test* is to detect the presence of an unobserved effect. /*If the p-value is below 0.05, then reject the hypothesis, else accept. If the *BPLM test* is rejected, proceed with the Hausman test.
	----------	----------
	eststo fe1: xtreg blev1 l.prof l.growth l.size l.tang l.risk l.gdp, fe ***eststo re1: xtreg blev1 l.prof l.growth l.size l.tang l.risk l.gdp, re*** ***hausman fe1 re1*** ***estadd scalar hausman = r(p)*** ***eststo hausman1***	/*Run Fixed Effects then Random Effects. /**Hausman test* is to check whether the estimated coefficients are significantly different from each other. If the p-value is below 0.05, then reject the hypothesis, else accept. A rejection favors *Fixed Effects* over *Random Effects*.
	----------	----------
	eststo fe1: xtreg blev1 l.prof l.growth l.size l.tang l.risk l.gdp, fe ***xttest3*** ***estadd scalar hettest = r(p)*** ***eststo hettest1***	/*Run Fixed Effects. /*The *heteroskedasticity* test calculates a modified Wald statistic for groupwise heteroskedasticity in the residuals of a Fixed Effect regression model. If the p-value is below 0.05, then reject the hypothesis, else accept. A rejection shows the presence of *heteroskedasticity*.

Output	Output results ***esttab bplm1 hausman1 hettest1 bplm2 hausman2 hettest2 using*** /// ***log using "<working directory>\ <file name>.rtf"*** /// ***replace b(3) se(3) r2(3) ar2(3) scalars(bplm hausman hettest) obslast nogap title ("<any name>")*** /// ***mtitle("BPLM1" "Haus1" "Het1") label starlevels(* 0.10 ** 0.05 *** 0.01) compress varwidth(20) brackets nonum page*** ***log close*** ***estimates clear***	/*Tell Stata to produce publication-style table(s) that display(s) the estimation results. /*Output in .rtf file format; provide path and file name. /*(*title*) Title of the table; provide any name. /*(*mtitle*) Title(s) of each model(s), provide any name. /*Tell Stata to close the log-file. /*Tell Stata to drop all stored estimation results.
To-Do	Run the regression model for each *country*/*industry* separately. (see examples for US and Technology) ***eststo re1: xtreg blev1 l.prof l.growth l.size l.tang l.risk l.gdp if idm==1, re*** ***eststo re1: xtreg blev1 l.prof l.growth l.size l.tang l.risk l.gdp if idi==9000, re***	/*In the *country* sample, use id 1, 2, 3, 4, 5, 6, and 7 for *US*, *UK*, *CA*, *JP*, *SK*, *TW*, and *IN*, respectively. /*In the *industry* sample, use id 1, 1000, 2000, 3000, 9000, 4000, and 5000 for *OILG*, *BMAT*, *IND*, *CGDS*, *TECH*, *HCARE*, and *CSRV*, respectively.
	Market Leverage	/*The process resembles book leverage. Run for the *overall (pooled)* sample and each *country* and *industry* separately, using the model (14).
	Pecking Order Theory (POT)	/*The process resembles leverage regression. Run for the *overall (pooled)* sample and each *country* and *industry* separately, using the model (23) and model (24).

Table G.7: Correlation Matrix and Multicollinearity Test.

Reference(s)	**Table 5.5, Table C.8 in Appendix C (Leverage Regression), and Table D.8 in Appendix D (POT Regression)**	**Notes/Comments**
Pre-Set	***set more off, permanently*** ***xtset code year, yearly***	/*Tell Stata not to pause or display the – more – message. /*Declare data set as a panel data, whereby *code* represents "firms" and *year* represents "time series".
Command	Pairwise-Correlation Matrix	
	pwcorr blev1 mlev1 prof growth size tang risk gdp, star (5)	/*Both dependent variables (*blev and mlev*) and all independent variables.
	Multicollinearity Test – VIF (Variance Inflation Factor)	
	Step 1: Run the regression model. ***reg blev1 prof growth size tang risk gdp*** Step 2: Run Variance Inflation Factor. ***vif***	/*Use the model (13) but in the current form ($_t$).

Table G.8: Auto-/Serial Correlation Test.

Reference(s)	**Table B.4 in Appendix B (Leverage Regression), and Table F.7 in Appendix F (POT Regression)**	**Notes/Comments**
Pre-Set	***set more off, permanently*** ***xtset code year, yearly***	/*Tell Stata not to pause or display the – more – message. /*Declare data set as a panel data, whereby *code* represents "firms" and *year* represents "time series".
Command	Book Leverage	Example: *overall (pooled)* sample
	xtserial blev1 prof growth size tang risk gdp /**overall (pooled)* ---------- ***xtserial blev1 prof growth size tang risk gdp if idm==1*** /**country* ***xtserial blev1 prof growth size tang risk gdp if idm==6*** /**country* ---------- ***xtserial blev1 prof growth size tang risk gdp if idi==1*** /**industry* ***xtserial blev1 prof growth size tang risk gdp if idi==9000*** /**industry*	/*Use the model (13) but in the current form ($_t$). ---------- /*In the *country* sample, use id 1, 2, 3, 4, 5, 6, and 7 for *US*, *UK*, *CA*, *JP*, *SK*, *TW*, and *IN*, respectively. ---------- /*In the *industry* sample, use id 1, 1000, 2000, 3000, 9000, 4000, and 5000 for *OILG*, *BMAT*, *IND*, *CGDS*, *TECH*, *HCARE*, and *CSRV*, respectively.
To-Do	Market Leverage	/*The process resembles book leverage. Run for the *overall (pooled)* sample and each *country* and *industry* separately, using the model (14) in the current form ($_t$)
	Pecking Order Theory (POT)	/*The process resembles leverage regression. Run for the *overall (pooled)* sample and each *country* and *industry* separately, using the model (23) and model (24).

Table G.9: Test of Strict Exogeneity (Endogeneity Test).

Reference(s)	**Table B.5 in Appendix B (Leverage Regression)**	**Notes/Comments**
Pre-Set	***log using "<working directory> \<file name>.log", replace*** ***set more off, permanently*** ***xtset code year, yearly***	/*Tell Stata to protocol the log-file; provide path and file name. /*Tell Stata not to pause or display the – more – message. /*Declare data set as \a panel data, whereby *code* represents "firms" and *year* represents "time series".
Command	Book Leverage	Example: *overall (pooled)* sample
	Run the regression model with future values of all independent variables. ***eststo all: xtreg blev1 prof growth size tang risk f.prof f.growth f.size f.tang f.risk, fe vce (cluster code)*** ---------- ***eststo us: xtreg blev1 prof growth size tang risk f.prof f.growth f.size f.tang f.risk if idm==1, fe vce (cluster code)*** ---------- ***eststo og: xtreg blev1 prof growth size tang risk f.prof f.growth f.size f.tang f.risk if idi==1, fe vce (cluster code)*** ---------- ***eststo te: xtreg blev1 prof growth size tang risk f.prof f.growth f.size f.tang f.risk if idi==9000, re vce (cluster code)***	/*Use the model (13). ---------- /*In the *country* sample, use id 1, 2, 3, 4, 5, 6, and 7 for *US*, *UK*, *CA*, *JP*, *SK*, *TW*, and *IN*, respectively. ---------- /*In the *industry* sample, use id 1, 1000, 2000, 3000, 9000, 4000, and 5000 for *OILG*, *BMAT*, *IND*, *CGDS*, *TECH*, *HCARE*, and *CSRV*, respectively. /*For Technology (*TECH*), idi==9000, the estimation selection process (see Table B.3 in Appendix B) identified Random Effects as the suitable estimator; hence we use "re".

Output	Output results ***esttab all us og te using*** /// ***log using "<working directory>*** ***<file name>.rtf"*** /// ***replace b(3) se(3) r2(3) ar2(3) scalars(N_g) obslast nogap title*** ***("<any name>")*** /// ***mtitle("BLev-All" "BLev-US" "BLev-OILG" "BLev-TECH") label*** ***starlevels(* 0.10 ** 0.05 *** 0.01) compress varwidth(20)*** ***brackets nonum page*** ***log close*** ***estimates clear***	/*Tell Stata to produce publication-style table(s) that display(s) the estimation results. /*Output in .rtf file format; provide path and file name. /*(*title*) Title of the table; provide any name. /*(*mtitle*) Title(s) of each model(s), provide any name. /*Tell Stata to close the log-file. /*Tell Stata to drop all stored estimation results.
To-Do	Market Leverage	/*The process resembles book leverage. Run for the *overall (pooled)* sample and each *country* and *industry* separately, using the model (14).
Hypothesis	If the "lead" variable's coefficient (i.e., *t+1*) is significant, it indicates that the variable might be *endogenous,* otherwise *predetermined*. GDP variable is not added because it is *exogenous* by default.	Stata provides time-series operators L. F. D. S., which specify lags, leads (forward values), differences, and seasonal differences, respectively. We use "f."

Table G.10: Leverage Regression – *Overall (pooled)*.

Reference(s)	**Table 5.6 and Table E.2 in Appendix E (Leverage Regression)**	**Notes/Comments**
Pre-Set	***log using "<working directory>\<file name>.log", replace*** ***set more off, permanently*** ***xtset code year, yearly***	/*Tell Stata to protocol the log-file; provide path and file name. /*Tell Stata not to pause or display the – more – message. /*Declare data set as a panel data, whereby *code* represents "firms" and *year* represents "time series".
Command	Shari'ah Compliant Sample (SC) *(dsc==1)* Shari'ah Non-Compliant (SNC) Sample *(dsc==0)*	
	Book Leverage	Example: *overall (pooled)* sample
	Run the regression model for SC and SNC firms separately. ***eststo bsc: xi:xtreg blev1 l.prof l.growth l.size l.tang l.risk l.gdp i.year if dsc==1, fe vce (cluster code)*** ***eststo bsnc: xi:xtreg blev1 l.prof l.growth l.size l.tang l.risk l.gdp i.year if dsc==0, fe vce (cluster code)***	/*Use the model (13). /*SC firms (dsc==1) /*SNC firms (dsc==0)
Output	Output results ***esttab bsc bsnc using*** /// ***log using "<working directory>\ <file name>.rtf"*** /// ***replace b(3) se(3) r2(3) ar2(3) scalars(N_g) obslast nogap title ("<any name>")*** /// ***mtitle("BLev-SC" "BLev-SNC") label starlevels(* 0.10 ** 0.05 *** 0.01) compress varwidth(20) brackets nonum page*** ***log close*** ***estimates clear***	/*Tell Stata to produce publication-style table(s) that display(s) the estimation results. /*Output in .rtf file format; provide path and file name. /*(*title*) Title of the table; provide any name. /*(*mtitle*) Title(s) of each model(s), provide any name. /*Tell Stata to close the log-file. /*Tell Stata to drop all stored estimation results.
To-Do	Market Leverage	/*The process resembles book leverage. Run for the *overall (pooled)* sample and each *country* and *industry* separately, using the model (14).

Table G.11: Time Breakdown Regression – *Overall (pooled)*.

Reference(s)	**Table D.1 in Appendix D (Leverage Regression)**	**Notes/Comments**
Pre-Set	***log using "<working directory>*** ***<file name>.log", replace*** ***set more off, permanently*** ***xtset code year, yearly***	/*Tell Stata to protocol the log-file; provide path and file name. /*Tell Stata not to pause or display the – more – message. /*Declare data set as a panel data, whereby *code* represents "firms" and *year* represents "time series".
Command	Shari'ah Compliant Sample (SC) *(dsc==1)* Shari'ah Non-Compliant (SNC) Sample *(dsc==0)*	
	Book Leverage	
	Run the regression model for SC and SNC firms separately. ***eststo bsc1: xi:xtreg blev1 l.prof l.growth l.size l.tang l.risk l.gdp i.year if dsc==1, fe vce (cluster code)*** ***eststo bsnc1: xi:xtreg blev1 l.prof l.growth l.size l.tang l.risk l.gdp i.year if dsc==0, fe vce (cluster code)*** ---------- ***eststo bsc2: xi:xtreg blev1 l.prof l.growth l.size l.tang l.risk l.gdp i.year if dsc==1 & inrange(year, 2004, 2007), fe vce (cluster code)*** ***eststo bsnc2: xi:xtreg blev1 l.prof l.growth l.size l.tang l.risk l.gdp i.year if dsc==0 & inrange(year, 2004, 2007), fe vce (cluster code)*** ---------- ***eststo bsc3: xi:xtreg blev1 l.prof l.growth l.size l.tang l.risk l.gdp i.year if dsc==1 & inrange(year, 2008, 2009), fe vce (cluster code)***	/*Use the model (13). /*SC firms (dsc==1) /*SNC firms (dsc==0) /*Apply *inrange* to specify the time frame. /*Years: 2004–2007 (Pre-Crisis) /*Years: 2008–2009 (Crisis) /*Years: 2010–2014 (Post-Crisis)

(continued)

Table G.11 (continued)

Reference(s)	**Table D.1 in Appendix D (Leverage Regression)**	**Notes/Comments**
	eststo bsnc3: xi:xtreg blev1 l.prof l.growth l.size l.tang l.risk l.gdp i.year if dsc==0 & inrange(year, 2008, 2009), fe vce (cluster code) ---------- ***eststo bsc4: xi:xtreg blev1 l.prof l.growth l.size l.tang l.risk l.gdp i.year if dsc==1 & inrange(year, 2010, 2014), fe vce (cluster code)*** ***eststo bsnc4: xi:xtreg blev1 l.prof l.growth l.size l.tang l.risk l.gdp i.year if dsc==0 & inrange(year, 2010, 2014***), fe vce (cluster code)	
Output	Output results ***esttab bsc1 bsnc1 bsc2 bsnc2 bsc3 bsnc3 bsc4 bsnc4 using*** /// ***log using "<working directory>\<file name>.rtf"*** /// ***replace b(3) se(3) r2(3) ar2(3) scalars(N_g) obslast nogap title ("<any name>")*** /// ***mtitle("BLev-SC-All" "BLev-SNC-All" "BLev-SC-Pre" "BLev-SNC-Pre" "BLev-SC-Cr" "BLev-SNC-Cr" "BLev-SC-Post" "BLev-SNC-Post") label starlevels (* 0.10 ** 0.05 *** 0.01) compress varwidth(20) brackets nonum page*** ***log close*** ***estimates clear***	/*Tell Stata to produce publication-style table(s) that display(s) the estimation results. /*Output in .rtf file format; provide path and file name. /**(title)* Title of the table; provide any name. /**(mtitle)* Title(s) of each model(s), provide any name. /*Tell Stata to close the log-file. /*Tell Stata to drop all stored estimation results.
To-Do	Market Leverage	/*The process resembles book leverage. Run for the *overall (pooled)* sample and each *country* and *industry* separately, using the model (14).

Table G.12: Leverage Regression – *Country*.

Reference(s)	**Table D.2 and Table D.3 in Appendix D, and Table E.3 and Table E.4 in Appendix E (Leverage Regression)**	**Notes/Comments**
Pre-Set	***log using "<working directory>\<file name>.log", replace*** ***set more off, permanently*** ***xtset code year, yearly***	/*Tell Stata to protocol the log-file; provide path and file name. /*Tell Stata not to pause or display the – more – message. /*Declare data set as a panel data, whereby *code* represents "firms" and *year* represents "time series".
Command	Shari'ah Compliant Sample (SC) *(dsc==1)* Shari'ah Non-Compliant (SNC) Sample *(dsc==0)*	
	Book Leverage	Example: *US and Taiwan* (SC) and *UK and India* (SNC)
	Run the regression model for SC and SNC firms separately. ***eststo bscus: xi:xtreg blev1 l.prof l.growth l.size l.tang l.risk l.gdp i.year if idm==1 & dsc==1, fe vce (cluster code)*** ***eststo bsctw: xi:xtreg blev1 l.prof l.growth l.size l.tang l.risk i.year if idm==6 & dsc==1, fe vce (cluster code)*** ---------- ***eststo bsncca: xi:xtreg blev1 l.prof l.growth l.size l.tang l.risk l.gdp i.year if idm==2 & dsc==0, fe vce (cluster code)*** ***eststo bsncin: xi:xtreg blev1 l.prof l.growth l.size l.tang l.risk l.gdp i.year if idm==7 & dsc==0, fe vce (cluster code)***	/*Use the model (13). /*SC firms (dsc==1) /*Note: GDP for Taiwan is not available. ---------- /*SNC firms (dsc==0) /*In the *country* sample, use id 1, 2, 3, 4, 5, 6, and 7 for *US*, *UK*, *CA*, *JP*, *SK*, *TW*, and *IN*, respectively.

(continued)

Table G.12 (continued)

Reference(s)	**Table D.2 and Table D.3 in Appendix D, and Table E.3 and Table E.4 in Appendix E (Leverage Regression)**	**Notes/Comments**
Output	Output results ***esttab bscus bsctw bsncca bsncin using*** /// ***log using "<working directory>\<file name>.rtf"*** /// ***replace b(3) se(3) r2(3) ar2(3) scalars(N_g) obslast nogap title ("<any name>")*** /// ***mtitle("US SC" "Taiwan SC" "Canada SNC" "India SNC") label starlevels(* 0.10 ** 0.05 *** 0.01) compress varwidth(20) brackets nonum page*** ***log close*** ***estimates clear***	/*Tell Stata to produce publication-style table(s) that display(s) the estimation results. /*Output in .rtf file format; provide path and file name. /*(*title*) Title of the table; provide any name. /*(*mtitle*) Title(s) of each model(s), provide any name. /*Tell Stata to close the log-file. /*Tell Stata to drop all stored estimation results.
To-Do	Market Leverage	/*The process resembles book leverage. Run for the *overall (pooled)* sample and each *country* and *industry* separately, using the model (14).

Table G.13: Leverage Regression – *Industry.*

Reference(s)	**Table D.2 and Table D.3 in Appendix D, and Table E.3 and Table E.4 in Appendix E (Leverage Regression)**	**Notes/Comments**
Pre-Set	***log using "<working directory>\ <file name>.log", replace*** ***set more off, permanently*** ***xtset code year, yearly***	/*Tell Stata to protocol the log-file; provide path and file name. /*Tell Stata not to pause or display the – more – message. /*Declare data set as a panel data, whereby *code* represents "firms" and *year* represents "time series".
Command	Shari'ah Compliant Sample (SC) *(dsc==1)* Shari'ah Non-Compliant (SNC) Sample *(dsc==0)*	
	Book Leverage	Examples: CGDS *and TECH* (SC) and *HCARE and CSRV* (SNC)
	Run the regression model for SC and SNC firms separately. ***eststo bsccg: xi:xtreg blev1 l.prof l.growth l.size l.tang l.risk l.gdp i.year if idi==3000 & dsc==1, fe vce (cluster code)*** ***eststo bscte: xi:xtreg blev1 l.prof l.growth l.size l.tang l.risk l.gdp i.year i.idm if idi==9000 & dsc==1, re vce (cluster code)*** ---------- ***eststo bsnchc: xi:xtreg blev1 l.prof l.growth l.size l.tang l.risk l.gdp i.year i.idm if idi==4000 & dsc==0, re vce (cluster code)*** ***eststo bsnccs: xi:xtreg blev1 l.prof l.growth l.size l.tang l.risk l.gdp i.year if idi==5000 & dsc==0, fe vce (cluster code)***	/*Use the model (13). /*SC firms (dsc==1) ---------- /*SNC firms (dsc==0) /*Estimator selection procedure in Panel A, Table B.3 in Appendix B, favored Random Effects (RE) for *TECH* and *HCARE*. We use *re*. Control for *country fixed effects* by adding the dummy *i.idm* on the Random Effects (RE) regression models. /*In the *industry* sample, use id 1, 1000, 2000, 3000, 9000, 4000, and 5000 for *OILG*, *BMAT*, *IND*, *CGDS*, *TECH*, *HCARE*, and *CSRV*, respectively.

(continued)

Table G.13 (continued)

Reference(s)	**Table D.2 and Table D.3 in Appendix D, and Table E.3 and Table E.4 in Appendix E (Leverage Regression)**	**Notes/Comments**
Output	Output results ***esttab bsccg bscte bsnchc bsnccs using*** /// ***log using "<working directory>\<file name>.rtf"*** /// ***replace b(3) se(3) r2(3) ar2(3) scalars(N_g) obslast nogap title (“<any name>”)*** /// ***mtitle("CGDS SC" "TECH SC" "HCARE SNC" "CSERV SNC") label starlevels(* 0.10 ** 0.05 *** 0.01) compress varwidth(20) brackets nonum page*** ***log close*** ***estimates clear***	/*Tell Stata to produce publication-style table(s) that display(s) the estimation results. /*Output in .rtf file format; provide path and file name. /**(title)* Title of the table; provide any name. /**(mtitle)* Title(s) of each model(s), provide any name. /*Tell Stata to close the log-file. /*Tell Stata to drop all stored estimation results.
To-Do	Market Leverage	/*The process resembles book leverage. Run for the *overall (pooled)* sample and each *country* and *industry* separately, using the model (14).

Table G.14: Target vs. Actual Leverage Ratio – *Overall (pooled)*.

Reference(s)	**Figure 6.1, Figure 6.2, and Table D.4 in Appendix D**	**Notes/Comments**
Pre-Set	***log using "<working directory>\<file name>.log", replace*** ***set more off, permanently*** ***xtset code year, yearly***	/*Tell Stata to protocol the log-file; provide path and file name. /*Tell Stata not to pause or display the – more – message. /*Declare data set as a panel data, whereby *code* represents "firms" and *year* represents "time series".
Command	Shari'ah Compliant Sample (SC) *(dsc==1)* Shari'ah Non-Compliant (SNC) Sample *(dsc==0)*	
	Book Leverage	
	Step 1: Run the regression model for SC and SNC firms separately. ***eststo bsc: xi:xtreg blev1 prof growth size tang risk gdp i.year if dsc==1, fe vce (cluster code)*** Step 2: Predict the fitted model after regressing and follow the following commands. ***predict <anyname> if dsc==1, xb*** ***tabstat BSC if year==2004*** ***tabstat BSC if year==2005*** ***tabstat BSC if year==2006*** ***tabstat BSC if year==2007*** ***tabstat BSC if year==2008*** ***tabstat BSC if year==2009*** ***tabstat BSC if year==2010*** ***tabstat BSC if year==2011*** ***tabstat BSC if year==2012*** ***tabstat BSC if year==2013*** ***tabstat BSC if year==2014***	/*Use the model (13) in the current form (not in the lag form). /*Prediction must be made for each sub-sample separately (i.e., BLEV/SC and BLEV/SNC). Therefore, run with SC firms *dsc==1*, then with SNC firms *dsc==0*. /*e.g., predict *BSC*, xb /*This Stata procedure is for the *Target Leverage*. The *Actual Leverage* means can be retrieved from Table 5.2 (descriptive statistics).
To-Do	Market Leverage	/*The process resembles book leverage. Run for the *overall (pooled)* sample and each *country* and *industry* separately using the model (14).

Table G.15: Direct Measure – Dynamic Trade-Off Theory Regression.

Reference(s)	**Table D.5 and Table D.6 in Appendix D, and Table E.7 and Table E.8 in Appendix E**	**Notes/Comments**
Pre-Set	***log using "<working directory>\<file name>.log", replace*** ***set more off, permanently*** ***xtset code year, yearly***	/*Tell Stata to protocol the log-file; provide path and file name. /*Tell Stata not to pause or display the – more – message. /*Declare data set as a panel data, whereby *code* represents "firms" and *year* represents "time series".
Command	Shari'ah Compliant Sample (SC) *(dsc==1)* Shari'ah Non-Compliant (SNC) Sample *(dsc==0)*	
	Speed of Adjustment (Partial Adjustment Model)	
	Book Leverage	
	Run the regression model for the *overall (pooled)* sample with SC and SNC firms separately. ---------- ***eststo bscall: xi:xtabond2 blev1 l.blev1 l.prof l.growth l.size l.tang l.risk l.gdp i.year i.idm i.idi if dsc==1, gmm (l.blev1 l.prof l.growth l.size l.tang, lag(2 .)) iv(l.risk l.gdp i.year i.idm) twostep robust orthogonal*** ---------- Run the regression model for the *country* sample with SC and SNC firms separately.	/*Use the model (18). ---------- /*Control for *country/industry fixed effects* by adding the dummies *i.idm/i.idi* on the *system GMM* regression models. ---------- */*Example: United States, idm==1*

	eststo bscus: xi:xtabond2 blev1 l.blev1 l.prof l.growth l.size l.tang l.risk l.gdp i.year i.idi if dsc==1 & idm==1, gmm (l.blev1) iv(l.prof l.growth l.size l.tang l.risk l.gdp i.year) twostep robust ---------- Run the regression model for the *industry* sample with SC and SNC firms separately. ***eststo bscbm: xi:xtabond2 blev1 l.blev1 l.prof l.growth l.size l.tang l.risk l.gdp i.year i.idm if dsc==1 & idi==1000, gmm (l.blev1, collapse) iv (l.prof l.growth l.size l.tang l.risk l.gdp i.year i.idm) twostep robust orthogonal***	/*In the *country* sample, use id 1, 2, 3, 4, 5, 6, and 7 for *US*, *UK*, *CA*, *JP*, *SK*, *TW*, and *IN*, respectively. /*Control for *industry fixed effects* by adding the dummy *i.idi* on all *system GMM* regression models. ---------- /**Example: Basic Materials, idi=1000* /*In the *industry* sample, use id 1, 1000, 2000, 3000, 9000, 4000, and 5000 for *OILG*, *BMAT*, *IND*, *CGDS*, *TECH*, *HCARE*, and *CSRV*, respectively. /*Control for *country fixed effects* by adding the dummy *i.idm* on all system GMM regression models.
	IMPORTANT NOTE: We followed Roodman (2009) and applied the authors' recommendations as strictly as possible. /*Before running any model, check the Endogeneity Test results in Table B.5 in Appendix B and, if deemed fit, start applying the suggested *endogenous* and *predetermined* variables under ***gmm*** and first ***iv***, respectively. (Remember: Table B.5 in Appendix B results, use them ***only*** as guidance) Furthermore, we initially set the instruments restricted to two lags ***(2 2)***, but if the serial correlation of the second-order, i.e., AR(2), was present, or if the Sargan/Hansen test failed, then lags of the third and higher-order was set. Apply ***(. .)*** when the maximum available instruments are desired. – ***gmm*** ([lag]dependent variable and all *endogenous and predetermined variables* [in the lag-form]) – ***lag (x y)*** (specify desired lags) – ***iv*** (all *exogenous variables* [in the lag-form])	

(continued)

Table G.15 (continued)

Reference(s)	**Table D.5 and Table D.6 in Appendix D, and Table E.7 and Table E.8 in Appendix E**		**Notes/Comments**
Output	Output results ***esttab bscall bscuk bscbm using*** ***log using "<working directory>*** ***<file name>.rtf"*** ***replace b(3) se(3) scalars*** ***("j #instruments" "N_g #groups" "ar1p Arellano-Bond: AR(1)"*** ***"ar2p Arellano-Bond: AR(2)" "hansenp Hansen test (p-val)")*** ***obslast nogap*** ***title ("<any name>") mtitle("B-All" "B-UK" "B-BMAT")*** ***label starlevels(* 0.10 ** 0.05 *** 0.01) compress varwidth(20)*** ***brackets nonum page*** ***log close*** ***estimates clear***	 /// /// /// ///	/*Tell Stata to produce publication-style table(s) that display(s) the estimation results. /*Output in .rtf file format; provide path and file name. /**(title)* Title of the table; provide any name. /**(mtitle)* Title(s) of each model(s), provide any name. /*Tell Stata to close the log-file. /*Tell Stata to drop all stored estimation results.
To-Do	Market Leverage		/*The process resembles book leverage. Run for the *overall (pooled)* sample and each *country* and *industry* separately, using the model (19).

Table G.16: Direct Measure – TOT Regression, Alternative Approach (Remedy).

Reference(s)	Table D.7 in Appendix D	Notes/Comments
Pre-Set	***log using "<working directory>\<file name>.log", replace*** ***set more off, permanently*** ***xtset code year, yearly***	/*Tell Stata to protocol the log-file; provide path and file name. /*Tell Stata not to pause or display the – more – message. /*Declare data set as a panel data, whereby *code* represents "firms" and *year* represents "time series".
Command	An alternative approach to remedy those models with unsuccessful results denoted with ×.	
	Interactive-Dummy for Shari'ah Compliance (*iblev=1* represents SC; *iblev=0* represents SNC)	
	Speed of Adjustment (Partial Adjustment Model)	
	Book Leverage	
	Run the regression model denoted as ×[1] (see Table D.5 in Appendix D)* ---------- ***eststo bca: xi:xtabond2 blev1 l.blev1 l.iblev1 l.prof l.growth l.size l.tang l.risk l.gdp i.year i.idi dsc if idm==3, gmm (l.blev1) iv(l.prof l.growth l.size l.tang l.risk l.gdp i.year i.idi) twostep robust*** ***lincom l.blev1+l.iblev1***	/*Use the model (18). ---------- /**Example: Canada, idm==3* /*Control for *industry fixed effects* by adding the dummy *i.idi* on all *system GMM* regression models. /*It is crucial to control *Shari'ah Compliance (SC)* in general; hence dummy variable *dsc* is added in all models. Note(s) => see IMPORTANT NOTE in Table G.15.

(continued)

Table G.16 (continued)

Reference(s)	**Table D.7 in Appendix D**	**Notes/Comments**
	IMPORTANT NOTE: The coefficient of the variable *l.blev1* represents SNC firms, and the variable *l.iblev1* represents "the comparative difference" between SC and SNC. However, to identify the coefficient results for SC firms per se, it is the sum of *l.blev1* and *l.iblev1*. The *lincom* command is convenient as it computes point estimates, standard errors, *t* or *z* statistics, *p-values*, and confidence intervals for linear combinations of coefficients after any estimation command. Consequently, we applied *lincom* directly after each regression, as shown in the first remedy example ✖[1].	
Output	Output results ***esttab bca using*** /// ***log using "<working directory>*** ***<file name>.rtf"*** /// ***replace b(3) se(3) scalars("j #instruments" "N_g #groups" "ar1p*** ***Arellano-Bond: AR(1)" "ar2p Arellano-Bond: AR(2)" "hansenp*** ***Hansen test (p-val)") obslast nogap*** /// ***title ("<any name>") mtitle*** ***("B-Canada")*** /// ***label starlevels(* 0.10 ** 0.05 *** 0.01) compress varwidth(20)*** ***brackets nonum page*** ***log close*** ***estimates clear***	/*Tell Stata to produce publication-style table(s) that display(s) the estimation results. /*Output in .rtf file format; provide path and file name. /**(title)* Title of the table; provide any name. /**(mtitle)* Title(s) of each model(s), provide any name. /*Tell Stata to close the log-file. /*Tell Stata to drop all stored estimation results.
To-Do	Check Table D.7	/*The process resembles the example for Canada. For all book leverage models, use the model (18), and for all market leverage models, use the model (19).

Table G.17: Direct Measure – Pecking Order Theory Regression.

Reference(s)	**Table D.10 and Table D.11 in Appendix D (current period *t* and lag period *t-1*), and Table F.8 in Appendix F (current *t*)**	**Notes/Comments**
Pre-Set	***log using "<working directory>\<file name>.log", replace*** ***set more off, permanently*** ***xtset code year, yearly***	/*Tell Stata to protocol the log-file; provide path and file name. /*Tell Stata not to pause or display the – more – message. /*Declare data set as a panel data, whereby *code* represents "firms" and *year* represents "time series".
Command	Interactive-Dummy for Shari'ah Compliance (*idef=1* represents SC; *idef=0* represents SNC)	
	Debt and Equity Issues (current period *t*)	
	Run the regression model for the *overall (pooled)* sample. ---------- Debt Issues ***eststo dall1: xi:xtreg debtissue def idef i.year dsc, fe vce (cluster code)*** ***lincom def + idef*** ***estadd scalar deficit r(estimate)*** ***estadd scalar stderr r(se)*** ----------	/*Use model (23). /*Fixed Effects (FE), therefore, no dummies added. /*Important, the coefficient of the variable *def*, represents SNC firms. To identify the coefficient results for SC firms, we apply the *lincom* command directly after each regression. ----------

(continued)

Table G.17 (continued)

Reference(s)	**Table D.10 and Table D.11 in Appendix D (current period *t* and lag period *t-1*), and Table F.8 in Appendix F (current *t*)**	**Notes/Comments**
	Equity Issues ***eststo eall1: xi:xtreg debtissue def idef i.year dsc, fe vce (cluster code)*** ***lincom def + idef*** ***estadd scalar deficit r(estimate)*** ***estadd scalar stderr r(se)***	/*In the *country* sample, use id 1, 2, 3, 4, 5, 6, and 7 for *US*, *UK*, *CA*, *JP*, *SK*, *TW*, and *IN*, respectively. /*Control for *industry fixed effects* by adding the dummy *i.idi* on all OLS and Random Effects (RE) regression models.
	---------- Run the regression model for *country* sample. ***eststo duk1: xi:reg debtissue def idef i.year i.idi dsc if idm==2, vce (cluster code)*** ***eststo euk1: xi:reg debtissue def idef i.year i.idi dsc if idm==2, vce (cluster code)***	---------- /*In the *industry* sample, use id 1, 1000, 2000, 3000, 9000, 4000, and 5000 for *OILG*, *BMAT*, *IND*, *CGDS*, *TECH*, *HCARE*, and *CSRV*, respectively. /*Control for *country fixed effects* by adding the dummy *i.idm* on all OLS Random Effects (RE) regression models.
	---------- Run the regression model for *industry* sample. ***eststo dind1: xi:xtreg debtissue def idef i.year i.idm dsc if idi==2000, re vce (cluster code)*** ***eststo eind1: xi:xtreg debtissue def idef i.year i.idm dsc if idi==2000, re vce (cluster** code)	/*Before running any model, check the estimator selection procedure in Panel C, Table B.3 in Appendix B, and apply the favored estimator. /*It is crucial to control *Shari'ah Compliance (SC)* in general; hence dummy variable *dsc* is added in all models.
	IMPORTANT NOTE: The coefficient of the variable *def* represents SNC firms, and the variable *idef* represents "the comparative difference" between SC and SNC. However, to identify the coefficient results for SC firms per se, it is the sum of *def* and *idef*. The *lincom* command is convenient as it computes point estimates, standard errors, *t* or *z* statistics, *p-values*, and confidence intervals for linear combinations of coefficients after any estimation command. Consequently, we applied *lincom* directly after each regression, as shown in the *overall (pooled)* sample example.	

Output	Output results ***esttab dall1 eall1 duk1 euk1 dind1 eind1 using /// *** ***log using "<working directory>\<file name>.rtf" /// *** ***replace b(3) se(3) r2(3) ar2(3) scalars(N_g deficit stderr) obslast*** ***nogap title ("<any name>") /// *** ***mtitle("Debt-All" "Equity-All" "Debt-UK" " Equity-UK" "Debt-IND" "Equity-IND") label starlevels(* 0.10 ** 0.05 *** 0.01)*** ***compress varwidth(20) brackets nonum page*** ***log close*** ***estimates clear***	/*Tell Stata to produce publication-style table(s) that display(s) the estimation results. /*Output in .rtf file format; provide path and file name. /**(title)* Title of the table; provide any name. /**(mtitle)* Title(s) of each model(s), provide any name. /*Tell Stata to close the log-file. /*Tell Stata to drop all stored estimation results.
To-Do	Debt and Equity Issues (lag period *t*)	/*The process resembles Debt and Equity Issues (current period *t*). Run for the *overall (pooled)* sample and each *country* and *industry* separately, using the model (24).

About the Author

Dr. Ramazan Yildirim is the Managing Director of Upsite Consulting, located in the Kingdom of Bahrain. He has gained entrepreneurial and consulting experiences, especially in corporate governance areas, such as Business Process Management (BPM) and Corporate Risk Management (CRM), followed by a strong academic background in complex research environments. He provides his professional services globally to several multinational conglomerates among various industries such as Siemens, SAP, Software AG, SABIC, and many more. Born and raised in Stuttgart, Germany, Dr. Ramazan received his BBA in Information Systems and his MBA in International Management and Marketing (in cooperation with Nanyang Technological University, Singapore) from Pforzheim Business School, Germany. He obtained his PhD in Islamic Finance from the International Centre for Education in Islamic Finance (INCEIF), Kuala Lumpur, Malaysia.

Dr. Ramazan has authored and reviewed in international journals and publishing houses. He received the Best Paper Award from Pacific-Basin Finance Journal (PBFJ) at the Malaysian Finance Association (MFA) Conference 2017 for his paper titled *"Determinants of Capital Structure: Evidence from Shari'ah Compliant and Non-Compliant Firms"*. Furthermore, he presented his innovative idea titled *"Shari'ah Screening Methodology – New Shari'ah Compliant Approach"* at the 1st IF Innofest 2016 (Islamic Finance Innovation Festival/Competition) sponsored and organized by the Central Bank of Malaysia (Bank Negara) and INCEIF, respectively. He received the 1st Prize for his Idea Pitch (Exhibitor).

His research interests are in the areas of (but not limited to) Corporate Finance, Corporate Governance, Capital Markets, Portfolio Management, and Financial Economics from Islamic and conventional perspectives. Currently, he resides in the Kingdom of Bahrain, together with his two teenagers. Dr. Ramazan can be reached at ramy@upsiteconsulting.com and ramjumyas@gmail.com.

https://doi.org/10.1515/9783110713664-016

List of Abbreviations and Symbols

AAOIFI	Accounting and Auditing Organization for Islamic Financial Institution
BLEV	Book Leverage
BMAT	Basic Materials
BNM	Bank Negara Malaysia
CA	Canada
CAPEX	Capital Expenditures
CGDS	Consumer Goods
CSRV	Consumer Services
DJ	Dow Jones
DJGI	Dow Jones Global Index
DJIMI	Dow Jones Islamic Market Index
EBIT	Earnings before Interest, Taxes, Depreciation and Amortization
EBITDA	Earnings before Interest and Taxes
EPS	Earnings-per-Share
FE	Fixed Effects
FTSE	The Financial Times Stock Exchange
GCC	Gulf Cooperation Council
GDP	Gross Domestic Product
GFC	Global Financial Crisis
GMM	Generalized Moments Method
GROWTH	Growth Opportunity
HCARE	Health Care
ICB	Industry Classification Benchmark
IFI	Islamic Financial Institutions
IFSB	Islamic Financial Services Board
IIFA	International Islamic Fiqh Academy
IN	India
IND	Industrials
IPOM	Islamic Pecking Order Model
JP	Japan
MLEV	Market Leverage
MM	Modigliani–Miller theorem
MSCI	Morgan Stanley Capital International
MTB	Market-to-Book
NDTS	Non-Debt Tax Shield
NPV	Net Present Value
OILG	Oil and Gas
POT	Pecking Order Theory
PROF	Profitability
R&D	Research and Development
RE	Random Effects
REIT	Real Estate Investment Trust
RISK	Business Risk (Earnings Volatility)
RIEM	Ramy Islamic Equity Market
S&P	Standard and Poor's
SAC	Shari'ah Advisory Council

https://doi.org/10.1515/9783110713664-017

SC	Shari'ah Compliant or Shari'ah Compliance
SIZE	Firm Size
SNC	Shari'ah Non-Compliant or Shari'ah Non-Compliance
SK	South Korea
SPV	Special Purpose Vehicle
TOT	Trade-Off Theory
TANG	Tangibility
TW	Taiwan
UK	United Kingdom
US	United States

List of Figures

https://doi.org/10.1515/9783110713664-018

List of Figures (appendices)

https://doi.org/10.1515/9783110713664-019

List of Tables

https://doi.org/10.1515/9783110713664-020

List of Tables (appendices)

https://doi.org/10.1515/9783110713664-021

Index

https://doi.org/10.1515/9783110713664-022